Frommer's®

Chile & Easter Island

2nd Edition

by Nicholas Gill, Caroline Lascom & Christie Pashby

Here's what the critics say about Frommer's:

"Amazingly easy to use. Very portable, very complete."
—BOOKLIST

"Detailed, accurate, and easy-to-read information for all price ranges."
—GLAMOUR MAGAZINE

"Hotel information is close to encyclopedic."
—DES MOINES SUNDAY REGISTER

"Frommer's Guides have a way of giving you a real feel for a place."
—KNIGHT RIDDER NEWSPAPERS

WILEY
Wiley Publishing, Inc.

Published by:
WILEY PUBLISHING, INC.

111 River St.
Hoboken, NJ 07030-5774

ISBN 978-0-470-43514-4

Editor: Jennifer Reilly
Production Editor: Eric T. Schroeder
Cartographer: Liz Puhl
Photo Editor: Richard Fox
Production by Wiley Indianapolis Composition Services

Front cover photo: Lago San Rafael: Kayaker on lake
Back cover photo: Rapa Nui, Easter Island: Stone Maoi statues at Rano Raraku

For information on our other products and services or to obtain technical support, please contact our Customer Care Department within the U.S. at 877/762-2974, outside the U.S. at 317/572-3993 or fax 317/572-4002.

Wiley also publishes its books in a variety of electronic formats. Some content that appears in print may not be available in electronic formats.

Manufactured in the United States of America

5 4 3 2 1

CONTENTS

4 SUGGESTED CHILE ITINERARIES 53

5 THE ACTIVE VACATION PLANNER 64

6 SANTIAGO 76

7 AROUND SANTIAGO: THE CENTRAL VALLEY, PEAKS & COASTAL REGION 126

8 LA SERENA & THE ELQUI VALLEY 190

9 THE DESERT NORTH 208

10 THE CHILEAN LAKE DISTRICT 244

11 CHILOÉ 311

12 THE CARRETERA AUSTRAL 328

13 SOUTHERN PATAGONIA & ANTARCTICA 363

LIST OF MAPS

ABOUT THE AUTHORS

Writer and photographer **Nicholas Gill** (Chilean Lake District, Chiloe, The Carretera Austral, and Easter Island chapters) is based in Lima, Peru and Brooklyn, New York. His work appears in publications such as *Conde Nast Traveler, Islands, Forbes Traveler,* World Hum, and *The Columbus Dispatch.* He has also authored numerous travel guides on Latin American countries. Visit his personal website (www.nicholas-gill.com) for more information.

Caroline Lascom (front of book chapters, as well as Santiago, Around Santiago, La Serena & the Elqui Valley, and the Desert North chapters) has spent much of the last decade traveling through Latin America, working as a freelance travel writer. She has authored and contributed to many guidebooks. Her credits include *Footprint* guides to Havana, Lisbon, Mexico, and Costa Rica, the *Rough Guide* to Mexico, and *Insight Guide* Chicago.

Christie Pashby (Southern Patagonia & Antarctica) is the author of *Frommer's Banff & Jasper National Parks* and co-author of *Frommer's Argentina, Frommer's Chile* and *Frommer's Best Hikes in BC.* Christie divides her time between the Canadian Rockies and Bariloche, Argentina. A freelance journalist and translator, she also somehow finds the time to run a small guiding business with her husband, and cram in two ski seasons a year. Her websites include www.patagoniatravelco.com and www.patagonialiving.com.

ACKNOWLEDGMENTS

I'd like to thank everyone at Posada de Mike Rapu for their help in getting around the island and Bertha at LAN airlines for her logistical help. In the Lakes District, a big thanks goes out to Alberto Becker for conquering two flat tires to help get me to the Cliffs. In Patagonia, thanks to Jasnaa, Perla, Carolina, and everyone at Nomads of the Seas for their help in reaching several remote locations, as well as Damanio and everyone at Hacienda Tres Lagos for their kind assistance.

—Nicholas Gill

When I was a child, my Grandpa gave me a copy of *National Geographic* magazine that had a photo of Torres del Paine in it, and I've been mad for Patagonia ever since. I would also like to thank Jennifer Reilly and the crew at Frommer's. And *gracias* to my husband Max, for asking so many questions.

—Christie Pashby

AN INVITATION TO THE READER

In researching this book, we discovered many wonderful places—hotels, restaurants, shops, and more. We're sure you'll find others. Please tell us about them, so we can share the information with your fellow travelers in upcoming editions. If you were disappointed with a recommendation, we'd love to know that, too. Please write to:

Frommer's Chile & Easter Island, 2nd Edition
Wiley Publishing, Inc. • 111 River St. • Hoboken, NJ 07030

AN ADDITIONAL NOTE

Please be advised that travel information is subject to change at any time—and this is especially true of prices. We therefore suggest that you write or call ahead for confirmation when making your travel plans. The authors, editors, and publisher cannot be held responsible for the experiences of readers while traveling. Your safety is important to us, however, so we encourage you to stay alert and be aware of your surroundings. Keep a close eye on cameras, purses, and wallets, all favorite targets of thieves and pickpockets.

FROMMER'S STAR RATINGS, ICONS & ABBREVIATIONS

Every hotel, restaurant, and attraction listing in this guide has been ranked for quality, value, service, amenities, and special features using a **star-rating system.** In country, state, and regional guides, we also rate towns and regions to help you narrow down your choices and budget your time accordingly. Hotels and restaurants are rated on a scale of zero (recommended) to three stars (exceptional). Attractions, shopping, nightlife, towns, and regions are rated according to the following scale: zero stars (recommended), one star (highly recommended), two stars (very highly recommended), and three stars (must-see).

In addition to the star-rating system, we also use **seven feature icons** that point you to the great deals, in-the-know advice and unique experiences that separate travelers from tourists. Throughout the book, look for:

Finds	Special finds—those places only insiders know about
Fun Facts	Fun facts—details that make travelers more informed and their trips more fun
Kids	Best bets for kids, and advice for the whole family
Moments	Special moments—those experiences that memories are made of
Overrated	Places or experiences not worth your time or money
Tips	Insider tips—great ways to save time and money
Value	Great values—where to get the best deals

The following **abbreviations** are used for credit cards:

AE American Express	**DISC** Discover	**V** Visa
DC Diners Club	MC MasterCard	

FROMMERS.COM

Now that you have this guidebook to help you plan a great trip, visit our website at **www.frommers.com** for additional travel information on more than 4,000 destinations. We update features regularly to give you instant access to the most current trip-planning information available. At Frommers.com, you'll find scoops on the best airfares, lodging rates, and car rental bargains. You can even book your travel online through our reliable travel booking partners. Other popular features include:

- Online updates of our most popular guidebooks
- Vacation sweepstakes and contest giveaways
- Newsletters highlighting the hottest travel trends
- Podcasts, interactive maps, and up-to-the-minute events listings
- Opinionated blog entries by Arthur Frommer himself
- Online travel message boards with featured travel discussions

What's New in Chile

While Chile may be South America's richest, most stable nation, with a mature democracy and a solid infrastructure that garners a buoyant tourist industry, a sense of dynamism remains, ensuring that each year Chile tops the hot lists for its stellar inventory of world-class hotels, state-of-the-art wineries, and culinary wizardry. Here are some highlights related to new hotels, restaurants, and attractions that you'll find in this edition of the book.

SANTIAGO

The introduction of a new integrated public transport system, known as **Transantiago,** in 2007 was a fiasco that resulted in transport mayhem for Santiago's rush-hour commuters. Avoiding the Metro during the early morning and late afternoon should allow you to steer clear of any inconvenience, however.

Travelers on a budget have excellent new hostel choices. **Andes Hostel** (**© 2/632-9990;** www.andeshostel.com) is the sister hostel of the superb **Orly Hotel** (**© 2/231-8947;** www.hotelorly.cl), which continues to shine as the best midrange hotel in the city, combining European flair with Latin hospitality. Both the **Chillhotel** (**© 2/264-0643;** www.chillhotel.cl) and **Vegas Hotel** (**© 2/632-2514;** www.hotelvegas.net) offer a warm ambience and well-maintained rooms in convenient locations that defy their wallet-friendly prices.

The dining trend toward all things fusion continues with the opening of **Sukalde** (**© 2/665-1017;** www.sukalde.cl), in Providencia, featuring imaginative dishes from globetrotting Chilean chef and TV celebrity Matías Palomo, who studied under food god Ferrán Adria at Spain's El Bulli; plan ahead as reservations are currently hard to come by. Purists will prefer the sleek, minimalist **Infante 51** (**© 2/264-3357**), where Basque chef and part owner Xabier Zabala serves platters of unadulterated fish and seafood dishes ranging from white tuna to grilled breca from the Juan Fernandez islands.

For more information on Santiago, see chapter 6.

AROUND SANTIAGO

It's worth applauding when a charming boutique hotel comes on the scene that positively oozes style and sophistication. At the moment, accolades should go to the new **Zerohotel** (**© 2/211-3113;** www.zerohotel.com), a restored mansion with dreamscape views and gratifying attention to detail. Among this book's notable finds for budget travelers is the artsy **Camila 109** (**© 32/249-1746;** www.camila109.cl), which encapsulates the raw bohemian spirit of Valparaíso that has been diluted by the city's gentrification. Valpo continues to blaze the trail in terms of the region's gastronomic kudos.

Newcomers that excel in terms of modern fusion cuisine and jaw-dropping vistas are **Concepción,** (**© 32/249-8192**) and **Montealegre** (**© 2/657-3950;** www.hotelcasahigueras.cl).

For more information on this region, see chapter 7.

LA SERENA & THE ELQUI VALLEY

La Serena is the only town in Chile that still lives and breathes its colonial Spanish heritage. La Serena's rough-and-tumble neighbor Coquimbo has continued to experience a renaissance as a nightlife hub and boasts Chile's biggest outdoor fair, La Pampilla. The beaches at La Serena here have now eclipsed Viña del Mar as the sun-worshippers' hot spot.

As much of the country becomes enveloped by tourism, the Elqui Valley remains an untouched, stunning landscape of pastel-streaked mountains and lush valleys, which unfurl beneath the clearest skies in the hemisphere. Go now while you can still enjoy the solitude and wonderful, affordable accommodations options. The best at the moment is the delightfully holistic **Misterios de Elqui,** (**© 51/451126;** www.misteriosdeelqui.cl), which offers designer cabins with breathtaking views, a gorgeous pool, and tasty home-style cooking, all for less than $100 (£67) per night.

For more information on this region, see chapter 8.

THE DESERT NORTH

In the midst of this beautiful "wasteland," in the tiny emerald oasis of San Pedro, two new hotels were unveiled to much fanfare from the travel industry arbiters of style: **Awasi** (**© 888/880-3219** in the U.S., 2/233-9641 in Chile; www.awasi.cl) is the ultimate in rustic chic, with stylish rooms and superlative amenities and service; **Tierra Atacama** (**© 800/829-5325** in the U.S., 55/555977 in Chile; www.tierra atacama.com) offers more affordable luxury than its iconic rival, the explora. While more and more hotels and backpacker hostels are springing up in San Pedro each year, these tasteful, new adobe and stone constructions blend harmoniously with the landscape and the town has managed, so far, to maintain its low-key, pueblo vibe.

For more information on this region, see chapter 9.

THE LAKE DISTRICT

The new dining hot spot in Valdivia is **Santo Pecado** (**© 63/239122;** www.santopecado.cl), with its funky Pop-art decor and cool lounge scene. Fortunately, this is not a case of style over substance; the menu is as creative and imaginative as the interior design.

In Puerto Varas, **Merlin** may have closed, but the whimsical **Govinda Restaurant & Living Bar** (**© 65/233080;** www.govinda.cl) is proving a worthy replacement. The sleek service and charming atmosphere provide a warm backdrop for the delicious Peruvian accented cuisine, best appreciated with a cocktail or one of the Cork artisan beers served on tap.

About an hour from Puerto Montt, the **Cliffs Preserve** (**© 888/780-3011;** www.cliffspreserve.cl) is a prototype resort from a U.S.-based luxury community development company. The setting, nestled amid primary coastal rainforest, is idyllic. Active excursions, ranging from horseback riding to whale-watching trips, are arranged by qualified guides and naturalists. An additional 12 villas are under construction and are slated to open late in 2010.

One of the world's great small-scale luxury tourism operations, **Nomads of the Seas** (**© 866/790-4560** from the U.S., 2/414-4600 in Santiago; www.nomadsoftheseas.com) offers a once-in-a-lifetime cruise aboard the *Atmosphere.* The astronomical price tag grants you an exclusive tour to the farthest reaches of Patagonia; you will see only the best of the best. Nomads is planning ground operations in the Andes and Atacama in 2010.

For more information on this region, see chapter 10.

CHILOE

The much anticipated **Palafitos Hostel** (© **65/531008;** www.palafitohostel.com) has finally opened in the renowned Gamboa district; it perfectly embodies Castro's architectural style with a rich profusion of wood and picture windows that flood the public spaces with light, illuminating the contemporary art decking the walls.

For more information on this region, see chapter 11.

THE CARRETERA AUSTRAL

In May 2008, the town of **Chaiten** was engulfed by the violent eruption of the Chaiten volcano. The town has essentially been destroyed and, at press time, the government was still deciding how best to restore services. There are a couple of ferries that still visit the area and a handful of small inns have reopened, but tourism has ground to a halt. Tentative government plans to rebuild the road to Caleta Gonzalo from Chaiten should enable the southern half of Pumalin Park to reopen for the 2009–10 summer; however, new volcanic activity in February 2009 may cause further delays.

South of Coyhaique, the highway has been improving and tourist traffic has been increasing at a steady clip. Idyllic, off-the-beaten-path towns such as **Caleta Tortel** and **Villa O'Higgins** are finally getting their due.

For more information on this region, see chapter 12.

SOUTHERN PATAGONIA & TIERRA DEL FUEGO

Torres del Paine, Chile's crown jewel and most important national park, keeps drawing more and more visitors—in 2008 the park saw an average of 700 visitors a day, with more than 1,000 during the peak month of January. The most interesting new lodging option here is the **Patagonia Camp** (© **2/335-6898;** www.patagoniacamp.com) just outside the park, on the newly opened western access road, which cuts a half-hour off the trip from Puerto Natales into such places as the explora and Hosteria Lago Grey. Inside the park, the traditional **Hosteria Las Torres** (©/fax **61/363636;** www.lastorres.com) has expanded into a sprawling hotel complex complete with stables and a spa.

In **Punta Arenas,** the port area is undergoing a major renovation that will include a new hotel and casino, slated for late 2009. In the meantime, the new **Hotel Diego de Almagro** (© **61/208800;** www.dahoteles.com) is a good bet right on the shores of the Magellan Straight.

On the Argentine side of southern Patagonia, the tiny trekking hub of **El Chaltén** now has kayaking and multisport options, and a lovely little inn, **Senderos Hostería** (© **2962/493336;** www.senderoshosteria.com.ar). **El Calafate** continues to sprawl with many sub-standard hotels, but there are a few gems as well, such as the **Hotel Edenia** (© **2902/497021;** www.edeniahoteles.com.ar) and the luxurious **Casa los Sauces** (© **2902/495584;** www.casalossauces.com), owned by Argentina's President Cristina Fernandez de Kirchner.

On the island of Tierra del Fuego, **Ushuaia** continues to be a hub for cruise ships, both those rounding the tip of South America en route from Buenos Aires to Santiago, Chile and more expedition-style ones heading to Antarctica. There are, frankly, too many new hotels here, most of which are decidedly mediocre. However, **Los Cauquenes Resort** (© **2901/441300;** www.loscauquenes.com), right on the Beagle Channel, is a remarkable exception.

Across the channel in **Puerto Williams,** Chile, a new hotel called **Lakutaia** (© **61/621733;** www.lakutaia.cl) has started selling multiday, multisport adventures in the hard-to-access Isla Navarino.

EASTER ISLAND

On the world's most remote island, **explora's Posada de Mike Rapu** (**© 866/750-6699** in the U.S., 2/206-6060 in Santiago; www.explora.com), designed by Germán de Sol, opened in December 2007, replacing its smaller incarnation. With stunning, modernist architecture, refined cuisine, and day treks led by native Rapa Nui guides, the new explora offers the ultimate in luxury and opens up a world of unforgettable experiences.

The new owners of **Haka Kanu** (**© 32/255-1677**), previously known as El Jardin de Mau, have injected a more modern feel to the place. With its infectiously amiable ambience, it's a must-visit for mouthwatering sashimi.

For more information on this region, see chapter 14.

The Best of Chile

Chile's tremendous length covers a hugely diverse array of landscapes, from the desolate moonscape of Chile's Atacama Desert, to the fertile vineyards of the Central Valley, to the lush rainforests of the Lake District, down to the magnificent glaciers and peaks of Patagonia—not to mention more than 4,830km (3,000 miles) of coastline and Easter Island. It's truly mind-boggling to think of how many different experiences a traveler can have in just 2 or 3 weeks in this South American nation. The following is a list of the best Chile has to offer, including hotels, restaurants, and outdoor activities—so read on and start planning!

1 THE MOST UNFORGETTABLE TRAVEL EXPERIENCES

- **Discovering the Madcap Streets of Valparaíso:** The ramshackle, colorful, and sinuous streets of Valparaíso offer a walking tour unlike any other. Antique Victorians and tin-walled buildings cling to steep hillsides, roads and walkways wind haphazardly around the slopes like a rabbit's warren, and rickety funiculars lift visitors to the tops of hills. Beyond the fun of exploring this city, a handful of the region's best restaurants and boutique hotels can be found here, too. Poetic, chaotic, and enigmatic, Valparaíso embodies the soul of its most famous denizen, Pablo Neruda, like no other. See chapter 7.
- **Visiting the Valley of the Moon:** The barren beauty of the Atacama desert presents a surreal odyssey that plays out the sci-fi fantasies of every youth. As the sun rises and falls upon this rarified, ethereal landscape of timeless volcanoes, serrated mountains, and striated mesas, some of nature's most foreboding glories are reinvented again and again as the palette shifts from beige and golden brown to improbable pinks, blues, and greens, and silhouettes recast the imagination to thoughts of lost civilizations. See chapter 9.
- **From Ocean to the World's Highest Lake:** Only 200km (124 miles) separate the Pacific Ocean from Lake Chungará, one of the world's highest bodies of water. Head up the lush Lluta Valley, dramatically hemmed in by desert walls featuring giant geoglyphs centuries old. Time crunches and space can be dizzying as you ascend high altitude terrain quickly. Take it slow, immersing yourself in the wondrous sights, from colonial churches to perfect snowcapped volcanoes and the world's highest trees along with teeming wildlife. See chapter 9.
- **Stargazing in the Southern Hemisphere's Clearest Skies:** Northern Chile's dry skies are some of the clearest in the world, which is why so many international research teams have flocked to this region to erect multimillion-dollar observatories. There are plenty of stargazing opportunities for the amateur, too. The area around La Serena has several observatories geared to casual visitors. A couple of hotels,

including Elqui Domos in the Elqui Valley, have their own telescopes; or you can book a night tour with a degreed guide who can point out Southern Hemisphere constellations and other celestial wonders. The stunning Elqui Valley also offers a handful of wonderful accommodations choices geared to travelers looking to immerse themselves in outdoor pursuits and achieve holistic equanimity. See chapter 8.

- **Sailing the Quiet Fjords of Southern Chile:** Quietly sailing through the lush beauty of Chile's southern fjords is an accessible experience that all can afford. Budget travelers get a kick out of Navimag's 3-day sail between Puerto Montt and Puerto Natales, mid-range travelers enjoy Skorpios's programmed journeys to hot springs and the Chiloé coast, and the luxury market loves the freedom of a chartered yacht. These pristine, remote fjords rival the drama and beauty of Norway's fjords, and often the camaraderie that grows between passengers, in the end, is what makes for such a fulfilling trip. See chapter 11.
- **Traveling to the End of the World:** It's a tough, crunchy drive along 1,000km (620 miles) of gravel road, but that is precisely why Chile's "Southern Highway" has kept the crowds at bay. This natural wonderland, saturated in green and hemmed in by jagged, snowcapped peaks, offers a journey for those seeking to travel through some of Chile's most remote and stunning territory. It can be done in a variety of directions and segments, but you'll need a rental car unless you have a lot of time. There are plenty of great stops along the way, including rainforest walks, the idyllic mountain valley of Futaleufú, the wet primeval forests of Pumalín and Parque Queulat, Puyuhuapi and its thermal spas, and the untouched wilds around Lake General Carrera. Top it off with Mt. Fitz Roy and Torres del Paine near the southern tip of the continent, crossing through Argentina. See chapters 12 and 13.
- **Glimpsing the Cuernos and Torres del Paine:** It's the iconic image of Patagonia, one of the most stunning horizons on the planet. Many make the arduous journey to the end of the world without ever actually seeing the majestic horns and towers that make up the Paine Massif. Those who are fortunate enough to be awarded with even a quick glance through the stormy clouds will never, ever forget the sight. See chapter 13.
- **Exploring Easter Island:** The poster child of Chile, Easter Island or "Rapa Nui," is famous for its ethereal moai sculptures that defy hyperbole, regardless of how many tourist brochure images of them you've seen. Traveling to the world's most remote island—it's located farthest away from land than any other island—will make for an unforgettable odyssey. The entire island is a veritable living museum; it boasts two gorgeous beaches, phenomenal scuba diving in indigo blue water, wild horses, and a rich Polynesian culture that has survived against all odds. See chapter 14.

2 THE MOST CHARMING SMALL TOWNS

- **San Pedro de Atacama:** Quaint, unhurried, and built of adobe brick, San Pedro de Atacama has drawn travelers the world over who have come to experience the mellow charm and New Age spirituality that waft through the dusty roads of this town. Its location in the driest desert in the world makes for starry skies and breathtaking views of the weird and wonderful land formations that are just a stone's throw away. A distinctive collection of adobe hotels, which embody so effortlessly the concept of rustic chic, completes the town's lost pueblo ambience. See chapter 9.

- **Putre:** At a breathtaking 3,500m (11,500 ft.), splendidly backed by the double summits of the 5,775m (19,000-ft.) Taapacá Volcano, this tranquil Aymara village is a compelling vision of Andean culture. With 17th- to 19th-century stone portals flanking doors at many houses and a charming central square, it's a pretty place, reminiscent of pre-colonial Inca villages. Putre is the gateway to Chile's altiplano, and many tiny colonial villages nearby are still well off the beaten track. See chapter 9.
- **Pucón:** Not only was Pucón bestowed with a stunning location at the skirt of a smoking volcano and the shore of a glittering lake, but it's also Chile's self-proclaimed adventure capital, offering so many outdoor activities that you could keep busy for a week. But Pucón also has plenty of low-key activities if your idea of a vacation is plopping yourself down on a beach. You'll find everything you want and need without forfeiting small-town charm (that is, if you don't come with the Jan and Feb crowds). Rough-hewn wood restaurants, pubs, and crafts stores fill downtown, blending harmoniously with the forested surroundings. See chapter 10.
- **Frutillar & Puerto Varas:** Built by German immigrants who settled here in the early 1900s, these neighboring towns bear the clear stamp of Prussian order and workmanship, from the crisp lines of trees to the picturesque, shingled homes and tidy plazas ringed with roses. If you're lucky, you can still catch a few old-timers chatting in German over coffee and *küchen* (cake). Both towns feature a glorious view of Volcán Osorno and a lakefront address, a picture-postcard location that makes for an excellent boardwalk stroll. If that isn't enough, both towns also offer above-par lodging and a few of the best restaurants in the country. See chapter 10.
- **Futaleufú:** Nestled in a green valley surrounded by an amphitheater of craggy, snow-encrusted peaks, Futaleufú is made of colorful, clapboard homes and unpaved streets, and is, without a doubt, one of the prettiest villages in Chile. The population of 1,200 swells during the summer, when the hordes descend for rafting adventures on the nearby Class V river; but it hasn't changed the town's fabric too dramatically, and locals rarely saunter past a visitor without a tip of the hat and a *"Buenas tardes."* See chapter 12.
- **Caleta Tortel:** This remarkable little logging town near the very end of the Carretera Austral is an unreal, S-shaped place suspended somewhere between the steep slopes of a cypress forest and the pistachio green waters at the mouth of the Baker River. Wood-shingled houses cling precariously to the hillside, and cypress wood walkways and boats are the only way to get around. Cars are banished to a lot at the end of the Carretera Austral—even the fire truck is a boat, just like in Venice. Hiking trails and fishermen's boats can take you to even remoter spots, including glaciers. See chapter 12.
- **Puerto Natales:** Set on the stunning shores of the Ultima Esperanza fjord, with the rugged steppe to the east and giant mountains to the north and west, this Patagonian outpost is a modern mecca for adventurers. Nestled within the wind-ravaged streets are cozy cafes, lovely inns, funky bistros, and bookstores, and nature-lovers can head into or out of one of the finest pieces of wilderness in the world, nearby Torres del Paine National Park. You may think it's just a jumping-off point, but you'll find Natales to be friendly, warm, and rich with memory-making moments. See chapter 13.

3 THE BEST OUTDOOR ADVENTURES

- **Skiing & Snowboarding the Andes:** Taking to the mountains not only has a certain cachet but also, in terms of exhilarating terrain, convivial ambience, and affordability, the Andes deliver awesome skiing and snowboarding opportunities in Chile from June to October. **Portillo** has been around for 54 years, and its steep chutes still raise fear in the hearts of those about to make the descent. **Valle Nevado** and **Termas de Chillán** have a full infrastructure that includes state-of-the-art spas. And, the après ski scene in the Andes is certainly ebullient. Heliskiing companies and **Ski Arpa,** a Snowcat-serviced resort, can get you to terrain where the only living thing you'll see is a condor sailing through the sky. See chapter 7.
- **Follow in Darwin's footsteps and hike to the summit of Parque Nacional La Campana:** Less than an hour's drive from Santiago, the precipitous lookout point of this lush national park was immortalized by Charles Darwin in *Voyage of the Beagle;* Darwin eulogized that never had he enjoyed a day so much than the one spent atop this mountain. It is a challenging but infinitely rewarding 8-hour trek to reach the summit at 5,905 feet. There are also several tamer trails which offer the unique opportunity to trek through dense concentrations of Palma Chilema, the world's southernmost species of palm tree. See chapter 7.
- **Summiting a Volcano:** There's something more thrilling about summiting a volcano than any old mountain, especially when the volcano threatens to blow at any given time. Chile is home to a large share of the world's volcanoes, some of which are perfectly conical and entirely feasible to climb, such as **Volcán Villarrica** in Pucón and **Volcán Osorno** near Puerto Varas. Active Villarrica is a relatively moderate climb to the gaseous crater, followed by a fun slide on your rear down a human toboggan chute. Osorno offers a more technical climb, roping up for a crampon-aided walk past glacier crevasses and caves. In the far north, perfect conical volcanoes include **Parinacota,** east of Arica, and **Licancabur,** near San Pedro, both on the border with Bolivia. And in southern Aysén, ice fields around **San Valentín** beckon adventurous climbers. See chapters 9, 10, and 12.
- **Rafting & Kayaking the Futaleufú River or Pacific Ocean:** With churning river sections that are frightening enough to be dubbed "Hell" and "The Terminator," the Class V Futaleufú River, or the "Fu," as it's known, is solemnly revered by rafting and kayaking enthusiasts around the world as one of the most difficult to descend. A little too much white-knuckle excitement for your nerves? Rafting companies offer short-section rafting trips on the Futaleufú and down the tamer, crystalline waters of the neighboring Espolón River—kayak schools use this stretch, too. The scenery here redefines mountain beauty. An alternative is sea kayaking along the Patagonian channels or around Isla Damas, at the southern fringe of the Atacama Desert, renowned for their teeming wildlife; see chapters 10 and 12.
- **Casting a Line for Jumbo Trout:** Chile has literally thousands of spots for fly-fishing, from the Lake District all the way down to the sub-Antarctic wilderness of Tierra del Fuego. Above all, the many lodges along the remote Carretera Austral draw fishing aficionados from

around the world to rivers and lakes full of trout, weighing in from a pound to the hefty 8- to 10-pounders around Villa O'Higgins at the end of the road. Remember that the farther south you go, the shorter the season gets. See chapters 5 and 12.

- **Trekking in Torres del Paine:** Torres del Paine is one of the most spectacular national parks in the world, with hundreds of kilometers of trails through ever-changing landscapes of jagged peaks and one-of-a-kind granite spires, undulating meadows, milky turquoise lakes and rivers, and mammoth glaciers. The park has a well-organized system of *refugios* and campgrounds, but there are also several hotels, and visitors can access the park's major highlights on a day hike. See chapter 13.

4 THE BEST SPLURGE HOTELS

- **Ritz-Carlton,** Santiago (✆ **2/470-8500;** www.ritzcarlton.com): If old-world grandeur, superlative service, and flawless attention to detail are at the top of your list, you'll want to stay at the Ritz. This hotel lives up to its luxurious brand name with such amenities as a heated pool (a novelty in Chile) and serene spa, plus a convenient location close to some of the city's finest restaurants. The glass-domed top floor affords beautiful panoramas of the city and the Andes. For the ultimate in decadence, soak in a bath of carmenère wine, prepared by your very own bath butler, then head down to the butch bar, brimming with brass, leather, and mahogany, which offers an unholy alliance of top shelf liquors, cigars, and delectable snacks well into the early hours. See p. 92.
- **Hotel del Mar,** Viña del Mar (✆ **32/250-0800;** www.hoteldelmar.cl.): Viña's new Sheraton pales next to the classic Hotel del Mar, with its central location, regal Greco-Roman decor, and Monte Carlo–style casino. Best of all, everything's within reach, including the beach, just a hop across the street. For families, there's a children's center and proximity to kid-pleasing carriage rides and ice cream stands. See p. 128.
- **Casa Higueras,** Valparaíso (✆ **2/657-3950;** www.hotelcasahigueras.cl): Clinging to a hillside above the emblematic city, this restored mansion is now a sumptuous boutique hotel that defies hyperbole: gorgeous decor, luxurious bathrooms, views, service, gourmet cuisine, and the only hotel swimming pool in town. See p. 147.
- **Hacienda Los Lingues,** near San Fernando (✆ **2/431-0510;** www.loslingues.com): For pure old-world faded grandeur, step back in time to the 17th century with a visit to one of Chile's oldest hotels, located in the rural heartland of the Central Valley south of Santiago. Los Lingues has been in the same family's hands for more than 400 years, and each venerable room has been lovingly and individually decorated, with personal touches such as family antiques, photos, and other collectibles. If you are looking for high class and idiosyncratic character—not a high-end contemporary resort—this antique property will live long in the memory. See p. 173.
- **Clos Apalta Casitas,** Santa Cruz (✆ **72/321-803;** www.closapalta.cl): If money is no object, a couple of nights staying in one of the four deluxe *casitas* at Clos Apalta's state-of-the-art winery are the perfect indulgence for any oenophile. Nestled on a gentle slope high above the expansive Apalta Valley in the Colchagua Valley, this is one of the country's

most exclusive lodgings. Each secluded, one-room cottage is pared-down yet sophisticated, and an adjoining deck provides what is certainly the best view from any lodging unit in Chile's wine country. Horseback riding, gourmet meals, wine tastings, and tours, and a bottle of Chile's finest wine are included in the package. See p. 176.

- **Hotel Awasi,** San Pedro de Atacama (© **2/233-9641;** www.awasi.cl): This luxury newcomer to the all-inclusive scene in San Pedro de Atacama combines effortless style, gracious service, and superlative amenities in a rustic adobe setting that blends harmoniously with the landscape. With your own private tour guide and 4×4 vehicle at your disposal, you are guaranteed the freedom to experience this stunning area without compromise. With one of the finest chefs in the region at the helm in the kitchen, dining under the stars doesn't get much better than this. See p. 220.
- **Hotel Antumalal,** Pucón (© **45/441011;** www.antumalal.cl): This low-slung, Bauhaus-influenced country inn is one of the most special places to lodge in Chile. Located high above the shore of Lake Villarrica and a sloping, terraced garden, the hotel literally sinks into its surroundings, offering a cozy ambience and an excellent view of the evening sunset. A warm welcome and a room with no lock are all part of making you feel at home. The inn has outstanding cuisine, too. See p. 261.
- **Hacienda Tres Lagos** (© **2/333-4122** in Santiago; www.haciendatreslagos.com): Nestled near the southwest corner of spectacular Lake General Carrera, this *estancia*-style resort has a lake—and beach—of its own. Accommodations vary from hotel suites in the main lodge to family-oriented, independent *cabañas* to romantic yet very modern luxury apartments, but all share the lakefront view of Lago Negro and the Patagonian Andes beyond, and all are finely decorated with great attention to detail. As befits its location, it offers plenty of outdoor activities on foot, horseback, boats, or farther afield to the Tamango Nature Preserve to try to glimpse the endangered huemul deer. See p. 360.
- **explora Patagonia Hotel Salto Chico,** Torres del Paine National Park (© **866/750-6699** in the U.S., or 2/206-6060 in Santiago; www.explora.com): This is the hotel that put Torres del Paine on the map and created a new sense of outdoor luxury, where great hiking and divine service go hand in hand. And while $600 (£400) per person per night may be tough to swallow, consider that your stay here includes everything from superb bilingual guides, hikes, and horseback rides to fresh-baked cookies, an excellent wine list, and a spa. Plush beds, soaker tubs, and all meals are also included. See chapter 13.

5 THE BEST MODERATELY PRICED HOTELS

- **Hotel Orly,** Santiago (© **2/231-8947;** www.hotelorly.cl): This is my all-around favorite for reasonable prices; an absolutely ideal location near the Metro, shops, and restaurants; cheerful service; and coziness. Like the Vilafranca (below), this former mansion has rooms of varying sizes, so book accordingly. See p. 90.
- **Vilafranca Petit Hotel,** Santiago (© **2/232-1413;** www.vilafranca.cl): Santiago's hectic pace slows down when you step into this delightful B&B. Steeped in French Provençal decor, this former

home has been converted into a boutique hotel that is economically priced and a cozy place to stay; note that some doubles are tight. See p. 91.

- **Hotel Agora,** Viña del Mar (✆ **32/269-4669;** www.hotelagora.cl): There is a plethora of midrange lodging options in Viña, but this Miami-style, art-deco confection has fresh, contemporary decor, a great location, and gracious hosts. The hotel is tucked away on a street just 3 blocks from the beach. See p. 135.
- **El Puesto,** Puerto Río Tranquilo (✆ **2/196-4555;** www.elpuesto.cl): One of Patagonia's top places to stay is this three-room boutique hotel in tiny Puerto Río Tranquilo, on Lake General Carrera. While not directly on the lakeshore, family-run El Puesto is the perfect place to relax after a day of wilderness activities, from hiking on glaciers, visits to the beautiful Marble Cathedral and Chapel in the lake, to soaring through forest canopies. The whole place exudes a cozy, light atmosphere. See p. 360.
- **Indigo,** Puerto Natales (✆ **61/413609**): To say this former backpackers' hangout has been transformed is a major understatement. It's a little too big to call it a boutique hotel, yet it is a jewel indeed, from top-floor whirlpool and sauna to the clean-cut intimacy of the rooms, accessed through a spider's web of eucalyptus, black steel, and concrete walkways. While it also has the finest views of the Last Hope Sound and glaciers beyond, it's the most convenient place for a stroll into town. The previous, rickety backpackers' haunt—still charmingly clad in weather-beaten shingles—now boasts a very contemporary ground-floor restaurant and second-story lounge in airy, pale woods. See p. 383.

6 THE BEST DINING EXPERIENCES

- **Aquí Está Coco,** Santiago (✆ **2/235-8649**): This place is wildly popular with foreign visitors, with good reason: The kitschy atmosphere is as fun as the food is mouthwatering. The restaurant is spread over two levels of a 140-year-old home and festooned with oddball and nautically themed gadgets and curios. Arrive a little early and enjoy an aperitif in the cavelike, brick cellar lounge. Seafood is the specialty here. See p. 101.
- **Astrid y Gastón,** Santiago (✆ **2/650-9125**): Astrid y Gastón is the best restaurant in Santiago—the reason you'll often need to make reservations days in advance. The chef uses the finest ingredients, combined so that each plate bursts with flavor and personality; here, you'll find French, Spanish, Peruvian, and Japanese influences, as well as impeccable service, an on-site sommelier, and a lengthy wine list. If you can afford it, don't miss dining here. See p. 101.
- **Sukalde,** Santiago (✆ **2/665-1017**). For adventurous diners who are not averse to inhaling their food and who revel in all things fusion, Suklade offers a culinary odyssey like no other in Santiago. Chef Matias Paloma graduated from the hallowed El Bulli in Spain to create his own dynamic menu, and it's made the critics froth by combining interesting and unexpected ingredients with aplomb. See p. 102.
- **Bar Liguria,** Santiago (✆ **2/235-7914**): The two Bar Ligurias in Providencia are equally lively and loads of fun, often filling up before 10pm and spilling out onto tables on the sidewalk. Everyone loves the Ligurias: actors,

artists, businessmen, and locals converge here in a vibrant mélange that always feels celebratory. The Chilean fare is hearty and delicious, and the sharply dressed waiters rushing to and fro provide quick, attentive service. See p. 103.

- **Pasta e Vino,** Valparaíso (© **32/249-6187):** There's no view of the city harbor, but the mouthwatering cuisine at Pasta e Vino makes this restaurant one of the top five in Chile—which is why you'll often need to book days, even weeks, in advance. With its limited opening hours—which serves to heighten its exclusivity all the more—it really is the Holy Grail of dining in Valparaíso. Pasta e Vino virtually launched the culinary revolution in Valparaíso, offering a warm, intimate ambience, with brick walls and wooden tables, gourmet Italian cuisine that is consistently good, a well-chosen wine list, and owner-attended service. See p. 149.
- **El Chiringuito,** Zapallar (© **33/741024**): El Chiringuito, located in the upscale beach enclave Zapallar, is surely the most famous restaurant along Chile's Central Coast, and with good reason. Is there any more delightful way to spend a sunny day than to dine alfresco on seafood while watching the waves crash and pelicans swoop about? Alternatively, head south to the tiny harbor at Maitencillo for ultrafresh shellfish sold at simple seafood stalls near the beach. See p. 154.
- **Maracuyá,** Arica (© **58/227600**): The Azapa and Lluta valleys are Chile's tropical fruit orchards, and this restaurant makes ample use of its namesake, the passion fruit (*maracuyá,* in Spanish). For seafood, it's Arica's best choice, with fruit flavored sweet-and-sour sauces for the varied choices on the menu. Couple this with its location, perched in a villa almost over the water on a rocky stretch of coastline near the Morro, and you have one fine restaurant indeed. See p. 234.
- **Latitude 42,** at the Yan Kee Way Lodge, Ensenada (© **65/212030**): Worth the drive from Puerto Varas, this gorgeous restaurant boasts superb views of the Volcán Osorno (Osorno Volcano) and delectable cuisine served in a beautiful dining room. The talented chef uses locally grown produce to create imaginative dishes that come as close to nouvelle cuisine as you're ever going to get in southern Chile. Service is impeccable and there's a cigar bar and a cellar for wine tasting, as well. See p. 300.
- **Última Esperanza,** Puerto Natales (© **61/411391**): Few places in Patagonia compare with this old favorite in Puerto Natales that boasts a roughly 20-year tradition. The decor is nothing to write home about, but restaurants are about food, right? Última Esperanza has the best food in Magallanes, even beating out its rivals in the big city of Punta Arenas. It makes the best of Puerto Natales' location—on the ocean but near Patagonian ranches—to combine meats and seafood in a mean *curanto,* also serving such fine fish as conger eel and the renowned *centolla,* or king crab. See p. 385.

7 THE BEST MUSEUMS

- **Palacio de la Real Audiencia/Museo Histórico Nacional,** Santiago (© **2/411-7010**): The National History Museum holds a superb collection of more than 70,000 colonial-era pieces, from furniture to suits of armor to home appliances. This fascinating grab bag of artifacts is laid out in 16 display rooms within the lemon-colored, neoclassical Palacio de la Real, built in

1807 and the historic site of the first Chilean congressional session. The museum will give you insight into the history of the lives of Chileans, and it's conveniently located on the Plaza de las Armas. See p. 108.

- **Museo Chileno de Arte Precolombino,** Santiago (✆ **2/688-7348**): More than 1,500 objects related to indigenous life and culture throughout the Americas make the Pre-Columbian Museum one of the best in Santiago. Artifacts include textiles, metals, paintings, figurines, and ceramics from Mexico to Chile. All objects are handsomely lit and mounted throughout seven exhibition rooms that are divided into the Mesoamerica, Intermedia, Andina, and Surandina regions of Latin America. The museum is housed in the old Royal Customs House built in 1807. If you need a break, there's a patio with a small cafe and a good bookstore to browse. See p. 110.
- **Iglesia, Convento y Museo de San Francisco,** Santiago (✆ **2/638-3238**): One step into this museum and you'll feel like you've been instantly beamed out of downtown Santiago. This is the oldest standing building in Santiago and home to a serene garden patio where the only sounds are a trickling fountain and the cooing of pigeons. The museum boasts 54 paintings depicting the life and death of San Francisco, one of the largest and best-conserved displays of 17th-century art in South America. On the altar of the church, you'll see the famous *Vírgen del Socorro,* the first Virgin Mary icon in Chile. See p. 112.
- **Casa Pablo Neruda,** Isla Negra (✆ **35/461-2844;** www.fundacionneruda.org): This was Nobel Prize–winning poet Pablo Neruda's favorite home, and although his other residences in Valparaíso and Santiago are as eccentric and absorbing, this is the best preserved of the three. The home is stuffed with books by his favorite authors and the whimsical curios, trinkets, and toys he collected during his travels around the world, including African masks, ships in bottles, butterflies, and more. The museum can be found in Isla Negra, south of Valparaíso. See p. 195.
- **Museo de Colchagua,** Santa Cruz (✆ **72/821050;** www.museocolchagua.cl): In terms of historical range and scope, this is arguably Chile's best museum. You'll find a stunning collection of everything from pre-Hispanic objects throughout the Americas and local Indian artifacts to Spanish conquest–era helmets and artillery and *huaso* ponchos, and more. This museum is a not-to-be-missed stop while visiting the wine country. Unbelievably, the museum is really the private collection of a local man who earned his fortune in bomb manufacturing and arms dealing, and because he cannot leave the country (and risk arrest by the FBI), he has reinvested in projects such as this in his hometown. See p. 178.
- **Museo Arqueológico Padre le Paige,** San Pedro de Atacama (✆ **55/851002**): This little museum will come as an unexpected surprise for its wealth of indigenous artifacts, such as "Miss Chile," a leathered mummy whose skin, teeth, and hair are mostly intact, as well as a display of skulls that show the creepy ancient custom of cranial deformation practiced by the elite as a status symbol. The Atacama Desert is the driest in the world, and this climate has produced some of the best-preserved artifacts in Latin America, on view here. See p. 217.
- **Museo Arqueológico San Miguel de Azapa,** Arica (✆ **58/205555;** www.uta.cl/masma): For anyone with even a minimal interest in history and archaeology, this small museum belongs to the top attractions in the Western

Hemisphere. Around 5,000 B.C.—long before even the Egyptians began to mummify their dead—the Chinchorro culture developed a technique of its own to preserve bodies for eternity. The displays outline the entire history of pre-Columbian cultures in the Arica area through Tihuanaco and the Inca periods. The museum also has a section devoted to recent and contemporary Aymara culture in the area. See p. 232.

- **Museo Regional de Magallanes,** Punta Arenas (✆ **61/248840**): The Museo Regional de Magallanes is the former home of one of Patagonia's wealthiest families. Tapestries, furniture from France, Italian marble fireplaces, hand-painted wallpaper—this veritable palace is a testament to the Braun family's insatiable need to match European elite society. Several small salons are devoted to ranching and maritime history, but the grandeur of this museum is really the reason for a visit. See p. 371.
- **Museo Salesiano Maggiorino Borgatello,** Punta Arenas (✆ **61/221001**): There's so much on display here that you could spend more than an hour wandering and marveling at the hodgepodge collection of archaeological artifacts, photo exhibits, petroleum production interpretative exhibitions, ranch furniture, industrial gadgets, and, best of all, the macabre collection of stuffed and mounted regional wildlife gathered by a Salesian priest. See p. 370.

8 THE BEST AFTER-DARK FUN

- **Barrio Bellavista,** Santiago: Santiago's bohemian district features various sultry jazz clubs that offer quality lineups of international and local talent. **La Casa en el Aire** (✆ **2/735-6680;** www.lacasaenelaire.cl) and **El Perseguidor** (✆ **2/777-6763;** www.elperseguidor.cl) are the city's current jazz hot spots, with nightly performances starting around 11pm and a smooth, romantic candlelit ambience. Or stop by the long-time favorite **Club de Jazz** (✆ **2/326-5065;** www.clubdejazz.cl), where Louis Armstrong once played and now crooning legends perform to a crowd of impassioned jazz devotees. See p. 122 and 123.
- **Catedral,** Santiago (✆ **2/664-3048**): The chic Catedral is one of the capital's most ebullient bars, and it's where the gilded and glamorous gather to preen and strut. Arrive early in the evening to claim one of the coveted outdoor seats on the rooftop patio. See p. 98.
- **Club de Jazz,** Coquimbo (✆ **51/288784**): La Serena's prosaic neighbor, Coquimbo, happens to have the best live jazz bar in Chile, outside of perhaps Santiago, home to another Club de Jazz. Locals would claim that this Club de Jazz, located in the attractive enclave of Barrio Inglés, is the nation's top jazz venue, however, with stellar musicians and a raw and authentic ambience that is lacking in the capital's version. See p. 123.
- **Mamas & Tapas,** Pucón (✆/fax **45/449002**): Graze on tapas and appreciate the excellent soundtrack at Pucón's number-one bar, which is never short on atmosphere or musical talent, often courtesy of hip local DJs during the peak summer season. See p. 267.
- **Termas Los Pozones,** Pucón (no phone): The natural setting, 24-hour schedule, and cheap prices of Los Pozones hot springs in Pucón prove a decadent lure for young Chileans and travelers who are keen to keep in a party spirit after the discos have closed up shop for the night. See p. 267.

- **Mama Rosa Bar at Indigo Hotel,** Puerto Natales (✆ 61/413609): After a day out in the blustering weather of Patagonia, slip behind the tall iron door into this converted hostel for a pisco sour (choose from 15 different options), some cool tunes, and warm vibes. Through giant windows, watch the sun set behind the fjords and mountains in the distance and toast the sense of adventure that just oozes through the air here. See p. 383.
- **Topatangi, Hanga Roa** (✆ **32/255-1554**): From Thursday to Saturday nights in Hanga Roa, the dance floor at Topatangi Pub floods with Rapa Nui 20- and 30-something island girls and guys grooving to the sounds of local bands that jam everything from traditional sounds to '70s American rock. Don't go before 10pm and don't leave before sunrise. See p. 442.

2

Chile in Depth

With its desert northern fringes, its toes dipped in the Antarctic, and its slender core spliced by the serrated peaks of the iconic Andes, Chile is a landmass which is at once as absurd to contemplate as it is extreme to experience. Unfathomable in its breathtaking diversity, which ranges from crystal blue lakes to majestic mountains, rugged wilderness, and planes that carpet infinitely lush vineyards and ethereal desert-scapes, Chile presents any traveler with an epic, stirring journey.

Unlike its more edgy neighbors, Chile also has a solid democracy and strong economy. Its excellent transport infrastructure, fine hotels, gourmet restaurants, and warm and inclusive denizens invite camaraderie at every turn and facilitate a smooth travel adventure. Fans of culture will have a surplus of sophisticated options in such cities as Santiago and Valparaíso. Adrenaline junkies will have plenty of chances to travel off the beaten path by rafting one of the wildest rivers in the world, hiking the sublime towers of Torres del Paine, or climbing the peaks of Parque Nacional Campana.

What follows is a historical and cultural introduction to a country where adventure, beauty, and hospitality await the receptive traveler.

1 CHILE TODAY

The Chilean economy is the strongest in Latin America, both admired and scorned by its envious neighbors. Chile is rich in natural resources—copper mining is booming with China's demand for the raw product—and forestry, salmon harvesting, agriculture, high-quality wines, and tourism are also economic heavyweights. But the country still has a long way to go to solve social problems such as poverty and lack of education. The minimum wage is still less than $300 (£200) a month, and even the country's top universities come under fire for not meeting international standards.

The global financial meltdown in 2008 presented serious challenges for Chile's economy. With the fall in commodity prices and a weakening peso, a slowdown in growth took its toll on many sectors of Chile's economy. In the municipal elections in October 2008, Chile's governing center-left Concertación coalition, which has ruled Chile ever since the end of General Augusto Pinochet's dictatorship in 1990 (see "Looking Back at Chile" later for info), faced its first-ever defeat. Countering South America's steady drift to the left, the center-right opposition, Alliance, won 41% of the vote for mayors, which was sufficient to win 8 of the 14 regional capitals. Riding high on the crest of victory, Alliance leaders frothed that their success augurs well for a presidential win in December 2009.

One-third of Chile's 16 million people live in the Santiago metropolis alone. This disproportionate centralization in a country that stretches 4,200km (2,600 miles) from north to south often leads to accusations that the government does more for the local populace than for residents in far-flung locales such as Punta Arenas.

About 90% of the population is *mestizo,* a mix of indigenous and European blood that includes Spanish, German (in the Lake District), and Croatian (in southern Patagonia). Other nationalities, such as Italian, Russian, and English, have contributed a smaller influence. In general, visitors will find that the average Chilean looks like a southern European. Indigenous groups such as the Aymara in the northern desert and the Mapuche in the Lake District still exist in large numbers, although nothing compared to their size before the Spanish conquest. It is estimated that there are more than a half-million Mapuches, many of whom live on poverty-stricken *reducciones* (literally "reductions"), where they continue to use their language and carry on their customs—if traveling through those areas you can't miss their trademark silver and nickel jewelry. In southern Chile and Tierra del Fuego, indigenous groups such as the Alacalufe and Yagan have been diminished to only a few people, and some, such as the Patagonian Ona, have been completely extinguished.

Defying the stereotype of the flamboyant and eternally gregarious Latino, Chileans tend to be more conservative than their Latin American counterparts, arguably the result of Chile's unique geography, cut off by the Andes and the Pacific Ocean. Elite Chileans have been accused of looking to the outside world for comparisons rather than looking within themselves for original inspiration in everything from architecture to fashion to cuisine. In spite of this, Chileans are enormously patriotic, evidenced by celebrations during the multiday festival surrounding Independence Day, when Chileans festoon streets and vehicles with Chilean flags and decorations in a display of national pride. In rural areas and small towns outside Santiago, Chileans are usually warmly affectionate and hospitable to strangers.

Though not inherently a racist country (there is little racial diversity here), Chile suffers from an unhealthy amount of classism. The elite are known as *cuicos,* and the poor as *rotos* or *ordinarios.* Chile's economy, which was booming until the 2008 meltdown, has produced a burgeoning middle class, evidenced by jam-packed shopping malls and new condominium buildings springing up around Santiago, yet few talented Chileans from middle-class and poor families stand a chance at rising to the top without the right connections, known as *pituto.*

Given the provinciality of Chileans and the country's former era of dictatorship and censorship, Chileans have created an art form out of gossiping; no topic, it seems, is out of bounds for a good dish, invented or real. Chileans also tend to be indirect: When asking for directions, you may find that Chileans use constructive guesswork, often sending you on a false path, rather than admitting that they can't help.

Most Chileans strongly value the family unit, and they love kids. Unless a young adult marries or travels outside his or her hometown to study, most leave home at a late age. It is common to see a young adult who is 25 or 27 still at home and without any pressure to leave. Because kids and young adults are coddled by their mothers and maids (especially males), travelers often remark that Chilean young adults seem more immature than their foreign counterparts. Because young adults live at home, you'll also see heaps of amorous couples kissing and strolling through parks. Most Chileans marry before 30 and have kids shortly thereafter, the reason why slightly less than half the population is under 25. Divorce was only recently pronounced legal, with Chile being the last Latin American country to grant dissolution of marriage.

Chilean Customs

Chileans generally save shorts and T-shirts for weekends or for wearing in casual, outdoorsy oriented towns like Pucón or while at the beach. If you're looking to fit in almost everywhere, skip the Hawaiian shirt.

Chileans tend to appreciate formalities, so always greet a Chilean with a *"Buenas días"* or *"Buenas tardes."* When two women, or a man and a woman, greet each other in a social setting, they do so with one kiss on the right cheek. Men greet each other with a handshake, or with a quick hug if they are intimate friends or family. The same is true in business, but Chileans understand that some North Americans are uncomfortable with this and will greet you with a handshake if they know you're a foreigner. Like most Latin Americans, Chileans require less personal space when talking to another person; it can feel a bit awkward, but try not to step away.

Punctuality is appreciated in business settings, but don't be surprised if your Chilean guest shows up 30 to 45 minutes late for a dinner party. In contrast to North America, the do-it-yourself spirit is not very esteemed in Chile; rather, your ability to hire help to do it for you is what people value. Live-in or daily maids are very common in Chile, which means that, as a guest staying with a well-to-do family, you are not expected to make your bed or help around the house. When entering a room, you are expected to greet everyone individually or as a group.

2 LOOKING BACK AT CHILE

EARLY HISTORY

Little is known of Chile's history before the arrival of the Spaniards. Archaeologists have reconstructed what they can of Chile's indigenous history from artifacts found at burial sites, in ancient villages, and in forts. Because of this, much more is known about the northern cultures of Chile than their southern counterparts: The north's extraordinarily arid climate has preserved, and preserved well, objects as fragile as 2,000-year-old mummies. Northern tribes, such as the Atacama, developed a culture that included the production of ceramic pottery, textiles, and objects made of gold and silver, but for the most part, early indigenous cultures in Chile were small, scattered tribes that fished and cultivated simple crops. The primitive, nomadic tribes of Patagonia and Tierra del Fuego never developed beyond a society of hunters and gatherers because severe weather and terrain prevented them from ever developing an agricultural system.

In the middle of the 15th century, the great Inca civilization pushed south in a tremendous period of expansion. Although the Incas were able to subjugate tribes in the north, they never made it past the fierce Mapuche Indians in southern Chile.

THE SPANISH INVADE

In 1535, and several years after Spaniards Diego de Almagro and Francisco Pizarro had successfully conquered the Inca Empire in Peru, the conquistadors turned their attention south after hearing tales of riches that lay in what is today Chile. Already flushed with wealth garnered from Incan gold and silver, an inspired Diego de Almagro and more than 400 men set off on what would become a disastrous journey that left many dead from exposure and famine. De Almagro found nothing of the fabled riches, and he retreated to Peru.

Three years later, a distinguished officer of Pizarro's army, Spanish-born Pedro de Valdivia, secured permission to settle the land south of Peru in the name of the Spanish crown. Valdivia left with just 10 soldiers and little ammunition, but his band grew to 150 by the time he reached the Aconcagua Valley, where he founded Santiago de la Nueva Extremadura on February 12, 1541. Fire, Indian attacks, and famine beset the colonists, but the town nonetheless held firm. Valdivia succeeded in founding several other outposts, including Concepción, La Serena, and Valdivia, but like the Incas before him, he was unable to overcome the Mapuche Indians south of the Río Biobío. In a violent Mapuche rebellion, Valdivia was captured and suffered a gruesome death, sending frightened colonists north. The Mapuche tribe effectively defended its territory for the next 300 years.

Early Chile was a colonial backwater of no substantive interest to Spain, although Spain did see to the development of a feudal land-owning system called an *encomienda.* Prominent Spaniards were issued a large tract of land and an *encomienda,* or a group of Indian slaves that the landowner was charged with caring for and converting to Christianity. Thus rose Chile's traditional and nearly self-supporting *hacienda,* known as a *latifundo,* as well as a rigid class system that defined the population. At the top were the *peninsulares* (those born in Spain), followed by the *criollos* (Creoles, or Spaniards born in the New World). Next down on the ladder were *mestizos* (a mix of Spanish and Indian blood), followed by Indians themselves. As the indigenous population succumbed to disease, the *latifundo* system replaced slaves with rootless *mestizos who were* willing, or forced, to work for a miserable wage. This form of land ownership would define Chile for centuries to come, and traces of this antiquated system hold firm even in modern Chilean businesses today.

CHILE GAINS INDEPENDENCE

Chile tasted independence for the first time during Napoleon's invasion of Spain in 1808 and the subsequent sacking of King Ferdinand VII, whom Napoleon replaced with his own brother. On September 18, 1810, leaders in Santiago agreed that the country would be self-governed until the king was reinstated as the rightful ruler of Spain. Although the self-rule was intended as a temporary measure, this date is now celebrated as Chile's independence day.

Semi-independence did not satisfy many *criollos,* and soon thereafter Jose Miguel Carrera, the power-hungry son of a wealthy *criollo* family, appointed himself leader and stated that the government would not answer to Spain or the viceroy of Peru. But Carrera was an ineffective and controversial leader, and it was soon determined that one of his generals, Bernardo O'Higgins, would prove more adept at shaping Chile's future. Loyalist troops from Peru took advantage of the struggle between the two and crushed the fragile independence movement, sending Carrera, O'Higgins, and their troops fleeing to Argentina. This became known as the Spanish "reconquest." Across the border in Mendoza, O'Higgins met José de San Martín, an Argentine general who had already been plotting the liberation of South America. San Martín sought to liberate Chile first and then launch a sea attack on the viceroyalty seat in Peru from

Chile's shore. In 1817, O'Higgins and San Martín crossed the Andes with their well-prepared troops and quickly defeated Spanish forces in Chacabuco, securing the capital. In April 1818, San Martín's army triumphed in the bloody battle of Maipú, and full independence from Spain was won. An assembly of prominent leaders elected O'Higgins as Supreme Director of Chile, but discontent within his ranks and with landowners forced him to quit office and spend his remaining years in exile in Peru.

THE WAR OF THE PACIFIC

The robust growth of the nation during the mid- to late 1800s saw the development of railways and roads that connected previously remote regions with Santiago. The government began promoting European immigration to populate these regions, and it was primarily Germans who accepted, settling and clearing farms around the Lake District.

Growing international trade boosted Chile's economy, but it was the country's northern mines, specifically nitrate mines, that held the greatest economic promise. Border disputes with Bolivia in this profitable region ensued until a treaty was signed giving Antofagasta to Bolivia in exchange for low taxes on Chilean mines. Bolivia did an about-face and hiked taxes, sparking the War of the Pacific that pitted allies Peru and Bolivia against Chile in the fight for the nitrate fields. The odds were against Chile, but the country's well-trained troops were a force to reckon with. The war's turning point came with the capture of Peru's major warship, the *Huáscar.* Chilean troops invaded Peru and pushed on until they had captured the capital, Lima. With Chile as the final victor, both countries signed treaties that conceded Peru's Tarapacá region and Antofagasta to Chile that, incredibly, increased Chile's size by one-third with nitrate- and silver-rich land, and cut Bolivia off from the coast. More than a century later, Bolivia and Peru are still rallying against the Chilean government for wider access to the coastal waters off northern Chile.

THE MILITARY DICTATORSHIP

No political event defines current-day Chile better than the country's former military dictatorship. In 1970, Dr. Salvador Allende, Chile's first socialist president, was narrowly voted into office. Allende vowed to improve the lives of Chile's poorer citizens by instituting a series of radical changes that might redistribute the nation's lopsided wealth. Although the first year showed promising signs, Allende's reforms ultimately sent the country spiraling into economic ruin. Large estates were seized by the government and by independent, organized groups of peasants to be divided among rural workers, many of them uneducated and unprepared. Major industries were nationalized, but productivity lagged, and the falling price of copper reduced the government's fiscal intake. With spending outpacing income, the country's deficit soared. Worst of all, uncontrollable inflation and price controls led to shortages, and Chileans were forced to wait in long lines to buy basic goods.

Meanwhile, the United States (led by Richard Nixon and Henry Kissinger) was closely monitoring the situation in Chile. With anti-Communist sentiment running high in the U.S. government, the CIA allocated $8 million (£5.3 million) to undermine the Allende government by funding right-wing opposition and supporting a governmental takeover.

On September 11, 1973, military forces led by General Augusto Pinochet toppled Allende's government with a dramatic coup d'état. Military tanks rolled through the streets and jets dropped bombs on the presidential palace. Inside, Allende refused to surrender and accept an offer to be exiled. After delivering an emotional radio speech, Allende took his own life.

Wealthy Chileans who had lost much under Allende celebrated the coup as an economic and political salvation. But nobody was prepared for the brutal repression that would haunt Chile for the next 17 years. Pinochet shut down congress, banned political parties, and censored the news media, imposed a strict curfew, and inexperienced military officers took over previously nationalized industries and universities. Pinochet snuffed out his adversaries by rounding up and killing more than 3,000 citizens and torturing 28,000 political activists, journalists, professors, and any other "subversives." Thousands more fled the country.

Pinochet set out to rebuild the economy using Milton Freeman–inspired free-market policies that included selling off nationalized industries, curtailing government spending, reducing import tariffs, and eliminating price controls. From 1976 to 1981, the economy grew at such a pace that it was hailed as the "Chilean Miracle," but the miracle did nothing to address the country's high unemployment rate, worsening social conditions, and falling wages. More importantly, Chileans were unable to speak out against the government and those who did often "disappeared," taken from their homes by Pinochet's secret police never to be heard from again. Culture was filtered, and artists, writers, and musicians were censored.

THE END OF THE MILITARY DICTATORSHIP

The worldwide recession of 1982 put an end to Chile's economic run, but the economy bounced back again in the late 1980s. The Catholic Church began voicing opposition to Pinochet's brutal human-rights abuses, and a strong desire for a return to democracy saw the beginning of nationwide protests and international pressure, especially from the United States. In a pivotal 1988 "yes or no" plebiscite, 55% of Chileans voted no to further rule by Pinochet, electing centrist Christian Democrat Patricio Alywin president of Chile, but not before Pinochet promulgated a constitution that allowed him and a right-wing minority to continue to exert influence over the democratically elected government. It also shielded Pinochet and the military from any future prosecution.

It is difficult for most foreigners to fathom the unwavering blind support Pinochet's followers bestowed upon him in spite of the increasing revelation of grotesque human rights abuses during his rule. Supporters justified their views with Chile's thriving economy as testament to the "necessity" of authoritarian rule and the killings of the left-wing opponents. Following Alywin's election, Pinochet led a cushy life protected by security guards and filled with speaking engagements and other social events. What Pinochet hadn't counted on, however, was the dogged pursuit by international jurists to bring him to trial, and when in London in 1998 to undergo surgery, a Spanish judge leveled murder and torture charges against the former dictator and issued a request for his extradition.

Sixteen months of legal wrangling ended with Pinochet's release and return to Chile, but the ball was set in motion and soon thereafter Chile's Supreme Court stripped Pinochet and his military officers from immunity in order to face prosecution. Pinochet began pointing fingers, and old age and dementia shielded him from prosecution—but not from public humiliation. In 2004, it emerged that Pinochet had stashed $28 million (£19 million) in secret accounts worldwide, quashing his support by even his closest allies given that Pinochet advocated austerity and rallied against corruption as proof of his "just" war. Endless international news reports and the publication of torture victims'

Neruda's Victory

Never, forever . . . they do not concern me. Victory leaves a vanishing footprint in the sand. I live a bedeviled man, disposed, like any other, to cherish my human affinities. Whoever you are, I love you.

—Pablo Neruda, "Evening" (from *One Hundred Love Sonnets,* 1960)

accounts furthered the humiliation that many believe caused Pinochet more harm than any trial ever could.

The election of Chile's first female president, Michele Bachelet, in 2006 grabbed headlines around the world and proved how far Chile had come since the brutal repression of Pinochet. Bachelet, a Socialist who was tortured and exiled during Pinochet's rule, is also a divorcee who worked her way up the political ranks, including a post as the Minister of Defense. Shortly after Bachelet's election, Pinochet died at age 91.

3 THE LAY OF THE LAND

CHILE'S ECOSYSTEMS

Sandwiched between the Andes and the Pacific Ocean with a width that averages just 180km (112 miles) and some 4,830km (3,000 miles) of land, stretching from the arid northern desert to the wild desolation of Patagonia, Chile encompasses a dazzling array of landscapes and temperate zones. It is hard to believe such variation can exist in just one country; in fact, the only zone not found here is tropical.

The central region of Chile, including Santiago and its environs, features a mild, Mediterranean climate, reminiscent of California, while the Atacama region claims the world's driest desert, a beautiful "wasteland" set below a chain of purple and pink volcanoes and high-altitude salt flats. The Atacama Desert sits at altitudes of 2,000m (6,560 ft.) and up. The extreme climate and the geological forces at work in this region have produced far-out land formations and superlatives such as the highest geyser field in the world.

Few destinations in the world rival the lush scenery of Chile's Lake District. Over 10,000 years ago, retreating glaciers formed barriers of rock producing magnificent lakes and perfect conical, snowcapped volcanoes that burst skyward from beneath the glacial shield here. Today the Lake District is a dense, temperate, rainforest ecosystem packed with thick groves of native forest and shimmering lakes. Across the sound from the emerald rolling hills of Chiloé sits Chile's "frontier" highway, commonly known as the Carretera Austral, where tiny villages are speckled among thick virgin rainforest and waterfalls descend from rugged peaks.

Also known as the Magallanes Region, Patagonia is characterized by vast open *steppe;* colossal Northern and Southern Patagonian Ice Fields and hundreds of mighty glaciers; the peaks of the Andes, fading into the southern Pacific Ocean at their terminus; emerald fjords; and wind, wind, wind. At lower altitudes, valley ecosystems comprised of granite rocks have been chafed by glaciations and sedimentary deposits. Vegetation here is characterized by temperate, evergreen forests. There is no dry season, and rainfall is constant.

Easter Island, or "Rapa Nui," is the most remote island in the world, located farthest away from land than any other.

With its distinctive ecosystem, comprised of subtropical forests and scant precipitation, this largely volcanic island is composed of three extinct volcanoes and a number of volcanic craters and caves, and is carpeted with grasslands. Recently, Easter Island has suffered from soil erosion as a result of mass deforestation that is denuding the landscape of its statuesque palm forests.

FLORA AND FAUNA

Chile's climatic and topographical features correspond to defined botanical regions that boast a rich diversity of flora. Ethereal Atacama, which extends from the far north into Bolivia, is a desolate, lunar landscape where at higher altitudes cacti provide the only vegetation. In the central regions, greater rainfall and a humid environment produce shrubbery and trees with leaves known as sclerohyllous ("hard" leaves that facilitate a greater absorption of water). Predominant tree species include the guayacan, litre, lun, and peumo. The central valley is also characterized by hard espinos, a species of cactus, as well as the endangered Chilean palm, which can be seen in abundance at Parque Nacional La Campana (p. 155).

Desert brush lands sweep the *altiplano* (a high Andean plateau comprised of intermontane basins), which yield to more verdant grasslands on the lower slopes of the Andes. In the region south of the Bío-Bío River, temperate rainforests with high precipitation have yielded over 45 species of endemic trees. Magnolias, laurels, oaks, conifers, and beeches thrive in the dense forests here, but perhaps the most striking is the distinctive monkey puzzle tree (araucaria), Chile's national tree.

The frigid temperatures and violent winds of Patagonia preclude a rich diversity of forestation. The coigüe, lenga, and ñirre are the three principal endemic tree species of Patagonian forests. The coicopihue (Philesia magellanica) yields Chile's national flower, the scarlet Chilean bellflower (copihue).

Only a handful of Latin America's characteristic fauna are to be found in Chile. Larger (and very elusive) mammals include the puma and the cougar, while the llama-like guanacos and vicuñas, the Patagonian mountain deer known as a huemul, the vizcacha rodent, and cunning chilla fox are more visible. The pudu, the world's smallest deer, inhabits dense forest regions along with several other species of marsupial, but they are very difficult to spot. Chile's waters harbor a rich variety of fish and an abundance of marine species and waterfowl ranging from frolicking seals and sea lions to playful dolphins and sea otters, magnificent whales, and penguins.

For info on environmental concerns in Chile, see p. 45–47 in chapter 3, "Planning Your Trip to Chile."

SEARCHING FOR WILDLIFE

Various animals in the forests here are predominantly nocturnal. When they are active in the daytime, they are usually elusive and on the watch for predators. Birds are easier to spot in clearings or secondary forests than they are in primary forests. The vast open spaces of the *altiplano* and immense *steppe* of Patagonia are especially conducive to wildlife-watching. In the Atacama region, many species—flamingos, vicuñas, and guanacos—are easily encountered close to water sources such as lagoons, lakes, and oases.

Here are a few helpful hints for wildlife-watching in Chile:

- **Listen.** Pay attention to rustling in the leaves; whether it's a Magellanic woodpecker in Torres del Paine National Park or a guanaco scurrying across the *altiplano,* you're most likely to hear an animal before seeing one.
- **Keep quiet.** Noise will scare off animals and prevent you from hearing their movements and calls.

- **Don't try too hard.** Soften your focus and allow your peripheral vision to take over. This way you can catch glimpses of motion and then focus in on the prey.
- **Bring binoculars.** It's also a good idea to practice a little first to get the hang of them. It would be a shame to be fiddling around and staring into space while everyone else in your group oohs and aahs over a condor.
- **Dress appropriately.** You'll have a hard time focusing your binoculars if you're busy swatting flies. Light, long pants and long-sleeved shirts are your best bet. Comfortable hiking boots are a real boon, except where heavy rubber boots are necessary. Avoid loud colors; the better you blend in with your surroundings, the better your chances are of spotting wildlife.
- **Be patient.** The forest isn't on a schedule. However, your best shots at seeing forest fauna are in the very early morning and late afternoon hours.
- **Read up.** Familiarize yourself with what you're most likely to see—most hotels and lodges have field guides to Chile.

4 CHILE IN POPULAR CULTURE: BOOKS, FILM & MUSIC

BOOKS

A History of Chile, by John L. Rector, chronicles the political history of Chile during the second half of the 20th century. Sara Wheeler's *Travels in a Thin Country* is the story of an Englishwoman's trip to Chile, but it can be frustratingly superficial. A better read is *Chile: A Traveler's Companion,* translated by Katherine Silver, which provides readers with a well-rounded collection of regionally based memoirs penned by Chile's best contemporary writers, and arranged geographically so that readers may "travel" through the country's diverse landscapes.

Popular titles by Chile's top literary artists Pablo Neruda, Gabriela Mistral, and Isabel Allende have been translated into English. Neruda's masterful *Canto General* and *The Heights of Machu Picchu* will make a poetry lover out of anyone. Mistral's extraordinary poetry can be found in *Selected Poems of Gabriela Mistral,* in Spanish and English, translated by Ursula K. Le Guin, and Mistral's story has been brought to life for children in the book *My Name is Gabriela* by Monica Brown and John Parra. See the box on Mistral later for more information. Isabel Allende is Chile's most famous contemporary writer, well known for such works as the love-it-or-hate-it *The House of the Spirits, Eva Luna,* and her memoirs of the country she was forced to leave in exile, *My Invented Country.*

While not specifically set in Chile, Chilean writer Ariel Dorfman's lauded play *Death and the Maiden* deals with the aftermath of an era of torture and "disappearings." Other works that debate the Allende years and the Pinochet dictatorship that, depending on whom you talk to, are either accurate or dishonest, are ex-Allende translator Marc Cooper's memoirs in *Pinochet and Me;* Roger Burbach's *The Pinochet Affair: State Terrorism and Global Justice,* a scholarly yet lucid account of Allende and Pinochet, with more sympathies for the former than the latter; and Thomas Hauser's *The Execution of Charles Horman: An American Sacrifice,* which was adapted for the 1982 film *Missing.*

FILM

The Pinochet regime placed various limits on artistic liberties, which resulted in a dearth of mainstream cinematic production in the country during much of the late 20th century. Movie production

Gabriela Mistral

In 1945, Gabriela Mistral became the first Latin American woman to win the Nobel Prize for Literature. While Pablo Neruda was embraced in Chile and throughout Latin America for his charisma, passion, and gregarious nature, Mistral was an enigma to her fellow countrymen, an introverted woman whose still waters ran very deep. Reserved, laconic, and stern, Mistral's tragic life found powerful expression in the wistful, haunting, and yearning sonnets for which she was internationally renowned. The dominant themes in Mistral's poetry are love, death, childhood, justice, motherhood, religion, and the power of nature.

Born Lucila Godoy Alcayaga in Vicuña, in 1889, the second daughter of a Basque mother and an Indian/Jewish father, who was both a poet and school teacher, Gabriela embodied a spirit of feisty, Spanish individualism and of Indian stoicism. Tragedy struck Mistral early in life when her father abandoned the family when she was just 3 years old, establishing a heartbreaking pattern of lost love that would haunt her childhood and early adult years.

Gabriela's schooling was short but profound. She began school at the age of 9 but completed just 3 years. However, it was during this time that she discovered her affinity for poetry and began to compose her own poems under the pen name of Gabriela Mistral. Gabriela's older sister Emelina was a teacher and she continued to school Gabriela at home and stirred her desires to become a teacher. At just 16 years old, Gabriela began to support her mother by working as a teacher's assistant.

In 1906, Gabriela moved to La Cantera, where she met a young railway worker named Romeo Ureta. She fell instantly in love with him, drawn to his sensitive and tortured soul. Less than 2 years after their relationship began, Ureta committed suicide, an event that affected Gabriela profoundly and from which she never recovered.

After receiving a teaching diploma in 1912, Gabriela began to teach elementary and secondary school to make ends meet until, in 1914, the publication of *Sonetos de la muerte* made her renowned throughout Latin America and earned her a national prize in poetry. In 1922, she published *Desolación* (Desolation), the first volume of her collected poems, an expression of her feelings toward suffering and death.

Tragedy struck again when Gabriela's nephew, whom she treated very much as her own son, committed suicide at the age of 17. An intensely private individual, Gabriela didn't welcome the fame that accompanied her art but she was, however, able to utilize it to full effect to attain her humanitarian ambitions. In 1922, Gabriela was invited by José Vasconcelos, Mexico's minister of education, to establish educational programs for the disadvantaged. One of her achievements was to allow greater access to literature for low-income people living in rural areas through such initiatives as mobile libraries.

In 1923, the Chilean government awarded Mistral the title "Teacher of the Nation." In 1957, Gabriela died in the U.S. Her body was repatriated and she was buried in Montegrande. On her tomb are inscribed her own words:

"What the soul is to the body, so is the artist to his people."

increased during the 1990s, but a lack of funding has so far precluded international exposure. At the moment, Chileans are renowned for preferring imported American movies (Hollywood movies that have been filmed or set here include *The Motorcycle Diaries, The Quantum of Solace,* and *Missing*) to home-grown independent productions. However, the success of Sebastian Silva's film ***La Nana (The Maid),*** which received international recognition at the 2009 Sundance Film Festival, seems to have ushered in a new era of cinematic pride and could be the start of a movie industry renaissance.

The Valdivia Film Festival takes place in Valdivia in October each year and features Chilean films and documentaries, many of which were prohibited during the Pinochet regime. Visit www.ficv.cl for information.

MUSIC

Nueva Canción (New Song) is the most significant musical genre in Chile. These lyrical songs first became popular in the 1960s in both Chile and Argentina via the work of troubadours **Atahualpa Yupanqui** and **Violeta Parra;** their songs were instilled with political messages and soon became known in other Latin American countries and the Caribbean. The art form has been highly influential in terms of its political and social impact, most notably during the Pinochet years when many Nueva Canción artists suffered persecution and even death. Perhaps the most legendary Nueva Canción songwriter and singer, **Victor Jara** was murdered by the Pinochet regime.

Because Nueva Canción's significance peaked during the analogue years, it is rather difficult to find CDs and digital recordings but the most popular ones follow. Jara's album *Manifesto* features the haunting love song *Te recuerdo Amanda* as well as *Estadio Chile,* which was later recorded by Violeta Parra as *Ay Canto,* and is the artist's final composition. *Canta a mi América* is the quintessential collection of Violeta Parra, who remains one of South America's most beloved artists. The group **Quilapayún** recorded the anthem *El Pueblo Unido Jamàs Sera Vencido,* which was one of the most influential Chilean songs of the 1970s.

Today, the folk group **Illapu,** which excels at Andean instrumentals and salsa-tinged ballads, is perhaps the most popular band in Chile. Other popular bands include the heavy rock band **Chancho en Piedra,** as well as indie rockers **Los Bunkers,** who enjoy a high profile in both the U.S. and the U.K. The immensely popular, Grammy-award-winning, pop rock band **La Lay** split in 2005, ostensibly to work on solo projects, but are still one of the most frequently played Chilean bands. Latin pop diva and darling of the press, **Myriam Hernández,** now in her 40s, has been topping the charts since she was catapulted into the spotlight, at age 11, as a child soap opera star before being named *Artista Revelación* (Best New Artist) by the Chilean music press at age 18.

5 EATING & DRINKING IN CHILE

Chilean gastronomy is coming into its own, but for now it's safe to say that you will not return from your trip raving about the country's cuisine. This is not to say that the food is mediocre; it's just that despite the bounty of wonderful ingredients at hand such as shellfish and fish, vegetables, and exotic fruits, Chilean food lacks creativity. Most restaurants rely on the same time-worn recipes; meat and fish are grilled, fried, or sautéed and served with rice or fries—not very memorable.

The exception to this is Chile's *cocina de autor* (nouvelle and fusion cuisine) found mostly in Santiago, restaurants in tourist-oriented destinations, and most major hotels that employ talented chefs and a long list of high-caliber wines. When ordering lunch, ask whether the restaurant has a *menú del día* or *menú ejecutivo,* a fixed-price lunch for $6 to $11 (£4–£7.30) that typically includes an appetizer, main course, beverage or wine, coffee, and dessert. The lunch *menú* is normally a cheaper and fresher alternative to anything listed on the *carta* (menu).

What beef is to Argentina, seafood is to Chile, and Chileans eat it all, from sole to sea urchin to conger eel. What's odd, however, is that Chileans dine on seafood in restaurants but rarely at home, which is why you'll see a larger selection of seafood at any given restaurant than you will in the local grocery store.

Chilean waiters operate at a languid pace, and foreign diners might have trouble adjusting to this. Waiters for the most part in Chile are not service-oriented, and often you'll find yourself craning your neck trying to catch the attention of a waiter who is busy chatting or hiding out in the kitchen. Also, waiters in Chile do not automatically bring the check—you'll have to request it. It is customary to tip 10%, which you may do in cash or by adding the tip onto the credit card slip *before* the card is run through.

The cost to dine in Chile is on the rise, with main courses ranging between $9 and $15 (£6–£10); cocktails retail for around $7 (£4.70), but then again barmen here make them doubly strong. In cities such as Santiago, dining categories are rated by the cost of a main course: Expensive is more than $15 (£10), Moderate is $10 to $15 (£6.70–£10), and Inexpensive is less than $10 (£6.70).

DINING CUSTOMS Every hotel, with the exception of dirt-cheap hostels, serves breakfast free with the room price, which may be a skimpy continental breakfast with coffee, juice, and a roll, or a full "American" breakfast with eggs. Few restaurants serve breakfast outside of major hotels. In Chile, lunch is served between 1 and 3pm, and it is considered the main meal of the day and taken very seriously. Businesses may close during the lunch hour, and it is difficult to reach anyone by phone during this time.

Americans need some adjusting to get used to the country's dinner hours. Dinner is typically very late; in small towns, you'll be hard-pressed to find an eatery that opens before 8pm. Most restaurants close before midnight, but on weekends they'll stay open until 2 or 3am. Even in private homes, families eat dinner around 9:30 or 10pm. This giant hunger gap between lunch and dinner has given rise to the Chilean tradition of *onces*—literally "elevenses," or afternoon tea. At home, a Chilean might have a cup of tea with a roll and jam, but you'll find *salones de té* throughout the country that serve complete *onces* that can include rich, sugary cakes, toasted cheese sandwiches, juice, ice cream, and more. Many Chileans have a light sandwich during this time and call it an early dinner.

FOOD

APPETIZERS *Entradas* are seafood appetizers, such as razor clams or *ceviche,* that are ordered before meals. Bar appetizers are known as *picoteos,* hearty platters with meat and cheese and other goodies.

SANDWICHES & SNACKS Chileans cling to the traditional heavy lunch, but many also lunch or snack on quick meals such as sandwiches or empanadas, those tasty fried or baked turnovers filled with shellfish, cheese, or a meat and onion mixture known as *pino.* Sandwiches are hefty and often require a knife and fork. A grilled ham and cheese is known as a *barros jarpa,* and a meat and melted cheese is known as a *barros luco.* Then there's the *completo,* a hot dog topped with mustard, mayonnaise, and sauerkraut, or the *italiano,* a hot dog with globs of mayonnaise, mashed avocado, and chopped tomato, an impossibly messy Chilean favorite. Cheap cafes, known as *fuentes de soda* or *schoperías* (from the word *schop,* or draft beer), serve fast snacks and sandwiches. One of the most common and inexpensive dishes is *cazuela,* a hearty soup made with either a chicken leg or hunk of beef, and potato, corn, rice, and green beans—*cazuela* is comfort food when you're sick or have stayed out too late the night before.

MEAT Although Chilean meat consumption is no match for the carnivores of Argentina, they do consume a lot of it. Chile also loves its lamb, especially in the Lake District and Patagonia regions where lamb is butterflied and tied to a spit and slowly roasted over a wood fire. Beef is the focal point for the social Chilean *asado,* or barbecue, that commonly begins with an appetizer of *choripan,* or savory sausage served in a roll. The tenderest cuts of steak are the *lomo* and the *filete. Costillar de cerdo,* or pork ribs, served with spicy mashed potatoes, is a classic Chilean dish. Chicken can be found on most menus but is considered an "inferior" meat here. You'll either love or hate *pastel de choclo,* a casserole of ground beef and chicken, topped with a sugary sweet corn crust baked golden brown.

SEAFOOD Fruits of the sea are this country's specialty, and the Chileans' love for the variety of weird and wonderful shellfish seems limitless. *Machas* (razor clams), the delicious but hard-to-get *loco* (a meaty, thick abalone), *choros* or *choritos* (mussels), *ostras* (oysters), *ostiones* (scallops), or the outstanding *centolla* (king crab) are familiar. Less familiar are *picorocos* (barnacles), the much-loved *erizo* (sea urchin), and the exotic *piure,* an iodine-rich, alien-looking red blob that attaches itself to rocks and is served in soups. The most common fish you'll see on the menu are salmon, the buttery *congrio* (conger eel), *merluza* (hake), *corvina* (sea bass), and increasingly, *mero* (grouper), *lenguado* (sole), and *atún* (yellowfin tuna). Popular Chilean-style seafood dishes are *paila marina* (shellfish stew), ceviche (fish cubes and onion "cooked" in lemon juice), *chupes* (a creamy casserole made with crab or abalone), or *caldillo* (a fish stew).

VEGETABLES Chile's Central Valley is the breadbasket of this slender country, producing the majority of the country's fruits and vegetables. In the southern regions that are prone to cold weather and heavy rainfall, vegetables are grown in greenhouses—in fact, it seems that every rural household has one in its backyard. In Patagonia, vegetables and fruit are very difficult to come by, and what you get is of secondary quality and very expensive. Most restaurants do not serve vegetables as a side dish; however, you can order just about any kind of vegetable in a salad, including beets, corn, green beans, and so on. The avocado, called *palta,* is ubiquitous, well loved, and cheap, as are the tomato and onion, both of which are combined to form an *ensalada chilena.* Vegetarian meals are gaining a

Sustainable Seafood

Much confusion and controversy surrounds the famed "Chilean sea bass," served less and less frequently in North American restaurants because over-fishing has brought the fish to the brink of extinction. Its real name is a lot less glamorous: Patagonian toothfish. Sea bass is really *corvina;* you'll want to avoid Patagonian toothfish if you're trying to eat sustainably.

foothold in Chile, especially in Santiago, but in rural restaurants you'll need to satisfy yourself with french fries and a salad.

FRUITS Chile harvests a rich, flavorful assortment of fruits in its central valley and citrus groves in the desert north, exporting a good percentage of its crops to North America and beyond. Apples, oranges, and bananas are common, but you'll want to sample exotic fruits such as the *chirimoya* (custard apple), *tuna* (cactus fruit), *pepino dulce* (a sweet pepper that tastes somewhat like melon), or *membrillo* (quince).

DESSERTS Chileans often order dessert after lunch and then again after dinner, even if it's just chopped fresh fruit or fruit from a can. Desserts to look out for are the gooey, sugary *suspiro limeño,* which originates from Peru. German immigration left its mark on Chile with dense cakes called *küchen,* a specialty throughout the Lake District. Nothing is more Chilean, really, than *mote con huesillo,* a dessert popular during the summer and in rural areas, which combines dried peaches soaked in a light syrup and served over barley grain. *Mil hojas* is a cake layered with a "thousand" flakey dough layers; and *lucuma,* a butterscotch-flavored fruit, is delicious in cakes and ice cream.

BEVERAGES

Chileans guzzle *bebidas* (soft drinks) such as Coca-Cola, Sprite, or the country's own fantasy flavors, the nuclear-red Biltz and lemon-yellow Pap—you'll just need to try them because their taste defies description. Fruit juice is very popular, sold either in boxes at the supermarket or served fresh in restaurants, cafes, and roadway stalls. These fresh juices are delightful and are usually made of *frambuesa* (raspberry), *naranja* (orange), or *durazno* (peach).

If you love coffee, you're in for a disappointment. High-end restaurants serve espresso drinks or brewed coffee, but even high-tab eateries occasionally try to get away with serving a packet of Nescafe and a cup of boiling water. Ask if a restaurant serves real *café-café,* or if they have an espresso machine.

The water in Chile is generally safe to drink except for San Pedro de Atacama, though travelers with sensitive stomachs and pregnant women should drink bottled water wherever possible. You'll find bottled water sold everywhere either as *agua mineral sin gas* (still water), or *agua mineral con gas* (sparkling water).

BEER, WINE & LIQUOR Start your meal the way Chileans do with a pisco sour, considered to be the national drink of Chile and made of the grape brandy *pisco,* fresh-squeezed lemon, sugar, and sometimes an egg white and a dash of bitters. Chileans and Peruvians are divided on who invented the pisco sour, but the drink was popularized in this country. Stick to a maximum of two—these babies are potent!

Chile has garnered worldwide recognition for its fine wines, the bulk of which are exported to outside markets. However, you will be able to get your hands on fine boutique wines not available or easily found in the U.S., so visit a *vinoteca* (wine store) and see what's on offer. Moderate-quality wines are lower in price by U.S. standards, but expect to pay premium for reserve and icon wines.

Chile's lager beers are (listed from lightest to strongest): Cristal, Becker, Austral, and Escudo, and the dark beer Morenita. The Peruvian beer Paceña is catching on, as is the Brazilian beer Brama. Chilean brewers have been toying with microbrews, but they're not yet the sensation they are in the U.S.—the best is Kunstman, followed by Capital. Otherwise, you'll find Corona, Budweiser, Heineken, and Guinness in most shops and restaurants.

6 SHOPPING IN CHILE

Chile doesn't have the diversity or quality of **handicrafts** *(artesanía)* that you will find in Peru or Bolivia, and the prices here are certainly considerably more expensive, especially in Santiago and the Central Valley. However, if you are a patient and savvy shopper and you know what you are looking for, you can certainly discover unique and beautiful traditional souvenir items in the craft markets *(ferias artesenales),* which are omnipresent throughout the country.

Look out for items made by the indigenous Aymara and Mapuche tribes; *zampoñes* (flutes), *kultrunes* (ceremonial drums), and *palos de agua* (rain sticks). In the altiplano region, especially around Arica, **alpaca sweaters, ponchos,** and **scarves** are the more readily available and eye-catching souvenirs (and most practical, given the high altitude chill), but they are of generally inferior quality to those across the border and therefore are most worthy of polite, but canny, bargaining. The best quality alpaca weavings are those produced by the Aymara people in Lauca National Park. In La Serena's crafts markets, the **leather** items are quite striking; you can find everything from saddles and stirrups to belts and boots—if you want to look the part, you can even pick up some idiosyncratic *huaso* (cowboy) items such as a straw hat or poncho.

Jewelry, ranging from copper bangles to stunning **lapis lazuli** and **Mapuche silverware,** is Chile's prize purchase. The semiprecious, indigo-blue *lapis lazuli* stone is found only in Chile and Afghanistan and is normally set in silver to form dazzling pendants, chokers, rings, earrings, and bracelets. While it is generally less expensive than in the U.S. and Europe, it is still a rather pricey investment—a pair of simple lapis lazuli stud earrings costs around $40/£27. It is always best to buy *lapis lazuli* from a reputable jewelry store (one exception being the excellent Pueblito de los Dominicos market, just west of Los Condes; p. 119), and always look for the deepest color stones, which are considered to be of superior quality. In Santiago, the area surrounding Patio Bellavista offers high quality stones and a variety of styles ranging from the simple to the ostentatious.

The Lake District is the best place to purchase **Mapuche silver ware.** Still worn by indigenous women, these striking silver designs and extravagant headdresses were originally designed to be a show of wealth; the artful fusion of the practical and the decorous in these pieces is both distinctive and dramatic.

Chilean **wine** is considered to be among the finest and best value of the New World wines. Don't get too carried away however; there are strict Customs limitations on how much you can take home. See p. 33 for info. If you plan to tour the **pisco** distilleries of La Serena and Pisco Elquí, you can learn about the nuances of the local pisco grapes and make informed decisions on the best bottle to take home for a cocktail-hour pisco sour. See chapter 8 for options.

Planning Your Trip to Chile

Chile, a gorgeous string bean of a country, is one of the hottest destinations in South America, given its solid tourism infrastructure, ethereal landscapes, and myriad outdoor activities. The country gives visitors the chance to pack a lot of diversity into a single trip. For a start in narrowing down your choices of where to go, see the "Suggested Chile Itineraries" and "Active Vacation Planner" chapters 4 and 5, as well as the "Best Of" selections in chapter 1.

Compared to much of Latin America, Chile is not a country that requires intense advance planning to visit. No vaccinations are required, and most foreign nationals do not require a visa. Politically, Chile is very stable, with an economy that is strong by regional standards with low inflation, although compared to its continental neighbors to the north, it is expensive. Yet some basic questions, like when to visit and what are the hotels like, need to be addressed right from the get-go. This chapter provides answers to these questions so that you can be prepared when you arrive in Chile.

For additional help in planning your trip, please turn to the "Fast Facts, Toll-Free Numbers & Website" appendix on p. 443.

1 VISITOR INFORMATION

You'll find a municipal tourism office in nearly every city and the national tourism board **Sernatur** (www.sernatur.cl) offices in major cities. The quality of service and availability of printed matter, such as maps and brochures, varies from office to office. Visitors are usually better off planning ahead via Internet research, booking a tour, or seeking the assistance of a hotel concierge than relying on the advice of a Sernatur clerk.

Most general travel sites in Chile have converted into for-profit booking centers; however, most top tourism destinations produce their own independent sites. Try the content-rich sites **www.sanpedroatacama.com** and **www.torresdelpaine.com**.

- **Turistel** (www.turistel.cl): Turistel, a Spanish-language road-guide series, has a website with route maps that can be downloaded by clicking on *mapas ruteros.* I strongly recommend that travelers renting vehicles arrive prepared, as many agencies will not provide detailed road maps.
- **ContactChile** (www.contactchile.cl): This Santiago-based agency assists foreigners with room rentals, internships, and Spanish-language courses. It also provides travelers with a beginner's guide to Chilean culture, cuisine, transportation, and other tourism-related topics.
- **Chilean Cultural Heritage Corporation** (www.nuestro.cl): Run by the nonprofit, philanthropic Chilean Cultural Heritage Corporation, this is Chile's most comprehensive guide to music, arts, literature, museums, and archaeological monuments. This is an essential

site for information about cultural news and events.

- **South American Explorers** (www.samexplo.org): The South American Explorers website includes up-to-date information about health and political crises, as well as frequently asked questions, travelogues, discounts, advice, and a quarterly journal. However, information is for members only, and it costs $50 (£33) to join.
- **Wines of Chile** (www.winesofchile.cl): This Santiago and U.K.-based promotional association for export wines offers information about its 85 member wineries, plus links to the five established wine routes. Or try **www.vinasdechile.cl** for wine-tasting reservation info for Chile's more traditional wineries and wine-related news.
- **AndesWeb** (www.andesweb.com): A blanket guide to ski resorts small and large in Chile and Argentina, with transportation information, snow conditions, and, best of all, a travel forum for swapping information and opinions.
- **Andes Handbook** (www.andeshandbook.cl): The definitive site for mountaineering in Chile, with guides to more than 150 peaks, including location, height, routes, and difficulty ratings. Climbers may also download topographical maps here.

2 ENTRY REQUIREMENTS

PASSPORTS & VISAS

For information on how to get a passport, go to "Passports" in the "Fast Facts, Toll Free Numbers & Websites" appendix—the websites listed provide downloadable passport applications as well as the current fees for processing passport applications. For an up-to-date, country-by-country listing of passport requirements around the world, go to the "Foreign Entry Requirement" Web page of the U.S. Department of State at **http://travel.state.gov**.

Citizens of the United States, Canada, the United Kingdom, Australia, and New Zealand need only a valid passport to enter Chile. Chile charges a **reciprocity fee** upon entry to citizens of the following countries: $131 for the U.S., $61 for Australians, $132 for Canadians, and $23 for Mexicans. Visitors from the U.K. and New Zealand do not pay a fee. The one-time fee is good for the life of a traveler's passport, and is charged when entering through the **Santiago airport only.** Travelers crossing over land do not pay this fee. You may pay this fee at the airport counter (to the left of Customs) with your credit card.

Before entering Chile, you'll need to fill out a tourist card that allows visitors to stay for 90 days. **Do not lose this card,** as you will need to present it to Customs when leaving the country. Also, many hotels waive Chile's 19% sales tax applied to rooms when the guest shows this card and pays with U.S. dollars or a credit card. The easiest (and free) way to renew your 90-day stay is to cross the border and return. For $100 (£67), tourist cards can be renewed for another 90 days at the **Extranjería,** Agustinas 1235, second floor, in Santiago (© **2/550-2400**), open Monday through Friday from 8:30am to 2pm (be prepared for excruciatingly long lines), or at any Gobernación Provincial office in the provinces. The extension must be applied for 1 month before the visa's expiration date. Bring the original card, your passport, and photocopies of the two.

Contact the Chilean consulate closest to you for information about children under age 18 traveling alone, with one parent, or with a third party. Child abduction awareness is on the rise, and I've heard of Customs agents preventing parents traveling solo to or from Chile with children. Play it safe and travel with a written authorization by the absent parent(s) or legal guardian granting permission, which must be notarized by the consulate or a reputable notary.

Lost Documents

If you lose your tourist card outside Santiago, any police station will direct you to the Extranjería police headquarters for that province (usually the nearest principal city). In Santiago, go to the **Policía Internacional,** Departamento Fronteras, General Borgoña 1052 (✆ **2/565-7893**), open Monday through Friday from 9am to 5pm.

If you lose your passport, you can get a passport replacement at your country's embassy. See p. 446 for a list. The embassy might require you to file a *constancia* with the police, but without Spanish skills, this can be difficult; call ahead and ask if this document can be waived. It is imperative that you carry a **photocopy of your passport** with you and another form of ID to facilitate the process.

CUSTOMS

What You Can Bring Into Chile

Any travel-related merchandise brought into Chile, such as personal effects or clothing, is not taxed. Visitors entering Chile may also bring in no more than 400 cigarettes, 500 grams of pipe tobacco, or 50 cigars, and 2.5 liters of alcoholic beverages per adult (ages 18 and up).

What You Can Take Home from Chile

U.S. Citizens

Returning U.S. citizens who have been away for at least 48 hours are allowed to bring back once every 30 days $800 worth of merchandise duty-free. You will be charged a flat duty fee for the next $1,000 worth of purchases. Beyond that, any dollar amount is dutiable at whatever rates apply. On mailed gifts, the duty-free limit is $200. Be sure to have your receipts or purchases handy to expedite the declaration process. ***Note:*** If you owe duty, you are required to pay upon arrival in the United States by cash, personal check, government or traveler's check, or money order, and in some locations, by Visa or MasterCard.

To avoid having to pay duty on foreign-made personal items you owned before you left on your trip, bring along a bill of sale, insurance policy, jeweler's appraisal, or receipt. Or register items that can be readily identified by a permanently affixed serial number or marking—think laptop computers, cameras, and CD players—to avoid problems with Customs. Take the items to the nearest Customs office or register them with Customs at the airport from which you are departing. You will receive, at no cost, a Certificate of Registration, which allows duty-free entry for the life of the item. There is little chance that Customs will seriously question personal items, but it's better to be safe than sorry.

For specifics on what you can bring back and the corresponding fees, download the invaluable free pamphlet *Know Before You Go* online at **www.cbp.gov**. (Click on "Travel," and then click on "Know Before You Go! Online Brochure"). Or contact the **U.S. Customs & Border Protection (CBP),** 1300 Pennsylvania Ave. NW, Washington, DC 20229 (✆ **877/287-8667**), and request the pamphlet.

Canadian Citizens

For a clear summary of Canadian rules, write for the booklet *I Declare,* issued by the **Canada Border Services Agency** (✆ **800/461-9999** in Canada, or 204/983-3500; **www.cbsa-asfc.gc.ca**).

U.K. Citizens

For information, contact **HM Customs & Excise** at ✆ **0845/010-9000** (020/8929-0152 from outside the U.K.), or consult the website at **www.hmce.gov.uk**.

Australian Citizens

A helpful brochure available from Australian consulates or Customs offices is *Know Before*

You Go. For more information, call the **Australian Customs Service** at ✆ **1300/363-263,** or log on to **www.customs.gov.au**.

New Zealand Citizens

Most questions are answered in a free pamphlet available at New Zealand consulates and Customs offices: *New Zealand Customs Guide for Travellers, Notice no. 4.* For more information, contact **New Zealand Customs,** The Customhouse, 17–21 Whitmore St., Box 2218, Wellington (✆ **04/473-6099** or 0800/428-786; www.customs.govt.nz).

3 WHEN TO GO

Brazilians and Argentines vacation during the summer from December 15 to the end of February, as well as the 2 middle weeks of July and Holy Week *(Semana Santa),* the week preceding Easter Sunday. These dates coincide with school vacations. In spite of cheaper deals during the off-season, nearly everyone from these three countries takes his or her vacation during high season, and consequently the teeming masses seen in popular destinations such as Pucón or Viña del Mar during this time can be overwhelming. If that weren't enough, consider that hotels and businesses in tourist areas jack up their prices in anticipation of vacationers who come with money to burn. If you travel to Chile during this time, book a room *well* in advance. Or you can do as most North American and Europeans do and come from late September to early December for the spring bloom, or from March to June, when the trees turn color; both seasons have pleasant weather, and destinations around Chile are less crowded, and in some cases completely empty of people. In fact, it's preferable to be in the extreme regions of Chile during these "off-seasons." In northern regions, such as San Pedro de Atacama, the searing heat during the summer is a killer. In Patagonia, the fierce wind blows from October to April but is most consistent in December and January.

The only exception to this high-season rule is in Santiago. Summer is in fact the most pleasant time to visit, as Santiaguinos head out for vacation, easing traffic, reducing smog, and dropping rates in most hotels.

CLIMATE

Chile's thin, drawn-out territory stretches over 38 degrees of latitude, encompassing every climate found in the world except tropical. In many areas there are microclimates, pockets of localized weather that can completely alter the vegetation and landscape of a small area.

The northern region of Chile is so dry that some desert areas have never recorded rain. Summer temperatures from early December to late February in this region can top 100°F (38°C), then drop dramatically at night to 30°F (–1°C). Winter days, from mid-June to late August, are crisp but sunny and pleasant; but, as soon as the sun drops, the temperature turns bitterly cold. Along the coast, the weather is mild and dry, ranging from 60° to 90°F (16°–32°C) during the summer.

The Santiago and Central Valley region features a Mediterranean climate, with rain during the winter only and temperatures that range from 32° to 55°F (0°–13°C) in the winter, and 60° to 95°F (16°–35°C) during the summer. Farther south, the Lake District and the Carretera Austral are home to sopping wet winters, and overcast days and rain are not uncommon during the summer, especially in the regions around Valdivia and Puerto Montt.

The Magellanic Region presents unpredictable weather patterns, especially during the summer, with extraordinary windstorms that can reach upwards of 120kmph (75 mph), and occasional rain. The windiest months are mid-December to late February, but it can blow any time between October and April. Winters are calm, with irregular snowfall and temperatures that can dip to 5°F (–15°C).

PUBLIC HOLIDAYS

Chile's national holidays are New Year's Day (Jan 1), Good Friday (late Mar or Apr), Labor Day (May 1), Remembrance of the War of the Pacific Victory (May 21), Corpus Christi (late May or early June), St. Peter & St. Paul Day (June 26), Asunción de la Virgen (Aug 15), Independence Day and Armed Forces Day, the major holiday of the year (Sept 18–19), Indigenous Day (Oct 12), All Saints' Day (Nov 1), Feast of the Immaculate Conception (Dec 8), and Christmas (Dec 25).

Virtually every business in Chile shuts on public holidays, as is the case with national and local elections (midnight–midnight). Alcohol is not sold on election days.

CHILE CALENDAR OF EVENTS

The following are some of Chile's major events and festivals that take place during the year. Contact **Sernatur** (www.sernatur.cl) for additional information.

February

Festival Costumbrista Chilote, Chiloé. The city of Castro hosts a celebration of the culture, history, and mythical folklore that makes the island unique. Part of this celebration is centered around making chicha from fermented apples and curanto, a slowly cooked combo of shellfish and pork steamed over hot rocks in the ground and covered with nalca leaves. Early February.

Semana Valdiviana, Valdivia. This grand weeklong event features a variety of maritime-theme activities, contests, expositions, and more. The highlight takes place on the third Saturday of February, the "Noche Valdiviana," when the Río Valdivia fills with festively decorated boats and candles, and the skies fill with fireworks. This is a very crowded event, and advance hotel reservations are essential. Mid-February.

Festival de la Canción, Viña del Mar. The gala Festival of Song showcases Latin American performers and usually one or two hot international acts during a 5-day festival of concerts held in the city's outdoor amphitheater. The spectacle draws thousands of visitors to an already packed Viña del Mar, so plan your hotel reservations accordingly. Late February.

March/April

Fiesta del Cuasimodo. This event is held mostly in towns in central Chile, in which huaso cowboys parade through the streets accompanied by Catholic priests who often pay visits to the infirm and people with disabilities. First Sunday after Easter.

June

Fiesta de San Pedro. Fishermen celebrate in towns along the coast of Chile to bring about good fortune, weather, and bountiful catches. They decorate their boats, light candles, arm themselves with an image of their patron saint, and drift along the coast. A great place to check out this event is Valparaíso. June 29.

July

La Tirana. Almost abandoned during most of the year, this tiny Atacama Desert village, east of Iquique, hosts Chile's most important traditional religious festivals, including La Tirana ("The Tyrant"), named after a legendary—and legendarily cruel—Inca princess who converted to Christianity and was martyred. Close to a quarter million of the faithful, including 207 religious associations in colorful costumes, swarm the town for the Virgen del Carmen commemorations. It's best to stay in Iquique, though the dancing goes on all night. Other major pilgrimages here occur January 5 and 6 (Three Wise Men or Magi), Holy Week, and Independence Day. July 10–19.

Virgen del Carmen. The patron saint of the armed forces is celebrated with military parades throughout the country, especially near Maipú, where Chile's liberators O'Higgins and San Martín defeated Spanish forces in the fight for independence. July 16.

Carnaval de Invierno. Two days' worth of parade floats and fireworks inject some cheer into the dank, dark, sub-Antarctic winter in Punta Arenas. Last week of July.

September

Independence Day. While serious, stiff official commemorative parades are held in Santiago and Valparaíso, everywhere in Chile around "El Dieciocho" (the 18th) and Armed Forces Day (the 19th), festivities abound in *fondas,* mostly outdoor fairs under *armadas,* tree branches and reeds offering shade or a place to string up multicolored light bulbs. The biggest celebration is La Pampilla, near Coquimbo. Grilled meats and *empanadas* abound, along with rivers of wine and pisco, and live traditional music adds to the merrymaking under ubiquitous national flags. September 18–19.

Rodeo season kick-off. Chile's rodeo season starts on Independence Day and culminates with a championship in the city of Rancagua around late March or early April. There are a variety of rodeo dates throughout the Central Valley, but September 18 and the championships are festivals in their own right, with food stalls, lots of chicha (a fermented fruit cider) drinking, and traditional cueca dancing. Contact the Federación de Rodeos in Santiago at ©/fax **2/420-2553,** or visit www.huasosyrodeos.cl for a schedule of rodeos throughout Chile. September 18.

December

Fiesta Grande. The remote mining village of Andacollo, south of La Serena, proudly boasts a purportedly miracle-working wooden statue of the Virgin Mary. In her honor, an astounding 400,000 pilgrims congregate here on December 26, following a tradition begun in 1584, with dancers drawing on pre-colonial traditions. A smaller commemoration takes place on the first Sunday in October. December 26.

4 GETTING THERE AND GETTING AROUND

GETTING TO CHILE

By Plane

Several major airlines serve Santiago's **Arturo Merino Benítez** airport (SCL) with direct flights from Miami, Atlanta, New York, Dallas–Fort Worth, Los Angeles, and Toronto. Turbulent times in the airline industry mean that fares can vary wildly depending on the time of year, departure location, and price wars that periodically break out. Most flights are red-eyes.

Note: LAN Airlines (see later) has a **South America Pass** for travelers who would like to visit more than one destination in Chile, or more than one country in South America. The pass gives travelers the opportunity to customize their own journey by purchasing one-way tickets to 49 cities in Argentina, Brazil, Chile, Colombia, Ecuador, Peru, Paraguay, and Uruguay. The glitch is that travelers must produce a round-trip air ticket to South America aboard LAN or any other "oneworld Alliance" airlines, and there is a minimum of three legs that must be purchased. Check the website to build a flight combination, then contrast the fare with your travel agent's fare or any other Web-generated fare; a promotional deal might be cheaper than the South America Pass's fixed prices for its routes. Visit the website for more information and for suggested itineraries.

See the "Fast Facts, Toll-Free Numbers & Websites" appendix on p. 443 for additional help in booking your air travel to Chile.

FROM NORTH AMERICA The country's national air carrier **LAN Airlines** (✆ **866/435-9526;** www.lan.com) has daily flights to Santiago from New York and Los Angeles, and nonstop flights from Miami. Check its website on Wednesdays for cheap, last-minute (and heavily restricted) fares from Miami. **American Airlines** (✆ **800/433-7300;** www.aa.com) has daily nonstop flights from Miami and Dallas–Fort Worth, with connections from Vancouver, Toronto, and Montreal. **Delta** (✆ **800/221-1212;** www.delta.com) offers nonstop daily flights from Atlanta. Costa Rica's **Lacsa** airline, of the parent company Taca (✆ **800/535-8780;** www.taca.com), has flights from San Francisco, Los Angeles, New York, or Miami with a stopover in Costa Rica or El Salvador. **Air Canada** offers nonstop service from Toronto to Santiago (✆ **888/247-2262;** www.aircanada.com). ***Tip:*** The airline with the most gracious service and the best planes (domestically and internationally) is LAN Airlines, by a long shot.

FROM EUROPE & THE U.K. **LAN Airlines** (✆ **0800/917-0572** in the U.K.; www.lan.com) serves London to Santiago via Madrid, in partnership with Iberia and British Airways, or try booking directly with **Iberia** (✆ **800/772-4642** in the U.S., or 0870/609-0500 in London; www.iberia.com) or with **British Airways** (✆ **0870/850-9850;** www.ba.com). **Air France** (✆ **0870/142-4343;** www.airfrance.com/uk) has two to five daily flights from London to Santiago via Paris. **KLM** (✆ **0870/142-4343;** www.klm.com) and **Lufthansa** (✆ **0870/8377-747;** www.lufthansa.com) also serve Santiago.

FROM AUSTRALIA & NEW ZEALAND **Qantas** (✆ **13-13-13** in Australia, or 0800/808-767 in New Zealand; www.qantas.com) works in conjunction with LAN, offering four flights per week from Sydney and Auckland to Santiago. **Aerolíneas Argentinas** (✆ **2/9234-9000** in Australia, or 9/379-3675 in New Zealand; www.aerolineas.com) has three weekly direct flights from Sydney and Auckland to Buenos Aires, Argentina, with a connecting flight to Santiago aboard LAN.

GETTING AROUND

By Plane

Given Chile's length, travelers, especially those short on time, must fly if planning to visit several destinations. **LAN Airlines** (✆ **866/435-9526** in the U.S., or 600/526-2000 in Chile; www.lan.com) is the leader of the airline pack in terms of destinations, frequency, and quality of service. LAN serves Arica, Iquique, Calama, Antofagasta, Concepción, Temuco, Valdivia, Osorno, Pucón (Dec–Feb only), Puerto Montt, Coyhaique (Balmaceda), and Punta Arenas. **Sky Airline** (✆ **600/600-2828;** www.skyairline.cl) is another Chilean domestic carrier, with daily flights to all major cities. The Spanish-owned **Aerolineas del Sur** (✆ **800/710-300;** www.aerolinasdelsur.cl) offers daily economical Santiago–Punta Arenas flights, and flies to Puerto Montt, Calama, Antofagasta, and Iquique.

If you're planning to visit several countries within South America, remember to check out LAN's **South America Air Pass,** which allows travelers to custom-book one-way flights around the continent and within Chile, for typically lower prices.

By Car

Car rentals for Santiago are totally unnecessary, but they do offer immense freedom if you are in the Lake District or wish to drive along the coast. Weekly rates for a compact vehicle, rented from and returned to the Santiago airport, average about $280 to $375 (£187–£250). Prices include basic insurance with no deductible and unlimited mileage, although some companies include full insurance in the price, with the exception of theft of car accessories such as a stereo. Each company sets its own policy, so comb carefully through the contract before signing it.

You may find cheaper rates by booking via an agency's website before you arrive. Most major American rental-car companies have offices in Chile, which are listed under the appropriate chapter for each company's location. To make a reservation from the United States, call **Alamo** (✆ **800/GO-ALAMO;** www.alamo.com), **Avis** (✆ **800/230-4898;** www.avis.com), **Budget** (✆ **800/472-3325;** www.budget.com), **Dollar** (✆ **800/800-4000;** www.dollar.com), or **Hertz** (✆ **800/654-3001;** www.hertz.com). If you haven't made a reservation, you can still rent from an agency kiosk at the airport.

Don't overlook a few of the local car rental agencies for cheaper prices; you'll sometimes find better value with the smaller operations. (See the "Getting Around" sections throughout this book for names of operators.) ***Note:*** If you plan to take the car over the border to Argentina, you'll need to make a request 3 to 4 days ahead of time for the proper paperwork to be set up, and pay $90 to $110 (£60–£73) extra for a stay of up to 14 days in Argentina. In this case, you'll need to reserve locally, not through a company's general website in your home country.

You don't need an international driver's license to rent a vehicle—your current driver's license suffices. It's a disappearing practice, but the police, or *carabineros,* are allowed to stop motorists without reason, which they frequently do under the guise of "control." They usually just ask to see your license and then let you pass through their checkpoint.

Driving in Santiago is better than driving in some other capitals, but you'll find more considerate motorists outside of the capital. Drivers use their horn and indicators constantly to signal where they are turning or that they are passing another vehicle—you should, too. On the highway, car and especially truck drivers signal to advise you that it's safe ahead to pass, but don't put your entire faith in the other driver's judgment, and give yourself ample space, as Chilean drivers have lead feet. The concept of "merging" is entirely foreign to Chilean drivers—you'll need to be a little aggressive to get into another lane, or wait until all traffic passes by to enter. Right turns on red are forbidden unless otherwise indicated.

Outside Santiago, especially on roads off the Pan-American Highway (Carretera Panamericana), your major concern will be keeping an eye out for bicyclists and farm animals along the road. The Panamericana underwent a huge expansion and modernization program in 2001, and drivers must now pay for it via **periodic tollbooths** on the highway and at most highway exits. Tolls, or ***peajes,*** are expensive, ranging from $1.20 to $6 (80p–£4; note that tolls are higher from 5pm on Fri to midnight on Sun). Most country roads off the Panamericana are dirt, either smoothed with gravel or washboard bumpy and pothole scarred. Gasoline is sold in liters and is called ***bencina,*** and comes in three grades: 93, 95, and 97.

Car-rental agencies provide emergency road service. Be sure to obtain a 24-hour number before leaving with your rental vehicle. The **Automóvil Club de Chile** also offers services to its worldwide members, including emergency roadside service. For more information, contact the offices in Santiago, at Av. Andrés Bello 1863 (✆

2/431-1000, or toll-free in Chile **600/464-4040**; www.automovilclub.cl).

Maps can be hard to come by; **Copec,** the gas station chain, sells Automapa's *Rutas de Chile* road maps at most of its larger stations; however, maps often sell out. Hertz offers complete maps to renters, but many rental agencies don't; request one ahead of time and fully expect them to fall through on their promise. If they do, a few shops in the airport sell maps or the excellent **Turistel** guidebooks (also sold at most bookstores and a few kiosks on popular intersections in Santiago). They are in Spanish but provide detailed road maps, city maps, and visitor information—you can even download and print maps from the website **www.turistel.cl** before you leave for your trip.

By Train

The company **Empresa de los Farrocarriles del Estado (EFE)** offers high-speed train service from Santiago to Chillán aboard modern and comfortable coaches, stopping along the way in Rancagua, San Fernando, and Talca, and passing through beautiful, pastoral landscapes along the way. Call EFE or check the website for updated information (© **600/585-5000;** www.efe.cl), or check with your travel agent or hotel for a reservation.

By Bus

Traveling by bus is very common in Chile, and there are many companies to meet the demand. Fortunately, most Chilean buses are clean and efficient and an excellent choice for traveling shorter distances. Longer distances, Santiago to Calama, for example, can be excruciating, so reevaluate taking a flight, and check www.lan.com for last-minute flights if price is an issue. The main bus companies in the country are **Pullman** (© **2/334-6683;** www.pullman.cl), **Tur Bus** (© **2/490-7500**), **Expreso Norte** (© **2/777-4462**), and **Cruz del Sur** (© **2/335-8358;** www.busescruzdelsur.cl).

If you decide to travel for more than a few hours by bus, it helps to know your options. Standard buses go by the name *clásico* or *pullman.* An *ejécutivo* or *semi-cama* is a little like business class: lots of legroom and seats that recline farther. At the top end of the scale is the *salón cama,* which features seats that fold out into beds. A *salón cama* is an excellent way to get to a region such as the Lake District, as riders sleep all night and arrive in the morning. Fares are moderately priced and seats fill up fast, so buy a ticket as far in advance as possible. Ask what is included with your fare, and whether they serve meals or if they plan to stop at a restaurant along the way.

By Ferry & Local Cruises

Navimag offers an exceptional 3-day journey from Puerto Montt (Lake District) to Puerto Natales (Patagonia) or vice versa aboard a passenger/cargo ferry that introduces travelers to remote, virgin fjordland unseen outside of Norway. The journey is very popular with backpackers with a lot of time on their hands and who enjoy the camaraderie that often develops among passengers during the journey. Navimag is not a luxury liner, but there are berths that provide enough standard comfort for even finicky travelers.

Transmarchilay has cargo ferries for vehicles that link Puerto Montt and Chiloé with the Carretera Austral. **Andina del Sud** and **Cruce de Lagos** work together to provide countless visitors with a full-day cruise between Argentina and Chile in a boat-bus-boat combination through Vicente Pérez Rosales National Park near Puerto Varas and Nahuel Huapi Lake at Bariloche, Argentina. The demanding traveler will find ample comfort aboard the small cruise ships provided by the following companies.

Skorpios has 4- and 7-day cruises from Puerto Montt or Puerto Chacabuco, stopping at Castro and Quellón in Chiloé before or after the Laguna San Rafael Glacier; they also have a dock in Puerto Natales that takes passengers to Pío XI Glacier (the only advancing glacier off the Southern Ice Field) and the remote village Puerto Eden. The ship ***Mare Australis*** offers an unforgettable journey through the untouched wilderness of Tierra del Fuego, either as a round-trip journey from Punta Arenas to Ushuaia and back, or one-way. For more information, see "Ferry Journeys Through the Fjords to Laguna San Rafael," near the end of chapter 12, and chapter 13.

For private yacht rental in Patagonia, see "Activities A to Z" in chapter 5.

5 MONEY & COSTS

CURRENCY

The unit of currency in Chile is the **peso.** The value of the peso has held steady at around 620 pesos to the American dollar and 880 pesos to the British pound; prices in this book are listed in U.S. dollars and pounds. ***Note:*** In Chile, the peso is indicated with "$" while amounts in U.S. dollars are preceded by "US$" or "$US." In this book, rates are quoted in U.S. dollars with just the "$," and pesos are quoted only rarely because of the high conversion rate. Bills come in denominations of 1,000, 2,000, 5,000, 10,000, and 20,000 pesos. There are currently six coins in circulation, in denominations of 1, 5, 10, 50, 100, and 500 pesos; however, it's unusual to be issued 1 peso or even 5. In colloquial Spanish, Chileans frequently call 1,000 pesos a *luca,* as in "It cost *cinco lucas*" (5,000).

Chile levies a steep 19% **VAT tax,** called IVA *(Impuesto al Valor Agregado)* on all goods and services. Foreigners are exempt from the IVA tax when paying in dollars for hotel rooms and vacation packages; however, you might find this is not the case with low-budget hotels and hostels. Do a little math when offered a price in dollars as the peso rate might be cheaper due to a proprietor's improper or inflated exchange rate.

Carry small peso bills and coins with you when traveling around Chile, as corner shops, taxis, kiosks, and other small businesses rarely have change for anything over 5,000 pesos. Consider keeping the change separate from your larger bills, so that it's readily accessible and you'll be less of a target for theft.

ATMs

A Chilean ATM is known as a *cajero automático,* or more commonly as a **Redbanc,** which is advertised on a maroon-and-white sticker. Redbancs are compatible with a variety of networks, including Visa/Cirrus and MasterCard/PLUS. Before you travel, be sure your ATM can be used overseas and that you know your daily withdrawal limit. ***Note:*** Chilean banks do not charge a fee to use their ATMs, but your bank may impose a fee that can be higher for international transactions (up to $5/£3.30 or more) than for domestic ones (where they're rarely more than $2/£1.30). For international withdrawal fees, ask your bank. You'll find ATM Redbancs in banks, grocery stores, gas stations, and pharmacies.

TRAVELER'S CHECKS

Traveler's checks are accepted at larger hotels but few other places, though they can be changed in most cities and towns. Some travelers feel safer carrying a few traveler's checks just in case, and they can be bought at most banks in denominations of $20, $50, $100, $500, and sometimes $1,000. Generally, you'll pay a service charge ranging from 1% to 4%. Try **American Express** (✆ **800/807-6233,** or

What Things Cost in Chile	US$	UK£	Australian $ [A$]	Canadian $ (C$)
Cup of coffee	$2.50	£1.50	A$3.90	C$3.10
A movie ticket	$7.50	£4.75	A$12	C$9.40
Taxi from airport	$24.00	£15.00	A$37	C$30
Gallon of gas	$4.00	£1.75	A$6.20	C$5
Price of moderate, 3-course dinner for one sans alcohol	$16.00	£11.00	A$25	C$20

800/221-7282 for cardholders; the latter number accepts collect calls, offers service in several foreign languages, and exempts Amex gold and platinum cardholders from the 1% fee); **Visa** (© **800/732-1322** or 866/339-3378, where AAA members can obtain Visa checks for a $9.95 fee for checks up to $1,500); and **MasterCard** (© **800/223-9920**). Keep a record of the serial numbers separate from your checks in the event that they are stolen or lost. You'll get a refund faster if you know the numbers.

Traveler's checks, dollars, and euros can be exchanged at a ***casa de cambio*** (money-exchange house) for a small charge; *casas de cambio* are generally open Monday through Friday from 9am to 6pm (closed 1–3pm for lunch), and Saturday until 1pm.

CREDIT CARDS

Visa, MasterCard, and American Express are widely accepted throughout Chile, and Diner's Club isn't far behind. Many Chilean businesses are charged a 2% to 4% service fee and will pass that cost on to you, so expect cheaper deals with cash. Smaller hostels and hotels often do not accept credit cards at all.

You can withdraw cash advances from your credit cards at banks or ATMs (provided you know your PIN), but this is an expensive option considering that you'll pay interest from the moment of your withdrawal, even if you pay your monthly bills on time. Also, note that many banks now assess a 1% to 3% "transaction fee" on *all* charges you incur abroad (whether you're using the local currency or your native currency).

6 HEALTH & SAFETY

STAYING HEALTHY

Chile poses few health risks to travelers, and no special vaccinations are required. In fact, there are no poisonous plants or animals in Chile. Nevertheless, standard wisdom says that travelers should get tetanus and hepatitis boosters before leaving.

DIETARY AILMENTS Few visitors to Chile experience anything other than run-of-the-mill traveler's stomach in reaction to unfamiliar foods and any microorganisms in them, but even this is uncommon. As a general rule, it's best to eat shellfish only in reputable restaurants or those that are near the sea and receive fresh supplies daily.

In many large cities and towns, Chile's tap water is clean and safe to drink. Seek local advice, if you are in doubt; or, to be on the safe side, drink bottled water—it's widely available throughout Chile. In San Pedro de Atacama, ***do not under any circumstances drink tap water,*** as it contains trace amounts of arsenic.

ALTITUDE SICKNESS Altitude sickness, known as *soroche* or *puna,* is a temporary yet often debilitating affliction that affects about a quarter of travelers to the northern *altiplano,* or the Andes at 2,400m (7,872 ft.) and up. Nausea, fatigue, headaches, shortness of breath, sleeplessness, and feeling "out of it" are the symptoms, which can last from 1 to 5 days. If affected, drink plenty of water, take aspirin or ibuprofen, and avoid alcohol and sleeping pills—or better yet, avoid the condition by acclimatizing yourself by breaking the climb to higher regions into segments.

SUN & THE OZONE LAYER Do not take this lightly. Chile's ozone layer, especially in the southern region and Patagonia, is thinner than in the U.S. or Europe, and you'll burn a lot faster here, especially if you're in high altitudes. In Patagonia, "red alert" days (Sept–Nov) mean that fair-skinned visitors can burn within *10 minutes.* Protect yourself with sun block, a long-sleeved shirt, a wide-brimmed hat, and sunglasses. Slap sunscreen on even when at the beach in Viña.

General Availability of Health Care

Contact the **International Association for Medical Assistance to Travelers** (**IAMAT;** ✆ **716/754-4883** or, in Canada, 416/652-0137; **www.iamat.org**) for tips on travel and health concerns, and for lists of local, English-speaking doctors. The U.S. Embassy in Santiago (✆ **2/232-2600;** www.usembassy.cl) also has a list of English-speaking doctors that you can download from the website. The United States **Centers for Disease Control and Prevention** (✆ **800/311-3435;** www.cdc.gov) provides up-to-date information on health hazards by region or country and offers tips on food safety. The website **www.tripprep.com**, sponsored by a consortium of travel medicine practitioners, may also offer helpful advice on traveling abroad. You can find listings of reliable clinics overseas at the **International Society of Travel Medicine** (www.istm.org).

What To Do If You Get Sick Away From Home

Medical care in Santiago is world-class, and many doctors are English-speaking. In smaller towns, always visit a private clinic instead of a public hospital. Some rural areas have only a basic clinic, and you'll need to travel to the nearest large town for more complicated procedures. We list **hospitals** and **emergency numbers** under "Fast Facts" throughout this guide.

If you suffer from a chronic illness, consult your doctor before your departure—especially if planning to visit high altitudes. Pack **prescription medications** in your carry-on luggage, and carry them in their original containers, with pharmacy labels—otherwise they won't make it through airport security. Carry the generic name of prescription medicines, in case a local pharmacist is unfamiliar with the brand name.

For travel abroad, you may have to pay all medical costs up front and be reimbursed later. See "Medical Insurance," under "Travel Insurance," on p. 443. We list **additional emergency numbers** in the "Fast Facts" appendix, p. 443.

STAYING SAFE

Chile is one of the safest countries in Latin America, with little political unrest, corruption, or violent crime. A traveler's principal concerns are pickpockets and break-ins, which are on the rise in cities like Santiago. Never leave valuables in your rental car, and always keep a close eye on your belongings when in public.

Police officers wear olive-green uniforms and are referred to as *carabineros,* or colloquially as *pacos.* Never, ever, think about bribing a police officer—you'll be taken straight to the *comiseria* (police station).

Chile's police force is fair and courteous to travelers, if just not very effective when it comes to petty crime. If you've been robbed, your insurance company will most likely ask for a police report, called a *constancia,* which you can get at any police station.

7 SPECIALIZED TRAVEL RESOURCES

TRAVELERS WITH DISABILITIES

There are more options and resources out there than ever before for travelers with disabilities, and here in Chile it is increasingly common to see hotels and restaurants that are wheelchair-accessible. It's best to call ahead (especially with restaurants) to inquire about an establishment's facilities.

Many travel agencies offer customized tours and itineraries to Chile for travelers with disabilities. Among them are **Flying Wheels Travel** (✆ **507/451-5005;** www.flyingwheelstravel.com); **Access-Able Travel Source** (✆ **303/232-2979;** www.access-able.com); and **Accessible Journeys** (✆ **800/846-4537** or 610/521-0339; www.disabilitytravel.com). **Avis Rent a Car** has an "Avis Access" program that offers such services as a dedicated 24-hour toll-free number (✆ **888/879-4273**) for customers with special travel needs; special car features such as swivel seats, spinner knobs, and hand controls; and accessible bus service.

Organizations that offer assistance to travelers with disabilities include **MossRehab** (www.mossresourcenet.org); the **American Foundation for the Blind** (✆ **800/232-5463;** www.afb.org); and **SATH** (Society for Accessible Travel & Hospitality; ✆ **212/447-7284;** www.sath.org).

AirAmbulanceCard.com is now partnered with SATH and allows you to preselect top-notch hospitals in case of an emergency.

For more information and resources on travel for those with disabilities, see www.frommers.com/planning.

GAY & LESBIAN TRAVELERS

Gays and lesbians visiting Chile will most likely not encounter any prejudice or outward intolerance. However, public displays of affection between same sexes are rare, even in metropolitan cities such as Santiago. In general, attitudes, especially those of Chilean men, toward gays and lesbians are not very liberal, owing in part to the Catholic, conservative nature of their society. Homosexual relationships have only recently been declared officially legal, and many gays and lesbians are not actively open about their orientation outside their own circles. In Santiago, the two most gay-friendly neighborhoods are Bellavista and Parque Forestal (also known as Bellas Artes).

The best source for information is the website **www.santiagogay.com**, a resource directory that covers gay issues and provides information about travel, gay-oriented businesses and bars, employment, and more. **Gay Adventure Tours, Inc.** (✆ **888/206-6523;** www.gayadventuretours.com) occasionally offers trips to Chile. **The International Gay and Lesbian Travel Association (IGLTA;** ✆ **800/448-8550** or **954/776-2626**; www.iglta.com) is the trade association for the gay and lesbian travel industry, and offers an online directory of gay- and lesbian-friendly travel businesses; go to the website and click on "Members."

For more gay and lesbian travel resources visit www.frommers.com/planning.

SENIOR TRAVELERS

Seniors, referred to in Chile as *tercera edad,* or "third age," will find plenty of discounts at museums and attractions, but not much else. Members of **AARP,** 601 E St. NW, Washington, DC 20049 (✆ **888/687-2277;** www.aarp.org), get discounts on hotels, airfares, and car rentals. AARP offers members a wide range of benefits, including *AARP The Magazine* and a monthly newsletter. Anyone over 50 can join.

Many reliable agencies and organizations target the 50-plus market. **Elderhostel** (✆ **877/426-8056;** www.elderhostel.org) arranges outstanding study programs in Chile for those ages 55 and over. **ElderTreks** (✆ **800/741-7956;** www.eldertreks.com) offers small-group tours to off-the-beaten-path or adventure-travel locations, restricted to travelers 50 and older. **INTRAV** (✆ **800/456-8100;** www.intrav.com) is a high-end tour operator that caters to the mature, discerning traveler (not specifically seniors), with trips around the world that include guided safaris, polar expeditions, private-jet adventures, and small-boat cruises down jungle rivers.

For more information and resources on travel for seniors, see www.frommers.com/planning.

FAMILY TRAVELERS

Chileans love kids, and family-friendly lodging and kid's specials are the rule, not the exception. Many hotels feature playgrounds, swimming pools, child care, and attached rooms or space for additional beds, and some resorts offer full-scale kids' activities, giving parents a breather and a little "adult time." Few, if any, hotels (such as luxury hotels) refuse children, but be sure to check their policy anyway when booking. To locate accommodations, restaurants, and attractions that are particularly kid-friendly, refer to the "Kids" icon throughout this guide. For special travel requirements for children, see "Passports & Visas" earlier in this chapter.

When choosing lodging, check to see if a suite is cheaper than booking two connecting rooms. Most suites have a sofa bed, or at the very least the hotel can add an extra cot-style bed. A good bet for families spending several days in a destination is an *apart-hotel* or a *cabaña,* which are self-catering units with living areas and kitchens—these options are frequently less expensive than a hotel room. Hotel chains such as the Radisson and the Sheraton occasionally offer specials for families with kids, but as a general rule, kids are either free when sharing a room with their parents, or are charged a minimal fee for an extra bed.

For a list of more family-friendly travel resources, visit www.frommers.com/planning.

WOMEN TRAVELERS

Chilean men are more "macho" than their Argentine counterparts, but they do not tend to whistle and make boisterous comments to women the way that Argentine men do. Chilean men instead leer, which can be annoying, creepy, or both. My advice is to just ignore the situation, as any kind of remark just seems to egg them on. Hitchhiking in rural areas by single women is common, but exercise caution. A lift up to a ski resort or into a national park that does not have public transportation is okay, but longer trips up and down the Pan-American Highway are best undertaken aboard one of the country's cheap and plentiful long-distance buses.

For general travel resources for women, go to www.frommers.com/planning.

STUDENT TRAVELERS

You'd be wise to arm yourself with an **International Student Identity Card (ISIC),** which offers substantial savings on plane tickets and entrance fees in Chile. It also provides you with basic health and life insurance and a 24-hour help line. The card is available from **STA Travel** (✆ **800/781-4040** in North America; www.sta.com or www.statravel.com; or www.statravel.co.uk in the U.K.), the biggest student travel agency in the world. If you're no longer a student but are still under 26, you can get an **International Youth Travel Card**

(IYTC) from the same people, which entitles you to some discounts (but not on museum admissions). **Travel CUTS** (✆ **800/667-2887** or **416/614-2887**; www.travelcuts.com) offers similar services for both Canadians and U.S. residents. Irish students may prefer to turn to **USIT** (✆ **01/602-1600;** www.usitnow.ie), an Ireland-based specialist in student, youth, and independent travel.

For more information on traveling as a student, go to www.frommers.com/planning.

SINGLE TRAVELERS

On package vacations, single travelers are often hit with a dreaded "single supplement" to the base price. To avoid it, you can agree to room with other single travelers or find a compatible roommate before you go, from one of the many roommate-locator agencies.

Travel Buddies Singles Travel Club (✆ **800/998-9099;** www.travelbuddiesworldwide.com), based in Canada, runs small, intimate, single-friendly group trips and will match you with a roommate free of charge. **TravelChums** (✆ **212/787-2621;** www.travelchums.com) is an Internet-only travel-companion matching service with elements of an online personals–type site, hosted by the respected New York–based Shaw Guides travel service. **Backroads** (✆ **800/462-2848;** www.backroads.com) offers more than 40 active-travel solo trips to destinations worldwide, including Chile.

For more information on traveling single, go to www.frommers.com/planning.

8 SUSTAINABLE TOURISM

The principal environmental problems that confront Chile are deforestation and air, water, and land pollution. Santiago is one of Latin America's most polluted cities, and air pollution there has become an acute problem; children and the elderly and infirm are frequently advised to stay indoors for days on end due to dangerous levels of toxic pollutants that enshroud the capital. Rapid urban expansion, industrial emissions from the copper mining sector, and the increased volume of car traffic are cited as the main causes of Santiago's air pollution. Mining is responsible for releasing the chief air and water pollutants, including sulfur dioxide and arsenic. In 2000, the city faced an unprecedented pollution emergency when over 200,000 vehicles were prohibited from driving on the roads and offending industries were shut down. Fortunately, in the last few years, environmental issues have taken a more prominent role in domestic politics and, while the pace is slow, government initiatives have gone a long way to improving the situation.

The indiscriminate logging of Chile's temperate forests has resulted in the tragic disappearance of thousand-year-old forests. The most publicized case of illegal logging, which has been taken up by environmental agencies, including Greenpeace, is that of the rare alerce tree, which is found in the Andes and can live for up to 3,500 years. Similar to Californian redwood trees, its robustness and impermeability make it an extremely valuable commodity; a cubic meter can sell for as high as $5,300/£3,533 on the international black market. Under Pinochet, logging of the alerce reached its sickening nadir, and while new laws introduced in 1974 have protected the species under international law, logging still exists due to a loophole that allows for the extraction and commercialization of trees that were cut before the law was passed. Greenpeace has denounced CONAF, the Chilean National Parks and Wildlife Service, for its complicity in the illegal logging industry and has made persistent calls for the Chilean government to declare a national moratorium on alerce logging permits.

Many animals are in serious risk of extinction throughout the country, as well. As of 2001, of the 91 listed mammals in Chile, some 16 species were registered as endangered. Almost 5% of Chile's 298 breeding bird species are threatened with extinction, most notably the tundra peregrine falcon, the Chilean woodstar, and the ruddy-headed goose. Also threatened are four types of freshwater fish and over 250 plant species. See "Sustainable Seafood" in chapter 2 for tips on eating sustainably in the country.

Chile hasn't made great strides in the sustainable accommodations arena. Patagonia, and to a lesser extent Easter Island, are the only areas with truly environmentally conscious hotels. Hotels in the Patagonia region are some of the most innovative on the continent when it comes to sustainability. The striking **Remota Hotel** (p. 384) in Puerto Natales has natural grasses planted on the roof, simplified heating from appropriate sun exposure, energy-efficient lighting, and low-consumption water systems. At press time, the **explora Salto Chico Hotel** (p. 394), in nearby Torres del Paine, was midway through receiving prestigious LEED certification from the United States Green Building Council.

Nearby, **Indigo Patagonia** (p. 383) includes an advanced insulation system that requires no central heating for most of the spring and summer, and bright natural solar lighting that reduces the need for bulbs. Inside the hotel, there's extensive recycling. The new **Patagonia Camp** (p. 395) was built completely on stilts so as to have a minimal impact, and houses a graywater treatment system and solar-powered lighting.

With their near-nothing eco-footprint, the colorful domes at **Eco-Camp Patagonia**, inside Torres del Paine National Park, have been awarded the rigorous Swiss-based ISO 14001 certification. It's the only property in Patagonia to garner this award for its eco-efforts, including using alternative energy, waste water processing, and compost toilets.

In 2009, the **explora Posada de Mike Rapu** (p. 435) in Easter Island became the first hotel in Latin America to attain LEED certification from the U.S. Green Building Council and the 13th in the world to achieve this distinction. Construction followed LEED recommendations while protecting the delicate surroundings of the island.

As the popularity of **Antarctic tourism** has boomed over the past few years, so have concerns about the safety of both the local ecology and the tourists who are venturing to see the continent. A handful of incidents involving expedition ships sinking, running aground, or hitting rock or ice in Antarctic waters have set off alarm bells. Controversial calls in mid-2009 for stricter regulations, including drastic limits on visitor numbers and ship sizes, could have a serious impact on tourism. A proposal to ban ships carrying more than 500 passengers from any landing sites, and to limit the number going ashore at any time to 100, was recently approved by members of the Antarctic Treaty. Remember, though, that these regulations are voluntary under international law, since the Antarctic has no internationally-recognized governance body.

See "Volunteer Opportunities" under "Special-Interest Trips" (p. 48) for info on volunteer trips to Chile.

In recent years, **dog-sledding**, a popular activity in southern Chile, has become shrouded in controversy as global animal rights activists have launched a series of campaigns highlighting the brutal effects of pushing the dogs too hard under extreme conditions. For information on this and other animal-friendly issues in Chile, visit **Tread Lightly** (www.treadlightly.org).

Tips It's Easy Being Green

Here are a few simple ways you can help conserve fuel and energy when you travel:

- Each time you take a flight or drive a car, greenhouse gases release into the atmosphere. You can help neutralize this danger to the planet through "carbon offsetting"—paying someone to invest your money in programs that reduce your greenhouse gas emissions by the same amount you've added. Before buying carbon offset credits, just make sure that you're using a reputable company, one with a proven program that invests in renewable energy. Reliable carbon offset companies include **Carbonfund** (www.carbonfund.org), **TerraPass** (www.terrapass.org), and **Carbon Neutral** (www.carbonneutral.org).
- Whenever possible, choose nonstop flights; they generally require less fuel than indirect flights that stop and take off again. Try to fly during the day—some scientists estimate that nighttime flights are twice as harmful to the environment. And pack light—each 15 pounds of luggage on a 5,000-mile flight adds up to 50 pounds of carbon dioxide emitted.
- Where you stay during your travels can have a major environmental impact. To determine the green credentials of a property, ask about trash disposal and recycling, water conservation, and energy use; also question if sustainable materials were used in the construction of the property. The website **www.greenhotels.com** recommends green-rated member hotels around the world that fulfill the company's stringent environmental requirements. Also consult **www.environmentallyfriendlyhotels.com** for more green accommodations ratings.
- At hotels, request that your sheets and towels not be changed daily. (Many hotels already have programs like this in place.) Turn off the lights and air-conditioner (or heater) when you leave your room.
- Use public transport where possible—trains, buses, and even taxis are more energy-efficient forms of transport than driving. Even better is to walk or cycle; you'll produce zero emissions and stay fit and healthy on your travels.
- If renting a car is necessary, ask the rental agent for a hybrid, or rent the most fuel-efficient car available. You'll use less gas and save money at the tank.
- Eat at locally owned and operated restaurants that use produce grown in the area. This contributes to the local economy and cuts down on greenhouse gas emissions by supporting restaurants where the food is not flown or trucked in across long distances.

9 SPECIAL-INTEREST TRIPS

COOKING CLASSES

Food and travel writer **Liz Caskey** (✆ **2/632-2015;** www.lizcaskey.com) runs customized culinary programs that include tours to wineries, markets, and farms around Santiago. Day classes and week-long courses are available.

Many tour operators run culinary tours through Santiago and the surrounding wine country that focus on visiting local farmers' markets, followed by a demonstration of the cooking techniques and discussion of the fresh produce that define Chilean gastronomy, all nicely rounded off with a gourmet lunch. **Santiago Adventures** (© **2/244-2750;** www.santiagoadventures.com) charges $143 (£95) for such a trip, per person based on two people.

LANGUAGE CLASSES

There is no shortage of Spanish language schools in Santiago and with the beach and mountains a short ride away, the city provides a great base for an active student life. Most of the city's reputable language schools are located in the residential areas of Providencia and Las Condes and offer total immersion programs with homestays that are usually a 20- to 30-minute journey on public transport from the school. Tuition and accommodations prices are considerably more expensive than other countries in Latin America; expect to pay between $2,500 and $3,000 (£1,667–£2,000) per month, including lessons (4–6 hr. per day) and accommodations in a private room with a host family, with two meals daily.

AmeriSpan (© **800/879-6640;** www.amerispan.com) is well established in South America and takes the hassle out of planning; the school, lodging, airport pickup, and other services are all prearranged. Their Santiago school is located in a renovated 18th-century building in Providencia and group classes are limited to seven people. Prices also include organized activities per week. Another big player with a strong reputation is **Spanish Abroad** (© **888/722-7623;** www.spanishabroad.com). Their school is also in the quiet neighborhood of Providencia, a few blocks from the Metro. Four classes are run daily, with a maximum of six students per class. **Bridge Abroad** (© **866/574-8606;** www.bridgeabroad.com) offers 4 hours of group lessons and 2 hours of private lessons at their school in Providencia; they also host family accommodations and can arrange a number of activities and excursions.

VOLUNTEER OPPORTUNITIES

There are literally hundreds of volunteer organizations operating in Chile. Most opportunities are aimed at gap year students and young adults taking work sabbaticals. Opportunities range from teaching English in small towns (TEFL certificates are usually required) to working in orphanages, building schools, community development, environmental conservation, and wildlife and research programs. Accommodations and meals are usually included.

South American Explorers (www.saexplorers.cl) is a wonderful nonprofit organization that has earned cult status among seasoned backpackers, especially those traveling solo with its outreach community feel and volunteer programs. Offices throughout South America provide fact sheets (available online) detailing hotels, transport information, entry requirements, travel advisories, and tour ideas. You are required to become a member of the club ($60/£40 per year), but if you are a regular visitor to the continent or just an armchair travel junkie, it's well worth it.

Also check out the following websites for details on volunteer programs in Chile:

- ELI (www.eliabroad.org)
- Mondo Challenge (www.mondochallenge.org)
- United Planet (www.unitedplanet.org)
- VE Global (www.ve-global.org)
- Volunteer Abroad (www.volunteerabroad.com)
- Volunteer Adventures (www.volunteeradventures.com)

10 STAYING CONNECTED

TELEPHONES

You won't have to walk far to find a **public phone** box in most large towns and cities. Most phone boxes accept coins, but you will often find them jammed; it's much more efficient to buy a **phone card,** available from newsstands or Metro stations. **Call centers** are also omnipresent in Santiago and larger cities; they are often much cheaper and more comfortable than using a public phone, especially if they are privately operated. A local phone call requires 100 pesos; phone cards sold in kiosks offer better rates. Phone cards have individual instructions on long-distance dialing, and phone booths at telephone centers will provide instructions on dialing according to the carrier they use.

To place a call from your home country to Chile, dial the international access code (011 in the U.S. and Canada, 0011 in Australia, 0170 in New Zealand, 00 in the U.K.) plus the country code (56), plus the Chilean area code, followed by the number. For example, a call from the United States to Santiago would be 011+56+2+000+0000. **To place a local call within Chile,** dial the number; for long-distance national calls, dial a carrier prefix, then the area code, and then the number. (To place a collect call, dial a prefix and then 182 for an operator.) **To place a direct international call from Chile,** dial a carrier prefix followed by 0, then the country code of the destination you are calling, plus the area code and the local number.

Cellular numbers are seven digits with a prefix of **9, 8,** or **7.** Here's the tricky part. When dialing from a local landline to a cellphone, you must dial an additional prefix of 09 (for example, 099+000+0000); but this is not the case when dialing from cellphone to cellphone (for example, 9+000+0000) or from outside Chile (011+56+9+000+0000). To dial a landline from a cellphone, you must first dial 02 (for example, 02+2+000+0000 for a number in Santiago), but landline to landline you simply dial the number (for example, 2+000+0000).

CELLPHONES

Chile's two largest phone companies, Entel and Telefónica, operate on a GSM 1900 MHZ frequency. Any dual or multiband GSM cellphone will work in Chile, but you'll pay expensive roaming rates; check with your cellphone company before leaving. (In the U.S., T-Mobile and AT&T/Cingular use this quasi-universal system; in Canada, Microcell and some Rogers customers are GSM.)

If your cellphone does not have this capability, you can rent a phone, either before you leave home or upon arrival in Chile. Pre-departure, North Americans can rent a phone from **InTouch USA** (✆ **800/872-7626;** www.intouchglobal.com) or **RoadPost** (✆ **888/290-1606** or **905/272-5665**; www.roadpost.com). InTouch will also, for free, advise you on whether your existing phone will work overseas; simply call ✆ **703/222-7161** between 9am and 4pm EST, or go to **http://intouchglobal.com/travel.htm**.

In Chile, you can rent a phone at the **Entel** or **Telefónica kiosks** located on the arrival level at the Santiago airport and insert your own SIM card; you'll still pay regular roaming rates. Considering that Entel and Telefónica earn money when you dial using roaming rates, they do not rent phones with prepaid calling cards; however, they do sell phones for as low as $55 (£37), which includes a calling card with $19 (£13) in calls. Local calls average 50¢ (35p) and receiving calls is free; however, this option does not allow you to dial internationally. Both kiosks at the airport

Online Traveler's Toolbox

Veteran travelers usually carry some essential items to make their trips easier. Following is a selection of handy online tools to bookmark and use.

- **Airplane Food** (www.airlinemeals.net)
- **Airplane Seating** (www.seatguru.com and www.airlinequality.com)
- **Foreign Languages for Travelers** (www.travlang.com)
- **Maps** (www.mapquest.com)
- **Subway Navigator** (www.subwaynavigator.com)
- **Time and Date** (www.timeanddate.com)
- **Travel Warnings** (http://travel.state.gov, www.fco.gov.uk/travel, www.voyage.gc.ca, www.smartraveller.gov.au)
- **Universal Currency Converter** (www.oanda.com)
- **Weather** (www.intellicast.com and www.weather.com)

can be found in the arrival level, and are open daily from 6am to 9pm.

INTERNET ACCESS

Nearly every hotel in Chile has an Internet station, but if for some reason they don't, **cybercafes** are commonplace and clustered around all commercial areas in every city's downtown area. Midrange and upscale hotel guest rooms have dataports, and more and more frequently, hotels, cafes, and retailers are signing on as Wi-Fi (wireless fidelity) "hotspots." The Santiago airport has **Internet kiosks** scattered throughout its gates for a per-minute fee.

11 TIPS ON ACCOMMODATIONS

In most cities and towns throughout Chile, you will usually find a broad range of accommodations choices. Low-cost hostel options start at $15/£10 per night while a budget hotel room will cost between $20 and $40 (£13–£27) per night. There are several great-value gems (which I have listed in the guide), but for the most part medieval dimensions and a paucity of services are the rule. Midrange hotels start at around $75/£50 and offer a more salubrious aura, dapper service, and plusher rooms. Expensive and luxury hotels will set you back at least $150/£100 per night and include some of the finest hotels on the continent, the Ritz, Hyatt, and explora groups being the flag bearers for sheer indulgence. A new wave of charming adobe-style lodges and decadent spas also provides a perfect fusion of style and substance.

It is imperative that you consider Chile's high season when planning your trip, as prices are sky-high and reservations are hard to come by without advance planning. High season runs from December 15 to the end of February, Easter week, and for 2 weeks around the middle of July, and hotels in tourist regions may extend their high season to include November and March. Some hotels drop their prices by as much as 50% in the off season. Hotel price ranges listed in this guidebook reflect low to high season rates.

House-Swapping

House-swapping is becoming a more popular and viable means of travel; you stay in their place, they stay in yours, and you both get an authentic and personal view of the area, the opposite of the escapist retreat that many hotels offer. Try **HomeLink International** (Homelink.org), the largest and oldest home-swapping organization, founded in 1952, with over 11,000 listings worldwide ($75 for a yearly membership). **HomeExchange.org** ($49.95 for 6,000 listings) and **Inter-Vac.com** ($68.88 for over 10,000 listings) are also reliable. Many travelers find great housing swaps on Craigslist (www.craigslist.org), too, though the offerings cannot be vetted or vouched for. Swap at your own risk.

The prices listed in this book are also **rack rates**—that is, a hotel's standard or advertised rate. Don't be shy about negotiating a discount with a hotel. Owners are accustomed to paying a 20% commission to tour operators, so they will often consider dropping the price slightly during the off-season (or for multiday stays). Alternately, check a hotel's website or simply ask if there is a promotion or package deal being offered that you're not aware of. Remember that if you pay in Chilean pesos for a room that's quoted in U.S. dollars, you'll often have to pay an IVA tax. Sometimes euros may also be accepted, but don't expect to be able to pay in any other foreign currency. See "Currency" on p. 40 for more info.

A sales tactic that is creeping its way into the cheap hotelier's lingo is the "bed-and-breakfast," but don't buy it. The term is redundant because every hotel, with the exception of the dirt-cheap hostel, includes breakfast in its price. Expect a continental breakfast at inexpensive and moderately priced hotels and an "American" or buffet breakfast at larger, high-end hotels.

Note: Air-conditioning is not necessarily a given in many hotels throughout the country. In general, this is not a problem. Cooler nights and a well-placed ceiling fan are often more than enough to keep things pleasant.

HOTEL OPTIONS

APART-HOTEL This amalgam is exactly what it implies: an "apartment-hotel," or a hotel room with an additional living area and kitchen. Found primarily in Santiago and other large cities, they offer a wider range of services than a *cabaña.* Some are bargains for their price and come with maid service. However, some are nothing more than a hotel room with a kitchenette tucked into a random corner.

CABAÑAS *Cabañas* are a versatile lodging option. They are commonly found in resort areas and are popular with families and travelers seeking an independent unit. They resemble cabins or chalets and range from bare-bones to deluxe, although all come with fully equipped kitchens, and most have maid service.

HOSTERIAS An *hostería* is a guest-house or hotel attended by its owner, typically found in a country setting.

RESIDENCIALES & HOSTELS These lodging options are for budget travelers. *Residenciales* are private homes whose owners rent out rooms, and they range from simple, clean rooms with a private or shared bathroom to ugly spaces with creepy bathrooms. In towns that see more tourists, a hostel can be a hip and very comfortable place run by foreigners or Chileans, typically from Santiago. Some hostels are private homes that use their living area as a common area, and some of them can be very comfortable.

REFUGIOS *Refugios,* which are common in Patagonia, are remote and rustic lodges that are similar to cabins. They are wonderful places to mix and mingle with fellow trekkers, and allow you to hike without a heavy pack loaded with a tent. Still, you'll want to bring your own sleeping bag, and book your bunk at *refugios* months ahead of time to secure your spot.

4

Suggested Chile Itineraries

Chile is home to a staggering array of formidable landscapes, each beautiful in its own way and offering a broad spectrum of otherworldly attractions and adrenaline-infused activities that will live long in the memory.

Whatever your passions or desires, Chile has it all: glistening salt flats; gorgeous wine country framed by an Andean backdrop; wild whitewater rapids; sea kayaking; country lanes perfect for biking; trekking and skiing in the stunning Andean peaks; surreal cityscapes in poetic Valparaíso; and more. Of course, there are also plenty of relaxing destinations for travelers who just want to kick back with a good book on a chaise lounge or spend their afternoons taking long walks along the beach. Fly-fishermen seeking to spend their days reeling in trout might plan their entire journey to Chile around this sport. Multisport resorts with their own guides have been popping up around Chile, providing guests with a home base and a roster of activities as varied as hiking, horseback riding, and mountain biking. These resorts can be found in outdoors meccas such as Patagonia and San Pedro de Atacama, and are usually quite pricey. Your other option is to book a hotel and arrange day activities with local operators, or have a tour company put the whole thing together for you.

Whatever the amount of time you plan to spend in Chile, remember that this is one heck of a long country, and you'll lose half a day traveling from one destination to another, and in the case of Patagonia you'll lose a full day traveling from Santiago. Flying is simply the most logical, although expensive, way to get around the country; with three domestic airlines, there are plenty of daily flights to all major cities. Many travelers spend little or no time in Santiago, while others use it as a base for exploring the lush vineyards, coastal resorts, and national parks of the Central Region. I recommend you spend at least 1 night in Santiago to visit the handful of historical attractions, which can be easily seen in 1 or 2 days, and develop an understanding of the psychology of a country with a compelling history.

Driving is the ideal way to experience the wine country or the coast, since it allows you the freedom and flexibility that the region's sensorial pleasures implore. The Lake District also provides plenty of photo-worthy sightseeing drives. DIY travelers who are not planning to take long hikes can also rent a vehicle in Punta Arenas and explore southern Patagonia on their own. You'll never need a vehicle in Santiago. See "By Car" under "Getting Around Chile," in chapter 3, for more information about driving in Chile.

The following itineraries are blueprints for memorable vacations that can be adhered to explicitly, modified according to your desires and likes, or even expanded if you're lucky enough to have an extended vacation.

1 REGIONS IN BRIEF

Sandwiched between the Andes and the Pacific Ocean, Chile's lengthy, serpentine shape at first glance seems preposterous: nearly 4,830km (3,000 miles) of land stretching from the arid northern desert to the wild desolation of Patagonia, and a width that averages 180km (112 miles). Chile encompasses such a breathtaking array of landscapes and temperate zones (the only zone not found here is tropical), it is hard to believe such variation can exist in just one country.

SANTIAGO & THE CENTRAL VALLEY The central region of Chile, including Santiago and its environs, features a mild, Mediterranean climate, which reminds many of California. This is Chile's breadbasket, with fertile valleys and rolling fields that harvest a large share of the country's fruit and vegetables; it also is the site of world-famous Chilean wineries. Santiago's proximity to ski resorts, beach resorts, and the idyllic countryside with its campestral and ranching traditions and colonial estates, offers a distinct variety of activities that make the Central Valley an excellent destination. See chapters 6 and 7.

LA SERENA & THE ELQUI VALLEY Aside from tiny villages in the Atacama Desert, La Serena is the only town in Chile that still lives and breathes the colonial Spanish heritage. La Serena's rough-and-tumble neighbor Coquimbo is experiencing a renaissance as a nightlife hub and boasts Chile's biggest outdoor fair, La Pampilla; and numerous beaches make this one of Chile's top summer holiday destinations, particularly for families. But it's not just beach-hopping and watersports: An array of attractions (including some of the world's greatest astronomical observatories, archaeological sites, religious festivities, nature preserves, and the relaxing Elqui Valley in the Andes) offers something for anyone seeking a quiet country rest or a desert, ocean, or mountain adventure—in other words, a little bit of everything. See chapter 8.

THE DESERT NORTH This region claims the world's driest desert, a beautiful "wasteland" set below a chain of purple and pink volcanoes and high-altitude salt flats. The most popular destinations here, including the Atacama Desert, sit at altitudes of 2,000m (6,560 ft.) and up. The extreme climate and the geological forces at work in this region have produced far-out land formations and superlatives such as the highest geyser field in the world. The earth here is parched, sun-baked, and unlike anything you've ever seen, but it gives relief through many of its tiny emerald oases, such as San Pedro de Atacama and Valle del Elqui. See chapter 9.

THE LAKE DISTRICT Few destinations in the world rival the lush scenery of Chile's Lake District, and for that reason it's the most popular destination for foreigners visiting Chile. This region is packed with a chain of conical, snowcapped volcanoes; glacier-scoured valleys; several national parks; thick groves of native forest; hot springs; jagged peaks; and, of course, many shimmering lakes. Temperatures during the summer are idyllic, but winter is characterized by months of drizzling rain. It's an outdoors-lover and adventure-seeker's paradise, especially in Pucón and Puerto Varas, offering biking, hiking, kayaking, rafting, fly-fishing, and more, but it is also a low-key destination for those who just want to kick back and enjoy the marvelous views. See chapter 10.

CHILOE The island of Chiloé is as attractive for its emerald, rolling hills and colorful wooden churches as it is for the unique culture that developed after 300 years of geographic isolation. Picturesque fishing hamlets and views that stretch from the Pacific to the Andes make for fine sightseeing drives, and Chiloé National Park offers ample opportunity for hiking along the island's untamed coastal rainforest. See chapter 11.

THE CARRETERA AUSTRAL Across the sound from Chiloé sits Chile's "frontier" highway, commonly known as the Carretera Austral, a dirt road that stretches nearly 1,000km (620 miles) from Puerto Montt in the north to beyond Coyhaique in the south. Along the way, this relatively new road passes through virgin territory visited by few travelers: tiny villages speckled among thick virgin rainforest, and rugged peaks from which waterfalls descend. This area could be one of Chile's best-kept secrets. See chapter 12.

PATAGONIA & TIERRA DEL FUEGO Also known as the Magallanes Region, Patagonia has soared in popularity over the past decade, drawing visitors from all over the world to places such as Torres del Paine National Park. Patagonia is characterized by vast open pampa similar to a prairie, the colossal Northern and Southern Ice Fields and hundreds of mighty glaciers, the peaks of the Andes as they fade into the southern Pacific Ocean at their terminus, emerald fjords, and wind, wind, wind. Getting here is an adventure—it usually takes 24 hours if coming directly from the United States or Europe—but the singular beauty of the region renders the journey worth it. Cruise through emerald fjords, walk across a glacier, stroll through frontierlike immigrant towns such as Puerto Natales, and, without a doubt, visit Chile's national jewel, Torres del Paine.

Tierra del Fuego, South America's largest island, sits across the Strait of Magellan and is shared by both Chile and Argentina. There is one town here on the Chilean side, Porvenir; the rest of the island is populated with more beavers than people. See chapter 13.

EASTER ISLAND Easter Island, or "Rapa Nui," is the world's most remote island, located farthest away from land than any other island. Annexed by Chile in 1888, the island is famous for its moai sculptures that dot the landscape and awe every visitor. Easter Island offers much more by the way of archaeology—the entire island is a veritable living museum—and there are two dreamy beaches, phenomenal scuba diving in the island's crystal-clear, periwinkle blue water, wild horses, and a people whose Polynesian culture is thriving despite having been nearly decimated. This is a destination that will exceed all expectations, but you'll need to come with a hang-loose attitude. See chapter 14.

2 CHILE IN 1 WEEK

Plenty of travelers head to Chile for 1 week only on a ski vacation, but it's a shame to come all this way and not experience anything other than the snowy Andean peaks. If you're not skiing and really only have 1 week to see Chile, your best bet is to pick one destination only: Patagonia, the Central Region, or San Pedro de Atacama. These three destinations offer the most "Chilean" experiences. For the Atacama or Patagonia, read those chapters and tailor your own journey to fit the confines of 1 week; it's very doable in this time frame, and you'll be able to fit a night in Santiago on your first or last night. The following itinerary is centered on the Central Region, because here you'll be able to pack the most diverse activities possible into 7 days. You might consider renting a car and striking out on your own when following this itinerary.

ONE WEEK *(above)*

Day 1 Santiago
Day 2 The Andes
Days 3 & 4 Wine Country
Days 5 & 6 The Central Coast
Day 7 From Valparaíso/Viña del Mar to Santiago/airport

TWO WEEKS *(right)*

Day 1 Santiago
Days 2–4 San Pedro de Atacama
Day 5 Punta Arenas
Days 6–10 Torres del Paine
Days 11–13 Puerto Varas or Pucón
Day 14 Santiago

Day ❶: Santiago

Arrive and get settled in **Santiago.** Chances are your flight arrived early in the morning; once you've rested and freshened up, head to **Cerro San Cristobal** and its **Metropolitan Park** (p. 114) for sweeping views of the city and to get your bearings. Afterward, take a stroll around the bohemian Barrio Bellavista and pay a visit to **La Chascona** ★★★ (p. 115), the former home of Pablo Neruda and now a museum. Head to the **Mercado Central** ★★★ (p. 114) for a typical Chilean seafood lunch and watch fishmongers shuck and fillet. Once refueled, walk to the **Plaza de Armas** (p. 107) to visit the city's best museum, the **Museo Chileno de Arte Precolombino** ★★★ (p. 110). Take a peek at the **Palacio de la Moneda** ★★ (p. 111), at Plaza de la Constitución, before heading over to the streets of **Bellavista** ★★ (p. 114), where you can peruse the artists' galleries and shops before enjoying an afternoon cocktail at one of the area's bars. Later that evening, order a frosty pisco sour and dine on traditional Chilean bistro food at **Bar Liguria** ★★★ (p. 124).

Day ❷: The Andes

During the summer, there's no shortage of adventurous activities, especially in the mountain valley **Cajón de Maipo,** located between 45 minutes and 2 hours (depending on how far up the valley you travel) from Santiago. Raft the Class III and IV rapids on the Maipo River; pretend you're Butch Cassidy or the Sundance Kid and horseback ride along Andean ridges that open out to sweeping views; or put on a pair of hiking boots and trek to a glacier in **El Morado National Park** (p. 157). Oenophiles will enjoy a scenic drive, perhaps stopping off at one of the region's gorgeous wineries. If it's winter, grab a shuttle and head high into the iconic **Andes Mountains** to one of the three ski resorts, for a day of skiing or snowboarding. **Valle Nevado** (p. 183), **La Parva** (p. 184), and **El Colorado** (p. 184) all lie within 1 to 1½ hours from the city, and you can rent gear when you get there.

Whatever you decide to do during the day, head back to your hotel in Santiago to indulge in an exquisite dinner at one of the city's finest restaurants, such as **Astrid y Gastón** (p. 106) or **Europeo** (p. 101).

Days ❸ & ❹: Wine Country

The **Colchagua Valley** is shaping up as Chile's version of Napa Valley, and what better way to get a taste of Chile than through its wine? Head out early from Santiago for the scenic 2½-hour drive following the jagged Andes south. Before entering Santa Cruz, stop at one of the region's oldest wineries, **Casa Silva** ★★ (p. 175), where you can sample excellent wines paired with a delicious lunch. Or, aspiring vintners can enroll in **Viña Viu Manent**'s "Winemaker for a Day" program" ★★★ (p. 177). Check into your room at the **Hotel Santa Cruz Plaza** ★★ (p. 180), and spend the afternoon strolling around the typical rural town of **Santa Cruz** (p. 162); dine that night in the hotel. If you really want to splurge, stay at the luxurious **Clos Apalta** (p. 176), one of the world's most talked about wineries, and revel in the luxurious facilities and fabulous array of activities on offer. The next day, don't miss the breathtaking **Clos Apalta** ★★★ (p. 176), have lunch at **Pan Pan Vino Vino** ★ (p. 181), then visit **Montes** ★★★ (p. 176) winery for a tour, tasting, and carriage ride.

Days ❺ & ❻: The Central Coast

This day involves driving north and then west from Santa Cruz to **Valparaíso** ★★★ (p. 138), a 3½- to 4-hour drive. Along the way, you have the option of stopping just outside of San Fernando for a wine tasting at **Casa Silva** ★★ (p. 175). Spend the afternoon getting lost along the kooky, twisty streets of Valparaíso, soaking up the old port town ambience, and reveling in sublime views over a light lunch at **Café Turri** ★★ (p. 150). Then visit **La Sebastiana** ★★★

(p. 142), the former home of Pablo Neruda. If it's the weekend, have dinner at the city's best restaurant, **Pasta e Vino** ★★★ (p. 149), or otherwise enjoy a romantic meal with dazzling panoramas at **Montealegre** ★★ (p. 151). If you are enticed by the notion of a lively beach scene, you will want to spend you next day in Viña or even spend the night at the fabulous **Hotel Del Mar** ★★★ (p. 128).

Day 7: Valparaíso or Viña to the Airport

The last day, rest up for your flight back at the beach in Viña, take a scenic coastal drive, or, if you haven't already had your fill of Chilean wine, stop at the **Viñedos Orgánicos Emiliana** ★★ (p. 167) and **House of Morandé** ★★ (p. 168) wineries on the road back to the airport. Arrive in time for your evening flight out of Santiago.

3 CHILE IN 2 WEEKS

Travelers with 2 weeks will be able to visit their choice of Chile's highlights and travel at a pace that allows some relaxation—unless, that is, you intend to visit multiple long-distance destinations, for example from Patagonia to Easter Island and then Atacama, in which case you'll spend a lot of time traveling and little time actually *visiting.* The following itinerary is geared toward both the adventurous traveler and the low-key traveler. All destinations listed offer something for everyone, or low-key travelers might consider following the 1-week itinerary described earlier and combining it with a visit to Patagonia, San Pedro de Atacama, or Easter Island. Adrenaline junkies will not want to miss the adventure mecca of Pucón. The following itinerary includes Patagonia, the Lake District, and the Atacama, but the Atacama could easily be replaced with a 4-day journey to Easter Island. Easter Island does not offer arduous trekking, but it does claim some of the best scuba diving in the world, has powerful waves to surf, and offers great mountain-biking terrain. Another option for this itinerary is to skip the Lake District and spend more time in the Atacama and Patagonia. This "classic" itinerary takes you to Chile's extremes, in terms of distance, culture, and landscapes.

Day 1: Santiago

Spend as described in "Chile in 1 Week: Day 1," earlier.

Days 2, 3 & 4: San Pedro de Atacama

Continue your 2-week holiday in the north, at the eerily beautiful **San Pedro de Atacama** (p. 214). Take an early morning, 2-hour flight to Calama, then drive 1 hour to San Pedro. Check into your hotel and spend the afternoon getting to know the artsy colonial town, or walk or rent a bike and pedal out to the **Pukará de Quitor** ★★ (p. 219). During the next 2 days, you can take your pick from a host of tranquil activities: visiting the archaeological ruins of **Aldea de Tulor** ★★ (p. 219) and touring the town's outstanding archaeological museum; admiring the sunset at **Valle de la Luna** ★★ (p. 218); or floating on salty water at **Laguna Sejar** ★ (p. 217). Travelers with more gusto can take the early morning tour (4am) to the high-altitude **Geysers del Tatio** ★★ (p. 218), finishing with a soak in the hot springs called the **Baños de Puritama** ★★ (p. 218). Adventure lovers can mountain bike or horseback ride in the **Valle de la Muerte,** join a 4×4 trip up to the high-altitude lakes **Meñique** and **Miscanti,** or even climb a high-altitude volcano (this must be done on the fourth day, in order to acclimatize beforehand).

Day 5: Punta Arenas

You'll need to climb aboard an early morning flight out of Calama to **Punta Arenas** (p. 364); it's more or less 7 hours travel time, but you'll get in early enough to tour the sights in this far-flung city. If you are visiting between November and January, don't miss the chance to waddle on out to the **Seno Otway penguin colony** (p. 373) or **Isla Magdalena** ★ (p. 373). Afterwards, if time permits, visit Punta Arenas' poignant **city cemetery** ★★ (p. 370), where funereal sculpture reaches its heavenly zenith, or the **Museo Salesiano Maggiorino Borgatello** ★★ (p. 370), which presents vivid geographical and ethnographical exhibits. End your evening with dinner at **Damiana Elena** ★★ (p. 377).

Days 6, 7, 8, 9 & 10: Torres del Paine

Leave early the following morning for Chile's star attraction, **Torres del Paine National Park** ★★★ (p. 386); the contrast between this southern park and the Atacama is striking. As a traveler, you have a few lodging options: Lodge in Puerto Natales and take day trips to the park, enjoying town life at night; lodge at one of the park's hotels or a working estancia outside the park and take day hikes; or camp and hike the W trail (you'll need to be a fit hiker to complete the W trail; you can choose to bunk in the park's series of *refugios,* or cabins, in lieu of pitching a tent). During these 5 days, you'll want to hike to **Las Torre/The Towers** ★★ (or horseback ride with local gauchos), walk to the **French Valley,** and hike or ride a ferry to **Glacier Grey.** Impassioned hikers will need an extra week to complete the **Circuit,** a weeklong (mostly flat) trek around the entire massif.

Days 11, 12 & 13: Puerto Varas or Pucón

Many flights from Punta Arenas to Santiago stop in **Puerto Varas** ★★ (Puerto Montt airport; p. 289) and **Pucón** ★★ (Temuco airport; p. 254)—why not take advantage of this stopover and break your trip up? Both towns are virtually identical in terms of activities, and both boast a backdrop of a perfectly conical volcano and are surrounded by lush, temperate rainforest. Spend your last days recuperating from trekking in Torres del Paine at the lakeshore beach, soaking in the hot springs, and visiting one of the regional spas. Or, keep the action going with a climb to the top of the smoking **Volcán Villarrica** or **Volcán Osorno;** fly-fish, raft, or kayak the Río Trancura rapids; hike to the top of a forested peak; zip through the trees on a canopy line; and more.

Day 14: Santiago

Plan your last-day flight to connect with your outbound flight from Santiago back home. If you can get an afternoon flight, spend your last day shopping for souvenirs for family and friends.

4 CHILE FOR FAMILIES

Chile is a veritable traveler's paradise for families. Chileans love kids, and the tourism industry goes out of its way to cater to people with kids, including offering children's rates, kids' menus, jungle gyms, and scheduled activities; many larger resorts offer free babysitting for young children. While the long-distance travel can be tiring, Easter Island is a fun place for children, with its easy walks, beaches, and ocean water that is noticeably warmer than the coast of Chile, fun forays to visit *moai* sculptures, caves to explore, and snorkeling. To include Easter Island in the following itinerary, spend Day 1 in Santiago,

Days 2 to 4 in Pucón, Day 5 in transit from Pucón to Easter Island, Days 6 to 8 on the island; return to Santiago on Day 9, and see the city's sights on Day 10 before catching your evening flight home.

Days ❶ & ❷: Santiago

Arrive and get settled in **Santiago.** If you can, stay in a hotel with a swimming pool like the family-friendly **La Sebastiana Apart Hotel** ★★ (p. 94). An inspired way to lift the jet-lag haze is to lose yourself to the city's dramatic setting. If it's a hot summer's day, dip into one of **Metropolitan Park**'s (p. 114) lovely public swimming pools; or take your kids first up the funicular there, ride the gondolalike *telesférico* across the hill, and on your way out stop for a visit at the city zoo, or **Jardín Zoológico** (p. 115). Here your kids can view animals endemic to Chile, such as the puma, condor, and guanaco. There is also a beautifully landscaped public swimming pool here. Kids should next get a kick out of checking out the weird seafood displayed at the **Mercado Central** ★★★ (p. 114); after lunch or an early dinner there, you can visit **Parque Quinta Normal** (p. 116) with its kid-friendly museums and beautiful gardens. For more kid-oriented activities in Santiago, see "Especially for Kids" in chapter 6.

Day ❸: The Andes

A trip to Chile wouldn't be complete without heading high into the famous **Andes Mountains** that tower above Santiago. If it's winter, grab a shuttle and head up to one of the three ski resorts that lie within 1 to 1½ hours of the city: **Valle Nevado** (p. 183), **La Parva** (p. 184), or **El Colorado** (p. 184). You can rent gear when you get there, and resorts offer ski lessons tailored to kids. During the summer, there's no shortage of kid-friendly activities, especially in the mountain valley **Cajón de Maipo** (p. 156), located roughly 45 minutes or 2 hours (depending on how far up the road you travel) from Santiago. Raft the Class III rapids section of the **Maipo River,** or horseback ride along **Andean ridges** that open out to sweeping views. If it's warm out, book a cabin at **Cascada de las Animas** ★ (p. 158), which has an outdoor pool, horses, and hiking trails, and spend the night.

Days ❹, ❺, ❻ & ❼: The Lake District

Hop on a flight to Temuco, gateway to the idyllic mountain village **Pucón** (p. 254). During January and February, Pucón is packed to the rafters with vacationing families, and though it's busy during this time, there are certainly a lot of other kids for your children to meet. Book a self-catering *cabaña,* rent a car, and spend your days taking easy to moderate hikes through lush forest, bike riding around town, relaxing and swimming at **Lake Villarrica**'s beach (p. 254), or visiting a fun hot spring such as **Termas Geométricas** ★★★ (p. 271). Three activities your kids will love are Pucón's canopy adventure; a horseback ride and farm visit at **Huifquenco Fundo** ★★★ (p. 255); and rafting the **Trancura River** (p. 259). The beauty of Pucón is that you can do as little or as much as you'd like, and there are plenty of outstanding restaurants and shops. Full-service hotels such as the **Gran Hotel Pucón** (p. 260) and **Las Cabañas Metreñehue** ★ (p. 262) have children's activities and are located next to the lakeshore.

Days ❽ & ❾: Viña del Mar

Kids love the beach any time of the year, and 2 days in **Viña del Mar** (p. 128) gives you a chance to relax; visit a couple of kid-friendly museums, such as the **Museo de Arqueología e Historia Francisco**

Chile for Families

Days 1 & 2	Santiago
Day 3	The Andes
Days 4–7	The Lake District
Days 8 & 9	Viña del Mar
Day 10	Viña to Santiago/airport

Chile for Wine Lovers

Day 1	Santiago
Day 2	Maipo Valley
Day 3	San Antonio Valley
Day 4	Cachapoal Valley
Days 5 & 6	Colchagua Valley
Days 7 & 8	Aconcagua Valley
Day 9	Casablanca Valley

Fonck ★★ (p. 132); take a buggy ride; or play in a park. The **Hotel San Martín** ★★ (p. 134) has reasonably priced suites that work well for families, or pay a little extra for the **Hotel del Mar** ★★★ (p. 133), which has a children's entertainment center and on-site day care.

Day ⑩: From Viña to the Airport

Viña is a convenient last-day destination as the airport lies on the highway back to Santiago, meaning you can max out your day with fun (and tire your kids out), in preparation for the flight home in the evening.

5 CHILE FOR WINE LOVERS

Chile's wine industry has come a long way during the past decade, and no other travel segment here has seen more growth than wine travel. In just 5 years, wineries have built hotels and B&Bs; opened gourmet restaurants, spas, and tasting facilities with normalized operating hours; and created such complementary activities as horse-and-buggy rides through vineyards, bicycling, and hiking. Prices are only slightly less than in comparable wine regions such as Napa Valley; however, in Chile the wine region has not yet been overtaken by the masses, and you can still enjoy wine tasting without the crowds, and savor the antique charm and slow pace of the colonial towns for which the Central Valley is known. The following 10-day itinerary covers the top wine-growing regions, concentrating on wineries that currently produce the best varieties today in Chile.

Day 1: Santiago

Arrive and get settled in **Santiago**—this will be your base for the next 3 nights. Spend the first part of your day as described in "Chile in 1 Week: Day 1," earlier. Before heading back to your hotel, take a stroll through picturesque **Parque Forestal** (p. 113). Enjoy a fine Italian meal and excellent service on the terrace of the chic **Nolita** ★ (p. 105), a favorite haunt of Las Condes' gilded denizens.

Day 2: Maipo Valley

Begin where it all started, at the **Maipo Valley** (p. 168), where Chile's first vines were planted in the mid-1500s. Drive or hire a cab to visit **Concha y Toro** ★★★ (p. 170), Chile's largest and best-known winery, now offering tastings of its full range of wines, including the top Almaviva. Tours take visitors through the lovely hacienda and gardens of the Concha y Toro family, and you can order appetizers in their wine bar. Later, head to Chile's oldest winery, **Cousiño-Macul** ★★ (p. 170), where you can appreciate one of the Maipo Valley's most characteristic wines while you lord amid a stunning estate with French-style gardens. In the evening, continue the old-world theme and dine at **Europeo** ★★★ (p. 106), in Vitacura, one of Santiago's most elegant restaurants.

Day 3: San Antonio Valley

This full-day journey visits Chile's hottest new wine-growing valley, **San Antonio** (p. 166), home to top boutique wineries located near the coastal city of the same name. Plan to visit **Matetic Vineyards** ★★★ (p. 166) first, producer of highly rated syrahs and an architectural gem to boot. After your tour, have a gourmet lunch at their restaurant. Continue west to **Viña Casa Marin** ★ (p. 167), the winery closest to the coast and producer of the country's top rated sauvignon blanc. Head back to Santiago for your final night there and dine at **Opera** ★★★ (p. 98), followed by cocktails upstairs at the hip **Catedral** ★★★ (p. 98).

Day 4: Cachapoal Valley

Arrange a tour or, even better, rent a vehicle and journey south to the **Cachapoal Valley** (p. 171), spread at the foot of the Andes. Bring along a picnic lunch. Arrive for your 10:30am wine-tasting tour at **Altaïr** ★★★ (p. 171), a unique winery launched to craft a distinctively Chilean grand cru. Enjoy your picnic (let them know you're bringing one when you book), and then carry on to **Chateau Los Boldos** ★★ (p. 172), a century-old vineyard with French owners and makers of fine wines and specialty liquors; book a tour or just stop off at their Boutique de Vino just off the highway. Your accommodations this evening are at **Hacienda Los Lingues** ★★★ (p. 173), one of the oldest and best-preserved haciendas in Chile, and gilded in antique splendor. If you arrive early enough, you can take a short horse ride atop one of their Arabian steeds.

Days ❺ & ❻: Colchagua Valley

Eulogized as the "Wine Valley of the Year" by *Wine Enthusiast* magazine in 2005, the **Colchagua Valley** (p. 174) is known as the Napa Valley of Chile, with a well-designed tourism infrastructure. Before you arrive at Santa Cruz, stop outside San Fernando for a wine tasting at the magnificent **Casa Silva** ★★ (p. 175). Carry on to just before Santa Cruz and stop next at **Viña Viu Manent** ★★ (p. 177) for a gourmet lunch, followed by a wine tasting and a horse-and-buggy ride through their vineyards. If you have kids in tow, you may prefer to spend a few hours touring Viña Santa Cruz, the Disneyland of the Chilean wine world, with its mock indigenous village and astronomical facilities. Check into your room at the **Hotel Santa Cruz Plaza** ★★ (p. 180), and spend the late afternoon strolling around the typical rural town of Santa Cruz or lounging by the pool; dine that night in the hotel.

The following day, tour the state-of-the-art winery **Clos Alpalta** ★★★ (p. 176), soak in the pastoral scenery, and taste their award-winning blends. Visit the **Montes** ★★★ (p. 176) winery for a tour and tasting of this well-known producer of fine varietals; if you are traveling in a group, Montes will arrange a delicious lunch for you; otherwise, eat at the rustic **Pan Pan Vino Vino** ★ (p. 181), which is steeped in historical ambience.

Days ❼ & ❽: Aconcagua Valley

Leave early in the morning for the 4-hour drive to the **Aconcagua Valley** (p. 164), with its stunning Andean views and tiny colonial villages. Lodge at the old-fashioned **Casa St. Regis** ★ (p. 165) or the luxury spa **Termas de Jahuel Hotel & Spa** ★★ (p. 165), and spend the afternoon visiting **Von Siebenthal** ★ (p. 164) winery. Dine at your hotel, and the next morning visit the venerable **Errazuriz** ★★ (p. 164) winery, with its pretty trellised terraces and historic winery. Later, drive to **Valparaíso** ★★★ (p. 138) to spend the night at the chic and central **Zerohotel** ★★★ (p. 147), or alternatively, stay in **Viña del Mar** (p. 92); spend the afternoon exploring one of the two towns.

Day ❾: Casablanca Valley

The following morning, pick up your exploration of either Viña or Valparaíso, pack your bags for the last time, and head back toward Santiago, stopping in the **Casablanca Valley** (p. 166) on the way. Here, you'll enjoy a lengthy tasting at **Viñedos Orgánicos Emiliana** ★★ (p. 167), an organic winery with excellent guides and winemakers who serve cheese and nuts while walking you through a relaxing tasting. Follow this visit with lunch at **Restaurante Viña Indomita** ★★ (p. 168), then make a final stop at the slick **Veramonte** ★ (p. 167) winery to taste their specialty white wines. Then it's on to the airport, where you'll catch your flight back home. Stop in the **La Vinoteca** store at the airport (p. 121) to pick up a 6- or 12-bottle case of wine if you haven't bought any yet. See p. 33 for tips on getting the wine back home.

5

The Active Vacation Planner

Chile is an active travel mecca. There are few countries where you can trek through primordial rainforests, ascend some of the world's highest peaks, kayak pristine lakes and fjords, raft one of the world's top-rated rivers, mountain bike on hushed country lanes lined with tall poplar trees, ski or snowboard where the powder lasts for days, not hours; climb a smoking volcano, or gallop across the Patagonian pampa like a true gaucho. Further boosting Chile's kudos as a breathtaking land of natural highs, many of Chile's national parks and reserves are so underrated and underappreciated that they are, for the most part, empty.

Adventure and active travel journeys can be pieced together as day excursions or your trip can be planned from start to finish by a tour operator. The latter option is often more expensive, but undoubtedly these planned journeys put far more emphasis on personalized attention and service than a run-of-the-mill day-tour operator. A handful of all-inclusive resorts and lodges also plan daily excursions that are sometimes included in the price of a room. Some of these resorts have their own horses, guides, and/or equipment, while others subcontract a local outfitter.

1 ORGANIZED ADVENTURE TRIPS

The advantages of traveling with an organized group are plentiful, especially for travelers who have limited time and enjoy the security of knowing in advance how each day will look. Tour operators take the headache out of planning a trip and can help transcend any cultural and linguistic barriers. A guide can also interpret the culture and history of Chile and the natural surroundings of your destination. Most tours include guides, ground transportation, accommodations, meals, and gear. Independent travelers tend to view organized tours as antithetical to the joy of discovery and too prescriptive, but leaving the details to someone else does free up substantial time to concentrate on something else.

The best tours limit group size to 10 to 15 people, which allows for personal attention and a bit of breathing room—this is appreciated after a week on the road together. Of course, most tour operators can book a custom trip for a family or small group, but the cost will be far higher than a regularly scheduled tour. Ask about difficulty levels when you're choosing a tour. Most tours are focused on "soft" adventure, with light excursions that are suitable even for couch tubers; be truthful with yourself when considering more difficult journeys. A multiday adventure that includes trekking through virgin jungle might look great on paper, but are you physically up to it? Tour operators are responsible for their clients' well-being and safety, but that doesn't let you off the hook in terms of your own personal responsibility. Inquire about your guide's experience, safety record, and insurance policy. Remember, no adventure trip is 100% risk-free.

NORTH AMERICA–BASED TOUR OPERATORS

These agencies and operators specialize in well-organized, 7- to 15-day tours that allow travelers to pack a lot of action into a short period of time. (***Tip:*** There's really no point in booking a tour that takes you to an all-inclusive lodge with its own guides and transportation, unless you just want someone to solve any glitches from start to finish.) A few of the operators include luxury accommodations and gourmet dining as part of the travel itinerary, and are therefore *very* expensive. Remember, the tours shown below do not include international or internal airfare. Solo travelers in most cases will be charged the dreaded single supplement that can run an additional $500 to $1,500 (£333–£1,000). For more specific activity-oriented tours, such as biking, see "Activities A to Z." Destination-specific chapters list local guide services or tour operators.

- **Abercrombie & Kent** (**✆ 800/550-7016;** www.abercrombiekent.com), an award-winning tour operator that caters to the luxury market (world-class hotels and gourmet dining), offers mostly set trips that combine Argentina or Brazil with Chile, and many tailored trips for families and independent groups. Their Wonders of Chile, Brazil, and Argentina tour takes travelers from Santiago to Puerto Montt, Bariloche, Buenos Aires, Iguazú Falls, and Río de Janeiro for $11,365 (£7,577) per person; their Chile Signature Series includes wine tasting, Patagonia, and the Atacama Desert for $8,825 (£5,648) per person.
- **Backroads Active Vacations** (**✆ 800/462-2848** or 510/527-1444; www.backroads.com) concentrates on active travel, leaning toward easy-going adventures, paired with stays at luxury hotels and inns. Backroads has two trips in Chile: a walking/biking tour through the lake districts of Chile and Argentina, with stops in Puerto Varas, Bariloche, and Villa la Angostura (with an afternoon of rafting); and hiking in Torres del Paine and Perito Moreno national parks. The 9-day biking trip costs $4,898 (£3,265) per person ($1,400/£933 extra for single supplement).
- **Bike Hike Adventures** (**✆ 888/805-0061;** www.bikehike.com) is a Toronto-based company specializing in multisport adventures for travelers who are at least in moderate shape. Their 7-day "A Pure Natural High" takes place around Puerto Varas and Ensenada, rafting the Petrohue, climbing to the peak of Volcán Osorno, horseback riding, and an 8-mile hike through Alerce Andino Park, with stays in moderate hotels and 1 night in a mountain refuge ($1,899/£1,266 per person). Bike Hike also has a 7-day, mountain refuge–based "Best of Patagonia" hiking trip, including Chile and Argentina ($1,999/£1,333).
- **Country Walkers** (**✆ 800/464-9255;** www.countrywalkers.com) focuses on easy to moderate, 5- to 12-mile day hikes through the highlights of the Lake District and Patagonia, including Vicente Pérez and Alerce Andino national parks, the emerald isles of Chiloé, and Torres del Paine, with overnights in high-end hotels. The 11-day trip costs $5,998 (£3,999) per person, with a single person supplement of $875/£583, and operates as early as October.
- **Gap Adventures** (**✆ 800/708-7761;** www.gapadventures.com) is a Canadian company that provides young adventurous travelers with journeys that steer clear of "traditional tourism," offering trips tailored to all lower budgets. Gap's "Roam" trips are a good bet for independent travelers who want to hit the road at leisure, stay in local homes, and tour with local operators, but are unsure how to go about planning their trip. The 13-day "Southern Sejorne," from Santiago to Buenos Aires, includes rafting in Pucón; paragliding, hiking, and skiing in Bariloche; and tango dancing in Buenos

Ecotourism

You can find eco-friendly travel tips, statistics, and touring companies and associations—listed by destination under "Travel Choice"—at the **TIES** website, www.ecotourism.org. **Ecotravel.com** is part online magazine and part eco-directory, which lets you search for touring companies in several categories (water-based, land-based, spiritually oriented, and so on). Also check out **Conservation International** (www.conservation.org).

Aires. Accommodations are simple (no meals included), and there are two night bus rides, for $600 (£400).

- **Mountain-Travel Sobek** (✆ **888/MTSOBEK** [687-6235] or 510/594-6000; www.mtsobek.com) are the pioneers of organized adventure travel; their trips involve a lot of physical activity and combine camping with hotel stays, with an average of 12 nights. Sample trips include the 10-night "Trekking the Paine Circuit," which costs, per person, $4,695 (£3,130) for five to eight guests, and $4,390 (£2,926) for 9 to 12 guests. Sobek is a pricey outfitter, but the guides carry gear and set up camp for guests, and Sobek is known for its knowledgeable and competent guides.
- **Wilderness Travel** (✆ **800/368-2794** or 510/558-2488; www.wildernesstravel.com) offers the most complete tour of the Lake District, visiting little-known national parks such as Conguilillo and Puyuehue. In addition to hiking in Patagonia, they have a hiking trip in the remote Futaleufú region with lodging in wooden cabins and tree houses, as well as a pricey cruise to Easter Island. The cost for the Lake District hiking tour is $3,995 (£2,663) per person for 4 guests, and $4,395 (£2,930) per person for 2 or 3 guests. Accommodations upgrades are possible for an additional charge.

U.K.-BASED TOUR OPERATOR

Journey Latin America (✆ **020/8747-3108;** www.journeylatinamerica.co.uk) is the U.K.'s largest tour operator that specializes in Latin American travel with a plethora of tailor-made and group tours. You'll really need to browse their website for ideas, which can be "Classic Tours" or "Original Adventures," focusing on active travel with stays in moderately priced lodging and public transportation often included. The 14-day "Pure Patagonia" tour costs $3,827 (£2,551). Other trips include luxury hotels and dining.

CHILE-BASED TOUR OPERATORS

Remember that international tour operators without their own local offices often subcontract local tour operators or book stays in all-inclusive hotels. Operators based in Chile typically offer a wider variety of tours here—after all, they operate within their own country. The following operators run a multitude of trips throughout the country; also see "Activities A to Z," later, for specialized tour operators.

- **Altué Expediciones** (✆ **2/232-1103;** www.altue.com) is the oldest and most respected tour outfitter in Chile. Their specialties are rafting (rivers Futaleufú, Maipo, and what's left of the Bío-Bío) and horseback riding (Central Andes, La Campana National Park, Patagonia), as well as their terrific kayaking operation/lodge based in Chiloé (with trips around Chiloé and Parque Pumalín). They have exceptionally friendly guides, a solid operation, and very reasonable prices. They can put together any kind of cultural tour or custom tour, including wine tasting, fly-fishing, and archeological tours.

- **Azimut Expediciones** (© **2/235-1519;** www.azimut.cl), a French and Chilean-run operation, is a top choice for adventure travel and traditional tours with an "avant-garde" itinerary—that is, travel that takes you to off-the-beaten-path locations and overland tours. Like Latitud 90 (below), this is a good choice for day tours and longer, more challenging expeditions in the Atacama Desert.
- **Latitud 90** (© **2/599-4664;** www.latitud90.com) is the most complete tour operator in Chile, offering soft and hard adventure trips and more traditional excursions such as wine tasting and cultural visits to areas outside of Santiago. It's a good outfit for mountaineering, and they also specialize in tailor-made trips, and incentive and group tours.

OTHER GENERAL-INTEREST TOUR AGENCIES & PACKAGE DEALS

- **Chile Discover** (© **866/369-8046;** www.chilediscover.com) puts together "Self-Guided" tours, whereby they book the car rental, hotels, and any other reservations; provide you with a map; and send you on your way on an independent tour. Research the hotels that they suggest as part of their itinerary—they may not be the best available.
- **Discover Latinamerica** (© **888/887-8869;** www.discoverchile.com) is owned by Chile's largest and most respected tour operator, Turismo Cocha, which often secures cheaper prices for hotels and other packages. Discover Chile is another excellent resource, offering complete trip planning and set packages, custom tours, and lower-cost deals on flights.
- **Ladatco Tours** (© **800/327-6162;** www.ladatco.com) organizes preprogrammed and custom tours in all regions of Chile, including theme-oriented tours such as wine tasting, fly-fishing, glaciers, and more. Ladatco has operated as a Central and South America tour operator for 30 years. The epic, 25-day "Ultimate Chile" tour includes luxury accommodations and costs $14,995 (£9,596) per person based on double occupancy.
- **PanAmerican Travel** (© **801/364-4359;** www.panamtours.com) is an outstanding company staffed by Latin Americans with firsthand knowledge of Chile. The company specializes in reasonably priced custom trips with unique itineraries, not set trips or standardized packaged vacations.

2 ACTIVITIES A TO Z

This section is divided by activity, with listings of the prime destinations in Chile for practicing each activity, and the tour operators and outfitters who tailor their trips around each activity. Tour operators bring with them local knowledge, and more importantly, they provide guides and in most cases equipment. If you are planning to focus your trip to Chile around one specific activity, these tour operators and outfitters are your best bet. The companies listed under "Chile-Based Tour Operators" above offer outstanding trips based around many of the following activities, so check them out and note that some of the following activities will refer you to the specific region for more information about outfitters.

Adventure travel carries risks, and travelers should be well aware of dangers before participating in any activity. The tour operators mentioned in this chapter have been chosen for their safety and reputation, but ask questions on your own. For example, if your adventure involves trekking, how strenuous are the trails? What safety gear will be carried along, and what experience do your guides have? Tour operators in Chile have had their share of accidents, either fatal or just serious, and you'll want to know the background details of said accidents and make your decision to book accordingly.

BIKING

Mountain biking has grown quickly in Chile, with tour companies now offering a variety of programmed trips throughout the country, and with the publication of the magazine *Contrapedal* (www.contrapedal.cl) available in kiosks. On main roads, stay alert for traffic, as many Chileans have a tendency to speed, pull out of lanes without signaling, and rarely demonstrate driving etiquette when its comes to cyclists. Most country roads are dirt and in varying states of ruggedness; the main traffic you'll encounter on these roads are horseback riders and livestock—so ride with caution around blind curves. Keep in mind that strong gales make biking difficult in Torres del Paine. Tourism-oriented towns such as Pucón and San Pedro de Atacama have bicycle rental shops and maps and information for bicycle routes in their region, which are listed in regional chapters within this book.

In **Santiago,** the most popular and safe bike-riding area is the **Cerro San Cristobal/ Parque Metropolitano** hill, which has winding paved roads—and pretty spectacular views to boot. Your best bet for bike rental here is **Bike 'n Views** (✆ **2/226-9231;** www.bikeandviews.cl), which rents mountain bikes and city bikes. Bike 'n Views also plans bike outings in and around the city, such as full-day trips through the coastal mountains and biking through the Cajón de Maipo, as well as a 2-day trip in the Reserva Nacional Los Cípreses with an overnight at the Termas de Cauquenes hotel.

An American-owned company based in Futaleufú, **Expediciones Chile** (✆ **888/488-9082;** www.exchile.com) specializes in mountain-biking trips that can be part of a multisport vacation (they are also well-known for their rafting and kayaking trips) on mountain trails around Futaleufú and Palena, and trips around Valle del Elqui in the Norte Chico region. **Pared Sur** (✆ **2/207-3525;** www.paredsur.cl) has three summer trips: from Chile to Argentina, in the Lake District; the Carretera Austral; and a bike-and-trekking journey in Torres del Paine.

BIRD-WATCHING

In Latin America, countries such as Panama or Brazil overshadow Chile when it comes to bird-watching, but Chile truly delights bird lovers for its nearly 300 species that include unusual birds such as the ostrichlike rhea and the Andean condor, pink flamingos, Magallenic woodpeckers, black-necked swans, torrent ducks, and Chilean flickers. Patagonia, especially **Torres del Paine,** is the perfect venue for bird-watching and home to the aforementioned birds. **Seno Otway** and **Isla Magdalena,** near Punta Arenas, are two sanctuaries for the amusing Magellanic penguins, who gather at both locations from September through March; the best viewing time, however, is November through January. Humboldt penguins can be viewed at the **National Humboldt Penguin Reserve** near La Serena, at the coast at **Maitencillo,** and at the penguin reserve at **Chiloé.** The Chilean Sea is rich with nutrients thanks to the Humboldt Current, attracting sea birds and such pelagic as boobies, albatrosses, and oystercatchers; you can see these birds virtually anywhere along the **Central Coast.**

The **Carlos Anwandter Nature Sanctuary** near Valdivia, renown for its wetlands that teem with birds such as grebes, ducks, and wigeons, took a major hit in 2005 when a pulp mill devastated its formidable black-necked swan population; you can still see these elegant birds and dozens of other marsh species at the nearby **Río Cruces Nature Sanctuary,** wetlands that remain prime marsh bird–viewing sites. In the nothofagus forests of the Lake District, especially in parks such as **Puyehue** and **Pumalin,** bird-watchers may spot (or hear the distinctive cluck) of a tapaculo called the *chucao,* and even clap eyes on a Magellanic woodpecker. The Lake District and Chiloé draw splendid ringed kingfishers and flocks of noisy ibis and wigeons. Other birding hot spots include the pink flamingo sanctuary at the **Atacama Salt Flat,** near San Pedro de Atacama, and **Lauca National Park.**

Few hotels, even those that are geared toward nature, offer bird-watching as a regular activity, but with some advance planning they should be able to hire a bird-watching guide for you. You might want to contact a Chile-based bird-watching tour operator for a professional guide and short trips. The American-owned company **Alto Andino Nature Tours** (✆ **9/282-6195;** www.birdingaltoandino.com) covers the northern region including Lauca National Park with day trips from San Pedro de Atacama and even ornithology courses. Farther south, try **Hualamo** (www.hualamo.cl; no phone) for day trips and custom multiday trips that center around the Central Andes and coast, the Río Cruces Nature Sanctuary, and the Lake District. The U.S.-based **Field Guides** (✆ **800/728-4953** or 512/263-7295; www.fieldguides.com) is a specialty bird-watching travel operator with highly esteemed and friendly guides. They offer an all-inclusive program, "The Heart and Sole of Chile," which covers Santiago to Chiloé, while the more comprehensive 2-day program spans northern Chile to Patagonia and costs $6,375 (£4,250) per person, not including internal flights, and the group maximum is 14. **Victor Emanuel Nature Tours** ★★ (✆ **800/328-8368** or 512/328-5221 in the U.S.; www.ventbird.com) is a well-respected tour operator and the largest company in the world specializing in bird tours. VENT offers a 13-day October trip to Torres del Paine, and around Tierra del Fuego aboard the *Mare Australis* cruise; the cost is $5,995 (£3,997).

CRUISING & YACHTING

No single activity has taken off in Chile like cruising, with scores of travelers hopping aboard for a circumnavigation of the southern cone. Most large cruise lines begin in Valparaíso or farther north in Peru and end in Buenos Aires or even Río de Janeiro. In Chile, stops can include Arica, Valparaíso, Puerto Montt, Puerto Chacabuco, and Punta Arenas.

Of course, as a cruise-ship passenger you won't spend a lot of time getting to know Chile, but there is something to be said for experiencing the lush Chilean fjords, and some cruises visit the Laguna San Rafael glacier and sail around Cape Horn. Also, if you begin or end your trip in Valparaíso, you can tack on a couple of extra days and visit Santiago, the coast, or wine country.

MAINSTREAM CRUISE LINES These cruise lines offer something for everyone: **Celebrity Cruises** (✆ 800/722-5941; www.celebritycruises.com); **Holland America** (✆ 877/724-5425; www.hollandamerica.com); **Norwegian Cruise Lines** (✆ 866/234-7350; www.ncl.com); **Oceania Cruises** (✆ 800/531-5619; www.oceaniacruises.com); **Orient Lines** (✆ 800/333-7300; www.orientlines.com); **Princess Cruises** (✆ 800/421-0522; www.princess.com); and **Royal Caribbean** (✆ 800/398-9819; www.rccl.com).

LUXURY LINERS Options include: **Crystal Cruises** (✆ 888/722-0021; www.crystal cruises.com); **Regent Seven Seas Cruises** (formerly Radisson; ✆ 877/505-5370; www. rssc.com); **Seabourn Cruise Line** (✆ 800/929-9391; www.seabourn.com); and **Silversea Cruises** (✆ 800/722-9955; www.silversea.com).

SPECIALTY CRUISES **Lindblad Expeditions** (✆ **800/397-3348;** www.lindblad expeditions.com) has educational cruises that focus on culture and the environment.

Travel agencies and tour operators that specialize in cruises buy in bulk and are often capable of offering lower rates than those advertised by cruise lines, and they stay on top of special deals and promotions. Try the **Cruise Company** (✆ **800/289-5505;** www.the cruisecompany.com) or **World Wide Cruises** (✆ **800/882-9000;** www.wwcruises.com).

CHARTER YACHTS This is the newest way to cruise the Chilean fjords, and Sausalito-based **Ocean Voyages** (✆ **800/299-4444;** www.oceanvoyages.com) is the company to call for customized yacht vacations for groups of up to 10 people aboard one of its 24m, 27m, or 30m (80-, 90-, or 100-ft.) yachts. Their *Tiffara* is based in the Strait of Magellan from December to March and sails from Punta Arenas to Ushuaia.

Chile-based Small Cruises & Yachting

Travelers experience a more intimate journey aboard cruise lines based in Chile rather than aboard one of the long-haul cruise lines mentioned above. Smaller ships foster more personalized attention, and smaller crowds allow guests to interact more closely with their natural surroundings.

Navimag Ferries is the cheapest option for sailing the Patagonia fjords, with comfortable but no-frills accommodations popular with backpackers and budget travelers. The Chilean company's M/N *Magallanes* passenger and freight ferry offers a 3-day journey from Puerto Montt to Puerto Natales and vice versa, which I recommend to travelers with a lot of time on their hands. See p. 39.

Small cruise operations based in the Chilean fjords include **Patagonia Express** (p. 357), which works in conjunction with the Puyuhuapi Lodge & Spa (formerly known as Termas de Puyuhuapi), leaving from Puerto Chacabuco and including a 2-night stay at the hotel and 1 night in Puerto Chacabuco. Contrasted with Navimag, it's a premium excursion, by it's not as luxurious as they might suggest. **Skorpios Cruises** is a deluxe (but not luxury) operation with three routes in Patagonia: the Aysen region, with visits to Chiloé and the fjords; Laguna San Rafael; and the Pio XI glacier, leaving from Puerto Natales. Cruises run from 4 to 7 days; see p. 39. **Catamaranes del Sur** (p. 357) is a catamaran service to Laguna San Rafael that works in conjunction with the Hostería Loberías del Sur hotel in Puerto Chacabuco. They offer packages that include a stay here, or 1-day journeys for travelers not lodging at the hotel. Catamaranes has their own private park, Aikén del Sur, which they visit for a half-day tour included in their 2- to 3-night packages.

The **Nomads of the Seas** cruise puts a different spin on luxury adventure cruising in the Chilean fjords—and in the world. It's not cheap, but given the tony interiors, degreed guides, onboard helicopter to reach out-of-the-way trout rivers and take fly-overs, and gourmet cuisine, it's worth every penny. Though the cruise focuses on fly-fishing, they cater to all outdoor pursuits; see p. 309.

FISHING

Chile is a world-class fly-fishing destination renowned for its trout-rich rivers, with shores that are blissfully empty of other anglers. Famous actors, such as Robert Redford and Harrison Ford, are fly-fishing fans who've thrown lines in here in Chile, and with so many outstanding fly-fishing lodges and quality tour operators, it's an easy trip to plan. Rivers and lakes suitable for fly-fishing can be found in the southern Lake District and Patagonia, centering around the Carretera Austral area. Lodges are not cheap, but they are attuned to the most demanding of tastes, offering highly qualified guides, deluxe lodging, and gourmet meals. See chapter 12 for a full guide to lodges and guides, and be sure to check out Chile's fly-fishing venture under "Chile-Based Small Cruises & Yachting" above for **Nomads of the Seas,** a luxury yacht that specializes in this sport.

Fishing Lodges

Chucao Fishing Lodge ★★ (✆ **2/201-8571;** www.chucaolodge.cl) is a newer lodge just 45 minutes from Chaiten, on the shore of the Yelcho Lake, and it is owned by Chilean Gonzalo Cortéz who authored the book *Fly Fishing in Chilean Patagonia.* The rough-hewn wood lodge offers comfort and views, and outstanding fly-fishing opportunities, given its location at the mouth of the Yelcho River. It costs $3,990 (£2,660) per week, including all meals and drinks.

El Patagon Lodge ★★ (✆ **65/212030;** www.southernchilexp.com) is the "backcountry" version of the Yankee Way Lodge, located in a remote area south of Futaleufú, that puts anglers closer to the goods for longer fly-fishing days. High-quality service and more rustic accommodations in wooden cabins, with a yurt dining room and outdoor hot tub, are the hallmarks of this lodge. El Patagon also offers a 10-day camping adventure program that includes hiking, horseback riding, and rafting; it costs $3,000 (£2,000).

Heart of Patagonia Lodge ★★ (✆ **67/334906;** www.heartofpatagonia.com) caters to foreigners, and is owned by an ex-editor of *Angling Report.* The lodge, a remodeled 1930s home built by an Austrian, is close enough to the Río Simpson to take advantage of the morning and evening hatch, but still close enough to Coyhaique, making this a good bet for fishermen with nonfishing companions. It costs $4,250 (£2,833) for 7 nights, all-inclusive.

Isla Monita ★★★ (✆ **800/245-1950** in the U.S.; www.islamonita.cl) is an English-run lodge that caters to distinguished clientele. It has access to some of the most diverse fly-fishing conditions found in Chile, and it's located on an exclusive island in the beautiful Yelcho Lake. Check the website for great deals during their off-season.

Mincho's Lodge ★★ (✆ **67/233273;** www.michoslodge.com) offers guided fly-fishing from their lodge near Coyhaique, but they offer plenty of other excursions for nonfishing visitors (such as geological tours), and even charge by the night, not by the package. It's good for visitors whose focus is not exclusively on fly-fishing.

Yankee Way Lodge ★★★ (✆ **65/212030;** www.yankeewaylodge.com) is the most luxurious choice, and its location at the foot of conical, snowcapped Volcán Osorno can't be beat. The lodge offers more creature comforts than its peers and soothes the senses with chalets and bungalows, a small spa, and gourmet dining. In addition to the renowned fly-fishing, accessed by boat or horseback, the lodge offers multisport packages.

GOLF

The beauty of playing golf in Chile lies in its Andean backdrop; the golf courses Coya and Pucón undoubtedly offer some of the most stunning views from any golf course in the world. However, golf in Chile is an exclusive sport played by the country's elite on private courses. There are, however, a few courses open to the public, and also the tour operator **Discover Chile** (✆ **888/887-8869;** www.discoverchile.com), whose parent company is the Chilean-based Cocha, can provide travelers with a guide who has access to private courses.

Public courses include the often mosquito-infested **Golf Mapocho** (✆ **2/7476-4800;** www.golfmapocho.cl), just outside of Santiago, near the airport; **Marbella Resort** (✆ **32/772020;** www.marbella.cl), at the coast near Maitencillo, which has ocean views; **La Serena Golf** (✆ **2/496-7200;** www.laserenagolf.com), which is also a coastal resort farther away from Santiago than Marbella, but with a better and more beautiful course; and Pucon's **La Peninsula** 8-hole course (✆ **45/443965**), which is open to the public and a good way to gain access to the sweeping views from the privately owned peninsula.

HORSEBACK RIDING

Chile was settled on horseback, and horseback riding's romantic lore includes even the tale of Butch Cassidy and the Sundance Kid, who rode trusty steeds through the Andes when on the run from the law. *Huasos* from the Central Region, and *baquedanos* or *gauchos* in Patagonia, are Chile's answer to the cowboy, and much of these regions' culture is centered on these two groups of wild and weathered Chileans. Two outfitters, **Cascada de las Animas** and **Altué Expediciones,** offer day horseback-riding trips in the Andes just outside of Santiago that are easy-going lopes up to lookout points with sweeping views of the Santiago Valley. See "What to See & Do" in section 4 of chapter 7.

Two excellent lodges specialize in horseback riding. One is **Hacienda los Andes** (✆ **53/691822;** www.haciendalosandes.com), located near La Serena and run by Austrian Manuela Paradeiser and German Clark Stede, offering visitors a chance to envelop themselves in Chilean culture and a hacienda lifestyle. You can choose from 4- or 8-day riding adventure packages or just book a room in the lovely hacienda on a nightly basis. Manuela also operates **Ride Chile** (✆ **53/691822;** www.ridechile.com), which specializes in 2- to 10-night horseback-riding trips in the Central Region and Patagonia. The second lodge is **Estancia Cerro Guido** (✆ **2/196-4807;** www.cerroguido.cl), located outside Torres del Paine National Park and within a converted *estancia* (ranch), with unique 4-day programs that include 2 days in the park and rides to Indian cemeteries at Sierra Baguales. The two **explora Hotels** in the Atacama and Torres del Paine have stables and include horseback riding as part of their activities.

Horseback riding hot spots include the **Atacama Desert, Central Andean Region, Colchagua Valley, Lake District,** and **Patagonia.** You'll find horseback operations in nearly every destination within Chile, so check each chapter for contact information. The following are a few of the best picks (the quality of the horses varies considerably; experienced riders may be frustrated), and they usually can put together multiday trips for riding fanatics. In San Pedro de Atacama, contact **Rancho Cactus** (✆ **51/851506;** www.rancho-cactus.cl), which offers day and overnight trips through stunning desertscapes. In Pucón, the two companies to contact are: **Campo Antilco** (✆ **9/713-9758;** www.antilco.com), a German-run business with day rides and 5- to 7-night trips to hot springs and Andean heights; and the **Huifquenco Fundo** (✆ **45/415040;** www.fundohuifquenco.cl), a working ranch with family-friendly farm tours and day rides paired with a Chilean-style barbecue. In Puerto Varas, visit the stunning **Campo Aventura** (✆ **65/232910;** www.campo-aventura.com), offering day rides and overnight trips, from 2 to 10 nights, based out of their modest lodge nestled in the rainforest near Vincente Pérez Rosales National Park. The trips also offer opportunities for rafting and canyoning.

KAYAKING & WHITEWATER RAFTING

It shouldn't come as a surprise that Chile has world-class rafting and kayaking, given the hundreds of pristine rivers that descend from the Andes and the country's Pacific Coast border. One of the most captivating and wildest rivers to raft in the world is the renowned **Futaleufú,** which means "Big River" in local indigenous Aracauria and sports Class III to Class V rapids with such daunting names as the Terminator and Hell Canyon. (Unfortunately, the Futaleufú is being threatened by an electro hydraulic dam slated for construction after 2012.) Local and international tour operators organize multiday rafting journeys based around mountain refuges and camping, and can be found in chapter 12. Just 45 minutes from Santiago at the Cajón de Maipo, the **Maipo River** is a quick city escape for moderate, Class III rafting from November to February, and tamer floats suitable for families the rest of the year; see "Chile-Based Tour Operators" earlier in this chapter. The **Petrohue River** with Class III and IV rapids is equally spellbinding for its impossibly emerald waters and the majestic Volcán Osorno that rises high in the distance. To raft this river, contact **Alsur Expeditions** (© **65/232300;** www.alsur expeditions.com).

While cruising the hushed Chilean fjords is a memorable experience, kayaking puts you closer to nature and the feeling of being enveloped in an emerald wonderland. Paddling journeys take travelers past cascading falls, along picturesque coves at Chiloé, and past sea lion rookeries, often stopping at a natural hot springs along the way. **Altué Expediciones** (© **2/232-1103;** www.altue.com) pioneered sea kayaking in this region; their modest but cozy lodge based at Chiloé has dynamite views, and their support vessel takes travelers wherever they want to paddle. **Yak Expeditions** (© **9/299-6487;** www. yakexpediciones.cl) specializes in low-impact trips with overnights in tents in natural settings, and they can also plan day trips around the lakes near Puerto Varas. The "official" tour operator for Pumalín Park is **Alsur Expeditions** (© **65/232300;** www.alsur expeditions.com), which has a support vessel, a traditional Chiloé boat, and kayak tours around the park, with overnights in tents. Note that while tent camping is a dream for nature lovers, a downpour, common in this region, can be uncomfortable, and support vessels are not usually large enough to accommodate groups indoors. If you're not specifically seeking out kayaking but would like to include the sport in your trip, check out **Austral Adventures** (© **65/625977;** www.australadventures.com) and their cruises, which sleep guests inside their boat and bring along a few kayaks for fun.

The company **Kayak Australis** (© **2/650-8264;** www.kayakaustralis.com) offers river and sea kayak courses and trips throughout the length of Chile, even across the Inca Lake at Portillo.

MOTORCYCLING

The romantic tale of Che Guevara and his epic journey through South America has enticed legions of travelers to Chile, seeking to follow Guevara's famous route. But, don't be swept away by the romance of the movie and book *The Motorcycle Diaries:* many of the roads in Patagonia are unpaved and rife with potholes. Lengthy motorcycle trips are for those with a true spirit for adventure and who are mentally and physically up to the demand, and reservations must be made far in advance for organized journeys. The Texas-based company **MotoDiscovery** (© **800/233-0564** in the U.S.; www.moto discovery.com) has a 32-day, January/February ride leaving from Viña del Mar and heading to Tierra del Fuego and back through Argentina, crossing over at Mendoza to finish in Santiago; the cost is $10,879 (£7,253) for a rider and $8,795 (£5,863) for a passenger.

SKIING

Chile's awesome Andean terrain and world-class resorts are no longer just a summer refuge for ski fanatics and foreign ski teams—it's now a hot destination for even recreational skiers, especially in August. A guide to Chile's ski resorts can be found in chapter

7 ("Ski Resorts in the Central Andean Region" and "Chillán & Termas de Chillán Resort"). With the exception of the Snowcat-serviced resort Ski Arpa, the resorts listed on these pages are the country's largest, and pull in the lion's share of foreign skiers. But adventurous skiers and snowboarders are finding that heliskiing (p. 183) lets them put tracks down where no one has before, and others are striking out and visiting the country's unsung, smaller resorts such as Corralco (p. 252), where they find intimate settings and a more "Chilean" experience. **PowderQuest Tours** (© **888/565-7158** toll-free in the U.S., or 206/203-6065; www.powderquest.com) offers complete ski and snowboard tour packages that take guests on an 8- to 16-day tour of Chilean and Argentine ski resorts, and they offer snowboard and heliski camps. The group maximum is eight, and they focus on off-*piste* and backcountry terrain with qualified, responsible guides. Their 9-day guided ski trip staying in upscale accommodations at the major ski resorts costs $3,525 (£2,350). Of the handful of ski tours out there, I trust PowderQuest more than any other.

For trip planning, call **Moguls Mountain Vacations** (© **888/767-0679;** www.southamerica.skitrips.com) or **Ski Organizers** (© **800/283-2SKI** [283-2754]; www.skiorganizers.com); both are specialists in ski and snowboard vacations in Chile and Argentina, and they can put together an entire package, including flights and transfers. These guys offer the best prices and the most knowledgeable information about what resort is right for you.

SPAS

Chile's geographic faults produce geothermal activity and mineralized, naturally hot water that has given birth to a long tradition of facilities offering *baños termales* (thermal baths). Some of the country's century-old facilities have been renovated to appeal to modern spa tastes, others offer a historical traipse back in time, with their marble tubs and vigorous massages. Count on nearly every world-class hotel to provide guests with services such as massage, a gym, a sauna, and sometimes a steam room. In Santiago, try the sleek spa **Balthus,** in Vitacura (© **2/410-1423;** www.balthus.cl), a spa within the city's toniest gym. For a Santiago getaway, try the Viña's luxury hotels, the **Sheraton Miramar** (which has a Balthus spa; p. 133) or the **Hotel del Mar** (p. 133). In Pucón, the **Almoni del Lago Resort Spa** (p. 261) offers a variety of massage and body treatments. Here are a few highlights of spas in Chile.

Puyuhuapi Lodge & Spa ★ (formerly known as Termas de Puyuhuapi; ©/fax **2/225-6489;** www.patagonia-connection.com) is the best-known spa in Chile, and its breathtaking location on the Puyuhuapi fjord is part of the draw, too. It takes time to get here, but the remote location is close enough to cruise to the Laguna San Rafael glacier, which the spa features as part of its package. A massive indoor pool and three fern-fringed outdoor pools complement a full range of spa services such as massage, facials, and body treatments. A 4-day "body and soul" package costs from $1,670 to 1,820 (£1,113–£1,213).

Termas de Cauquenes ★ (© **72/899010;** www.termasdecauquenes.cl) draws visitors more for its award-winning restaurant, antique hacienda-style architecture, and lovely alpine setting than its spa facilities and guest rooms. The 200-year-old spa is Chile's oldest, having hosted the likes of Charles Darwin, and it was inspired by France's Vichy Spa. While the spa's Gothic-designed thermal pavilion is striking, the ancient marble tubs do not inspire a soak.

Termas de Chillán ★★★ (© **866/237-4119;** www.termasdechillan.cl) is the best all-in-one spa destination for families or a group, and the beech forests and craggy peaks that envelope the area are simply lovely. More than a spa, it is a full-scale destination resort with all the trimmings, including a ski resort, golf course, casino, and three hotels—plus their state-of-the-art spa was totally renovated in 2006. Along with massage, aromatherapy, facials, and other body treatments, Termas de Chillán boasts outdoor thermal pools and even a natural pool reached by a hike through the peaks.

Termas de Puyehue ★ (✆ **2/283-1010;** www.puyehue.cl) draws mostly Chileans for its "tropical" indoor pool; herbal, mud, sulfur, and marine salt baths; massage; and family-friendly activities such as horseback riding and farm tours. The facade reminds visitors of a traditional European spa, and the services are not as modern as those found elsewhere in the country. The real perk here is the nearby Antillanca ski resort.

Termas Geométricas ★★★ (✆ **2/214-1214;** www.termasgeometricas.cl) is not a "spa" but a series of slate-tiled hot springs that descend through a jungle-draped ravine. It's an utterly divine and exotic attraction and well worth the 45-minute drive from Pucón.

SURFING

The powerful swells and consistent breaks off the Pacific Ocean along Chile's 4,186km (2,600-mile) coast draw surfers from around the world—but man, it's *cold* swimming out there, and you'll need a wetsuit (4/3 mm during the winter, 3/2 mm during the summer), booties, and even a hood when surfing south of the northern region. Surfing is good year-round, and a majority of left-breaking waves makes Chile a goofy-foot paradise. In the north, expect a few beach breaks but mostly board-breaking, Hawaiian-style reef breaks; here the best spots for surfing are Iquique and Arica. The Central Region's best (and most popular) spots for surfing include Chile's surfing mecca Pichilemu, with three surfing areas: La Puntilla, a 2-minute walk from town; Infernillo, which, when conditions are right, can produce a 2.4m-plus (8-ft.-plus) tube; and Punta de Lobos, considered Chile's most consistent break and a long left break with mixed conditions producing tubes and powerful waves. Lastly, Puertocillo is a renowned point break that's fast and has excellent tubes. Though this spot is closed to the public without a permit, you can access this beautiful cove by booking a room at the **Pacifika Surf Lodge**; they offer surf classes and trips to surf spots around the area, and are open year-round.

WELLNESS ACTIVITIES

While there is a paucity of lodges and spas dedicated to yoga practice in Chile, several adventure tour operators run annual 7- to 10-day-long yoga retreats that include daily yoga sessions complimented with river rafting, horseback riding, and a myriad of other wilderness activities that promise rejuvenation of the body and soul. The acclaimed **Bio Bio Expeditions** (✆ **800/246-7238;** www.bbxrafting.com) offers a comprehensive 9-day "Yoga Adventure Patagonia" program, with eco-camp style accommodations options in both Argentina and Chile. At around $3,200 (£2,133) per person, there is nothing very zen about the price, however. **Expediciones Chile** (✆ **888/488-9082** in the U.S., 2/570-9885 in Chile; www.exchile.com) offers a more economical 9-day program (for $2,195/£1,463) based on the Futaleufú river, which includes beach yoga, rafting the Terminator section of Futaleufú, sea kayaking, hiking, and horseback riding. These vacations are not advised for yoga devotees who wish to dedicate the majority of their day to yoga practice; rather these vacations offer an excellent compromise for couples and friends who may have varied interests, including yoga.

6

Santiago

Santiago, one of South America's most sophisticated cities, is a thriving metropolis that's home to over six million people, a third of Chile's entire population. In spite of being the civic, cultural, and historical nucleus of the country, Santiago is one of Chile's least-popular tourist destinations, and most visitors use the city only as a jumping-off point to locations such as Patagonia (see chapter 13) or the Lake District (see chapter 10), or as a base while exploring the central region.

You won't find a rich, vibrant culture, graceful architecture, an impassioned sensuality, or an endless list of things to do or see in Santiago. The city's neighborhoods are divided by prosaic malls, monolithic skyscrapers, and frenetic thoroughfares; visitors cannot wander freely from district to district, as they can in more vibrant cities like Río or Buenos Aires.

Yet as memories of the stifling Pinochet dictatorship fade, Santiago is reinventing itself. Perhaps nothing embodies Santiago's embrace of the avant garde more strikingly than the city's new modernist cultural center, La Moneda. Nightlife is decidedly low key and centers upon intimate bars and convivial live music clubs. The restaurant scene, which languished for so long under the mantel of mediocrity, has never been better, with a wave of innovative chefs working their culinary magic at restaurants throughout town. Add to this the city's historical attractions and its proximity to ski resorts and wineries, and you can see why the capital city deserves at least a 1-day visit.

Santiago's salient feature is its one-of-a-kind location sprawled below some of the highest peaks of the Andes range, providing a breathtaking city backdrop when the air is clear and the peaks are dusted with snow. Visitors are unfortunately not always treated to this view, as dust and smog is a chronic problem in Santiago, especially during the winter months from May to August. From December to late February, when Santiaguinos abandon the city for summer vacation and the city is blessed with breezier days, the smog abates substantially. These are the most pleasant months to tour the city.

Architecturally, Santiago's city planners have shown indifference to continuity of design during the last century. Rather than look within for a style of its own, Chileans have been more inclined to copy blueprints from other continents: first Europe and now the U.S. Earthquakes have flattened many of Santiago's colonial-era buildings, and what remains has been left to decay to the point that tearing down an antique mansion is cheaper than restoring it to its former glory. Thus, it isn't uncommon to see a glitzy skyscraper or crackerbox apartment building towering over a 200-year-old relic, or to see cobblestone streets dead-end at a tacky 1970s shopping gallery. Some neighborhoods look as though they belong to entirely different cities. The residential areas of Providencia and Vitacura are exceptions. Here you will find lovely leafy streets, manicured lawns, and attractive single-family homes divided by parks and plazas—but even these two neighborhoods are being threatened by an unprecedented boom in condominium construction.

1 ORIENTATION

ESSENTIALS

Getting There

BY PLANE Santiago's **Comodoro Arturo Merino Benítez Airport** (SCL; © **2/690-1900;** www.aeropuertosantiago.cl) is served by LAN, Air Comet, Aerolínea Principal, and Sky, in addition to most major international carriers. The relatively new airport has plenty of restaurants (the best dining options are to be found when you have passed through the security and immigration checks) and souvenir stands, and a Vinoteca wine shop for last-minute purchases.

Once you pass through Customs, there is a small **currency exchange** kiosk. To the left and right of the passenger gate there are cash machines. Men in olive jumpsuits at the arrival gate and the outdoor-departure curb work as airport bellhops, and they will assist you with your luggage for a 1,000 to 2,000 peso tip (about $1.70–$3.40/£1.15–£2.25).

Depending on traffic, your Santiago destination, and how you get there, the city can be reached in 20 to 45 minutes. Most hotels offer a private car or van pickup for about $25 (£17). An official **taxi** to Santiago costs between $25 and $30 (£17–£20), depending on your destination. ***Tip:*** A gauntlet of taxi drivers vie for business at the exit gate, but play it safe and buy a taxi ride at one of the official counters located just as you exit the gate, to avoid getting ripped off. More economical options are the minivan transfer shuttles **TransVip** (© **2/677-3000;** www.transvip.net) and **Tur Transfer** (© **2/677-3600;** www.turtransfer.cl) that charge, per person, $8 (£5.30) for downtown Santiago and $10 (£6.70) to Las Condes. Tickets can be purchased in both the domestic and international arrivals areas. For outbound passengers leaving Santiago for the airport, both companies prefer that reservations are made 1 day in advance. The drawback with this service is that you may stop at several other destinations before arriving at your own. Cheaper yet are bus services that depart from the far ends of the arrival curb and drop passengers downtown, from where they can take the Metro or a taxi. Hotels can also arrange taxis on a fixed fare basis which, depending on your hotel and negotiation skills, tends to be much cheaper, at about $23 (£15). The blue bus **Centropuerto** leaves every 10 minutes from 6am to 11:30pm and drops passengers at Los Héroes Metro station on the main avenue Alameda. **Tur Bus** leaves every 30 minutes from 6:30am to midnight, dropping passengers off at Terminal Alameda at the Universidad de Santiago Metro station. The cost is $2.50 (£1.70).

BY BUS There are four **bus stations** in Santiago. The station for international arrivals and departures to and from destinations in southern Chile is **Terminal Buses Estación Central,** formerly known as the Terminal Santiago and not to be confused with the actual Estación Central train station and Metro stop; it's located at Alameda 3850 (© **2/376-1755;** Metro: Universidad de Santiago). The **Terminal Alameda** next door at Alameda 3750 is the terminal for the Pullman and Tur Bus companies, two well-respected, high-quality services. For departures to northern and central Chile, you'll go to **Terminal San Borja,** Alameda 3250 (© **2/776-0645;** Metro: Estación Central). The smaller **Terminal Los Héroes,** Tucapel Jiménez 21 (© **2/423-9530;** Metro: Los Héroes), has service to a variety of destinations in both northern and southern Chile as well as a clutch of international destinations.

Downtown Santiago Accommodations, Dining & Attractions

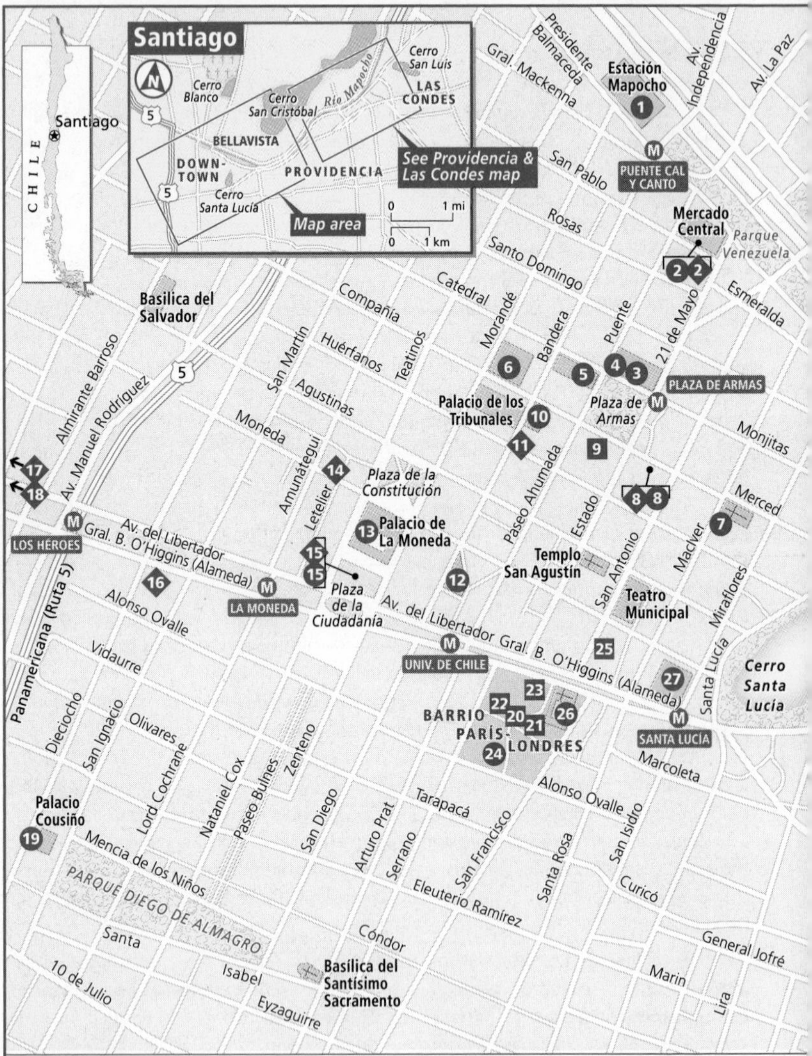

ACCOMMODATIONS ■
- Andes Hostel **28**
- Hostal Plaza de Armas **9**
- Hotel Del Patio **39**
- Hotel Fundador **22**
- Hotel Galerias **25**
- Hotel París Nuevo **21**
- Hotel Plaza San Francisco **23**
- Hotel Vegas **20**

DINING ◆
- Ambrosía **8**
- Amorío **44**
- Azul Profundo **45**
- Barandiaran **40**
- Bar Nacional **11**
- Confitería Torres/Café Torres **15, 16**
- El Caramaño **38**
- El Toro **33**
- Etniko **43**
- Frederick's Bistro **14**
- Galindo **46**
- Gatopardo **31**
- Il Siciliano **47**
- Japón **30**
- Opera & Catedral **35**
- Patagonia Café **29**
- Picada Ana María **18**
- Squadritto **32**
- Zully **17**

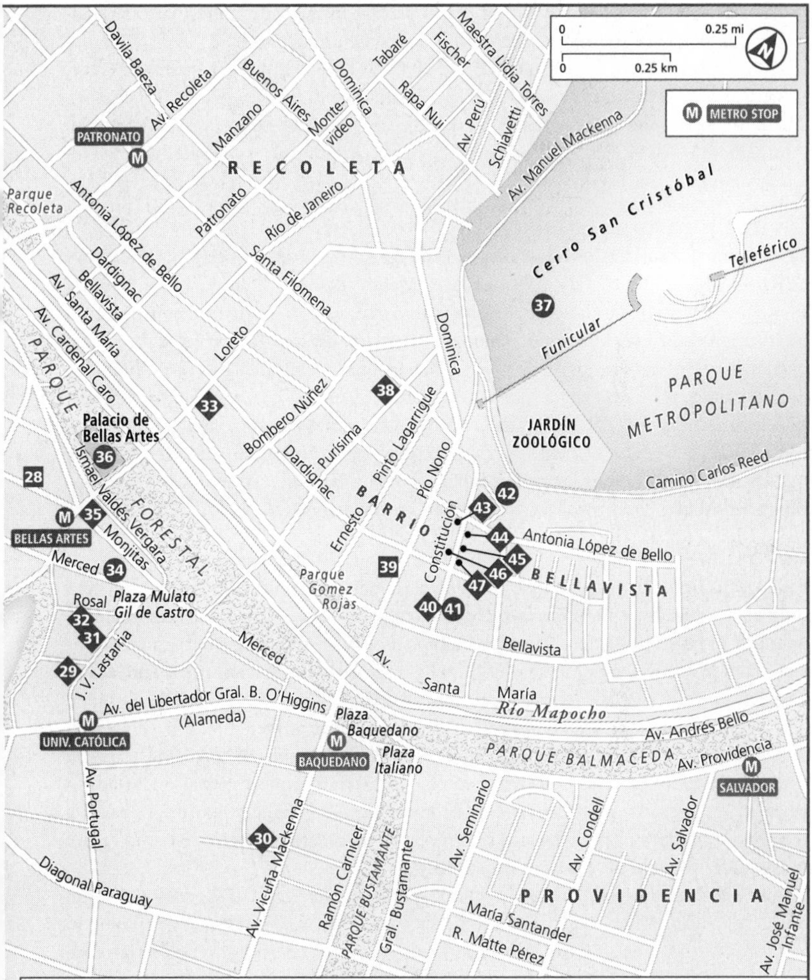

ATTRACTIONS

- Barrio París-Londres **24**
- Basílica de la Merced **7**
- Biblioteca Nacional **27**
- Calle Dieciocho and Palacio Cousiño Macul **19**
- Calle Nueva York & the Bolsa de Comercio **12**
- Casa Colorada & Santiago Museum **8**
- Catedral Metropolitana and Museo de Arte Sagrado **5**
- Centro Cultural Palacio La Moneda **15**
- Cerro San Cristóbal **37**
- Correo Central and Museo Postal **4**
- Estación Mapocho **1**
- Ex-Congreso Nacional and Palacio de los Tribunales **6**
- Iglesia, Convento y Museo de San Francisco **26**
- La Chascona **42**
- Mercado Central **2**
- Museo Chileno de Arte Precolombino **10**
- Museo de Artes Visuales/ Museo Anthropología **34**
- Palacio de Bellas Artes & Museo de Arte Contemporaneo (MAC) **36**
- Palacio de la Real Audiencia/ Museo Histórico Nacional **3**
- Palacio La Moneda **13**
- Patio Bellavista **41**

BY TRAIN Santiago is serviced by the state owned **Empresa de los Farrocarriles del Estado (EFE),** which provides modern and comfortable service to Chillán, stopping first in Rancagua, San Fernando, and Talca, and passing through beautiful, pastoral landscapes. For reference, prices in 2008 from Santiago to Chillán were $13 to $15 (£8.70–£10) one-way for "salon" class, and $26 to $28 (£17–£19) one-way for "preferred" class, which has seats that recline to 140 degrees. Tickets purchased online are 10% cheaper. There is a snack and beverage service car. Call EFE or check the website for updated information (✆ **600/585-5000;** www.efe.cl), or check with your travel agent or hotel for a reservation.

Visitor Information

The **National Tourism Service (Sernatur)** office is at Av. Providencia 1550 (✆ **600/SERNATUR** [737-6288]; www.sernatur.cl; Metro: Manuel Montt), open Monday through Friday from 9am to 6pm, Saturday from 9am to 2pm. Sernatur also has a small information desk, with hotel information and maps, on the departure level of the airport open daily from 9am to 5pm (no phone). The Santiago Municipality has an **Oficina de Turismo** inside the Casa Colorada at Merced 860 (✆ **2/632-7783**), with limited information about downtown Santiago attractions only. Also downtown, at the south side of Cerro Santa Lucía at Avenida Alameda, is a tourism office (✆ **2/664-4216**). The **Yellow Pages** has detailed maps of the entire city of Santiago, or you can pick up a pocket guide to the city, called **Map City** (www.mapcity.com), sold at newsstands and kiosks, for $7 (£4.70).

CITY LAYOUT

Santiago incorporates 32 *comunas,* or neighborhoods, although most visitors will find they spend their time in just a few. **Downtown,** or *el centro,* is the thriving financial, political, and historic center of Santiago, although it has been losing clout as more companies opt to locate their offices in burgeoning neighborhoods such as **Providencia, Las Condes,** and the tiny area that separates the two, **El Golf** (also known as El Bosque). These upscale, modern neighborhoods are residential areas centered on a bustling strip of shopping galleries, restaurants, and office buildings. *El centro* is older and scruffier, with the exception of the small but charming **Lastarría/Parque Forestal** micro-neighborhood, an up-and-coming arts and cafe community. Still, while it may not be easy on the eye or the nerves, *centro* remains the city's microcosm and the most rewarding place to get under the skin of Santiago's urban matrix.

The well-heeled residential neighborhood **Vitacura,** north of Las Condes and south of the Mapocho River, and spliced by the thoroughfare Avenida Kennedy, is home to Santiago's luxury shopping and many gourmet restaurants. The sleepy, middle-class residential communities **Ñuñoa** and **La Reina** offer few attractions and, therefore, little of interest to the visitor, with the exception of Plaza Ñuñoa and its booming restaurant and bar scene. Santiago is bisected by the Río Mapocho, a muddy river that alternately rushes or trickles down from the Andes and is bordered through downtown and Providencia by the grassy Parque Forestal. On the north side of the Mapocho rises the hill Cerro San Cristóbal, a 880m (2,886-ft.) forested park with lookout points over the city. At the foot of the hill is the bohemian neighborhood **Bellavista,** another restaurant haven and happening night spot. Note that the principal avenue that runs through downtown is called Avenida Alameda by absolutely everyone, but its official moniker is Avenida Libertador Bernardo O'Higgins.

Accommodations, Dining & Attractions in Providencia & Las Condes

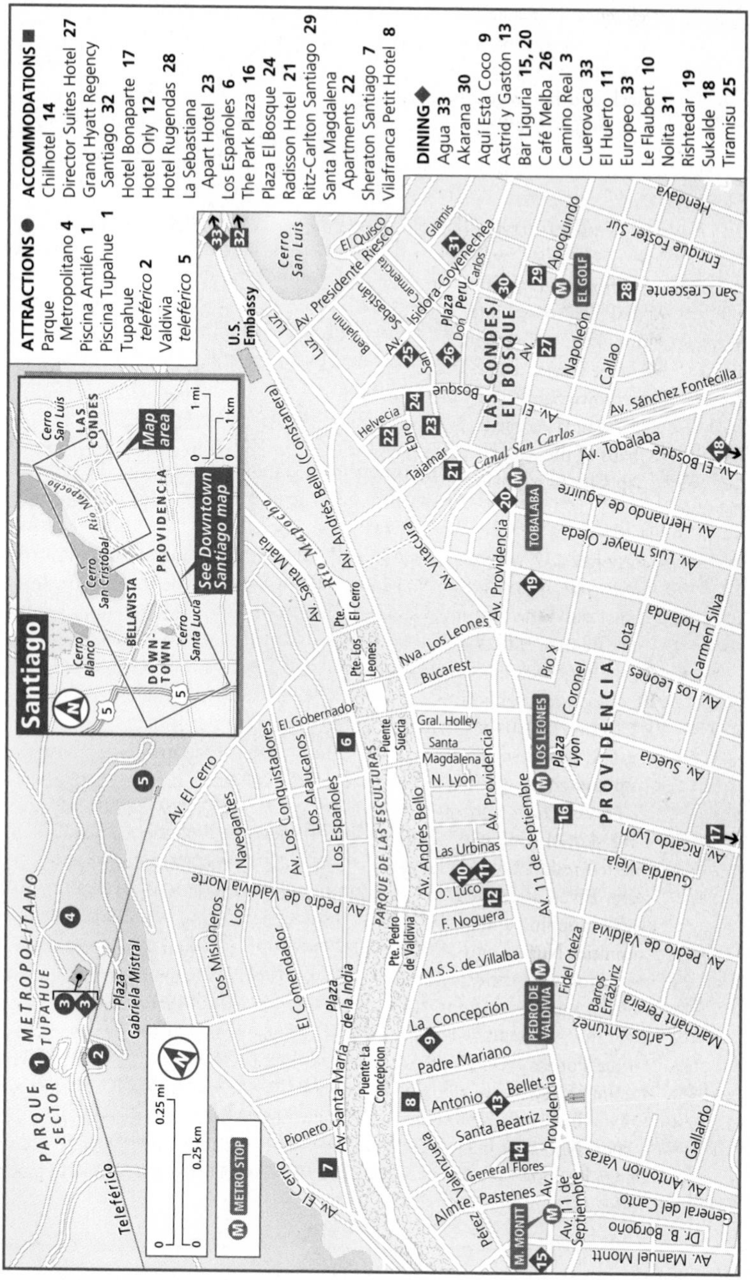
ATTRACTIONS
Parque Metropolitano 4
Piscina Antilén 1
Piscina Tupahue 1
Tupahue teleférico 2
Valdivia teleférico 5
ACCOMMODATIONS
Chilhotel 14
Director Suites Hotel 27
Grand Hyatt Regency Santiago 32
Hotel Bonaparte 17
Hotel Orly 12
Hotel Rugendas 28
La Sebastiana Apart Hotel 23
Los Españoles 6
The Park Plaza 16
Plaza El Bosque 24
Radisson Hotel 21
Ritz-Carlton Santiago 29
Santa Magdalena Apartments 22
Sheraton Santiago 7
Vilafranca Petit Hotel 8
DINING
Agua 33
Akarana 30
Aquí Está Coco 9
Astrid y Gastón 13
Bar Liguria 15, 20
Café Melba 26
Camino Real 3
Cuerovaca 33
El Huerto 11
Europeo 33
Le Flaubert 10
Nolita 31
Rishtedar 19
Sukalde 18
Tiramisu 25
Santiago
Cerro Blanco
Cerro San Cristóbal
Cerro San Luis
Cerro Santa Lucía
BELLAVISTA
DOWN-TOWN
PROVIDENCIA
LAS CONDES
Map area
See Downtown Santiago map
PARQUE METROPOLITANO
SECTOR TUPAHUE
Plaza Gabriela Mistral
Teleférico
0.25 mi
0.25 km
METRO STOP
U.S. Embassy
Río Mapocho
Canal San Carlos
PARQUE DE LAS ESCULTURAS
LAS CONDES/ EL BOSQUE
PROVIDENCIA
Av. Providencia
Av. 11 de Septiembre
Av. Andrés Bello
Av. Santa María
Av. Apoquindo
Av. Vitacura
Av. Tobalaba
Av. Pedro de Valdivia
Av. Los Leones
Av. Presidente Riesco
Av. Isidora Goyenechea
M. MONTT
PEDRO DE VALDIVIA
LOS LEONES
TOBALABA
EL GOLF

BY METRO

Cheap, clean, and efficient, the Metro subway (www.metrosantiago.cl) is by far the fastest and most agreeable way to get around the city. It's also an attraction in its own right—stations are adorned with murals painted by some of Chile's most important artists. Unfortunately, it is now the most congested transport option, especially during rush hour from 7 to 10am and 5 to 7pm, when critical mass reaches an estimated six users per square meter. The Metro is considered to be generally safe; however, pickpocket incidents are on the rise with the new influx of passengers, so keep a sharp eye on your belongings.

There are five Metro lines. Line 1 is the principal Metro line for travelers, as it runs from Las Condes to attractions and bus stations downtown. Line 2 transfers from Line 1 at Los Heroes and stops at Cal y Canto (near the Mercado Central). Lines 4 and 4a are residential lines connecting Avenida Alameda with La Reina. Line 5 takes travelers transferring at Baquedano to Plaza de Armas and the Quinta Normal park. ***Note***: Lines 3 and 6 are not scheduled for completion until 2015.

A prepaid *bip* card is the only way to pay for travel on Santiago's existing public transport system. Cards *(tarjetas)* can be purchased at Metro stations, various banks (Banco de Chile and Banco Santander), various commercial locations throughout the city, and designated *Punto bip* centres. Minimum *Tarjeta bip* credit is 800 pesos ($1.35/90p) going up to a maximum of 2,500 pesos ($43/£29). A one-way bus fare costs 380 pesos (65¢/45p), permitting three transfers within 120 minutes. If you then transfer from the bus to the Metro, you will be required to pay an additional 40 pesos (5¢/3p). If you begin your journey on the Metro, the initial fare costs 420 pesos (70¢/45p). You must validate your *Tarjeta bip* card prior to each journey or else risk being charged for fare evasion.

See the inside front cover of this guide for a map of the city's Metro system.

Transantiago: Mass Transit Mayhem

Arguably the most loathed word in the Chilean lexicon, Transantiago, the integrated transport system introduced in February 2007, has provoked chaos on an unprecedented scale. The most ambitious transport reform undertaken by a developing country, Transantiago was introduced via a "big bang" approach rather than as a gradually phased-in scheme. The ensuing mayhem was reflected in President Michelle Bachelet's approval rating, which fell from 55.2% to 42.7% in the month following the system's introduction. With decreased bus routes, an increased route network, and insufficient infrastructure to deal with the complexities of a prepay system, travelers have opted to use the more efficient Metro. Since 2007, the Metro has been overwhelmed by increased passenger numbers (riders jumped from 1,300,000 to 2,200,000 that year). Government initiatives imply that the flaws in the system will be gradually smoothed out, dispersing the congestion to an expansion of the bus route network, however.

BY BUS

The Santiago bus system has undergone an overhaul in the last few years. Old yellow buses have been replaced with new gleaming white-and-green "Transantiago" coaches, which you cannot ride without a *bip* transit card. See "By Metro" above for info. If you do not have a *bip* card, you can still pay cash on the local feeder buses, but at a higher rate and without the possibility of free transfers.

BY TAXI

Taxis are reasonably priced and plentiful. They are identifiable by their black exterior and yellow roof; there's also a light in the corner of the windshield that displays a taxi's availability. Always check to see that the meter is in plain view, to avoid rip-offs. Drivers do not expect tips. Do not confuse taxis with ***colectivos,*** which are similar in appearance but without the yellow roof—these are local, shared taxis with fixed routes that are too confusing to visitors to recommend taking one.

Fares are low compared to North American and European cities. The starting fare is 250 pesos (40¢/25p), then 60 pesos (10¢/5p) for every subsequent 200m. Drivers are permitted to charge more at night, so always check the rates (usually indicated on the window) before you get in; also try to get a verbal estimate of your fare and have small bills handy to avoid scams, which are frequent. It doesn't hurt to research your route in advance, either, as many taxi drivers don't have special knowledge of the city's layout.

BY CAR

Do not rent a vehicle if staying within metropolitan Santiago, but consider doing so if you are an independent traveler seeking to visit the coast, Cajón de Maipo, or wine country. Santiago's slick new Costanera Norte (an express transit tunnel that runs from La Dehesa and Las Condes to the Pan-American Hwy. and the airport) has entrances and exits along the River Mapocho, but finding one can be confusing, so check out the website www.costaneranorte.cl for a map, or ask your rental agency or hotel to guide you. The city's "TAG" system (TAG stands for an automatic toll that is charged electronically to the vehicle) is included in the rental price. Downtown Santiago, and the entire length of Avenida Alameda/Avenida Providencia are not recommended for timid drivers. Buses and other drivers steadfastly refuse to let other vehicles merge into their lane, so be prepared early to turn or exit a highway.

RENTALS At the airport you'll find most international rental agencies, such as **Alamo** (© 2/690-1370; www.alamo.com), **Avis** (© 2/690-1382; www.avis.com), **Budget** (© 2/690-1233; www.budget.com), **Dollar** (© 2/202-5510; www.dollar.com), **Hertz** (© 2/601-0977; www.hertz.com), and local agency **Rosselot** (© 800/201298). All agencies have downtown or Providencia offices. Generally, Rosselot and Dollar are lower in cost. Many hotels also offer competitive rates and can pick up and drop off the car.

DRIVING TIPS On weekdays, the two yellow lanes running the length of Avenida Alameda (which changes its name to Providencia, 11 de Septiembre, and Apoquindo in other neighborhoods) are bus lanes, and drivers of vehicles may enter only when preparing to make a right turn. Take care with speed limits (120kmph) on the main highways out of town, especially Ruta 5 where *carabinieros* (police officers) wield radars and purvey hefty fines.

It's a good idea to arrive in town with some maps, as gas stations are often sold out of maps and rental agencies usually do not stock any, especially regional maps. The Turistel road guide website (www.turistel.cl) has helpful route maps that can be printed.

PARKING Every hotel, with the exception of budget hostals, offers on-site, free parking. There is no street parking downtown except Saturdays and Sundays, although there are underground lots called *estacionamientos* that are recognizable by a blue sign marked with a giant E. In Providencia, along Avenida Providencia, there is a series of expensive underground lots. Santiago meters busy streets in Providencia and Bellavista, which is done by an official meter maid who waits on the street and times and charges drivers—he or she will leave a white ticket on your windshield. On commercial streets where there is no meter maid, you'll find the *cuidador*, an unofficial, ragtag "caretaker" who will "watch" your car for you. You're expected to give him or her a tip of 100 to 300 pesos (15¢–50¢/10p–35p) when you leave your space. *Cuidadores* can be aggressive if you elect not to pay them.

Do not under any circumstances leave valuable items in your car if you park on the street; break-ins are frequent in all of Chile. Car theft is common, too, so always park your vehicle in a lot overnight.

ON FOOT

Santiago is not laid out on a perfect grid system; however, the neighborhoods most visitors stick to run along the length of the Mapocho River, making the river a good point of reference. Always carry a map with you. Saturday afternoons and Sundays are quieter days to explore neighborhoods such as downtown. Pedestrians should be alert at all times and never stand too close to sidewalk curbs because buses roar by dangerously close to sidewalks. Drivers are not always polite enough to give the right of way to pedestrians, so cross streets quickly and with your eyes wide open.

Fast Facts Santiago

American Express The American Express office is at Av. Isidora Goyenechea 3621, Piso 10 (© **2/350-6700**); open Monday through Friday from 9am to 2pm and 3:30 to 5pm. Twenty-four-hour customer service in the U.S. is at © **800/545-1171**, although you will be charged for the call if you call from outside of the United States.

Banks Banks are open from 9am to 2pm Monday through Friday, closed on Saturday and Sunday. You don't have to look hard in the downtown area to find an ATM, referred to as "Redbancs" and identified by a maroon-and-white logo sticker. Many commercial outlets also have ATMs. These machines accept Visa/PLUS and MasterCard/Cirrus. Redbancs can also be found in most gas stations and pharmacies.

Business Hours Commercial business hours are Monday through Friday from 10am to 7pm, closing for lunch between 1 and 1:30pm and reopening between 2:30 and 3pm. Most stores are open from 10am to 2pm on Saturday and closed on Sunday, with the exception of shopping malls.

Currency Exchange All major banks exchange currency, but most charge a commission that is higher than a money-exchange house *(casa de cambio)*. In downtown, there are numerous exchange houses on Agustinas between Ahumada and Bandera: Bombero, Ossa 1053 (✆ **2/698-1703**); Transpacific, Augustinas 1028 (✆ **2/232-1176**). In Providencia, exchange houses are around Avenida Pedro de Valdivia at Avenida Providencia. In Las Condes, there are a couple on Avenida El Bosque Norte near Avenida Apoquindo. Exchange houses are generally open Monday through Friday from 9am to 2pm and 4 to 6pm, Saturday from 9am to 1 or 2pm. Hotels exchange dollars at an unfavorable rate.

Emergencies For a **police** emergency, call ✆ **133.** For **fire,** call ✆ **132.** To call an **ambulance,** dial ✆ **131.**

Hospital The American Embassy can provide a list of medical specialists in Santiago. The best hospitals in Santiago are private: **Clínica Las Condes,** Lo Fontecilla 441 (✆ **2/210-4000**); **Clínica Alemana,** Vitacura 5951 (✆ **2/210-1111**); and **Clínica Indisa Santa María,** Av. Santa María 01810 (✆ **2/362-5555**).

Internet Access Every hotel has a computer with Internet connection for its guests, and many hotels (mostly large chains) now offer free Wi-Fi in guest rooms or in public areas. There is an abundance of Internet centers in the downtown area; popular cafes include **Café.com,** at Alameda 143, and **Sonnets Internet Café,** at Londres 43.

Outdoor Equipment Parque Arauco mall has a **North Face** clothing store (✆ **2/201-3679**). Locally produced, high-quality outdoor gear company **Doite** (✆ **2/213-1223**) is in the Alto los Condes mall; **Patagonia Sport** is in Providencia at Almirante Simpson 77 (✆ **2/222-9140**). The best outdoor equipment and info can be found at **La Cumbre,** Apoquindo 5220 (✆ **2/220-9907;** www.lacumbreonline.cl), which is open Monday through Friday 11am to 8pm and Saturday 11am to 4pm.

Pharmacies Pharmacies are ubiquitous in Santiago, and can even be found in gas stations along major highways. They're generally open from 8am to midnight; however, the following branches are open 24 hours: **Farmacias Ahumada** (✆ **600/222-4000;** Av. El Bosque 164); and **Farmacias Salco Brand** (✆ **600/360-6000;** Av. Padre Hurtado, at Av. Las Condes). Both of these pharmacies deliver for a nominal fee.

Post Office The main post office is on Plaza de Armas (Mon–Fri 8:30am–7pm; Sat 8:30am–1pm). There are other branches at Moneda 1155, in downtown, and Av. 11 de Septiembre 2239, in Providencia. **FedEx** is at Av. Providencia 1951, and in the Dimacofi center at Moneda 792 (✆ **2/361-6000;** Mon–Fri 9am–7pm).

Telephone Tourists are offered cheaper rates from phone centers than from their hotels. The centers are predominately run by **Entel** (at Morandé btw. Huérfanos and Compañía) and **Telefónica CTC Chile** (found inside the Metro stations Universidad de Chile and Moneda, and in Providencia at the Mall Panorámico at Av. 11 de Septiembre 2155). Most phone centers have fax service and Internet access as well. Alternatively, you can buy a phone card at any kiosk, gas station, corner store, or telephone center, but ask your hotel if you are charged for the local connection—chain hotels can really stick it to you even though you're using a phone card. Also see the "Telephone" section in "Fast Facts: Chile" in Appendix A for info.

3 WHERE TO STAY

Given Santiago's mélange of architectural styles and socioeconomic levels, where you stay could very well shape your opinion of the city. The cheapest accommodations are in the downtown area, *el centro,* and this is the obvious choice if proximity to museums and historical attractions is important to you. However, *el centro* is noisily congested with people and traffic during weekdays, and it is altogether a grittier neighborhood, with many buildings weathered by age and neglect. Still, there's a lot of character found in this part of town, and the Lastarría/Parque Forestal neighborhood, located nearby on the east side of Cerro Santa Lucía, is simply lovely.

Some travelers enjoy the upscale ambience of Las Condes, while others find it to be too antiseptic and devoid of local color, in addition to being a longer (although direct) Metro ride to downtown (around 15–20 min.). Providencia is a happy medium between the two, with leafy streets, restaurants, and shops. Energetic types can also reach downtown on foot heading directly east along Avenida Providencia (around 45 min.). Remember that it is a snap to get around town via the Metro, no matter where you stay. Nearly all hotels with 100-plus rooms are international chain hotels; the concept of boutique hotels or B&Bs has not taken off here as it has in many other major cities, but there are a few solid choices for hotels with a more intimate ambience. See the maps on p. 78 and 81 to locate the hotels reviewed below.

Parking at Santiago hotels is free unless otherwise indicated below. High and low seasons differ from hotel to hotel (if they do indeed adhere to price changes), and are individually noted in each review.

DOWNTOWN SANTIAGO

Very Expensive

Hotel Fundador Extensive renovations by acclaimed Chilean architect Germán de Sol have injected the Fundador's traditionally frumpy European decor with a vibrant dose of contemporary style to bring this reliable downtown standby in line with its sister hotel, Remota (p. 384). In the lobby, a hallucinogenic palette prevails with lime green leather sofas, egg yolk Louis XI-style chairs, and rustic, monochrome Andean tapestries and murals. The sharply decorated rooms are now awash with handpainted murals and the stained, worn carpets have been stripped away to reveal wooden floors warmed by Andean rugs. Rather soft beds are draped with crisp Peruvian cotton bedspreads. The buffet breakfast is decent. The location, on the edge of the atmospheric Barrio París-Londres, is a comfortable walk to the city's attractions and Lastarría's cafe society. This area can be noisy, though, and is not recommended for travelers looking for a peaceful day's retreat from the urban jungle.

Paseo Serrano 34. ✆ **2/387-1200.** Fax 2/387-1300. www.hotelfundador.cl. 150 units. $149–$164 (£99–£109) double; $187–$233 (£125–£155) suite. AE, DC, MC, V. Valet parking. Metro: Univ. de Chile. **Amenities:** 2 restaurants; bar; concierge; indoor pool; health club; sauna; room service; babysitting; laundry service; Wi-Fi (free). *In room:* A/C, TV, Wi-Fi, minibar, hair dryer.

Hotel Plaza San Francisco ★★ Value Following an exhaustive $5-million renovation in 2008, rooms at the Plaza are now comfortable, if rather homogenous—all sport the neutral tones and Pottery Barn–esque furnishings that are clearly the decor of choice in the Santiago hotel industry today. While it may not exude the class and style of its luxury peers, the prices here are more affordable than the competition most of the year (the exception is in Oct or Nov).

The Hotel Plaza is on bustling Avenue Alameda, but behind the hotel lie the tranquil pedestrian streets of the Barrio París-Londres micro-neighborhood, and guest rooms have double-paned windows to muffle noise. The hotel's proximity to downtown attractions and the shops and cafes of the Lastarría Street area is a definite perk, especially if you are only in town for a day or two. The hotel has a long list of amenities, but note that their "spa" is really a fitness center with a sauna and massage services. The **Bristol Restaurant** has been lavished with national gastronomic awards.

Alameda 816. ✆ **2/639-3832.** Fax 2/639-7826. www.plazasanfrancisco.cl. 155 units. $149–$230 (£99–£153) standard double; $310–$350 (£207–£233) executive suite. AE, DC, MC, V. Metro: Univ. de Chile. **Amenities:** Restaurant; bar; indoor heated pool; heath club; concierge; room service; laundry service. *In room:* A/C, TV, Wi-Fi, minibar.

Expensive

Hotel Galerias ★★ Kids Just when it seemed that hoteliers had all but given up on the downtown area, up pops this gem. The hotel, like its sister hotel Plaza Santa Cruz in the Colchagua Valley, is known for its heavy dose of themed decor, throughout the public spaces, representing the various cultures and regions of Chile. Altogether it's a delightful oasis in bustling downtown, and its location provides visitors with more authentic Chilean urban surroundings than Las Condes. The guest rooms, renovated only a few years ago, are modern and functional with a pared-down style colored in varying earth tones. Any tendency toward sterility is offset by marshmallowy beds topped with crisp white duvets and soft lighting, and wide windows (double-paned to keep the street noise out). Rooms are spacious enough for a couple of chairs and a small table, and suites are double the size, with a sofa bed for kids. The hotel has 12 floors and interior balconies that wrap around the main living area and a sixth-floor pool, surrounded by palm trees and pretty gardens.

San Antonio 65. ✆ **2/470-7400.** www.hotelgalerias.cl. 168 units. $130 (£87) double; $210 (£140) suite. AE, DC, MC, V. Rates include breakfast. Metro: Santa Lucía. **Amenities:** Restaurant; bar; outdoor pool; sauna; laundry service. *In room:* A/C, cable TV, Wi-Fi, minibar, hair dryer.

Inexpensive

Hostal Plaza de Armas ★ Moments You couldn't ask for a more evocative view than the one from this pleasant, well maintained backpacker's hostal, which looks out over the palm-studded Plaza de Armas and the historical buildings that surround it. The hostal is reached by passing through a hectic strip of cheap food stands, then by ascending to the sixth floor in a manually operated elevator. A cheerful staff and an even cheerier ambience await. The lively common areas and BBQ area invite traveler camaraderie. The owners of the hostal preserved the antique splendor of the building's hardwood floors, high ceilings, and a long balcony overlooking the plaza, but spruced the interiors up with hip, postmodern colors and furniture. What's odd about the hostal, though, is that rooms are freestanding, roofed "cubicles" that stretch the length of a loftlike space, which is hardly conducive to peaceful slumber. The best room here is a private double tucked away near a common patio. Three of the five rooms are shared dorms, and bathrooms are shared.

Compañía 960. ✆ **2/671-4436.** www.plazadearmashostel.com. 5 units. $32 (£20) double; $11–$14 (£7.30–£9.30) per person shared dorms. AE, DC, MC, V. No parking. Metro: Plaza de Armas. Continental breakfast $3 (£2). **Amenities:** Cafe; self-service laundry; Wi-Fi. *In room:* Kitchenette (in some), no phone.

Hotel París Nuevo ★ (Value) It's worth paying the extra few dollars to stay in the new annex of this eclectic European-style budget hotel, which would not look out of place amid the decaying Belle Epoque of Paris's Latin Quarter. Despite its functional flaws, this mansion-turned-hotel is showing its age gracefully with a range of eccentric and cozy rooms, some appointed with oriental rugs, antiques, and mahogany molding, which lead off from winding, creeky stairs. The rooms in the older annex are resolutely for backpackers. When booking, ask for a room with a terrace and a TV, because they are the same price and tend to be larger. Continental breakfast costs $3 (£2).

París 813. ✆ **2/664-0921.** Fax 2/639-4037. carbott@latinmail.com. 40 units. $30 (£20) double new wing; $23 (£15) double old room. AE, DC, MC, V. Parking across the street $3–$5 (£2–£3.30) per day. Metro: Univ. de Chile. **Amenities:** Cafe; laundry service. *In room:* TV (in some rooms).

Hotel Vegas ★ On a calm, cobblestone street, the popular Hotel Vegas stands out for its distinctly Chilean feel, traditional decor, and bargain rates. With its wood paneling, beamed ceilings, taxidermy, chandeliers, and frosted glass, it feels more like a mountain lodge circa 1970 than an urban hotel, but the overall effect is salubrious and rather charming. The spacious rooms are flooded with light and have soaring ceilings, wood-paneled walls, and window alcoves. The beds could be firmer, the carpeting doesn't invite barefoot rambling, and you won't find marble and double vanities in the bathrooms; but if it's quirky charm and old world eclecticism that you are looking for, this fits the bill. Travelers who prefer to sightsee on foot will revel in the location, at the epicenter of the París-Londres neighborhood, which is a great base for exploring the city. Check online for even cheaper rates.

Londres 49. ✆ **2/632-2514.** Fax 2/632-5084. www.hotelvegas.net. 20 units. $81 double (£54); $95 (£63) triple. AE, DC, MC, V. Metro: Univ. de Chile. **Amenities:** Cafe; bar; room service. *In room:* A/C, TV, Wi-Fi, minibar, hair dryer.

BELLAVISTA

Hotel Del Patio ★★ This immaculate boutique hotel marries an artistic flair with literary spirit sufficient to stir poetic yearnings in the most prosaic of souls. The hotel occupies the second floor of a 19th-century mansion, which has been beautifully restored and infuses stately grandeur with contemporary Zen touches. A grand staircase winds up to a galleried lobby, where soaring ceilings, expansive windows, lanterns, and hardwood floors set the tone for the pristine rooms—each a haven of tasteful simplicity, with soothing, muted decor, and understated furnishings offset by splashes of vibrant peacock colored paint, satine bedspreads, and mosaic-tiled bathrooms. The staff are courteous and knowledgeable, without being intrusive. A deliciously healthy continental breakfast is served on the rooftop terrace that overlooks the charming Bellavista Patio with its chi chi array of shops, restaurants, and coffee shops; it makes for a lively social scene that can be rather intrusive for sensitive sleepers, and is less than ideal for wary single travelers. The physically challenged should also take note that there are plenty of stairs to be negotiated.

Pio Nono 61. ✆ **2/732-7571.** www.hoteldelpatio.cl. 10 units. $120 (£80) double. AE, DC, MC, V. Metro: Baquedano. **Amenities:** Restaurant; bar; room service; laundry service. *In room:* Fan, TV, Wi-Fi, hair dryer.

PROVIDENCIA

Very Expensive

The Park Plaza ★ The Park Plaza calls itself a boutique hotel, but the uniformed bellhops and traditional decor (not to mention 104 rooms) make it a midsize hotel known for its personalized service. The hotel's salient feature is its perfect location on a tree-lined street just 1 block from Providencia's shops and services. The hotel has a traditional decor, with Oriental rugs, brocade fabrics, wingback chairs, and wood-paneled walls. While the hotel is kept spotlessly clean, its claim of luxury guest rooms is a stretch, and many of the guest rooms and bathrooms are musty and are beginning to show wear and tear. Still, the rooftop pool is a nice perk, and you simply can't beat the location. If you are looking for a little more independence, the Plaza's **Park Suite Apartments** around the corner (Lota 2233) are a good deal at $100 (£64) for a one-bedroom. They each come with fully furnished kitchenettes, seating areas, and full use of the hotel facilities. Prices are reduced for multiday stays.

Ricardo Lyon 207. ✆ **2/372-4000.** Fax 2/233-6668. www.parkplaza.cl. 104 units. $175 (£117) standard double; $250 (£167) suite. Parking available. Metro: Los Leones. **Amenities:** Restaurant; bar; indoor rooftop pool; health center; sauna; concierge; Internet access; room service; babysitting; laundry service. *In room:* A/C, TV, Wi-Fi, minibar, hair dryer.

Sheraton Santiago ★ With its crystal chandeliers, marble floors, and voluminous lobby, the Sheraton Santiago is all about glamour. The Sheraton is actually two hotels: the older Sheraton with standard rooms, and the luxurious **San Cristóbal Tower ★★★** with conference centers and executive rooms. The upside to the Sheraton are its spectacular views of Santiago and the Andes (any room on the 10th floor and up), but the downside is that the hotel is cut off from Providencia by the Río Mapocho and a busy thoroughfare, meaning you must take a cab or walk to the nearest intersection, then cross and continue on for 5 blocks (about 15 min. to the nearest Metro station).

I recommended that you only consider rooms in the San Cristóbal Tower due to the worn state of the standard rooms in the older wing. Executive guest rooms and suites in the Tower complex are top-notch, with plush beds and polished furnishings; each floor has its own butler, and there's a private lounge for breakfast or tea on the 21st floor. The Sheraton occasionally sells out to visiting conventioneers. Note that the restaurants are pricey; it's better to grab a cab and dine in Providencia or Bellavista.

Av. Santa María 1742. ✆ **2/233-5000.** Fax 2/234-1066. www.sheraton.cl. 379 units. Sheraton: $180 (£120) double standard; San Cristóbal Tower: $220 (£147) double, $525 (£350) deluxe executive suite. AE, DC, MC, V. Metro: Pedro de Valdivia. **Amenities:** 3 restaurants; bar; outdoor and indoor pools; tennis courts; sauna; concierge; babysitting; laundry service. *In room:* A/C, TV, Wi-Fi, minibar, hair dryer, stereo.

Expensive

Hotel Bonaparte ★★ On a leafy street in poised Providencia, the European-style Bonaparte is a reliable midrange choice. While the classically designed lobby promises old world grandeur, the interior doesn't quite meet such lavish pretentions. Guest rooms are modern and Scandinavian in their streamlined simplicity and unwavering functionality—passing the litmus test for firm beds and good water pressure—and despite the generic overtones, they are very relaxing and cheery. Avoiding the anonymity of its larger peers, the Bonaparte provides truly personalized service, with courteous staff on hand to cater to every whim. The small, Mediterranean outdoor pool area is a welcome addition, although swimming laps is logistically challenging. The restaurant features a much praised breakfast buffet, and a drink on the flower-strewn terrace bar is a pleasant way to kick-start any evening. There are great weekend special offers available (check the website for details), with double rooms, including breakfast, for $100 (£67).

Mar del Plata 2171 ✆ **2/796-6900.** Fax 2/204-8907. www.hotelbonaparte.cl. 65 units. $180 (£120) double; $190 (£127) junior suite, $240 (£160) suite. AE, DC, MC, V. Metro: Los Leaones. **Amenities:** Restaurant; bar; outdoor pool; health club; concierge. *In room:* A/C, TV, Wi-Fi, hair dryer.

Hotel Orly ★★★ (Finds This French-influenced boutique hotel is the city's most charming choice. What makes it shine is its combination of everything a traveler looks for: a friendly staff that bends over backward to help, an unbeatable location, a reasonable price, an eye-catching decor, and local color and charm. The Orly is housed in a renovated mansion that's meticulously maintained and warmly decorated. The lobby has a few cozy nooks with reading lights for relaxing and a small, glass-roofed patio; there's also a bar and a dining area for breakfast. The interiors are a restful white and accented with contemporary art and ambient light. Room sizes vary; doubles come with two twins or a full-size bed and are of average size, while singles are Lilliputian. All junior suites have a sitting area; however, if you are staying for a few nights, the king room is most recommended for its spaciousness. For those who need peace and quiet, request a room in the back as rooms overlooking the street can be noisy. Book well in advance during the peak summer season.

Av. Pedro de Valdivia 027. ✆ **2/231-8947.** Fax 2/334-4403. www.hotelorly.cl. 28 units. $110 (£73) double; $125 (£83) king room; $140 (£93) junior suite. AE, DC, MC, V. Metro: Pedro de Valdivia. Airport transfer $23/£15. **Amenities:** Cafe; bar; room service; laundry service; shower room. *In room:* A/C, TV, Wi-Fi, minibar, hair dryer.

Radisson Hotel ★★ The Radisson Hotel is housed within the glitzy World Trade Center building, one of the more interesting, avant-garde skyscrapers in Santiago. The location is very convenient for tourists and business travelers alike because it is close to Las Condes–district businesses and the El Bosque restaurant row, as well as a few good bars. Best of all, the guest rooms were freshly renovated in January 2007, with a smart, contemporary decor that updated what used to be seriously frumpy guest rooms, and gave them what they needed: a synergistic pairing with the modernity of the hotel's glass high-rise exterior. Get a room that faces the Andes (seventh floor and up). At night, the towering ultramodern buildings that surround the hotel provide glittering nighttime views. The health club and pool on the rooftop have panoramic views.

Av. Vitacura 2610. ✆ **800/333-3333** in the U.S., or 2/203-6000 in Santiago. www.radisson.cl. 159 units. $144 (£96) double. AE, DC, MC, V. Metro: Tobalaba. **Amenities:** Restaurant; 2 bars; indoor pool; sauna; concierge; babysitting; laundry service. *In room:* A/C, TV, Wi-Fi, minibar, hair dryer.

Moderate

Chilhotel (Kids (Value Price and location are the major draws for this functional, no-frills lodging, tucked away on a quiet street. A medley of basic rooms, which vary from prissy to spartan, are weaved through the labyrinthine corridors of an eccentric, rambling old house. While certain areas of the place could do with upgrading (like the carpets), the sizeable rooms are all crisp, clean, and comfortable. The *laissez-faire* common areas are more akin to a hostel than a hotel, with travelers hanging out and exchanging stories over beer and pisco sours. Chilhotel is an especially good choice for families, large groups, or for skiing enthusiasts looking for a convenient launchpad for the slopes. Ask to see a few rooms before you commit; and, if you are noise sensitive, be sure to request a room overlooking the tranquil courtyard. The location, in the thick of the action, just a block away from the Manuel Montt Metro, is hard to beat. Rooms come in four sizes, each with a private bathroom, and sleep up to five people.

Cirujana Guzmán 103. ✆ **2/264-0643**. Fax 2/264-1323. www.chilhotel.cl. 32 units. $58–$65 (£39–£43) single; $65–$75 (£43–£50) double; $85 (£57) triple; $95 (£63) quad. Rates include breakfast. AE, DC, MC, V. Metro: Manuel Montt. **Amenities:** Cafe; laundry service. *In room:* A/C (superior rooms only), TV, Internet access (superior rooms only), fridge.

Los Españoles ★ This is a good hotel for travelers seeking generic comfort. Los Españoles is part of the Best Western chain, although it has been run by the same family for 26 years—in fact, the hotel is their old family home, and their friendliness really makes you feel at home yourself. The rooms are spotless, comfortable, and modern, though each is sized differently and some are dark and smaller, so let them know what kind of room you want. Top-floor suites have attached terrace patios. This hotel sits beside the Mapocho River in a quiet residential area and is a 10-minute walk to the commercial center of Providencia and the closest Metro station. It also faces a lengthy park that's a good place for a run or a walk.

Los Españoles 2539. ✆ **2/232-1824.** Fax 2/233-1048. www.losespanoles.cl. 50 units. $130 (£87) double; $150 (£100) suite. AE, DC, MC, V. Metro: Pedro de Valdivia. **Amenities:** Restaurant; bar; sauna; babysitting; room service; laundry service. *In room:* A/C, TV, minibar, hair dryer.

Vilafranca Petit Hotel ★★★ *Finds* I can't stop gushing about this "petit" B&B. Oddly, boutique hotels and B&Bs never quite caught on in this city, but with the introduction of Vilafranca, my guess is that will change soon. Housed in a superbly refurbished old mansion, the Vilafranca provides travelers with a more personalized lodging option, brimming with character and coziness, at a price that's reasonable. As with any B&B, the feeling that you're bunking in an old home is clearly evident, yet the young Spanish owners who launched this hotel in 2004 have a penchant for French Provençal design, and they have bestowed the interiors with lovely old antique armoires and nightstands, fresh white linens, and walls painted in soothing tones of ecru and decorated with dried sprigs of flowers and simple sketch art. And what a value—for such a gorgeous hotel, it is hard to believe that a double costs just $80 (£53) a night, but then many rooms are very small. Common areas include a living room with overstuffed sofas, and a cobblestone patio fringed in greenery.

Perez Valenzuela 1650. ✆ **2/232-1413.** www.vilafranca.cl. 8 units. $80 (£53) double with a double bed; $89 (£59) double with 2 twins. AE, DC, MC, V. Metro: Manuel Montt. Rates include breakfast. **Amenities:** Cafe. *In room:* A/C (some rooms), Wi-Fi, TV, hair dryer.

Inexpensive

Andes Hostel ★★★ *Finds* If you thought your hostelling days were over, it may be time to think again. The sister hostel of the superlative Orly Hotel, this lively lodging is the best budget option in town. At the pumping heart of the fashionable and energetic Barrio Bellas Artes, the hostel's location is ideal for the eclectic diversions of Lastrarria. Sleeping choices include dorm rooms with communal bathrooms, sleeping four to six guests, or slightly more expensive single and double rooms with private facilities. The spic and span, folksy rooms are freshly painted and certainly a cut above most hostels, with embroidered sheets and duvets, lanterns, muslin drapes, and colorful artworks. Unlike most hostels, all sheets and towels are provided and daily cleaning is included. The cheerily inviting communal living room feels more like an art-house cafe with a vibrant retro mélange of leopard print rugs, pop art, and postmodern furnishings. Astonishingly, here you pay for your room what you would pay for breakfast in one of the luxury hotels, and at the Andes, a morning feast is included, too.

Monjitas 506. ✆ **2/632-9990.** www.andeshostel.com. 16 units. $17–$18 (£11–£12) shared room sleeping 4–6; $34 (£23) single/double with shared bathroom per person; $50 (£33) double with private bathroom per person. AE, DC, MC, V. Metro: Bellas Artes. **Amenities:** Cafe; bar; room service. *In room:* A/C, TV, minibar, hair dryer, minibar.

Very Expensive

Grand Hyatt Regency Santiago ★★★ If the Ritz is old-world glamour, the Hyatt is pure nouveaux riche and, not surprisingly for one of the Hyatt's flagship hotels, the amenities are without peer. The expansive foyer surrounds a 24-story atrium tower with two adjacent wings and four glass elevators that whisk guests up to their split-level rooms and terraced suites. Nestling among tranquil, colorful gardens, there is a large palm-and-fern-fringed pool complete with a plunging waterfall and poolside bar. Guests in suites enjoy their own 16th-floor private lounge for lingering over breakfast and soaking up the spectacular view. With all manner of sporting activities on hand and the best gym/spa of any hotel in Santiago, the Hyatt is a joy for weary travelers keen to devote themselves to serious relaxation and pampering. Should you choose to leave, however, you'll need to take a taxi because the location at the head of a crazy traffic loop makes it difficult to walk anywhere from here.

Av. Kennedy 4601. ✆ **2/950-1234.** Fax 2/950-3155. www.hyatt.cl. 336 units. $340 (£227) grand deluxe double; $500 (£333) grand suite. AE, DC, MC, V. **Amenities:** 3 restaurants; bar; outdoor pool; health club; sauna; tennis courts; concierge; room service; massage; babysitting; laundry service. *In room:* A/C, TV, minibar, hair dryer.

Plaza El Bosque ★★★ This exclusive hotel provides high-end accommodations with contemporary flair, a plethora of amenities, a convenient location, and a much-praised rooftop restaurant with sweeping, panoramic views. Best of all, given its local ownership, it has a more Chilean flavor than its chain-hotel counterparts, without skimping on cheerful, bilingual service.

The spacious guest rooms are warm and comfortable, and come with a living area with a sliding door, and their executive suite has a fully stocked kitchenette that provides an urban *pied-à-terre* for both business and leisure travelers. The chic rooftop terrace, pool, and restaurant are the highlights here, however. The hotel is less suited for young children, but their billiard room is a great bonus for teens. Located in the heart of El Bosque and close to every service imaginable, the hotel's entrance is on a quiet tree-lined street and not on the main drag.

Ebro 2828. ✆ **2/498-1800.** Fax 2/498-1801. www.plazaelbosque.cl. 179 units. $240 (£160) single suite; $340 (£227) executive suite. AE, DC, MC, V. Metro: Tobalaba. **Amenities:** 2 restaurants; bar; rooftop pool; gym; sauna; spa; game room; concierge; business center; room service; babysitting; laundry service. *In room:* A/C, TV, kitchenette (in executive suites), minibar, hair dryer, safe.

Ritz-Carlton Santiago ★★★ While the exterior of the Ritz-Carlton is utilitarian, this is undoubtedly Santiago's poshest and most intimate luxury hotel, with the most adept staff. Most important, this Ritz is more economical than its counterparts elsewhere, and it enjoys a more convenient location than the Hyatt given its proximity to fine restaurants, a Metro station, and a thriving economic hub of Santiago.

The guest rooms are luxurious in a home-spun floral kind of way; some Ritz devotees may be disappointed by the lack of butch glamour and antiquity that characterizes the Ritz brand. Still, each spacious room is quiet, spotless, and blessed with heavenly beds. The hotel has a fabulous rooftop health center under a glass dome that boasts a view of the city and the Andes. The spa offers reasonably priced massages, or you can request a bath butler who will prepare a decadent bath for you—a soak in carmenère wine. The hotel's impressive lobby, which has a two-story rotunda, leads to the hotel lounge and a plush (usually smoky) wine bar. The Ritz's bar/restaurant 345 has quite possibly the best wine list in Santiago, and they've taken to hosting special weekend cocktail hours.

El Alcalde 15. ✆ **800/241-3333** from the U.S., or 2/470-8500. Fax 2/470-8501. www.ritzcarlton.com. 205 units. $429 (£286) double room; $500 (£333) club room. AE, DC, MC, V. Metro: El Golf. Rates include breakfast. **Amenities:** 3 restaurants; bar; indoor rooftop pool; health club; spa; sauna; concierge; room service; babysitting; laundry service. *In room:* A/C, TV, minibar, hair dryer.

Expensive

Director Suites Hotel (Kids) This monolithic apart-hotel may not be easy on the eyes, nevertheless it has garnered a loyal following owing to its congenial service, swanky environs, and reasonable rates. In the residential El Golf district, surrounded by a myriad of glitzy bars, shops, and restaurants, it's just a 15-minute Metro ride (El Golf Metro stop is just 100m from the hotel) to the downtown area. While the fusty decor and gloomy furnishings could do with a style injection, the spacious, well-appointed rooms are perfectly comfortable and salubrious. Because they have kitchenettes and a sitting area, they are also well suited for families with children. Bathrooms are functional, but rather clinical. A buffet breakfast is served in the cafeteria-style dining room. Check the website for great deals, with discounts for 3-night stays and alluring single room rates of less than $40 (£26) per night.

Carmencita 45. ✆ **2/498-3000.** Fax 2/498-3010. www.director.cl. 49 units. $115 (£76) double; $156 (£104) executive room; $240 (£160) penthouse. AE, DC, MC, V. Metro: El Golf. **Amenities:** Restaurant; bar; health club; room service. *In room:* A/C, TV, Wi-Fi, minibar.

Hotel Rugendas ★ The Tuscan-style Hotel Rugendas is a high-quality choice in Las Condes for its location near El Bosque restaurants and services; it's on a leafy residential street several blocks from busy Avenida Apoquindo. During the week, businessmen are the hotel's primary clients, meaning the price drops on weekends, so ask for promotions when booking a Friday or Saturday stay. Rooms on the 10th floor are newer and the same price; however, all guest rooms are cozy and neatly maintained. Junior suites are small but worth the extra money. For views, book anything on the seventh floor up and ask for a room oriented toward the Andes.

Callao 3123. ✆ **2/370-5700.** Fax 2/246-6570. www.hotelrugendas.cl. 51 units. $140 (£93) double. AE, DC, MC, V. Metro: El Golf. **Amenities:** Restaurant; bar; health club. *In room:* A/C, TV, minibar, hair dryer.

Santa Magdalena Apartments ★ These modern, streamlined apartments with a nod to Danish discretion are ideal for independent travelers in search of homey amenities who'd rather mingle with local Santiaguinos than with their compatriot travelers. Occupying the upper levels of a modern high-rise in the busy El Bosque Norte commercial area—some rooms have wonderful cityscape views with the Andes as the backdrop—each of the unfussy, one- or two-bedroom apartments is spacious and well equipped with a living and dining area, separate kitchen, and a terrace. There is a fresh and comfortable feel throughout, with crisp, white linens, scattered rugs, drapes, and store-bought art. The spotless, modern bathrooms come with all the necessary accoutrements for beautification, and such nice touches as plants and flowers offset any tendency toward sterility. The small rooftop pool is more for a paddle than a swim.

Helvecia 244. ✆ **2/374-6875.** Fax 2/233-1048. www.santamagdelana.cl. 40 units. $115 (£77) 1-bedroom apartment; $130 (£87) 2-bedroom apartment. AE, DC, MC, V. Metro: Tobalaba. **Amenities:** Outdoor pool; health club; dry cleaning service. *In room:* A/C, TV, Wi-Fi, hair dryer.

Moderate

La Sebastiana Apart Hotel ★★ Kids Value A relative newcomer in the Las Condes neighborhood, this apart-hotel is just what it says: hotel rooms with living areas and kitchens. It's attractive and fresh and decorated with inexpensive but trendy furniture and store-bought art; the owners clearly have an eye for design. Rooms come in three sizes: studio, one-bedroom (standard), and a two-bedroom (superior), the latter of which has a sofa bed for a total of six guests. It's an ideal place for long-term visitors (who pay a discounted rate for stays of 2 weeks or longer), and families with young children; and you can't beat the price or the location close to shops and restaurants, nor the outdoor, rooftop pool (summer only).

San Sebastian 2727. ✆ **2/658-7220.** www.lasebastiana.cl. 45 units. $72 (£48) studio; $80 (£53) standard; $125 (£83) superior. AE, DC, MC, V. Metro: Tobalaba. **Amenities:** Outdoor pool; business center w/Wi-Fi; laundry service. *In room:* A/C, cable TV, kitchenette, minibar, CD player.

4 WHERE TO DINE

Santiago's gastronomic scene has undergone a culinary revolution during the past decade or so, with an influx of ethnic restaurants and trendy eateries serving fusion-style, creative cuisine commonly known as *cocina de autor.* The culinary scene is now fertile enough to persuade the city's most talented chefs to stay rather than flee to Europe or the U.S. High-end, haute-cuisine restaurants are predominately springing up in the eastern edge of Santiago's swanky Vitacura neighborhood north of Las Condes and closer to the Hyatt Hotel. While it's gratifying to see young Chileans these days study to become "chefs" rather than "cooks," when compared with other world class cities, Santiago continues to fall short when it comes to producing consistent and tasty midrange meals. If you strike out on your own, don't expect the Parisian security of walking into an unassuming bistro and reveling in innovative dishes conjured using the finest ingredients. Beyond the clique of elitist establishments, meals in Santiago are generally devoid of flair, spice, and culinary wizardry.

Downtown, civic center area eateries cater principally to office workers, meaning they're open for lunch only and closed on weekends (there are several exceptions, listed later). The Lastarría neighborhood, on the east side of Cerro Santa Lucía, has a much more cosmopolitan feel with patio seating and all day drinking and dining. For lunch in the downtown area, cheap meals can be found at *picadas,* or diners, that line the pedestrian walkways Ahumada and Huerfanos; they offer a fixed-price lunch called a *menú del día, menú ejecutivo,* or *coloación* for about $6 to $10 (£4–£2.50) that includes an appetizer, main course, beverage, coffee, and dessert. *Autoservicios,* or self-service restaurants, also abound, and most restaurants advertise their prices on sandwich boards or on signs posted near the front door.

In the peculiar Chilean fashion of concentrating similar businesses in one neighborhood (Av. 10 de Julio, for example, is lined for blocks with auto mechanics), restaurant "clusters" have been popping up like mushrooms around the city. Bellavista is perhaps the best neighborhood to see this phenomenon, with its mind-boggling number of hip restaurants, from Chilean to Cuban to Mediterranean to Asian. Both Avenida El Bosque Norte and its sister street, Avenida Isidora Goyenechea, are lined with a mélange of upscale eateries and American chain restaurants, and now the Avenida Italia area in Providencia and the Lastarría/Parque Forestal areas are forging ahead as the new dining hot spots. A few of the local favorites from these neighborhoods are listed below, but you could really just stroll the streets until something strikes your fancy. All major hotels have outstanding—though pricey—restaurants open to the public. Highlights are the Hyatt's **Senso** and **Matsuri** restaurants, the Ritz-Carlton's **Adra** restaurant, and the Sheraton's **El Cid** restaurant. Chile is to seafood what Argentina is to beef, yet Chileans consider seafood a delicacy and rarely eat it at home. "Dining out" to Chileans often means dining on seafood, one reason why you'll find such a bountiful selection in Santiago restaurants.

Santiago is not a cafe society; however, following are a couple of recommendations. **Café Tavelli** (**© 2/333-8481**) has two branches, and both are plum spots for people-watching. The branch at the corner of Tenderini and Agustinas in downtown occupies the northeastern corner of the Municipal Theater building; this is where you come to see executives, politicians, and society ladies. Lofty ceilings give the cafe a sense of grandeur, but the outdoor tables are where to watch the city street action. There is another bustling Café Tavelli on Andres de Fuenzalida 36 in Providencia, with a more artsy and middle-class crowd. For rich desserts, ice cream, and other sweet delights, try the chain **Coppelia** (**© 2/232-1090**) in Providencia, with locations at Manuel Montt 2517, Av. Providencia 2211, and Av. Ricardo Lyon 161. In general, the best bet for cafes is in the Lastarría/Parque Forestal area (see below).

See the maps on p. 78 and 81 to locate the restaurants reviewed below.

DOWNTOWN

Restaurants in the Lastarría Street/Plaza Mulato Gil de Castro micro-neighborhood offer evening dining if you are staying downtown and would rather not wander too far. Lastarría, also known as Parque Forestal, is a burgeoning artsy, cafe-oriented neighborhood that has undergone a revival in the past few years, and it is undoubtedly the most charming neighborhood in Santiago. A few cafes to check out in this area are **Emporio La Rosa** (corner of Monjitas and Merced; **© 2/638-9257;** Mon–Wed 8am–9pm and Thurs–Sun 9am–10pm), for tasty homemade ice cream, sandwiches, and outdoor seating; **La Pérgola de la Plaza** (Plaza Mulatto Gil de Castro; **© 2/639-3604;** Mon–Fri 11am–midnight, Sat 11am–2am, Sun 11am–4pm), a pretty little cafe with a good fixed-price lunch menu and outdoor seating; and **"R"** (Plaza Mulatto Gil de Castro; **© 2/664-9844;** Mon–Sat 12:30–4:30pm and 7:30pm–1:30am), a cozy spot for wine and conversation, although the ambience is far better than the food. **Mosqueto Café** (corner of Villavicencio and Lastarría; **© 2/639-1627;** daily 8:30am–10pm), serves coffee, cakes, and sandwiches in a gorgeous, meticulously restored antique building that also houses the cultural center and crafts shop El Observatorio (see "Shopping," p. 118). ***Tip:*** "R" and Emporio La Rosa are two of the best places in Santiago to sit outdoors and watch an eclectic group of locals meander by. You can park your rental car in the garage at Merced 317.

Expensive

Squadritto ★★ ITALIAN Squadritto provides the most formal and elegant dining experience in the Lastrarría neighborhood. The Tuscan-style dining room is accented with dark wooden furnishings, ochre painted walls, plants, and ambient lighting. The well-executed menu pays homage to classic northern Italian staples with menu stalwarts such as fried calamari and eggplant parmesan followed by seafood risotto and king crab ravioli. The dishes are rather rich, with cream making its way into many of the pasta entrees but, then again, the pasta portions are hardly monumental—they can easily be split as an appetizer should you wish to sample one of their fish-and-meat specialties as an entree. These fish-and-meat dishes change according to the season and tend to be simpler in presentation. My only complaint with Squadritto is that a misplaced snobbery prevails among the staff members, who often appear to cater to suited businessmen on expense-account lunches rather than casual travelers.

Resal 332. ✆ **2/632-2121.** Reservations recommended. Main courses $9–$15 (£6–£10); tasting menu $20 (£13). AE, DC, MC, V. Mon–Fri 1–4pm and 7pm–midnight. Metro: Univ. Católica.

Zully ★★ Moments INTERNATIONAL Chic yet true to the utterly charming, historical Concha y Toro neighborhood in which it is located, Zully is one of those places travelers delight in discovering. Brimming with architectural flair and suffused with a historical aura, Zully was once home to Chilean poet Vicente Huidobro. Spread over four floors of a lovingly restored old mansion, each of Zully's four dining rooms features whimsical decor, with trendy murals, halogen lights, white leather stools, and inviting chaise longues. There's also an interior patio on the ground floor and a wine-tasting cellar. While the menu is ostensibly Chilean, the chef continually fine-tunes the seasonal offerings by adding inventive fusion-style dishes that are not generally as consistent as the more purist fish and meat dishes—the seared Easter Island tuna or seafood risotto will not disappoint. The recent addition of a sushi bar and jazz lounge has only served to increase Zully's hipster credentials. While the terrace, unfortunately, is only open to parties of 20 or more, it's worth asking if you can pop up there to get a good view of the city. It's best to take a taxi here at night because it's a walk from the Metro.

Concha y Toro 34. ✆ **2/696-3990.** Reservations recommended for dinner. Main courses $16–$21 (£11–£14). AE, DC, MC, V. Mon–Fri 1–4pm and 8pm–1am; Sat 8pm–2am (when the last guest leaves; either slightly earlier or later). Metro: República.

Moderate

Ambrosía ★★ INTERNATIONAL Tucked behind the Casa Colorado Museum (enter the museum and cross the patio to get here), Ambrosía is a thoroughly modern and chic, family-run restaurant that would not be out of place in London or Manhattan. A quiet haven from the boisterous downtown streets outside, Ambrosía draws businessmen with furrowed brows, bejeweled ladies-who-lunch and museum weary travelers in equal measure. Young, boho chef Carolina Bazán has created a well conceived menu that is resolutely all things to all men, with an eclectic offering of Asian, Peruvian, French, and Italian dishes. The *panko* breaded shrimp or Thai spring roll appetizers inject an oriental note, while the ceviche is a more delicate precursor to classic entrees to the tune of lamb in mint sauce and salmon risotto. There are also fresh salads, and a few wild cards such as a BLT sandwich and a hummus pita. Ambrosía, true to its name, also offers a repertoire of heavenly desserts, including mousse and cheesecake renditions artfully swirled with fruity coulis. With its patio dining, this restaurant is ideal for summer days.

Merced 838 A. ✆ **2/697-2023.** www.ambrosia.cl. Main courses $8–$11 (£5.30–£7.30). AE, DC, MC, V. Mon–Fri 9am–6pm. Metro: Plaza de Armas.

Bar Nacional CHILEAN Bar Nacional is an institution in downtown Santiago, having drawn locals for more than 50 years for simple, hearty Chilean fare served by grumpy old-timers in bow ties. It's well known on the tourist map, so expect inflated prices for what are essentially no-frills staples. Located on Calle Bandera next to the Pre-Columbian Museum and also on Paseo Huérfanos, both diners are virtually identical in style. This is where you come to sample national favorites guaranteed to cause midriff havoc: Empanadas, *cazuela* (a hearty chicken soup), *pastel de choclo* (maiz casserole), and the cholesterol-boosting *lomo a lo pobre* (steak and fries topped with sautéed onions and a fried egg). On any given day they offer only two dozen main courses from their voluminous menu. There are plenty of local and imported beers, spirits, and wines to choose from, as well as delicious *licuados* (fresh fruit juices).

Bar Nacional 1: Huérfanos 1151. ✆ **2/696-5986.** Bar Nacional 2: Bandera 371. ✆ **2/695-3368.** Main courses $7–$11 (£4.70–£7.30); sandwiches $3–$4 (£2–£2.70). AE, DC, MC, V. Mon–Fri 7:30am–11pm; Sat 7:30am–4pm. Metro: Plaza de Armas.

Confitería Torres ★★ **(Moments)** CHILEAN Saved from the wrecker's ball, Confitería Torres, Santiago's oldest restaurant, first opened its doors in 1879, and has been splendidly reborn as a contemporary eatery serving a sophisticated crowd. This restaurant was the haunt of intellectuals, writers, politicians, and poets for decades, including former president Barros Luco (for whom the eponymous melted cheese and slab of steak sandwich served throughout Chile is named) and poets Rubén Darío and Vincente Huidrobo. More recently Plácido Domingo developed quite a taste for the pisco sour here. The Chilean couple who invested in this project rescued the original Art Deco–style oak bar, reset the great clock that had stopped years ago, and refurbished the original Queen Anne chairs and tables. Cherry-red booths and smart white tablecloths have spruced up what was once a rather fatigued ambience.

The chef rescued traditional recipes from high society during the late 1800s and gives them a modern flair, turning out dishes such as beef marinated in cilantro, and conger eel with a barnacle sauce—simple but tasty. On Fridays and Saturdays, the restaurant has live tango music; in the afternoon, the restaurant is a good bet for tea and cakes. Confitería Torres recently inaugurated a **restaurant/cafe** within the Centro Cultural (p. 111), offering the same menu but in a more masculine, modish ambience, with leather booths and a sun-filled nonsmoking area. It's an attractive place for lunch, but for the real deal, visit their locale on Avenida Alameda.

Alameda 1570. ✆ **2/688-0751.** www.confiteriatorres.cl. Main courses $7–$12 (£4.70–£8). AE, DC, MC, V. Mon–Sat 11am–midnight (later Fri–Sat). Metro: Univ. de Chile.

Gatopardo ★ FRENCH Tasty nouvelle cuisine served in a sophisticated space flooded with light and adorned with a fine collection of contemporary art has made this restaurant a local favorite—especially for lunch. If you are looking for sophisticated gastronomy that doesn't cost an arm and a leg, their fixed-price lunch menu, which can include stuffed calamari, steamed mussels, steak frites, or lamb chops with rosemary, in addition to a run through the excellent salad bar (a unique concept in Chile and a vegetarian's dream) with the wine and dessert included, makes $10 (£6.60) seem like a steal. While Gatopardo labels itself as modern French, the menu certainly dips its toes into the Mediterranean and occasionally goes native with some expertly grilled local fish. The airy, handsome interior is lit by a glass atrium supported by giant oak trunks felled by an earthquake in the south of Chile.

Lastarría 192. ✆ **2/633-6420.** Main courses $9–$15 (£6–£10). AE, DC, MC, V. Mon–Fri 12:30–3:30pm and 7:30pm–midnight; Sat 7:30pm–1am. Metro: Univ. Católica.

Japón ★★ SUSHI/JAPANESE This is hands-down Santiago's best restaurant for sushi, principally because of the quality and freshness of their fish, and the fact that they don't run out of harder-to-get varieties such as tuna. Owned and operated by Japanese immigrants, this is Chile's oldest Japanese restaurant. On any given day, at least half the clientele are visiting Japanese—a good sign the food hits the mark. Also on offer are udon soups, tempura, teriyaki meats, and so on. The restaurant has a handsome sushi bar and table seating. To get here, from the Baquedano Metro station, head south on Vicuña Mackenna and turn right on Baron Pierre De Coubertin street.

Baron Pierre De Coubertin 39. ✆ **2/222-4517.** Rolls \$4–\$7 (£2.70–£4.60). AE, DC, MC, V. Mon–Sat 12:30–3:30pm and 7:30–10:30pm (Fri–Sat until midnight). Metro: Baquedano.

Opera & Catedral ★★★ CONTEMPORARY FRENCH/CHILEAN Wildly popular with a young artistic crowd, Opera and Catedral were the forerunners in bringing sophistication and delicacy to the downtown dining experience. Opera is a polished, fine-dining establishment, with exposed-brick walls, contemporary paintings, and white linen tablecloths, and it is small enough to require reservations far in advance. It pays homage to French cuisine, serving fabulous dishes such as a delicate foie gras, chicken breast poached in broth and served with truffles, and a "tasting" of five kinds of crème brûlée. Like the name says, this is an ideal place for a post-opera dinner. Upstairs at inexpensive Catedral, the look is minimalist, with gun-battle-gray walls, wicker chairs, and a couple of leather couches that are difficult to nab unless you arrive before 6pm. Really, you'll want to get here before the 9pm mob arrives—this place is smoking hot and crazy-busy most nights. There is also an outdoor terrace for summer evenings. Cathedral serves modern takes on Chilean classics, with a few Asian-influenced dishes, gourmet sandwiches, and a very tasty *crudo,* or steak tartare.

Both located at the corner of Merced and José Miguel de la Barra. ✆ **2/664-3048.** www.operacatedral.cl. Reservations required at Opera; reservations not accepted at Catedral. AE, DC, MC, V. Opera: Main courses \$15–\$21 (£10–£14). Mon–Fri 1–3:15pm and 8–10:30pm; Sat 8–10:30pm. Catedral: Main courses \$5–\$11 (£3.30–£7.30). Mon–Wed 12:30pm–2am; Thurs–Sat 12:30pm–5am. Metro: Bellas Artes.

Patagonia Café ★★ ARGENTINE It calls itself a cafe, but this unpretentious eatery is much more than that. Patagonia is warm and inviting during colder months, with rough-hewn wood interiors and a floor-to-ceiling wine rack boasting excellent varieties. When the weather heats up, you can't beat their outdoor seating for dining on simple yet surprisingly good food and catching a few rays. This is one of only a handful of restaurants in Santiago that serves a brunch buffet (Sat, Sun, and holidays 10am–5pm), with cold meats and seafood, quiches, salads, and the cafe's outstanding cakes and pastries. The menu focuses on unadulterated meats, seafood, and sandwiches prepared with Patagonian-style recipes, plus warming stews and soups during the colder months; their lamb is especially good. On weekdays, there is a fixed-price lunch from noon to 4pm for \$10 (£6.60). This restaurant fills up quickly during the lunch hour, so arrive early or late.

Lastarría 96. ✆ **2/664-3830.** Reservations not accepted. Main courses \$8–\$13 (£5.30–£8.70); brunch \$14 (£9.30) per person. No credit cards. Mon–Fri 8am–1am; Sat–Sun 9am–1am. Metro: Univ. Católica.

Picada Ana María ★ Finds TRADITIONAL CHILEAN This little-known, old-fashioned restaurant is quintessentially Chilean, and they specialize in wild game entrees such as boar, venison, and pheasant. The Picada started out as a *picada,* which is Chilean for a restaurant that serves simple, inexpensive meals, but its popularity prompted the owners to break out the tablecloths and open a full-service restaurant. Located within a handsome antique home with just a tiny sign by the door to orient you, the uniqueness of this establishment draws politicians and businessmen at lunch and families on weekends, making it a good place to people-watch. The restaurant is on the other side of the Pan-American Highway and far from the Metro, so take a cab—it's about a 5-minute drive from Plaza de Armas outside of rush hour.

Club Hípico 476. ✆ **2/698-4064.** Main courses \$7–\$12 (£4.70–£8). AE, DC, MC, V. Mon–Sat noon–4pm and 7pm–midnight; Sun noon–4pm.

BELLAVISTA

Moderate

Amorío ★★ CONTEMPORARY CHILEAN Amorío is part of the Mori Cultural Center that, along with a theater and art cinema, is housed inside a beautifully recycled old mansion and has swiftly become a Bellavista institution. The city's elite flock here, owing in part to the celebrity kudos of its flamboyant owners, Benajamín Vicuña and Gozalo Valenzuela, and for the stunning dining area, which has one of the chicest ambiences in Santiago: Think retro-style hibiscus-flower wallpaper, white leather banquettes, exposed brick walls, refurbished Louis XIV chairs, candelabras, parquet floors, and lots of soft halogen lighting. The first floor is more formal, with a full menu that includes delicate dishes such as tuna with mint, or more earthy *asado de tiro estofado* (a tender stewed beef), and for vegetarians, a pumpkin potage with goat cheese. The second floor is more casual and offers a tapas menu and cocktails. While the food is certainly decent, its experimental philosophy falls far short of Sukalde and Puerto Fuy in terms of presentation and execution. Still, it is much easier on the wallet and a couple hours spent in the dining room here is memorable in itself.

Constitución 181. ✆ **2/777-1454.** Main courses $10–$15 (£6.70–£10). AE, DC, MC, V. Tues–Fri 1–4pm and 8pm–midnight; Sat 8pm–midnight; Sun 1–4pm. Metro: Baquedano.

Azul Profundo ★ Kids SEAFOOD Seafood lovers will find their mecca at the "Deep Blue" in the bohemian Bellavista neighborhood. The menu is divided into four regions: fish and shellfish from south, central, and northern Chile, as well as fresh yellowfin tuna and vidriola fish from Easter Island, served grilled, or *a la plancha* (sizzling on a cast-iron plate). Add just a squeeze of lemon or choose one of five sauces. If there are two of you, you might opt for a shared dish such as *curanto,* the surf-and-turf stew from Chiloé, or a Tabla Marina, a selection of shellfish and salmon served with grilled vegetables. Everything on the menu is appealing; therefore, decisions are not easily made. Try getting started with an appetizer of one of eight different kinds of ceviche, the crowd-pleaser razor clams Parmesan, or the killer fish soup. A cozy nautical theme complete with fish nets, a wooden siren hanging from a mock ship's bow, and bathroom doors that look like they lead to a sailor's bunk lend a theme park vibe to the restaurant, which makes this a gem of a place for young families. Rarely do kid-friendly restaurants serve such mouthwatering cuisine.

Constitución 111. ✆ **2/738-0288.** Main courses $9–$16 (£6–£11). AE, DC, MC, V. Daily 1–4:30pm and 7:30pm–12:30am (Fri–Sat until 1:30am). Metro: Baquedano.

Barandiaran ★★ PERUVIAN Peru is widely regarded as home to the best cuisine in Latin America after Mexico, and far and away the best place in Santiago to sample the country's spicy, delicious concoctions is Barandiaran. The eponymous Chef Marco Barandiaran launched his career as the chef in residence at the Peruvian embassy before graduating to become a charismatic TV personality in addition to an acclaimed gastro entrepreneur. This is the third and the newest Barandiaran restaurant, and the best in terms of service, its attractive yet casual ambience, and location. Because it is tucked away in the Patio Bellavista arts-and-crafts market, you can shop till you drop and then refuel on superbly prepared *ceviche,* fried calamari, *parihuela* (sea bass stew), or tender lamb in a cilantro puree. There's also lots of patio seating. Contrary to popular belief here in Chile the pisco sour originated in Peru, and the potent exemplars served here—blended with an egg white—will knock your socks off.

Constitución 38 (inside Patio Bellavista). ✆ **2/737-0725.** Reservations recommended Sat–Sun. Main courses $8–$10 (£5.30–£6.70). AE, DC, MC, V. Daily 1pm–midnight. Metro: Baquedano.

El Toro ★ CHILEAN/LIGHT FARE An enduring favorite among hipsters, artists, and actors alike, El Toro is the kind of restaurant you expect to see in San Francisco's Mission District, or London's Shoreditch. The ambience is laid-back, service is friendly, and a whimsical 1970s decor with disco balls, paper menus, and crayon graffiti scrawled on the walls sets the irreverent mood. El Toro's sister restaurant in Providencia has the same style and the same menu. The international culinary repertoire won't win any medals for originality, but each dish, ranging from bountiful Caesar salads to crepes oozing with mushroom and cheese and simply grilled salmon, is flavorful and satisfying.

Bellavista location: Loreto 33. ✆ **2/737-5937.** Providencia location: Santa Beatriz 280. ✆ **2/235-5012.** Reservations recommended for parties of 4–6. Main courses $7–$13 (£4.70–£8.70). AE, DC, MC, V. Mon–Sat 1–4pm and 7:30pm–midnight. Metro: Baquedano.

Etniko ★★ ASIAN/SUSHI Etniko is one of Santiago's hippest restaurants, serving Asian-influenced cuisine in a trendy and sophisticated space frequented by Santiago's stylish young adults and expats. Soberly attired waiters will guide you through the menu's eclectic selection, but the regulars laud over the 40 varieties of sushi (don't miss the Easter Island tuna). Also on offer are Japanese tempura and Chinese and Vietnamese stir-fries. The best part of Etniko is its stunning open-air atrium seating area, and it also features one of the liveliest bars in town. As the evening accelerates, the dining room pulsates to the modern beat of house music played by talented resident DJs. The front door is always shut (not to be taken as a sign of pretentious exclusivity), so ring the bell to enter, and don't expect the place to fill until 9 or 10pm.

Constitución 172. ✆ **2/732-0119.** Reservations recommended. Main courses $8–$15 (£5.30–£10). AE, DC, MC, V. Mon–Sat 8pm–midnight (Fri–Sat until 2am). Metro: Baquedano.

Inexpensive

El Caramaño TRADITIONAL CHILEAN From the outside, this may look like a den of iniquity, but this unassuming hole in the wall, tucked away on Purisima Street, is one of the most spirited, genuinely Chilean places in town. With walls covered in graffiti and, not for the shy, marauding, often intoxicated, musicians who are likely to serenade you passionately with their dulcet tones, this is a fun and warm place to enjoy good value, traditional Chilean dishes served in a no-nonsense manner. There is no sign; to enter the restaurant, ring the doorbell.

Purisima 257. ✆ **2/737-7043.** Main courses $6–$11 (£4–£7.30). AE, DC, MC, V. Mon–Sat 10am–2am. Metro: Baquedano.

Galindo TRADITIONAL CHILEAN This local favorite is a hit for its cheap prices and its *comida casera:* simple, hearty dishes like your mother used to make—if your mother were Chilean, that is. Virtually any kind of typical meal served in Chilean homes can be found here, including *pastel de choclo* (a ground beef and chicken casserole) and *cazuela* (chicken soup with vegetables). The atmosphere is folksy and casual; in the evening, the restaurant serves as a meeting place for writers, artists, and other local folk to share a bottle of wine and good conversation. There's additional seating outside on the sidewalk, and it's open late into the evening, even on weekdays.

Dardignac 098. ✆ **2/777-0116.** Main courses $6–$9 (£4–£6); fixed lunch $5 (£3.30). AE, DC, MC, V. Mon–Sat 10am–2am. Metro: Baquedano.

PROVIDENCIA

Ask a cab driver or hotel clerk where to dine or drink in Providencia, and oftentimes their knee-jerk reaction is Avenida Suecia (at Av. Providencia). Don't listen to them. Apart from a few reasonably quiet bars, the 3-block radius is like a frat house gone wild on weekends, and reports of violent crime fueled by alcohol are on the rise in this oddball neighborhood. Most call it *gringolandia,* for its resemblance to the United States and its handful of restaurants serving typical American food.

Expensive

Aquí Está Coco ★★ SEAFOOD This eclectic restaurant not only serves some of the city's freshest seafood, but it's also a fun place to dine. Housed in a 140-year-old home, the restaurant is owned by charismatic Jorge "Coco" Pacheco, who gave the place its name: "Here's Coco." Coco traveled the world for several years and culled hundreds of nutty maritime knickknacks that he used to decorate the interiors, giving the place a decidedly kitschy atmosphere. But it's the fish that brings them back every time. An oversize menu offers every kind of seafood available in Chile, including hake, swordfish, cod, sea bass, tuna, and shellfish, and a host of tantalizing seafood appetizers such as crab cakes or broiled scallops in a barnacle sauce. I recommend the trout stuffed with king crab and a *thermidor* (lobster bechamel) sauce—I order it every time I eat here. Attentive service and a menu in English are reasons you'll see many gringos here, but Chileans love Aquí Está Coco, too. Note that the restaurant has a good selection of meat dishes for those not fond of seafood.

La Concepción 236. ✆ **2/235-8649.** www.aquiestacoco.cl. Main courses $12–$20 (£8–£13). AE, DC, MC, V. Mon–Sat 1–3pm and 8–11pm. Metro: Pedro de Valdivia.

Astrid y Gastón ★★★ INTERNATIONAL Immediately after Astrid and Gastón flung open the doors at their eponymous restaurant in Santiago in 2000 (their flagship restaurant is in Lima, Peru), critics and gourmet food lovers alike scrambled like mad to get a reservation, having previous knowledge of Gastón's reputation of something of a food god in his native Peru. In 2008, despite strong competition, Astrid and Gastón was named the best restaurant in Santiago by the city's prestigious *Guía Culinaria.*

Gastón and his wife Astrid are experts at sourcing the most luxurious ingredients and combining them in unexpected ways to present some of the most exciting and provocative flavor combinations you are likely to taste anywhere. Refreshingly, there are no gimmicks, the focus here is on artful simplicity, and the dining experience is as satisfying as it is adventurous. The brightly lit dining room may preclude romantic dining, but the ambience is elegant, stately, and discreet, and affords views of the chef and kitchen staff conjuring their culinary delights. Try the *ceviche,* a colorful stack of octopus, calamari, and swordfish sweetened with corn kernels and slivers of sweet potato or the crab shell filled with bucatini pasta and draped in an *ocopa* sauce (a milk, cheese, and chili concoction). The desserts are a seductive blend of the decadent and exotic; orders must be placed along with the entrees so that the kitchen staff can make each one from scratch. The service at Astrid y Gastón is flawless, and there is an on-site sommelier and one of the city's most interesting and varied wine lists.

Antonio Bellet 201. ✆ **2/650-9125.** Reservations required. Main courses $13–$19 (£8.60–£13). AE, DC, MC, V. Mon–Fri 1–3pm and 8pm–midnight; Sat 8pm–midnight. Metro: Pedro de Valdivia.

Camino Real ★ (Moments) INTERNATIONAL/CHILEAN There's nothing quite like dining in Santiago with the city lights twinkling at your feet. This restaurant/wine bar and museum is nestled in gardens atop Cerro San Cristóbal park, affording sweeping views across the valley and up to the Andes. Smog is an issue if you come for lunch, but even bad air can't mask the thousands of lights at night. The menu is imaginative but there are certainly better restaurants below; what you're here for is the view, and it's worth the splurge. Menu examples include lamb chops with lentils and bacon, grilled sole with barnacle ravioli, and chestnut pudding with cream. The hacienda style of the restaurant has outdoor seating around a central patio, and an indoor dining area.

Parque Metropolitano, Cerro San Cristóbal. ✆ **2/232-1758.** Reservations required. Main courses $11–$20 (£7.30–£13); fixed-price lunches/dinners $25 (£17). AE, DC, MC, V. Daily 12:30–4pm and 7–11pm. Metro: Pedro de Valdivia.

Infante 51 ★★★ SEAFOOD This sleek relative newcomer serves über fresh fish and seafood dishes that are a purist's dream. The well-versed, debonair staff will guide you passionately through the menu, describing in intricate detail the origins, flavors, and even the oceanic habits of each fish. The menu is an ever-changing roll call that can feature as many as 20 specialties, ranging from white tuna and meaty but sweet kana from Easter Island, deep and earthy grilled breca from the Juan Fernandez islands, and rich and smooth cojinova austral from Puerto Montt, each simply grilled or sautéed. The focus of the dining experience is the exquisite taste of each fish, pure and unadulterated—if you like experimental sauces and rich accompaniments this isn't the place for you. Basque chef and part owner Xabier Zabala is clearly fanatical about the chastity of taste: "I don't like girls who wear makeup," he is reputed to have said in relation to his cooking style. Even the minimalist decor, with its whitewashed walls, sober furniture, and its muted aura, is designed to not steal the glory of the fish.

Jose Miguel Infante 51. ✆ **2/264-3357.** Reservations recommended. Lunch 1–3:30pm, dinner 8–11:30pm. Main courses $10–$19 (£6.70–£13). AE, DC, MC, V. Metro: Pedro de Valdivia.

Sukalde ★★★ FUSION After studying under prestigious food god Ferrán Adria and putting in time at Spain's El Bulli and NYC's Dania, globetrotting Chilean chef Matías Palomo opened Sukalde in 2006 to much critical fanfare. If you can get a reservation, Sukalde will offer you a truly memorable dining experience. The focus is on tasting portions of dishes created from unusual ingredients and prepared in unconventional ways; you need to be an adventurous diner to truly enjoy a meal here. The tasting menu changes frequently but is never short on publicity-stirring gimmicks. One menu was inspired by the last meal served on the Titanic and featured dishes to the tune of tuna tartare topped with soy sauce beads and lemon peel puree, followed by grilled Konzo, a rare Pacific fish doused with apple puree spiked with cilantro and "curry air." It has to be said that much of the fuss about inventive cooking may be lost on seasoned diners familiar with inhaling their appetizer. The dining room is a shrine to gastronomic innovation, simply decorated with quasi-religious purity—white walls, soaring ceilings, archways, dark wooden floors, and a harmonious ambience aim to prepare the diner for gastronomic transcendence.

Av. Bilbao 460. ✆ **2/665-1017.** www.sukalde.cl. Reservations recommended. Daily 1–4pm, 8–11:30pm. Main courses $12–$20 (£7–£12). AE, DC, MC, V. Metro: Pedro de Valdivia.

Moderate

El Huerto ★ VEGETARIAN With its organic decor, peaceful ambience, and creative vegetarian dishes, El Huerto is the culinary equivalent of a pair of Birkenstocks. For all its natural kudos, it offers a hip, metropolitan dining experience with a wonderful outdoor terrace on a quiet leafy street in the heart of Providencia. Breakfast features omelets, granola, fruit smoothies, and freshly baked bread, but it's El Huerto's lunch and dinner menu that really allows the chef's skills to shine through—traditional veggie staples are reinvented with enough panache to abate the fleshy cravings of even the most die-hard carnivores. From the cheesy asparagus strudel to an artichoke tart and an eye-catching Asian salad featuring a mélange of peas, avocado, soybeans, quinoa, and baked tofu drizzled with an Asian peanut dressing, El Huerto's dishes are healthy and delicious—until you get to the dessert menu, that is. The double cheesecake sampler and brownie à la mode are wickedly rich and creamy. You can get back on the wagon before you break away by purchasing healthy condiments, herbal teas, and even a pair of sandals in the adjoining eco-products shop.

Orrego Luco 054. ✆ **2/233-2690.** www.elhuerto.cl. Main courses $6–$9 (£4–£6). AE, DC, MC, V. Restaurant Mon–Thurs 12:30pm–midnight; Fri–Sat 12:30pm–1am. Cafe Mon–Sat 9am–1pm. Metro: Los Leones.

Le Flaubert ★★ Finds FRENCH/CHILEAN Have you ever had a favorite haunt that you felt inclined not to promote in fear of letting the secret out? This is mine. Le Flaubert is a petite French/Chilean bistro with an understated elegance and romantic, Provençal-style ambience that make it the ideal address for a date or intimate meal among friends. The plant-filled outdoor dining area in the back patio is soothing and cool on a hot day, and the waitstaff is mindful without being overbearing. Le Flaubert offers five appetizers and as many main dishes presented on a chalkboard, with delicious fare such as duck confit, crab casserole, and a recommended sea bass with a shrimp and avocado sauce. From Monday to Friday there is a fixed-price lunch with appetizer and main course for $11 (£5.25), and Le Flaubert offers a daily afternoon tea from 4:30 to 8pm, with cakes and scones. Their on-site "Emporio" shop sells local cheeses, marmalades, and other handmade foodstuffs. This is one of the only restaurants in Providencia that is open on Sunday; they have a takeout service, and will deliver for free if you're within 2 blocks of the restaurant.

Orrego Luco 125. ✆ **2/231-9424.** www.leflaubert.cl. Main courses $9–$15 (£6–£10). AE, DC, MC, V. Mon 12:30–4:30pm and 7:30–11:30pm; Tues–Sat 12:30–11:30pm; Sun noon–9pm. Metro: Pedro de Valdivia.

Inexpensive

Bar Liguria ★★★ Moments CHILEAN/BISTRO The city's two convivial Bar Ligurias are vibrant, warm, and eternally popular with actors, writers, businesspeople and just about everyone else who comes to soak up the kitschy, bohemian atmosphere. The newest Liguria at Luis Thayer Ojeda Street has been a phenomenal success since opening day, due to its large and lofty upstairs dining room. The eclectic clientele chat and philosophize loudly at rickety tables draped with red-and-white check tablecloths surrounded by a gallery of floor-to-ceiling posters, paintings, maps, and memorabilia. At lunchtime and on weekends after 9pm, you'll usually have to wait 10 to 15 minutes at the bar before you get a table. The Manuel Montt location recently expanded and now has two bars and three dining areas, without compromising its coziness. A fleet of bow-tied waiters provides entertaining, if rather lackadaisical, service. The Liguria serves ample portions of emblematic Chilean meat dishes in addition to a handful of Italian dishes, such as vegetarian lasagna, spaghetti with meatballs, and goat cheese ravioli, as well as hefty sandwiches and salads that are reasonably priced. If you're looking for an all-in-one dinner and drinking spot, this is your place.

Ojeda location: Luis Thayer Ojeda 019. ✆ **2/231-1393.** Providencia location: Av. Providencia 1373. ✆ **2/235-7914.** Reservations not accepted. Main courses $6–$9 (£4–£6). AE, DC, MC, V. Mon–Sat noon–1am (Fri–Sat till 3am). Metro: Los Leones (Ojeda branch), and Manuel Montt (Providencia branch).

Rishtedar INDIAN With just eight tables, this intimate and colorful neighborhood joint serves bountiful dishes of piquant Indian food. The select menu features Pakistani and Northern Indian dishes—choose from chicken, lamb, or shrimp draped with either a spicy biryani sauce or a smoother, sweeter masala. For the budget conscious, the daily special menu includes a drink and dessert. The vegetarian options, including saag aloo (spinach curry with fried potatoes) are rather heavy, especially served alongside the requisite crispy samosas, doughy naans, and fluffy basmati rice, which for carb lovers make a fine meal in themselves. Refreshing, lighter options include a minty Goan salad and a Bangladesh salad served with garlic and shrimp. With its Bollywood music videos and laissez faire vibe, Rishtedar is a hot spot for trendy 20-something Chileans who follow up dinner with conversation over a fruit flavored *shisha* (hookah). If you are trying to budget, beware that while the entrees here are extremely reasonable, the bottles of wine are pretty exorbitant ($15/£10 minimum) for a restaurant in this price range.

Holanda 160. ✆ **2/231-3257.** Main courses $6–$9 (£4–£6). AE, DC, MC, V. Mon–Sat noon–1am (Fri–Sat till 3am). Metro: Los Leones.

LAS CONDES/ EL BOSQUE NORTE

El Bosque Norte and Isidora Goyenechea streets are two gastronomic gauntlets that connect at Avenida Vitacura; occasionally you'll hear the area referred to as El Golf, for the Metro stop nearby. Virtually every business on these two streets is a restaurant, food shop, or cafe. American chain restaurants are concentrated here, such as **T.G.I. Friday's,** with the usual fattening menu, at Isidora Goyenechea 3275 (✆ **2/234-4468**); **New York Bagel,** Roger de Flor 2894 (✆ **2/246-3060**); or **Starbucks,** Isidora Goyenechea 2940 (no phone).

Expensive

Akarana ★★★ PACIFIC RIM Capitalizing on the packed-to-the-rafters success of Café Melba, owner Dell Taylor, a transplant from New Zealand, decided to take things up a notch by launching a stylish eatery with a philosophy that's unique in Santiago—small plates. The broad menu highlights the flavors of the Mediterranean and the Pacific Rim with a couple of Middle Eastern, Indian, and New Zealand creations thrown in. Couples may opt to share five or six "tapas" dishes to the tune of Korean beef kebabs or pan-fried squid with a rich herb tomato sauce served with hunks of ciabatta for dunking. The entree menu is equally globetrotting, with a beer-battered sea bass served with thick cut chips and imaginatively dressed thin-crust pizzas. Some dishes, however, are less successful; the curried rabbit is surprisingly bland. The highlight of the dessert menu is the chocolate *Bomba,* a decadent warm-center chocolate pudding served with ice cream. Akarana is an excellent place to enjoy well-prepared afternoon cocktails, when a DJ spins mellow music; occasionally the restaurant hosts live music on the patio. Be sure to reserve ahead to ensure a table outside; Akarana's contemporary, all-white interiors are chic and airy but lack the patio's atmosphere.

Reyes Lavalle 3310. ✆ **2/231-9667.** Reservations recommended. Tapas $4–$5 (£2.70–£3.30). Main courses $10–$18 (£6.70–£12). AE, DC, MC, V. Daily noon–midnight. Metro: El Golf.

Moderate

Café Melba ★★ INTERNATIONAL This bustling yet unassuming cafe is simply *the* best spot in El Bosque for lunch, the reason why you'll have to wait 15 minutes or so for a table if you arrive after 1:30pm. On any given day, at least a quarter of the clientele are American or British expats who come for Café Melba's inventive meals and good-natured ambience. The restaurant also serves American/English-style breakfasts, a rarity in Santiago, and doors open early at 7:30am on weekdays, 8:30am on weekends. More thought is put into the lunch menu here than at nearby competing restaurants, with a seasonally changing menu that features pastas, salads, meats, and seafood. There's an Internet cafe and a covered outdoor seating area.

Don Carlos 2898. ✆ **2/232-4546.** Reservations not accepted. Main courses $6–$9 (£4–£6). AE, DC, MC, V. Daily 8am–3:30pm. Metro: El Golf.

Nolita ★★ ITALIAN/AMERICAN Taking its cue from Northern Italy and New York (yes, its name was borrowed from the NYC neighborhood), Nolita specializes in cuisine from the former and style from the latter. The El Bosque neighborhood is often referred to as "Sanhattan," and so a restaurant like Nolita only makes sense with its cosmopolitan atmosphere, poised service, and refined cuisine created by a chef with roots in the U.S. The pasta dishes are rich and decadent with specialties such as ravioli stuffed with ricotta and wild boar draped in a mushroom sauce, but the menu highlights are the classic seafood dishes: shrimp with garlic tossed over linguini or trout stuffed with spinach and drizzled with a creamy shrimp sauce. With the exception of such indulgent appetizers as caviar and oysters, the prices here are very reasonable for a restaurant of this caliber in this neighborhood.

Av. Isidora Goyenechea 3456. ✆ **2/232-6114.** Reservations required after 9pm on weekends. Main courses $9–$21 (£6–£14). AE, DC, MC, V. Mon–Sat 1–3:30pm and 8–11pm (until midnight Fri–Sat); Sun 1–3:30pm. Metro: El Golf.

Inexpensive

Tiramisu ★ PIZZA/ITALIAN This gourmet pizzeria began as a hole-in-the-wall but spread into three dining areas to accommodate the growing throngs of admirers. Its rough-hewn wood and checkered-tablecloth ambience make it the perfect spot for dining when you don't feel like getting dressed up, although shorts are not recommended. Tiramisu serves thin-crust pizzas baked in a stone oven that are large enough for two when ordering an accompanying salad. With dozens of combinations, from margherita to arugula with shaved Parmesan and artichokes, you'll have a hard time choosing your pie. The restaurant has killer cocktails, too, and desserts that, of course, include tiramisu. The restaurant will prepare pizzas to go, if you're looking to take one back to your hotel.

Av. Isidora Goyenechea 3141. ✆ **2/335-5135.** www.tiramisu.cl. Pizzas $7–$12 (£4.70–£8); salads $5.80–$12 (£3.80–£8). AE, DC, MC, V. Daily 1–4pm and 7pm–midnight. Metro: El Golf.

VITACURA

The apex of Santiago's burgeoning gourmet scene is here in Vitacura, a neighborhood known for its art galleries, Rodeo Drive–style shopping, expensive homes, and prime real estate bordering the Mapocho River. In fact, the restaurant complex **BordeRio** (Av. Monseñor Escrivá de Balaguer 6400; ✆ **2/218-0100;** www.borderio.cl) means just that, "bordering the river." BordeRio is a cluster of nine upscale restaurants housed in a modern, Spanish-influenced complex built of white stucco and terra-cotta tile. Certainly there are a few fine restaurants here, but my take is that it feels prefabricated, like a shopping mall. In the absence of an efficient public transport option, it is worth having a taxi drop you off so that you may wander around until you find a place to suit your mood—with the exception of Fridays and Saturdays, the place rarely seems full.

BordeRio has everything from Italian to Japanese to steakhouse fare. My pick is **Zanzibar** (✆ **2/218-0118**). With sparkling chandeliers and mosaic pillars, it feels like walking into a palace in Marrakech; but the best thing about this restaurant is the rooftop Moroccan lounge, where you can savor a soft breeze and the Andean view. It's best for an early evening cocktail and appetizers—make a reservation and prepare yourself for slow service. The owners of Zanzibar also own a BordeRio nightspot, **Lamu Lounge** (p. 125).

Agua ★★★ FUSION Sleek and minimalist, at the turn of the millennium Agua was a pioneer in fashionable dining among Santiago's well-to-do, who clambered for reservations in what was then *the* place to see and be seen. Aqua still bustles with beautiful people, and although its founding chef has since moved on, the restaurant remains at the apex of culinary innovation and creativity, with a menu that focuses on top Chilean products such as Magellanic lamb, king crab, shellfish, tuna from Easter Island, and more. The current chef, by the way, is a former apprentice of Thomas Keller's Per Se. Foodies will delight in Agua's four fixed-price lunch menus, which change daily and include three courses for $15 (£7.50), not including wine or beverages. A sample menu could include a choice between smoked salmon salad, beef filet with herbs and squash risotto, and a *lucuma* mousse (a natural fruit that tastes like butterscotch). Service, unfortunately, is the weak point here: While impeccable in terms of attention, that attention can often come without a smile.

Nueva Costanera 3467. ✆ **2/263-0008.** www.aguarestaurant.cl. Reservations recommended. Main courses $12–$19 (£8–£13). AE, DC, MC, V. Mon–Fri 12:30–3pm and 7:30pm–midnight; Sat 8:30pm–midnight.

Cuerovaca ★★★ STEAK Santiago's top steakhouse focuses on providing carnivores with the finest cuts of meat available in Santiago, including *wagyu,* the Japanese-origin Kobe beef, lamb from the Falklands Island, and locally produced Angus and Hereford beef. If you're not a beef eater, there are seafood dishes that specialize in Easter Island imports and locally produced salmon. Cuerovaca strives to educate diners and build a "culture" around the appreciation of fine beef, and they'll happily provide you with background information about your cut. The ambience is urban-contemporary, with flagstone walls, wood, and glass, and they feature an outstanding wine list. Note that accompaniments and salads are an additional cost to prices listed below.

El Mañío 1659. ✆ **2/206-3911.** www.cuerovaca.cl. Reservations recommended. Beef cuts $13–$16 (£8.70–£11); Kobe beef cuts average $44 (£29); seafood courses $11–$17 (£7.30–£11). AE, DC, MC, V. Daily 1–4pm and 8–11:30pm.

Europeo ★★★ CONTINENTAL Since it nudges up against a Louis Vuitton store, it's no great surprise that Europeo reigns supreme as the best restaurant in Santiago, at least as far as the city's arbiters of style are concerned. As the name implies, Europeo specializes in European-influenced cuisine, although native Swedish chef Carlos Meyer has expanded his global range by adding a dab of Asia here and there to liven things up. You'll find dishes such as foie gras, steak tartare on rye, or a "strudel" of lobster and spinach on vanilla-infused bisque, as well as more classic steak and lamb specialties. Before diners yield to the temptation of dessert, waitstaff serve a complimentary exotic sorbet as a palate cleanser. The dining area is polished and sophisticated, yet its compact size and individual hanging lamps create warmth and intimacy. Europeo is also one of the few restaurants in the city that imparts the knowledge of a superb sommelier—Jose Riffo can describe over 180 wines in intimate detail. For a more affordable bistro-style meal or a light alfresco lunch, try Europeo's **La Brasserie,** which remains true to Europeo's outstanding quality.

Alonso de Córdova 2417. ✆ **2/208-3603.** Reservations recommended. Main courses $16–$25 (£11–£17) Europeo, $8–$13 (£5.30–£8.70) La Brasserie. AE, DC, MC, V. Mon–Fri 1–3pm and 8–10:30pm; Sat 8–11pm.

5 WHAT TO SEE & DO

Visitors with little time can pack in a lot of attractions in just 1 day, given that most of the city's highlights are found in a localized area that runs along the length of the Mapocho River. I recommend that visitors begin in *el centro,* the city's historic center and home to museums, cathedrals, cultural centers, and civic institutions. Pick a few attractions that pique your interest, then walk over to the Barrio París-Londres neighborhood. Cross back over Avenida Alameda to the Cerro Santa Lucía hilltop park, and take a stroll through the charming streets of Parque Forestal, Santiago's burgeoning arts-and-cafe neighborhood. From here, it is just a short walk across the Mapocho River to the bohemian Bellavista neighborhood and Cerro San Cristóbal. If you still have time, wander around the shopping district of Providencia by crossing back over the river.

Now, if you do indeed have only 1 day, you're going to have to hustle and get a very early start, or narrow attractions down to only those that really interest you. Travelers with 2 or 3 days can take this tour at a more leisurely pace, and visit more off-the-beaten-track attractions such as the Quinta Normal Park or Barrio Brasil.

See the maps on p. 78 and 81 to locate the attractions reviewed below.

DOWNTOWN HISTORIC & CIVIC ATTRACTIONS

Plaza de Armas

Begin your tour of Santiago at the grand **Plaza de Armas** ★★★ (Metro: Plaza de Armas). Pedro de Valdivia, who conquered Chile for the Spanish crown, founded this plaza in 1541 as the civic nucleus of the country and surrounded it with the Royal Court of Justice (now the Natural History Museum), the Governor's Palace (now the Central Post Office), the Metropolitan Cathedral, and the venerable homes of early Chile's movers and shakers. The square became the epicenter of public life and the stage for markets, festivals, and even bullfights. In the mid-1800s, the somber plaza was spruced up with gardens and trees, creating a promenade that became a social center for fashionable society. Though fashionable society has since moved uptown, the plaza still ranks as one of Santiago's most enjoyable areas to sit and watch the world go by. Between the hustle and bustle of city workers, there is an eclectic mix of characters that spend the better part of their day here: soap-box speakers and shoe shiners, comedians and preachers, garrulous old men playing chess, young couples embracing on park benches, and street photographers and artists hawking paintings.

Catedral Metropolitana and Museo de Arte Sagrado ★★ The corpulent Metropolitan Cathedral stretches almost an entire city block. This is the fifth cathedral to have been erected at this site because of fire and seismic damage to earlier ones. The cathedral began construction in 1748 following Bavarian Jesuit designs (you can admire their handiwork in the church's brawny cypress doors and silver frontal). It was during the cathedral's fourth restoration in 1780 that Italian architect Joaquín Toesca bestowed his signature harmony and unity, fusing the structure's baroque and neoclassical features with aplomb. It's worth taking a look inside to view the opulent main altar, dripping with white marble, bronze, and lapis lazuli. In 2005 and 2006, the main altar of the cathedral was completely remodeled; in the process, workers discovered the tomb of the lost body of Diego Portales, one of the founding fathers of Chile. Dozens of other Chilean luminaries and archbishops are buried here, too. The Cathedral's **Museum of Sacred Art** highlights more of the Jesuit's silver handiwork; the collection's two outstanding pieces are a silver lectern and tabernacle. There is also an ad-hoc ensemble of religious paintings and furniture which pales in comparison to those exhibited in the Iglesia San Francisco's museum (p. 112). Don't miss the ethereal courtyard, a paradigm of faded grandeur. The museum is reached through the bookstore neighboring the cathedral.

Paseo Ahumada, on the west side of the plaza. No phone. Free admission. Mon–Sat 9am–7pm; Sun 9am–noon. Metro: Plaza de Armas.

Correo Central and Museo Postal The pastel-pink Central Post Office was built in 1882 on the remains of what was once the colonial Governor's Palace and the post-independence Presidential Palace. After the building succumbed to fire in 1881, workers rebuilt it, incorporating several of the old building's walls. In 1908, architect Ramón Feherman added a third floor and an extravagant glass cupola. Unless you have postcards to mail or a fondness for Renaissance-period architecture, there isn't much to see here.

Calle Puente, north side of the plaza. © **2/601-0141.** Free admission. Mon–Fri 9am–5pm. Metro: Plaza de Armas.

Palacio de la Real Audiencia/Museo Histórico Nacional The Historical Museum offers an in-depth look into Chile's history—from the conquest to present day—in a size and scope that doesn't feel overwhelming. The museum is housed in the elegant, lemon-colored Palacio de la Real, built by the Spanish between 1804 and 1807 to house the royal court of justice. Just 8 years later, it became the seat of government, where Chile held its first congress following independence. The museum winds around a central courtyard, beginning with the conquest, and finishing with a photo montage depicting modern political turmoil and literary and artistic accomplishments in Chile. Along the way, visitors can view weapons, agricultural tools, traditional costumes, household appliances, oil paintings depicting early Chile, and reproductions of home life during the 18th and 19th centuries. There are, unfortunately, no tours in English, all interpretative information is in Spanish, and the randomness of the exhibits precludes a sense of true enlightenment. Plan to spend 1 hour here.

Plaza de Armas 951. © **2/411-7010.** Admission $1.25 (80p) adults, 60¢ (40p) children 17 and under; free Sun and holidays. Tues–Sun 10am–5:30pm. Metro: Plaza de Armas.

Near the Plaza de Armas

Paseo Ahumada, at the southwest corner of the Plaza de Armas, and its sister street **Paseo Huérfanos,** which bisects Paseo Ahumada a block away, are bustling pedestrian walkways that offer the visitor a good feel for downtown Santiago and the people who work there. Dozens of newspaper kiosks, musicians, and street performers entertain passersby who race to and fro the almost continual line of shops and restaurants. It can get frenzied during the lunch hour here; when it does, keep an eye on your belongings.

Basílica de la Merced ★ A church was originally built on this spot in 1566 by the Order of the Blessed Virgin Mary of Mercy (Mercedarians) who arrived with the first discovery expedition to Chile. Following the earthquakes of 1647 and 1730, which destroyed the old colonial structure, the present, two-towered, neo-Renaissance structure

Coffee with Legs

Downtown Santiago is home to a curious phenomenon known as *Café con Piernas* ("Coffee with Legs"), cafes manned by waitresses done up in skimpy ensembles and thick makeup, serving ogling businessmen from behind a stand-up bar. **Café Haiti** (✆ **2/737-4323;** locations at Ahumada 140 and 336, Huérfanos 769, and Bandera 335) and **Café Caribe** (✆ **2/695-7081;** locations at Ahumada 120 and Huérfanos 796, 945, and 1164) are local institutions and tamer affairs than otherwise raunchier versions (recognizable by darkened windows and men sheepishly slinking in or out the door). Café Haiti and Café Caribe are patronized by women as well as men.

was completed in 1736. Rather incongruously sited on the periphery of the prosaic Alameda, the church's interior is something to behold, with a stunning baroque Bavarian pulpit and an altar displaying a 16th-century image of the Virgin Mary, which was brought by the first Mercedarian priests to the city. What is most striking about the museum is the realization that all relics associated with Christ are not the exclusive patrimony of the Vatican. Here at the Basílica de la Merced, under a protective crystal dome next to a money collection box, is what is said to be a sliver of the actual cross. How did it get here? The story goes that Spain's King Alfonso XIII donated the artifact in 1912 to Chilean mercenaries. As intriguing are the Basilica's neo-Renaissance architecture and the church's religious museum. Oddly enough, it boasts a sizable collection of Easter Island art (more artifacts than you'll find at the Hanga Roa museum on that island, anyway), including a rongorongo tablet, one of only 29 left in the world, as well as smatterings of religious kitsch in the form of baby Jesus figurines in bell glasses.

MacIver 341, corner of Merced. ✆ **2/633-0691** (church); ✆ 2/664-9189 (museum). Admission: Church free; museum $2 (£1.30) adults, $1 (70p) students. Church hours: Mon–Fri 6:30am–1:30pm and 3–8:30pm; Sat–Sun 9:30am–1:30pm and 6–9pm. Museum hours: Mon–Fri 10am–1:30pm and 3–9pm; Sat 10am–1pm. Metro: Plaza de Armas.

Casa Colorada & Santiago Museum Overrated The Casa Colorada (Red House) is regarded as the best-preserved colonial structure in Santiago, having survived devastating earthquakes and the whims of modern developers. The structure was built between 1769 and 1779 as a residence for the first president of Chile, Mateo de Toro y Zambrano. Inside, the missable (unless you have kids to entertain) Santiago Museum depicts the urban history of the city until the 19th century using amateurish scale models. Still, architecturally, the Casa Colorada is worth a look, and you can grab lunch or a coffee at Ambrosía (p. 96) behind the museum. There is also a **visitor center** with information about Santiago here.

Merced 860. ✆ **2/633-0723.** Admission 50¢ (30p). Tues–Fri 10am–6pm; Sat 10am–5pm; Sun 11am–2pm. Metro: Plaza de Armas.

Ex-Congreso Nacional and Palacio de los Tribunales ★ Before ex-dictator Pinochet seized power and moved the National Congress to Valparaíso, Congress met inside a handsome, French neoclassical edifice, with Corinthian pillars and lush gardens—a far cry from the Stalinesque monstrosity the government built for Congress in that port town. Today the building houses the foreign ministry and is not open to the public. Across the street, the Palace of the Courts of Justice stretches the entire block. The palace is home to the Supreme Court, the Appeals Court, and the Military Court, and it was the site of the birth of the First National Government Assembly. Interestingly, the building's stern exterior belies one of the most beautiful interiors found in Santiago, with vaulted metal and glass ceilings that run the length of the building, dappling the walls with soft light. Leave your ID at the front, and take a quick stroll through this exquisite foyer if you've got the time.

Compañía at Morandé. No phone. Free admission. Mon–Fri 9am–2pm. Metro: Plaza de Armas.

Museo Chileno de Arte Precolombino ★★★ Heading back on Merced and past the plaza to Bandera, you'll find the excellent Chilean Museum of Pre-Columbian Art, housed in the elegant 1807 ex-Royal Customs House. This is one of the better museums in Chile, both for its varied collection of pre-Columbian artifacts and its handsome design. There are more than 1,500 objects on display here, including Chinchorro mummies, pottery, jewelry, and ceramic art spread throughout seven exhibition rooms. The collection is encompassing but not as extensive as, say, the Anthropological Museum of Mexico; the exhibition does offer a vivid glimpse of indigenous life and culture before the arrival of the Spanish. The material spans from Mexico to Chile and is arranged according to the regions of Latin America; Mesoamérica, Area Intermedia, Andes Centrales, and Andes del Sur. Plan to spend about 90 minutes here. If you are short on time, head for the Area Mesoamérica, which showcases one of the museum's highlights, a compelling statue of the God of Spring Xipé-Totec. The Area Intermedia covers Ecuador, Nicaragua, Panama, Costa Rica, and Colombia and focuses upon early examples of Valdivia pottery that date to 500 B.C. Be sure to leave time for the museum's textile collection, located in the Area Andes Centrales. There's also a well-stocked store that sells music, videos, and reproductions of Indian art, textiles, and jewelry. Docents offer guided tours in English by appointment.

Bandera 361. ✆ **2/688-7348.** www.museoprecolombino.cl. Admission $3 (£2) adults, free for students and children, free Sun and holidays for all. Tues–Sun 10am–6pm; holidays 10am–2pm. Metro: Plaza de Armas.

Plaza Constitucion & The Commerce Center

The poster child of Santiago, the graceful **Palacio de la Moneda ★★** is considered one of the finest neoclassical structures in Latin America. Located between Plaza de la Constitución and Plaza de la Libertad and extending for an entire block, it was built between 1784 and 1805 to house the royal mint by revered Italian architect Joaquín Toesca. In 1848, it became the residential palace for the presidents of Chile starting with Manuel Bulnes and ending with Carlos Ibáñez de Campo in 1958, when it became the official seat of government rather than the president's home.

The palace's harmony and symmetry are best viewed from Plaza de la Constitución's northern side. The building regularity is truly striking—the same set of windows is repeated 14 times along the length of the main facade, each divided by uniform columns—and the overarching feel is of order and stability rather than grandeur. Fittingly, this is the only presidential headquarters in the world that allows civilians to simply stroll through the main archway and wander around the inner courtyards. Patio de los Cañones is named for the two centerpiece 18th-century canons while the Moorish-style Patio de los Naranjos is more reminiscent of the Alhambra Palace in Granada with a cluster of orange trees surrounding a serene 17th-century fountain. Take a walk inside; you may not see the president but it's quite an experience to glimpse the rush of ministers and journalists. There are also several art and sculpture exhibitions inside. Try to plan your visit at 10am to watch Chilean soldiers perform a somber **changing of the guard** to the Chilean national anthem; it takes place every other day.

Beyond aesthetic appreciation, the palace has symbolical and historical resonance. Most infamously, the Palacio was the site of the 1973 Pinochet-led coup that ousted Salvador Allende. For several generations of Chileans, the scratchy black-and-white images of La Moneda being blitzed by General Pinochet on September 11, 1973, ushered in a brutal period in the history of Chile. Today, it is the presidential palace and offices of Chile's first female president, Michelle Bachelet, who was herself imprisoned and tortured by the Pinochet regime. See p. 18.

Calle Nueva York & the Bolsa de Comercio ★★ Walk east on Moneda Street from the Plaza Constitución, and you'll immediately notice a marked increase in business suits—this is the financial apex of Santiago, home to the city's Stock Market (Bolsa de Comercio). The Stock Market occupies one of Santiago's most architecturally interesting buildings, a 1917 triangular stone French-style edifice, built of Roman pillars and topped with an elegant dome cupola. Few people are aware that you can observe the stock-market action Monday through Friday from 9am to 5pm (you'll need to leave your passport or photo ID at the door), even though much of the romantic air of the building's interior has been upgraded with cold technology. Surrounding the Bolsa are the sinuous, cobblestone streets of Nueva York, La Bolsa, and Club de la Unión—if you're downtown, you won't want to miss a stroll through these picturesque streets.

Calle Nueva York. ✆ **2/399-3000.** www.bolsadesantiago.cl. Free admission. Mon–Fri 9am–5pm. Metro: Plaza de Armas.

Centro Cultural Palacio La Moneda ★★★ Chile's most exciting arts and cultural center in decades opened with great fanfare in 2006 as an early public works celebration of Chile's bicentennial in 2010. The subterranean Centro is located below the Plaza de la Ciudadania (Citizen's Plaza), and can be accessed by walking down a ramp at either Teatinos or Morandé street. Capacious as an airport hangar and a sensational example of urban-contemporary design, the center displays revolving exhibitions of Latin American modern and historical art and photography. The center also has a permanent exhibition of arguably the highest quality regional *artesanía,* or arts and crafts, textiles, clothing, and jewelry, from around Chile with detailed maps indicating the artisans' origins. Within this exhibition, there is a store with a small selection for sale. The center also has an art-house cinema, library, educational center, and the sleek **Cafe Torres** (p. 97). Check the website for upcoming exhibitions and events, and plan to spend about 30 minutes here.

Plaza de la Ciudadanía (underground). ✆ **2/355-6500.** www.ccplm.cl. Admission $1 (70p) adults, 60¢ (40p) students and seniors, kids 4 and under free, Sun free for all. Tues–Sun 10am–9pm. Metro: La Moneda.

Attractions off the Alameda

The formal moniker of Santiago's principal avenue is Avenida Libertador Bernardo O'Higgins, but everyone calls it *La Alameda.* O'Higgins is Chile's founding father, and his remains are buried under a monument dedicated in his honor across from the Plaza de la Ciudadanía. La Alameda is a congested and harried thoroughfare, characterized by throngs of people and screeching buses, and there are few crosswalks—remember that you can cross the avenue via an underground Metro station. The following attractions can be found on or just off the Alameda.

Barrio París-Londres ★★ This incongruous neighborhood is just a few blocks in diameter and was built between the 1920s and 1930s on the old gardens of the Monastery of San Francisco. The neighborhood oozes charm: Mainly because with its cobblestone streets and gracefully decaying buildings, it looks as if a chunk of Paris's Latin Quarter was airlifted and dropped down in the middle of downtown Santiago. There are no sights as such but a wander along its hushed streets provides a soulful respite from the surrounding '70s-style *gallerias* and other mismatched buildings around the neighborhood's outskirts.

The streets btw. Prat and Santa Rosa, walking south of Alameda.

Biblioteca Nacional The principal attraction of the country's National Library is the French neoclassical stone building that houses it, which spans an entire city block. Inside its handsomely painted interiors are over six million works, as well as historical archives and a map room. The Jose Medina reading room offers a glimpse into an early-20th-century library, with antique books stacked in tiers, leather-topped reading desks, and a giant spinning globe.

Av. Bernardo O'Higgins 651. ✆ **2/360-5259.** Free admission. Mon–Fri 9am–6pm; Sat 9:15am–2:30pm. Metro: Cerro Santa Lucía.

Calle Dieciocho and Palacio Cousiño Macul ★ During the turn of the 20th century and before Santiago's elite packed it up and moved away from the downtown hubbub, Calle Dieciocho ranked as the city's toniest neighborhood. The tourism board touts Calle Dieciocho as a step back in time, but neglect has taken its toll, and the only site really worth visiting here is the **Palacio Cousiño Macul,** once the home of Chile's grandest entrepreneurial dynasties, the Goyenechea-Cousiño family. A visit here (by guided tour only) provides a unique opportunity to appreciate how Santiago's elite lived during the late 1800s. Once completed in 1878, the palace dazzled society with its opulence: lavish parquet floors, Bohemian crystal chandeliers, Italian hand-painted ceramics, and French tapestries. Much of the building was destroyed by fire in the 1960s but what remains provides a dizzying insight into the excellence of European craftsmanship at the turn of the 19th century. To get here, you can either take a taxi or the Metro (Estación Toesca). If you'd like to take a walk, then by all means do begin at Avenida Alameda and head down Calle Dieciocho for 15 minutes, until you reach the Palace (you might begin with lunch at the legendary Confitería Torres and then walk it off down Dieciocho). Also, take a 10-minute detour around the corner from Cousiño Macul (east on San Ignacio) to Parque Almagro, a scruffy park that nevertheless affords a view of the little-known, almost Gaudiesque **Basílica del Santísimo Sacramento** church, constructed between 1919 and 1931 and modeled after the Sacre Coeur in Montmartre, Paris.

Dieciocho 438. ✆ **2/698-5063.** Admission $2.50 (£1.70) adults, $1.50 (£1) children 11 and under. Bilingual tours Tues–Fri 9:30am–11:30pm and 2:30–4pm; Sat–Sun 9:30am–12:30pm. Metro: Toesca.

Iglesia, Convento y Museo de San Francisco ★★ The Church of San Francisco, built between 1586 and 1628, is the oldest standing building in Santiago, having miraculously survived three devastating earthquakes. At the altar sits the famous *Virgen del Socorro,* the first Virgin Mary icon in Chile brought here to Santiago by Pedro de Valdivia, the conquistador of Chile. Valdivia claimed the icon had warded off Indian attacks. The highlights, however, are the museum and the convent, the latter with its idyllic patio planted with flora brought from destinations as near as the south of Chile and as far away as the Canary Islands. The garden, with its bubbling fountain and cooing white doves, is so serene you'll find it hard to believe you're in downtown Santiago. The tiny museum houses a collection of one of the largest and best-conserved examples of 17th-century art in South America. A sizable percentage of colonial-period furniture, keys, paintings, and other items on display were crafted in Peru, when it still was the seat of the Spanish government in Latin America.

Av. Bernardo O'Higgins. ✆ **2/638-3238.** Admission to convent and museum $2 (£1.30). Tues–Sat 10am–1pm and 3–6pm; Sun and holidays 10am–2pm. Metro: Santa Lucía.

Cerro Santa Lucía & Plaza Mulato Gil de Castro

Materializing as if out of nowhere on the edge of the city's downtown limits, the lavishly landscaped and historically significant **Cerro Santa Lucía** ★★★ is a triangular-shape hilltop park, and one of the more delightful attractions in Santiago. This is where Pedro de Valdivia, the conqueror of Chile, founded Santiago in 1540 for the crown of Spain. For centuries, the rocky outcrop was seen as more of an eyesore than a recreational area (the Mapuche Indians called it *Huelén,* or "curse"), until 1872, when 150 prisoners were put to work landscaping the hill and carving out walkways and small squares for the public to enjoy. Today, office workers, tourists, couples, schoolchildren, and solitary thinkers can be seen strolling along leafy terraces to the Caupolicán Plaza for a sweeping view of Santiago. It's open daily from 9am to 8pm from September to March, 9am to 7pm from April to August; admission is free, though you'll be asked to sign a guest registry when entering. Enter at Avenida Alameda and St. Lucía, or St. Lucía and Merced; alternatively, you could take the elevator to the top on St. Lucía Street at Agustinas. At the top of the hill is the Castle Hidalgo, which operates as an event center. The **Centro de Exposición de Arte** has indigenous crafts, clothing, and jewelry from all over Chile for sale, but you'll find better deals across the avenue at the bustling crafts and junk market, the **Centro Artesanal de Santa Lucía,** with handicrafts, T-shirts, and more.

Santiago's burgeoning arts-and-cafe scene centers around the tiny **Plaza Mulato Gil de Castro** ★★, located at José Victorino Lastarría and Rosal streets. The fine examples of early 1900s architecture at the plaza and the handful of streets that surround it provide visitors with a romantic step back into old Santiago. From Thursday to Sunday, antiques and book dealers line the plaza, but the highlights here are the **Museo de Artes Visuales (MAVI)** ★★★ and the **Museo Anthropología (MAS)** ★★ (✆ **2/638-3502;** $1.60/£1 adults, 85¢/60p children; Tues–Sun 10:30am–6:30pm). Many of Chile's most promising contemporary artists exhibit their work at MAVI. The MAS offers archaeological displays of artifacts produced by indigenous peoples throughout the length of Chile. The collection at MAS is extensive, but the museum is small and takes no more than 10 minutes to peruse.

Parque Forestal

This slender, manicured park, landscaped in 1900 with rows of native and imported trees, skirts the perimeter of the Río Mapocho from Vicuña Mackenna at the Metro station Baquedano to its terminus at the Mapocho station. The winding path takes walkers past several great attractions and makes for a pleasant half-hour to 1-hour stroll, especially on a sunny afternoon when the air is clear. If you plan to walk the entire park, try to finish at the Mercado Central (see below) for lunch.

Estación Mapocho ★ Built in 1912 on reclaimed land formed by the canalization of the Río Mapocho, this beautiful, Beaux Arts building served as the train station for the Santiago-Valparaíso railway until the late 1970s, and it was built as part of the country's

100-year celebration. After a decade of abandonment, the Chilean government invited architects to sketch a renovation of the building as part of a contest, and the building was redesigned as a four-story, grand cultural center with a 40-ton copper, marble, and glass roof and seats made of Oregon pine. The center hosts events such as rock concerts and the International Book Fair, and within its handful of salons, visitors can view exhibitions of local art and a permanent installation of the popular "Painted Bodies," visit an arts-and-crafts store, and grab a coffee at one of two cafes. The Metro station Cal y Canto is also here, making this a perfect stop before visiting the Mercado Central.

Bandera and Río Mapocho. ✆ **2/787-0000.** www.estacionmapocho.cl. Daily 9am–5pm; other hours according to events. Metro: Calicanto.

Mercado Central ★★★ It's the quintessential tourist stop, but the colorful, chaotic Mercado Central is nevertheless a highlight for visitors to Santiago. A large share of Chile's economy depends on the exportation of natural products such as fruits, vegetables, and seafood, and the market here displays everything the country has to offer. Lively and staffed by pushy fishmongers who quickly and nimbly gut and fillet while you watch, the market displays every kind of fish and shellfish available along the Chilean coast. Depending on your perspective, the barking fishmongers and waitresses who harangue you to choose *their* zucchini, *their* sea bass, *their* restaurant can be entertaining or somewhat annoying. Either way, don't miss it, especially for the market's lofty, steel structure that was prefabricated in England and assembled here in 1868. Try to plan your visit during the lunch hour, for a rich bowl of *caldillo de congrio* (a thick conger eel soup) or a tangy *ceviche* at one of the many typical restaurants (see "Where to Dine," earlier in this chapter).

Vergara and Av. 21 de Mayo. No phone. Daily 7am–5pm (some stalls stay open later). Metro: Cal y Canto.

Museo Nacional de Bellas Artes (MNBA) & Museo de Arte Contemporaneo (MAC) ★★ The Palacio de Bellas Artes is the city's fine arts museum, housed in a regal, neoclassical building inaugurated on the eve of Chile's centennial independence day in 1910. The palace has a noteworthy glass cupola that softly lights the vast lobby. The importance of the permanent installations in the Fine Arts museum may be debatable (an uneven mix of Chilean and international artists' works since the colonial period), but lately they've been hosting temporary exhibitions of international artists such as Damian Hirst, Henri-Cartier Bresson, and David Hockney, to name a few, so it's worth stopping by to see what is on offer. Within the same building, but entering from the back, is the Museo de Arte Contemporaneo (MAC), the city's modern art museum and part of the University of Chile. This museum hosts temporary exhibitions of national and international modern art, yet such heavyweights as Hirst are typically shown in the Fine Arts Museum.

Parque Forestal, by way of Jose Miguel de la Barra. MNBA: ✆ **2/633-4472.** www.mnba.cl. MAC: ✆ **2/977-1741.** www.mac.cl. Admission MNBA and MAC $1.25 (80p) adults, 75¢ (50p) students (visitors must pay separately for each museum), free for all Sun. Tues–Sun 10am–7pm. Metro: Bellas Artes.

Barrio Bellavista ★★ & Parque Metropolitano (Cerro San Cristobal)

One of the city's most enigmatic neighborhoods, Bellavista, Santiago's bohemian quarter, is to Santiago what Montmartre is to Paris. Nestled at the foot of Cerro San Cristóbal and its Metropolitan Park, Bellavista positively buzzes with a sense of excitement and creativity, with new hip restaurants, boutiques, and avant-garde galleries occupying loft spaces and lordly mansions that punctuate tree-lined streets awash with colorful antique homes. Many of the city's esteemed intellectuals and artists live in Bellavista, following in the footsteps of its most famous denizen, Pablo Neruda. The shopping/dining area **Patio Bellavista** (see "Shopping," later) is a pleasant place for an afternoon stroll; in the evening, Bellavista pulses to the beat of music pouring from its many discos and bars. On weekends, there is an evening handicrafts market that runs the length of Pío Nono.

Cerro San Cristóbal ★★★ The lacerating Andean peak of San Cristóbal rises to 860m (2,820 ft.) and affords unrivalled views of the city (on a clear day), rendering this attraction one of the best in the city. To get here, head to the Plaza Caupolican at the end of Calle Pío Nono, where you'll encounter a 1925 **funicular** (not for the faint of heart) that lifts visitors up to a lookout point watched over by a 22m-high (72-ft.) statue of the **Virgen de la Inmaculada Concepción.** If you prefer a challenge, the rewarding ascent on foot takes about 90 minutes. Along the way, the funicular stops at the disappointing **Jardín Zoológico.** Below the statue is the **Tupahue *teleférico*** (cable car) that connects the two sections of the park—Cumbre and Tupahue, both of which are accessed by car, cable car, funicular, or on foot. The *teleférico* is a lot of fun, especially for kids, but it can be sweltering in the summer heat.

At Tupahue, which means "place of God" in the native Mapuche language, you'll find the **Piscina Tupahue** and **Piscina Antilén.** A far cry from your run-of-the-mill YMCA pools, these beautifully landscaped and meticulously maintained pools are an ideal place to cool off on a hot summer day and watch the Santiaguinos at play. In the case of Piscina Antilén, which sits atop the peak of Cerro Chacarillas, you can take in panoramic views of the city while you swim. You'll need a cab to Antilén, or you can walk northeast past the Camino Real to get here, about a 10-minute walk. From Tupahue, you can either head back on the tram to Cumbre and the funicular or take the **Valdivia *teleférico*** down, which will drop you off at the end of Avenida Pedro de Valdivia. It's about an 8-block walk down to Avenida Providencia. It's possible to take a taxi up Cerro San Cristóbal, but you'll need to pay the park entrance fee as well as the fare.

Cerro San Cristóbal/Parque Metropolitan. ✆ **2/730-1300.** www.parquemet.cl. Sun–Thurs 8am–10pm; Fri–Sat 8am–midnight. Free admission. Metro: Baquedano. Funicular: Mon 1–6pm, Tues–Sun 10am–6:30pm. $2 (£1.30) adults, $1 (70p) children 3–13. Teléferico: Mon 1:30–5:30pm, Tues–Sun 11:30am–5:30pm. $4.75 (£3.20) adults, $2.50 (£1.60) children. Admission for vehicles $2 (£1.30). Pools (no phone; Nov 15–Mar 15 Tues–Sun 10am–7pm; $7/£4.60 adults, $5/£3.30 children).

La Chascona ★★★ Bellavista's prime attraction is one of three homes once owned by Chile's most famous literary artist, the Nobel Prize–winning poet Pablo Neruda. Located a block east of the Plaza Caupolican (the entrance point to the Parque Metropolitano), Neruda lived here with his third wife, Matilde Urutia (the woman with the red, tousled hair for whom the house was named) between 1955 and 1973. As with Neruda's other two homes, La Chascona was built to resemble a ship, with oddly shaped rooms that wind around a compact courtyard. It's fascinating to wander through Neruda's quirky home and observe his collection of precious antiques and whimsical curios collected during his travels. Neruda's library is especially interesting, and it holds the antique encyclopedia set he purchased with a portion of his earnings from the Nobel Prize. The home is headquarters for the Fundación Pablo Neruda, which provides guided tours.

Fernando Márquez de la Plata 0192. ✆ **2/777-8741.** www.fundacionneruda.cl. Admission $4.75 (£3.20) adults Spanish tour, $6.75 (£4.50) English tour, Sun free. Jan–Feb Tues–Sun 10am–7pm; Mar–Dec Tues–Sun 10am–6pm. Call to make a reservation; otherwise, if you just show up, you may need to wait until a guide frees up. Metro: Baquedano.

Parque Quinta Normal

Santiago's loveliest and most graceful park commenced in 1841 as a plant-acclimatization nursery for imported species, when the area was still outside the boundaries of Santiago. The park grew to include 38 hectares (96 acres) of grassy lawns, dozens of varieties of trees (splendid mature examples of Monterey pine, Douglas firs, Sequoias, Babylonian willows, and more), sporting facilities, and a lagoon with paddle boat rental. It is truly one of Santiago's most underrated attractions; however, I wouldn't recommend the park as a top destination if you only have 1 day in the city, unless you have children. The park's four museums are kid-friendly, including the **Natural History Museum** (**© 2/680-4615;** www.mnhn.cl), open Tuesday through Saturday from 10am to 5:30pm, Sunday from noon to 5:30pm (Nov–Mar), and 11am–4:30pm (Apr–Sept); admission is $1.25 (80p) adults, 75¢ (50p) children 17 and under, Sundays and holidays free. The museum's handsome neoclassical exterior belies a rather fusty and underfunded collection. However, in 2008, renovations began (and are likely to continue through 2009) and a new Rapa Nui exhibition, which showcases a 17th-century moai named Kava Kava, augurs well for a more compelling and informative museum befitting of its status as the oldest natural history museum in Latin America.

Worth a visit is the **Artequín Museum ★★**, Av. Portales 3530 (**© 2/682-5367;** www.artequin.cl), open Tuesday through Friday from 9am to 5pm, and Saturday, Sunday, and holidays from 11am to 6pm. The museum is closed throughout February; admission is $1.40 (90p) adults, 75¢ (50p) students and children, free on Sundays. Housed in a fascinating cast-iron building accented with a kaleidoscope of colorful glass, it was first used as the Chilean exhibition hall at the 1889 Parisian centenary of the French Revolution. Workers took the building apart, shipped it to Santiago, and reassembled it here. The museum displays only reproductions of famous paintings by artists from Botticelli to Rubens, Picasso to Monet, and even Andy Warhol's *Marilyn* and Francis Bacon's *Study after Velázquez's Portrait of Pope Innocent X.* The idea is to introduce kids to important works of art.

A popular museum with kids here is the **Museo de Ciencia y Tecnología (Museum of Science and Technology) ★★** (**© 2/681-6022;** www.museodeciencia.cl), whose engaging, interactive, and hands-on displays provide a worthy initiation into the basic precepts of astronomy, geology, and physics. It is open Tuesday through Friday from 10am to 6pm, Saturday and Sunday from 11am to 6pm; admission is $1.40 (90p) adults and $1.25 (80p) students. At the southern end of the park, on Avenida Portales, is the fourth museum here, the **Museo Ferroviario (Railway Museum) ★** (**© 2/681-4627;** www.museodeciencia.cl/homeferroviario.htm), with railway exhibits that include 14 steam engines and railway carriages, including the train that once connected Santiago with Mendoza until 1971. It's open Tuesday through Friday from 10am to 6pm, Saturday and Sunday from 11am to 6pm; admission is $1.25 (80p) adults and 75¢ (50p) students.

ESPECIALLY FOR KIDS

In addition to the following recommendations, the Parque Metropolitano Zoo, the aerial tram at Cerro San Cristóbal, the Museum of Science and Technology, the Artequín Museum, the Natural History Museum, and the Railway Museum described earlier are all ideal for kids.

The spacious **Parque Bernardo O'Higgins** is a tired, worn-down park frequented by blue-collar Santiaguinos who come to fly kites and barbecue on the weekends; there's nothing worth seeing here except the modern amusement park **Fantasilandia** (**© 2/476-8600;** www.fantasilandia.cl). Admission is $10 (£6.60) adults, $5 (£3.30) children. It's open April 1 through November 9 on Saturday, Sunday, and holidays only from noon to 7pm. It's the largest amusement park in Chile, with four stomach-churning roller coasters, a toboggan ride, and a haunted house. If you are in town, the Halloween theme night is not to be missed.

The **Museo Interactivo Mirador (MIM)** ★★ and the **Santiago Aquarium** ★★ (two entrances: Sebastopol 90 and Punta Arenas 6711; ✆ **2/828-8000;** www.mim.cl; $6/£4 adults, $4/£2.70 children; combo ticket with aquarium $8/£5.30 adults, $6/£4 children) are neighbors within an 11-hectare (27-acre) park in the La Granja barrio. Inaugurated in 2000, MIM dedicates itself to providing children with an introduction to the world of science and technology. Adults will be fascinated by MIM, too. The ultramodern museum has more than 300 exhibits, mostly interactive displays that cover the range of paleontology, computer animation, robotics, and 3-D cinema. In 2008, MIM proudly unveiled its latest permanent exhibition, "Protecting the Ozone Layer." You could spend nearly a full day here if you choose to check out the aquarium which, while far from world class, has over 200 species of primarily Chilean marine life and an eternally crowd-pleasing sea lion show. Buy a combo ticket for both if you have enough time. To get here, take Metro Line 5 to the Mirador stop.

ORGANIZED TOURS

Major hotels work with quality tour operators and can recommend a tour even at the last minute; however, you'd be better off planning ahead and reserving a tour with an operator who can show you the more interesting side of Santiago or who is more attuned to foreign guests' desires or needs (that is, a guide who is truly bilingual). The following tours are operated by Chilean-American outfits.

Culinary Tour: Hip Santiago Centro presents a way to see, and taste, a different side of Santiago. Tours are led by American expat Liz Caskey. The tour kicks off with a walking tour through a typical farmers' market in the old-fashioned Brasil neighborhood, followed by a visit to the Mercado Central and a walk through the picturesque Parque Forestal neighborhood, and then to Liz's spacious apartment overlooking the park for a three-course lunch expertly paired with fine wines. Guests are welcome to join in on the cooking if they wish. Tours are available Monday through Saturday and depart at 10:30am. The tour lasts about 4 to 5 hours. For more information and a price quote, contact ✆ **2/226-6939** or 9/821-9230, or visit www.lizcaskey.com.

Santiago Adventures offers a half-day historical and cultural tour of the city, beginning in the Plaza de Armas and visiting La Moneda, the París-Londres neighborhood, the San Francisco colonial church, the Bellavista neighborhood, and the Cerro San Cristóbal. Daily tours are half-day (4 hr.) and visitors may choose one museum to visit: Cousiño Macul museum, the Pre-Columbian Museum, or Pablo Neruda's house. Tours cost $85 (£57) per person, based on two people (price goes down as group size grows), and includes entrance fees, a bilingual guide, transportation, and bottled water. Santiago Adventures can be reached at ✆ **2/244-2750** or www.santiagoadventures.com.

SPECTATOR SPORTS & RECREATION

HORSE RACING Two racetracks hold events on either Saturday or Sunday throughout the year: the recommended **Club Hípico,** Blanco Encalada 2540 (✆ **2/683-9600;** www.clubhipico.cl), and the **Hipódromo Chile,** Avenida Vivaceta in Independencia (✆ **2/270-9200;** www.hipodromo.cl). The Hípico's classic event, El Ensayo, takes place the first Sunday in November and always provides a colorful Chilean spectacle as attendees arm themselves with grills and barbecue meat in the middle of the racetrack oval. The

Hipódromo's classic St. Leger is the second week in December, but it takes longer to get to than the Club Hípico.

POOLS Your best bet are the public pools **Tupahue** and **Antilén,** atop Cerro San Cristóbal; see "Barrio Bellavista & Parque Metropolitano" above for details.

SKIING For information about skiing in the area, see chapter 7.

SOCCER (FOOTBALL) Top football (as soccer is called here) games are held at three stadiums: **Estadio Monumental,** Avenida Grecia and Marathon; **Universidad de Chile,** Camp de Deportes 565 (both are in the Ñuñoa neighborhood); and **Universidad Católica,** Andrés Bello 2782, in Providencia. Check the sports pages of any local newspaper for game scheduling. Though *fútbol* is popular in Chile, fans aren't quite as maniacal as they are in Argentina and Brazil.

6 SHOPPING

SHOPPING CENTERS

Santiago is home to two American-style megamalls: **Parque Arauco,** Av. Kennedy 5413, open Monday through Saturday from 10am to 9pm, Sunday and holidays from 11am to 9pm; and **Alto Las Condes,** Av. Kennedy 9001, open Monday through Saturday from 10:30am to 9pm, and Sunday and holidays from 11am to 9pm. Both offer a hundred or so national brands and well-known international chains, junk-food courts, and multiscreen theaters (Parque Arauco is closer to Providencia), but Parque Arauco has the edge with its "Boulevard" shopping area with hip shops and (unbelievably) some of Santiago's better restaurants. The best way to get to Parque Arauco is by cab (about $5–$6/£3.30–£4 from Providencia). Note that weekends are jam-packed with shoppers. There are no Metro stops near Alto Las Condes.

Like most Latin American nations, Chile has many shopping *galerías,* labyrinthine mini-malls with dozens of compact shops that independent vendors can rent for considerably less money than a regular storefront. Most are cheap to midrange clothing stores, upstart designers with fun styles but so-so fabrics, or importers of crafts, antiques dealers, tailors, and so on. A vibrant, bustling example is the **Mall Panorámico,** Avenida Ricardo Lyon and Avenida 11 de Septiembre (Metro: Pedro de Valdivia), with 130 shops and a department store across the street. For funky boutiques, try the "Drugstore," on Avenida Providencia between Las Urbinas and Avenida de Fuenzalida (walk back to where the cafe seating is and go left).

CRAFTS MARKETS

Crafts markets can be found around Santiago, as either permanent installations or weekly events, but two stand out as do-not-miss markets for travelers seeking souvenirs and gifts for friends and family back home. The bonus with these two markets is that with so much on offer, you could do all your shopping in one fell swoop. The beautifully designed **Patio Bellavista ★★** (btw. Constitución and Pío Nono sts., a half-block from Dardignac; ✆ **2/777-4766;** www.patiobellavista.cl) is a collection of shops hawking high-quality arts and crafts, jewelry, woolens, and woodwork, and centered around a cobblestone patio with a couple of cafes and outstanding restaurants. Patio Bellavista is open Wednesday through Sunday from 10am to 9pm, and Thursday through Saturday from 10am to 10pm. Heading toward the mountains, east of Las Condes, **Pueblito de**

los Dominicos ★★, at Apoquindo 9085, is one of the most enjoyable and convenient shopping experiences in Santiago. If you can get past the rather tacky, theme park–pueblo setting, a wealth of crafts, often made in workshops on site, can be perused. You'll find everything from souvenir items such as lapis lazuli jewelry, alpaca scarves, and quirky knickknacks to investment pieces ranging from stunning sculptures, beautiful woodwork, and modern art by up-and-coming Chilean artists. With over 100 stalls, you could quite easily spend a couple of hours here. To get here from Providencia, a taxi will cost around $6 (£4).

The cheapest place for locally produced crafts is the **Feria Santa Lucía,** at Cerro Santa Lucía (on the other side of Alameda; Metro: Santa Lucía). The outdoor market is hard to miss, with its soaring billboards and sprawl of stalls hawking clothing, jewelry, and arts and crafts—even some antiques and collectibles. Hours vary, but it's generally open Monday through Saturday (sometimes Sun) from 10am to 7pm.

SHOPPING FROM A TO Z

Antiques

The antiques stalls at **Anticuarios Mapocho,** at Mapocho and Brasil streets (daily 10am–late afternoon) near Parque Los Reyes, sell a high-quality selection of antique furniture, paintings, sculptures, jewelry, and one-of-a-kind keepsakes at very affordable prices. For large, heavy items, always check shipping costs (which can be excruciatingly expensive) before you buy; many stallholders will be able to arrange shipping. The market is within the confines of one huge red warehouse on the other side of the Panamericana, so a taxi here is about $4 (£2.70) from the Plaza de Armas; or take the Metro to Santa Ana station, head west on Catedral Street for 3 blocks to Avenida Brasil, turn right, and walk north 8 blocks until you reach Mapocho Street.

On Saturdays and Sundays, the parallel streets of Bío Bío and Franklin are transformed into a lively flea market. If you have the patience and luck, amid the bric-a-brac you can often discover eclectic antiques and handicrafts. Take the Metro to Franklin and then walk north to the intersection with Victor Manuel.

A collection of antiques stores can be found clustered around Malaquias Concha and Caupolican streets, between Condell and Italia avenues. Considering that there are only a few shops, however, I recommend visiting only if you have a lot of time or are seeking an enjoyable walk; the neighborhood here is antique and a very pleasant place for a stroll. In Vitacura, at Candelería Goyenechea 3820, the ground floor of the Anfiteatro Lo Castillo has two dozen antiques stores with beautiful European antiques at astronomical prices and more than a whiff of pretentiousness. Another pricey collection of antiques shops can be found at Calle Bucarest and Avenida Providencia, selling paintings, china, furniture, and nearly every knickknack imaginable. Lastly, the Plaza Mulato Gil de Castro, on Lastarría Street at Rosal, has a small antiques fair (mostly china, purses, and jewelry) on Saturday and Sunday from about 9am to 5pm.

Arts & Crafts

Artesanías de Chile, Av. Bellavista 0357 (© **2/777-8643;** www.artesaniasdechile.cl), is the public face of the Chilean Crafts Foundation, which promotes and sells the work of local artisans. The store offers simply stunning arts and crafts and other handiwork, including intricate hand-woven textiles from the Aymara Indians, clay pottery from Pomaire, Mapuche silver jewelry, hand-woven baskets, and woodcarvings. Artesanías has a small stand within Patio Bellavista, and a branch in the Centro Cultural (p. 111) with interpretative information and a small store.

Two stores specializing in less-traditional *artesania,* with arts and crafts produced by contemporary artists, are **Observatorio Lastarría,** at Lastarría 395 (✆ **2/632-4588;** www.elobservatorio.cl), and **Ona Chile ★★**, at Victoria Subercaseaux 295, across from Cerro Santa Lucía (✆ **2/632-1859**). Driven by a commitment to cultural and environmental conservation, the Observatorio has books, clothing made from local fibers, and ceramics for the home, and the shop is part of a larger arts center that often features temporary exhibitions, a sleek cafe and "La Cava," a wine cellar offering tastings, and workshops. Ona has a beautiful range of high-quality and unique artesanía, including alpaca shawls, *cacique* ponchos, ceramics, paintings, sculptures, jewelry, and other Patagonia and Ona Indian–themed art pieces.

Books

Surprisingly, English language books are far from ubiquitous and most stores have a limited selection of bestsellers. You'll find the largest selection of English-language books at the **English Reader,** Av. Los Leones 116 (✆ **2/334-7388;** www.englishreader.cl), a bookstore with hundreds of new and used titles and a small selection of U.S. magazines. They also have a cafe which is quite the bohemian hangout. **Librería Inglesa** sells English-language literature, nonfiction, and children's books in shops at Av. Pedro de Valdivia 47 (✆ **2/231-6270**); Paseo Huérfanos 669, Local 11 (✆ **2/632-5153**); and Vitacura 5950 (✆ **2/219-2735**). For the largest selection of books in Spanish, the **Feria Chilena del Libro,** Paseo Huérfanos 623 (✆ **2/345-8300**), is your best bet, and it sells local and national maps. It has a smaller branch in Providencia at Santa Magdalena 50 (✆ **2/232-1422**). Also in Providencia, **Libro's,** Pedro de Valdivia 039 (✆ **2/232-8839**), is the place to come for an array of U.S. and English magazines, with everything from *Vogue* and *Vanity Fair* to *The Face* and *GQ.* It also has a small selection of other English-language titles.

Fashion

The fashionista set flock to Bellavista, a neighborhood filled with shops stocking quirky and original garments. Try **Hall Central,** José Victorino Lastarria 316 (✆ **2/664-0763**), a flamboyant fashion store located in a stately 20th-century mansion. For feminine attire with Asian flair, **Kebo,** Av. Ismael Valdés Vergara 490 (✆ **2/639-5537**), purveys the designs of local fashion diva Carla Godoy. **Tampu,** Av. Merced 327 (✆ **2/638-7992**), presents modern renditions of the traditional weaving techniques of the Mapuche, Aymara, and Ona tribal cultures, with a funky range of sweaters and jewelry.

In Providencia, centered upon General Holley, Suecia, and Bucarest streets, you'll find the city's more expensive, upscale clothing boutiques. Chile's version of Rodeo Drive is Alonso de Córdova in the Vitacura neighborhood, where you will find the familiar designer-label fashion houses in addition to small chi chi boutiques featuring the work of established Chilean designers.

Food & Wine

If you're in Bellavista, try to make a stop at the **Emporio Nacional,** Av. Bellavista 0360 (✆ **2/481-3820;** www.emporionacional.cl). Built to resemble a late-1800s-era emporium, this shop is utterly charming, and it is the only shop in Santiago with specialty food products from all over Chile, including cured meats, jams, pickled vegetables, smoked salmon, dried nuts and fruits, plus a boutique wine shop. ***Tip:*** Emporio Nacional is the perfect one-stop shop for picnic supplies. Visit this shop in tandem with the Artesanías de Chile (above), as it's nearby.

Supermarkets offer a wide selection of more traditional wines at cheaper prices than specialty shops. For those hard-to-get wines you won't find back in the U.S., try **El Mundo del Vino** at Av. Isidora Goyenechea 2931 (✆ **2/584-1172;** www.elmundodelvino.cl), open Monday through Wednesday 10:30am to 8:30pm, Thursday through Saturday 10am to 9pm, and Sunday 11am to 6pm. El Mundo del Vino has an extensive selection and knowledgeable staff, but my pick for wine stores is undoubtedly **La Vinoteca** (✆ **2/334-1987**), at Av. Isidora Goyenechea 3520, and open Monday through Friday from 10am to 9pm, Saturday 10am to 8pm. La Vinoteca's sales team really know their stuff, and the shop specializes in boutique and hard-to-find wines. Also, La Vinoteca has a shop in the airport; if you buy a case here, they'll wrap it up so you can check it like luggage. For tips about shipping wine or bringing wine back with you on the plane, see p. 169 in chapter 7.

7 SANTIAGO AFTER DARK

Residents of Santiago adhere to a vampire's schedule, dining as late as 11pm, arriving at a nightclub past 1am, and diving into bed before the sun rises. But there are many early-hour nighttime attractions if you can't bear late nights. The newspaper *El Mercurio* publishes a Friday weekend-guide supplement called "Wiken" as does *La Tercera* and its "Guía Fin de Semana." Both contain movie, theater, and live music listings and special events.

THE PERFORMING ARTS

Santiago is known for its theater, including large playhouses and small-scale, independent theater groups. Rarely do newspapers give reviews and descriptions of theater productions, so it might be difficult to find a production that interests you. Ask around for recommendations, or ask the staff at your hotel.

Well-established theaters with high-quality, contemporary productions and comedies in an intimate setting include **Teatro Bellavista,** Dardignac 0110 (✆ **2/735-2395;** Metro: Salvador) and **Teatro Alcalá,** Bellavista 97 (✆ **2/732-7161**). As the name implies, the nearby **Teatro La Comedia,** Merced 349 (✆ **2/639-1523;** Metro: Baquedano), hosts comedy, but it is better known for cutting-edge productions. The cultural center **Estación Mapocho,** at the Plaza de la Cultura s/n (✆ **2/787-0000;** Metro: Cal y Canto), hosts a large variety of theater acts, often concurrently. The **Centro Mori** (✆ **2/777-6246;** www.centromori.cl), at Constitución 183, hosts well-respected, avant-garde theater acts that change weekly, and occasionally, live music; the center's hip restaurant, Amorío (p. 99), fronts the theater.

But now, let's be realistic. If you do not speak Spanish, even the city's current hit production is going to be a waste of your time and money. Stick to something more accessible, such as a symphony, ballet, or opera at the city's gorgeous, neoclassical **Teatro Municipal** ★, located downtown at Agustinas 749 (✆ **2/463-1000;** www.municipal.cl; Metro: Univ. de Chile). The jewel in the crown of Santiago's art scene, it is worth a visit alone to marvel at the lavish interior, dripping with marble, red velvet, and crystal. The National Chilean Ballet holds productions from April to December, including contemporary and classic productions such as *The Nutcracker.* There are musical events and special productions throughout the year; the best way to find out what's on is to check the theater's website. Tickets are expensive, with prices comparable to the U.S. and Britain;

For Theater Lovers

Santiago's largest summer festival, **Festival Teatro a Mil,** draws international theater troupes, clowns, mimes, and puppeteers from around the world in January to participate in a month-long celebration of the performing arts. Special productions take place in more than 15 playhouses, and the cost is a wallet-friendly 1,000 pesos ($1.70/£1.15) to enter most shows. See www.stgoamil.com for a list of events and venues.

The splendid **Teatro Municipal** was built in 1857 with the collaboration of architect Charles Garnier, who designed the Paris Opera; his influence is seen in the theater's elegant, baroque style and classic French colonnades. Beyond attending a performance here, you can also visit this venerable theater on an hour-long, English-language historical and "behind-the-scenes" tour offered exclusively by Senderos del Sur, every day, for $6 (£4) per person (**© 2/511-5778;** 24-hr. reservation required).

check the website for special promotions offering discounted tickets of up to 50%. You can **reserve and buy tickets** on the website, and select a seat from a diagram. Tickets are also sold over the phone Monday through Friday from 10am to 6pm, or can be bought in person at the theater itself from Monday through Friday from 10am to 7pm, and Saturday and Sunday from 10am to 2pm. Tickets are sold beginning 1 month before the show's starting date.

Visiting orchestras, the Fundación Beethoven, and contemporary acts play at the **Teatro Oriente,** Av. Pedro de Valdivia 099 (**© 2/334-2234**); buy tickets at the theater or by Ticketmaster (see below). **Teatro Universidad de Chile,** Av. Providencia 043 (**© 2/634-5295;** http://teatro.uchile.cl), hosts ballet and symphony productions, both national and international, throughout the year. You may buy tickets at the theater near Plaza Italia or by phone. **Ticketmaster** sells tickets for nearly every act in Santiago at Cine-Hoyts cinemas, at Falabella department stores, via their website, or by calling **© 2/690-2000** from 10am to 7pm.

THE CLUB, MUSIC & DANCE SCENE

Crowd-pulling national and international megabands typically play in the **Estado Nacional,** the **Espacio Riesco,** or the **Estación Mapocho.** Espacio Riesco is on the road to the airport, about a 15-minute drive from Las Condes, and with no public transportation available, you'll need a taxi. Note that Espacio Riesco also hosts electronic music festivals; check the website at www.espacioriesco.cl for the weekly lineup of events. Both Espacio Riesco and Estación Mapocho are infamous for their tinny sound system. You'll find listings for concerts in the daily newspaper or the *El Mercurio*'s website, **www.emol.com,** under "Tiempo Libre."

If you're looking for mellow night out, **Bellavista** is a good bet. Try **La Casa en el Aire ★**, Antonia López de Bello 0125 (**© 2/735-6680;** www.lacasaenelaire.cl), for a candlelit ambience and nightly live music on weekdays and Saturdays at 10pm and Sundays at 9pm. La Casa en el Aire's other location, within the Patio Bellavista complex, between Pío Nono and Constitución at Dardignac, has nightly tango, bolero, and jazz music beginning at 9 or 10pm. The center also hosts occasional readings and screens primarily art-house Latin American movies every Monday night at 8pm; check the website for the full schedule of events at both locations. Across the street, at López de Bello 0126, is **El Perseguidor** ★ (✆ **2/777-6763;** www.elperseguidor.cl), a happening jazz club with nightly performances starting around 11pm.

There are dozens of smaller music venues spread across the city, but the one that attracts the best bands and has the most variety is **La Batuta,** Jorge Washington 52 (✆ **2/274-7096;** www.batuta.cl), located in the Ñuñoa neighborhood, about a 10- to 15-minute taxi ride from downtown and Providencia. The atmosphere is underground, but the crowd profile depends on who's playing. If you arrive after 10pm, there won't be a seat in the house at **Mr Ed,** Suecia 0152 (✆ **2/231-2624**), a lively bar in the otherwise avoidable and tacky Suecia micro-neighborhood, which plays host to an impressive roll call of popular Chilean rock and folk bands and solo artists on the weekends. In Providencia, at Manuel Montt 1684 (✆ **2/269-5942**), **Casino Royale** is a sleek venue that showcases up-and-coming bands on Thursdays, Fridays, and Saturdays in addition to comedy nights, performance art, and literary soirées. The **Club de Jazz** ★★, José Pedro Alessandri 85 (✆ **2/326-5065;** www.clubdejazz.cl), has been jamming since 1943, and it's one of the city's more traditional night spots. Louis Armstrong once played here, and the club continues to pull in talented acts from around Latin America and the world. Live music happens on Thursdays and Fridays, beginning at 10:30pm, and there are two shows at 7pm and 10:30pm on Saturdays. The cover charge is $7 (£4.70).

Santiago's club scene caters to an 18- to 35-year-old crowd, and it all gets going pretty late, from midnight to 6am, on average. If you like electronica, you might check out "fiestas" publicized in the weekend entertainment sections of newspapers that list 1-night-only raves and live music, or, in Bellavista, try **La Feria** at Constitución 275, in an old theater, open Thursday through Saturday. **Blondie,** Alameda 2879 (✆ **2/681-7793;** www.blondie.cl), is a goth/'80s revival/electronic dance club, depending on the night. I recommend **Galpón 9** (no phone) for occasional live bands, a dance floor and bar, and music that ranges from hip-hop to pop to electronica. It's sometimes referred to as "Pub la Casa," and is near the Pablo Neruda museum in Bellavista at Chucre Manzur 9; doors open at 11pm from Thursday to Saturday.

THE BAR SCENE

For the amount of pisco and wine that Chileans drink, bars have never caught on. You'll see a lot of "resto bars," which are restaurants by day and bars by night, many of which still look like restaurants posing as bars at night, with table seating and no "bar" in sight. Bars that also feature live music can be found in "The Club, Music & Dance Scene," earlier. Most bars have happy hours from around 5 to 8pm.

Downtown

Downtown bars are all located in the Parque Forestal/Lastarría/Plaza Mulato Gil area near Cerro Santa Lucía, except for **Confitería Torres,** Av. Alameda 1570 (✆ **2/698-6220**), a renovated turn-of-the-20th-century restaurant/cafe that has live music on weekends. The upmarket, trendy **Catedral** ★★★ (p. 98) is the most happening bar in Santiago and the place to see and be seen. A word to the wise: Get there early, before 9pm, or prepare yourself to wait forever for a table or a place at the bar. Catedral has outdoor seating on the rooftop patio. Nearby, Lastarría Street is lined with cafes and restaurants that are popular for a quiet drink and light conversation. Near the Plaza Mulatto Gil de Castro is **Bar Berri,** Rosal 321, a pub frequented by locals and college students; for even more ambience, walk a block down the dead-end street off Rosal (called "Rosal Interior" a half-block from Lastarría) for **Café Escondido** (✆ **2/632-7356**), a "hidden" cafe/bar with cozy, rough-hewn wood interiors and soft music. A more underground scene (a relative term in Santiago) takes place at **Club Piso 33** at Alamada 1966 (no phone; www.piso33.cl), a rather self-conscious bar and restaurant with a dance floor where techno music and energy drinks spiked with liquor—think Vodka Red Bull—set the scene; it's thoroughly entertaining to behold, even if it does feel passé.

Providencia

The **Bar Liguria** ★, Luis Thayer Ojeda 019 (✆ **2/231-1393**) and Av. Providencia 1373 (✆ **2/235-7914**), has guaranteed broad appeal with a welcoming, infectious atmosphere and entertaining scenery. The two Ligurias are the most happening bars/restaurants in town; both are open until 2am on weeknights, until 5am on weekends, and are closed Sunday, and they serve food practically until closing time. The chic **Bar Yellow,** General Flores 47 (✆ **2/946-5063**), is a hole-in-the-wall where the city's best martinis are shaken and stirred; they also mix mean cocktails from imported liquor—but they're not cheap. Bellavista, long the hot spot for nightclubs mobbed by teens and university students, is now drawing in a more refined (and older) crowd with cosmopolitan bars, many of which are restaurants by day. **Santo Remedio,** Roman Díaz 152, provides one of the funkier atmospheres in Santiago, and it is the only bar open on Sunday nights (except for hotel bars).

In Bellavista, **Etniko** (p. 100) is a standby for a lively, sophisticated crowd, DJ music, a full bar, and an airy atrium that's ideal on a summer evening. Across the street at Constitución 187 is **Ozono** (✆ **2/735-3816**), a bar/restaurant within the old adobe walls of an antique *casona* that has all-white interiors, chill-out music, and outdoor seating. **Constitución,** at Constitución 61 (✆ **2/244-4569**), is the place where industry night owls head when they hang up their aprons for the night. With its casual chic ambience, theatrical bartenders, quality live musicians, and guest DJs, it's the epitome of Bellavista bohème. Around the corner, at Antonio Lopez Bello 0135, is **Off the Record** (✆ **2/777-7710**), a bohemian pub/bar that attracts literary types and has interiors that hearken back to the early 1900s; the walls here are adorned with photos of famous Chilean artists, past and present.

The Suecia micro-neighborhood is a conglomerate of themed restaurants and trashy bars popular with college-age party animals, and recent spates of serious crime here do not make this a recommended place for a cocktail late at night.

Las Condes & Vitacura

The **Ritz-Carlton Bar** (p. 92) bartenders are cocktail experts, and they offer more than 100 varieties of martinis. The bar hosts a Friday-night cocktail party with a DJ, but call ahead to reserve a table. The **Hotel Plaza el Bosque** (p. 92) is the best spot in town for their reasonably priced happy hours and dynamite city views from their 17th floor, with indoor and outdoor seating. **Flannigans's Geo Pub,** Encomenderos 83 (✆ **2/233-6675**), is an Irish pub with the usual pints on draft, and a hit with expats and the Santiaguinos who like to rub shoulders with them. It's open until midnight on weeknights, 2am on weekends. During the summer, you can't beat a table on the outdoor patio of **Akarana** (p. 104), which has an outstanding wine list, well-made cocktails, and mellow live (or DJ) music.

If it's a summer evening and you're looking for a calming place to have a cocktail with a crowd in their 30s and up, head to **Zanzibar,** in the multirestaurant complex BordeRío at Avenida Escrivá de Balaguer (about a $5/£3.30 taxi ride from Las Condes; ✆ **2/218-0120**). This Mediterranean/Moroccan restaurant and bar has an outdoor, candlelit terrace on the second floor furnished with pillows and banquettes, and a relaxing ambience with light chill-out music. Reservations are recommended; Zanzíbar is open at night Monday to Saturday 6:30pm to 1am (until 2am Fri–Sat). Also within the BordeRío is the sexy **Lamu Lounge** (no. 11; ✆ **2/218-0119**), with an African-Asian ambience, DJ music Wednesday to Saturday, and the widest selection of alcohol in Santiago. Lamu Lounge caters to a crowd in their late 20s to mid-40s, and is open Monday through Saturday from 7pm to 2am; reservations are necessary Thursday to Saturday.

CINEMAS

Megaplexes such as CineHoyts and Cinemark, with their multiscreened theaters, feature the widest variety of movies and a popular Monday-to-Wednesday discount price. More avant-garde and independent films can be found in "Cine Arte" theaters, such as **Cine Alameda,** Alameda 139 (✆ **2/664-8842**), and **El Biógrafo,** Lastarría 181 (✆ **2/633-4435**). The entertainment sections of *El Mercurio* and *La Tercera* newspapers list titles, times, and locations, or check www.emol.com.

7

Around Santiago: The Central Valley, Peaks & Coastal Region

Santiago is an excellent jumping-off point for a wealth of distinctive attractions and destinations: Fine beaches, an eccentric port town, nature preserves, serrated mountains, hot springs, and wineries are just a few examples of what's nearby. You'll also find a multitude of outdoor activities, including skiing at world-renowned resorts, hiking, rafting, biking, horseback riding, and more. Although some of the destinations listed in this chapter require an overnight stay, most attractions are within a half-hour to 2-hour drive from Santiago, meaning it is possible to pack a lot of action into just a few days.

This chapter proposes ideas for 1-day or multiday adventures outside of Santiago. You'll find information about where to find the best ski resorts, where to go wine-tasting, where to see Chile's rural traditions and old-world haciendas, and where to take a soak in a hot spring or visit a spa.

EXPLORING THE REGION

Many wineries, ski resorts, and coastal communities are close enough to Santiago to be explored on day trips, but your travel experience will be enriched if you opt to spend the night high in the Andes at a ski resort, or at a cozy B&B in the wine country. This way you'll spend less time in a vehicle and more time enveloping yourself in truly beautiful natural environments. A rental car provides a lot of freedom to explore at your own pace, especially if you are heading to the coast or visiting wineries. I've known more than a few travelers who, upon arrival or departure from Santiago, rent a vehicle at the airport, drive to the coast or the wine country, return the rental at the airport, and then taxi into Santiago (or vice versa). A good road map is essential. Once you exit the main highways, signposting is generally poor and Chileans will likely send you in the wrong direction than admit ignorance or an inability to help you.

Taking a bus is not a bad option either—in fact, Santiago's national coach system is better than that of the U.S. Buses are modern and clean, and there are usually a dozen or so daily departures to most major destinations. Bus terminals are located downtown but can by reached by Metro. Taxis wait at regional bus terminals to deliver you to your hotel or wherever you need to go.

1 THE COASTAL REGION

Beach retreats are the Chileans' favorite weekend getaway, and this chapter covers, in depth, Chile's better-known coastal cities, boisterous **Viña del Mar** and intriguing **Valparaíso.** Other smaller villages that dot the coast have their own strongly defined characteristics (and clear-cut socioeconomic levels), and visitors with a rental car will take

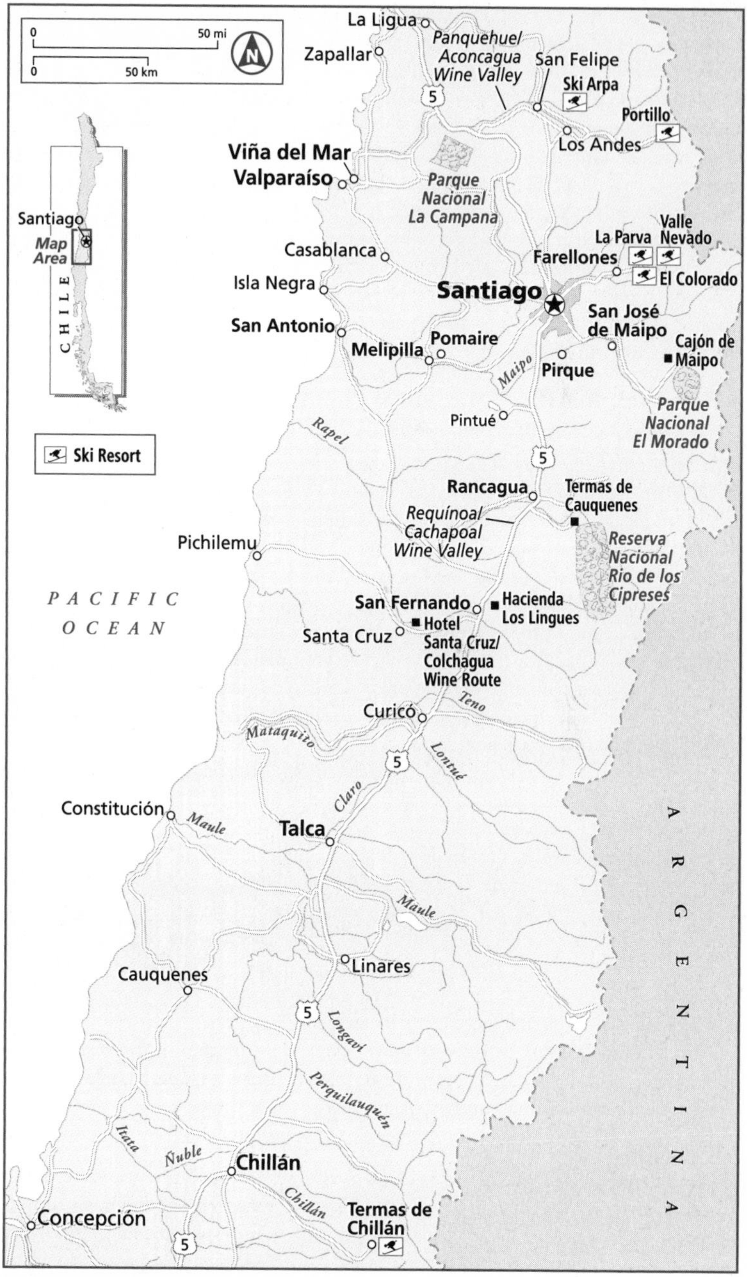
0
50 mi
0
50 km
N
Santiago
Map Area
CHILE
Ski Resort
PACIFIC OCEAN
La Ligua
Zapallar
Panquehue/ Aconcagua Wine Valley
San Felipe
Ski Arpa
Portillo
Los Andes
Viña del Mar
Valparaíso
Parque Nacional La Campana
Valle Nevado
La Parva
Farellones
El Colorado
Casablanca
Isla Negra
Santiago
San Antonio
San José de Maipo
Pomaire
Melipilla
Cajón de Maipo
Maipo
Pirque
Parque Nacional El Morado
Pintué
Rapel
Rancagua
Termas de Cauquenes
Requínoa/ Cachapoal Wine Valley
Reserva Nacional Río de los Cipreses
Pichilemu
San Fernando
Hacienda Los Lingues
Hotel Santa Cruz/ Colchagua Wine Route
Santa Cruz
Teno
Curicó
Mataquito
Lontué
Claro
Constitución
Maule
Talca
Maule
ARGENTINA
Linares
Cauquenes
Longaví
Perquilauquén
Itata
Ñuble
Chillán
Chillán
Termas de Chillán
Concepción
5

pleasure in discovering each new village around the bend. You can also arrange a tour to coastal destinations that are not part of the "usual" itinerary.

Zapallar is home to Chile's moneyed elite, and it's the prettiest cove in the region. **Cachagua** and **Maitencillo** are where the upper-middle and middle classes own their second homes. **Con Con** is where you'll find the cheapest—and the freshest—seafood restaurants, and a Radisson resort; **Reñaca** is where the young and gregarious socialize and loll in the sun. Farther south is another middle-class hub, **Algarrobo** (nothing much to see here), and down-at-the-heels **Cartegena,** the oldest seaside resort in Chile, which has now fallen out of favor (to give you an idea, Chileans commonly use the phrase "tackier than a honeymoon in Cartegena"). A popular destination on the tourist map these days is **Isla Negra,** because Pablo Neruda spent most of his time in his house here, which is now a museum (p. 153), and you can visit the up-and-coming San Antonio wine region on the way. The port city of San Antonio, south of Isla Negra, is a grim, desolate place that is often unavoidable for travelers who pass through due to restricted coastal access north of Isla Negra.

VINA DEL MAR

120km (74 miles) NW of Santiago; 8km (5 miles) N of Valparaíso

Viña del Mar is Chile's largest and best-known beach resort town. The city was founded in 1874 as a weekend retreat and garden residence for the wealthy elite from Valparaíso and Santiago, and it has remained a top destination for Santiaguinos ever since, although the ultrafashionable are now electing to build their second home in less-developed and therefore more exclusive coastal areas such as Tunquen and Quintay. Viña's manicured lawns, monolithic 1960s apartment buildings, and sandy beaches filled with sunbathers are an extreme contrast to the ramshackle streets of Valparaíso. Most Chileans call Viña del Mar simply "Viña"; you'll call it "chaos" if you come any time between December and late February, when thousands of vacationers arrive, crowding beaches and snarling traffic. On the other hand, there exists a heightened sense of excitement during these months with so much activity happening in the area. If the lure of the ocean is compelling for you, remember that Viña is certainly no beach paradise. The ocean is icy and too rough for swimming, and the characterless and crowded beaches pale in comparison to the Mediterranean or Caribbean. But, having said that, if you enjoy the overarching indulgence and expectation that such resorts imbue, a couple of days in Viña may be to your liking—especially if you reside for a night at the superlative Hotel del Mar.

Along the coast of Viña are plenty of fine beaches, but the beach to see and be seen at is in Reñaca, about 6km (3¾ miles) north of Viña (see "What to See & Do," later in this section). Unfortunately, the Humboldt Current that travels up the coast from Antarctica makes for chilly swimming conditions, even during the summer, but regardless of the season, Viña is a wonderfully relaxing place to spend 1 or 2 days.

The city is divided into two sectors: downtown and the beachfront. Travelers are happiest lodging near the beach; however, the downtown area is a tad more "Chilean," and you're really only a 15- to 20-minute walk from the beach.

ESSENTIALS

Getting There

BY CAR Viña is 134km (83 miles) from Santiago and is reached by the highway Rte. 68. Driving to Viña from Santiago is quite easy: Simply hop onto the Costanera Norte headed west, and follow it all the way to the coast (the Costanera turns into Rte. 68).

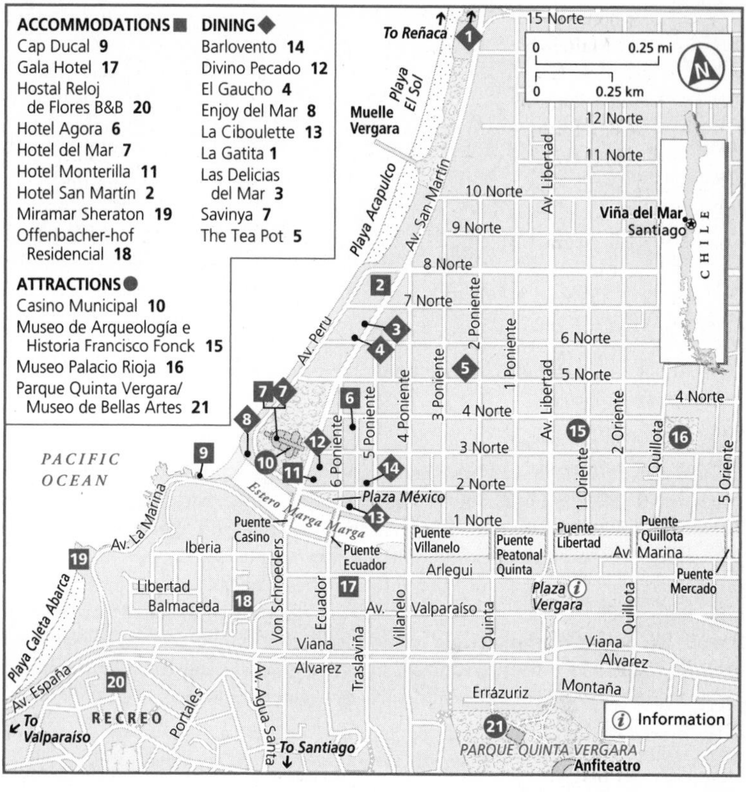

There are two tolls along the way that each cost 1,200 pesos ($2.05/£1.35) from Monday to 5pm on Friday, and 1,900 pesos ($3.25/£2.15) from 5pm Friday to Sunday. Note that **street parking** in Viña is scarce in January and February.

BY BUS **Tur Bus** (✆ **600/660-6600;** www.turbus.cl) and **Pullman** (✆ **600/320-3200;** www.pullman.cl) leave from the Terminal Alameda in Santiago, located at Av. Alameda 3750 (Metro: Univ. de Santiago), every 15 minutes from 6:30am to 10:30pm (Tur Bus), and 6:10am to 10:10pm (Pullman); the cost is $6.75 (£4.50) one-way. During weekends, especially December through March, it is strongly recommended that you buy your ticket in advance from any Tur Bus or Pullman office in Santiago (your hotel can give you the address of the nearest office). The trip takes around 1½ hours. The bus terminal in Viña is located at Avenida Valparaíso and Quilpué, near the main plaza, and there are taxis available.

BY TRAIN The **Metrotren** (also known as the "Merval"; ✆ **32/238-1500**) connects Viña with Valparaíso, leaving every 5 to 10 minutes from 7:30am to 10pm during weekdays, and every 15 to 20 minutes from 9:30am to 9pm on Saturdays, Sundays, and holidays. To ride the train, you must first make a one-time purchase: a rechargeable card for $1 (70p) that you then charge with enough money to cover the cost of your trip. If you're with friends or family, you need only purchase one card for your group.

Getting Around

All attractions in Viña can be reached on foot with streets organized according to a grid layout that is easy to navigate. Taxis are inexpensive and are available either by hailing one in the street or calling **Taxi Alfonso** (© **32/288-1870**) or **ABA Taxi** (© **32/297-9399**). The town is divided into two sections along the Marga Marga, a former lagoon, swaths of which now form the town's main parking lot. North of Marga Marga, you'll find the casino and access to the 3.5km (2.1 miles) of coastline fronted by monolithic condominiums, rowdy bars, and theme restaurants catering primarily to tourists. South of Marga Marga stretches Avenida Valparaíso, the main shopping avenue punctuated with all the familiar global brand stores and fast-food outlets. Sleek designer stores and shopping malls are concentrated along the 5 blocks west of Plaza Vergarda; just walk west toward the ocean as far as Calle Ecuador. A taxi to Valparaíso costs between $6 and $9 (£4–£6) one-way. A couple of blocks south, the exotic Quinta Vergara Park is ideal for an afternoon stroll.

Visitor Information

The **Oficina de Turismo de Viña** is on Plaza Vergara, next to the post office near avenidas Libertad and Arlegui (© **800/800-830** toll-free in Chile; www.visitevinadelmar.cl). Summer hours are weekdays from 9am to 9pm, Saturday and Sunday from 10am to 9pm; off-season hours are weekdays from 10am to 7pm (closed 2–3pm), and Saturday and Sunday from 10am to 7pm. The helpful staff speaks English and can provide visitors with maps, events details, and accommodations information, including private cabin rentals. The **Sernatur office,** located on the third floor (office no. 303), at Av. Valparaíso 507 (© **2/268-3355;** www.sernatur.cl), is also very helpful and has information and maps on the entire region. It's open Monday through Friday 8:30am to 5:30pm.

SPECIAL EVENTS Every second or third week of February, Viña plays host to the **Festival de la Canción,** a weeklong gala event held at the Quinta Vergara Park amphitheater. It's Chile's largest music festival, drawing nearly 30,000 spectators nightly. Apart from national and international Latin acts such as Daddy Yankee and Fito Paez, past festivals have booked such wild cards as Tom Jones and Franz Ferdinand as part of the lineup. Viña bursts at the seams during this event, and hotel reservations are imperative. During the second or third week of October, Viña hosts the acclaimed **Festival Cine Viña del Mar** film festival (www.festivalcinevinadelmar.cl). Nearly 90% of films showcased during this event are of Latin American origin and in Spanish and Portuguese only.

Fast Facts Viña del Mar

Banks Most major banks can be found on Avenida Arlegui, and although they're open Monday through Friday from 9am to 2pm only, nearly all have ATMs (Redbancs).

Car Rentals Try **Alamo,** Agua Santa 402 (© 32/262-5297; www.alamochile.com); **Avis,** Arlegui 201 (© 32/268-7037; www.avischile.cl); **Budget,** 7 Norte 1023 (© 32/268-3420; www.budget.cl); **Rosselot,** Av. Libertad 892 (© 32/238-2373; www.rosselot.cl), and Av. Alvarez 762 (© 32/238-2888); **Hertz,** Av. Quillota 766

(✆ 32/238-1025; www.hertz.com); or **Verschae Rent-A-Car,** Av. Libertad 1045 (✆ 32/226-7300; www.verschae.cl). Daily rental prices average $50 (£33) per day for a compact car, and $75 (£50) for a midrange vehicle.

Currency Exchange *Cambios* (money-exchange houses) are open in the summer Monday through Friday from 9am to 2pm and 3 to 8pm, and Saturday from 9am to 2pm; and in winter Monday through Saturday 9am to 2pm and 4 to 7pm, and Saturday from 9am to 2pm. Several *cambios* can be found along Avenida Arlegui.

Emergencies For **police,** dial ✆ **133;** for **fire,** dial ✆ **132;** and for an **ambulance,** dial ✆ **131.**

Hospital For medical attention, go to **Hospital Gustavo Fricke** on calles Alvarez and Simón Bolívar (✆ **32/267-5067,** or 32/652328 for emergencies).

WHAT TO SEE & DO

The Coastline

Just south of the Marga Marga, the whimsical **Castillo Wulff,** with its Bavarian-style turrets, is quite the architectural anachronism. Built for coal baron Gustavo Adolfo Wulff in the early 20th century, the Maritime Museum that was housed here for many years has been transformed into a cultural center; it's worth taking a stroll around inside to view the eccentric interior. Just south, **Playa Caleta Abarca** beach is in a protected bay near the entrance to Viña del Mar, next to the town's poster-child "flower clock," a meticulously landscaped flower-bed complete with working dials and flanked by exotic palms. On weekends, Playa Caleta beach is an animated scene, with groups of friends and families setting up shop for the day with picnic tables, barbecues, and boom boxes.

In the northeast, fronting rows of terraced high-rise apartment buildings, you'll find **Playa Acapulco, Playa Mirasol,** and **Playa Las Salinas** (the latter is near the naval base). The sea here tends to be too rough for swimming. These beaches also see throngs of vacationers and families in the summer. **Reñaca,** just 6km (3.7 miles) up the coast, is *the* coastal hot spot. The first stretch of the beach is popular with families, while the end is the "cool" spot frequented by the young for its sleek cocktail bars and ebullient discos. There are several glass-enclosed beach cafes along the principal road here for a snack and plenty of cheap seafood restaurants. Because Chileans party late into the night, you won't see many people on any beach until about noon. To get here, take a taxi (about $4–$7/£2.70–£4.70 one-way) or a bus (nos. 1, 10, or 111 at av. Libertad and 15 Norte).

It's also worth taking a drive north for 10km (6.2 miles) to **Concón,** for splendid coastal views and a chance to see fat sea lions sunning themselves on the rocky shore. Follow the coastal road Avenida San Martín until it becomes Avenida Jorge Montt, and continue along the winding, two-lane road as it hugs the shore. When you tire of the drive, simply turn around and head back the same way. This run-down fishing village, overlooked by smug, pristine villas and mansions, makes for a fascinating contrast to the airs of Viña. It's worth strolling down to the frenetic quay here, La Boca, where *marisquerías* purvey über fresh fish, shellfish, and crustaceans.

The Top Attractions

Casino Municipal ★ Built in 1930, the Casino Municipal was the most luxurious building in its day and is worth a visit even if you're not a gambler. The interior has been remodeled over time, but the facade has withstood the caprices of many a developer and is still as handsome as the day it opened. Semiformal attire is required to enter the gaming room: no T-shirts, jeans, or sneakers. Minimum bets of 5,000 pesos ($8/£4) may deter some budget travelers, although there are slot machines and video poker. The casino holds periodic art exhibits on its second floor, and there are three bars if you're looking for nightlife that's a step up from the teen clubs in Viña.

Plaza Colombia, btw. Av. San Martín and Av. Perú. ✆ **32/250-0600.** www.hoteldelmar.cl. Hours vary, but generally in winter game room Mon–Thurs noon–4am, Fri–Sun 24 hr.; in summer daily 24 hr.

Museo de Arqueología e Historia Francisco Fonck ★★ Founded in 1937, this highly recommended natural history museum is named after German doctor Francisco Fonck (1830–1912), a pioneer in the archaeological exploration of Central Chile, who bequeathed his extensive collections of artifacts from Chile, Peru, and Ecuador to the Chilean government. The natural history display at the Museo Fonck spans the entire second floor, but what really warrants a visit here is the museum's 1,400-piece collection of Rapa Nui (Easter Island) indigenous art and archaeological artifacts, including one of the only six Moai sculptures found outside the island (the others are in England, the U.S., Paris, Brussels, and La Serena in Chile). This monumental piece brought from Easter Island in 1950 stands majestically in the garden by the museum's entrance. The display is more complete than the archaeological museum on Easter Island itself. Also on display are art and archaeological remnants of all cultures in Chile, and the size of the museum is just right to not grow tiresome—you'll need about 45 minutes here. There is also an on-site store selling jewelry, Easter Island art replicas, woolen goods, and more.

Av. 4 Norte 784. ✆ **32/268-6753.** www.museofonck.cl. Admission $2.70 (£1.80) adults, 45¢ (30p) children. Mon–Fri 10am–6pm; Sat, Sun, and holidays 10am–2pm (Oct–Mar Sat 10am–6pm).

Museo Palacio Rioja ★★ The lushly landscaped grounds that surround this grand Belle Epoque stone mansion are only a fraction of what they once were when wealthy Spaniard banker Fernando Rioja took residence in 1910. Originally spanning 4 blocks, with a classical facade dominated by stout Corinthian columns, this palace took opulence to a new level during its time. It's well worthwhile taking one of the daily tours (around 30 min., in Spanish only) to absorb the grandeur of elite life during the early 20th century. The rich interiors, made of oak and intricately carved stone, feature a split double staircase and baroque, rococo, and Chesterfield furniture imported from Spain and France. The palace hosts a range of classical concerts and theater performances in addition to screening movies.

Quillota 214. ✆ **32/248-3664.** Admission $1 (70p) adults, 50¢ (30p) children. Tues–Sun 10am–1:30pm and 3–5:30pm.

Parque Quinta Vergara/Museo de Bellas Artes ★★ A compact but absolutely lovely park, the Quinta Vergara pays homage to the future with its spaceshiplike music amphitheater, and to the past, with its converted 1910 Venetian-style palace, the former home of historical heavyweights the Alvarez/Vergara family, now converted into a fine arts museum. Quinta Vergara was originally the site of an early 19th-century hacienda, which was acquired by Portuguese shipping magnate Francisco Alvarez and his wife Dolores in 1840. Dolores was a keen botanist and in between bouts of pre-Raphaeilite languor, she transformed the gardens into an exotic Eden featuring many exotic plants brought from Europe and Asia by her seafaring son, Salvador. Taking center stage in the park, the striking Italianate Palacio Vergara was built in 1906 by Blanca Vergara, Salvador's granddaughter. When Blanca's mother married José Francisco Vergara, the man who founded Viña del Mar in 1874, two of Chile's most influential families were united. The mansion now houses the family's collection of baroque European paintings, as well as oil paintings of Chilean VIPs during the 19th and early 20th century. Every February, this park fills with music lovers who come for the annual Festival of Song, which features largely Latin pop boy bands hotly pursued by cadres of screaming groupies. The rest of the year the park is an idyllic spot for a quiet stroll.

Near Plaza Parroquia. Museum: ✆ **32/225-2481.** Admission 75¢ (50p) adults, 35¢ (25p) children. Tues–Sun 10am–2pm and 3–6pm. Park: Free admission. Daily 7am–6pm (until 7pm in summer).

WHERE TO STAY

Very Expensive

Hotel del Mar ★★★ Kids Moments For many travelers, reason alone for staying a couple of nights in Viña is the opportunity to revel in the unbridled luxury, exquisite taste, and superlative amenities of this, the city's finest hotel. The Greco-Roman style Hotel del Mar presents one of those unmissable opportunities to experience five-star luxury at a price that won't break the bank. Nestled in the heart of the action near restaurants and shops and fronting the beach, the hotel is also adjacent to the city's historic, 1930s-era casino. Sun worshippers will delight in basking glamorously on the sweeping terrace, which curves like an amphitheater above the ocean. If the beach is too crowded for your liking, the spectacular glass-enclosed indoor pool with Roman pillars affords panoramic views of the ocean. The guest room aesthetic is sober and understated, decorated in neutral tones of gray, chocolate, and mahogany; standard and deluxe rooms are on the north and south ends of the hotel with city/sea views, while suites are in the center, offering a wide-open view of the sea. All rooms have balconies. The city's best restaurant, Savinya (see "Where to Dine," later) is here, too.

Av. San Martín 199. ✆ **32/250-0800.** Fax 32/250-0801. www.hoteldelmar.cl. 60 units. $250–$300 (£167–£200) double standard Sun–Thurs, $231–$285 (£154–£190) Fri–Sat; $330–$390 (£220–£260) suite Sun–Thurs, $377–$446 (£251–£297) Fri–Sat. AE, DC, MC, V. Valet parking. **Amenities:** 4 restaurants; bar; indoor pool; solarium; health club; children's game room; 24-hr. room service; babysitting; laundry service. *In room:* A/C, plasma TV w/pay-per-view movies, DVD and CD player, hair dryer.

Miramar Sheraton ★★★ Glittering in white-and-glass minimalism, Viña's newest world-class hotel flung open its doors with grand fanfare in 2006, promising luxury, sweeping ocean views, a state-of-the-art spa and fitness center, and an endless range of high-end services. On paper, it certainly delivers. The Sheraton's guest rooms are gorgeous and plush, seductively enticing you to linger in the room longer than you normally would at any given hotel. Every detail, from the silky cotton sheets to the pricey, stylish furniture, is impeccable. All guest rooms come with ocean views, with small terraces. (Book a corner room facing Valparaíso for additional privacy.) The Sheraton's downfall resides in its aloof aura and echoing interiors. Though a little more warmth has been creeping into the design, the Sheraton still lacks the personalized service of its world-class peers. The hotel's location, immediately across from Viña's famous flower clock, a 10-minute walk to beachfront restaurants, is also not quite as central as it could be. If you're a spa lover or are seeking pool time, this is your place, however.

Av. Marina 15. ✆ **32/238-8600.** www.starwoodhotels.com/sheraton. 142 units. $269 (£179) double; $585 (£390) suite. AE, DC, MC, V. Valet parking. **Amenities:** 2 restaurants; bar; indoor and outdoor pools; state-of-the-art health club and spa; concierge; 24-hr. room service; babysitting; laundry service. *In room:* Plasma TV, minibar, hair dryer.

Expensive

Gala Hotel ★ The high-rise Gala hotel is a contemporary hotel within walking distance of the beach, offering a myriad of facilities that facilitate affordable pampering. The rooms are your average beachside rooms with generic art and flimsy, IKEA-style furnishings, but they are light, breezy, and kept spotlessly clean. Most travelers find that the array of facilities, as well as the location and price, compensates for the generic overtones. The hotel often plays host to large conferences, which precludes a sense of intimacy and escapism.

Arelegui 273, Viña del Mar. ✆ **32/232-1500.** Fax 32/268-9568. www.galahotel.cl. 64 units. $145 (£97) standard double; $163 (£109) suite. AE, DC, MC, V. **Amenities:** Restaurant; bar; outdoor heated pool; sauna; business center; babysitting; laundry service. *In room:* A/C, cable TV, minibar, hair dryer.

Hotel San Martín ★★ Kids The Hotel San Martín's spotless guest rooms bear a whiff of '50s modern with clean lines, polished wood, and chrome fixtures, but the salmon pink or floral bedspreads and coordinated drapery may prove too fusty and garish for those with minimalist tastes. At these prices, it's worth paying extra for the terra-cotta-hued suites, which are more sophisticated and spacious. Double rooms here are tight; if you need a lot of room consider their suites or opt against staying here. Light sleepers should also be forewarned that there is a lack of effective soundproofing; noise from the street and the beach can be particularly bothersome, day and night. Polished parquet floors with carpet runners and halogen lighting lend the hotel's public spaces coziness. The hotel has five rooms adapted to wheelchair users. Only the north wing has sea views, and those rooms come at a higher price. The hotel's central location is very convenient; and, while there's no pool, with the beach at your feet, who needs one?

Av. San Martín 667. ✆ **32/268-9191.** Fax 32/268-9195. www.hotelsanmartin.cl. 160 units. $145 (£97) double with street view; $160 (£107) double with sea view; $200 (£133) suite. AE, DC, MC, V. **Amenities:** Restaurant; bar; tiny gym; sauna; room service; laundry service; rooms for those with limited mobility. *In room:* Cable TV, Wi-Fi, minibar, hair dryer, safe.

Moderate

Cap Ducal ★ Built to resemble a ship moored to the shore, this offbeat hotel has been a Viña institution since 1936. The hotel's location perched above the coastline affords views of the pounding surf from all of its 25 rooms, which cantilever out over the ocean. Balconies afford prime viewing territory for the rich profusion of birdlife and sea lions. Inside, the nautical theme continues, with narrow halls with wood-paneled walls and brass handrails; the low-slung rooms look and feel much like a ship's berth. On the downside, potential irritations do lurk beneath the hotel's overarching coziness. The hot water can be sporadic and the hotel's age clearly shows in its worn furnishings; the carpet could stand to be replaced and some rooms reek of smoke (ask for a nonsmoking room). Still, it's an overall welcoming and clean place to spend the night. The beach is a 10- to 15-minute walk away. The restaurant is well known for its superb seafood dishes.

Av. Marina 51, Viña del Mar. ✆ **32/262-6655.** Fax 32/266-5471. www.capducal.cl. 25 units. $100–$120 (£67–£80) standard double; $125–$150 (£83–£100) junior suite. AE, DC, MC, V. **Amenities:** Restaurant; cafe; laundry service. *In room:* Cable TV, minibar.

Hotel Monterilla ★★ Kids Finds This delightful, family-run boutique hotel, located near the beach and casino, is an excellent value and one of the best-kept secrets in Viña del Mar. Cheerful service and a central location are definite draws, but the hotel's contemporary decor is what really makes the Monterilla special. Chromatic furniture contrasted against white carpet, and walls adorned with colorful postmodern art, provide crisp, eye-catching surroundings, and though the guest rooms are not huge, they're fresh and comfortable. There is one apartment with a kitchenette for four guests, a good bet for families staying longer than a few days. Despite its central location, the hotel is tucked away on 2 (Dos) Norte Street and feels far from the hubbub. The Monterilla offers frequent promotions for parents with kids.

2 Norte 65, Plaza México, Viña del Mar. ✆ **32/297-6950.** Fax 32/683576. www.monterilla.cl. 20 units. $113 (£75) standard double; $157 (£105) suite. AE, DC, MC, V. **Amenities:** Cafeteria; bar; laundry service. *In room:* Cable TV, Wi-Fi, minibar, hair dryer.

Inexpensive

Hostal Reloj de Flores B&B ★ Dollar for dollar, the Hostal Reloj de Flores offers decent value. There's nothing fancy about the place, but guest rooms, especially those with private bathrooms, are clean, comfortable, and brightly decorated. It's just a hop, skip, and a jump to the Caleta Abarca Beach (but a healthy walk to restaurants along the beachfront). As a converted home, rooms are differently sized and decorated—some are contemporary, with colorful duvet comforters, and others have antique headboards. Two rooms have shared bunks, and some private rooms have shared bathrooms. Try to nab their only room with a balcony, as it is the same price. As with most B&Bs, service is exceptionally friendly, and there's a shared kitchen and barbecue area. The staff will also help to arrange tours in the area.

Calle Los Baños 7. ✆ **32/248-5242.** Fax 32/262-1063. www.hostalrelojdefloresbb.com. 13 units. $50 (£33) double with shared bathroom, $54 (£36) double with private bathroom. No credit cards. **Amenities:** Cafe; shared kitchen; Internet access; babysitting; laundry service. *In room:* Cable TV, no phone.

Hotel Agora ★ This pristine art deco hotel is an absolute gem, a paradigm of tasteful simplicity and low-cost chic tucked away on a peaceful street just a 15-minute walk to the ocean. With its stark, rectilinear form and white and pastel color scheme, it creates the immediate impression of a tropical playground. A true rarity in Viña, rooms are a blaze of hallucinogenic color with acid greens, ocean blues, and egg yolk yellows contrasting with polished wooden floors and minimalist bed frames. Rooms are discreetly appointed with TVs, minifridges, and reading lights.

Poniente 253, Viña del Mar. ✆ **32/269-4669.** Fax 32/269-5165. www.hotelagora.cl. 16 units. $55 (£37) standard double. AE, DC, MC, V. **Amenities:** Cafeteria; bar; laundry service. *In room:* Cable TV, minibar, hair dryer.

Offenbacher-hof Residencial ★ Housed in a Victorian house dating to 1905, perched high atop Cerro Castillo, the Offenbacher has sweeping views of the city and the hills beyond, and a splendid glass-enclosed patio. It is by far one of the more interesting and best value places to lodge, and its location on this historic hill puts you near some of the city's oldest homes—a delightful location, but guests must either grab a taxi to reach the beach, or hoof it. The mix-and-match decor is on the funky side, but it's hard to balk at the flea market furniture when you consider the panoramic views. Superior doubles are worth the extra $10 (£5) for better views and substantially more space. Their three doubles that open onto the patio are darker and less private. The German-Chilean family that runs the Offenbacher is cheerful, helpful, and always on hand to provide comprehensive information on cultural tours and activities throughout the region.

Balmaceda 102, Cerro Castillo, Viña del Mar. ✆ **32/621483.** Fax 32/662432. www.offenbacher-hof.cl. 15 units. $60–$66 (£40–£44) standard double; $70–$76 (£47–£51) superior double. AE, DC, MC, V. **Amenities:** Cafe; bar; gym; whirlpool; sauna; tours and airport transfers; laundry service; solarium. *In room:* Cable TV, Wi-Fi.

Valparaíso has taken the lead as the gastronomic nucleus of the central coastal region, leaving Viña in the dust. Frankly, it's a mystery as to why there are so few good restaurants here considering its importance as a tourism destination. Expect a lot of fast-food joints, beer halls, and theme restaurants with loud music and wine-barrel decor.

If you are spending a few days in town, I recommend you take a drive up the coast one afternoon to Concón (16km/10 miles from Viña) or one of the tiny hamlets before it—this is where the locals go for fresh seafood in one of the many *picadas* (something like a dive—cheap but hearty and delicious). One of the best *picadas* is **La Gatita,** Avenida Borgoño in Higuerillas (✆ **32/281-4235;** Sun–Wed noon–4pm and Thurs–Sat noon–midnight), a wildly popular restaurant with an agonizingly long wait if you arrive any time between 1:30 and 3pm on weekends. There is no street number, so look for a small fish market on the left-hand side of the road just after passing the yacht harbor (when driving north). Try Chile's famous *caldillo de congrio* (conger eel soup) here. Another local favorite is **Las Delicias,** Av. Borgoña 25370, in Concón (no phone; daily 11am–5pm), which only sells greasy-good fried empanadas, specializing in seafood empanada fillings such as crab, shrimp, and a delicious *macha pino,* or razor clams sautéed in onions.

Most restaurants in Viña are centered on Avenida San Martín along the coast. For afternoon tea, try **The Tea Pot,** 5 Norte 475 (✆ **32/268-7671;** Mon–Fri 10am–2pm and 4:30–9pm, Sat 10am–9pm), which offers more than 60 kinds of tea and delicious pastries. Also consider trying the seafood restaurant at **Cap Ducal** (see "Where to Stay" earlier).

Expensive

La Ciboulette ★ Finds BELGIAN/CHILEAN An altogether unwelcoming facade keeps tourists away from this tiny restaurant, but La Ciboulette is a local favorite and has won various culinary awards for its home-style, Belgian-influenced cuisine prepared by old fashioned restaurateurs who are passionate about the delicate balance of each dish; ask for a substitution at your peril. The chalkboard menu changes seasonally so that every element is very fresh, and their wine list is quite good. Each dish is flavorful and transcends the homely quality of a traditional, local Belgian bistro; snails are drenched in a rich sauce of Camembert, almonds, and Noilly Prat while the rib-eye steak is doused with a light oriental pepper sauce. For dessert, try the juicy strawberries laced with pepper and served with homemade ice cream.

1 Norte 191-A. ✆ **32/269-0084.** Reservations recommended. Main courses $17–$21 (£11–£14). No credit cards. Tues–Sun 1–3:30pm and 8pm–midnight.

Savinya ★★★ INTERNATIONAL Savinya is part of the Hotel del Mar and known for its outstanding haute cuisine. It's Viña's most refined and expensive restaurant, and the place to go if you're looking to blow your budget on a special meal. Still, when compared to restaurants of the same caliber in the U.S., the prices at Savinya could be considered quite reasonable. The menu changes seasonally, but owing to the chef's Italian heritage, the cuisine tends to be slanted toward richly elegant pasta creations, impeccably executed and blending uncommon flavors and textures that work surprisingly well together. A white truffle infusion here and a foie gras sliver there add a lavish decadence that transforms an otherwise hearty Mediterranean staple into haute cuisine. For purists, the unadulterated meat dishes provide intense flavors and a silken texture. Attentive, agreeable service comes with the price, as does an elegant-chic ambience, and gigantic picture windows that offer a gorgeous view overlooking the ocean.

Av. Perú and Los Héroes. ✆ **32/250-0800.** www.hoteldelmar.com. Reservations recommended for dinner. Main courses $16–$24 (£11–£16). AE, DC, MC, V. Daily 12:30–3:30pm and 8pm–12:30am.

Moderate

Barlovento ★ MODERN CHILEAN Barlovento is a perfect distillation of Viña's thoroughly modern night scene. The menu features casual, well-prepared dishes that are ideal for late night munchies and shared plates. There are a few heartier dishes, such as a very cheesy onion soup, fettuccine with seafood, and ginger-marinated salmon, but stick to what Barlovento does best: wraps, sandwiches, salads, and appetizer platters to share among friends. Another major draw for Barlovento is that the bartenders here really know how to make a proper cosmopolitan, dry martini, and a Bloody Mary, a skill not often well honed in Chile. Barlovento's minimalist look of cement, steel, glass, and wrap-around windows is quite the architectural anachronism. Barlovento's live DJ music on weekends packs in a young, lively adult crowd of hipsters. If you are in the mood for something a little more refined, there is a subterranean wine cellar for tastings.

2 Norte 195. ✆ **32/297-7472.** www.barlovento.cl. Reservations accepted for groups. Main courses $8–$14 (£5.30–£9.30); sandwiches and wraps $6 (£4). AE, DC, MC, V. Daily 6pm–2am.

Divino Pecado ★★ ITALIAN This is hands-down my favorite restaurant in Viña del Mar because it combines all the elements of an enjoyable dining experience: owner-attended, a pleasant waitstaff, delectable fresh pastas and seafood, and a trattoria-style dining area that's cheery during the day, and romantic at night. For an aperitif, order a pisco sour—this restaurant is known for its delicious Peruvian variety. Also, the wine list is extensive and offers excellent value for the price. Don't expect traditional Italian home-style cooking; each dish promises to be a taste sensation with interesting and unusual combinations of traditional Italian ingredients infused with ethnic herbs and spices and some modern European twists. "Black" raviolis are made with calamari ink and stuffed with curried shrimp, while the fettuccine with lamb is garnished with aromatic clumps of rosemary. Divino Pecado specializes in specialty fish such as sole, the delicate *mero* (grouper), and Easter Island tuna, and there are meats such as filet mignon. Pastas here are served very al dente, so let your waiter know if you'd like your noodles cooked some other way.

Av. San Martín 180 (in front of casino). ✆ **32/297-5790.** divinopecado@terra.cl. Reservations recommended. Main courses $11–$16 (£7.30–£11). AE, DC, MC, V. Daily 12:30–3:30pm and 8–11pm (Sat–Sun until 1am).

El Gaucho ★ ARGENTINE/STEAK Carnivores will find a home at El Gaucho, which dishes out succulent cuts of just about any kind of meat, served sizzling off their huge indoor *parrilla* (grill). The Argentine-style "interiors" appetizers include blood sausage, sweetbreads, and crispy intestines. If that doesn't make your mouth water, try starting with grilled provolone cheese with oregano. Entrees include beef loin, ribs, chicken, sausages, and other grilled items and salads. Wood floors and brick walls create a warm, comfortable ambience.

Av. San Martín 435. ✆ **32/269-3502.** Main courses $8–$14 (£5.30–£9.30). AE, DC, MC, V. Daily 12:30–3:30pm and 7:30–11pm (Fri–Sat until 1am).

Las Delicias del Mar SEAFOOD Las Delicias serves inspired seafood dishes in a comfortable, plant-filled environment, with attentive service. The restaurant is one of the best bets in town for fresh fish dishes, which former TV chef Raul Madinagoitía executes with flair and imagination. Each recipe has a story; the *crema de almejas* soup is an homage to a humble Hamptons clam chowder, while the Corvino Dicaprio—sea bass steamed with crab, mussels, shrimp, and white wine—was baptized in honor of the eponymous Leonardo following his recent visit. The excellent paella, prepared according to a centuries-old traditional Spanish recipe, is always a hit. The wine list is also one of the most discriminating in Viña and the classic desserts, such as the crème brûlée, have the power to stir heavenly rapture. There is also a sister restaurant in Reñaca.

Av. San Martín 459. ✆ **32/290-1837.** Main courses $13–$17 (£8.70–£11). AE, DC, MC, V. Daily 12:30–4pm and 7pm–midnight.

Inexpensive

Enjoy del Mar ★★ INTERNATIONAL The best alfresco dining venue in Viña is on Enjoy del Mar's open-air deck, with the sea breeze in your face and a cold glass of chardonnay in your hand. The restaurant is part of the Hotel del Mar, but it is located across the street on the beach. The few main courses on the menu strive for gourmet caliber, but it never quite achieves that; instead, the best bet here is their barbecue, which allows for a choice of steak, chicken, or ribs, and includes soup, a salad bar, wine, or beer and dessert, for a very reasonable $14 (£9) per person. There are also sandwiches, burgers, and an ice cream parlor. The restaurant is always open, from the early morning until the wee hours, and they host live music on weekends.

Av. Peru 100. ✆ **32/268-7755.** Main courses $5–$10 (£3.30–£6.70). AE, DC, MC, V. Daily 9am–1am (Thurs–Sat until 3 or 4am).

2 VALPARAISO ★★★

115km (71 miles) NW of Santiago; 8km (5 miles) S of Viña del Mar

Valparaíso is Chile's most captivating city, and, accordingly, it is the most popular coastal destination and an obligatory cruise ship port of call. During the 19th century, Valparaíso ranked as a port town of such wealth that few others in the world could compare, but in the years following the completion of the Panama Canal, Valparaíso sunk into poverty. Like a penniless aristocrat, the city clung for decades to its glorious past, yet only traces of the architectural splendor and riches the city once knew could still be seen. Today, especially on hills such as Cerro Concepción and Cerro Alegre, the city's run-down buildings are experiencing a rebirth. With so many gourmet restaurants and boutique hotels opening at such a fast pace, Valparaíso is quickly becoming *the* choice destination for dining and lodging on the coast. The historical importance of this city, paired with the vibrant culture of local *porteños,* is far more intriguing than Viña—a reason why UNESCO designated Valparaíso a World Heritage Site in 2002.

Much like San Francisco, the city is made of a flat downtown surrounded by steep hills, but unlike that city, the irregular terrain in Valparaíso presented far more challenges for development. The jumble of multicolored clapboard homes and weathered Victorian mansions that cling to sheer cliffs and other unusual spaces are testament to this, and you could spend days exploring the maze of narrow passageways and sinuous streets that snake down ravines and around hillsides. Given the lack of towering high rises on the hillsides, the city is frequently described as "stadium seating"—providing breathtaking views no matter where you are.

Valparaíso has spawned generations of international poets, writers, and artists who have found inspiration in the city, including the Nobel Prize–winning poet Pablo Neruda,

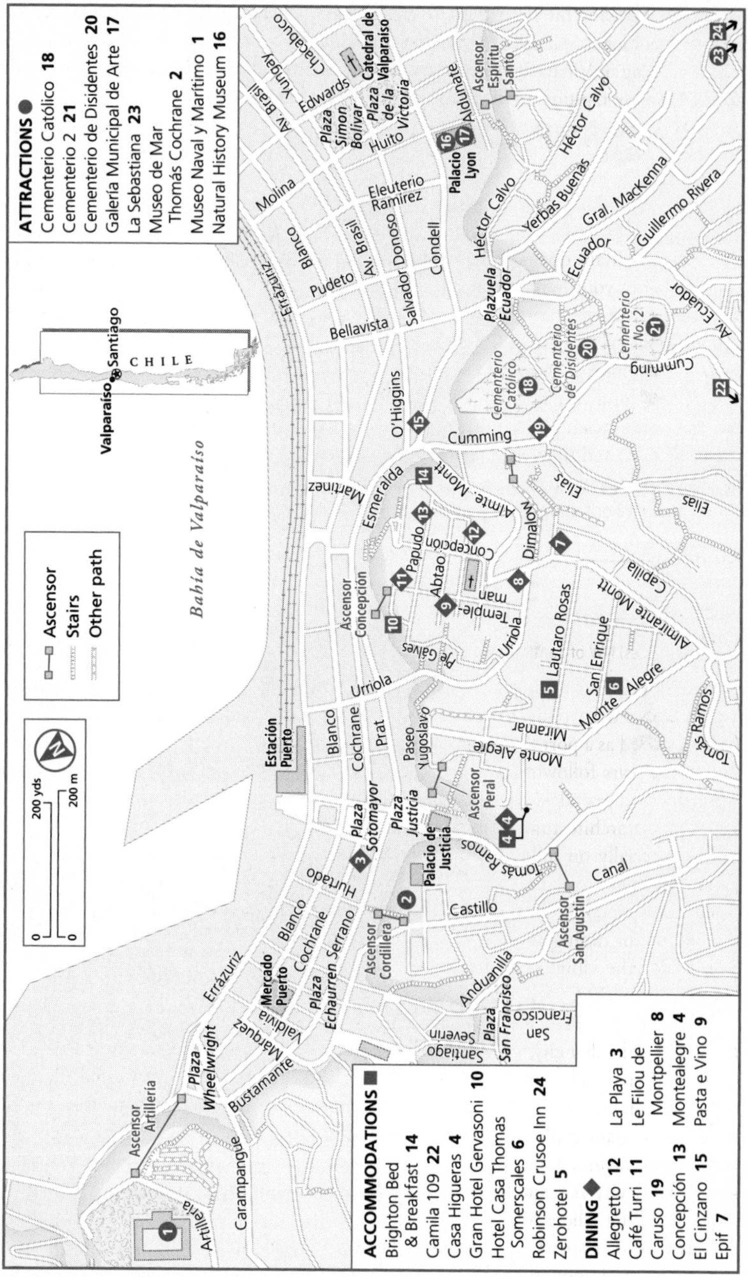
ATTRACTIONS
Cementerio Católico 18
Cementerio 2 21
Cementerio de Disidentes 20
Galería Municipal de Arte 17
La Sebastiana 23
Museo de Mar Thomás Cochrane 2
Museo Naval y Marítimo 1
Natural History Museum 16
ACCOMMODATIONS
Brighton Bed & Breakfast 14
Camila 109 22
Casa Higueras 4
Gran Hotel Gervasoni 10
Hotel Casa Thomas Somerscales 6
Robinson Crusoe Inn 24
Zerohotel 5
DINING
Allegretto 12
Café Turri 11
Caruso 19
Concepción 13
El Cinzano 15
Epif 7
La Playa 3
Le Filou de Montpellier 8
Montealegre 4
Pasta e Vino 9
Ascensor
Stairs
Other path
0 200 yds
0 200 m
Bahía de Valparaíso
CHILE
Valparaíso
Santiago
Estación Puerto
Mercado Puerto
Plaza Sotomayor
Plaza Justicia
Palacio de Justicia
Plaza Echaurren
Plaza Wheelwright
Plaza San Francisco
Plaza Simon Bolívar
Plaza de la Victoria
Catedral de Valparaíso
Palacio Lyon
Plazuela Ecuador
Cementerio Católico
Cementerio de Disidentes
Cementerio No. 2
Ascensor Artillería
Ascensor Cordillera
Ascensor San Agustín
Ascensor Peral
Ascensor Concepción
Ascensor Espíritu Santo
Paseo Yugoslavo
Artillería
Carampangue
Bustamante
Márquez
Valdivia
Errázuriz
Blanco
Cochrane
Serrano
Hurtado
Prat
Urriola
Anduanilla
Castillo
Canal
Tomás Ramos
Santiago Severín
San Francisco
Monte Alegre
Miramar
Lautaro Rosas
San Enrique
Almirante Montt
Capilla
Elías
Dimalow
Templeman
Abtao
Papudo
Concepción
Pje Gálvez
Esmeralda
Martínez
Almte. Montt
Cumming
O'Higgins
Bellavista
Pudeto
Av. Brasil
Salvador Donoso
Condell
Molina
Eleuterio Ramírez
Huito
Edwards
Yungay
Chacabuco
Aldunate
Héctor Calvo
Yerbas Buenas
Gral. MacKenna
Guillermo Rivera
Ecuador
Av. Ecuador

who owned a home here. The city is also known for its bohemian and antiquated bars that stay open into the wee hours of the morning.

But the real attraction here is the city's streets, where you can admire the angular architecture that makes this city unique, and ride the century-old, clickety-clack *ascensores,* or funiculars, that lift riders to the tops of hills. If you're the type who craves character and culturally distinctive surroundings, this is your place.

ESSENTIALS

Getting There

BY BUS **Tur Bus** (✆ **600/660-6600;** www.turbus.cl) and **Pullman** (✆ **2227-3125;** www.pullman.cl) leave from the Terminal Alameda in Santiago, located at Av. Alameda 3750 (Metro: Univ. de Santiago), every 15 minutes from 6:30am to 10:30pm (Tur Bus), and 6:10am to 10:10pm (Pullman). The trip takes about 1 hour and 15 minutes, depending on traffic, and costs $8 (£5.30). In Valparaíso, you'll disembark at the terminal at Avenida Pedro Montt; taxis are available and a good idea at night—it's possible to walk to the Cerro Concepción funicular in approximately 20 to 30 minutes, but the neighborhood surrounding the bus depot is pretty grimy. Microbuses and collectives also run frequently from outside the station to the city center (60¢/40p) During weekends, especially from December to March, it is strongly recommended that you buy your ticket in advance from any Tur Bus or Pullman office in Santiago (your hotel can give you the address of the nearest office).

BY CAR Valparaíso is reached by Rte. 68, a four-lane highway in good condition. Driving to Valparaíso from Santiago is quite easy: Take the Costanera Norte headed west, and follow it all the way to the coast (the Costanera turns into Rte. 68). There are two tolls along the way that each cost 1,200 pesos ($2.05/£1.35) from Monday to 5pm on Friday, and 1,900 pesos ($3.25/£2.15) from 5pm Friday to Sunday. At Km 105, follow the signpost for Valparaíso, taking Avenida Santos Cossa. You'll enter Valparaíso and turn onto Avenida Argentina, then turn onto Avenida Pedro Montt, which will take you to downtown. Hotels offer street parking only. If visiting for the day, park in the underground garage on Calle Errázuriz, across from the Plaza Sotomayor, or at Avenida Brasil and Bellavista. Do not leave possessions in your car if you park it on the street at night, as break-ins are common.

BY TRAIN The very sleek **Metrotren** (also known as the "Merval"; ✆ **32/238-1500**) connects Viña with Valparaíso (Plaza Sotomayor), leaving every 5 to 10 minutes from 7:30am to 10pm during weekdays, and every 15 to 20 minutes from 9:30am to 9pm on Saturdays, Sundays, and holidays. To ride the train, you must purchase a rechargeable card for $1 (70p) that you then charge with enough money to cover the cost of your trip. If you're with friends or family, you need only purchase one card for your group. During summer, you can also purchase a *Tarjeta Turista* ($8/£5.30), which gives unlimited travel on the "Merval" for 3 days.

Getting Around

Walking is really the only way to see Valparaíso; hilltop streets are confusing and very tight to drive, so park downtown and ride a funicular up. The only exception, considering the strenuous uphill walk, is the Pablo Neruda museum (La Sebastiana) and the City Cemetery. There are 15 *ascensores* (funiculars) that operate daily from 6am to 11pm (15¢–30¢/10p–20p). The *ascensores,* which most travelers will wind up taking at some point, are: Cerro Concepción, which runs from Calle Prat, opposite the Turri clock tower, to the gilded residential enclave of Paseo Gervasoni; Ascensor Artillería, which runs from Plaza Aduana to Paseo 21 de Mayo and usually packs in tourists with mouths agape at the sublime vistas; and the vertiginous Ascensor Polanco, which runs from Calle Almirante Simpson to Calle Latorre.

Visitor Information

The city's municipality has closed its main tourist office and opened two **information kiosks,** located in the center of Plaza Sotomayer and Plaza Anibal Pinto (✆ **32/293-9695;** www.municipalidaddevalparaiso.cl), open Monday through Friday from 10am to 2pm and 3:30 to 5:30pm, and Saturday and Sunday from 10:30am to 5:30pm. There's also an information kiosk at the bus station, open daily from 8:30am to 5:30pm.

Santiago Adventures, in the Providencia neighborhood of Santiago, at Av. Guardia Vieja 255 (✆ **2/244-2750;** www.santiagoadventures.com), offers day trips from Santiago to Valparaíso (combined with Viña) for $160 (£107) per person, based on two passengers and including transportation, lunch, and a bilingual tour. A cheaper option is **Turis Tour** (✆ **2/488-0444;** www.turistour.com), which runs tours from Santiago to Valparaíso and Viña for $60/£40 and up. Given the efficiency, frequency, and comfort of bus transportation from Santiago to the coast, however, you may prefer to travel to both cities on your own. See the "Walking Tour" later for information about picking up a detailed walking guide.

The first bank in the country was in Valparaíso, on Plaza Sotomayor, so it's not surprising to discover that the city has no shortage of financial services. **Banks** and **currency exchange** can be found along Calle Prat and Esmeralda Street. Opening hours are more limited than in Santiago; banks are open Monday to Friday from 9am until 4pm. Most ATMs *(cajeros automáticos)* are open 24 hours. For medical emergencies, **Hospital Carlos Van Buren** is at Av. San Ignacio 725 (on the corner of Colón; ✆ **32/220-4000**).

SPECIAL EVENTS Valparaíso's famed **New Year's Pyrotechnic Festival** is an event so spectacular even Chileans consider it something they must see at least once in their lives (during the 2007 New Year, the city shot for the Guinness Book of World Records for the largest amount of fireworks exploded in one evening—16,000). Thousands of partiers crowd the streets and hilltops to take in the radiant lights that explode over the shimmering bay. You'll want to stake out your "corner" early atop one of the hills. Savvy Chileans arrive in the early afternoon and bring chairs, barbecues, and a day's ration of food and drink to save their viewing platform for the nighttime fireworks display.

WHAT TO SEE & DO

The city's **Natural History Museum,** Av. Condell 1546 in the Palacio Lyon (✆ **32/245-9056**), has been closed for desperately needed renovations for the last few years, and continues to shut down for construction—check on the off chance that it is open (usual hours are Tues–Sat 10am–1pm and 4–9pm; Sun and holidays 10am–2pm; admission $1/70p, or free Wed and Sun). The **Galería Municipal de Arte,** in the basement level of the Palacio Lyon at Av. Condell 1550, features paintings and sculptures by regional artists, usually arranged thematically and related to the Valparaíso area. It's open Tuesday through Sunday, with erratic hours dependent on the current exhibition.

Cementerio 1, 2 & De Disidentes ★★ A walk through Valparaíso's cemeteries is not only worthwhile for its utterly fascinating, baroque antique mausoleums, but it also provides visitors with some of the best views in the city. Focus your visit on the Cementerio de Disidentes; this is where the tombs of British and European immigrants lie, having been shunned from the principal cemeteries for not being Catholic (the reason why it is called the Cemetery of the "Dissidents"). This cemetery is by far more intriguing than the other two for its matter-of-fact gravestones spelling out often dramatic endings for (usually very young) adventurers who arrived during the 19th century. It's a short, but hearty, walk up Ecuador Street to get here, and worth the effort—or just grab a cab.

Btw. Av. Ecuador and Cumming (Cerro Panteón). No phone. Free admission. Daily 10am–5pm.

La Sebastiana ★★★ Kids La Sebastiana is one of poet Pablo Neruda's three quirky homes that have been converted into museums honoring the distinguished Nobel laureate's work and life. Neruda is Chile's most beloved poet, and the country's most famous literary export. Even if you haven't familiarized yourself with Neruda's work, this museum is worth visiting to explore this eccentric home and view the whimsical knickknacks he relished collecting while traveling in Africa, Asia, and Europe. Neruda searched for poetry in the most mundane of objects. From a carousel horse brought from Paris to a chest of drawers wrenched from a ship, Neruda developed a collector's zeal for what most people would view as junk. The poet called himself an "estuary sailor"; although terrified of sailing, he nevertheless was spellbound by the sea, and he fashioned his homes to resemble boats, complete with porthole windows. Neruda named the house after its architect, a "poet of construction" Sebastián Collado, who had searched relentlessly for a site that would afford a panoramic view of the city. When Collado died, Neruda bought the house and in September 1961 it became the home where he would spend a great deal of time during the last decade of his life. The organized chaos that characterizes this home is a perfect microcosm of Valparaíso itself. While Neruda's house at Isla Negra is the most authentic, revealing more poignantly Neruda's spirit and lifestyle, at La Sebastiana visitors are able to wander freely at their own pace—something you can't do at Neruda's other museums. There are self-guiding information sheets that explain the significance of important documents and items on display. A cultural center is here too, with a gallery and a gift shop.

The walk from Plaza Victoria is a hike, so you might want to take a taxi. From Plaza Ecuador, there's a bus, Verde "D," or the *colectivo* no. 39.

Calle Ferrari 692 (Cerro Bellavista). ✆ **32/225-6606.** www.lasebastiana-neruda.cl. Admission $5 (£3.30) adults, $1.75 (£1.20) students. Mar–Dec Tues–Sun 10am–6pm; Jan–Feb Tues–Sun 10:30am–6:50pm.

Museo de Mar Thomás Cochrane ★ The main reason for visiting this maritime museum, built to house the impressive display of model ships that belonged to British navy hero Lord Cochrane, is to revel in one of the best panoramic views in the city. High atop Cerro Cordillera, this stately mansion, now a national monument, was built by one Juan Mouat, an English immigrant who designed the house in 1841 in colonial style with all the trimmings. The residence even had its own observatory—the first in Chile.

Calle Merlet 195 (via the Ascensor Cordillera). ✆ **32/293-9486.** Free admission. Tues–Sun 10am–6pm.

Museo Naval y Marítimo ★★★ This museum merits a visit even if you do not particularly fancy naval and maritime-related artifacts and memorabilia. The museum is smartly designed and divided into four salons: the War of Independence, the War against the Peru-Bolivia Confederation, the War against Spain, and the War of the Pacific. Each salon holds antique documents, medals, uniforms, and war trophies. Of special note is the Arturo Prat room, with artifacts salvaged from the *Esmeralda,* a wooden ship that sank while valiantly defending Valparaíso during the War of the Pacific.

Paseo 21 de Mayo, Cerro Artillería. ✆ **32/283749.** Admission $1 (70p) adults, 50¢ (35p) children 11 and under. Tues–Sun 10am–2pm and 3pm–6pm.

START: Muelle Prat (Prat Pier).
FINISH: Ascensor Concepción or Calle Esmeralda.
TIME: 1 to 3 hours.
BEST TIMES: Any day except Monday, when most museums and restaurants are closed.

The **Fundación Valparaíso** has done an exceptional job of mapping out a "Bicentennial Heritage Trail," a looping 30km (19-mile) walking tour divided into 15 thematic stages. I urge visitors to pick up a copy of the trail guide to supplement the walking tour described below; the guide can be found at the **Gato Tuerto bookstore,** located at Héctor Calvo 205 (Espíritu Santo Funicular), or bookstores (if you are cruising, you may find the book at the Baron's Pier shopping gallery). Or better yet, download a copy of the map on their website at www.senderobicentenario.cl, although this option does not come with interpretive information, only the map. Each stage takes approximately 90 minutes to 3 hours to walk, and the guide provides historical data, literary gossip, architectural information, and fun anecdotes about the city. To help you navigate, the *fundación* has placed arrows on the street at various stages of the trail. For visitors with limited time in the city, the walking tour outlined below will take you to the city's finest viewpoints and top attractions.

1 Muelle Prat (Prat Pier)

Begin at the Prat Pier. There is quite a bit of hullabaloo at the dock here, with skippers pitching 20-minute boat rides around the bay to tourists aboard one of their rustic fishing skiffs. It's not a very professional operation, but for $2 (£1.30) per person, what do you have to lose? There are few places in the world where you can get so close to commercial ships (docked here in the harbor). Valparaíso has changed little in the past century, and to view the city from this perspective is to see the city as many a sailor did when arriving here for the first time after a long journey around Cape Horn. A row of curio shops line the dock, which are packed with tourists when a cruise ship docks in Valparaíso.

Head away from the pier and cross Errázuriz to reach:

2 Plaza Sotomayor

Until the late 1800s, the sea arrived just a few feet from the edge of this plaza, lapping at the gates of the Naval Command Headquarters on the west side of the plaza. Built in 1910, the grand neoclassical building was once the summer residence for several of Chile's past presidents. At the plaza's entrance you'll encounter the **Monument to the Heroes of Iquique.** The heroes of the War of the Pacific—Prat, Condell, and Serrano—are buried underneath this monument. This tremendous battle in 1879 pitted Chile against a Peru-Bolivia confederation, and Chile's victory against the two resulted in the capture of the mineral-rich northern territory, cutting Bolivia off from the sea and extending Chile's size by nearly a third (to learn more about the war, visit the Naval Museum). Underneath the plaza, where you now stand, are shipwrecks and remains of the old pier, which you can view at the tiny underground museum (at the plaza's center, daily 10am–6pm). The pier and artifacts such as anchors, ballast, and cannons were discovered while excavating land to build the parking garage at the northeast edge of the plaza. Next to the old post office is the "American Fire House," the first volunteer fire station in Latin America. There is also a visitor kiosk here. Cross the plaza toward the Justice Palace.

To the left of the plaza, next to the Palacio de Justicia, ride the Ascensor Peral (ca. 1902) for 15¢ (10p) to the top of Cerro Alegre and there you'll find:

❸ Paseo Yugoslavo

Nitrate baron Pascual Baburizza built this pretty terrace walkway and dubbed it Yugoslavian Promenade in honor of his heritage.

Continue along the terrace until you pass:

❹ Palacio Baburizza

This Art Noveau palace was built in 1916 for Ottorino Zanelli and later sold to nitrate baron Pascual Baburizza, who lived here until his death in 1941. The palace is a fine display of the best European handiwork available during the early 1900s; today it is the city's Fine Arts Museum, housing a collection of 19th- and 20th-century Chilean and European paintings. The museum is most interesting for its paintings of early Valparaíso by local artists Juan Mauricio Rugendas and Thomas Somerscales. ***Note:*** The museum has periodically closed for reparations, and at press time it was busy seeking funds to continue; hard to say if it will be open when you visit, but hours are generally Tuesday through Sunday from 10am to 6pm, and admission is free.

Continue along Paseo Yugoslavo, past the La Colombina restaurant. The road curves to the right around a tiny plaza; follow it until you reach Calle Alvaro Besa. Take Alvaro Besa as it winds down the hill, or take the shortcut down Pasaje Bavestrello, a cement stairway at the left. Continue until you reach Calle Urriola, which you'll cross, then walk up 20m (66 ft.) and turn left into another stairway, Pasaje Gálvez. The narrow walkway twists and turns, passing the colorful facades of some of the most striking homes in Valparaíso. At Calle Papudo, climb the stairway and turn left into:

❺ Paseo Gervasoni

Another of Valparaíso's characteristic promenades, this *paseo* fronts a row of stately 19th-century mansions.

At the end of the walkway, you'll find Café Turri, a popular Valparaíso restaurant and a good spot for a snack or coffee. Before the cafe, to the right, is the:

❻ Casa Mirador de Lukas

This museum is dedicated to the much-loved "Lukas," aka Renzo Pecchenino, a brilliant cartoonist and satirist who worked for years for the newspaper *El Mercurio.* Lukas dedicated his career to drawing Valparaíso and the eccentric characters found here; a collection of his drawings is available for sale, *Apuntes Porteños,* which makes an excellent Valparaíso souvenir. The museum is open Tuesday through Sunday from 11am to 7pm; admission is $2 (£1.30). It is possible to terminate the walking tour here and descend via Ascensor Concepción, but I recommend that you keep walking.

Continue around Gervasoni until you reach Papudo. You can take a detour here 2 blocks up Calle Templeman to visit the:

❼ Anglican Church of St. Paul

Built in 1858, this Anglican church was not officially recognized until 1869, when the Chilean government repealed a law banning religions other than Catholicism. The church houses a grand organ donated by the British in 1901 in honor of Queen Victoria. You can hear this magnificent instrument at work at 12:30pm every Sunday.

Double back to Calle Papudo, head southeast (turning right if returning from the church) until reaching:

❽ Paseo Atkinson

At the entrance to Paseo Atkinson, you'll pass the city's Lutheran church, built in 1897 for the large German population here in the early 19th century. Paseo Atkinson is another breathtaking pedestrian walkway, bordered by antique homes with zinc facades and guillotine windows popular with the British in the early 20th century. Continue down the pedestrian stairway until you reach Calle Esmeralda and the end of the walk. You can also descend by doubling back and riding the Ascensor Concepción to Calle Prat.

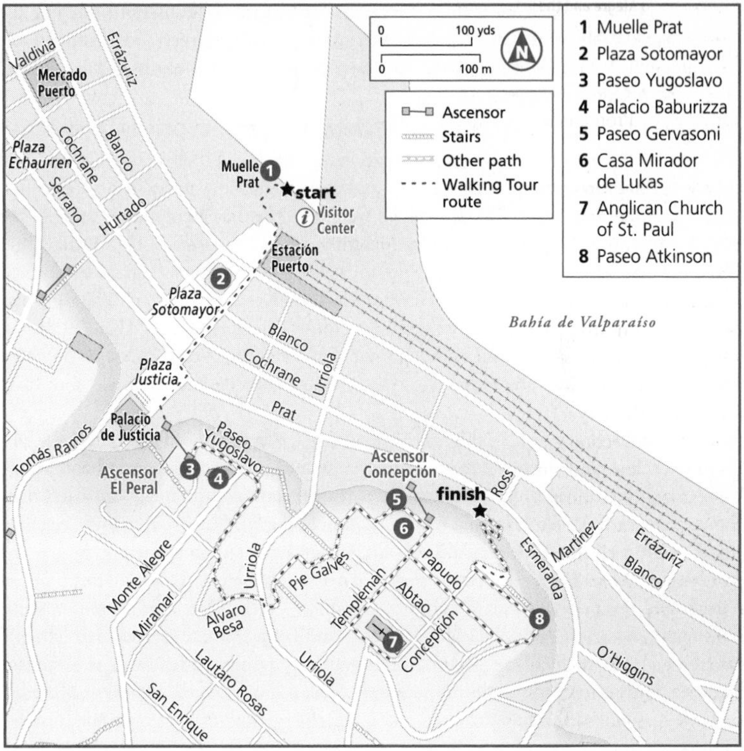

Other Walks

At the southwest corner of the Anglican church, walk up Templeman and left on Urriola. Just past the El Desayunador cafe on the left is a barely perceptible promenade, called Dimalow. Halfway down the esplanade, you will encounter one of the **best viewpoints** in Valparaíso, a truly spectacular vista of the bay, the tall steeple of the Lutheran church, and the colorful, tumbledown homes clinging to the hills. Bring your camera. The Queen Victoria Funicular is here, and you can ride it down to Cumming Street, head left 1 block to the Plaza Aníbal Pinto, then down Esmeralda until reaching the Plaza Sotomayer.

The coastline of Valparaíso, accessible at Muelle Baron (parking 50¢/35p for 30 min.), has an attractive jogging/walking path that hugs the shoreline, offering splendid views for visitors seeking a little exercise. Also at Muelle Baron is **Puerto Deportivo** (**© 32/259-2852;** www.puertodeportivo.cl), which offers kayak rental for $7 (£4.70) for a half-hour, which includes gear, kayak, and use of their showers.

THE PORT NEIGHBORHOOD Begin at the **Customs House (Aduana),** the grand, colonial American–style building built in 1854 and at the north of town at Plaza Wheelwright at the end of Cochrane and Calle Carampangue. To the right, you'll find the

Ascensor Artillería, built in 1893; it costs 15¢ (10p). The wobbly contraption takes visitors to the most panoramic pedestrian walkway in Valparaíso, **Paseo 21 de Mayo.** Don't miss the view of the port from the gazebo. Follow the walkway until reaching the **Museo Naval y Marítimo** (described in "What to See & Do," earlier). To return, double back and descend via the *ascensor,* or head down the walkway that begins at the cafe, and take a left at Calle Carampangue.

RUTA BELLAVISTA: FROM PLAZA VICTORIA TO THE CASA DE PABLO NERUDA (LA SEBASTIANA) The recent incarnation of the "Ruta Bellavista—Culture and Poetry" is the result of businesses, artists, and the Fundación Valparaíso on Cerro Bellavista banding together to offer a mapped walking route that incorporates some of the city's highlights, including La Sebastiana (described in "What to See & Do," earlier), and Plaza Victoria, where in the late 1880s elegant society met, and whose grand trees, trickling fountain, and sculptures imported from Lima recall that era's heyday. The Ruta also includes the **Open Air Museum,** a public art display featuring more than 20 murals painted on cement retainer and building walls along winding streets. Pick up a brochure with a map at most restaurants, hotels, or at the visitor kiosk on Plaza Sotomayor or Plaza Aníbal Pinto.

Really, the best way to walk this route is downhill (unless you need the exercise—Calle Ferrari is Valparaíso's steepest street), beginning high up at La Sebastiana and continuing down along Ferrari, veering left onto Héctor Calvo and taking a quick duck left onto Temuco to see the Villa Hispania castles. Continue down Héctor Calvo until reaching the outstanding **Gato Tuerto bookstore** and arts-and-crafts shop at the Fundación Valparaíso (Héctor Calvo 205); there is also Internet service here and a cafe. Turn right on Pasteur and make an immediate right onto Guimera for the Open Air Museum, which continues down along Rudolph, looping back onto Ferrari, where, if you head left, will take you down to the Plaza Victoria at Edwards and Independencia. The **Ascensor Espíritu Santo** allows you to ride up to simply catch a glimpse of the Open Air Museum, and can be found on Aldunate Street; take a left after getting off and continue the walk at Rudolph Street (as earlier).

Shopping

Travelers searching for that unique something to bring home should make a beeline to **Tuten,** Esmeralda 1140 (© **32/221-7941;** www.tuten.cl), a new collective for regional artists and craftsmen of the Valparaíso area. Within the walls of Tuten, you'll find beautifully crafted, original, and high-quality carved wood items; jewelry handmade of glass, copper, and gold; glassware such as vases and plates; folksy art representing the Valparaíso area; children's items; copper; and gold. It's open Monday through Saturday from 9am to 9pm.

For books, guides, and maps, head to the Fundación Valparaíso's **Gato Tuerto Café & Bookstore,** Héctor Calvo 205 (© **32/222-0867;** Espíritu Santo Funicular), which also has a small arts-and-crafts store. **Design For Valparaíso,** Concepcion 154B (© **32/259-1868**), has original designs of textiles and clothing woven from natural fibers found in Chile.

Plaza O'Higgins, close to the Congreso Nacional, hosts a weekend **flea market** purveying all manner of collectibles ranging from knickknack memorabilia to books, homemade jams, Neruda-themed souvenirs, and electrical items. You will also find local artistes selling their wares at stalls clustered close to the Neruda museum and along the Paseo Gervasoni.

WHERE TO STAY

Less than a decade ago, decent lodging was so scarce in Valparaíso that even the city's own tourism board recommended travelers lodge in Viña. Today, Valparaíso is the epicenter of stylish boutique lodging, whereas Viña is known more for full-scale hotels and resorts with all the bells and whistles and beach access. You'll still spot a few *hostales* whose pretty, flower-boxed facades belie awful conditions within, but even these establishments are being bought up by hoteliers who see the potential in Valparaíso becoming the next hot tourism destination rather than just a character-rich—but down-at-the-heels—city suited only for a day visit.

Expensive

Casa Higueras ★★★ Moments Clamped to the hillside of Cerro Concepción, Casa Higueras is without a doubt one of the finest hotels in Chile. It's the ideal choice for anyone with an eye for style and a desire to relax and be pampered. One of Chile's star interior designers renovated this former mansion, using lots of dark wood flooring and paneling, and minimal, but well-placed, designer furniture. The guest rooms have panoramic windows, and they feature only a touch of color from heavy yellow or rose-colored curtains and photos of Valparaíso life, plus 300–thread count sheets on heavenly soft beds, plasma TV screens, and balconies; the mosaic-tiled bathrooms are splendidly appointed with fluffy robes and walk-in showers with rainfall showerheads.

Outside, the three-story hotel descends over a rectangular pool and hot tub that is attractively landscaped into the hillside. There is also a minispa for unwinding after a day tromping up and down Valparaíso's hills. If you bore of your view, and it's hard to imagine you would, you can kick back on their rooftop terrace, or the hotel restaurant's patio.

Higueras 133, Cerro Concepcion. ✆ **2/657-3950.** www.hotelcasahigueras.cl. 20 units. $210–$238 (£140–£159) double standard; $265–$322 (£177–£215) suite. AE, DC, MC, V. **Amenities:** Restaurant; outdoor pool; sauna; whirlpool; Internet access; limited room service; massage; laundry service. *In room:* Plasma TV/DVD, Wi-Fi, minibar, hair dryer.

Zerohotel ★★★ This beautiful blue mansion with white shutters and corrugated metal siding was extensively renovated in 2005 and repositioned as a poised boutique hotel, a perfect romantic enclave from which to experience this poetic city. The epitome of graceful simplicity, the blue-and-white color scheme continues throughout the guest rooms, which have vertiginous ceilings, polished parquet floors, crisp 400–thread count Egyptian cotton sheets, and stylish slate tile bathrooms complete with all the requisite pampering accoutrements. It's worth paying extra for one of the four rooms overlooking the bay—the views of the town mosaic cascading down the hillside and stretching toward the bay are just sublime. The "colores" rooms overlook the colorfully restored houses of the streets of Cerro Alegre. While breakfast is a little disappointing compared to the lavish spread at Casa Higueres (see earlier), it is served in the glorious winter garden conservatory from which steps lead down to three heavenly terraces, which invite relaxation with sun loungers and a small pool.

Lautaro Rosas 343, Cerro Alegre. ✆ **2/211-3113.** www.zerohotel.com. 9 units. $230 (£153) city view; $320 (£213) port view. AE, DC, MC, V. **Amenities:** Bar; Wi-Fi; limited room service; massage; laundry service. *In room:* CableTV, Wi-Fi, hair dryer.

Moderate

Hotel Casa Thomas Somerscales ★★★ Value This exquisite hotel is housed in the former home of Valparaíso's most famous painter, Thomas Somerscales, renowned for his portraits of the city and the War of the Pacific. It is old enough to be on the National

Heritage Registry, and this historical focus and the lovingly restored interiors makes the Somerscales one of the most unique places to stay in Valparaíso. Guest rooms are immaculately clean and fresh, and feature crisp white linens and curtains, 19th-century antiques, and period ornaments. The stairwell is cheerfully lit by a two-floor stained-glass window, and the front patio still has its black-and-white checkered tiles. If you consider a luxury hotel too impersonal and a typical B&B too homespun, this is a happy medium. Guests often get to know each other over breakfast, but you can always sleep in and have it served to you in bed.

San Enrique 446, Cerro Alegre. ✆ **32/233-1006.** www.hotelsomerscales.cl. 8 units. $85 (£57) double; $145 (£97) double with terrace and bay view. AE, DC, MC, V. **Amenities:** Cafeteria; Internet. *In room:* TV, minibar, safe.

Gran Hotel Gervasoni ★ With sweeping views from the crest of Cerro de Concepción, this boutique hotel is a Victorian gem. The glorious mansion was built in the 1870s and is replete with original features including hardwood floors, delicate cornicing, stained-glass windows, and shimmering chandeliers. From the plush, gilded lobby, the hushed salon with its velvet drapes, oriental rugs, and antiques gives way to an elegant dining room and terraces with dazzling views of the ocean and the topsy-turvy alleyways of Valparaiso. Rooms vary in size and character but all are tastefully furnished, with interior brick and stonework. Each room discreetly maintains the 19th-century aura while at the same time being thoroughly functional and well planned.

Paseo Gervasoni 1. ✆/fax **32/223-9236.** www.hotelgervasoni.com. 15 units. $158 (£105) double. AE, DC, MC, V. **Amenities:** Restaurant; Internet access; limited room service; laundry service. *In room:* TV, Wi-Fi, hair dryer.

Robinson Crusoe Inn ★★ (Finds Valparaíso's first boutique inn was the brainchild of an American-Chilean who saw the potential in tourism here long before many others made the plunge. After purchasing several neighboring and run-down homes, he enclosed the properties in zinc and wood and gave the interiors a dose of antique-chic charm, blending period furniture with a vaguely nautical decor and other bric-a-brac. The top floor was converted into a glass-enclosed terrace with an absolutely knockout view of the city; upon arrival you're given a complimentary bottle of wine, and one could hardly fathom a better place to drink it than overlooking the twinkling lights of the city.

The rooms are cozy, with antique armoires and fluffy comforters; most have a bay view, and their Sky Suite has panoramic views but is pricey considering its folksy decor. I must rave about the breakfast here: Few hotels bother to serve such a hearty and diverse breakfast when it's included in the price. The hotel is several blocks up from the Espíritu Santo funicular, and close to the Pablo Neruda museum.

Héctor Calvo 389, Cerro Bellavista. ✆ **32/249-5499.** www.robinsoncrusoeinn.com. 14 units. $90 (£60) double; $110 (£73) suite; $235 (£157) loft suite with panoramic views. AE, DC, MC, V. **Amenities:** Cafe; airport transfer at additional cost; Internet access; laundry service. *In room:* TV.

Inexpensive

Brighton Bed & Breakfast ★★ (Value Location, location, location—wow, does this little hotel have it. Perched vertiginously high atop a cliff on Cerro Concepción, this canary-yellow hotel provides all-embracing views of the harbor and the city center below (although only the suite and three doubles have the view). Because this is a converted old Victorian, room sizes vary: All are on the small side with the exception of rooms 1 and A; rooms with a sea view are 1, A, E, and X. Expect simple decor with polished parquet floors and white duvets. The Brighton has a popular cafe on the first floor with two terrace patios that seem to hang over the city; it's mesmerizing and encourages you to linger long after you've finished breakfast. Otherwise, the food is mediocre, although it is one of the only places open on Sunday evenings. On weekends, the cafe has live bolero and tango music, and it stays open until 4am.

Paseo Atkinson 151–153, Cerro Concepción. ✆/fax **32/222-3513.** www.brighton.cl. 9 units. $60 (£40) double without sea view; $78 (£52) double with sea view. AE, DC, MC, V. **Amenities:** Cafe. *In room:* Cable TV, no phone.

Camila 109 ★★ Finds Valparaíso's best B&B is stylish and intimate and provides warm, personalized service from a very hospitable owner. Precipitously located on Cerro La Loma, next to the fine arts school, this modern home with huge picture windows has sweeping views over the bay from its rooftop terrace. The three double rooms are impeccable and very urban in feel with minimalist furnishings, polished wooden floors, and huge windows. Red and blue linen adds a flash of vibrancy to an otherwise Zen simplicity. From the crisp linens to the delicious coffee, quality and simplicity are the overarching themes. For travelers keen to explore beyond the more manicured areas of town, this is a great base and, because of its proximity to La Sebastiana, a raw, artistic vibe prevails.

Calle Camila 109, Cerro la Loma. ✆ **32/249-1746.** www.camila109.cl. 3 units. $45 (£30) double. AE, DC, MC, V. **Amenities:** Internet access; laundry service.

WHERE TO DINE

The culinary scene in Valparaíso is hot, hot, hot—not even Santiago can compete with the gastronomic explosion currently taking place in this port town. Valparaíso's bohemian flair, its concentration of talented young chefs, and its constant supply of adventurous and demanding diners have all combined to inspire a synergistic food culture found in few regions of Chile. The bistro reigns here in Valparaíso, those intimate eateries housed in recycled old Victorians that are typically owner-attended and offer inventive cuisine in lieu of the fish-and-fries fare and grumpy service that reigned in this city for decades. Valparaíso, it can be said, shows a newfound respect for diners. Of course, you won't want to miss dropping into one of the century-old establishments in Valparaíso that have played host to generations of revelers, if only for the antique architecture and a whiff of the city's formidable and colorful history. Note that most restaurants are either closed or open for lunch only on Sundays.

Valparaíso has quite a few charming cafes for a snack or *onces,* Chile's famous afternoon tea. **Café Riquet,** located at no. 1199 in the Plaza Anibal Pinto, is a local institution in Valparaíso and a popular point of reunion for writers and artists and a host of characters, and they have reasonably priced fixed-price lunches. **Café del Poeta,** no. 1181, is a good spot for coffee and pastries, and they serve *onces.* **Café Harté,** just to the right of the El Peral funicular on Cerro Alegre, is the cafe to go to for a spectacular view.

Expensive

Pasta e Vino ★★★ CONTEMPORARY ITALIAN The day Pasta e Vino opened its doors to the public, it became immediately clear what Valparaíso had been missing all these years: a warm, intimate ambience, fabulous cuisine, and owner-attended service. Pasta e Vino virtually launched the culinary metamorphosis in Valparaíso, and it remains the best restaurant in this city—the reason why you'll need to make reservations days in advance. Pasta e Vino is the brainchild of a young Chilean and his Italian wife, the restaurant's chef and a woman who really understands flavor combinations and technique. Standout menu items include ginger-lime clams, squid risotto, plump salmon ravioli, and fresh green salad. The ambience is exposed brick walls and sophisticated chic, but wooden tables and a lively atmosphere keep the restaurant down-to-earth.

Templeman 352. ✆ **32/249-6187.** pastaevino@hotmail.com. Reservations required. Main courses $9–$15 (£6–£10). AE, DC, MC, V. Wed–Sat 8pm–midnight; Sun 1–5pm.

Moderate

Café Turri ★★ (Moments FRENCH/CHILEAN Valparaíso's emblematic restaurant has—at last!—changed ownership, and the nasty waiters, fluorescent lights, and awful food are thankfully a thing of the past. This restaurant has always reigned as the city's best spot for alfresco dining, and it's well located at the top of the La Concepción funicular and close to other points of interest. The new owners (a French/Chilean pair who once owned La Fourchette in Viña) have preserved the restaurant's lovely antique interiors, but they've given them a contemporary update. They've also hired a cheery waitstaff. That said, while the food is night-and-day better than before, it still isn't as good as the fare at such places as Pasta e Vino. The French-influenced fare includes duck confit, steak tartare, grilled fish and meats, salads, and appetizers such as grilled Camembert cheese. At press time, the owners planned to open a wine/tapas bar on the ground floor, serving even super premium wine by the glass. For a primo table, book at least a day ahead on weekends.

Calle Templeman 147 (Cerro Concepción; take the Concepción lift). ✆ **32/236-5307.** www.cafeturri.cl. Reservations recommended for outdoor seating. Main courses $10–$14 (£6.70–£9.30). AE, DC, MC, V. Daily 10am–midnight, but closed Mon Apr–Nov.

Caruso ★ (Finds SEAFOOD A fun little restaurant, Caruso is located on the newly gentrifying hill Cerro Cárcel. The folksy restaurant, with whitewashed walls, local art, and wooden tables, specializes in seafood, especially rock fish such as *vieja* and *tomollo,* delicious varieties caught by local fishermen with harpoons and not commonly seen on Chilean menus. Given the scarcity and freshness of Caruso's ingredients, their chalkboard menu changes daily, and sometimes throughout a single day. Dishes boast hints of Peruvian-style cooking, with some straight-out Peruvian dishes such as *aji de gallina,* a creamy chicken stew. The relaxed ambience of Caruso captures the city's eclectic rhythm, but note that service here is slow, so don't come if you're in a hurry. Given their excellent wine list, it's a good place to wait, however.

Av. Cumming 201, Cerro Carcel. ✆ **32/259-4039.** caruso@vtr.net. Reservations recommended. Main courses $8–$12 (£5.30–£8). AE, DC, MC, V. Lunch Tues–Sun 1–4pm; dinner Thurs–Sat 8:30pm–midnight.

Concepción ★★ INTERNATIONAL The 8 tables at this sleek new restaurant sit in one of the prettiest gardens in the city. With its enviable port views, and a something-for-everyone menu, it's a wonderfully relaxing place to while away a sunny afternoon or enjoy a romantic dinner. The mood hits the right note between casual and elegant, with pristine white tablecloths and conscientious staff but an informal ambience. The bread service, which includes doughy home-baked bread served with herb-infused olive oil and tapenade, is a treat in itself. The eclectic menu is slanted toward seafood, with excellent ceviche and sashimi on order, along with large green salads dressed with hunks of goat cheese, olives, and pearly shrimps. Other standout items are the conger filet served atop an eggplant strudel; the grilled sea bass with polenta; and the king crab ravioli, a perennial favorite in Valparaíso. Save room for the delicious chocolate desserts. The only downside with this place is that the service can be so laid back that you can easily end up waiting an hour for your meal to arrive.

Papudi 541, Cerro Concepción. ✆ **32/249-8192.** Reservations recommended. Main courses $9–$13 (£6–£8.70). AE, DC, MC, V. Lunch Tues–Sun 1–4pm; dinner Thurs–Sat 8:30pm–midnight.

Montealegre ★★ INTERNATIONAL Casa Higueras' elegant restaurant not only has a wonderful view, especially at night as the cruise ships pull out of the bay and the hillside is transformed into a dazzling cascade of twinkling lights, but it also has the advantage of being open on Sundays and Mondays when most other places are closed. The short menu offers some interesting flavor combinations; the tender venison loin is encrusted with olives, and slivers of foie gras are perched atop silky veal. For an appetizer, you might try the barnacle salad or the king crab casserole, a rich confection of cream, tomato, and small flakes of crab. The pasta dishes, especially the goat cheese and pancetta tortellini, are tasty and are best as a shared appetizer as the servings are insubstantial for a main course. In fact, most of the artfully presented dishes here are small compared to other restaurants of this caliber. The fig cheesecake and the lúcuma mousse make for great desserts, if you're still hungry after the main course. Service is friendly and attentive and the mood very conducive to winding down.

Higueras 133, Cerro Concepcion. ✆ **2/657-3950.** www.hotelcasahigueras.cl. Reservations recommended. AE, DC, MC, V. Main courses $8–$10 (£5.30–£6.70). Daily 1–4pm; 8pm–midnight.

Inexpensive

Allegretto ★ DELI/PIZZERIA A cheery, retro ambience reminiscent of an old emporium, a jukebox that spins old rock and English punk, wooden booths, and friendly service make Allegretto a truly enjoyable place for a casual meal. The large stone-baked, thin-crust pizzas, which can be customized with a medley of ingredients, are the highlight of the menu; avoid the gloopy gnocchi and risotto dishes, which have a mass-produced flavor and texture. What's great about Allegretto is that you can get out the door having spent less than $20 (£13) for two, with wine included. They even deliver. Allegretto has a selection of packaged specialty foods from around Chile for sale, too. Come for the locally brewed draft beer, but skip the premade pisco sours.

Pilcomayo 529 (Cerro Concepción). ✆ **32/296-8839.** Pizzas $8 (£5.30). No credit cards. Daily noon–4pm and 7–11pm.

epif VEGETARIAN Veggies and vegans will find a home at epif, located a few steps from the top of the Reina Victoria funicular. The young Chilean-American couple who own epif (which is short for epiphany, by the way), are great fun and very friendly—probably because they gave up Boston for Valparaíso and couldn't be happier. There is a funky, antiques-filled dining area and a brighter interior patio, which is an ideal spot for their weekend brunch. It's a very relaxed environment, and most diners come as much for the inexpensively priced veggie burgers, gazpacho, and tofu burritos as they do for its lively nightlife.

Calle Dr. Grossi 268 (Cerro Concepción). ✆ **32/259-5630.** www.epif.cl. Main courses $4–$6 (£2.70–£4). No credit cards. Wed–Thurs 7pm–1am; Fri–Sat 8pm–2am; Sun 1–4pm.

La Playa CHILEAN As young restaurateurs scramble to open the next "it" gourmet restaurant on Cerros Alegres and Concepción, the La Playa restaurant, located on the edge of downtown's Plaza Sotomayer, keeps drawing in a steady clientele of diners and drinkers just like they have for more than 100 years. It is one of Valparaíso's oldest bars/

restaurants, and no other establishment in this city oozes more old-world, bohemian charm, with its long oak bar, dusty marine memorabilia, lofty ceilings, and antique mirrors rescued from the Seven Mirrors brothel that shut down decades ago. While digging into an inexpensive meal of crab soup or steak *a la pobre,* it's easy to sense the ghosts of sailors past who frequented this restaurant during the city's heyday, in search of nighttime adventure. After 10pm, the restaurant converts into a pub popular with young adults and college students, with live jazz or blues music kicking off around midnight and shutting down at a respectably late hour for a bar like this—5am.

Serrano 568. ✆ **32/259-4262.** Reservations not accepted. Main courses $5–$9 (£3.30–£6). No credit cards. Mon–Wed 10am–10:30pm; Thurs–Sat 10am–5am.

Le Filou de Montpellier ★ FRENCH If the fashion for all things fusion is starting to wear a little thin then head to Le Filou, a bastion of French gastronomic ingenuity. A local favorite and one of the first restaurants on Cerro Concepción, Le Filou started out serving a Saturday lunch special that grew so popular the chef had no choice but to open his bistro full time. The dining room is cozy, charming and buzzes with chatter, a reflection of the gregarious spirit of the charming French owner who may even be your waiter for lunch. The ideal way to sample the chef's bistro classics is to relax over one of the inexpensive fixed-price lunches, which change daily but always feature well-executed, simple, and truly authentic Gaelic delicacies; try an appetizer of Parma ham with couscous followed by melt-in-your-mouth medallions of beef tenderloin in a Port wine sauce and a gooey chocolate crepe for dessert. Dinner is served only on Fridays and Saturdays. There is another venue on Almirante Montt 51, which is more of a cafeteria serving wholesome snacks, quiche, salads, and fresh juices.

Almirante Montt 382. ✆ **32/222-4663.** montpellier@hotmail.com. Reservations recommended Sat–Sun. Fixed-price lunch $7 (£4.70) Tues–Wed, fixed-price lunch Thurs–Sun and dinner $11 (£7.30). No credit cards. Tues–Sun 1–3pm; Fri–Sat dinner 8–10:30pm.

Poblenou ★ SPANISH/TAPAS This hole-in-the-wall tapas bar is one of the cozier places for a light meal and glass of wine. Low ceilings, a fireplace, candles, and wooden tables create a mellow ambience, making Poblenou an easy place to relax and converse. The menu centers around Spanish appetizers such as *montaditos,* or toasted bread, with a variety of choices for toppings such as chicken with orange and Gouda cheese; salads; crepes; and vegetable and meat kebabs. Portions are generally larger than your average tapas serving.

Urriola 476 (Cerro Alegre). ✆ **32/249-5245.** Tapas $1.50–$6.50 (£1–£4.35). AE, DC, MC, V. Tues–Sun 6:30pm–midnight (Sat opens at 8:30pm).

VALPARAISO AFTER DARK

Valparaíso is nationally famous for its bohemian pubs and bars where poets, writers, tango aficionados, sailors, university students, and just about everyone else spend hours drinking, dancing, and socializing well into the early morning hours. In fact, most restaurants and bars do not adhere to a set closing hour, but instead close "when the candles burn down."

That said, given the Valparaíso University here, a lot of these nighttime watering holes draw in a disproportionate amount of young adults. The **Cinzano,** facing Plaza Aníbal Pinto on Calle Esmeralda (✆ **32/221-3043**), is an exception. This traditional and unabashedly kitschy bar/restaurant is known for its kooky tango singers who break out the mic Thursday through Saturday after 10pm. But you need to get here earlier, or you'll end up waiting for a table. **La Colombina** (✆ **32/223-6254**) is frequented by an adult/young adult crowd for its comfortable ambience, live jazz and bolero music, and view of the glittering lights of Valparaíso that spread out below; take a cab or the funicular Ascensor Peral and walk down Paseo Yugoslavo. The **Brighton Bed & Breakfast** has live music on Fridays and a bar ambience most nights on their hanging terrace (see "Where to Stay," earlier). **La Playa,** Serrano 568 (✆ **32/259-4262**), is one of Valparaíso's legendary bar/restaurants, and it draws an eclectic mix of characters who come to eat, drink, and listen to live music or poetry readings well into the early morning.

My pick for a venue dedicated to nightlife action is **La Piedra Feliz** ★, Av. Errázuriz 1054 (✆ **32/256788**). The bar/dance club is housed within the old storehouse of a shipping company, and it has something for everyone: a trendy subterranean lounge and club with DJs (lounge Thurs–Sat), a salsa room, tango room, pub, and a stage for live music. Twenty- and thirty-somethings sweat to electronic music at the ultracool **Mundo Pagano,** Blanco 236 (✆ **32/223-1118;** www.mundopagano.cl), which has nightly dance parties and occasionally live music. On Cerro Concepción, one of the hippest bars is **Gremio,** Pasaje Gálvez 173 (✆ **32/222-8394;** www.gremio.cl), with periodic arts exhibitions and snacks. **Deck 00,** Muelle Barón (✆ **32/259-2852**), a glass cube building at the end of the dock, offers a waterfront view and occasional lounge parties, but you'll need to check their website for info as they open and close on a whim. **Bitácora,** Cumming 68 (✆ **32/222-6412**), is a popular cultural center featuring local artists; there's a bar on the first floor and a second-floor salon dedicated to theater and music.

3 EXCURSIONS OUTSIDE VALPARAISO & VINA DEL MAR

ISLA NEGRA

125km (78 miles) W of Santiago

Isla Negra is mostly known as "the place where Pablo lived"—Pablo Neruda, that is. His third—and favorite—home is here, perched high above the sand and sea that inspired him, and it is now a museum. The endearing little town is about 1½ hours south of Valparaíso, and anyone planning to spend the night in that city might consider this recommended destination as a first stop. Another idea is to include a visit to Isla Negra before or after a tour of the San Antonio wine region (see section 5, later in this chapter). After lunch here at one of two good restaurants, you can head north for a beautiful coastal drive to Valparaíso. The **Casa Museo Pablo Neruda** ★★★, at Calle Poeta Neruda s/n (✆ **35/461-2844;** www.fundacionneruda.org), has been afforded quasi-mythical status by many Chileans. Larger than Neruda's other two homes, ethereally perched on a cliff overlooking the crashing waves of the Pacific, it harbors a remarkable depository of travel mementoes: glass bottles, wooden sirens salvaged from ships' bows, butterflies, shells, African masks, Hindu carvings, ships-in-bottles, and more. Neruda, it seems, when not penning verse, liked to travel, hunt out treasures, and spend a lot of cash. The museum is a wonderful place to visit, and kids love it, too. The tomb of Neruda and his wife is also on view here. Tours in English cost $7 (£4.70), and reservations must be made in advance. It's open Tuesday through Sunday from 10am to 6pm.

At the back of the museum is **Café del Poeta** (✆ **35/461774**), with pleasant outdoor seating and a direct view of the rocky beach and crashing waves below. You'll find good pisco sours, seafood dishes, and fixed-price lunches here. If you are tempted to stay, **Hostería La Candela,** Calle de la Hostería 67 (✆ **35/461254;** www.candela.cl), is a charming, rustic little hotel and restaurant owned by a local filmmaker and his musician wife. Neruda photographs and memorabilia line the walls of the lobby and stand as testament to the author's time here. The rooms are all decorated differently, in theme with Neruda's "20 Poems of Love"; a few have balconies with sea views and fireplaces. The restaurant is open all day and serves primarily simply prepared seafood.

The coastal strip of Isla Negra has been declared a *Zona Típica* (Heritage Zone) to preserve the area from becoming overrun by multistoried apartment buildings. You can get here from Valparaíso by bus with **Tur Bus** (✆ **600/660-6600;** www.turbus.cl) and **Pullman** (✆ **600/320-3200;** www.pullman.cl), which leave from the Terminal Alameda in Santiago, located at Av. Alameda 3750 (Metro: Univ. de Santiago). I recommend that visitors rent a car, stop along the way in Pomaire (see "Pomaire: The Clay Village," on p. 158) or wine taste, visit Isla Negra, and return to Santiago or head up to Valparaíso. To get here by car from Valparaíso, drive back out toward Santiago on Rte. 68 and follow the sign to Algarrobo (Isla Negra is south of Algarrobo); the trip should take about 2 hours.

ZAPALLAR, MAITENCILLO & COLCHAGUA

Continuing north along the coast road, some 80km/50 miles from Viña del Mar you will reach Zapallar, which is a refuge of Chile's moneyed elite. The stalwart residents who have lived here over the past century have lobbied successfully to keep the riffraff out and construction to a minimum. Accordingly, it is the loveliest residential cove along the shore of the Central Coast. Each home flourishes with exotic landscaping, and the beach is so pristine, it looks as though it has been raked with the meticulousness of a Zen master.

All this aside, Zapallar is also where you'll find one of the region's most popular restaurants, **El Chiringuito** ★★ (✆ **33/741024**), on the south end of town. Birthed from humble beginnings, Chiringuito serves the same tasty but simply prepared seafood dishes it always has, so bring your bourgeois manners and your proletarian bite; the crashing sea views and outdoor seating here encourage you to linger for a long lunch. Credit cards aren't accepted, and reservations are strongly recommended for weekends and during the summer. The place to spend the night here is the **Hotel Isla Seca,** Rte. F-30 E, no. 31 (✆ **33/741224;** www.hotelislaseca.cl). The hotel has 38 handsome, comfortable guest rooms, two swimming pools, and a full-service restaurant. Rates are $150 to $180 (£100–£120) for a standard double, $185 to $220 (£123–£147) for a double with a terrace and ocean view.

Neighboring Zapallar is Colchagua and farther south, Maintencillo, two middle-class weekend retreats for Santiaguinos. In this region, individual private cabins and weekend homes are really the only lodging options here, with one exception: **Cabañas Hermansen,** one of the more interesting places to bunk for the night (Av. del Mar 592; ✆ **32/277-1028;** www.hermansen.cl). These self-catering, Swiss Family Robinson–style cabins are handcrafted to be individually different and are scattered amid thick foliage on a hilly slope. Although perfectly comfortable and a hit with kids, you've got to have a sense of adventure to stay here and a rental car to get around. The cost is $50 to $70 (£33–£47) for two people, $60 to $125 (£40–£83) for six; no credit cards are accepted.

A few attractions in this area stand out. At the northern end of the beach in Cachagua, there is a rocky pathway that takes visitors past the **Island of Cachagua Nature Sanctuary,** where you can view Humboldt penguins and sea lions (try to bring binoculars if you can).

In Maitencillo, at Playa Caleta, there is a **fishermen's market** with a dozen stands hawking shellfish and fish just pulled from the sea. This is as fresh as it gets: Order a plate of raw clams or live scallops, and watch the fishmongers expertly fillet the catch of the day.

PARQUE NACIONAL LA CAMPANA ★

Parque Nacional La Campana is located in the dry coastal mountains, 110km (68 miles) from Santiago, close enough for a day visit or as a stop on the way to or from Valparaíso. Immortalized by Charles Darwin in *Voyage of the Beagle,* the park's jagged peaks afford the most spectacular views in Chile as well as a rich profusion of Palma Chilena *(Jubaea chilensis),* the southernmost species of palm tree in the world. It was from the summit of the 1,800m-high (5,904-ft.) Cerro La Campana that Darwin professed that he never so thoroughly enjoyed a day as the one he spent atop this summit. It does indeed offer the best 360-degree summit lookout point in the central region, but it's a *strenuous* hike to get to it (see later for more info).

While Parque Nacional La Campana may not offer the diverse array of activities that you find in Cajón de Maipo, it is wonderful hiking territory. There are three sectors with separate entrances. **Sector Ocoa** has the largest concentration of palms and is a lovely day hike winding through palm groves and ending at a 30m (98-ft.) waterfall. The trail is mostly flat and about 6km (3.75 miles) long. The stout-trunk palms that you see here grow very slowly and live as long as 800 years. Hundreds of thousands once blanketed the central region, but they were nearly harvested to extinction for their sap, which was used to make *miel de palma,* something like a pancake syrup. You can reach this sector from the Pan-American Highway; the signs for the park exit are very visible.

In the Sector **Cajón Grande,** the Sendero Plateaux is a 4.2km (2.6-mile) trail through oak groves (best viewed in the autumn) that is easy to moderate and takes around 2 hours to complete. Also in the Cajón Grande sector, the Sendero Portezuelo Ocoa is a 5.5km trail (3.4 miles) which meanders through magical woods with *miradores* that overlook the valley.

Far and away the park's most popular sector is **Granizo,** where you'll find Sendero Andinista, the trail head for Darwin's climb to Cerro La Campana. The trail is very steep in parts, especially the last 90 minutes, and can be slippery due to loose rock; if you can hack it, the view at the end is breathtaking, with sweeping views of the Andes mountain range and the coast. The trail is 7km (4.25 miles) and takes approximately 8 hours to complete. For a more tranquil ramble, the Sendero Los Peumos is a 4km (2.6 mile) walk through lush woodlands, which connects with the Sendero Portezuelo Ocoa Sector in the **Cajón Grande** sector. The Conaf station at Granizo is the most equipped, with knowledgeable rangers providing comprehensive, well-designed information. Both sectors Grande and Granizo are in the park's southern region, with both entrances close to the pleasant town of Olmué. There are campsites in all three sectors, which cost $10 (£6.70) per night for one to six people. If you plan to stay for a couple of nights, you'll find more creature comforts at the immaculate and welcoming **Hostería Copihue,** Diego Portales 2203 (✆ **33/441-544**), which has pleasant, if spartan, rooms nestled in manicured grounds with swimming pools, a gym, and a good restaurant.

Admission to the park is $2 (£1.35) for adults and 75¢ (50p) for children; it's open year-round Saturday to Thursday from 9am to 5:30pm, and Friday from 9am to 4:30pm. Call ✆ **33/441342** for more info. It is possible to reach the park by taking a bus from Santiago, Valparaiso, and Viña del Mar. From the San Borja terminal in Santiago, *Golondrina* run daily services every 30 minutes to Olmué, which connect with the local *Agdabus* bus service every 10 minutes—this will drop you off at the park entrance at Granizo.

From Valparaíso, the route is much more direct with *Ciferal* Express services running every 2 hours, leaving from Playa Ancha and 1 Norte in Viña del Mar and dropping you off less than half a kilometer from the park entrance at Granizo. For more freedom, rent a car, or contact **Santiago Adventures** (p. 164), which runs day tours.

4 CAJON DE MAIPO

San Alfonso: 65km (40 miles) E of Santiago

Cajón de Maipo is part *huaso* (a cowboy from the Central Valley), part artists' colony, part small-town charm tucked into a valley in the foothills of the Andes. From Santiago, it's less than 1 hour to the heart of the Cajón, the reason so many city denizens come to exchange the city smog and cement for the area's rugged, pastoral setting of towering peaks, freshly scented forest slopes, and the roar of the Maipo River as it descends along its route to the sea. If you have a day and would like to get a feel for the Andes and its rugged beauty, I highly recommend a visit here.

The highlight of this area is **El Morado National Park,** which offers ideal opportunities for day hiking, but it is certainly not a requisite destination. Cajón de Maipo boasts a wide array of outdoor activities, such as rafting, horseback riding, hiking, climbing, and more, but it also offers a chance to linger over a hearty lunch or picnic, stroll around the area, and maybe even lay your head down for the night in one of the charming little hotels or *cabañas* that line the valley.

The well-paved road through this valley follows the path of the Maipo River. Along the way you'll pass dozens of stalls set up by locals who sell fresh bread, honey, *küchen* (a dense cake), empanadas, *chicha* (cider), and chocolate to passersby.

Then you'll pass the tiny hamlets of Vertientes and San José de Maipo, the principal city of the area, founded in 1792 when silver was discovered in the foothills. Colonial adobe homes and an 18th-century church still stand at the traditional plaza in the center of town. Continuing southeast, the road curves past San Alfonso and eventually reaches a police checkpoint where drivers register before continuing on the dirt road to El Morado. About a half-hour farther (due to the condition of the road), there are fabulous clay-pool hot springs surrounded by soaring alpine peaks. ***Note:*** The weekends are packed with day-trippers, the hot springs are overflowing with people, and traffic on the way back is horrible. Plan to come on a weekday, if you can.

GETTING THERE

BY BUS Getting here by bus is cheap, but takes forever. First you'll need to take the Metro Line 4 toward Puente Alto and get off at the Las Mercedes station. You'll come out on Avenida Concha y Toro, and from here buses pass by every 10 minutes for San Jose de Maipo; if you're headed to San Alfonso, you can take a *taxi colectivo* (shared black taxis) from San Jose for 75¢ (50p) once you get there.

BY TAXI This is a faster option than the bus. Take the Metro as stated above; outside the Metro station await the *taxis colectivos,* which leave every 10 minutes from 7am to 8pm and cost $2 (£1.35) per person. Regular taxis (with the yellow roof) from the Mercedes Metro station can run anywhere from $13 to $19 (£8.70–£12.70) depending on your destination in the Cajón. Always negotiate a price with the driver beforehand.

BY CAR The fastest and easiest way from Las Condes or Providencia is to take Avenida Vespucio Sur and head south until the avenue turns into a highway. Exit at Las Tores and continue straight along the lateral road and make your first left, heading under the freeway. After turning left, get in the right lane and veer right immediately onto Avenida La Florida. Continue along this road for 12km (7$^1/_2$ miles) until you see the road fork at Puente Alto; head left at the sign pointing toward San José de Maipo. If you are downtown, follow Vicuña Mackenna Street until you hit Departamental, and head left (east) until you run into Avenida La Florida. Take a map and count on snarling weekend traffic. If you plan to go to El Morado, note that there is a police checkpoint where drivers are sometimes asked to show their documents, including a passport.

WHAT TO SEE & DO

EL MORADO NATIONAL PARK This 3,000-hectare (7,410-acre) park is 90km (56 miles) from Santiago. It takes its name from the sooty-colored rock of the Morado mountain (*morado* means "purple" or "bruised"). At 5,060m (16,596 ft.), the views at El Morado are stunning, and a relaxing spot to take in all this beauty is the Tyrolean mountain lodge **Refugio Lo Valdés ★**, San José de Maipo (✆ **9/220-8525;** www.refugiolovaldes.com). The *refugio* (meaning "refuge," but really a rustic lodge made of stone) serves truly delicious food and a fixed-price lunch and dinner. This is hands-down my favorite place for lunch in the Cajón de Maipo, since you can sit out on their stone patio and gaze out at the snowcapped peaks. The *refugio* is owned by the same people as La Cumbre mountain store in Las Condes (see "Fast Facts: Santiago" in chapter 6), and they offer outdoors activities such as day hiking or overnight climbing trips, horseback riding, mountain biking, visits to the hot springs, nature tours, and even fossil hunting. There are clean, simple accommodations (all bathrooms are shared) should you decide to spend the night, including three doubles with a queen-size bed, four doubles, three triples, and a few bunk rooms, and a cozy dining area warmed by a wood stove. Rates are $27 (£18) per adult, $22 (£15) per child age 6 to 12, and $16 (£11) per child age 1 to 5; breakfast is included.

You'll find the Conaf park ranger hut at **Baños Morales.** The park is open daily October through April from 8:30am to 6pm, and costs $2.50 (£1.70) to enter. There is just one trail, which runs for 8km (5 miles) and varies between easy and intermediate terrain, eventually passing by an alpine lake and a glacier with a profile view of the El Morado mountain. This is a first-rate day hike (about 6 hr. average round-trip), and there is a place to camp near the lake. The reserve provides a haven for an array of bird species, including hummingbirds, austral thrush, and the cometocino. The raggedy little village of Baños Morales has several very hot spring pools open daily from 8:30am to 8pm during the summer and from 10am to 4pm April through September, but they are not particularly inviting, and they're crammed with Santiaguinos during the peak of summer. Better natural hot springs are at **Termas de Colina,** in the form of clay pools descending a slope. The expansive alpine setting adds a sense of grandeur to the experience. It takes time to get here due to the condition of the road; continue past Lo Valdés for 12km (7$^1/_2$ miles). If you don't have a car, **Manzur Expediciones** (✆ **2/777-4284**) offers round-trip transportation for $18 (£12) per person, which includes the entrance fee, leaving Santiago at 7:30am and returning at 8pm. However, they operate only on weekends (unless you have a group and rent the whole minivan), and that is when the hot springs are at maximum capacity. The entrance fee is $7 (£4.70) per person.

RAFTING Rafting the Maipo River is very popular among Santiaguinos and foreigners alike. It is just incredible that this activity exists so close to a major metropolitan city. Although the season runs from September to April, the river really gets going from

Pomaire: The Clay Village

Every region in the Central Valley has a specialty good that it produces with pride, and Pomaire's is ceramic pottery. Pomaire is a small, dusty village 65km (40 miles) west of Santiago that was known as a *pueblo de indios,* a settlement the Spanish created for Indians. The area is rich in brown clay, and the main street (almost the only street here) overflows with shops hawking vases, funny little figurines, decorative pieces, and pots, plates, and other kitchen crockery—all at reasonable prices. This is also the place to sample homespun, country cooking (try San Antonio or Los Naranjos restaurants) such as the stews *cazuela* and *charquicán,* and Pomaire's famous half-kilo empanada; some restaurants even have *cueca* shows, the national dance of Chile.

Most tour companies offer this excursion, or you can rent a car or take **Buses Melipilla** (✆ **08/584-6812**), which has several daily trips from the San Borja Terminal in Santiago at Alameda O'Higgins 3250. The bus will leave you at the end of the road to Pomaire, where you'll have to take a *colectivo,* or shared taxi, into town. To get here by car, take the Pan-American Highway to the turnoff for Rte. 78 to San Antonio; follow the highway until you see the sign for Pomaire 3km (1¾ miles) before Melipilla. Note that Pomaire is shut down on Monday, and weekends are crowded.

November to February, when rafters can expect to ride Class III and IV rapids. Two companies offer half-day rafting excursions: **Cascada de las Animas** (✆ **2/861-1303;** www.cascadadelasanimas.cl) is based in the Cajón, and they arrange rafting trips from their tourism complex in San Alfonso (see "Where to Stay," later), but it's best to reserve beforehand. Another highly respected, and much friendlier, outfitter is **Altué Expediciones,** in Santiago, Encomenderos 83 (✆ **2/232-1103;** www.altue.com). They are based in Santiago and can arrange transportation for you to the Cajón de Maipo.

HORSEBACK RIDING The same two companies above offer horseback riding in the Cajón de Maipo, either for the day or for multiday riding (with themes such as "Following Darwin's Footsteps"). I can't express enough how enjoyable a horseback ride in the Andes is: the sweeping views from high, the grassy meadows, galloping home . . . There is an indefinable magic about crossing the Andean peaks the way Butch Cassidy and the Sundance Kid did. Cascada de las Animas has tours through its own private chunk of the Andes (see later), but verify that your guide is bilingual when booking as they like to send out old ranch hands who just lope quietly along with you. Horseback rides are suitable for families and even those with little experience.

WHERE TO STAY

Cascada de las Animas ★ (Kids) This tourism center is run by the Astorga-Moreno family, who own a monster swath of land outside San Alfonso. Within their complex are 80 campground and picnic sites scattered about a lovely wooded hillside. There are also eight log cabins set amid sylvan, leafy surroundings and uniquely built with carved wood details; they're rustic but enchanting, with fully equipped kitchens and wood-burning stoves. Owned by the same family, the tiny **Hostal La Casa Grande** in San Alfonso, (Vicuña Mackenna 90; (✆ **2/222-7347;** www.hostalcasagrande.cl), just 4 blocks from the entrance to their complex, offers tasteful simplicity in a welcoming hostel housed in a renovated 1930s home and surrounded by greenery. While the cabins are great for a group of four to six, the hostel is more economical ($34/£23 for a double with private bathroom) for a couple, and rooms are brightly painted, spotless, and very comfortable. Only two of the four rooms are en suite. Breakfast is included at the hostel, but not for the cabins; however, guests in both lodging options receive a discount on excursion prices (see "What to See & Do"). From April to August Monday through Thursday, there is a 20% discount for cabins.

There is a small grocery store in San Alfonso, and Cascada has a **restaurant** with dynamite views overlooking the Maipo River. The food is tasty, with lots of vegetarian options, but my major caveat with Cascada is that their staff seems unenthusiastic to the point of being aloof, and service is agonizingly slow.

Camino al Volcán 31087 (San Alfonso). ✆ **2/861-1303.** www.cascadadelasanimas.cl. 8 units. $70 (£47) *cabaña* for 1–4 people; $122 (£81) for 8. AE, DC, MC, V. **Amenities:** Restaurant; outdoor pool; sauna; game room; horseback riding; guided activities. *In room:* Kitchenette (cabins), no phone.

La Bella Durmiente Located at the end of a steep dirt road, these *cabañas* seem as if they've jumped out of the tale *Sleeping Beauty,* which is what the name means—but the word *durmiente* also refers to the thick wooden railroad planks used in the cabins' construction. Each *cabaña* is distinct, but all are handcrafted from wood and stucco and set among a grove of trees. While they may not offer many creature comforts, they are cozy idyllic places to relax a couple of nights. Each cabaña has a kitchen and barbecue, which can prove cost effective for independent travelers. Given the setting and amenities, such as the lovely palm-fringed swimming pool and games room with ping-pong and pool, the cabins are especially popular with young Chilean families. Try to get the "honeymoon" cabin—it's the best here.

Calle Los Maitenes 115, San Alfonso. ✆ **2/861-1525.** www.labelladurmiente.cl. 5 units. $55 (£37) cabin for 2; $76 (£51) cabin for 4. AE, MC, V. **Amenities:** Restaurant; outdoor pool (summer only); game room. *In room:* TV, kitchenette.

WHERE TO DINE

Casa Bosque Restaurant ★★ Kids STEAK If you don't eat at Casa Bosque, stop here quickly anyway to check out the restaurant's fabulously outlandish architecture. The local artist who designed Casa Bosque has left his mark on many buildings in Cajón de Maipo, but none as dramatically as here: Polished, raw tree trunks are kept in their natural shape, forming madcap door frames, ceiling beams, and pillars; oddly shaped windows and stucco fill in the gaps. It's pure fantasy, and adults will love it as much as kids. Casa Bosque is a *parrilla,* and it serves succulent grilled beef, chicken, and sausages from a giant indoor barbecue, which you can pair with fresh salads, creamy potatoes, or a grilled provolone cheese, along with a few vegetarian dishes. During the weekend lunch hour, this restaurant can get packed, mostly with families with lots of kids, and service can be absent-minded and slow.

Camino el Volcán 16829. ✆ **2/871-1570.** Main courses $5–$10 (£3.30–£6.70). AE, DC, MC, V. Mon–Thurs 12:30–6pm; Fri–Sat 12:30pm–midnight; Sun 12:30–7pm.

La Petite France Restaurant & Hotel ★★ Finds BISTRO The walls of La Petite France's restaurant, with its Edith Piaf posters and ads for French products, are pure kitsch. In spite of its incongruity here in the Chilean Andean foothills, the locals love this little restaurant, especially for the pastries and pretty outdoor deck. La Petite blends classic French bistro fare with flavorful Chilean and international dishes. On offer are dishes such as filet mignon in a puff pastry with Roquefort sauce, and turkey breast stuffed with almonds, plums, and apples in a cactus sauce. Of course, there's also pâté, escargot, and croque monsieur. During teatime on weekends, mouthwatering desserts are laid out enticingly across a long table: Tarte tatin, crème brûlée, and chocolate layer cake are just a few choices.

La Petite also runs a small hotel above the restaurant—a level high enough to provide guest rooms with sweeping views of the mountains. I love the setting here, especially the garden and the outdoor pool, and the nine rooms, while simple, are perfectly comfortable and have private bathrooms and TVs (but no phone). Amenities include an outdoor pool, laundry service, and Internet access; guest rooms are $65 (£41) double occupancy.

Camino el Volcán 16096. ✆ **2/861-1967.** Main courses $7–$11 (£4.70–£7.30). AE, DC, MC, V. Tues–Sun noon–6pm and 8pm–midnight.

Trattoria Calypso ★★ ITALIAN Owned and operated by a Genovese family who immigrated to this region more than a decade ago, Trattoria Calypso serves delicious homemade pastas and, on Saturdays and Sundays only, crispy stone oven–baked pizzas. Everything is made using organic and local farm ingredients, such as the mozzarella bought from a family in Cajón de Maipo and smoked here at the restaurant. Pastas include ravioli, cannelloni, fungi fettuccine, and pesto lasagna, but you might want to nibble an antipasti platter with fresh focaccia bread. The cozy restaurant has indoor and outdoor seating at wooden tables; the staff gives a warm welcome to all who pass through the doors. It's open Friday through Sunday only, but if you're in the area during one of these days, don't miss a stop here.

Camino el Volcán 9831. ✆ **2/871-1498.** Main courses $7–$12 (£4.70–£8). No credit cards. Fri–Sun 12:30–10pm; Sun 12:30–6pm.

5 WINE, SPAS & RURAL TRADITION IN THE CENTRAL VALLEY & ACONCAGUA REGIONS

Just outside the city limits of Santiago, the scenery opens into a patchwork of poplar-lined agricultural fields and grapevines, and tiny towns hearken back to a quieter, colonial era where it is common to see weathered adobe homes, horse-driven carts, and dirt roads. This is Chile's breadbasket, a region that boasts a mild, Mediterranean climate, fertile soil, and plenty of irrigation thanks to the Andes, and testament of this natural bounty can be seen at the myriad of roadside stands hawking fresh fruit and vegetables and unbelievably cheap prices.

There is much to see and do here, but what travelers really come to do is tour vineyards, the reason why this section is divided into the main wine regions, featured chronologically from north to south, and encompassing hotels, spas, and rural and colonial historical highlights found within each area.

WINE IN CHILE: THE FACTS

The international popularity of Chilean wine has grown dramatically over the past 10 years, and because Chilean wine has moved slowly up the ladder into the premium and ultrapremium bracket, it is now capturing the attention of wine enthusiasts and collectors worldwide. Chile's wine tradition dates back to the days of the Spanish conquest, although modern winemaking techniques and technology were only introduced in the late 1970s, when the Spanish winemaker Miguel Torres imported the first stainless-steel wine tanks. Yet given this long tradition of winemaking, the Chileans themselves have been slow to appreciate their wines, and consequently many winegrowers export the bulk of their product to Europe, the United States, Canada, and Asia.

Chile is a winemaking paradise. Mother Nature has blessed the country with a natural geography that creates the perfect *terroir*—that is, a combination of local climate and geology. Central Chile's Mediterranean-like climate produces lots of luminosity and minimal but sufficient rainfall outside the winter months. During the past few years winemakers have learned which grapes grow better and produce better wines in which valleys. For example, white grape production has been moved from the Colchagua Valley to the Casablanca Valley, a cooler region that has produced far superior sauvignon blancs and chardonnays, and vintners have identified which micro-regions are ideal for producing premium wines, such as Apalta.

What is unique about Chilean wine is that vintners imported their rootstock from Europe more than a century ago, long before European roots were affected with *phylloxera,* a pest that nearly wiped out the whole of the European wine industry. Chilean rootstock, having not been affected by this plague, is therefore the oldest original European rootstock in the world. Another unique fact is that Chileans only discovered the **carmenère** grape in 1994, intermingled with its merlot vines. Outside Chile there are very few hectares of carmenère planted in the world due to the difficulty in growing the grape and its late harvest. Carmenère is now Chile's flagship grape variety, even though it is more commonly used in blends.

What you're now seeing in Chile is direct foreign investment and partnerships with American and European companies, such as Gran Marnier, Château Lafite, Baron Philippe de Rothschild, and Kendall Jackson, who have recognized Chile's ideal growing conditions and cheaper land and labor costs as a potential to produce world-class wines.

The Regions in Brief

In 1994, the Chilean government defined specific viticultural regions, known as appellations, and their sub-regions: **Atacama** (Copiapó and Huasco valleys); **Coquimbo** (Elqui, Limarí, and Choapa valleys); **Aconcagua** (Aconcagua, Casablanca, and San Antonio valleys); **Central Valley** (Maipo, Rapel, Curicó, and Maule valleys); and the **South** (Itata, Bío-Bío, and Malleco valleys).

Of Chile's five grape-producing regions, currently the two most important in winemaking are the **Aconcagua** and **Central Valley** regions, beginning about 100km (62 miles) north of Santiago and stretching south past Talca, a little less than 300km (186 miles) from Santiago. Within these two regions lie seven sub-regions (or appellations), composed of the Aconcagua, Casablanca, San Antonio, Maipo, Rapel, Curicó, and Maule valleys. Within these valleys, finer distinctions have been divided into sub-appellations and even micro-valleys. Such is the case of the Rapel Valley being split into the Cachapoal and Colchagua valleys.

The traditional wineries of Chile (Cousiño Macul and Concha y Toro) and a few up-and-coming boutique wineries are located within 35km (22 miles) of Santiago, meaning it is possible to spend a day wine-tasting without having to travel very far. Even the Casablanca Valley is less than an hour away. The valleys covered in this guide are: Aconcagua, Casablanca, San Antonio, Maipo, Cachapoal, and Colchagua. Of these, the best

Tips Reservations at Wineries

Only a few wineries are open to anyone who walks through the doors between 9am and 5pm. Most wineries require reservations for English-speaking tours, or even just to pay a visit. Call to confirm if you have your heart set on visiting a certain winery; unfortunately some Chilean wineries still lack professionalism, and reservations are occasionally canceled at the last minute, or private tours are not honored and visitors must join the regular group tour. More popular wineries such as Concha y Toro can accommodate tour groups of up to 30 people, yet other wineries limit the number of guests to create a more intimate experience. If you'd like a personalized tour, ask to have one set up for you; it will cost extra, but it is usually worth it.

known outside Chile is the **Colchagua Valley,** Chile's answer to Napa Valley, and centered around the curious town of Santa Cruz, a Wild West town but with all the poise of a village in Bordeaux, about a 2½-hour drive from Santiago.

TOURING THE WINE COUNTRY & THE RURAL HEARTLAND

Be sure to pick up Turiscom's excellent English-language ***Guía de Vinos*** wine guide series sold at bookstores and wine shops (also sold in the Vinoteca wine store in the airport), which comes with a detailed map of the entire Chilean wine region. Or purchase a copy online at **www.turistel.cl**. Many of these routes combine nature, culture, and historical attractions as part of the tour.

Established Wine Routes

The Aconcagua, Cachapoal, Casablanca, Curicó, Colchagua, and Maule wine valleys and their corresponding wineries have banded together to offer travelers organized "wine routes," with maps, a reservation center, bilingual guides, and transportation, and a few extra road signs to navigate independent travelers. However, the concept is still in its infancy, and really the only truly well-established wine route is in the Colchagua Valley, and it is recommended above all others.

Half-day wine route tours include visits to two wineries, and full-day tours include a visit to a third winery and lunch either at a winery or a local restaurant. Visitors may either rent a vehicle and visit wineries on their own, having made reservations through the wine route office, or pay an additional fee for transportation from the route's meeting point (in the case of Colchagua, in Santa Cruz), and a bilingual guide. This guide simply leads the group and is an additional cost; tastings and tours are provided by winery staff members, so you may want to forego the guide unless you'd like to learn about the regional culture and history.

Given the growing popularity of wine-tasting in Chile, the wine routes now divide their tours into "wine lovers," "connoisseurs," and "fanatics" tours, which essentially refers to the cost and the caliber of wines offered for tasting: varietals and reserve wines; grand reserve and premium; and ultrapremium/icon wines. Of course, prices vary with "fanatics" tours costing more than three times the basic tour. The cost for tours without transportation and lunch are per person, regardless of the group size; the per-person cost for tours that include transportation and lunch drops as the group size grows.

- **Ruta del Vino, Colchagua Valley,** Plaza de Armas 298, Santa Cruz (© **72/823199;** www.colchaguavalley.cl), incorporates some of the most important wineries in Chile, including **Viña Montes, Viu Manent, Casa Silva, Emiliana Orgánica,** and **Casa Lapostolle's Clos Apalta.** Reservations are required 24 hours in advance. A bilingual guide costs an additional $55 (£37) for a half-day, $96 (£64) for a full day. Tours are as cheap as $32 (£21) per person for a half-day without transportation and lunch, or $300 (£200) per person (based on two guests) for an all-inclusive fanatics tour. The full-day tour can be three wineries, or two wineries and a stop at the **Museo de Colchagua** (p. 178). The included lunch for the full-day tour is at the Hotel Santa Cruz, Casa Silva, Pan Pan Vino Vino, or Hacienda Lolol.
- **Ruta del Vino, Valle de Casablanca,** Av. Portales 90, Casablanca (© **32/274-3933;** www.casablancavalley.cl), is a new wine route with the perk that they provide round-trip transportation to and from Santiago. Still, they've yet to embrace the wine route concept, and are often disorganized—better to visit this region on a privately organized wine tour or on your own, especially when headed to Valparaíso. The Casablanca Wine Route includes the wineries **William Cole, Morandé, Casas del Bosque, Emiliana Orgánicas, Viña Mar,** and **Indómita.** Half-day tours include two wineries, a guide, and transportation for $75 (£50) per person; full-day tours visit three wineries and include lunch for $95 (£63) per person. Prices are for a minimum of five people and require reservations made a week in advance.
- **Ruta del Vino, Valle de Aconcagua** (© **9/479-0278;** www.aconcaguavinos.cl) is the least visited wine route and not as organized as Colchagua. However, they do offer a full-day tour to two wineries via bicycle: They pick you up in Santiago and transport you to the region, provide the bicycles and a guide, and include lunch at the Casa St. Regis (p. 165). The cost is $100 (£67), with a minimum of five guests. Half-day tours cost $75 (£50) per person, based on four guests. Wineries that are part of the tour include **Errázuriz, Von Siebenthal, San Esteban,** and **Sanchez de Loria;** reservations must be booked 48 hours in advance.
- **Ruta del Vino, Alto de Cachapoal,** Calle Comercio 435, Requínoa (© **72/553684;** www.cachapoalwineroute.cl), is relatively unconsolidated as a whole, so arm yourself with a good sense of adventure. The wineries below the Andes (known as "Alto Cachapoal") have more paved roads than their counterparts on the western side of the Pan-American Highway. Guided tours are "Basic," with a visit to two wineries; "Classic," which adds lunch at Hacienda Los Lingues (including a horse show and tour of the hotel); and "Gastronomy," with one winery visit and a full country-style lunch at **Viña Gracia** or a Chilean-style barbecue at **Chateau Los Boldos** (barbecue minimum is 11 guests). The costs, respectively, per person and based on four people, are $33 (£22), $95 (£63), and $54 (£36) or $70 (£47) for the barbecue. Another winery here is **Altaïr** (p. 171), a state-of-the-art winery with glorious views.

Private & Independently Planned Tours

Guided tours make a lot of sense if you want to leave the headache of planning a tour to someone else, or if you'd like a personalized tour tailored to your interests. Private tours open a lot of doors to an "insider's" view, including visits with a winemaker and visits to wineries that are otherwise closed to the public. Wine fanatics seeking to only visit wineries that "matter" will need a private tour.

Before you book an expensive trip through an international wine tour operator, remember that many wine tour companies outside of Chile subcontract local operators and charge you extra, or take you to the biggest wineries for basic tastings. For a tailored experience, go directly to the local source. **Liz Caskey Culinary & Wine Experiences** (✆ **904/687-0340** in the U.S., or **2/632-2015** in Chile; www.lizcaskey.com) specializes in custom-made gastronomic and wine tours to the region's wine-growing valleys, including Mendoza, Argentina. Wine connoisseurs can build a tour according to their tastes; for new wine enthusiasts, the tours are a perfect way to taste and learn about both premium wines and local culture. The founder, an American expat and sommelier, combines winery explorations with visits to artisan olive oil plants, colonial bakeries, sea salt beds, cheese makers, and handicraft stores; tours can include active and wellness options such as hiking, biking, horseback riding, and yoga. They also offer trip extensions to such destinations as Patagonia, San Pedro de Atacama, and Easter Island.

If you're the more independent type who savors hitting the open road alone, but are loathe to make the reservations or are nervous planning your journey in a foreign land, contact **Santiago Adventures** (✆ **2/244-2750;** www.santiagoadventures.com). Santiago Adventures specializes in self-drive tours: You provide them with a little information about what you're looking for, they build the itinerary and book the car rental, hotel, and winery reservations for you. Upon arrival in Santiago, the company gives a meet-and-greet to review the itinerary and supply you with a map and driving instructions, a wine guidebook, your hotel reservations, and your rental car, plus a 24/7 emergency number. Santiago Adventures also offers guided trips with transportation that either focus entirely on wine, or that combine cultural visits, to places such as Valparaíso, with wine-tasting.

THE ACONCAGUA VALLEY

Spread across the feet of the Andes, this is the narrowest wine-growing valley with the steepest slopes, offering visitors one of the most stunning wine country tours in terms of scenery. The Aconcagua is characterized by winter rains and cool breezes entering from the Pacific Ocean, and is particularly well adapted for growing syrah, or blends based on syrah. The Aconcagua is ideal for visitors headed to Argentina or skiers visiting Portillo or Ski Arpa resorts, and there is a spa and lots of picturesque rural adobe architecture. Beyond the restaurants listed below, note that the Portillo resort is open year-round for lunch, and is worth the extra 1½-hour round-trip drive from Los Andes for its majestic Alpine views.

Errazuriz ★★ One of Chile's oldest and most respected wineries, Errazuriz was founded in 1870 by Don Maximiano Errazuriz, a member of one of Chile's most illustrious families, as it includes four presidents as well as a number of diplomats and writers. The particular appeal of this lovely winery resides in its Spanish-style architecture that dates to 1850, and there are sweeping views of the valley and the Andes and an impressive underground barrel cellar. This vineyard is renowned for its natural techniques and delicate production methods, which are employed to create complex and elegant wines. Both their cabernet sauvignon and La Cumbre syrah are ranked internationally as some of Chile's best wines. Tour 1 visits the cellar and estate ($20/£13 per person, with two tastings), and Tour 2 adds a walk to the top of La Cumbre for views ($25/£17 per person, with three tastings). Groups can book lunch, but you'll need to book far in advance. For driving details, print out the map on their website under "Wine Stores & Tours."

Calle Antofagasta s/n, Panquehue. ✆ **34/590139.** www.errazuriz.cl. Reservations required. Tours offered Tues–Sat 10am–6pm.

Von Siebenthal ★ Finds One of the valley's upstarts, this boutique winery was founded by Swiss attorney Mauro Von Siebenthal in the late 1990s. Mention Von Siebenthal in local wine crowds and you will get a consistent thumbs-up on the overall quality of the vineyard's cabernet sauvignon, merlot, and carmenère to cabernet franc, petit verdot, and syrah. Varied soils allow the winery to grow all their grapes on site. Given the winery's limited production, its top wines include the super premium Montelig, premium Carabantes and Parcela 7, and carmenère reserva, which won the prestigious Concours Mondial de Bruxelles 2005 Tastings, with Von Siebenthal's sommelier provide the sort of personalized attention most visitors crave. Tours cost $10 (£6.70) per person.

Av. O'Higgins s/n, Panquehue. ✆ **34/591827.** www.vinavonsiebenthal.com. Reservations required. Tours Thurs–Fri 9am–5pm. From Los Andes, located on the road to San Esteban at Km 77.

Where to Stay & Dine

Casa St. Regis ★ Finds Take a step back in time and immerse yourself in history at this converted 19th-century hacienda, one of the more unique lodging options in the Central Valley. The former manor home of an expansive 16,000-hectare (40,000-acre) estate, Casa San Regis is now a bed-and-breakfast, but really little has changed given that the hacienda features all the original parquet floors, antique furnishings and flair—and guest rooms that are turn-of-the-20th-century simple. The hacienda's intimate character and the warm hospitality bestowed by the house-proud owners Marcela and Alexis are the main reasons to stay here. With the exception of the "Aconcagua" suite and Los Cobres guest room, most rooms have twin beds and shared bathrooms. The roaring fireplace in the living room is an excellent place to unwind after a long day of wine-tasting, and there's an outdoor pool. The family delights in organizing horseback-riding excursions, wine-tasting forays, and teaching guests about the hacienda's agricultural production. The Chilean-style meals are very good, and are served family-style at their grand dining room table; breakfast is included, and lunch and dinner cost $13 (£8.70) each.

La Chaparrina 791. ✆ **34/481052** or 9/252-5133. www.casasanregis.cl. 5 units. $42–$67 (£28–£45) single; $85 (£57) standard double; $96 (£64) suite. No credit cards. **Amenities:** Meals; outdoor pool; game room; organized tours; cable TV room. *In room:* No phone.

Termas de Jahuel Hotel & Spa ★★★ Kids Central Chile's spa tradition dates back to the turn of the 20th century, but Termas de Jahuel is the only spa resort that has renovated its facilities for the 21st century. Nestled in the foothills of the Andes near San Felipe, Termas de Jahuel was built in 1912 with Oregon Pine that had been used as ballast in cargo ships sailing to Valparaíso from the U.S. To classify the hotel as luxurious is an overstatement and frequent visitors to spa resorts in the U.S. will be sadly disappointed by the mediocre accommodations options. Improvements have been made recently, however; the hotel was restored in 2005, updating the guest rooms, which are now spacious and comfortable, if devoid of sophistication.

It is well worth paying the extra $20/£13 for a room in one of the new wings, even if you sacrifice a view of the valley. The resort is very popular with weekender Santiaguinos who come to enjoy the salubrious setting, state-of-the-art spa facilities, and Olympic outdoor pool, which is actually a hot springs with mineralized water. There are also short trails winding around the resort that afford stunning views of the valley. Meals, especially breakfast, are generally of a higher standard than you would expect, and the format varies between an all-you-can-eat buffet or a three-course set menu with a couple of choices.

Jahuel s/n, San Felipe. ✆ **2/411-1720** or 2/421-2400. www.jahuel.cl. 82 units. $265 (£177) Classic Double; $295 (£197) Superior Double; $325 (£217) VIP Double. Rates include full board, and are per room, not per person. AE, DC, MC, V. **Amenities:** 3 restaurants; bar; outdoor and indoor heated thermal pools; full-service spa; games; guided treks. *In room:* Satellite TV, minibar, hair dryer, CD player.

THE CASABLANCA & SAN ANTONIO VALLEYS

The Casablanca and San Antonio valleys are often compared to California's Sonoma and Russian River valleys. Although they neighbor each other, their wines and their wineries couldn't be more distinct. Casablanca is centered around the Rte. 68 highway that connects Viña del Mar and Valparaíso with Santiago. Until recently, the region was mostly dairy farms. Winemaker Pablo Morandé saw parallels here to California's Carneros region, and in 1982 he planted 20 hectares (49 acres) of chardonnay, riesling, and sauvignon blanc. His hypothesis proved right: Today Casablanca is considered *the* great discovery in wine valleys in the modern era of winemaking, and it now produces most of Chile's white wines and some pinot noirs. The Casablanca Valley is known for its slick wine-tasting facilities, high-volume visitor capacities, and a couple of stylish restaurants. Many visitors stop here on the way out to Viña del Mar or Valparaíso.

San Antonio is the newest, tiniest, and most "happening" wine appellation in Chile, with only four boutique wineries that focus on quality, not quantity, producing Chile's finest pinot noir, sauvignon blanc, and syrah. Plan your visit here in conjunction with a visit to Pablo Neruda's museum in Isla Negra.

Casas del Bosque ★ Founded in 1993 by Chilean businessman Juan Cuneo Solari, this boutique winery produces just 70,000 cases of wine a year and provides a more intimate approach to oenotourism. Located just 12 miles from the Pacific, the winery is widely applauded for its delicious and crisp sauvignon blanc and chardonnay. Although the house specialty is white wine, their creative winemaking team was the first in the valley to plant merlot. Also in their red wine repertoire is a fresh, peppery syrah that is worth a sip. Reservations are necessary for tours of the winery, which can be customized: $10 (£6.70) per person for the basic tour, $15 (£10) per person for a visit to the vineyard lookout point for a tasting and appetizer; there are also horse-drawn carriage rides. Or, you can simply stop off at their sleek **Tanino** restaurant which offers a course tasting menu paired with wine.

Alejandro Galvaz s/n. ✆ **2/377-9431.** www.casasdelbosque.cl. Reservations required. Tours Mon–Sat 9:30am–5:30pm, Sun 10am–5pm. Restaurant Tues–Sun 10am–5pm. Exit at the Casablanca/Lo Vasquez sign, cross over the hwy., and continue to Alejandro Galvaz. Turn right and drive about 1km (2/3 mile) until you see the winery on the left-hand side.

Matetic Vineyards ★★★ Kids Located within its own 11,000-hectare (27,000-acre) valley not far from the Pacific, Matetic's state-of-the-art multimillion-dollar, gravity-flow winery is sunken into a sloping hill, and it is one of the most architecturally avant-garde wineries in Chile. They are also experts in determining just the right *terroir* to produce Chile's EQ syrahs, judged one of the world's top 100 wines by *Wine Spectator* magazine in 2006 in addition to being named a *Decanter* gold medal winner the same year. Matetic is simply one of the most exciting and swish wineries in Chile to visit. For a treat, have lunch at the gourmet restaurant (Tues–Sun) where chef Matiás Bustos creates innovative recipes using the freshest local ingredients. The guest home is plush and charming, but overpriced (see "Where to Stay & Dine," later). Apart from wine tours, Matetic's agrotourism offerings include horseback riding, harvest tours, and blueberry picking, making this winery a good bet for kids. Wine tours range from $14 (£9.30) per person for a basic tour to $28 (£19) per person for advanced tours. To find how to get here, download a map from their website.

Fundo Rosario, Lagunillas. ✆ **2/232-3134** or 2/595-2661 www.matetic.cl. Reservations required 24 hr. in advance. Tours Tues–Sun 11am–3:30pm. From road to Algarrobo, take Lagunillas exit and continue to Rosario, where you'll see the winery's sign.

Veramonte ★ This is perhaps the most "Californian" of all Chile wineries due to its founders, the Hunees family, who have their roots in Napa Valley—in fact, Veramonte's first vintages (1995–97) were bottled in California! More than 85% of their wine is exported to the U.S. Veramonte's vineyards are designed for mechanical harvest, and their state-of-the-art facility is capable of crushing 75 tons of grapes per day. Wine tours begin out in the vineyards with a detailed explanation of the characteristics of the grapes and the features of the terrain before proceeding to an explanation of the manufacturing process, and finishing in the attractive tasting room, which has a soaring rotunda and glass walls that let you peek into the barrel caves below—still, it's a "stand-up" winery that's better for a quick tasting, not a tour. Tastings cost $2 (£1.35) for two wines, or $3 (£2) for a tasting of their top cabernet-merlot blend, Primus.

Rte. 68, Km 66, Casablanca. ✆ 32/232-9999. www.veramonte.cl. Tasting room Mon–Fri 9am–6pm; Sat–Sun 9am–3pm. Tours Mon–Fri 10:30am, 2:30 and 3pm. Sat–Sun 10:30am and 12:30pm.

Viña Casa Marin ★ Finds This winery holds the distinction of being closest to the Pacific Ocean; it is also the proud producer of Chile's best sauvignon blanc (Los Cipreses 2005), quite the victory for a winery that has been around only since 2003. Casa Marin is the brainchild of winemaker María Luz Marin, ex-head of production at the gargantuan Viña San Pedro. Marin's pet project focuses exclusively on pinot noir and white varieties such as its sauvignon blanc, and riesling, gerwurztraminer, and sauvignon gris. The vineyards here are slope-planted and take advantage of varying soils and orientations—producing outstanding results. Tours cost $17 (£11) per person, including one wine, and $28 (£19), including two wines. Premium tours can also be arranged (Sat only), which include a personal tour of the winery by Casa Marin owner and CEO María Luz Marin and a tasting of all Casa Marin wines ($120/£80).

Another reason to pay a visit here is Casa Marin's **Corazón Vinospas** ★, undoubtedly one of the finest spas in Chile, offering high-end treatments such as massages that blend Hawaiian Lomi Lomi, reiki, and energy healing, $75 (£50), and body treatments and facials, $60 (£40). Afterward, you can recline on their deck with a glass of wine (included in the price). The spa is open from early November to late April Monday through Saturday from 9am to 6pm, and Sundays by appointment only.

Camino Lo Abarca s/n. ✆ **2/657-1530.** www.casamarin.cl. Reservations required. Tours Mon–Sat. From Rte. 78 toward San Antonio, turn right at the Malvilla exit.

Viñedos Orgánicos Emiliana ★★ Chile's pioneer in organic and biodynamic wines also prides itself on service-oriented tastings. Like Veramonte, it's one of the few wineries in Chile where you can just pull over and visit during open hours, yet it's best to call ahead for the full, sit-down wine-tasting with cheese and fruit. Emiliana's main winery and cellar is located in Colchagua; the Casablanca vineyards are for white wine production, and here they have a contemporary, glass-and-wood tasting facility and wine shop surrounded by a grassy park. Groups of 10 or more can book a gourmet lunch for $38 (£25) per person (1-week advance reservation required). Emiliana's premium wine, Coyam, is the highest-rated assemblage in the country, and their recently released Gê is the country's only biodynamic icon wine. Basic hour-long tours with tastings are $13 (£8.70) per person for three wines. Reservations aren't required.

Rte. 68, Km 61, Casablanca. ✆ **9/327-4019.** www.voe.cl. Tasting room daily 10am–6:30pm. Tours Wed–Sun 10:30am, noon, 3 and 4:30pm.

Matetic Guesthouse & Restaurant ★★★ One imagines that more and more wineries will jump on the bandwagon with the wine tour/boutique hotel/gourmet restaurant concept, but for now this is the only place in the Casablanca Valley to spend the night. And, if you have ever dreamed of owning your own vineyard, this is the place to live the fantasy. It comes at a premium price, but if you've got the funds you won't be disappointed. The modest early 20th-century colonial-style hacienda belies three lavishly appointed, French country-chic guest rooms, replete with parquet floors, antique furniture, and French doors that open onto a patio terrace and a lovely garden. As an exclusive guesthouse, it is not a full-service hotel with all the trimmings (like room service), but then hardly a guest would complain given the sylvan surroundings and the gorgeous interiors. Rates include breakfast, and lunch or dinner, a wine tour and tasting, and horseback riding.

Day-trippers will certainly want to carve out 1½ hours for a sumptuous meal at Matetic's restaurant. Chef Matías Bustos is a pro at creating innovative meals with local ingredients and artful presentation, without going over the top.

Fundo Rosario, Lagunillas. ✆ **2/232-3134** or 32/274-1500. www.matetic.cl. 3 units. $400 (£267) double. AE, DC, MC, V. **Amenities:** Restaurant; wine tours. *In room:* Hair dryer, safe, no phone.

Where to Dine

House of Morandé ★★ Viña Morandé's stylish eatery is located right off Rte. 68 at Km 61, and is therefore a convenient stopping point for lunch. There is a glass-and-wood indoor dining area, and pleasant patio dining overlooking a grassy expanse and grapevines—still, you can hear the faint whoosh of cars whizzing by. The well-balanced menu features lots of seafood, such as classic Parmesan razor clams, three kinds of *ceviche,* king crab lasagna, and hard-to-obtain fish such as tuna, tilapia, and grouper, but there are also meats and salads. Save room for their "tasting" of three desserts. The staff is all smiles, and they are well educated to provide suggestions for wine pairings. Although House of Morandé offers a selection of Casablanca wines, I say skip their tour and tasting, and try their wine varieties over lunch. They have an on-site wine shop if you want to take home a bottle.

Rte. 68, Km 61. ✆ **32/275-4701.** www.morande.cl. Reservations recommended for Fri dinner. Main courses $11–$12 (£7.30–£8). AE, DC, MC, V. Tues–Sun 11am–5pm (Fri until midnight).

Restaurante Viña Indómita ★★ (Moments You can't miss Indómita. Just look for the Hollywood-style lettering and a giant white castle perched on a knoll above a spread of grapevines. The food is outstanding and the sweeping views of the Casablanca Valley even more so. And the wine? Well, two out of three ain't bad. They charge more for a soft drink than for a glass of their wine, so soak up the view, bring a camera, and prepare yourself for epic dining. Tender osso buco cooked in pinot noir and served with coriander gnocchi is a longstanding favorite, while the pistachio-encrusted beef tenderloin served with a date and wild mushroom strudel is wonderful. The ambience at Indómita is sophisticated and, like most of the wineries in wine country, serves reinvented Chilean meats and seafood, appetizers, and fresh salads.

Rte. 68, Km 63. ✆ **32/275-4400.** www.indomita.cl. Main courses $13–$18 (£8.70–£12). AE, MC, V. Daily 12:30–4:30pm.

THE MAIPO VALLEY

Chile's "classic" valley is home to the most traditional wineries in the country, including heavyweight winemaker Concha y Toro. The huge advantage of visiting wineries here is

Tips Shipping & Carrying Wine Back Home

Ever since the ban of liquids on flights, many visitors aren't sure how to get their wine home. Here are several points to consider.

- First, check to see if you can buy the wine at home for less money. Chilean wines are often cheaper in the U.S., for instance, as the VAT (sales) and alcohol tax exceeds 35% in Chile. Generally speaking, though, you won't find boutique gems outside of Chile.
- Shipping wine is expensive: around $250 (£160) per 12-bottle case. Most wineries that ship abroad by air use **Hot Express** (✆ **2/687-3410;** www.hotexpress.cl), who are experts in shipping wine and have special wine cases fitted with Styrofoam to protect bottles, which you can pick up at their office or coordinate to have dropped off at your hotel. Plan ahead at least 2 or 3 days.
- Despite the myth, corks do not explode, and bottles will not break if some care and common sense are taken when packing. If you can't get your hands on a Hot Express Styrofoam case, any sturdy 12-bottle cardboard wine case will do. Pack each bottle firmly in bubble wrap (or your underwear and socks) and place in the case so that they don't move. For 6 bottles in a 12-bottle case, for example, stagger the bottles so there's an open place between them so they don't bang against each other. Close and reinforce with packing tape. Put your name, address, and a "fragile" label on the box. You can shrink-wrap your box at the airport if it gives you peace of mind. Check the box as a normal piece of luggage.
- While you may be able to get wine out of Chile, make sure you can get it *into* your home. In the U.S., some states like Pennsylvania and Arizona have stringent alcohol laws. In some cases you will have to pay duty, and in some states your wine may be confiscated. U.K. residents can take home a maximum of 4 liters of still table wine (per adult) without paying customs duty. New Zealand residents can enter with 4.5 liters of wine, while Australian residents are limited to 2.25 liters of duty-free alcohol total. Canadian travelers may return from Chile with just 1.5 liters of wine, *or* 1.14 liters of liquor, *or* 24 12-ounce cans or bottles of beer or ale, including beer coolers over 0.5% alcohol. For updated information, check your home country's customs regulations before you travel.
- Once your wine is safe in your home, you'll need a couple of weeks to let it rest. Wine gets "stressed" when traveling, and it can actually taste off if you don't give it time to let the molecules settle.

their proximity to Santiago. In fact, you can simply taxi over to wineries like Concha y Toro or Cousiño Macul. The Maipo is the king of red wine production, with cabernet sauvignon occupying more than 70% of the total hectares planted here. This valley was recently divided into the sub-appellations **Alto Maipo** and **Isla de Maipo.**

For a taxi to Concha y Toro or Cousiño Macul, call a private radio taxi with executive vehicles, such as **Radio Taxi Chile** (✆ **2/699-4303**), or ask your hotel concierge to call one rather than flagging down a street cab. Often you'll need the bare minimum of Spanish, as drivers do not speak English. Rates cost approximately $28 (£19) one-way from downtown, and $26 (£17) one-way from Las Condes. Ask the driver to wait for you. A taximeter is used for all cars and the per-hour cost of having the driver wait is $7 to $10 (£4.70–£6.70); negotiate directly with the driver if you can for the entire cost of the journey.

Concha y Toro ★★★ Chile's largest and best-known winery accounts for 33% of all national wine sales, and they produce the lion's share of export wines—from inexpensive table reds to some of Chile's high-end, traditional cabernet sauvignons such as Don Melchor, which was recently acknowledged by *Wine Spectator* as the best wine in Chile. Founded in 1883 by the eccentric mining magnate Don Melchor Concho y Toro, this gorgeous estate, which resembles an English country manor, is part of the attraction, with gardens large enough to require eight full-time gardeners, a sculpted lake, eucalyptus-lined pathway and antique *bodegas* whose interiors include the famous "Castillero del Diablo," a folkloric tale featuring a cellar haunted by a devil, invented to scare workers away from stealing the owner's prize wines. There is a huge wine shop with wine, souvenirs, arts and crafts, and books, too. If you want to skip the tour, Concha y Toro's smart wine bar has tastings of all wines, including Almaviva (see later), paired with appetizers, and is open Monday through Saturday from 10am to 6pm. Group tours cost $12 (£8) and include a souvenir glass. You can even take the Metro here: Ride to the Tobalaba station, transfer to Line 4, and ride it to Plaza de Puente Alto station; from here, a taxi gets you there in 5 minutes.

Virginia Subercaseux 210, Pirque. ✆ **2/476-5269.** www.conchaytoro.com. English tours Mon–Sun at 10 and 11:30am, noon, and 3pm.

Cousiño-Macul ★★ The first vines in Chile were planted here in 1546, but the winery itself was founded by the Cousiño family in 1856. Of its peers established at the same time (such as Concha y Toro, earlier), Cousiño Macul is the only one that continues in the hands of the original founding family, now in its sixth generation. In 2005, the Guia de Vinos de Chile gave top honors to Cousiño-Macul's 2003 Antiguas Reservas Chardonnay, which, at less than $15 (£10) per bottle, is also an excellent value. Using entirely estate-grown grapes, Cousiño-Macul's wines are known around the world for their distinctive Maipo characteristics and fruit. To celebrate its 150th birthday, the winery recently launched its first icon wine, Lota. The beautiful estate, with its lush, French-designed gardens, is worth a visit to see this grand original in the history of Chilean wine. Tours cost $10 (£6.70) and include a souvenir wine glass and tastings of two wines.

Av. Quilin 7100, Peñalolen. ✆ **2/351-4175.** www.cousinomacul.cl. Tours Mon–Fri at 11am and 3pm; Sat 11am. Sat tours in English and Spanish. To get here, head south on Americo Vespucio until the Rotunda Quilin; from here, head east toward the Andes. The winery is on the left-hand side.

Odfjell Vineyards ★ A newcomer to the Isla de Maipo scene, this winery is the creation of Norwegian shipping magnate Dan Odfjell and his son, an architect who sketched out the winery's stylish, minimalist look and narrow ceiling, which gives the sensation of being in a ship's hull. Although "boutique" by Chilean standards, Odfjell is by no means a small operation, producing 50,000 cases per year in different price ranges and lines. In 2008, Odfjell purchased a new 7-hectare vineyard of cabernet sauvignon and carmenère grapes in the Colchagua Valley. The wines routinely score high on the

Wine Spectator scale, but it's the sylvan setting, design, quirkiness of the winery, and Mrs. Odfjell's Norwegian ponies that make this a worthwhile visit. There is a terrace with a sprawling view of the vineyard and the Andes. A basic tour costs $20 (£13) and includes two wines; an advanced tour costs $40 (£27), including four wines.

Camino Viejo a Valparaíso 7000. ✆ **2/811-1530.** www.odfjellvineyards.cl. Reservations required. Tours Tues–Thurs by appt. only. Follow the Camino Melipilla west until crossing under Americo Vespucio. Continue for 14km (8⅔ miles) until you see the sign for Odfjell on the right.

Viña Almaviva ★★★ Almaviva is Chile's top winery, a world-class joint venture between Baron Philippe de Rothschild S. A. and Viña Concha y Toro. Almaviva seeks to create an exceptional Franco-Chilean premium wine under the concept of the French grand cru. The winery's slick design for its cellars and tank areas reminds one vaguely of Opus One in Napa. The wine itself is phenomenal; their 2005 carmenère, cabernet franc, and cabernet sauvignon blend was awarded 95 points by *Wine Spectator.* It is worth the visit just to try a glass of this nectar, which they include in the $25-per-person (£17) tour price (a bottle of Almaviva retails for about $100/£67). The tours are sleek and very Americanized. Almavira winery can be visited in tandem with Concha y Toro.

Av. Santa Rosa, Paradero 45, Puente Alto. ✆ **2/852-9300.** www.conchaytoro.com. Reservations required at least 1 week in advance. Tours Mon–Fri. Take Americo Vespucio to Santa Rosa exit, head south just past Paradero 45; you'll see Almaviva on your left near the Shell station.

Where to Stay

Villa Virginia Fundación Origen ★ This is the only decent place to spend the night in the Maipo Valley. The charming, country-style boutique hotel is part of the Fundación Origen, a non-profit agro-ecological school in Pirque that offers training for local youth and adults. The hotel grounds feature a sprawling lawn and garden with towering Chilean Araucaria and purple Jacaranda trees that frame a shimmering pool. There are two sleeping options: the main house, a 100-year-old villa; or in a more modern pagoda-style building. The hotel focuses on de-stressing via their hot tub, visits to the ecological school, a meditation room, and yoga classes. But be prepared to be jolted awake with an early wake-up call, courtesy of a local rooster.

Virginia Subcaseaux 2450, Pirque. ✆ **2/853-1818.** 24 units. www.fundacionorigen.cl. $78 (£52) double. AE, DC, MC, V. **Amenities:** Restaurant; outdoor pool. *In room:* No phone.

CACHAPOAL VALLEY

This valley was for years included along with the Colchagua Valley, but the split came when differences between climate and topography became too distinct to ignore. The Alto Cachapoal near the Andes produces world-class cabernet sauvignon with a freshness and natural elegance derived from its alluvial, infertile soils and cool breezes. To the west, carmenère has thrived, achieving a perfect maturity. Other grapes that are producing interesting results are viognier, syrah, merlot, and cabernet franc. In addition to wine, the Cachapoal Valley is home to a couple of fascinating attractions such as one of the oldest haciendas in Chile, the deepest copper mine in the world, and an old-world spa modeled after Vichy. ***Tip:*** The drive from the Pan-American Highway (Rte. 5) up to Termas de Cauquenes along the "Copper Highway" is one of my favorite drives in Chile for its utterly spectacular Andean views.

Altaïr ★★★ Situated in the foothills of the Andes in Alto Cachapoal, Altaïr is a joint venture between Viña San Pedro and France's Chateau Dassault, launched in 2001 to craft a uniquely Chilean grand cru. The winery itself is understated yet majestic, made

A Copper Mine & a Nature Reserve

Close to Rancagua, **El Teniente** is the world's largest underground copper mine and a supremely fascinating journey into the bowels of the earth. El Teniente began in 1905 and once employed 15,000 workers, who, at the time, lived at the mine in the town **Sewell** (www.sewell.cl). Dubbed the "city of stairs" for its location on a mountain slope, it is now a ghost town and a UNESCO World Heritage Site, and a superb example of old company towns that fused know-how from industrialized nations with local labor. Many of the old homes have been restored as interpretive museums. About 3,000 Chileans still work at El Teniente in shifts, 24 hours a day, and a tour here puts you in safety gear and shows you how they do their job. You will be blown away by the immense size of this mine; however, claustrophobia sufferers should think twice about this tour. The minimum age is 14. **VTS Tours** (✆ **72/210290;** www.vts.cl) has Spanish-only tours and transportation here leaving at 10:30am from the Rancagua train station.

While in the area, you'll want to pay a visit to the underrated **Reserva Nacional Rio Los Cipreses,** a little-known nature reserve 14km (8¾ miles) from Cauquenes; it's open daily from 8:30am to 6pm (until 8pm Dec–Feb); admission is $3 (£2). There is a park administration center with information, including trails and a guide to the flora and fauna of the reserve. Here it is possible to watch wild parrots swoop from trees and tiny caves high on cliffs; there are also rabbitlike *vizcachas* and red foxes, and, of course, a blanket of cypress trees.

You'll need your own car to get here. If you plan to stay at Termas Cauquenes (or Hacienda Los Lingues), have them plan a visit for you.

of natural stone culled from the surrounding area, and their "quincho" (pavilion) and tasting room boast a 360-degree view of the patchwork valley below and the hills. This is without a doubt the Cachapoal Valley's finest winery, and both their Altaïr and Sidera cabernet blends are elegant yet powerful. All Altaïr wines have been rated over 90 points by *Wine Advocate.* There is a range of inspired tour programs, including horseback riding through the foothills ($45/£30 per person). A basic tour and tasting costs $22 (£15) per person.

Fundo Totihue, Requínoa. ✆ **2/477-5555.** www.altairwines.com. Reservations required. Tours daily at 10am, noon, 3 and 5pm. From the Panamericana, exit at Requínoa and head left until you reach a dead-end intersection; turn right and follow the road until Camino a Pimpinela, turn left and continue 10km (6 miles).

Chateau Los Boldos ★★ Founded in 1990 by the Massanez family, a French family whose primary business was in specialty liquors and spirits, Chateau Los Boldos was originally a century-old vineyard whose rocky soils, it was found, produce quality wine with extreme ripeness. Of course, the outstanding quality of their wines comes from a lot of French know-how, too. Chateau Los Boldos also elaborates spirits and a unique pear-in-a-bottle liqueur, all handmade and bottled on-site. It is possible to book a tour, or simply stop at their Boutique de Vino just off the Pan-American Highway (eastern side) at Km 112 in Rosario. Tours cost $10 (£6.70) for a tasting of two wines.

Camino Los Boldos s/n, Requinoa. ✆ **72/514929.** www.chateaulosboldos.com. Reservations required for tours, Mon–Fri. Boutique de Vino daily 10am–8:30pm. For directions, see Altair above; the winery is next door.

Where to Stay & Dine

Hacienda Los Lingues ★★★ Moments Nestled among poplar-lined country fields and rolling hills lies one of the most special places to stay in Chile, the Hacienda Los Lingues, one of the oldest and best-preserved haciendas in Chile. Though more luxurious, newer lodging options are around, nothing comes close to this hotel's character, charm, and sumptuous natural surroundings. King Phillip III bestowed this lovely estate to the first mayor of Santiago in 1599, and it has remained in the same family for 400 years.

Every room is accented with crystal chandeliers, Oriental rugs, and antique furniture, and is literally brimming with decorative pieces, family photos, collector's items, and fascinating odds and ends. The guest rooms are decorated individually with antique armoires and tables, and iron bed frames and crocheted bedspreads. Other delightful features are an antique chapel, a patio with a bubbling fountain shrouded in greenery, an organic garden, a library, and a rodeo ring. Meals in the antique dining area employ fresh vegetables from the organic garden as well as home-grown cheese, honey, and eggs, and are extra: Breakfast is $27 (£18), lunch $52 (£35), and dinner $69 (£46).

If you can't stay overnight, consider a **day tour** ($56/£37 per person) that includes a welcome cocktail, tour of the hacienda, lunch in the cavernous wine *bodega,* horse demonstration, and optional use of their swimming pool. Los Lingues boasts a prestigious horse-breeding farm, with Arabic horses originally brought from Spain in the 1700s. Horseback riding is an additional cost, and recommended for sweeping views of the Central Valley. For day tours, rent a car or have the hotel arrange a shuttle (two to six people, about $200/£133 round-trip), or take the Metro to Estación Central and take a "Metro Train" toward San Fernando (get off at Pelequén). The hotel will send a taxi (arrange this first, for about $10/£6.70 one-way).

Reservations in Santiago: Av. Providencia 1100, no. 205. ✆ **2/431-0510.** Fax 2/431-0501. www.loslingues.com. 21 units. $267 (£178) double. $491 (£327) suite. AE, DC, MC, V. **Amenities:** Outdoor pool; 2 clay tennis courts; horseback riding; game room; room service.

Hotel Il Giardino ★★★ Finds There are few hotels in Chile with an interior design as tasteful and beautiful as the Il Giardino, and at less than $100/£50 per night, it's a steal. Tucked behind a brick wall, with a sizable garden centered around an outdoor pool, this boutique hotel is frequented more by traveling businessmen in the wine and copper industry than by tourists, which is odd given that the hotel is so perfectly suited as a base when exploring the area. From the outside, it's the spirit of rural Chile, but on the inside it is a blend of modernism and French country: A soothing muted palette of cream and soft beige offsets the mahogany bed frames, fluffy white duvets, toile curtains, and velvet settees. The view's better up at Cauquenes, but the rooms are 50 times better down here. A copious breakfast is included and afternoon high tea, served on the terrace, makes for a very civilized ritual.

Carretera del Cobre, Km 7. ✆ **72/281301.** www.hotelilgiardino.cl. 9 units. $62–$96 (£41–£64) double. AE, DC, MC, V. **Amenities:** Restaurant; bar; outdoor pool; laundry service. *In room:* A/C (some rooms), TV, minibar, hair dryer, safe.

Termas de Cauquenes ★ Tucked away in the foothills of the Cachapoal Valley and boasting one of the most gorgeous alpine settings in Chile, this old-fashioned spa and hotel is a relaxing sanctuary that is a good base for wine tasting, nature walks, and a visit to historic Sewell (see the "A Copper Mine & a Nature Reserve" box, earlier). The 200-year-old spa is Chile's oldest, having hosted the likes of Charles Darwin and Chile's founding father Bernardo O'Higgins in the early 1800s, and its style was inspired by France's Vichy Spa. The spa's centerpiece is a lovely, Gothic-designed thermal pavilion offset with colorful stained glass, marble floors, and antique marble soaking tubs; the hotel rooms are part of a converted hacienda that beams with antique splendor. In the central patio is a vine-trellised walkway and fountain, and the spa's surrounding gardens are delightful places for soaking in the peaceful ambience. Given the exterior beauty, it is a mystery as to why the guest rooms have not been renovated in more than a decade. Expect very basic comfort, midrange quality beds, and frumpy, cheap furniture—if you're looking for luxury, look elsewhere. Still, the bucolic setting and historical appeal of Cauquenes is attractive in its own right.

The current owners are Swiss and professional chefs, and their **restaurant** is hailed by critics for its fine cuisine. In my opinion, the food is quite good, but their ranking as an epicenter of gourmet cooking is a touch overrated. The changing menu features fresh seafood and meats that embrace regional recipes, and the voluminous, old-world dining area, flooded with light from the floor to ceiling windows, makes for an interesting option for lunch if you're just touring the area. A fixed, four-course lunch costs $25 (£17). On weekends, the spa offers massage and other beauty services to guests and the public by advance reservation, but their swimming pool is for guests only. Note that the original soaking tubs are tiny and ancient, but they also have a few modern whirlpools with mineralized water. I recommend driving a rental car here, because the road connecting the highway with the hotel passes through stunning vistas and many photo-taking opportunities.

Road to Cauquenes, near Rancagua. ✆/fax **72/899010.** www.termasdecauquenes.cl. 50 units. $115 (£77) per person double for full pension and use of spa baths; $63 (£42) per person double for breakfast only and spa baths. AE, DC, MC, V. **Amenities:** Restaurant; bar; outdoor pool (guests only); massage. *In room:* TV, minibar.

COLCHAGUA VALLEY

Proclaimed the Wine Valley of the Year by *Wine Enthusiast* magazine in 2005, the Colchagua Valley has been compared by many to Napa Valley in California, and it is home to many of Chile's top red wines and the most developed tourism infrastructure. Colchagua's hot climate is due to the steep hills surrounding both sides of the valley that extend from the Pacific Coast east to the Andes. These hills block the cool breezes entering from the Pacific trapping the daytime heat, and making Colchagua a paradise for "big" red wines, and, in particular, carmenère, a variety that needs a lot of heat and sun to mature correctly. Syrah, cabernet, and malbec have also found their home in the valley. All these grape varieties express themselves quite differently than in other valleys, with ripe flavors, high alcohol levels (here they can top 15 degrees), and tannins with a firm, silky feel that is almost like a chocolate candy. However, beyond Santa Cruz, vintners like Montes are now exploring cooler areas to the west near the coast in Lolol and Marchigue, with such new plantings as pinot noir, and always searching for a different expression of wines.

Getting There

BY BUS **Expresos Santa Cruz** (✆ **2/764-4717**) leaves from the **Terminal Buses Estación Central** (ex-Terminal Santiago and not to be confused with the actual Estación Central train station and Metro stop, located at Alameda 3850), which can be reached via the Universidad de Santiago Metro station. Buses run every 20 minutes Monday

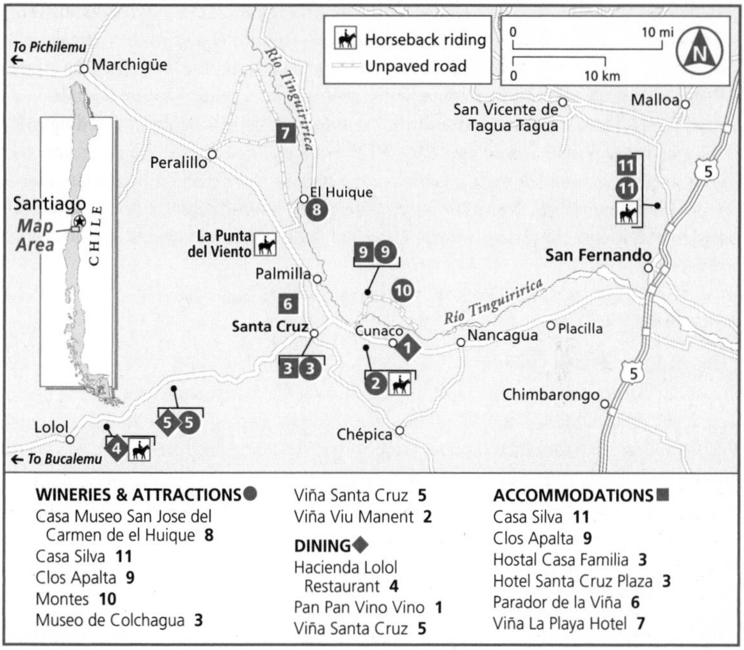

through Saturday from 8:10am to 9:15pm, and Sundays 1 to 10pm. The cost is $7 (£4.70) one-way.

BY CAR Leaving Santiago, take the Pan-American Highway (Rte. 5) and drive south toward San Fernando for 142km (88 miles). There is one $3 (£2) toll on Rte. 5 along the way. Pass the first exit for San Fernando and exit on the road to Pichilemu, or the "Carretera del Vino," (Wine Hwy.). Pay a 50¢ (35p) toll, and continue toward Santa Cruz 37km (23 miles).

BY PLANE **AirAdventure** (✆ **2/363-0870;** www.airadventure.cl) works in tandem with the wine route by offering a half-day and full-day program that includes round-trip transportation from your hotel to the Tobalaba aerodrome, flight to Santa Cruz, and wine tasting at two wineries. The full-day tour includes lunch at the Hotel Santa Cruz (p. 180), a visit to the museum, and an overflight of the wine country and the coast. Half-day tours leave at 8:30am and 2:30pm; full-day tours leave at 8:30am and return at 5:30pm. The maximum is three guests; the cost for a half-day is, per person, $900 (£600), $500 (£333), and $360 (£240) for one, two, or three guests, respectively. Full-day tours cost, per person, $1,200 (£800), $700 (£467), $520 (£347), for one, two, or three guests, respectively.

Touring the Wineries

Casa Silva ★★ Originally founded and planted by the Frenchman Emilio Bouchon in 1892, this winery has some of the oldest vines in Colchagua. The Silva family grew bulk wines until the 1990s, when the family son Mario Pablo Silva had an idea to revolutionize the winery to focus on fine bottled wines. Silva wines are now known for their excellent price-quality ratio and consistency. The winery's vineyards are dispersed around the Colchagua Valley, but it is here in Los Lingues that the Silva family established its gorgeous wine-tasting facilities and idyllic B&B and restaurant (see "Where to Stay") that follow the style of whitewashed adobe walls, red-tiled roofs, and old-world ceramic patterned floors. Hour-long tours to visit the facilities cost $8 (£5.30), $14 (£9.30) with a tasting of three reserve wines, and $18 (£12) for a tasting of three gran reserve wines ("gran reserve" wines must meet specific criteria such as using the best barrels in order to get the prestigious label). More comprehensive tours, which include a horse-drawn carriage ride through the estate, stopping at the polo pitch and rodeo arena, can be arranged.

Hijuela Norte, Casilla 97, San Fernando. ✆ **72/716519.** www.casasilva.cl. Reservations required. Tours daily at 10 and 11am, noon, and 3, 4, and 5pm.

Clos Apalta ★★★ (Moments) Few wineries in Chile have been talked about more than Clos Apalta's facility, and rightfully so. It took Casa Lapostolle, the parent of this icon wine, 4 years to blast tons of granite bedrock on a sloping hillside in order to build a $10-million, six-story, gravity-flow winery that descends deep underground. Was it worth it? Well, the property is now simply one of the most stunning wineries in the world. Spanning five levels, the winery is entirely gravity-fed. Three levels have been chiseled from the granite hillside to create a naturally cool environment for cellaring and ageing. The pundits have certainly made their opinions clear; Clos Apalta rates about 95 points in *Wine Spectator* and, in 2008, it was furnished even greater kudos by *Wine Spectator* when it elected Clos Apalta 2005 its Wine of the Year. Much of the blasted granite was reused for flooring, and the arced wooden ceilings made of native *rauli* wood in the cellar are equally simple yet intricate and just beautiful. The winery's spiral staircase, reminiscent of the Guggenheim in New York, was made to resemble wine swirling in a glass.

This is not a run-of-the-mill winery suitable for large groups or those who hold an incipient interest in wine; this is a highlight on any wine connoisseur's tour. Basic tours cost $20 (£13) per person with a minimum of four people, and include tastings of Clos Apalta and other lines of the Casa Lapostolle brand. Tours, including lunch paired with Clos Apalta wine, cost $60 (£40). The Clos Apalta lodge (p. 179), located near the winery, has four casitas designed in harmony with the winery.

Hijuela Villa Eloisa, Camino San Fernando a Pichilemu, Km 36. ✆ **72/321803.** www.casalapostolle.cl. Reservations required. Tours daily at 10am, noon, and 3:30pm. On the road to Santa Cruz from San Fernando, turn right just after the Casa Lapostolle winery at the sign for the Apalta valley.

Montes ★★★ Montes is a true Chilean winery success story. Twenty years ago, four partners with little capital and a big dream set out to make premium wines, something unheard of at the time in this country. Today it is one of the best-known premium wines out of Chile in the U.S. (Costco is the biggest buyer of their Alpha wine, for example). Montes struck gold here in the Apalta micro-valley, benefiting from an ideal climate and soil that bestowed the winery with spectacular reds—particularly their Montes "M," Folly, and the cultish Purple Angel, a carmenère–petit verdot blend. The Apalta valley is more temperate than the rest of the Colchagua valley and produces cabernet sauvignon, syrah, merlot, carmenère, petit verdot, cabernet franc, and mouvedre. The tour of Montes itself is an adventure. Informative and entertaining guides lead guests through the modern winery and its gravity-flow winemaking facilities, and then taken on a tractor ride through the sloping vineyards to an observation deck with a panoramic view, and finally back in the tasting room to try three different wines, including the Alpha ($25/£17 per person). Montes has a botanical trail to a lookout point with sweeping views, which will appeal to visitors who need a little vigorous exercise. For larger parties, Montes can arrange lunch for you.

La Finca de Apalta, Parcela 15, Apalta. ✆ **72/825417.** www.monteswines.com. Reservations recommended. Tours daily at 9:30am, noon, 3 and 5pm.

Viña Santa Cruz ★ Kids Just outside the picturesque village Lolol, this Disneyland-esque winery is one of the most curious wineries in the world: It's a mock indigenous village, observatory, and museum all wrapped up into one. Launched in 2006 by local entrepreneur and one-man promoter of Santa Cruz, Carlos Cardoen, the Viña Santa Cruz focuses less on wine than most vineyards, to the chagrin of wine enthusiasts but to the relief of young families. The tour begins with a cable car ride—or as they like to call it, the "time machine"—that transports visitors to a hilltop to tour representations of the typical houses of the Mapuche, Aymará, and Rapa Nui indigenous groups of Chile. (Do not visit this winery after the Colchagua Museum to avoid artifact overkill.) Later, the guide herds the group through the gift shop, and then for a brief tasting. The winery's small observatory boasts the most powerful telescope in private hands in Chile; and, on Friday and Saturday nights, Viña Santa Cruz offers a highly recommended "tour through the cosmos," which allows visitors to star-gaze through the winery's high-powered telescopes.

Fundo El Peral s/n. ✆ **72/941090.** www.vinasantacruz.cl. Reservations required for observatory tour only. Tours daily 10am–6pm; observatory tours begin at 9:30pm. From Santa Cruz, take Rte. 72 southwest toward Lolol to Km 25.

Viña Viu Manent ★★★ Viu Manent has seized the potential of wine tourism, and they've done everything right. The winery was founded more than 70 years ago, and their house specialty is malbec, a wine normally associated with Argentina. In fact, their gran reserva wines are perennial favorites, and their lauded Viu 1 wine is Chile's only malbec icon wine. You can just drop in for a tasting, or go all the way with Viu Manent's "Winemaker for a Day" program, whereby amateurs can blend their own varieties, and even create their own labels, to be judged later by experts. Beyond wine tasting, visitors can take a leisurely ride in a horse-drawn carriage, or rent one of their bicycles for a spin through the vineyards, finishing off with a gourmet lunch in their colonial courtyard or a sandwich in their pretty cafe looking out over the vineyard. Horseback rides and riding lessons are available through their on-site equestrian club. A basic tour with carriage ride costs $16 (£11), with a tasting of four to five wines.

Road to Santa Cruz, Cunaco. ✆ **72/858350.** www.viumanent.cl. Tours 10:30am, noon, 3 and 4:30pm.

Santa Cruz Wine Train

If you're in San Fernando and seeking a ride to Santa Cruz, the languid **Santa Cruz Wine Train** (✆ **2/470-7403;** www.trendelvino.cl) may be rather pedestrian for some tastes, but hopping on board this 1913 coal-fired steam engine locomotive certainly beats taking a bus. An attraction not unlike the Napa Valley Wine Train, it's altogether touristy and very expensive compared to independent touring. Once aboard, there is a tasting of five lowly varietal wines, so pay a little extra for their tasting of gran reserva wines. There is also a folkloric dance show. There are several tour options to choose from. The basic, full-day tour departs from Santiago at 8:15am on Saturdays only and includes round-trip bus transportation to San Fernando, the wine train, lunch, a visit to the Colchagua museum, and the Santa Cruz winery. It's a heck of a lot of antiquity/museums/artifacts/history for 1 day, and you'll need to plan to spend the majority of your day aboard moving vehicles of one kind or another. It costs $108 (£72).

Historical Attractions

Casa Museo San Jose del Carmen de el Huique ★ If you're already in the neighborhood or are especially fond of antique architecture, it's worth a visit to this antique *casa patronal,* an estate home typical of wealthy Chilean hacienda landowners during the colonial period. Though interesting from a historical point of view, especially for the contrast between classes at this time, what makes this museum special is that it is the only *casa patronal* in Chile that is open to the public and bestowed with all its original finery. There are two tours: landowner family life and worker's life, and boy, what a difference it is. Tours are in Spanish only, and groups of more than two people should make a reservation ahead of time.

28km (17 miles) from Santa Cruz, near the Hotel La Playa. ✆ **72/933083.** Admission $3 (£2) adults, $2 (£1.30) children, $1 (70p) seniors. Tues–Sun 10am–5pm.

Museo de Colchagua ★★★ Kids Arguably one of Chile's best museums for its scope and handsome design, you'll be flabbergasted when you consider that this is the collection of one man, Carlos Cardoen, who also owns the Hotel Santa Cruz, the Viña Santa Cruz, the Wine Train, and so on. Cardoen is a controversial figure wanted by the FBI for arms trading, and to bide his time while he's prohibited from leaving Chile, he's launched a mind-boggling spending spree that has doubled the size of this museum over the past few years. Wander the halls and admire exhibits that include paleontology, pre-Columbian artifacts from all of Latin America, colonial household items, indigenous clothing, and colorful *huaso* ponchos. The Pavilion of Arms presents the country's finest and broadest collection of weapons, which span the pre-Columbian epoch through to World War II and includes arms used by the Third Reich. The Jewels from the Andeas collection is a dazzling display of Maya, Olmec, Aztec, and Inca jewels. Step outside to view the collection of carriages—the 1800s funeral carriage is simply astonishing—as well as farm machinery. This is a don't-miss attraction that should be given 1 to 2 hours to explore. Audio guides are available in Spanish and English at an additional cost of $4.50 (£3).

Av. Errazuriz 145. ✆ **72/821050.** www.museocolchagua.cl. Admission $4.70 (£3.10). Daily 10am–7pm.

Outdoor Fun

BIKING **Viu Manent** (p. 177) has bicycles for rent for either independent riding through their vineyards, or guided tours.

HIKING **Montes** (p. 176) offers a new botanical trail for hiking, with guided tours leaving at 9am every day, and lasting about 4 hours total. Plan this hike with a tasting upon your return—you've earned it.

HORSEBACK RIDING The Colchagua Valley isn't just about wine—it's about rural tradition and *huasos,* and historically the only way to get around the valley was by horseback. It makes sense, then, to see this beautiful region from atop a saddle. **Hacienda Lolol** (✆ **72/941077;** pradera@cmet.net) offers three rides—Adventure, Family, and Basic—that include riding, a Chilean-style lunch at the old-fashioned Hacienda, and a tour of the quaint village of Lolol. Prices per person are: Adventure tour $65 (£43) adults,

$55 (£37) kids; Family tour, $50 (£33) adults, $40 (£27) kids; and Basic tour, $38 (£25) adults, $28 (£19) kids.

Viña Viu Manent (✆ **72/379-0439;** www.viumanent.cl) boasts a certified equestrian club, and they offer a 45-minute tour through their vineyards for $33 (£22) per person, or a 1-hour ride from their vineyards in Peralillo to a spectacular lookout point for $58 (£39) per person. The rides are led by professional riding guides who are members of the club, and they also offer a 1-hour professional lesson for $23 (£15) per person.

La Punta del Viento (✆ **72/823599** or 9/639-5027; www.colchaguavalley.cl) has a minimum of four guests, but the unique thing about these rides is that not only do you ride high to a sweeping lookout point, but you can also program a wine-and-cheese tasting there, then descend for a typical Chilean barbecue. The cost for the 3-hour ride on stunning Chilean purebred horses alone is $50 (£33) per person, and the 5-hour ride with barbecue is $100 (£67) per person. La Punta can also organize a visit to Macho Overo, the finest saddle maker in the country.

Where to Stay

Expensive

Casa Silva ★★ Finds This enchanting B&B is a wistful paradigm of French country chic. The Silva family left the infrastructure of this old hacienda as is and spruced up its interiors with restrained elegance to create a Provincial style that leans heavily on the white, distressed-paint wood look on all of its beams, pillars, and furniture, and fitted the interiors with crystal chandeliers, four-poster beds, oriental carpets, and overstuffed couches. Guest rooms are spacious and homely without sacrificing style or flair. They are each decked out in a different color, such as lime, ruby, or with gingham-check wallpaper. Room 4 is particularly well conserved and features high ceilings. Considering its location, this B&B is more suitable for visitors with a rental car, as it is a 30-minute drive to Santa Cruz and not within walking distance to anything.

The **Casa Silva Restaurant** has the same rustic-chic decor as the hotel, and serves very tasty cuisine at decent prices, including meats, seafood, and salads. My only caveat is that during lunch they might or might not have patio seating; otherwise the restaurant is windowless (overlooking their barrel cellar). If you're not staying here, it's a good idea to join their wine tour, have lunch, and carry on to Santa Cruz. The restaurant is open Tuesday through Sunday from 1 to 3:30pm and 8 to 11:30pm (Sun lunch only until 3:30pm).

Rte. 5, Km 128. ✆ **72/913091.** www.casasilva.cl. 7 units. $140 (£93) double; $180 (£120) double deluxe. AE, DC, MC, V. **Amenities:** Restaurant; bar; wine tours. *In room:* TV, Wi-Fi, minibar.

Clos Apalta ★★★ Moments The dream child of Alexandra Marnier Lapostolle and her husband Cyril, Clos Apalta is the Colchagua Valley's most luxurious and exclusive lodging option and is without a doubt one of the most special places to stay in Chile. Few hotels in Chile provide guests with more bucolic, peaceful surroundings than Clos Apalta's four *casitas* or small individual units, each named for the primary red grape varietals planted on the property. The casitas (accessible by stairs or an electric "elevator") are nestled on a hillside near their winery and by the guesthouse, which is more or less the main body of the winery area itself and offers less privacy. All guest rooms are elegantly appointed and modernist in decor, with lots of dark wood, white and ecru-colored fabrics, freshly cut flowers, plush bathrooms, and, in the case of the *casitas,* with wooden decks that afford truly magnificent, wide-open views of the Apalta Valley. On the grounds is a heated infinity pool complete with a waterfall; horseback riding, tours of the winery, and gourmet meals—accompanied, of course, by a bottle of Clos Apalta's extraordinary wine—are included in the price.

Hijuela Villa Eloisa, Camino San Fernando a Pichilemu, Km 36. ✆ **72/321803.** www.casalapostolle.cl. $900 (£600) for 2, all-inclusive. AE, MC, V. **Amenities:** Gourmet restaurant; outdoor pool; wine tours; massage. *In room:* Wi-Fi.

Moderate

Hotel Santa Cruz Plaza ★★ Kids This was the Colchagua's first "wine country" hotel built for visiting oenophiles and amateur wine swillers, and it remains the best all-around hotel in terms of quality, services, and location. Sitting on the main plaza of Santa Cruz, the style is colonial, with terra-cotta tiles and lots of wrought iron and heavy doors, and there is a central patio area with an open-air restaurant, outdoor pool fringed with thick vegetation, a small villa-style dining area for breakfast, a boutique wine shop, and a gift shop. The location means you can walk anywhere around Santa Cruz, and enjoy the rhythm of the town plaza in the afternoon. Guest rooms are not luxurious, but they are clean and comfortable with a touch of faded grandeur lacking in your typical chain hotel; they are average size and feature French doors that open onto a tiny balcony. If you're planning on signing up for the wine route and do not have a rental car, this is definitely your hotel, as the wine route leaves from here and their offices are next door.

The hotel's **Restaurante Los Varietales** serves mostly Chilean fare, with a few international dishes, and it's undoubtedly one of the most popular restaurants here, more for its alfresco dining; the food is generally decent, especially the hearty Chilean fare, but it does tend to be inconsistent. It's open daily from 1 to 4pm and 8pm to midnight. For something more casual, **Pizzeria Chaman** is open from 1pm until midnight and serves very good wood-oven pizzas, Spanish-style tapas, and Mexican appetizers.

Plaza de Armas 286, Santa Cruz. ✆/fax **72/821010.** www.hotelsantacruzplaza.cl. 44 units. $212 (£141) double; $254–$332 (£169–£221) suite. Rates include breakfast. AE, DC, MC, V. **Amenities:** Restaurant; outdoor pool; sauna; babysitting; laundry service. *In room:* A/C, TV, Wi-Fi.

Viña La Playa Hotel ★★ Kids The 25-minute drive here from Santa Cruz is an inconvenience, but the compensation is arriving after a long day of wine tasting to a gorgeous pastoral setting, with a shaded patio with lots of overstuffed couches to enjoy a soft breeze, or an outdoor pool to loll around in the sun. Also, don't expect staff on hand; as a guesthouse, it's a quiet, discreet place, where you tend to be left very much to your own devices. The rooms, like the rest of the hotel, boast a country style without being frumpy, with floral curtains, comfy beds, and wood furniture. Rooms open onto a terrace or a balcony, and some even come with a fireplace. The hotel has a landing strip for guests arriving in a private plane (charters can be arranged from Santiago for $232 (£148), and there are bike rentals, tennis courts, horseback riding, and other activities for all ages, even kids.

Fundo San Jorge s/n, Camino a Calleuque. ✆ **9/020-7700.** www.laplayawine.com. 11 units. $140 (£93) double; $170 (£113) suite. AE, DC, MC, V. **Amenities:** Restaurant; bar; outdoor pool; tennis courts; bike rental; Internet access; pool table. *In room:* Cable TV, Internet access.

Inexpensive

Hostal Casa Familia If you are on a budget, consider this clean but no-frills hostel, which is the cheapest place to lodge in Santa Cruz. Rooms are basic and drab, but are nonetheless comfortable and functional compared to all other options in this price category. Considering it is family-run, service is very friendly and personal, and all rooms have private bathrooms with hot showers that have decent water pressure. Also, it has the added bonus of being just a 6-block walk to the main plaza in Santa Cruz.

Los Pidenes 421. ✆ **72/825766.** casafamilia@valledecolchagua.cl. 9 units. $60 (£40) double. No credit cards. **Amenities:** Breakfast cafe. *In room*: No phone.

Parador de la Viña ★ If you're looking to spend a little less in wine country, this Parador de la Viña is reasonably priced but doesn't skimp on service or quality. Located about a 5-minute drive from Santa Cruz, along a dusty road, the hotel is within a converted adobe hacienda built in 1930. Most rooms are on the small side, but they're clean and fresh, with floral bedspreads and whitewashed walls. The best room here is the "suite," a large double with views of the vineyard, and it's usually the same price as a king, so ask for it. There are plenty of patios and an outdoor pool for kicking back.

Camino Los Boldos s/n. ✆ **72/825788.** www.paradordelavina.cl. 6 units. $80 (£53) double. AE, DC, MC, V. **Amenities:** Cafeteria; outdoor pool. *In room:* TV, minibar, electric kettle, no phone.

Where to Dine

If you're here on a Saturday, try to make it to **Viña Santa Cruz**'s gastronomic center (see "Touring the Wineries") for their regionally famous coq au vin, served from 12:30 to 4pm in a dining area that provides a 360-degree view. The cost is $18 (£12) and includes several courses; drinks and wine are additional.

Hacienda Lolol Restaurant ★ (Kids) CHILEAN Country meals are the specialty here, and whether it's pot roast, lamb, goat stewed in wine, or roast pork, it all costs just $8 (£5.30). This lovely old hacienda is part of the allure of dining here, and it's a friendly, family-run place. Meals come with a choice of potatoes, salad, or rice. There is also a delicatessen next-door, if you're looking to stock up for a picnic.

Road to Lolol, Km 27. ✆ **72/941308.** haciendalolol@yahoo.es. Reservations recommended on weekends. Main courses $8 (£5.30). No credit cards. Mon–Sat noon–4pm and 7–11pm; Sun noon–4pm.

Pan Pan Vino Vino ★ CHILEAN This restaurant is steeped in history, having opened in 1860 as the grand bakery of the Cunaco Hacienda, and the old stone oven and rusticity of the dining room have been maintained, lending a lot of character. It's a cozy place on a cold day given their wood-burning stoves and exposed brickwork. The food, while it certainly won't blow you away with its originality, is satisfying and tasty; the Italian slant proves particularly favorable to vegetarians, who'll be happy with the selection of pasta dishes and even a vegetarian sampler platter. There is a varied wine list, and friendly, if rather slow, service.

Road to Santa Cruz from San Fernando, Km 31, near Cunaco. ✆ **72/84835.** www.panpanvinovino.cl. Reservations recommended on weekends. Main courses $8–$10 (£5.30–£6.70). AE, DC, MC, V. Tues–Sat 1–4pm and 8–11pm; Sun 1–4pm.

6 SKI RESORTS IN THE CENTRAL ANDEAN REGION

It's no longer just a summer getaway for skiing fanatics in search of the endless winter. In 2006, North American guests came close to ranking number one in client visits at the major Chilean ski resorts. The allure? Andean skiing delivers a combination of world-class terrain, glorious weather, and an exotic journey that is without peer. The novelty of skiing from June to October does have some cache, but skiers have also discovered that the Andean terrain has everything from easy groomers to spine-tingling steeps, and with so few people on the slopes here, that powder lasts for days, not hours. From mid-July to late September, a 3m ($9^3/_4$-ft.) base of snow is guaranteed. There are few lift lines, and passes are generally 50% cheaper than ski resorts in France, Austria, and Switzerland. The ambience is relaxed and conducive to making friends and waking up late. For families, the kids are on vacation, and most resorts offer reduced rates or free stays for kids under 12. Beware, however, that during the school holidays in July, when children in Chile are on vacation, prices can soar by as much as 80%.

The major resorts in Chile are top-notch operations with modern equipment and facilities. Resorts centered on the Farallones area, such as Valle Nevado, La Parva, and El Colorado, can be reached in a 1- to $1^1/_2$-hour drive from Santiago or the airport, and can be visited for the day. Note that Valle Nevado requires a minimum of a 5-night stay during high season if you'd like to spend the night. At a little over 2 hours from Santiago, the venerable, world-renowned Portillo can be visited for the day, but most skiers headed to that resort bunk in their all-inclusive hotel, which must be booked from Saturday to Saturday during most of the season. Don't overlook Termas de Chillán, even though it is a short flight and a $1^1/_2$-hour transfer shuttle away, or a $4^1/_2$-hour train ride followed by a 1-hour transfer; this wonderful resort offers tree skiing, a casino, and an extensive spa. Looking for wild adventure? Check out the box "Backcountry Bliss" on p. 185 for ideas about out-of-the-ordinary ski and snowboard adventures.

GETTING TO THE RESORTS Portillo organizes transfers through its own company, Portillo Tours & Travel, when you reserve. If you've booked a reservation for any resort through a U.S.-based tour operator (see chapter 5), they'll book your transportation for you. You do not need to rent a vehicle if you are planning to spend the night at any of the resorts listed in this chapter. **Ski Total** (**© 2/246-0156;** www.skitotal.cl) has transfer shuttles to El Colorado, La Parva, and Valle Nevado for $18 (£12) round-trip per person. The shuttles leave at 8:30am from their offices at Av. Apoquindo 4900, no. 42 (in the Omnium shopping mall in Las Condes—there's no Metro station nearby, so take a taxi), and no reservation for these shuttles is required. Round-trip transportation with hotel pickup costs $30 (£20) per person, and requires a reservation made 24 hours in advance; pickup time for this service is 8am. All return shuttles leave from the resorts at 5pm. Transfer shuttles to Portillo require a minimum of five people, and cost $35 (£24) per person for one of their 8:30am shuttles.

SKI PORTILLO

Internationally famous, Portillo is South America's oldest resort and one of the more singular ski destinations in the world. The resort is set high in the Andes on the shore of Lake Inca, a little more than 2 hours from Santiago and near the Argentine border. Unlike most ski resorts, there is no town at Portillo, just one sunflower-yellow lodge and two more economical annexes. Although open to the public for day skiing (call ahead—they're open to the general public only when conditions are optimal), Portillo really operates as a Saturday-to-Saturday, all-inclusive resort. The ski area is smaller than Valle Nevado and Termas de Chillán; however, Portillo boasts steeper terrain and fewer crowds. Champion skier Steve McKinney set world records here, and it was on the slopes of Portillo that a woman exceeded 100 mph for the first time. Portillo is billed as a "boutique resort" with a maximum of 450 people, giving visitors the sensation of skiing in their own private resort. Indeed, the camaraderie that grows over a week spent here brings many guests back to Portillo year after year.

Portillo is not for everyone, specifically groups with a member who does not ski. There is not a lot of terrain here suitable for intermediates, yet the ski school here is world-class and can greatly push you to boost your ability level. There are no TVs in the rooms, an attempt by owner Henry Purcell to stimulate social interaction among his guests, a gesture which, for the most part, is appreciated. The grand yet rustic hotel forgoes glitz for a more relaxed atmosphere encouraged by its American owners. Rooms are on the small side but comfortable; the best rooms are the sixth-floor doubles because they come with balconies and larger bathrooms. The Octagon annex has rooms with four bunks and a private bathroom; the Inca annex is for backpackers and has Lilliputian rooms with four bunks and a common bathroom. The Octagon and the Inca annexes offer a special price for only three people per room; otherwise, if you're less than four, you might share with strangers. The main dining area features hearty staples and is for hotel and Octagon guests only; Inca guests dine in the cafeteria or at the mountainside restaurant or snack bar on the slopes. Portillo loves a party, and on some nights the fiesta really cranks up with live music in the hotel bar, a thumping disco, and an off-site *cantina.*

There are 13 lifts, including five chairs, five Poma lifts, and three "slingshot" lifts that tow skiers to the top of vertiginous chutes. Heliskiing costs $195 (£130) per person for the first run, and $150 (£100) for the second run, based on three guests, and the cost of the guide (split btw. the guests) is $55 (£37) for the first run, $34 (£23) thereafter.

Where to Stay **Hotel Portillo**'s 7-day packages include lodging, lift tickets, four meals per day, and use of all facilities. Per person rates are: $1,450 to $2,650 (£967–£1,767) double with lake view; $2,000 to $4,700 (£1,333–£3,133) suites; $1,200 to $1,990 (£800–£1,327) family apartments (minimum four people). Children under 4 stay free, kids 4 to 11 pay half-price, and kids 12 to 17 pay about 25% less than adults.

For more information or to make reservations, contact the resort's office at Renato Sánchez 4270 in Santiago (✆ **2/263-0606;** fax 2/263-0595; www.skiportillo.com), or call the toll-free lines at **800/829-5325** in the U.S., or 800/514-2579 in Canada. Lift tickets cost $36 (£24) for adults, $28 (£19) for children under 13. Amenities at the resort include an outdoor heated pool, fitness center, sauna, child-care center, game room, salon, massage, laundry service, a full-court gymnasium, disco, cybercafe, and theater.

VALLE NEVADO

Valle Nevado sits high above Santiago, near El Colorado and La Parva resorts, and it is the only resort in Farallones (also called the Three Valleys) area that offers a full-service tourism infrastructure. The resort complex is not a town, but there are clothing, gear, and souvenir shops, seven restaurants, bars, a disco, and a full-service spa, making Valle a good destination for nonskiing guests accompanying their family or friends. The French-designed resort is Chile's answer to Les Arcs, with three hotels and two condominium buildings that straddle a ridge line. The terrain is large enough to entertain skiers for days, and they can purchase an interconnect ticket for an additional cost and traverse over to La Parva and El Colorado. The steeper runs are at Portillo, yet Valle is larger and the runs longer. Of all the resorts in Chile, Valle is the most snowboard-friendly, offering a terrain park and monster half-pipe, and the resort hosts the Nokia Snowboarding World Cup every year. There is a lot of intermediate off-*piste* terrain here, whereas most off-*piste* terrain at Portillo is for advanced skiers.

Many Santiaguinos visit Valle Nevado on weekends—note that traffic up the hill can back up for hours if there has been a recent snowfall, and the wait can be excruciating. Saturdays and Sundays bring long lift lines and crowded slopes in the morning, but everyone calls it a day after lunch and the runs in the afternoon are gloriously people-free.

WHERE TO STAY Valle Nevado offers all-inclusive packages that include lodging, ski tickets, breakfast, and dinner (lunch is an additional cost), which can be taken in any one of the resort's restaurants. Unlike Portillo, Valle's more economical hotel does not have shared rooms, and are more akin to a regular hotel room. Prices are per person, double occupancy. The elegant world-class **Hotel Valle Nevado** is, per night, $190 to $350 (£127–£233) for a standard double, and $280 to $460 (£187–£307) for a suite.

The midrange **Hotel Puerta del Sol,** which is popular with families, is $162 to $348 (£108–£232) a night for a double, and $183 to $319 (£122–£213) a night for a suite.

Hotel Tres Puntas has rooms with either two twins or four-bed bunks; and they are great values for their private bathrooms. The hotel is popular with younger guests and families; rates are $120 to $220 (£80–£147) per night.

The **Edificio del Sol** building has condos for up to six guests, for $340 to $600 (£227–£400) per night, not including meals or lift tickets; however, this lodging option can ultimately be cheaper for its fully equipped kitchens.

For more information or to make reservations, contact the resort's office at Av. Vitacura 5250, no. 304, in Santiago (✆ **2/477-7700;** fax 2/477-7736; www.vallenevado.com). Lift tickets cost $35 to $42 (£23–£28) for adults, $22 to $27 (£15–£18) for children under 13. Amenities for guests at the resort include an outdoor heated pool, full-service spa with fitness gym, massage and sauna, a child-care center, game room, room service, laundry service, a full-court gymnasium, and a cinema. For the public, there's a bank, high-end boutiques, and a minimarket.

LA PARVA

La Parva caters to Santiago's well-heeled skiers and snowboarders, many of whom have condos or chalets here. For visiting travelers, La Parva rents mediocre apartments that have not been updated since the 1970s, and there isn't the kind of infrastructure for tourism that you'll find at Valle Nevado. However, on weekends the center seems to take on the feel of a small village, and the ski center offers good off-*piste* skiing conditions and the steepest inbound terrain of the three resorts. Also, La Parva is closer to Santiago, if you're heading up only for the day.

There are four chairs and 10 surface lift runs, such as T-bars, and several on-slope cafes for lunch and a few at the base of the resort, including the yodely, fondue-style restaurant **La Marmita de Pericles, El Piuquen Pub** for pizzas, and the **St. Tropez** for breakfast, fine dining, and a bar with excellent pisco sours.

Condos have kitchens, living areas, and TVs; the cost is $1,700 to $2,600 (£1,133–£1,733) for six people, $2,700 to $3,650 (£1,800–£2,433) for eight people; maid service is an additional $20 (£13) per day. You'll need to buy groceries in Santiago. Lift tickets are $38 to $49 (£25–£33) for adults, $31 to $39 (£21–£26) for children. For more information, contact the resort (✆ **2/431-0420** in Santiago, or 2/220-9530 direct; fax 2/264-1575; www.laparva.cl).

EL COLORADO & FARELLONES

Farellones is a sprawl of chalets and small businesses spread across a ridge below the ski area El Colorado. This ski area is La Parva's blue-collar brother, an older, more economical option that is popular with beginning skiers, tubing aficionados, snowman builders, and the like. There is a wide variety of terrain, and fewer skiers and snowboarders on the slopes than the neighboring resorts, but the lift system is dated. If you are looking for cheaper lodging at the Three Valleys area, this is where you'll find it. There is even a backpacker's lodge.

Backcountry Bliss

Skiing beyond the cordoned-off limits of a commercial resort and into the backcountry is an awesome experience that every skier and snowboarder should try at least once in his or her life (with an experienced guide, of course). Here in Chile, it's just you, the spectacularly rugged Andean Mountains, condors soaring overhead, and lots of virgin powder snow. There are several options for backcountry skiing and snowboarding near Santiago, but you've got to be at least an intermediate/advanced level skier to join in. It's best to reserve ahead with the following companies, but sometimes they have a space open at the last moment.

- **Ski Arpa** (✆ **802/904-6798** in the U.S.; www.skiarpa.com), located just outside San Esteban, about 2 hours north of Santiago and owned by Austrian Toni Sponar, has two Snowcats, based at a picturesque mountain refuge at 2,700m (8,825 ft.), that carry skiers up to altitudes as high as 3,750m (12,500 ft.). At the top, Mt. Aconcagua, the highest in the Americas, rises in the near distance. Ski Arpa offers day trips from Santiago, and multiday trips with lodging at the Casa St. Regis or Termas de Jahuel (p. 165); cost for a day trip is $100 (£67) per person, based on four people, for a total of four runs, with an additional flat fee of $100 (£67) for a guide. Round-trip transportation from Santiago is available and costs extra if you do not have a rental vehicle.
- **Chile Unlimited** (✆ **08/429-6319;** www.chileunlimited.com) is run by an American expat with more than a decade customizing heliski trips throughout the Central Valley region, including Cajón de Maipo and even as far as Termas de Chillan. Guests can lodge in Santiago and head up for the day, or they can book a private home or lodge in the Andes. Chile Unlimited also runs Andes Snowboard Clincs—check the website for more information.

The resort has five chair lifts and 17 surface lifts. The El Colorado Apart-Hotel is modern and clean, with two- and three-bedroom units with kitchenettes for $198 to $336 (£132–£224) per person, double occupancy, including meals. They'll also take you to Valle Nevado or La Parva if you're looking to ski there. For more information, contact the resort (✆ **2/246-3344;** fax 2/206-4078; www.elcolorado.cl). In Farallones there is a backpacker's lodge with very basic accommodations, the **Refugio Alemán,** Cóndores 1451 (✆ **2/264-9899;** www.refugioaleman.cl), with shared accommodations in rooms with four, five, and six beds for $40 (£27) per person per night, which includes breakfast and dinner.

7 CHILLAN & TERMAS DE CHILLAN RESORT

407km (252 miles) S of Santiago

Chillán is a midsize city located 407km (252 miles) south of Santiago, and it is the gateway to the popular **Termas de Chillán,** one of South America's largest and most complete ski and summer resorts. A rustic but tidy city of 145,000, with five spruce plazas and hodgepodge, utilitarian architecture, bustling streets with open storefronts, and street dogs, Chillán looks like any other Chilean city in the Central Valley.

There is really only one reason to stop here when heading south on the Pan-American Highway, the **Feria de Chillán ★★**, one of the largest and most colorful markets in Chile, where you'll find baskets, *huaso* clothing and saddles, chaps and spurs, pottery, knitwear, blankets, caged birds, and Jurassic size fruit and vegetables. Bargaining is futile unless your Spanish is at the very least proficient. The Feria is located between Maipón, Arturo Prat, 5 de Abril, and Isabel Riquelme streets; across Maipón Street is the food market, with everything from pickled vegetables to dried fruit to Chillán's famous sausages.

Although Termas de Chillán is a full-service resort, it is the only ski resort in the Central Region with a neighboring town, **Las Trancas,** about a 10-minute drive from the resort base. Many choose to stay here rather than up at the resort, given that there are pubs and restaurants here, independent lodging in *cabañas,* and inexpensive lodging options that are more flexible with shorter stays.

ESSENTIALS

Getting There

BY PLANE Chillán is served by the **Aeropuerto Carriel Sur** (CCP; ✆ **041/748-879**) in Concepción, about an hour away. There are direct flights here from Santiago several times daily from **LAN** and **Sky Airline;** see the "Appendix A: Fast Facts, Toll-Free Numbers & Websites" for phone numbers. If you've made hotel reservations at Termas de Chillán, their transfer service will pick you up and take you directly there. If not, you must take a taxi to the bus terminal, where buses for Chillán leave every 20 minutes.

BY BUS **Línea Sur** and **TurBus** offer daily service from most major cities, including Santiago. The trip from Santiago takes about 5 to 6 hours and costs $11 (£7.35) one-way. The bus terminal in Chillán is located at Av. O'Higgins 010, and from there you can grab a bus for the Termas.

BY TRAIN **EFE** (Terrasur) offers a truly enjoyable 4½-hour train journey from Santiago, leaving from the Estación Central, and arriving in Chillán at the station at Calle Brasil (✆ **600/585-5000;** www.efe.cl). This modern train speeds through scenic orchards and farmland, much of it still tilled by horse, with changing views of the Andes. One-way fares cost $19 to $22 (£13–£15) for a *salón* coach, and $29 to $55 (£19–£37) for a *"preferente"* coach with reclining seats. There are three to five daily trips, and a dining car with snacks, sandwiches, and beverages.

Visitor Information

Sernatur can be found at 18 de Septiembre 455 (✆ **42/223272**); it's open Monday through Friday from 8:30am to 1:30pm and 3 to 6pm, and closed on weekends.

WHERE TO STAY & DINE

Few foreign visitors spend the night in Chillán (visitors to Termas de Chillán do not stay here and drive up daily), unless they're looking for a place to rest after driving along the Pan-American Highway. During the day, great local color and cheap prices can be found in abundance at the **Municipal Market** across the street from the Feria de Chillán, where simple restaurants serve seafood and local dishes, some featuring Chillán's famous sausages (though I've never figured out what the fuss is about—they're merely okay). Be forewarned of pushy waitresses who stalk the passageways and practically clobber you over the head and drag you into their restaurant; it can be very entertaining but a little overwhelming! The Feria is open every day. Cheap, hearty meals and hefty sandwiches are served at the **Fuente Alemán** (✆ **42/212720**), on the pedestrian walkway next to the Hotel Isabel Riquelme.

Gran Hotel Isabel Riquelme ★★ This hotel sat ignored and unloved for so many years, it was difficult to remember that it was, in its day, a "Gran" hotel. After a rebirth, its bar/restaurant fills with friends chatting over coffee and businessmen shaking hands and smoking cigars, and even the waiters just seem thrilled to be a part of such a lively center in this dreary old town. The lobby gleams, and the common areas are surprisingly stylish, with flagstone walls, ambient lighting, leather and wood furniture, and contemporary art, and the guest rooms are handsome in their shades of chocolate and beige, with floor-to-ceiling drapes and squeaky-clean bathrooms. If you don't stay here, eat here, as their restaurant serves creatively prepared Chilean food, and they have lighter fare and a decent wine list.

Arauco 600, Chillán. ✆ **42/434400.** Fax 42/211541. www.hotelisabelriquelme.cl. 70 units. $95 (£63) double; $155 (£103) suite. AE, DC, MC, V. **Amenities:** Restaurant; bar; room service; laundry service. *In room:* Cable TV.

Hotel Paso Nevado If you just need a clean and reasonably priced place to put your head down after long hours on the road, this is a good bet. Country furnishings, comfortable guest rooms, a pleasant outdoor patio for enjoying the continental breakfast (included in the price), and amicable service can be expected. Ask for a discount, as the hotel will often grant one. The hotel is located 3 blocks west of the main plaza.

Libertad 219. ✆ **42/237666.** Fax 42/211541. www.pasonevado.cl. 70 units. $66 (£44) double. AE, DC, MC, V. **Amenities:** Cafeteria; bar; laundry service. *In room:* Cable TV, hair dryer.

TERMAS DE CHILLÁN

The star attraction in the Chillán area is **Termas de Chillán,** a full-season resort 80km (50 miles) from the city that is principally known for skiing, although the resort is open year-round and offers excellent hiking, biking, and horseback riding opportunities in the summer. Visitors to Chile normally head to Pucón, Puerto Varas, or even Patagonia for those kinds of summer-season activities because they offer more uniquely beautiful landscapes than Chillán. However, you might find a world-class spa and the 5-hour drive from Santiago to be an appealing factor.

Termas de Chillán is nestled in a forested valley under the shadow of the 3,212m (10,535-ft.) Chillán Volcano, and unlike ski resorts in the north, this resort has a fair amount of tree skiing. The mountain feels monumental in size and the terrain is more suited to intermediates with trails winding along the volcano's ridge. There is also ample off-*piste* terrain, around the rolling terrain. The resort is notoriously anti-snowboarding, and will not allow snowboarders on certain Poma lifts. It can often snow more here than in the north; however, snow conditions change quickly throughout the day given its lower altitude. The resort has 29 runs, including the longest run in South America, and there's dog sledding, too.

Another huge bonus with this resort is its state-of-the-art spa and outdoor hot springs produced by the natural geothermal fissures in the area. The spa offers hydrotherapy, aromatherapy, mud baths, and massages, and is open to the general public during the ski season until 2pm, and to Gran Hotel guests only in the afternoon. Termas also has a new casino, significantly boosting what once was a rather tame nightlife scene.

Tips Come with Cash

Note that there are no ATMs anywhere in Termas de Chillán or Las Trancas, so do your banking beforehand and bring a credit card.

There are two hotels at the base of the resort: the luxury **Gran Hotel Termas de Chillán** with 120 rooms, and the basic **Hotel Pirigallo** with 48 rooms. Closer to Las Trancas is the midrange **Hotel Pirimahuida,** with free—but scheduled—transportation to and from the resort. The Hotel Pirimahuida is an attractive option for its low cost and proximity to the restaurants and bars in tiny Las Trancas. Rates include breakfast and dinner, lift tickets, and access to the resort's outdoor hot springs. The Pirigallo has an outdoor thermal pool; otherwise, guests must pay extra to use the Gran Hotel's facilities. Seven-night stays receive 6 hours of free group ski or snowboard instruction. Prices are per person, based on 7 nights and double occupancy: Gran Hotel $1,250 to $2,200 (£833–£1,467); Hotel Pirigallo $850 to $1,500 (£567–£1,000). The Hotel Pirimahuida is an excellent value at $650 to $980 (£433–£653), given that its interiors and guest rooms are far more attractive than the dated Hotel Pirigallo.

You might try one of the **condominium units** at the resort base for four to six guests; they cost $1,100 to $1,800 (£733–£1,200) per week, per condo, with meals and lift tickets costing extra. There is a small grocery store (bring specialty items with you from Santiago) in Las Trancas, or you can dine a la carte in the resort's restaurant or buy an additional meal plan. Lift tickets cost, per week, $230 (£153) for adults, and $155 (£103) for children.

Lodging Outside the Resort

Before reaching the resort, you'll pass through Las Trancas, a scattering of hotels, *cabañas,* restaurants, gear-rental shops, and other small businesses dependent on tourism. The party is rowdier here than the relatively tame nightlife at the resort, and prices here are cheaper than at the resort. None of the 10 or so restaurants is particularly memorable, so you might find renting a cabin with a kitchen a better proposition; but double-check before you rent that there's a dining and living area, or you'll have only a bed to kick back on. Also, hardly any property in Las Trancas has transportation to the resort, so verify this or else you'll be taking the once-a-day bus or be forced to rent a car.

Cabañas and Restaurant Rucahue ★ Kids Here you'll find comfortable cabins for 2 to 10 people, with kitchens and living areas. The best thing about these cabins is that they are part of a complete service complex, including a game room with video games and pool tables, a cybercafe, and a general store, and they also have the best restaurant in town, the **Restaurant Rucahue,** serving international and vegetarian dishes.

Km 72, Las Trancas. ✆ **42/236162.** www.rucahueescalador.cl. 6 units. $105 (£70) cabin for 4 (2 bedrooms). AE, DC, MC, V. **Amenities:** Restaurant; cybercafe; game room. *In room:* TV.

Hotel Robledal ★ This hotel is surrounded by oak and beech trees and serenaded by a babbling creek. It is a good choice "hotel" option for lodging outside the Termas de Chillán ski resort if you can't get a room at Termas de Chillan's Las Trancas–based Hotel Pirimahuida. One perk here is that the Robledal has a heated pool, and Pirimahuida does not, although the pool is covered by a plastic bubble, making it one hot, stuffy swim. The entrance is flanked on one side by an airy, comfortable lobby with a copper fireplace and bar, and on the other by a restaurant. Guest rooms feel like condominiums, starkly decorated but brightly lit by an abundance of windows; some have terraces.

8km (5 miles) from Termas de Chillán. ✆/fax **42/214407.** www.hotelrobledal.cl. 22 units. $120 (£80) per person, includes breakfast and dinner. AE, DC, MC, V. **Amenities:** Restaurant; bar; outdoor pool, Jacuzzi; babysitting. *In room:* Cable TV, minibar.

Mission Impossible Lodge ★ This is my favorite place to stay outside of the Termas de Chillán ski area. The young owners of MI Lodge, a French trio, found their home here in Las Trancas and built a lofty yet cozy and bright lodge for people who love to snowboard and ski, and kick back and enjoy warm camaraderie at night. The 360-degree views from here are the best in Las Trancas, and there is a wood fire–heated hot tub, swimming pool, snowmobiles, a climbing wall, and other toys. However, it is a long walk to the road, and you'll need to either have a car or rely on the lodge's transportation to get to Las Trancas (an additional cost). This is good place to have a rental vehicle. Solo travelers may or may not feel lonely here, depending on the lodge's occupancy at any given time. Wood-paneled rooms have comfortable beds and quad rooms for groups. The friendly, knowledgeable staff is the best in the area for tips on secret powder stashes and backcountry terrain, and you can hire a guide to lead you around for a day on the slopes. Prices include breakfast and dinner, and use of their facilities. There is also a snowboard/ski shop on the premises, with rentals.

Fundo Los Pretiles, Parcela 83, Sector C, Las Trancas. ✆ **9/623-0412.** www.misnowchile.com. 6 units. $60–$85 (£40–£57) per person, double occupancy. AE, DC, MC, V. **Amenities:** Restaurant; bar; outdoor pool; hot tub. *In room:* Wi-Fi.

8

La Serena & the Elqui Valley

Between the Mediterranean climate of Santiago and the bone-dry Atacama Desert runs a roughly 500km (310-mile) stretch of arid territory that Chileans call *Norte Chico,* or Little North. Though less famous overseas than the far north, the area surrounding La Serena, Chile's sole remaining colonial Spanish city, features much more in the way of beach fun, along with penguins and dolphins up the coast and a unique fog-fed mini–cloud forest to the south.

Get away from it all in the rustic Elqui Valley and sample its spirits—both brandy and its esoteric retreats. With 300 nights a year of some of the world's clearest skies, astronomers from around the globe are drawn to the region, a hub of state-of-the-art telescopes. With few travelers and a clutch of good value, holistic lodges, and plenty of outdoor activities ranging from hiking to horseback riding, it's a place to truly unwind and revel in the beautiful landscape. Norte Chico's most alluring attraction might be the *desierto florido* (flowering desert), which occurs only every few years, when above-average winter rainfall triggers a springtime explosion of wildflowers that turn the dusty desert into a multicolored feast for the eyes.

1 LA SERENA ★

474km (295 miles) N of Santiago

Founded in 1544 on a bluff just south of the Elqui River's entry into the Pacific, La Serena is Chile's second oldest city (the oldest is Santiago, established in 1541). Now home to some 150,000 inhabitants, it alone among the country's larger cities still sports more than just a few memories of Spanish architectural heritage; low-slung colonial houses, beautifully restored churches, and kaleidoscopic crafts markets are all on offer. La Serena is by far the most harmonious city in the entire country; and, with the bucolic and mystical delights of the Elqui Valley less than an hour's drive away and nature preserves both to the south and to the north, La Serena is a worthy destination in its own right.

Chile was one of Spain's poorest, remotest colonies, limiting what could be spent on architecture, and much of what at first glance appears old in La Serena in fact was built rather recently. The town's architecture fails to match the beauty of the colonial gems of the Andean countries, Mexico, or Cuba, but art fans will love the few, attractive Mannerist-style (late Renaissance) stone churches that survived the multiple pirate raids. Most of the city was built during the silver boom times of the 19th century or after 1950 in imitation baroque style, in the wake of the 1948 "neocolonial" plan hatched by President Gabriel González Videla, who hailed from the city. Church spires dominate the skyline, and even the shopping mall respects the traditional style. For several years, construction companies have been pushing for the right to build high-rises downtown. Fortunately, so far at least, city planners have resisted. Hopefully, La Serena will not suffer the same sad fate suffered by most Chilean cities. La Serena has seen notable improvement in the past

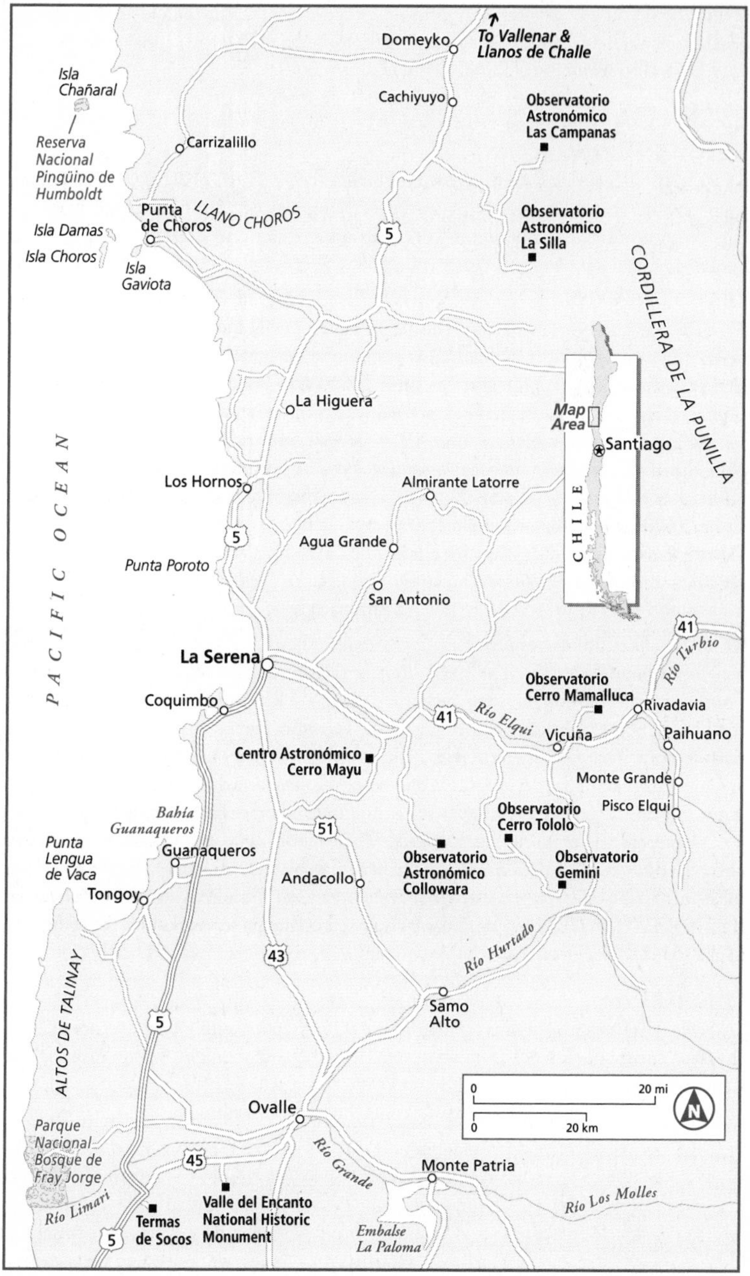

LA SERENA & THE ELQUI VALLEY 8 LA SERENA

few years—many of those ugly electrical and phone cables that mar so many towns have, at least in the city center, been buried under new stone paving—and nowhere else in the country will you get a better impression of what it was like in the old days. Plus, the beaches are among Chile's finest—having eclipsed Viña del Mar in terms of beach scene cachet—and in season, you'll find plenty of activities.

ESSENTIALS

Getting There

BY PLANE La Serena's **Aeropuerto La Florida** (LSC; © **51/272652**), 5km (3 miles) from downtown on Rte. 41, is served by **LANExpress** (© **600/526-2000;** www.lan.com) with up to three daily flights from the capital. Check for deep discounts on early bookings. A taxi to downtown costs around $8 (£5.30); airport transfer vans cost $3 (£2) per person to downtown, $4 (£2.70) to beachfront hotels on Avenida del Mar.

BY BUS It takes close to 7 hours to reach La Serena by bus from Santiago. You can make it an overnight trip, but that means a crack of dawn arrival as no buses leave Santiago later than shortly before midnight. **Tur Bus** (© **600/660-6600;** www.turbus.com) departs from Santiago's Terminal Alameda at Av. Alameda 3750 (Metro: Univ. de Santiago); prices for the five daily *semi-camas* are $20 (£13) one-way, $40 (£27) for the two *salón camas.* Note that if you want to head back to Santiago, you might prefer to board a bus that starts off in La Serena rather than way up north, because these are frequently delayed. **Pullman Bus** (© **600/320-3200;** www.pullman.cl) leaves eight times daily from Estación San Borja (Metro: Estación Central). Prices for a *semi-cama* are $11 (£7.30) one-way and $25 (£17) for *salón camas.* In general, prices are lower during the off-season. La Serena's bus terminal is just south of downtown at El Santo and Amunátegui.

BY CAR The trip up from Santiago takes about 6 hours on Rte. 5, a toll road (the trip will cost around $23/£15). The speed limit is 120km; beware of police radars. Coming from the south, stop and put some fuel in your tank at Pichidangui or Los Vilos as the next station is at Socos, a stretch on one tank all the way from Santiago and with frequent long waits to boot. That said, if you're renting, it probably makes more sense to pick up the car in La Serena than in Santiago. A car is the means of transport of choice in the Elqui Valley. You won't need a 4×4, though the drive out to Punta Choros is a little rough.

The airport has rental kiosks for **Avis** (© **600/368-2000** or 51/200921; www.avischile.cl), **Budget** (© **2/362-3200** or 51/270975; www.budget.cl); and **Hertz** (© **2/496-1000** or 51/200922; www.hertz.cl). Downtown, you'll find **Avis** on Av. Francisco de Aguirre 63 (© **51/227171;** laserena@avischile.cl); **Budget** at Av. Francisco de Aguirre 15 (© **51/218272**); and **Hertz** at Av. Francisco de Aguirre 225 (© **51/218925**).

Orientation

La Serena's square-grid colonial center lies on a bluff about a mile from the ocean, with the main square just a block from its western fringe and all the sights within easy walking distance. You'll need a taxi to travel to and from the beachfront hotels, which run north–south 12km (7½ miles) all the way down to the port of Coquimbo.

Visitor Information

Sernatur operates a visitor center with friendly, helpful staff (some English spoken) at Matta 461 on the west side of the plaza between Prat and Cordovez, almost across from the cathedral (© **51/225138**). In January and February, it's open daily from 8am to midnight; the rest of the year, Monday through Friday from 9am to 5:30pm, and Saturday from 10am to 1pm and from 2 to 4pm.

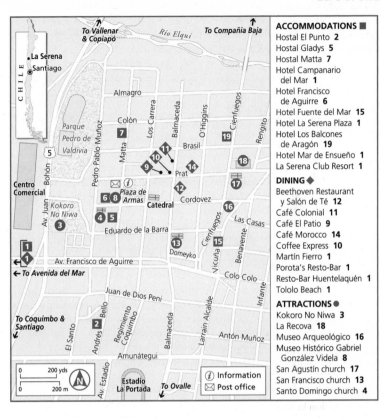

ACCOMMODATIONS ■
Hostal El Punto **2**
Hostal Gladys **5**
Hostal Matta **7**
Hotel Campanario del Mar **1**
Hotel Francisco de Aguirre **6**
Hotel Fuente del Mar **15**
Hotel La Serena Plaza **1**
Hotel Los Balcones de Aragón **19**
Hotel Mar de Ensueño **1**
La Serena Club Resort **1**

DINING ◆
Beethoven Restaurant y Salón de Té **12**
Café Colonial **11**
Café El Patio **9**
Café Morocco **14**
Coffee Express **10**
Martín Fierro **1**
Porota's Resto-Bar **1**
Resto-Bar Huentelaquén **1**
Tololo Beach **1**

ATTRACTIONS ●
Kokoro No Niwa **3**
La Recova **18**
Museo Arqueológico **16**
Museo Histórico Gabriel González Videla **8**
San Agustín church **17**
San Francisco church **13**
Santo Domingo church **4**

Fast Facts La Serena

ATMs & Currency Exchange Options include **AFEX,** Balmaceda 413 (✆ **51/217751;** www.afex.cl); **Cambios Inter,** Balmaceda 431 (✆ **51/224673**); and **Fides,** Balmaceda 460 no. 7 (✆ **51/214554**), all open Monday through Friday from 9am to 6:30pm and Saturday from 10am to 2pm. You'll find plenty of ATMs in the banks and pharmacies on Cordovez and Prat, as well as the shopping center west of downtown and the mall near the bus station.

Hospital The city's hospital is at Balmaceda 916 (✆ **51/200500**). For emergencies, dial ✆ **131.**

Internet Access There are plenty of Internet cafes downtown, including **Infernet,** Balmaceda 417 (daily 10am–midnight); **Netcafé,** Cordovez 285 (daily 11am–11pm); and **CyberCaféBar,** Matta 611 (daily 10am–10pm).

Laundry Some Laundromats to try in town are: **Lavaseco Supremo,** Balmaceda 851 (© **51/225195**); **Nevada Lavaseco,** Los Carrera 635 (© **51/216607**); and **Lavandería y Lavaseco Vicky,** Juan de Dios Pení 363-A (© **51/222746**).

Post Office **Correos de Chile** is at the corner of Prat and Matta (© **51/213753**). It's open Monday through Friday from 8:30am to 6:30pm.

WHAT TO SEE & DO

Many tour operators offer excursions in and around La Serena, including transportation to the observatories (see later). Check with your hotel regarding quality as some get poor reviews, notably Talinay and Intimahina. For day tours of the city or 2- or 3-night specialist packages, including visits to vineyards, nature preserves, and archaeological monuments, as well as a pisco tasting and astronomy lessons, check with **Ingservtur,** Matta 611 (© **51/220165;** www.ingservtur.cl), or **O.V.I. Travel,** Balmaceda 1126 (© **51/340541;** www.ovitravel.cl). For more athletic activities, including horseback riding, surf camps, ocean kayaking, mountain biking, and camping, contact **Chilesafari,** Matta 367 (© **51/225138;** www.chilesafari.com). There's also the little **Poisson** surfing school (© **9/894-9128**) right on the beach on Avenida del Mar.

Churches

La Serena's most recent urban renewal includes expensive, bilingual (Spanish/English), but ridiculously illegible glass historic markers on its main landmarks, including the most important of its 30-odd churches. Most, including the 1844–56 cathedral, date back to the 19th-century silver mining boom. Three attractive stone colonial churches bear special mention; admission is free but opening hours are irregular.

Mannerist, late-16th-century **San Francisco church** ★★ at Eduardo de la Barra and Balmaceda, was the only religious building to survive the destruction wreaked by English pirate Bartholomew Sharp in 1680. Supported by meter-thick walls, the stone facade (stone churches are a rarity in Chile) is beautifully carved with ornate Baroque flourishes.

Rebuilt in the mid-18th century in the wake of pirate Edward Davis's 1685 raid, **Santo Domingo church** ★★ is located on a small square on Cordovez just off the main plaza. It boasts a simple, airy interior, a 16th-century baptismal font, and an attractive courtyard; an ill-fitting, neo-Renaissance bell tower was attached in the early 20th century.

Following the expulsion of the Jesuits in the late 18th century, the Augustinians laid claim to **San Agustín church** ★, across from the Recova market on Cienfuegos. It has a similar Italian Renaissance style to that of Santo Domingo and was restored between 1985 and 1995 according to the original 17th-century plan.

Museums

Museo Arqueológico ★★ This smallish, crescent-shaped building houses a top-notch collection of pre-Columbian pottery from the Diaguita people who, originally from across the Andes, lived in the Norte Chico from around the year 1000 until largely disappearing in the wake of the Spanish conquest. The pottery alone makes it a must-see local attraction, but it also boasts a real *moai*—a giant anthropomorphic head from Easter Island—which was donated to the museum in 1952 as a result of the not-so-subtle persuasion of President Videla. It does a good job of tracing Chile's pre-Columbian history, but the museum has a major downside: All signs are in Spanish, and many of the museum's rooms are in dire need of renovation. The museum sells an odd assortment of expensive archaeology books and pottery, including clay dinosaurs and T-shirts.

At Cordovez and Cienfuegos. ✆ **51/215082.** Admission $1 (70p), half-price for seniors, free for all Sun. Tues–Fri 9:30am–5:50pm; Sat 10am–1pm and 4–7pm; Sun 10am–1pm.

Museo Histórico Gabriel González Videla Your ticket from the archaeological museum is also valid for the main collection in this two-story mansion—the former home of President Videla—on the main square (and vice versa). Along with modest contemporary Chilean painting and temporary exhibitions, the collection of course focuses on the museum's namesake and city's native son. The display of photographs, letters, and paintings related to the man responsible for exiling Chile's greatest poet, Pablo Neruda, is misleadingly positive and rather dull. You might even be the wiser skipping this place. Of course without that exile, we wouldn't have had the charming 1994 Italian movie, *Il Postino (The Postman).*

Matta 495. ✆ **51/217189.** Admission $1 (70p), half-price for seniors. Mon–Fri 10am–6pm; Sat 10am–1pm.

The Japanese Garden

Kokoro No Niwa ★ "Garden of the Heart," as the name translates, is a delightful, unique park whose manicured lawns, ponds, waterfowl, and Japanese pagodas and bridges are in stark contrast to the derelict Parque Pedro de Valdivia next door and its depressing zoo. Japanese architect Akira Ohira designed the 2.6-hectare (6½-acre) grounds in honor of La Serena's 450th anniversary.

Entrance off Av. Juan Bohón. ✆ **51/217013.** Admission $1 (70p). Daily 10am–6pm.

Shopping

One of Chile's best-known city markets, **La Recova ★**, lies on the square at the corner of Prat and Cienfuegos just 3 blocks from the plaza. Many of the handicrafts are pretty tacky and most feature goods imported from Peru or Bolivia, but you can sample some of the local sweets and liquors for an authentic taste of the area. You'll also find items in lapis lazuli and combarbalite, a unique, gray-green semi-precious stone found only around Combarbalá, a village to the south. In January and February, it's open Monday through Saturday from 10am to 10pm and Sunday from 10am to 5pm; during the rest of the year, Monday through Saturday from 10am to 9pm, and Sunday from 10am to 3pm.

Downtown, the main shopping area includes Cordovez and Prat streets departing from the plaza. You'll find several handicraft stalls selling local honey and folkloric dolls and knickknacks along Cordovez. A shopping mall straddles La Serena's colonial center to the south next to the bus station, while a large strip mall lies to its west just across the train tracks, each keeping the neocolonial style and each featuring retail chains common in Chile, including clothing and athletic goods stores. There's a jumbo supermarket of a similar ilk to Costco, with a little more polish—it's a convenient place to stock up on food or camping equipment. They also sell some electronics, such as memory cards and cellphone batteries, as do several stores in the downtown shopping district.

WHERE TO STAY

If you'd like to step outside your hotel in the evening, I recommend you stay on the beach, particularly if you're looking for a more upscale hotel; downtown, pickings in those categories are slim and nightlife is as serene as the city's name implies. The 6km (3¾-mile) string of accommodations running down Avenida del Mar isn't particularly attractive, but rooms are comfortable, and they're directly across the street from the beaches. The cuisine in this area by far outshines that offered downtown, too, and here you'll be able to sip a sunset cocktail on the beachfront. Plus you'll be much closer to the attractively restored English Quarter in Coquimbo, the region's newest nightlife hub.

Expensive

Hotel Campanario del Mar ★★ The Campanario del Mar is the most intimate hotel on the beachfront. Overshadowed a bit by the adjacent apartment building, it was built in Spanish colonial style, with tiled roofs below the namesake little belfry and an interior courtyard enlivened by a fountain. All rooms, including a triple and two suites, are on the second floor, have a view of the Pacific, and are recarpeted every season. They are decorated in a blue-and-white nautical color scheme with spartan furnishings including metal-framed beds and dressers. The white-tiled bathrooms with tubs are sterile but clean and quite spacious. The suites and superior rooms have kitchenettes and minibars. The restaurant offers open-air terrace seating with a view of the beach.

Av. del Mar 4600, La Serena. ✆ **51/245516.** Fax 51/245531. 14 units. www.hotelcampanario.cl. $113–$137 (£75–£91) double. AE, DC, MC, V. **Amenities:** Restaurant; bar; billiard room. *In room:* TV, Wi-Fi, kitchenette, minibar.

Hotel Francisco de Aguirre **Overrated** In theory, this is the top place in town, in a historic neoclassical three-story building a block from the main plaza. It promises swanky accommodations and a range of good amenities, but the place has been undergoing major noisy remodeling while remaining open for a couple of years and, as of mid 2009, there was no sign of it being completed.

Cordovez 210, La Serena. ✆ **51/222991.** 90 units. $110 (£73) double. AE, DC, MC, V. **Amenities:** Restaurant; bar; small outdoor pool; Internet access. *In room:* TV, minibar, safe.

Hotel La Serena Plaza ★ Don't be put off by the plain exterior of this hotel, which belies a pretty interior that is shaded by large palm trees and a good-size pool. Its conservative, tangerine yellow rooms are a 1970s throwback and range from smallish singles to big quadruple and junior suites. The rooms vary considerably in terms of polish and some are much more faded than others; be sure to ask for a nonsmoking room. While it's just across from La Serena's landmark faux lighthouse on Avenida del Mar, the stretch of beach closest to this hotel is neither particularly clean nor safe, so you'll need to walk a fair distance before you reach a good spot for a dip in the waves. The staff is friendly and helpful. The Plaza also has one of the biggest and best-equipped gyms of any hotel in Chile, but you'll have to share it with local members of the Pacific Fitness chain.

Av. Francisco de Aguirre 660, La Serena. ✆ **51/226913.** www.hotelserenaplaza.cl. 58 units. $80 (£53) double. AE, DC, MC, V. **Amenities:** Restaurant; bar; outdoor pool; Internet access; Wi-Fi in lobby area. *In room:* TV, Internet access, minibar, hair dryer, safe.

Hotel Mar de Ensueño This 15-year-old hotel looks a bit odd: The four-story main building is covered in thatch, as are the 10 family cabins on the grounds, while the large grassy garden around the pool has practically no shade and faces the avenue directly. The location does give all rooms an ocean view, most with a balcony, and all rooms except doubles and triples have kitchenettes with refrigerators. Still, for its plainness, this hotel is on the expensive side.

Av. del Mar 900, La Serena. ✆ **51/222381.** Fax 51/226177. www.hotelmarensueno.com. 50 units and 10 4-person cabins. $90–$150 (£60–£100) double; $210 (£140) cabin. AE, DC, MC, V. **Amenities:** Restaurant; bar; pool; Internet access. *In room:* TV, minibar, safe.

La Serena Club Resort ★★ (Kids) As beach resorts go in northern Chile, this is as good as it gets. The resort bears the style of the architects who designed the upscale Casa Piedra convention center in Santiago. The owners have been very creative with color and furnishings, giving smallish rooms a more spacious feel; suites can be booked together with doubles to connect rooms for families. The French-inspired restaurant serves good meals, but the highlight here is really the ocean view from the large windows. The central palm-lined pool and gardens offer plenty of room for the kids, with entertainment and aerobics on the beach during high season. The competent, attentive staff may well be the best in La Serena. Suites have terraces, with ocean views from the fourth floor.

Av. del Mar 1000, La Serena. ✆ **51/221262.** Fax 51/217130. www.laserenaclubresort.cl. 95 units. $95–$110 (£63–£73) double. AE, DC, MC, V. **Amenities:** Restaurant; bar; barbecue area; outdoor pool; clay tennis courts; massage. *In room:* TV, minibar, hair dryer.

Moderate

Hotel Fuente del Mar This is a brighter, more charming, and more economical alternative to the Balcones de Aragón (below), and it's run by a lady who moved here from Viña del Mar. You'll be surprised at the height of the courtyard inside as the colonial-style hotel appears much smaller from the outside. The cream-colored rooms are brighter and quieter than at the Balcones, but quite a bit smaller and more simply decorated.

Vicuña 210, La Serena. ✆ **51/222991.** 20 units. $60 (£40) double. No credit cards. **Amenities:** Cafeteria; Internet access. *In room:* TV.

Hotel Los Balcones de Aragón Walk into this downtown hotel and you'll immediately know this is an aging, midrange place. The hotel is on the expensive side for what it offers—though the friendly staff almost makes up for what's lacking. The rooms are fairly large and comfortable; go for the newer ones around the pleasant courtyard that are lighter and much quieter than the darker, heavily draped hunter green rooms facing the noisy street.

Cienfuegos 289, La Serena. ✆ **51/212419.** Fax 51/211800. www.losbalconesdearagon.cl. 30 units. $65 (£43) double. AE, DC, MC, V. Rates include a modest breakfast. **Amenities:** Restaurant; bar; Internet access. *In room:* TV, minibar.

Inexpensive

Hostal El Punto ★★ (Finds) This charming German-owned little hostel, located just beyond downtown, is extremely well run and oozes character. In many respects, El Punto is a much more appealing prospect than La Serena's bland midrange options, with pristine, whitewashed guest rooms with high ceilings and comfy, wood-framed beds. The six cheapest rooms share three bathrooms, while the most expensive have private bathrooms and balconies. El Punto's most endearing feature is the gorgeous garden courtyard, providing a shady spot to relax and read or enjoy a meal amid the flowers and cream-colored Mediterranean arches. Activities such as yoga add to the hostel's serene allure. It's also very convenient for those schlepping luggage from the bus station 2 blocks away.

Andrés Bello 979, La Serena. ✆ **51/228474.** 14 units. www.punto.de/en_index.html. $20–$25 (£13–£17) double with shared bathroom, $23–$44 (£15–£29) double with private bathroom. No credit cards. **Amenities:** Kitchen; Internet access; laundry services; yoga room. *In room:* TV.

Hostal Gladys ★ (Value) This nice little hostel has an excellent downtown location just off the main plaza on the square closed off by Santo Domingo, but you'll need to squeeze past a rather narrow entrance to find the surprisingly large, sky-blue rooms well above the usual backpacker's standard. You'll think you're staying in a friend's guest room with the stocked bookshelves, TV, stereo, and comfy bed facing the patio, and decorations that mix contemporary colors with some kitschy lamps and rugs. The simple bathrooms are shared.

Cordovez 247, La Serena. ✆ **9/540-3636.** 5 units. gladyslaserena@chile.com. $11 (£7.30) per person. No credit cards. **Amenities:** Kitchen; barbecue area; bike rental; Internet access. *In room:* TV.

Hostal Matta ★ Value This pleasant colonial-style hostel is hard to miss with its vibrant yellow and crimson exterior. Despite being centrally located just a couple of minutes' walk from Plaza de Armas, the hostel is on a quiet street and exudes a very peaceful vibe. The spotless, airy rooms are a step above the sterile functionality of most hostels and even have small kitchenettes and accessories such as hair dryers and irons. The staff is warm and extremely helpful and can arrange transfers to the bus station and airport. It's worth paying the extra $6/£4 for a room with a private bathroom. Advanced reservations are highly recommended from March through December, when the hostel gets busy with college students.

Matta 234, La Serena. ✆ **51/210014.** 12 units. www.hostalmatta.com. $28 (£19) double with private bathroom, $22 (£15) double with shared bathroom. No credit cards. **Amenities:** Kitchen; laundry; airport transfer. *In room:* TV, Wi-Fi, kitchenette, fridge, hair dryer, iron.

WHERE TO DINE

A few downtown cafes will give you a chance to take a break from your stroll. **Café Morocco ★**, Prat 566 (✆ **51/550444**), serves what may well be Chile's best-decorated *cortados* set in a lightly Arab-themed, intimate setting of wood-inlaid tables and exposed brick walls. It also has a few sidewalk tables, as does the larger, less stylish **Coffee Express** on the corner of Prat and Balmaceda (✆ **51/221673**). Half a block away on Balmaceda 475, **Café Colonial** has vegetarian dishes and offers set lunches for $5 (£3.30; ✆ **51/216373**). **Café El Patio,** in a courtyard at Prat 470 (✆ **51/210759;** www.cafeelpatio.4mg.com), is actually more of a jazz bar than a cafe and offers main courses around $7 (£4.70). None of these places is open on Sundays, but for an inexpensive lunch on any day of the week, head to the Recova market, where many second-floor restaurants prepare fresh seafood and hearty Chilean stews, or *cazuelas*.

Beethoven Restaurant y Salón de Té ★ INTERNATIONAL/CHILEAN This is one of the best restaurants downtown, as much for its broad menu as for its lovely location on the palm-shaded Patio Colonial courtyard. Nudging up against a handful of upscale arts-and-crafts shops with a decidedly European air, this artsy enclave provides a welcome respite from busy Avenida Balmaceda. The attentive staff serve a variety of international dishes leaning toward Italian (pasta and risotto) and crepes, but the restaurant also has some tasty, locally inspired dishes like the *lomo elquino*—not elk but grilled beef with Chilean papaya sauce and mushrooms.

Balmaceda 432. ✆ **51/218102.** Breakfast $4.50 (£3); afternoon tea $6.50 (£4.30); main courses $13 (£8.70). AE, DC, MC, V. Daily 10am–10pm.

Martín Fierro ★ ARGENTINE Tired of fish? This is the place to go for hearty meat dishes. Martín Fierro specializes in Argentine beef cuts—the jolly waitstaff are very happy to provide guidance on the various cuts of meat served—as the owners sought to make clear when naming the large restaurant after the legendary gaucho hero. Pork and lamb dishes along with homemade pasta also please a large appetite at a fair price. For the less carnivorous, there are several well-prepared fish dishes including sea bass, conger eel, and salmon carpaccio, which are served with a choice of different sauces and accompaniments. The restaurant has an average selection of Chilean wines to accompany the meals. It also has a small playground.

Cuatro Esquinas and Av. Pacífico. ✆ **51/219002.** www.martinfierro.cl. Main courses $9–$20 (£6–£13). AE, DC, MC, V. Daily 11:30am–4:30pm and 7pm–midnight.

Porota's Resto-Bar ★ INTERNATIONAL/CHILEAN The closest beachfront restaurant to downtown has a few outdoor tables and friendly service along with a varied, imaginative menu interspersed with Asian influences. It's expensive except for the salads, but the dishes are well portioned. Try the albacore—a white-fleshed tuna—with papaya jam spiced with aniseed and accompanied by mushrooms in port wine. The sauces accompanying the meat dishes tend to be a little on the heavy side, and the music blares way too early before its bar and lounge turn it into a trendy evening hangout.

Av. del Mar 900b. ✆ **51/210937.** Main courses $9–$14 (£6–£9.30). AE, DC, MC, V. Daily 11:30am–midnight.

Resto-Bar Huentelauquén ★★ (Kids) (Finds) ITALIAN This laid-back, ebullient restaurant has an extensive Italian menu served in a cozy and artistic setting. The dining area sits in a semicircular space built around several polished tree trunks and a central steel fireplace. Illuminated at night under conical lamps, most tables have windows facing the ocean, but you can also sit outside, either on top of the building itself or facing the sea. It's the imaginative varieties of oven-baked pizzas that draw the crowds, but the salads, which are composed of a bounty of fresh ingredients from the Elqui Valley, are as wholesome as they are delicious. The homemade pastas are decent, if rather rich. The restaurant gets its name from a unique cheese produced in the hamlet of Huentelauquén, about 200km (125 miles) to the south, and it's a great addition to all the Italian dishes. Huentelauquén is also very kid friendly; children will love to clamor on the playground wooden ship in between munching on pizza and tasty empanadas.

Av. del Mar 4500. ✆ **51/233707.** www.pizzeria-huentelauquen.cl. Reservations recommended in high season. Main courses $9 (£6), prix-fixe meal $11 (£7.30). AE, DC, MC, V. Daily 1pm–2am in summer; Fri–Sun 1pm–2am rest of year.

Tololo Beach ★★ SEAFOOD If you want to dine on fresh seafood with the sand between your toes, this is the place. The varied menu has plenty of local seafood entrees, including a good selection of native fish like albacore and rollizo that you won't often find elsewhere, omelets, meat dishes, and pizzas. They don't serve salmon, a farmed fish that has to be trucked in from hundreds of miles away. You can sit amid small palms right on the beach, but the most pleasant and comfortable seating is on the slightly oriental-style terrace, where you can rest your spine against the tall, leather-backed chairs and watch the pelicans dive into the Pacific against the backdrop of La Serena's port neighbor, Coquimbo. You can charge your cellphone for free in the individual lockers near the door.

Av. del Mar 5200. ✆ **51/242656.** Main courses $8–$18 (£5.30–£12); sandwiches $3–$4.50 (£2–£3). AE, DC, MC, V. Daily 11am–2am in summer; rest of year daily 11:30am–midnight.

NEAR LA SERENA

Through careful restoration of its 19th-century center, **Coquimbo,** a gritty, tough port city of 150,000, has captured the area's nightlife crowds, much to the chagrin of cross-town rivals in La Serena. Though Pedro Velásquez, the mayor pushing for the ambitious renewal, has run into trouble for misusing public funds, the turnaround has been remarkable, particularly in the **Barrio Inglés ★**, a neighborhood named for the mostly English foreigners who built the houses in the port's 19th-century heyday. It's like a little

Valparaíso, with old mansions turned into restaurants and bars, including the elegant **London House** ★, Argandoña 350, on Plaza Prat (✆ **51/323911;** www.londonhouse.cl); the **Club de Jazz** ★★ at Aldunate 739 (✆ **51/288784**), which is considered the best live jazz venue in Chile, outside of Santiago; **Blue Moon,** Sierra 51 (✆ **51/312110;** www.bluemoon.cl), an informal bar and dance club; and **De Costa a Costa,** at Aldunate 51 (no phone), a restaurant and bar with sweeping coastal views, serving a good selection of imported and draft beer, and hosting quality live music on the weekends.

Annually, Coquimbo hosts Chile's biggest popular festival, *La Pampilla,* during Independence Day festivities from September 18 to 20. It's a massive, utterly Chilean folk event with popular concerts, but it might be a little rough for those who are annoyed by heavy drinking. There's also a string of beachfront villages farther south, including **Guanaqueros** and **Tongoy,** popular for their wide, sandy beaches and seafood.

Conquimbo's sights include a small, restored 19th-century **fort** at the end of the peninsula, with an 1868 English cannon and a cafe; the swanky Barrio Inglés, a secluded enclave of restored mansions that were built by some of the finest craftsmen during the city's mining heyday; the **church** designed by famed French engineer Alexandre Gustave Eiffel in the Guayacán neighborhood; the **English cemetery** in the same neighborhood; and the 36m-tall (118-ft.) **mosque.** The mosque was built by Moroccan craftsmen at the behest of Mayor Velásquez and funded by King Mohammed VI of Morocco, though few Muslims actually live in town. It's near the bus station (**Rodoviario Coquimbo,** Av. Varela 1300; ✆ **51/326651**). The biggest and ugliest of Velásquez's latest projects is the gigantic hilltop **Cross of the Third Millennium,** a sculpture that was built to commemorate 2,000 years of Christianity and that now dominates the skyline.

The Observatories

The Norte Chico's dry, clear nights and skies, which are visible only from the Southern Hemisphere, have inspired a cluster of observatories that are among the most advanced in the world. You can visit these for free on Saturdays during the daytime, but must reserve via phone or e-mail weeks before your trip in order to do so.

Near Vicuña are **Observatorio Cerro Tololo** (✆ **51/205200;** www.ctio.noao.edu; Sat 9am–noon and 1–5pm) and **Observatorio Gemini** (✆ **2/365-4441;** www.gemini.edu; no scheduled tours). North toward Domeyko are **Observatorio Astronómico La Silla** (✆ **2/205200;** www.ls.eso.org; contact mbauerle@eso.org), open September through June on Saturday from 1:30 to 4:30pm, and **Observatorio Astronómico Las Campanas** (✆ **51/224680;** www.lco.cl), open Saturday from 2:30 to 5pm. Both Las Campanas and La Silla are quite a distance from La Serena—around a 90-minute drive.

You might prefer to look through a telescope yourself, and you can at three tourist observatories. The closest to La Serena is the **Centro Astronómico Cerro Mayu,** 27km (17 miles) east of La Serena (✆ **51/224508;** Tues–Sat 6pm–midnight); admission is $5 (£3.30) for adults, $3 (£2) for students and seniors. If you are staying in Pisco Elqui or Vicuña, your best option is **Observatorio Cerro Mamalluca** (✆ **51/411352;** www.mamalluca.org; daily 9am–8pm except Oct 30, Dec 24–25 and 31, and Jan 1); tours in English or Spanish cost $6 (£4) for adults, $3 (£2) for children. Tours are geared toward those with a basic knowledge and begin at 9pm and last for 2 hours (minibus transfers leave from Vicuña each night at 8:30pm). Tour groups are rather large (often as many as 30 people), which means that there is a lot of standing around in the cold while you await your turn to look through the telescope. Near Andacollo, 60km (37 miles) southwest of La Serena, is **Observatorio Astronómico Collowara** (✆ **51/432964;** www.collowara.cl; reserve at Urmeneta 599 in Andacollo); it costs $6 (£4) for adults, $3 (£2) for children.

Reserva Nacional Pinguino Humboldt ★★

Three rocky islands in the Pacific 110km (68 miles) north of La Serena form the **Reserva Nacional Pingüino de Humboldt,** a small 860-hectare (2,125-acre) preserve remarkable for its abundant marine wildlife, such as its namesake species of penguin, sea lions, sea otters, and bottlenose dolphins. Other cetaceans have also been sighted on occasion, including fin and blue whales and other species of dolphins. You can disembark on one of the islands, Isla Damas, which has two beautiful beaches and a small campsite (reserve at **Conaf** in La Serena; ✆ **51/272798**).

The friendly fishermen in **Punta de Choros** offer boat trips to the island, and the desert hamlet offers pleasant accommodations, including the rustic **Cabañas Amarilis** (✆ **9/447-5200;** www.ananucas.cl), charming, well equipped cabins close to the main square and the beach. **Memo Ruz** (✆ **9/534-3644;** www.puntadechorosmemoruz.cl) is a tourist center that organizes activities, including diving tours, and also has several sturdy, modern beachside cabins with terraces for rent. Tour agencies in La Serena offer day trips to the preserve. You can book a multiday sea-kayaking, scuba diving, or fishing trip to the islands through **Kayak Australis** (✆ **2/650-8264;** www.kayakaustralis.com) or **Yak Expediciones** (✆ **9/299-6487;** www.yakexpediciones.cl); book early as dates for these trips are limited. Note that trips in the winter months can be very windy, making for choppy water.

Desierto Florido ★★★

The phenomenon known as the **Desierto Florido,** or flowering desert, occurs when enough rain falls in the winter months to trigger an explosion of colors, carpeting hundreds of square kilometers of parched, barren desert with endemic wildflowers that appear almost hallucinogenic in color. There is really no way to predict when this will happen, especially because winter rainfall seems to be decreasing annually, but a rough guess would put the chances at every 4 or 5 years. Some 70 species, including the rare red lion's claw—protected in the **Llanos de Challe** national park—the violet guanaco's foot, or the blue field sigh, brighten the drab desert near **Vallenar,** a town 187km (116 miles) north of La Serena. They crop up with at least 35mm (1¹/₃ in.) of water; a good year demands some 55mm (2¹/₄ in.). When the desert blooms, you'll have from late July to October to visit, with flowers closer to the coast opening their petals later than those in the Central Valley.

Tours are available in season from La Serena, or drive north on the Pan-American Highway (Rte. 5), remembering to fill your tank before departing. From Vallenar, loop to the west to the coast, head north to Llanos de Challe national park, then back southwest to Vallenar.

Fray Jorge National Park ★

In an otherwise arid area, plants have clutched enough moisture from the desert fog *(camanchaca)* that regularly rolls in from the ocean to form vegetation amazingly similar to Patagonian rainforests. A UNESCO World Biosphere Reserve, Fray Jorge National Park is actually a remnant of those same forests that has held on from the end of the last ice age. Sadly, since its discovery in 1627 by Franciscan friar Jorge, settlers chopped down much of the original forest, leaving just 400 wooded hectares (990 acres) out of a total 9,959 hectares (24,610 acres) protected in the national park. Beyond a visitor center, a short hilltop trail leads through the forest and offers views of the steep drop to the Pacific. The best time to visit is late October and November, when its flowers bloom.

Park wildlife includes birds of prey, hummingbirds, guanacos, gray and culpeo foxes, along with sea otters and Humboldt penguins along the shore. Fray Jorge is about 100km (62 miles) due south from La Serena on the Pan-American Highway. Tours are available from La Serena. The park is open daily from 9am to 4pm, and an hour later in January and February. Admission for adults is $3 (£2) and $1 (70p) for children.

As the limited trail means your visit to Fray Jorge will likely be short, I recommend you combine it with a visit to the **Valle del Encanto National Historic Monument ★**, 14km (9 miles) from the Pan-American Highway. The park holds 30 petroglyphs chiseled into the stones by the El Molle culture from around A.D. 700, though objects dating from as far back as 2000 B.C. have been found. The park is open daily from 8am to 4:30pm; admission is 60¢ (40p) for adults, 20¢ (15p) for children. There are also thermal pools at the **Socos spa and hotel** (**© 53/198-2505**; www.termasocos.cl).

Farther inland from Fray Jorge are **Ovalle,** whose museum holds a very good collection of Diaguita pottery, and **Andacollo,** a mining village that hosts one of Chile's main religious celebrations. In honor of the Virgin Mary, an astounding 400,000 pilgrims congregate here on December 26, following a tradition begun in 1584. Including Fray Jorge, this 318km (197-mile) loop can be done in a day with a rental car, but it will be a long one as roads to Andacollo are not all paved and some have hairpin mountain turns. You might want to consider an overnight stay at Socos.

2 THE ELQUI VALLEY ★

Pisco Elqui: 104km (65 miles) SE of La Serena; 578km (359 miles) N of Santiago

A long, green garden in the arid Andes, enfolded by stunning mountains streaked with improbable hues of pink, silver, beige, and blue, the tranquil Elqui Valley faces the challenge of safeguarding its rural *huaso* soul amid expanding agro-industrial fruit production, distilleries, and an influx of Santiaguinos fleeing the capital's urban ills. Still a backwater until very recently, in the past few years miles of ugly plastic windbreaks have gone up around this valley to protect the fruit vineyards, but otherwise, the area's unspoiled nature under a clear and bright sky remains intact. A string of wholesome villages comprising colorful low-slung adobe houses punctuates the valley's serpentine roads, which weave through mountains where locals gather to sell fresh fruit and other food. While its list of attractions is short, the valley's salubrious aura, wonderful healthy food, and humbling natural setting will relax. Here, you'll be safe from the clamor of ring tones, and many places offer to soothe your spirit with massages, yoga, and other therapies. If meditating isn't your thing, hiking, mountain biking, and horseback riding will keep you busy, while pisco distilleries offer spirits of another kind. It can get very crowded in February at the height of the travel season, but the gentle climate makes the valley a great place to visit year-round.

ESSENTIALS

Getting There

BY CAR The journey from La Serena to Vicuña takes around 45 minutes on the excellent Rte. 41. To reach Pisco Elqui, turn south on Rte. 485 just past Rivadavia; it takes another 30 minutes along a serpentine mountain road. Vicuña has the only fuel station (Shell, on Rte. 41, just before the turnoff to town) beyond La Serena, as well as the last bank and ATM (often out of service). It's a relatively short trip on good roads, and a rental car is convenient as attractions are pretty far apart. For rental locations, see "Getting There: By Car" in "La Serena" on p. 192.

BY BUS For buses to La Serena, see "Getting There: By Bus" on p. 192. **Tur Bus** (✆ **51/411466** in Vicuña) and **Expreso Norte** (✆ **51/411348** in Vicuña) provide daily service to Vicuña's bus terminal at Prat and O'Higgins (✆ **51/441348**) from Santiago's San Borja terminal. The latest buses to La Serena leave Vicuña around 8:30pm. To Pisco Elqui, **Via Elqui** departs La Serena's terminal every half-hour Monday through Sunday from 6:30am to 8:30pm; some continue on to Alcohuaz at the end of the Claro Valley. Buses charge $2 (£1.30) for the La Serena–to-Vicuña and Vicuña-to–Pisco Elqui legs, while the direct trip from La Serena to Vicuña costs $3.20 (£2.15).

Orientation

The area popularly called Valle de Elqui actually includes the three valleys of the Elqui, Claro, and Cochiguaz rivers. **Vicuña,** 55km (34 miles) east of La Serena, is the main town, with services, a rural hospital, and four small museums, one in honor of Nobel Prize–winning poet Gabriela Mistral.

A string of villages continues on up to the higher reaches of the Claro, including (north–south) **Paihuano, Monte Grande** (Mistral's birthplace), and **Pisco Elqui,** a quaint, hillside place on the left bank of the river. All are easily navigable on foot but poorly lit in the evenings.

Visitor Information

In Vicuña, the municipality operates a **visitor center** in the landmark faux-medieval tower **Torre Bauer** on the plaza (✆ **51/209125**). In January and February, it's open daily from 8:30am to 9pm; the rest of the year, it's open Monday through Saturday from 8:30am to 5:30pm, and Sunday from 9:30am to 2pm. In Pisco Elqui, the Internet cafe and pool hall **Migrantes,** Prat 280 plaza (✆ **51/451-1917;** Tues–Sun 9am–2pm and 4–10pm), is the sole center with detailed information in the upper valleys, including maps. They also offer half-day to 4-day tours in the Andes, mountain biking, and horseback riding.

WHAT TO SEE & DO

For at least 400 years, people in what now are Chile and Peru have distilled a brandy from wine called **pisco,** named after the Peruvian port of the same name through which it was shipped to Spain. Still popular in both countries—particularly in the ubiquitous cocktail called pisco sour—the debate rages on regarding which side can actually claim the rights to the name. Nevertheless, to underscore the authenticity of Chile's claim, in the 1930s González Videla (you'll remember him from La Serena) pushed for the renaming of the village of La Unión to Pisco Elqui.

The valley produces most of Chile's pisco, and you can visit several distilleries. West of Vicuña is **Pisco Ruta Norte,** launched in 2004 by CCU, Chile's dominant beverage company (✆ **2/427-3012**); it's open in January and February daily from 10am to 6pm, and March through December on Tuesday from 10:30am to 5:30pm. Two kilometers (1¼ miles) east of Vicuña is the touristy **Capel,** a pretty colonial estate, which includes a contrived **Pisco Museum** (✆ **51/411251;** www.piscocapel.cl); it's open daily from 10am to 12:30pm and 2:30 to 6pm, and in January and February daily from 10am to 6pm. In Monte Grande, you'll find **Artesanos del Cochiguaz** (✆ **51/198-2649**), which is now part of the Capel cooperative, open daily from 10am to 1pm and 2:30 to 6pm, in January and February daily from 10am to 6pm.

There are two distilleries producing pisco that is relatively rare in Chilean supermarkets. One is **Tres Erres** (© **51/451358**), on Pisco Elqui's main square, named after Rigoberto Rodríguez, one of the region's first pisco producers who sold his trademark brand to one of the country's most important distilleries, called Control, based in La Serena. It's open March through December daily from 10:30am to 1pm and 2 to 5pm, but call ahead on a Sunday or Monday to see if it's open; January and February, it's open daily from 11am to 1:30pm and 2:30 to 8pm. The other is **Los Nichos** (© **51/451085**), located 3km (2 miles) south and open March through October daily from 10am to 1pm and 2 to 6pm, and November and December daily from 11am to 7pm.

Outdoor Activities

An excellent **hike** if you don't mind the steep, 2,000m (6,560-ft.) climb is the 6.5km (4-mile) *Cumbres de Elqui* or Elqui Peaks, departing from Pisco and marked by three statues on the way up; register with the police before setting out. Alternatively, for a more accessible, less challenging hike from Pisco, take Calle Baquedano (just north of the main square on the road to Alcoguaz) and follow the dirt track through the mountains. You are unlikely to pass another soul other than the odd herd of lonely goats, a few wild horses, and a couple of lone *huesos.* Experiencing the silent grandeur of the mountains with the flourishing valley below is a soulful way to spend a couple of hours. Take plenty of water, as cool mornings soon give way to torrid midday heat. Hotels often offer **horseback riding** throughout the valleys, and you can try your hand at **trout fishing** in the rivers. Winds over the artificial lake **Puclaro** west of Vicuña make it a great area for **watersports** such as wind or kite surfing; check at your hotel (El Tesoro de Elqui, reviewed later, is best). An entertaining spectator sport is the Chilean-style **rodeo,** held annually September 19 in the rickety-looking *media luna* or crescent stadium near Horcón.

Shopping

A government-sponsored investment scheme has helped local craftsmen set up a market in the hamlet of **Horcón** 10km (6 miles) past Pisco Elqui. They offer a wide range of goods from herbs, honey, and jams to musical instruments and crafts made of quartz, metals, and wood. It's open January and February daily from 12:30 to 8:30pm, and during the rest of the year Tuesday through Friday from 12:30 to 6:30pm, Saturday and Sunday 12:30 to 8pm.

WHERE TO STAY

You'll find plenty of campgrounds and *cabañas* catering to domestic tourists throughout the valley. Standards are improving, there are some great places to stay, and the hotel staff will be able to help you book excursions or relaxation therapies.

Expensive

Elqui Domos ★ One of the more futuristic and memorable accommodations choices in Chile, Elqui Domos is a hotel composed of six canvas geodesic domes that look like a hillside observatory. These are no ordinary tents. The split-level domes are large with a living room and bathroom on the first level and a bedroom complete with a detachable ceiling and your own telescope and astronomical literature so that you can gaze at the stars. Each dome can sleep up to four people. The domes are airy and the decor is minimalist—white lounge chairs, futon, and quilted bed—and each dome has a terrace with deck chairs. On the downside, most but the highest are a bit close for comfort and it can get chilly in the winter. Reserve in advance, as these book up quickly.

Sector Los Nichos s/n, 3.5km (2 miles) S of Pisco Elqui. ✆ **51/211453.** www.elquidomos.cl. 6 units. $90–$99 (£60–£66) double. MC, V. **Amenities:** Barbecues; bike rental; Internet access; Wi-Fi; astronomy lectures; horseback riding; outdoor terrace with tub and hammocks. *In room:* Minibar, free coffee and tea, hair dryer upon request.

Hostería Vicuña ★ This is a hacienda-style hotel with a 40-year tradition, which also means it could use a little sprucing up. Pricey but still the best hotel in Vicuña, it has relatively few rooms considering the size of the complex, which includes a swimming pool and a kiddie pool, tennis courts, and palm-lined grounds with pet llamas. Rooms are large and have high ceilings, with huge windows looking out on the pool and comfortable beds covered in flowery bedspreads.

Sargento Aldea 101, Vicuña. ✆ **51/411301.** www.hosteriavicuna.cl. 15 units. $75 (£50) single; $105 (£70) double; $150 (£100) quadruple. AE, DC, MC, V. **Amenities:** Restaurant; bar; large outdoor pool; wading pool; tennis courts; Internet access; laundry service. *In room:* TV, minibar, no phone.

La Casona Distante ★★★ **Value** If you are looking for peace and seclusion in a stunning setting with plenty of activities on hand, this "secluded ranch" is worth the journey. This is the best hotel in the valley and, as its name indicates, one of its most remote, all the way at the high end of the valley near Alcoguaz, 17km (11 miles) beyond Pisco Elqui. The owners have transformed the three-story 1940 hacienda, nestled amid 63 acres of lush valley, into a gorgeous eco-lodge in adobe, bay, and poplar. Rooms have high wooden ceilings, earthy adobe walls, and comfortable beds. Bathrooms are fancifully rustic and very stylish, and the outdoor pool is beautiful. Thick walls help keep the rooms cool in summer. All meals are included and the dining area and kitchen are integrated, so you can watch or participate—you can even cook your own trout from the river. Considering its service and amenities, it's an absolute bargain.

Fundo Distante s/n, Alcoguaz. ✆/fax **55/851149,** 55/851247, or 9/226-5440. www.casonadistante.cl. 8 units. $107 (£71) double; $120 (£80) suite with whirlpool. No credit cards. **Amenities:** Restaurant; bar; outdoor pool; bikes; fishing; hiking trails; horseback riding; massage room; laundry service; TV room. *In room:* TV and minibar (by request), hair dryer.

Moderate

Hotel El Galpón ★ La Serena artist Marcos Ramos has decorated this hotel with vaguely Mayan elements to reflect the mystical, esoteric side of the valley, with symbols for light, water, earth, and sun both on the outside of the main building and inside the rooms. The hotel gardens are a blaze of color and surround a good-size pool, which has plenty of chaises for sunbathing and sits at the foot of the mountains. The rooms are tasteful if simple, with white, thick adobe walls of natural stone, and beds with metal or wood frames and white bedding. It also has more traditionally decorated rooms in its five spacious, terraced cabins. On the downside, it is a dark 15-minute walk at night along a mountain road to get to Pisco Elqui, so most guests tend to dine at the hotel.

1km (half a mile) N of Pisco Elqui on the main hwy. ✆ **51/198-2554.** www.elgalpon-elqui.cl. 6 units. $95 (£63) double; $115–$130 (£77–£87) cabin. AE, DC, MC, V. Children are not accepted. **Amenities:** Restaurant w/Internet and Wi-Fi; bar; lounge w/fireplace. *In room:* TV, minibar, hair dryer.

Hotel Halley ★ This colonial hotel close to Plaza de Armas has old-fashioned rooms with Victorian-style furnishings and 1950s adornments. High ceilings and large windows alleviate the fussy trimmings. The main allure lies in the building's charming original features such as wrought-iron balconies and a verdant courtyard with a small pool, and the reasonable tariff. On the downside, the beds are rather soggy, rooms facing the street are noisy, and you don't always get service with a smile.

Gabriela Mistral 542, Vicuña. ✆ **51/412070.** 13 units. $46 (£31) double. AE, DC, MC, V. **Amenities:** Small outdoor pool; Internet access; laundry service.

Hotel Las Pléyades ★★ Finds Owner Soledad Donoso has elegantly transformed a large old house into the valley's only boutique hotel. Rooms are large and, like the living and dining areas, have a fine but rustic decor—plenty of wood and stone, and no two rooms are alike. It has an outdoor pool and a private beach on the river. Show Ms. Donoso this Frommer's guide and she'll give you a discount (as much as a 50% discount in the off-season). Monte Grande is 4km (2½ miles) from Pisco Elqui.

Calle principal s/n, Monte Grande. ✆ **51/451107.** www.valledeelqui.cl/laspleyades.htm. 5 units. $85 (£57) double. No credit cards. Children are not accepted. **Amenities:** Dining area; outdoor pool; laundry service. *In room:* Hair dryer.

Misterios de Elqui ★★ Finds Tasteful and utterly relaxing, this Santa Fe–style adobe hotel is a heavenly place to spend a couple of nights in the Elqui Valley. At the foot of the mountains, spacious cabins with jaw-dropping views are weaved through lush gardens that brim with color. The beautifully designed cabins are the epitome of rustic chic with fluffy, white cotton bedspreads, hand-carved mahogany bed frames, cream linen sofas, and well-appointed bathrooms with rainforest shower heads and slate tile showers. There are no TVs in the rooms, just dazzling views of star-studded skies. The pool area affords glorious mountain views and has sun loungers surrounded by verdant gardens, a barbeque, a putting green, and even a bustling little brook. The stylish reception area has a small bar and TV area and is decorated with local arts and crafts. The intimate restaurant is one of the best in the area. Convivial owner Jaime is helpful and as likely to be sunbathing next to you on the terrace as he is working the reception desk.

Arturo Prat s/n. ✆ **51/451126.** www.misteriosdeelqui.cl. 6 units. $87–$95 (£58–£63) double. AE, DC, MC, V. Rates include large breakfast. **Amenities:** Restaurant; outdoor pool; laundry service; TV room.

Inexpensive

El Tesoro de Elqui ★ Kids Value The beauty of its gardens sets this hotel apart from others in Pisco Elqui, and the place was designed with foreign tourists in mind. Its 10 *cabañas* and two double rooms vary widely, though all have their own bathrooms except for the dorm-type room. They also all have warm, tan adobe walls, most with wooden floors. You can view them all on the hotel's trilingual website. My favorite is the cozy, skylighted *Suspiro* (Sigh) that allows you to stargaze. The staff can also organize kite surfing on the Puclaro lake for you. The view of the Andes from the figure-eight pool is great.

Arturo Prat s/n, Pisco Elqui. ✆ **51/451069.** www.tesoro-elqui.cl. $58 (£39) double; $70–$81 (£47–£54) triple with kitchenette. AE, DC, MC, V. **Amenities:** Restaurant; bar; outdoor pool; laundry service.

Hotel Elqui ★ Value This centrally located hotel in a classic, carmine-on-buff mansion is the oldest in Pisco Elqui, with 5 decades under its belt. It's still run by the friendly Áviles family who give it a welcoming, homey atmosphere. It has eight simply decorated rooms sharing five clean bathrooms. It's a steal considering its amenities: attractive gardens with three pools to cool off in, balconies in some rooms, and hammocks. Plus, it has one of the better restaurants for traditional Chilean fare.

O'Higgins s/n (off the square), Pisco Elqui. ✆ **51/451130.** www.valledeelqui.cl/mainhotelelqui.htm. 8 units. $12–$20 (£8–£13) per person. No credit cards. **Amenities:** Restaurant; 3 pools. *In room:* TV by request.

Moderate

Donde la Elke ★ INTERNATIONAL An offshoot of a successful Santiago restaurant, Donde la Elke has the most extensive variety of cuisine in town. The rustic ambience and muted, natural decor serve as a perfect backdrop for an appealing menu of homemade pastas and quiches, along with fish and meats, the specialty of the friendly Argentine running the place.

Carrera s/n (on the corner of Manuel Rodriguez), Pisco Elqui. ✆ **51/451088.** Main courses $10–$20 (£6.70–£13). No credit cards. Thurs–Tues 1–5:30pm and 7–11pm (or later).

El Durmiente Elquino ★ CHILEAN In Pisco Elqui, this adobe building with terracotta walls decorated with local artworks and an outdoor terrace complete with a roaring fire pit is a heart-warming setting to try old-fashioned Chilean specialties, snack on decent thin-crust pizzas, or sample healthy salads made from local products (be sure to try the goat cheese from Horcón). If you are in the mood for a hearty staple, the *cazuela de ave* (chicken and vegetable stew) has hunks of fresh, succulent chicken, and a medley of locally grown vegetables, but lacks seasoning. As for libations, there is a well conceived selection of regional wines and, of course, the fitting precursor for any meal in Chile, a feisty pisco sour.

Las Carreras s/n, Pisco Elqui. ✆ **8/906-2754.** Main courses $7–$13 (£4.70–£8.70). AE, DC, MC, V. Tues–Sun 11am–1am.

Hacienda Miraflores ★★ Moments CHILEAN This is one of the few remaining family-owned haciendas in the valley, though the owners have switched to exporting grapes from making their own pisco. The Miraflores has splendid views through enormous windows. Its high-quality spit roasted meats will tempt all except for vegetarians, but it also serves pasta dishes. They offer good desserts, and it's one of a few places in the valley with real espresso. You can also head down to the river on the property, or spend a pleasant evening on the terrace. It is popular with tour groups, especially at lunchtime, so reservations are highly recommended.

Rte. 485, 2.5km (1⅔ miles) past Pisco Elqui. ✆ **51/285901.** Reservations recommended. Main courses $9–$16 (£6–£11). AE, DC, MC, V. Jan–Feb Tues–Sun 12:45pm–1am; rest of year Sat–Sun and holidays.

Inexpensive

Los Jugos ★ CHILEAN More a pub than a restaurant, this is Pisco Elqui's main nightlife hot spot. Famous for its fruit juices, it also serves La Serena sours, and pisco with papaya rather than lemon juice. It offers set menus along with good, large pizzas and a great onion soup perfect for a chilly evening. The soundtrack of indie rock music sits perfectly with the rustic decor.

Centenario s/n (on the main square), Pisco Elqui. ✆ **51/212182.** Set menu $7 (£4.70), pizzas $10–$16 (£6.70–£11). No credit cards. Daily 8am–11pm.

9

The Desert North

Almost a third of Chile's 6,000km (3,720-mile) length is the driest desert in the world; the Atacama is an area of red sand and stone so dry that NASA has picked it to conduct experiments for Martian exploration as some areas are practically devoid of any life at all. Death Valley is moist by comparison. Still, several rivers descend from the Andes—including Chile's longest, the Loa—and oases dot the region, giving life to picturesque villages steeped in native and colonial Spanish tradition, including, most famously, San Pedro de Atacama.

In this desert, you'll find literally breathtaking high-altitude landscapes, abundant wildlife, archaeological and architectural heritage, and multiple activities for sports enthusiasts. San Pedro's burst onto the travel scene has led to many improvements in infrastructure: The dusty village itself boasts some of the best hotels in the country amid a relaxed, laid-back atmosphere easily accessible to those with limited time. But the area also holds many more remote jewels to entice adventuresome travelers.

EXPLORING THE REGION

Calama, a scrappy boomtown served by frequent flights from Santiago, is the gateway to San Pedro de Atacama. Calama is usually experienced by travelers only from an airplane window, as an inspiring jumble tossed upon the dusty and inhospitable desertscape. It's not surprising that most visitors make a hasty exit and head to the more soulful oasis town of San Pedro. The only reasons to spend the night in Calama are to visit the immense Chuquicamata copper mine and to use it as a springboard to the border with Bolivia at Ollagüe. From **San Pedro,** you can take part in a multitude of day trips ranging from close encounters with ethereal natural phenomenon to soulful wanderings amid the colonial villages that dot the central desert. Plan for at least 4 days to visit this region's highlights, or 6 to 7 days to really explore it, if you're a fan of active travel. With a plethora of adobe-style accommodations, convivial restaurants where travelers gather around fire pits under star studded skies, and an artsy laissez faire vibe, it's easy to yield to San Pedro's wild mysticism. It's certainly nothing like home.

Arica, the coastal city on the border with Peru and home to the world's oldest mummies, is your first stop on the way to spectacular **Lauca National Park** and its unique villages, but it's also a fine place to unwind on the beach. The city and immediate environs can be explored in a day. While Lauca is less than 200km (124 miles) from Arica, take it easy because of the high altitude and allot at least 2 days for your visit, with an overnight stay in the pretty Aymara village of **Putre.**

Immense distances between sites of interest means that travelers should focus on one area of Chile's northern desert rather than trying to pack in too many stops. Many tour operators offer multiday excursions to a variety of additional locations in this otherworldly environment, some of which may not be highlighted in this book. Considering the compact size of the villages and the plentiful, very reasonably priced guided tours that are available to all destinations, a vehicle is unnecessary. However, if your intrepid spirit demands the freedom and spontaneity that a vehicle affords, safety considerations are

Valle de la Luna (Valley of the Moon) ★★ with its ethereal lunar landscape, mountains streaked with pink, and foreboding silence, is the poster child of the Atacama Desert. The valley is a depression surrounded by jagged spines of salt-encrusted hills, with an immense sand dune running between two ridges. Most tours include a 15-minute (tours depart at 3 or 4:30pm, depending on the season) stroll through the Cordillera de Sal (Salt Hill Range), where you will literally hear the rocks cracking, before ending at a lookout point reached by a 15-minute, fairly steep ascent along a sandy pathway at sunset. This is the best site to enjoy Atacama Desert's colors as they melt from violet to gold. You'll share this lookout point during the sunset hour with a hundred or more tourists, especially during the summer. For an unforgettable night, come on the eve of a full moon, when ghostly light casts shadows on an already eerie landscape. The Valle is 15km (9¼ miles) from San Pedro and can be reached by bicycle or vehicle. To get here, head west on the street Licancabúr toward Calama, and follow the left-turn sign for Valle de la Luna. Tour prices do not include admission to the national park, which costs $4.50 (£3). ***Warning:*** There's a minefield between the northern park gate and the main highway to Calama. Heed the warning signs, and don't wander off around the gate.

Heading south 38km (24 miles) from San Pedro, you will reach the oasis towns of Toconao, Camar, and Socaire. These three towns are not as picturesque as their counterparts in the Atacama Desert, so you might want to just continue on. What you should head for are the high altiplanic lakes, **Laguna Miscanti** and **Laguna Miñeques,** two stunning cobalt-blue lakes at the foot of their respectively named peaks, and the **Salar de Talar** and the **Laguna de Tuyajto,** where it is easier to spot flamingos than at the Salar de Atacama. This journey is recommended in order to view high-altitude lakes on a less strenuous trip than the **Salar de Tara** ★★★, near the Argentina/Bolivia/Chile border. More adventurous types are better off visiting Tara because the reserve is larger, the salt flat's colors are more intense, and there are no other tourists. The Salar de Tara (also part of the Flamingo Reserve) rates as one of the most memorable journeys in the Atacama area, but few visitors are aware of it. The trip requires a round-trip 200km (124-mile) drive mostly along bumpy roads in a 4×4, along with a moderate hike.

Geysers del Tatio/Baños de Puritama ★★

Without a doubt a highlight in the Atacama Desert, the **Geysers del Tatio (Tatio Geysers)** are nonetheless not the easiest excursion—there's not a lot of physical activity required, but tours leave at 4 or 5am (the geysers are most active around 6–8am). At 4,321m (14,173 ft.), these are the highest geysers in the world, and it is a marvelous spectacle to watch thick plumes of steam blow from holes in such a windswept, arid land. Interspersed between the geysers, bubbling pools encrusted with colorful minerals splash and splutter—but exercise extreme caution when walking near the thin crust; careless visitors burn themselves here frequently. Herds of *vicuñas,* the smallest camelid, with the animal kingdom's finest wool, graze in this area. There is a hot springs pool at the geyser site that most tours stop at, but I urge you to find a tour company that includes Baños de Puritama (see later). A lump of rusting metal at the geysers is what's left of a previous misguided attempt to industrialize the underground source of energy. The geysers are 95km (59 miles) north of San Pedro. I strongly recommend travelers with their own vehicle not drive here—even habitual drivers to the geysers can get lost in the dark amid myriad dirt roads. If you insist, buy a map at the military's geographic institute in Santiago and get an experienced driver to run you through details of the route, or hire a day

The army owns and operates the Morro's commemorative museum that explains the siege and combat in great detail, along with displaying uniforms and weapons of the war. Though former dictator Augusto Pinochet himself placed several plaques there that remain on display, it's not offensively nationalistic, but it also doesn't make much of an effort to explain the war itself.

Museo Histórico y de Armas. ✆ **58/254091.** www.museomorrodearica.cl. Admission $1 (70p) adults, 50¢ (35p) children. Mon–Fri 9am–8pm; Sat–Sun 9am–8pm.

Museo del Mar ★ In a pretty restored house, this "museum of the sea" is a bit misleadingly named as it focuses almost entirely on seashells alone. That said, it has some gorgeous specimens. The brainchild of a local private collector, the museum holds a 1,000-species collection of seashells, including fossils, many from Chile, others imported. It also has an aquarium featuring sea anemones.

Sangra 315. www.museodelmardearica.cl. Admission $2 (£1.30) adults, $1 (70p) children. Mon–Sat 10am–2pm and 4–8pm.

Shopping

With its proximity to Bolivia and Peru, a local Aymara Indian community, and thousands of years of history, you won't be surprised that Arica showcases plenty of Andean handicrafts. Stalls clog Bolognesi downtown, and a Bolivian-Peruvian market runs along Máximo Lira, between the entrance to the port and the Tacna train station. You'll find higher quality local products in the **Pueblo Artesanal,** a 12-hut replica of Parinacota, including a copy of its church that's worth a look. The high quality crafts include textiles, sculptures, alpaca knitwear, leather goods, and ceramics. The village entrance is at Hualles 2885, near the road entries to the Azapa Valley; it's open Tuesday through Sunday from 9:30am to 1pm and 3:30 to 7:30pm. Local products are absent from major supermarket chains, but available at **Sabores de Arica** downtown, on Bolognesi 317 (✆ **58/259101;** www.saboresdearica.cl).

Beaches

Arica's tourism is still principally geared toward domestic visitors and those from southern Peru and La Paz, who flock to its beaches mid-December through February. It certainly has plenty to offer at a noticeably warmer water temperature than that of the frigid ocean of the rest of Chile. Oddly, beachfront accommodations are comparatively rare and overpriced, with most hotels and small *residenciales* downtown.

North of downtown, the long **Chinchorro** beach will give you plenty of room for sunbathing, swimming, or in-season jet ski rental, and there are restaurants, cafes, parks, and an Olympic-size pool—it's open Tuesday through Sunday from 9am to 2pm and costs $1 (70p). Farther north, the undertow makes **Las Machas** too dangerous for swimming, but the waves are good for surfing. You might see the rusting remains of the U.S. steamer *Wateree* that an 1868 tidal wave ripped from anchorage in the harbor and shoved inland. It was little damaged and subsequently found use as a building, but the next tidal wave in 1877 destroyed it.

South of downtown are four popular beaches safe for swimming. *Micro* buses run along the length of Avenida San Martin. The closest to the center, just a 20-minute walk, and the most populated, is **El Laucho,** a pleasant cove of brown sand. The second and more attractive is **La Lisera,** about 20 minutes from downtown, followed by Playa Brava, and finally the dark sand expanses and curvaceous dunes of Playa Arenillas Negras, which has the benefit of being the quietest stretch, but the disadvantage of having ocean views marred by fish-processing plants. Farther south there are wilder, rockier beaches with a few cheap restaurants, which can be reached on an asphalt road that runs along the coast for 6km (4 miles) from the Morro. Where it ends, an easy, hour-long walk along the rocky shore will take you to a sea lion colony. You can camp and fish near the shore, but it's too dangerous for swimming.

The Azapa & Lluta Valleys

The lush valleys of fruit orchards and olive groves east of the city offer refuge from the dusty dryness of the Atacama and Arica's urban bustle. Enormous geoglyphs adorn the sandy hillsides, along with ruins of several native fortresses. Hundreds of mummies—the oldest found *anywhere*—have been unearthed and placed in the care of an excellent museum. The oldest artifacts found in Azapa date from 9000 B.C. But poor protection threatens these treasures just as they begin to capture the international spotlight.

Geoglyphs ★★★ Orange or yellow obelisks with red Indian symbols mark several archaeological sites in the Azapa and Lluta valleys, including gravesites, *pukarás* (pre-Columbian fortresses), and geoglyphs, giant depictions of people or animals scratched into the mountain or assembled in stones. Peru's Nazca Lines (200 B.C.–800 A.D.), some 800km/496 miles north, are the world's best known geoglyphs. More varied and covering a greater area, between Chug-Chug (near Calama) and Nazca in Peru, the Atacama geoglyphs were thought to have been built much later, between 600 A.D. and 1500 A.D., and in addition to possessing ritual and symbolic significance, these geoglyphs also served as route markers for desert caravans.

The geoglyphs of the Lluta Valley are the best preserved; the closer they are to Arica, the more they've been vandalized, grimly proving the fragility of the sites and their lack of protection. Binoculars are handy for viewing geoglyphs in the Lluta Valley, high above the valley floor. You can get much closer to the geoglyphs in the Azapa Valley and see them more clearly. Across the valley from the museum (see later), foundations remain of a *pukará* or village from the Tihuanaco period, with a great view of the emerald valley contrasting with the reddish desert.

Travelers who can't head to the Andean highlands for health reasons are able to do this excursion easily by booking a tour in Arica, but the Lluta geoglyphs will also be seen above the highway (Rte. 11) by those en route to Putre and the Lauca National Park—just use the obelisks for orientation.

Near Arica, at the mouths of the Azapa and Lluta valleys E and NE of town, respectively, and visible from a long distance away above the roads. For more specific information, ask at Sernatur downtown or the Museo Arqueológico San Miguel de Azapa (reviewed below).

Museo Arqueológico San Miguel de Azapa ★★★ For anyone with even a minimal interest in history and archaeology, this small museum, spanning 10,000 years of history, is one of the top attractions in all of Latin America. It outlines the entire history of pre-Columbian cultures in the Arica area through Tihuanaco and the Inca periods, but the standout attraction is the mummies on display. Around 5000 B.C.—long before even the Egyptians began to mummify their dead—the Chinchorro culture developed a technique of its own to preserve bodies for eternity. They removed the extremities, skin, and soft organs, dried and strengthened the bodies with sticks and clay, and later reassembled them and painted them black (5000 B.C.–3000 B.C.) or red (2500 B.C.–2000 B.C.). The accomplishment is all the more remarkable considering the tribes were fishers and gatherers, living on the Pacific coast from Ilo in Peru down to Antofagasta 6000 B.C. to 2000 B.C. The mummies in the museum were among 96 corpses discovered in 1983 just a few feet beneath the ground at the foot of the Morro, by members of Arica's water company who were laying new pipes. Earlier examples date to the 20th century when German archaeologist Max Ulhle became the first to understand that the preservation of these prehistoric remains involved a highly sophisticated form of mummification.

The fact that the museum displays only four mummies, a man, woman, and two children, is my lone issue with the museum. The other displays here include various types of artifacts like textiles, tapestries, pottery, and weapons, making it easier to trace the development of the distinct styles and periods. The museum also has a section devoted to recent and contemporary Aymara culture in the area, along with a giant olive oil press.

Camino Azapa, Km 12. ✆ **58/205555.** www.uta.cl/masma. Admission $2 (£1.30) adults, $1 (70p) children. Jan–Feb daily 9am–8pm; Mar–Dec daily 10am–6pm.

WHERE TO STAY

The overwhelming majority of hotels in Arica are small downtown *residenciales.* Other options are limited, perhaps with the exception of backpackers' hostels.

Expensive

Hotel Arica ★★ Kids The top option in the city, this resort hotel has a great location at the foot of the Morro between the El Laucho and La Lisera beaches, ideally perched for Pacific Ocean sunsets. Despite careful renovations, the rooms betray their 1970s utilitarian roots. Room sizes vary, but they're all decorated with cream-colored walls and appointed with bright orange and yellow bedspreads and drapes and chintzy furniture. The attractive cabins are darker, with funky crimson and white '70s tiles to help keep them cool. Service is friendly and professional, and the hotel offers plenty of amenities to keep the kids entertained in summer, including the "Happy Club," a schedule of daily events including volleyball and pilates, for adults and kids. The restaurant is one of the better options in town, but the gastronomic standards in Arica are quite low.

Av. San Martín 599, Arica. ✆ **58/254540.** Fax 58/231133. www.panamericanahoteles.cl. 114 units. $85 (£57) standard double; $99 (£66) superior double; $142 (£95) *cabaña* for 4; $199 (£133) suite. AE, DC, MC, V. **Amenities:** Restaurant; bar; outdoor pool; clay tennis courts; gym; massage/spa; babysitting; laundry service. *In room:* A/C, TV, minibar, safe.

Moderate

Hotel Bahía Chinchorro This Mediterranean-style hotel with white walls and red tiled roofs is the brainchild of the solid Latinorizons tour outfit. It's right on the ocean at the southern end of the Chinchorro beach, but the beach there is a bit scruffy, and the chain-link fence around the grounds is unattractive. Managers acknowledge the need to spruce up the garden. Still, this is one of few decent midrange options, with pleasant, airy rooms, and your breakfast will have an ocean view. It also has cheaper rooms with shared bathrooms and a six-person *cabaña.* English and French are spoken here.

Av. Luis Beretta Porcel 2031, Arica. ✆ **58/260676.** 16 units. $28–$50 (£19–£33). AE, DC, MC, V. **Amenities:** Restaurant; large outdoor pool; bike rental; horseback riding on the beach; excursions to Andes national parks; free Internet and Wi-Fi. *In room:* TV, no phone.

Hotel Savona ★ Value The Savona is a good downtown choice as it's within walking distance of all downtown sights. The prosaic two-story white building is set slightly away from the street, but the best rooms face the nearby Morro and attractive Mediterranean-style pool and terrace. The rooms themselves are moderate in size and fusty in decoration, with heavy wooden furniture and dowdy bedspreads mildly relieved by walls painted in varying pastel shades from cream to green. Large rectangular windows flood the place with light. The amenities are of a higher standard than most hotels in this category, making it a great value, even at full price.

Yungay 380, Arica. ✆ **58/231000.** Fax 58/256556. www.hotelsavona.cl. 31 units. $36 (£24) single; $49 (£33) double; $57 (£38) triple. AE, DC, MC, V. **Amenities:** Cafeteria; large outdoor pool; bicycles; Wi-Fi in lobby. *In room:* TV, hair dryer, safe.

Inexpensive

Hostal Sunny Days ★★ Kids Budget travelers will find this hostel in the peaceful Chinchorro neighborhood north of downtown very convenient, as it's close to the bus terminals and just a short walk from the beach. The hotel is an excellent value; simple rooms are good-size doubles or triples (one's a quadruple), with spotless bathrooms and all but one of the rooms on the airy second story. There is also a dormitory with seven single beds and a shared bathroom. Breakfast is copious, and Sunny Days is a great place to meet other travelers. The Chilean–New Zealander couple who own the place, Beatriz Carrasco and Ross Moorhouse, are very friendly and a great source of up-to-the-minute information. Reserve ahead, particularly during Chilean school holidays.

Tomas Aravena 161 and Pedro de Valdivia, Arica. ✆ **58/241038.** www.sunny-days-arica.cl. 7 units. $12–$15 (£8–£10); dorm room $10 (£6.70). No credit cards. **Amenities:** Bicycle rental; Internet access; kitchen use. *In room:* Wi-Fi.

WHERE TO DINE

Evenings start late in Arica, particularly on weekends, so seating shouldn't be difficult if you head off early. Despite its proximity to Peru, the food is heavily Chilean, with some of the better restaurants dabbling in regional cuisine. Peruvian influence is limited largely to the many roast chicken eateries and, interestingly, Chinese *chifas.* For people-watching, go to the cafes on 21 de Mayo downtown, or head to the places on Raul Pey, a stone's throw from the Chinchorro beach, which are lively deep into the night.

Expensive

Maracuyá ★★ SEAFOOD The Azapa and Lluta valleys are Chile's tropical fruit orchards, and this restaurant makes ample use of its namesake, the passion fruit. For fish and seafood, it's Arica's best choice, with fruit flavored sweet-and-sour sauces accompanying the varied choices on the menu. Try the salmon in a piquant pineapple sauce or the succulent sea bass with a light orange glaze. Couple this with its location, perched in a villa almost over the water on a rocky stretch of coastline near the Morro, and you have one fine restaurant indeed. The terrace can be a little drafty—dress accordingly if you wish to sit outside, especially at night.

Av. San Martín 321. ✆ **58/227600.** restaurantmaracuya@hotmail.com. Reservations recommended. Main courses $14–$22 (£9.30–£15). AE, DC, MC, V. Daily 11am–4pm and 8pm–1am.

Terra Amata ★★ INTERNATIONAL Downtown's best restaurant is housed in this partly circular, contemporary white Mediterranean building, which offers fine views of the historic squares, port, and Morro. The menu, though international, features interesting local and Peruvian cuisine. Try the local meat specialties such as a simply prepared lamb dish or quinoa pie filled with vegetables, or if you really want to go for protein, with beef (quinoa's grainlike seeds are also protein-rich). Watch where you put your hands: Hot metal plates allow you to join in the preparation of your meal. The desserts are equally tantalizing, especially the Boa Boa, a tropical fruit flambé that's drenched with ice cream. The restaurant also offers art exhibitions, and live music on weekends.

Yungay 201. ✆ **58/259057.** terraamata_arica@vtr.net. Reservations recommended. Main courses $11–$13 (£7.30–£8.70). AE, DC, MC, V. Daily noon–4pm and 8:30pm–3am.

Moderate

Chin Huang Tao ★ CHINESE One of the few Peruvian terms still used in Arica is *chifa,* slang for Chinese restaurant. Thousands of Chinese indentured servants toiled under Peruvian rule, and there's reason to believe they saw the Chileans as liberators. The many *chifas* in Arica provide some support to this theory, as does the surprising absence of other Peruvian cuisine in this city. Arica's best *chifa* is Chin Huang Tao, a roomy, pink-and-red downtown Cantonese spot sporting a feng-shui fish tank and just 10 tables. The food is authentic, flavorful, and of good quality—thousands of miles from where you might have expected.

Patricio Lynch 224. ✆ **58/232823.** Main courses $5–$10 (£3.30–£6.70). AE, DC, MC, V. Daily 6:30–11:30pm.

Inexpensive

Mata Rangi ★ (Finds) SEAFOOD This understated breezy fish restaurant inside the fishermen's harbor spot is a quirky, fun place for a seafood lunch. Upon entering you'll feel as though you have just stepped into a family kitchen; the family owned restaurant exudes a warm, relaxed but bustling experience. The seafood is of very good quality and simply prepared—grilled or fried—but the vegetables tend to be of the canned variety. Don't come after dark, or you'll lose out on one of its top attractions: watching the sea lions coast through the green sea water, the pelicans fly by, or even the gigantic tires from mining trucks being recycled as shock absorbers lining the docks. The owner also offers boat tours to view penguins and sea lions.

Máximo Lira 501, inside the port area. ✆ **9/682-5005.** www.turismomarino.com. Main courses $7–$9 (£4.70–£6). No credit cards. Daily 11:30am–10pm.

Pizzaiolia ★ PIZZA This chain-style pizza joint won't win any prizes for decor or ambience, but the specialty oven-baked pizzas—over two dozen varieties—are surprisingly good and certainly a hit with young Chilean families who converge here on weekends. The broad menu features sandwiches, salads, and vegetarian dishes as well as a very reasonable fixed-priced lunch. There is a good selection of Chilean wines and domestic and imported beers, as well as a pleasant terrace from which to watch Arica life unfold.

21 de Mayo 174. ✆ **9/256881.** Pizza $6–$8 (£4–£5.30). MC, V. Daily 9am–11:30pm.

Tortas y Tartas ★ CAFE There is no cafe society to speak of in Arica but this artful gem of a coffee shop is the perfect antidote to the omnipresent, fluorescent lit, no frills, snack joints that proliferate in town. With chic decor and a lively outdoor terrace providing great people-watching potential, Tortas y Tartas is an ideal place for a relaxing lunch or civilized afternoon tea. If you are in town for more than a couple of days, this is likely to become your daily fixture. The creative and appetizing menu of sandwiches, healthy salads, quiches, and empanadas is all freshly prepared and delicious, while the decadent display of scrumptious cakes and pastries is guaranteed to cause midriff havoc. If you are suffering withdrawal for a rich espresso or a frothy cappuccino, this is your place. Beer, wine, and cocktails are also served.

21 de Mayo 233. ✆ **9/258538.** Snacks $2–$4 (£1.30–£2.70). No credit cards. Daily 8:30am–10pm.

4 CHILE'S ALTIPLANO

Putre: 149km (61 miles) E of Arica; 2,202km (1,370 miles) N of Santiago

Rte. 11 will take you to the Andean highlands, first along the verdant Lluta Valley dotted by geoglyphs on its lower hills, later crossing a stretch of desert featuring pre-Columbian ruins 100km (62 miles) from Arica, including the *pukará* of **Copaquilla** and the *tambo* of **Zapahuira,** both visible from the highway. The Aymara influence is strongest here; this stretch of arid mountains is quite different from San Pedro and other places in the Atacama. Vast, centuries-old terracing surrounds tiny villages, and you can really feel that this area formed part of Peru until relatively recently. Higher up still, marvel at the spectacular landscape and unique flora and fauna along with one of the world's highest lakes and forests.

Note: Before heading off, make sure you have enough cash, as there are no ATMs beyond Arica.

PUTRE

Splendidly backed by the double summits of the 5,775m (19,000-ft.) Taapacá Volcano, this tranquil village of 1,200 people is the only real place to spend the first night upon arrival from the coast. Unfortunately, that first night likely won't be the most pleasant experience considering the jump in altitude: Putre is a vertiginous 3,500m (11,400 ft.) above sea level. Hikes in the vicinity of Putre are a good option to acclimatize, with ancient **cave paintings** at Incani and Wilaqawrani (unfortunately, partially vandalized). Later, you can head to the rustic **Jurasi hot springs** to relax; they charge $1 (70p), and tour agencies can offer transportation.

A picturesque mountain village, Putre was founded in 1580 and was once a center of Spanish settlement due to its healthier climate than that of then malaria-stricken Arica. Today the town has a charming central square and fine 17th- to 19th-century stone portals flanking many house doors. Some streets have central water runoffs reminiscent of pre-colonial Inca villages. The meek **San Ildefonso church** was restored in the late 19th century after suffering damage in an 1868 earthquake. The locals will tell you that the original church was a much more ostentatious affair, embellished with gold and silver.

High-Altitude Health Warning

What's true for San Pedro is even truer in Putre and beyond: The altitude here will slow you down, and it's tougher to deal with because at 3,500m (11,500 ft.), Putre is a quarter of a mile higher up from San Pedro. It's even higher than Cuzco in Peru, and Lake Chungará is one of the world's highest bodies of water and much higher still at 4,500m (14,760 ft.). Take it easy; even the young and the fit have fallen gravely ill after overexerting themselves. Consult your doctor before heading here if you have a heart or lung condition, and book only tours that carry emergency oxygen equipment. (Putre only has a small clinic.) Headaches and nausea are common occurrences at first; drink plenty of water and have some coca tea to help you adjust. Yes, it's perfectly legal; and no, you won't become a drug addict.

Census data show the Putre area lost a whopping third of its inhabitants between 1992 and 2002, many heading down to Arica, while the population of the villages farther to the north around Visviri has remained stable. Municipal and government offices are on the square, while most services are on Baquedano.

Essentials

Getting There

BY CAR From Arica, head north for 9km (6 miles), then east on Rte. 11, the sole option. The road is good until about 35km (22 miles) from the Bolivian border, at which point it suffers major and frequent potholes. With care, the secondary roads can be managed by normal cars, but check ahead for conditions. Trips south from the Surire Salt Flat need major preparation. Fuel up in Arica and invest in some gas canisters if you're planning a multiday outing, as the only place to get fuel in the altiplano is the hardware store in Putre, and it charges 30% more than the going price in Arica. For rental locations, see the "Arica" section, earlier.

BY BUS **La Paloma** (✆ **58/222710**) makes the daily trip from Arica to Putre, departing at 7am from Germán Riesco 2071 and returning from Putre at 2pm. From the international bus terminal, **Transportes Gutierrez** (✆ **58/229338**) departs Wednesdays and Fridays at 6:30am and Sundays at 7:30pm, returning to Arica Mondays, Wednesdays, and Fridays at 6pm. The fare is $3.50 (£2.30).

Visitor Information

In Putre, the municipality operates a **visitor center** on the main plaza, officially open Monday through Friday from 8:30am to noon and 3 to 6pm (✆ **58/252803**). You can also get information from the **tour agencies** on Baquedano, which are more likely to be staffed.

Fast Facts Putre

Currency Exchange There is a Banco Estado branch on the square that will exchange dollars, but it has no ATM.

Hospital Putre's clinic is near the village entrance at Baquedano 261 (✆ **58/200261**).

Internet Access A handful of spots offer Internet access, including the **public library** on Carrera and **Quipon@t** on the square. The best is the phone and Internet center at Baquedano 501. **Hotel Las Vicuñas** (see later) has Wi-Fi.

Post Office Located on Carrera just off the plaza's south side, the post office is open Monday through Friday from 9am to 1pm and Saturday from 10am to 2pm.

What to See & Do

For tours of the Putre area, there are several operators on Baquedano—including **Ankas Adventure,** at no. 439 (✆ **98/963-9599;** ankasadventure@hotmail.com); **Mayuru Tour,** at no. 411 (✆ **98/999-0173** and 98/963-9599; www.mayurutour.com); and **Tourandino,** at no. 340 (✆ **9/011-0702;** www.tourandino.com)—that offer tours of the surrounding areas and farther afield, including to the Lauca and Volcán Isluga national parks, to the colonial and Aymara villages of the area, and two day tours to the Salar de Surire. Tourandino also offers climbs to the area's high summits. Another experienced outfit, **Alto Andino** (✆ **9/282-6195;** www.birdingaltoandino.com), run by U.S. naturalist Barbara Knapton, focuses on wildlife, with programs in the altiplano and also along the coast. She also offers accommodations for tour participants.

Where to Stay

While a growing number of tour operators are touting Putre as "the next San Pedro," it's still so remote that there is a paucity of quality facilities for tourists. Even the more squalid accommodations offerings are often booked solid. I therefore recommend you book a room ahead of your arrival regardless of the category of hotel you seek.

Expensive

Hotel Las Vicuñas ★ Putre's best hotel option isn't exactly stylish but it's well managed, comfortable, and the staff are very helpful. Born out of a former mining camp, this large complex almost forms a mauve village of its own near the entrance to Putre proper, which is about a 5-minute walk away. The grounds lie at the foot of ancient terraces, with the Taapacá volcano looming as a backdrop. The wood-paneled main building and the 23 bungalows are pleasant and comfortable, and the staff is experienced and very friendly. The en-suite bungalow rooms are painted white, with solid beds and heating, but they're a bit small.

Baquedano s/n, Putre. ✆ **58/228564** or 9/999-5765. 100 units. $80 (£53) double; $120 (£80) triple. Rates include half-board. No credit cards. **Amenities:** Restaurant; bar; Internet access; Wi-Fi.

Moderate

Hotel Kukuli Just off Baquedano, Kukuli is a decent, clean place to stay. The rooms in the recently added north wing have a fresher feel while rooms facing the courtyard (a section of which is used as the parking lot) have little individual terraces. These make for nice spots to have your good-size breakfast (coca leaves for tea included), and gaze up toward the Taapacá summits. Rooms are a respectable size and airy, with high ceilings and comfortable beds. The hotel is on the noisy side, however, so if you're a light sleeper, I recommend earplugs.

Baquedano 301, Putre. ✆ **9/161-4709.** www.hotelkukuli.com/hotel.php. 16 units. $28 double (£19). No credit cards. **Amenities:** Bar. *In room:* No phone.

Inexpensive

Hostal Pachamama ★ (Finds) Among the very few hostels in Putre, this is the top choice. Owned by UKG, the company that also owns the Hotel Las Vicuñas, it's what a South American hostel should be: a charming colonial-style house, with rustic, three- to four-bedrooms grouped around a pretty, shady courtyard decked out in wicker chairs. The clean bathrooms are shared. The sole issue I have with it is that it's best to go for the rooms away from the entrance because, unfortunately, an obstinate neighbor often ties his horses just across the street, and you might get a whiff of them. UKG also has a large *cabaña* almost next door, suitable for up to eight people.

Lord Cochrane s/n, Putre. ✆ **58/228564** or 9/999-5765. 6 units. $10 (£6.70) per person. No credit cards. **Amenities:** Cafeteria; kitchen. *In room:* No phone.

Where to Dine

If you're here only for a brief stay, the altitude will likely stunt your appetite, which is perhaps as well since high altitude doesn't mean haute cuisine. The food is basic but authentically Andean. There are a handful of rustic restaurants in town; the godsend is **K'uchu Marka** on Baquedano, which caters mostly to tourists and has a cozy, rustic atmosphere. It has set meals for $7 (£4.70) featuring typical ingredients such as alpaca meat and quinoa, rabbit stew, and a couple of standout vegetarian dishes. It also offers sandwiches at $2 to $5 (£1.30–£3.30). **Rosamel** on the square is a bit cheaper with set meals for $3.60 (£2.40), but the food, including hearty stews and local meats, is generally bland and uninspired.

AYMARA & COLONIAL VILLAGES

Even little Putre dwarfs the tiny villages of the area, but these, too, deserve a visit. They are also very much off the beaten track. In fact, much of this area is still begging for proper archaeological study; pre-Columbian terracing abounds.

Socoroma, 27km (17 miles) south of Putre and also just north of Rte. 11, is a tiny Aymara village clinging to a promontory at 3,060m (10,040 ft.). Its adobe **San Francisco** church was built in 1560 and reconstructed in 1873, but it suffered some damage in the mid-2005 earthquake. It has a spectacular view of the mountains, overlooking ancient terraces which are now used for growing oregano, infusing the entire town with its heady aroma. At the desert rest stop of Zapahuira, take the dirt road toward Belén. Past the small power plant and village at Chapiquiña, note the frequent small trees with violet-colored trunks. They're *queñua,* an endangered, slow-growing species and possibly the tree that grows at the highest altitude anywhere.

Continuing on, make the detour down to the village of **Pachama,** 68km (42 miles) from Putre, greener than most of the others. The short road is in bad shape and the village almost abandoned, but its chalk-white late-17th-century church, **San Andrés ★★**, is a real gem of colonial architecture and painting. In typical Atacama style, the bell tower is separated from the church proper, surrounded by a wall with two arched entrances. If locked, make the effort to look for the person keeping the key—the very helpful locals will usually be able to point you in the right direction. The images of St. Andrew, the Virgin, and St. Peter above the door are unique—no other colonial church in the Atacama has exterior paintings. At the same time, they're just a hint of the fine polychrome 18th-century frescoes and painted altar you'll find inside. If you do venture inside, be sure to leave a tip.

A balmy climate and proximity to the route to Potosí led to the 1620 establishment of **Belén,** 77km (48 miles) from Putre and the only altiplano town founded by the Spanish, within proximity to an indigenous settlement. The smaller, older of the two churches here is on the higher ground of the main plaza; the more attractive is the 18th-century **Señora del Carmen ★**, most notable for the sculpted stone portal, featuring salomonic columns in an otherwise adobe structure. The interior holds polychrome baroque sculptures.

Within walking distance, besides the obvious and ubiquitous terraces, are two *pukarás,* Ancopachane near the cemetery and the adjacent Chajpa and Huaihuarani, the latter closest to a 5km (3-mile) stretch of the famous Inca road or *Camino del Inca.*

An attractive option for the return to Arica is to continue past Belén through Tignamar and Codpa, with plenty of petroglyphs, *pukarás,* and colonial churches along the way. The detour to Guañacagua is worthwhile for its baroque church, though it suffered some damage in the 2005 quake. This excursion can also be done as a day trip from Arica, if you have transportation of your own, though some tour agencies also offer the trip.

Aymara Indians

With a rich and complex history, the Aymara Indians are the second largest indigenous linguistic group in South America. They are believed to be the descendents of the ancient Tiahuanacan, the first great Andean empire that emerged in the Bolivian highlands around 600 B.C. and was centered around the southeastern side of Lake Titicaca.

Of the 2 million Aymara that remain, most communities or *ayllus* (traditional Aymara communes based on extended families living in single room, in gabled houses constructed of turf and thatched roofs) live in the altiplano regions of Peru, Bolivia, and Chile. Chile has the smallest number of Aymara people, around 45,000. Due to economic hardship and a propensity toward greater assimilation into typical Chilean life, many Aymara people have migrated from the altiplano to the coastal cities of Arica and Iquique and many small villages are now used only for ceremonial purposes.

Those who continue to carve out a subsistence existence from the desolate altiplano utilize 2,000-year-old traditions and techniques based on animal husbandry—the herding of sheep and llama—and agriculture, namely the cultivation of quinoa, potatoes, and barley. Rather contentiously, the Aymara have cultivated coca plants for centuries, using its leaves in traditional medicines, a fact which has brought the Aymara into conflict with the government, especially in Peru and Bolivia, since coca contains cocaine alkaloids, the basis for cocaine.

Social organization varies from community to community and leadership, based on a complex system of social prestige, is achieved through community service, sponsorship of fiestas, and extending ties beyond each *ayllu.* Patriarchal kinship is based on extended families and premised upon economic cooperation. Daughters tend to marry and move in with their husbands, while sons seek to establish a separate household within the same community as their fathers.

The Aymara have a profound respect for their ancient traditions, ancestors, and religion, and their ritualistic culture reveals a passionate adherence to their belief in a multispiritual world in which shamans, diviners, and magicians are a part. Festivals and rituals, which usually occur during harvest and to mark seminal life events such as baptism, marriage, and death, are ebullient community events involving frenzied dancing, singing, eating, drinking, and animal sacrifice. Each fiesta presents a compelling fusion of catholic and supernatural indigenous religious rituals. At the apex of the Aymara's mystical devotion is the goddess Mother Earth, known as Pachamama.

The Aymara dress is adapted to the harsh conditions of the high altitude altiplano. Men wear a *chullu* (a wool hat with ear-flaps) and striped ponchos over shirt and pants. Women wear bowler hats, ruffled blouses, brilliantly colored full skirts, sturdy boots, and an *aguayo* (a wool sling for carrying their baby on their backs).

LAUCA NATIONAL PARK ★★★

Stretching from Socoroma, Putre, and Belén eastward to the Bolivian border, Lauca National Park is one of the region's unquestionable highlights. The park comprises some of the most spectacular landscapes in the entire Andes, including the world's highest non-navigable lake, the stunning, emerald green Lago Chungará (at 4,500m/14,760 ft.), six peaks above 6,000m (19,700 ft.), volcanic calderas, and the famous altiplano village of **Parinacota.** Much of the 137,883-hectare (340,716-acre) park is accessible via the international highway and the secondary roads, though they're below the generally good standard of Chile's roads, affected as they are by heavy trucks and rain or snow in January and February during the "Bolivian Winter"—not a good time to visit. Wildlife is abundant and easy to see, from the cuddly viscachas to the lithe vicuñas—not to be confused with the larger, gray-faced guanacos you may see at lower altitudes—and over 130 species of birds, including the three species of flamingos that exist in Chile (the Andean, Chilean, and James's), along with rare hummingbirds.

Stop at **Las Cuevas,** which has a Conaf station (theoretically open daily 9am–12:30pm and 1–5:30pm), and take the path down toward the little hut that holds a rustic pool fed by a hot spring. On the way, you'll pass through a warren of mountain viscachas, long-tailed rodents with more than a passing resemblance to hares. They're easy to observe, and their slanted eyes and penchant to sit back on their haunches give them a positively relaxed expression.

A little farther along Rte. 11—past a ridiculous red, blue, and yellow pan-flute sculpture—you'll begin to approach the dramatic white cones of the 6,342m (20,807-ft.) Parinacota Volcano and the 6,282m (20,610-ft.) Pomerape. I recommend you head to the picturesque whitewashed village of **Parinacota** next, as the 17th-century church is more likely to be open in the morning; otherwise ask around for the caretaker at the crafts stalls in the little square. Most of the residents are evangelicals nowadays, hence Mass is rarely held. Much like the church at Pachama, but with more somber motifs of hell and the crucifixion, the interior boasts splendid frescoes, along with religious paintings reminiscent of the Cuzco school. There is also a macabre selection of priests' skulls and a table that—in deference to the town's supernatural proclivities—has been chained down to keep it from moving around town on its own accord. The exterior is walled in, with the square tower on one corner, and simple red sculptures (some bearing faces) on top of the walls. At 4,400m (14,430 ft.) and 36km (22 miles) from Putre, the village also holds the Conaf's administrative center of the park, which can provide maps and information, and there's a small campground and a 3km (2-mile) trail head behind this administrative center.

A poor road heads north toward other villages outside the park, notably Visviri at the northern tip of Chile. An **obelisk** north of the village marks the spot where Chile, Bolivia, and Peru meet in the high-altitude desert. On Sundays, an Aymara market drawing participants from the three countries takes place there.

The **Cotacotani lagoons** east of Parinacota form a mesmerizing, surreal landscape of dark lava and cinder cones piercing the green waters. A lookout point offers a good view from the highway, though it's spoiled a bit by power lines and litter. If you have time and have acclimatized, there's an easy but long 8km (5-mile) trail around them.

The view of **Lake Chungará,** finally, is the park's highlight. At daybreak, the summits are ablaze with orange, and when the wind is still, they reflect perfectly in its waters. Across the butterfly-shaped lake, you can see the 6,542m (21,460-ft.) Sajama, Bolivia's highest peak, among other mountains that almost encircle the lake. Some 150 species of birds inhabit the park, with many waterfowl species flocking to the lake, including native geese and duck species, giant coots, and of course flamingos. You will very likely also spot small herds of vicuñas that you can see from a short distance away, despite the proximity of the highway. A Conaf station near the lake is similar (unstaffed) to the one at Las Cuevas and has a small refuge and the most basic of restrooms (not recommended), along with a campsite. A short trail from the station's parking lot leads down to the lakeshore. A little farther on is the Chilean border station (note the visa reference in "Fast Facts: Arica," p. 228).

VICUÑA NATURE PRESERVE, SURIRE NATIONAL MONUMENT & VOLCAN ISLUGA NATIONAL PARK ★★

Because it's less accessible than Lauca National Park and has no public transport, your only option for exploring this remote area is to hire a 4WD or take an organized tour from Putre. However, this otherworldly altiplano landscape, dotted with the remains of ancient Aymara villages where graceful vicuñas roam beneath majestic snow-capped volcanoes, is nothing short of spectacular. This park has the largest concentration of the country's vicuña, some 20,000. In the 1980s, some were caught and exported to Ecuador to help reestablish a breeding population there. Vicuñas and guanacos—the wild form of the llama—almost never share a habitat, with the smaller, paler vicuña living at higher altitudes, because their unique wool provides protection against the nightly subzero temperatures. Near Las Cuevas, a minor road—A-235—turns south off Rte. 11. Marked with a sign for Guallatiri, the road is manageable without too much difficulty south until Surire, though the trucks that run to the borax mine near there can be an annoyance en route. Poaching remains an issue, but the preserve boasts one of Chile's few environmental success stories: the recovery of the vicuña population hunted to the brink of extinction for their wool, the world's finest.

At 83km (52 miles) from Putre, the pre-Hispanic village of **Guallatiri,** overshadowed by the active volcano of the same name, consists of some 50 houses and a white 17th-century Atacama church. The preserve also protects *queñua* along with the *llareta,* a very slow-growing shrub with leaves growing so tightly that, amazingly, it looks more like a rounded, moss-covered rock. Now rare and officially protected, it was previously burned for fuel in mining operations.

The far smaller **Surire National Monument** almost surrounds the salt lake of the same name, with beautiful views and relatively common rheas, ostrichlike birds called *suri* by the Aymara. It also has undeveloped hot springs at Polloquere. The borax plant at one side of the lake, however, is suspected of being responsible for a decline in flamingo hatchings; the company says it carries out periodic measurements with Conaf to make sure this isn't happening.

As an alternative to the road, consider heading back toward Putre via Itisa and Belén, which is also a long, bumpy ride of about 120km (75 miles).

Even worse and lonelier is the road that continues to the 174,744-hectare (431,600-acre) **Volcan Isluga National Park.** I don't recommend traveling this route alone; this is a trip best done on a multiday tour. One can travel there roundabout heading south from Arica, but the nearest village with services, the border post of **Colchane,** sports only the most basic accommodations. Many of the villages marked on maps are virtually abandoned, with the houses locked and the original inhabitants returning only for religious festivities. This is the case at **Isluga,** 205km (127 miles) from Putre, a tiny, picture-perfect village similar to Parinacota, boasting a 17th-century Atacama church. The Conaf ranger station is at Enquelga, 10km (6 miles) inside the park; there are hot springs nearby at Aguas Calientes. From Colchane, Arica is 401km (249 miles) via the paved road, but you can also travel to the seaside city of **Iquique,** 220km (137 miles) away.

10

The Chilean Lake District

South of the Bío-Bío River, Chile is transformed. The climate cools and becomes much more humid; dairy farms replace the vineyards; and lagoons, lakes, and emerald forests of ancient trees appear. The Andes lose altitude but more than make up for it in beauty, sprouting magnificent white-capped volcanoes. This is one of the most popular destinations in Chile, not only for its beauty, but also for the cultural and outdoor activities available, and its well-developed tourism infrastructure.

Only relatively recently did Chile manage to fully integrate the Lake District into the country. For some 350 years, the Mapuche Indians fiercely and successfully defended this land first against the Incas and later against the Spanish. Their influence spread into what is now Argentina, and only in the mid-1880s did Chile manage to subdue them. German-speaking settlers meanwhile had begun to clear land and fell timber for their characteristic shingled homes. Both ethnic groups have left their mark on the region through architecture, art, and food. In fact, German pastries have become so prevalent the German word for cake, *küchen,* has largely replaced the Spanish word *pastel* in Chilean usage.

Its natural wonders continue to provide the basis for the region's economy, harboring tourism, farming, salmon production, and forestry—a mix tough to manage, to the detriment of its once nearly impenetrable forests. But the many national parks and preserves give visitors a chance to immerse themselves in virgin forest unique for its stands of umbrella-shaped araucaria and 1,000-year-old alerce trees (see "The Alerce & the Araucaria: Living National Monuments," on p. 251).

EXPLORING THE REGION

The Lake District stretches 350km (215 miles) south from the Bío-Bío to the Reloncavi Sound, where Chile's Central Valley sinks into the Pacific. The northern third around **Temuco** forms the Mapuche heartland; farther south, lakes, forests, and volcanoes combine into a fairy-tale landscape almost too perfect to be true. Resorts—above all **Pucón** and **Puerto Varas**—draw thousands of tourists in the summer months of January and February, but it also has its charms in autumn when the leaves turn red, and in winter, you can soothe your limbs after a day of skiing with a soak in the area's numerous hot springs. The region's charm lies in its picturesque villages, boat rides, adventure sports, beaches, and kilometer after kilometer of bumpy dirt roads that make for lovely drives. An excellent alternative to the toll highway is the **Ruta Interlagos,** a dirt road that interconnects the numerous protected areas and lakes from near **Victoria** down to Puerto Varas. Another great draw here is the proximity to the **Argentine Lake District,** where you'll find the gorgeously located towns of Bariloche and San Martín de los Andes. If you're planning on visiting both countries, it makes sense to cross the border in the Lake District, where Chile and Argentina are separated by a 1- to 2-day boat ride or several hours by road, year-round.

1 TEMUCO

677km (420 miles) S of Santiago; 112km (69 miles) NW of Pucón

Few cities in southern Chile are old, and Temuco isn't among them. Founded in 1881 as a military outpost in the very heart of Mapuche territory, its creation sealed the Mapuches' fate and set the foundations for modern-day development—which, so far, hasn't been pretty. Temuco is near a handful of beautiful national parks such as **Conguillío** and **Villarrica,** and is the gateway to the wildly popular **Pucón.** But unless you've got an early flight or you are driving a long distance down the Pan-American Highway and need a rest, I do not recommend an overnight stay here; there are plenty of excellent options around Conguillío National Park and even more in the Pucón area. You'll need to fly here and transfer to Pucón during the winter; there is direct service to Pucón during the summer.

Temuco grew like a boomtown as Spanish, German, French, Swiss, and English immigrants poured into the region within the first few years of its foundation. Only traces of their architectural influence remain as rampant development has converted Temuco into yet another hodgepodge Chilean city. It's still one of the country's fastest-growing cities, as evidenced by the thundering buses, bustling downtown crowds, and increasingly poor air quality that threaten to absorb whatever charm remains. Most Mapuche today live in reservations *(reducciones),* west of the city in rural areas approaching the coast, but Temuco, along with the suburb of Padre Las Casas, is the best place to approach the proud culture of Chile's main native people.

ESSENTIALS

Getting There

BY PLANE **LANExpress** (✆ **600/526-2000** toll free, or 45/740375; www.lan.com) serves Temuco with an average of four daily flights from Santiago and one daily flight to Puerto Montt. **Sky Airline** (✆ **600/600-2828** toll free, or 45/747300; www.skyairline.cl) serves Temuco with two daily flights from Santiago and two weekly flights to and from Puerto Montt.

The **Maquehue Airport** (ZCO; ✆ **45/554801**) is about 8km (5 miles) from the city center. To get to Temuco, take a cab—about $10 (£6.70)—or arrange transportation with **Transfer & Turismo de la Araucanía** (✆ **45/339900**), a minivan service at the airport that charges $6 (£4) for door-to-door service. This transfer service has service to Pucón for $14 (£9.30) per person, but it might cost more if they are unable to arrange a group.

BY BUS To get to Temuco from Santiago by bus, **Tur Bus** (✆ **600/660-6600;** www.turbus.com) leaves from the Terminal Alameda at Av. Bernardo O'Higgins 3786; or **Cruz del Sur** (✆ **2/779-0607**) leaves from the Terminal Santiago at Av. Bernardo O'Higgins 3848. The trip takes 8 to 9 hours; a one-way economy ticket costs about $36 (£24), executive class $54 (£36). Most buses arrive at Temuco's **Terminal Rodoviario** at Vicente Pérez Rosales 01609 (✆ **45/225005**). From here, you can take a taxi to your hotel.

BY TRAIN **EFE** (✆ **2/585-5000** in Santiago, or 45/233416 in Temuco; www.efe.cl) offers one of the few train services in Chile, with salon and sleeper coaches. Unfortunately, a recent ambitious expansion plan has gone very wrong, making train service terribly unreliable, and Santiago-Temuco service has once again been interrupted. Instead, Lake District trains now run from Victoria (north of Temuco) down to Puerto

Montt; the daily trip costs $12 (£8) for a very long 8-hour ride. A connecting train does leave from Temuco three times a day (9:30am, and 4:10 and 8:30pm) to Victoria and vice versa; however, the time wasted during the transfer makes the bus much more attractive. It's safe to say that few take this route now and the Temuco station is languishing because of it. With things likely to continue in flux, check the website as you near your trip for updates (in Spanish only).

BY CAR The Pan-American Highway (Rte. 5) takes motorists to Temuco. Tolls cost $24 (£16) Santiago-Temuco; fuel prices tend to be about average along the highway. If you're heading to the national parks east of Temuco, fill up in town or on the highway as fuel prices in the villages are much higher.

Getting Around

Getting around Temuco is easy by foot. To get to outlying areas such as national parks, it's best to rent a car or go with a tour. To get to Pucón (see "Villarrica & Pucón," later in this chapter), try **Buses JAC,** corner of Balmaceda and Aldunate (✆ **45/231340**), which operates from its own terminal, leaving every half-hour on weekdays and every hour on weekends and holidays.

If you want to rent a car to see the outlying sights, Hertz, Avis, Budget, and Econorent all have kiosks at the airport. Outside of summer, it is possible for walk-ins to get a car easily. During the summer, it is important to reserve in advance. In downtown Temuco, **Hertz** can be found at Andrés Bello 792 (✆ **45/318585**), **Avis** at San Martín 755 (✆ **600/368-2000** toll free, or 45/237575), **Budget** at Vicuña Mackenna 399 (✆ **45/232715**), and **Econorent Car Rental** at Patricio Lynch 471 (✆ **45/214911;** fax 45/214911).

Visitor Information

Sernatur operates a well-stocked tourism office at the corner of Claro Solar and Bulnes streets at Plaza Aníbal Pinto (✆ **45/211969**). Hours from December to February are Monday through Saturday from 8:30am to 8:30pm, Sunday 10am to 2pm. The rest of the year, the office is open Monday through Friday from 9am to 2pm and 3 to 5pm.

Fast Facts Temuco

Currency Exchange There are *casas de cambio* and banks with 24-hour ATMs along Calle Bulnes at the main plaza. Try **Intercam,** Casa de Cambios, Claro Solar 780, Local 5; **Global,** Bulnes 655, Local 1; or **Comex,** Prat 427.

Hospital Temuco's highest-quality hospital is the **Clínica Alemana,** Senador Estébanez 645 (✆ **45/244244**).

Internet Try the Internet cafe **Kafé.com,** Bulnes 314, Local 8 (Mon–Sat 9am–10pm; Sun 10am–8pm); or the **Entel** office, Prat 505 (Mon–Fri 10am–8pm; Sat 10am–2pm).

Laundry **Marva** Laundromat has two locations: 415 and 1099 Manuel Montt (✆ **45/952200**).

Travel Agency Try **Agencia de Viajes y Cambios Christopher,** Bulnes 667 (✆ **45/211680**).

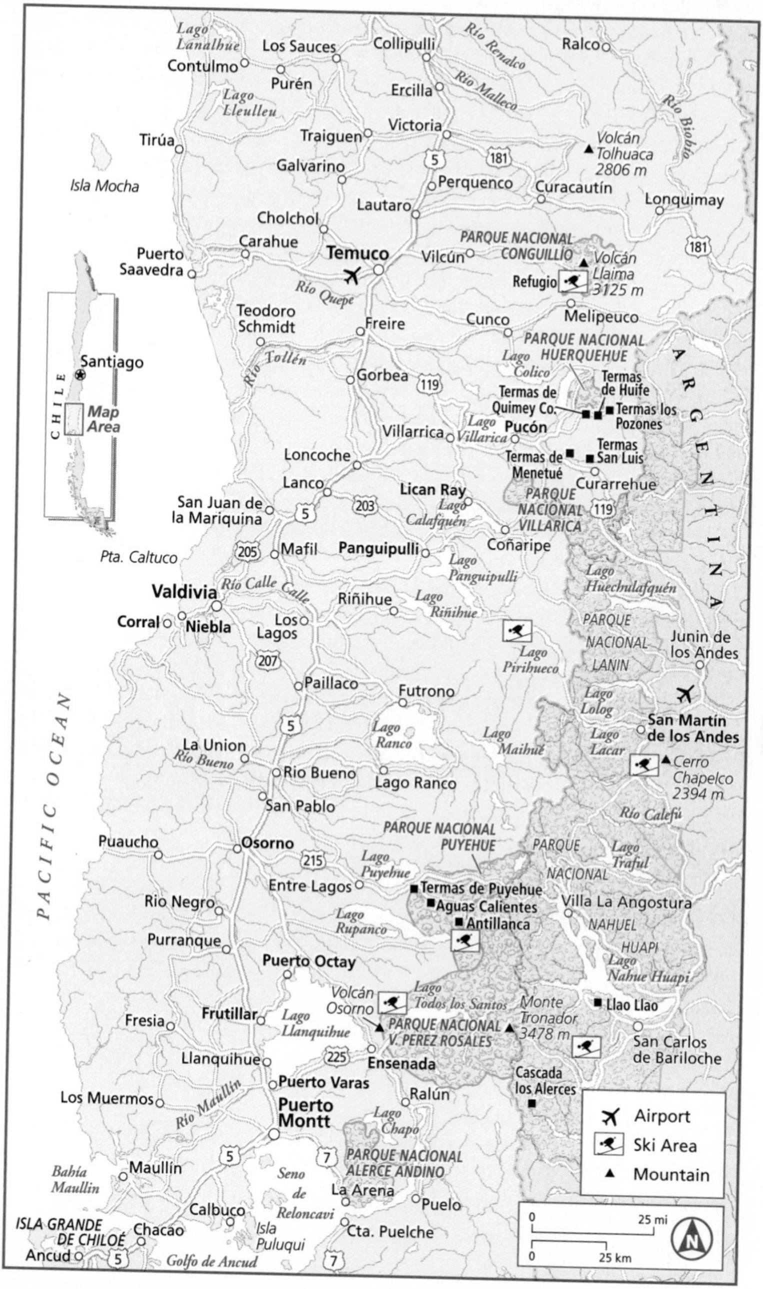
Lago Lanalhue
Los Sauces
Collipulli
Río Renalco
Ralco
Contulmo
Purén
Río Malleco
Ercilla
Río Biobío
Lago Lleulleu
Victoria
Traiguen
Tirúa
Volcán Tolhuaca 2806 m
5
181
Galvarino
Isla Mocha
Perquenco
Curacautín
Longuimay
Lautaro
Cholchol
PARQUE NACIONAL CONGUILLIO
181
Puerto Saavedra
Carahue
Temuco
Vilcún
Volcán Llaima 3125 m
Refugio
Río Quepe
Teodoro Schmidt
Freire
Cunco
Melipeuco
PARQUE NACIONAL HUERQUEHUE
Río Toltén
Lago Colico
Santiago
CHILE
Map Area
Gorbea
119
Termas de Huife
Termas de Quimey Co.
Termas los Pozones
ARGENTINA
Villarrica
Lago Villarica
Pucón
Termas de Menetué
Termas San Luis
Loncoche
Curarrehue
Lanco
Lican Ray
Lago Calafquén
PARQUE NACIONAL VILLARICA
119
San Juan de la Mariquina
5
203
Pta. Caltuco
205
Mafil
Panguipulli
Coñaripe
Lago Panguipulli
Lago Huechulafquén
Valdivia
Río Calle Calle
Riñihue
Lago Riñihue
Corral
Niebla
Los Lagos
PARQUE NACIONAL LANIN
Junin de los Andes
207
Lago Pirihueco
Paillaco
Futrono
PACIFIC OCEAN
Lago Lolog
5
Lago Ranco
Lago Maihue
Lago Lacar
San Martín de los Andes
La Union
Río Bueno
Rio Bueno
Lago Ranco
Cerro Chapelco 2394 m
San Pablo
Río Calefú
PARQUE NACIONAL PUYEHUE
Puaucho
Osorno
215
Lago Puyehue
PARQUE NACIONAL
Lago Traful
Entre Lagos
Termas de Puyehue
Aguas Calientes
Villa La Angostura
Rio Negro
Antillanca
NAHUEL HUAPI
Lago Rupanco
Purranque
Lago Nahue Huapi
Puerto Octay
Volcán Osorno
Lago Todos los Santos
Monte Tronador 3478 m
Llao Llao
Fresia
Frutillar
Lago Llanquihue
PARQUE NACIONAL V. PEREZ ROSALES
San Carlos de Bariloche
Llanquihue
225
Ensenada
Cascada los Alerces
Puerto Varas
Los Muermos
Río Maullín
Ralún
Puerto Montt
Lago Chapo
Airport
Ski Area
Mountain
5
7
PARQUE NACIONAL ALERCE ANDINO
Bahía Maullin
Maullín
Seno de Reloncavi
La Arena
Puelo
Calbuco
ISLA GRANDE DE CHILOÉ
Chacao
Isla Puluqui
Cta. Puelche
0
25 mi
0
25 km
N
Ancud
5
Golfo de Ancud
7

Within the manicured grounds of **Plaza Aníbal Pinto** in the city center, you'll find the sizable La Araucanía monument depicting the clash between the Mapuche and the Spanish. There's also a gallery here with temporary exhibits.

Walk up Calle Bulnes to Portales to enter one of Chile's best markets, the **Mercado Municipal ★★**, open Monday through Saturday from 8am to 6pm (8pm in summer), Sunday and holidays from 8am to 3pm; April through September, the market closes at 5pm. Rows of stalls sell high-quality woven ponchos, knitwear, textiles, woodwork, hats, *mate* gourds, and assorted arts and crafts, but what's really special here is the abundance of silver Mapuche jewelry. Around the perimeter, fishermen and food stalls aggressively vie for business, while butchers in white aprons hawk their meats from behind dangling sausages and fluorescent-lit display cases. Another market, the **Feria Libre,** at Aníbal Pinto, offers a colorful chaos of fruit and vegetable stands as well; the highlight here is the traditional Mapuche Indian vendors who come in from *reducciones* to sell their goods. The market is open Monday through Sunday from 8:30am to 6pm; from March to December, it closes at 5pm. ***Note:*** Watch out for pickpockets.

For a sweeping view of Temuco, take a taxi or hike up the heavily forested **Cerro Ńielol,** which also features four trails and a restaurant near the summit. It's open daily from 8am to 10pm; admission is $2 (£1.30) adults, $1 (70p) children (✆ **45/298222**). At the site marked LA PATAGUA, you'll find a plaque commemorating the agreement signed in 1881 between the Mapuche and the Chilean Army for peaceful settlement of Temuco.

Temuco also has a **Museo Regional de La Araucanía,** Alemania 084 (✆ **45/730062**), open Monday through Friday from 10am to 5:30pm, Saturday from 11am to 5pm, and Sunday from 11am to 2pm. The museum features exhibits charting Indian migration and history, along with displays of Mapuche jewelry and weapons; the Mapuche learned silver working from the Spanish, developing it into one of their most important forms of artistic expression. It also houses exhibits on immigration. Admission costs $1.50 (£1).

Railway buffs will like the **Museo Nacional Ferroviario Pablo Neruda,** Barros Arana 565 (✆ **45/227613;** www.temucochile.com), showcasing locomotives from 1908 to 1962 and the 1923 Presidential Coach, along with a working antique train sometimes used in short trips. It's open Tuesday through Sunday from 9am to 6:30pm; admission is $2 (£1.30).

WHERE TO STAY

Holiday Inn Express (Kids) Predictable in the way a Holiday Inn always is, this hotel is best used as an overnighter for those on their way out of Temuco. With clean rooms, comfortable beds, cable TV, and a location a half-block from an American-style shopping mall with the usual fast-food joints, you might feel like you're in the U.S. The principal drawback of this hotel is its distance from downtown; however, it is close to the highway. Kids under 18 can room with their parents for free, making this a good bet for families.

Ortega 1800, Temuco. ✆ **800/36666** or 45/223300. Fax 45/224100. www.holidayinn.cl. 62 units. $114 (£76) double. Children 17 and under stay free in parent's room. AE, DC, MC, V. **Amenities:** Small outdoor pool; exercise room; Jacuzzi; business center. *In room:* A/C, TV, coffeemaker, safe.

Hotel Aitué This family-owned and -operated hotel offers good value for the price, including a business center with an Internet connection and free airport pickup. Double rooms are average size; junior suites are substantially larger. Each well-lit room comes with mahogany furniture and fairly comfortable beds. The staff is knowledgeable and

Guided Tours in Temuco & Beyond

Multi Tour, Bulnes 307, (✆ **45/237913;** www.sur-expediciones.com) offers a wide variety of bilingual excursions, including city tours, day trips to Conguillío National Park, and cultural trips to indigenous communities. These cultural trips include visits to a *ruca,* a typical Mapuche home, and the opportunity to visit with Mapuches.

friendly, and strives to make guests feel at home. The hotel has a popular convention salon downstairs, and it also offers a small bar and lounge, as well as a fireside dining area serving breakfast and snacks.

Antonio Varas 1048, Temuco. ✆ **45/211917.** Fax 45/212608. www.hotelaitue.cl. 35 units. $75 (£50) double; $84 (£56) junior suite. AE, DC, MC, V. **Amenities:** Restaurant; bar; lounge; business center. *In room:* TV, minibar.

Panamericana Hotel Temuco ★★ This hotel, formerly called the Terraverde, is part of the Chilean Panamericana chain and is Temuco's top hotel, with excellent service geared primarily toward business travelers. At the foot of Cerro Ñielol but just 5 blocks from the main square, it's a modern, reddish, seven-story building amid pleasant green scenery, away from downtown's noise. It's not particularly exciting, but very comfortable from the outdoor pool to the very plushy tan carpeting in the rooms. Cream and brown colors—plus floral patterns on bedspreads and curtains—characterize the conservatively styled rooms. The larger, superior suites have views both of the Ñielol and of the Llaima volcano beyond. One floor is nonsmoking only. Wi-Fi is available in some rooms; check ahead of booking. As this is primarily a business hotel, it sometimes offers cheaper summer rates.

Av. Prat 220, Temuco. ✆ **45/239999.** Fax 45/233830. www.panamericanahoteles.cl. 74 units. $145 (£97) double; $215 (£143) suite. Rates include continental breakfast. AE, DC, MC, V. **Amenities:** Restaurant; bar; outdoor pool; sauna; Internet and Wi-Fi; laundry service; nonsmoking rooms. *In room:* TV, Wi-Fi (in some rooms), minibar, safe.

WHERE TO DINE

Head to the **Mercado Municipal,** open Monday through Saturday from 8am to 8pm and Sunday from 8:30am to 3pm, for a quick, inexpensive lunch at one of the market's dozen or so restaurants. To get there, enter at Portales at Bulnes or Aldunate streets. Waiters will harangue you until you're suckered into choosing their establishment, but the best bet is at **La Caleta** (Local 27). For sandwiches and other quick meals, try **Casa D'Empanada's** (no phone), at Mackenna 687.

Café Austral ★ INTERNATIONAL This modern international restaurant/bar does a good job of closing itself off amid the hubbub of downtown foot traffic. Because it's split into two glitzy levels with large windows facing the street, there's ample people-watching while you munch on sandwiches, grilled meats, full breakfasts, and pastries. A lively bar—particularly for after-work drinks when they have two-for-one specials—makes up most of the lower level. The three-course executive lunch menus are the best deal in the house.

Bulnes 880. ✆ **45/234880.** Main courses $8–$20 (£5.30–£13). AE, DC, MC, V. Mon–Fri 9am–11pm and Sat 11am–4pm.

Kokavi ★★ Finds CHILEAN This is probably the only restaurant in Chile featuring the cuisine of its main native people, but it's undeservedly unknown to almost everyone. Its uniqueness makes for an interesting visit, and its rock-bottom prices will lower the threshold for trying something new among those with less of an appetite for risk. Spicier than Chilean food in general, the food is liberal in the use of the deep red chili powder *merkén,* but also has a strong vegetarian slant, such as in the *pisku,* a heavy vegetable stew, or *millokin,* a kind of vegetable "meatball."

Rodríguez 1073. ✆ **45/951625.** Main courses $4 (£2.70). No credit cards. Mon–Sat 9:30am–10pm.

La Pampa ★ STEAK/ARGENTINE High-quality grilled meats, fresh salads, seafood, and an extensive wine list with export-only varieties make La Pampa a good place to dine. It was opened years ago by two Argentine transplants who came for a visit and never left. Try the trout with Roquefort sauce or one of the Argentine specialties such as *matambrito alla pizza,* thin meat rolled with spinach and egg. On weekends, there is an excellent *asado criollo,* thick ribs slowly grilled for 3 hours.

Caupolicán 0155. ✆ **45/329999.** Main courses $8–$18 (£5.30–£12). AE, DC, MC, V. Mon–Sat noon–4pm and 7:30pm–midnight; Sun noon–4pm.

Quick Biss Kids Value CAFE This modern cafeteria, with wooden booths and zebra-striped walls, is very popular with downtown workers for its reasonable priced meals. Diners fill their trays with items such as salads, hot dishes, sandwiches, soups, and desserts, or a simple empanada. Solo diners often sit at a large bar near the entrance where they watch the news or a soccer game while eating. The *autoservicio* (self-service) lunch runs from 12:30 to 4pm, dinner from 6 to 9pm, and there is also a simple menu offered all day.

Antonio Varas 755. ✆ **45/211219.** Main courses $4–$8 (£2.70–£5.30). AE, DC, MC, V. Daily 11am–11pm.

EAST OF TEMUCO

The Río Bío-Bío is born out of Lake Gualletue east of Temuco. Much of the upper river valley is protected in a series of preserves from the Ralco hydroelectric power plant southward, featuring beautiful araucaria forests and plenty of places to stay, including several spas. Three volcanoes—Tolhuaca, Lonquimay, and Llaima—dominate the landscape.

Conguillio National Park ★★★

One of Chile's finest national parks, Parque Nacional Conguillío surrounds the spectacular smoking cone of Volcán Llaima and features a dense forest of spindly araucaria trees, which the park was created to protect. It's a lovely park and a great attraction year-round due to several splendid hiking trails, a ski resort, and an outstanding park information center. Volcán Llaima is one of the most active volcanoes on Earth and has registered 40 eruptions since 1640, most recently in April 2009. In the southern section of the park, it is also possible to witness the tremendous destruction lava has wreaked on the surrounding forest. Conguillío is divided into three separate sectors with as many access points. The western side of the park is commonly known as Los Paraguas (the Umbrellas); the eastern side is accessed from the north in Sector Laguna Captrén, and the south at Sector Truful-Truful. Visitors will find the park's administration center, campgrounds, and most hiking trails here in the eastern sector.

The eastern access point is at the village **Cherquenco;** from here a 21km (13-mile) rutted road ends at the **Centro de Esquí Las Araucarias** (✆ **45/274141;** www.skiaraucarias.cl) in Los Paraguas. Las Araucarias is not well-known, and its four T-bars are

The Alerce & the Araucaria: Living National Monuments

The Lake District and its neighboring forests in Argentina are home to two of the oldest trees on the planet: the alerce and the araucaria, otherwise known as larch and monkey puzzle trees, respectively. The alerce is a sequoialike giant that grows less than 1 millimeter each year and can live for more than 3,000 years, making it the world's second-oldest tree after the California bristlecone pine. They are best viewed in the Alerce Andino National Park and Pumalín Park.

The araucaria, called *pehuén* by the Mapuche, is unmistakable for its gangly branches and thick, thorny leaves that feel waxy to the touch. Mature trees can grow as high as 50m (164 ft.) and take on the appearance of an umbrella, which is why they're often called Los Paraguas (the Umbrellas). They do not reach reproductive maturity until they are about 200 years old, and they can live as long as 1,250 years. They are best seen in Tolhuaca, Villarrica, and Conguillío national parks, but they're virtually everywhere around the Lake District. The araucaria seed *(piñón)*, an edible nut, was a principal source of food for the Mapuche; later the tree was coveted for its quality wood, and, as with the alerce, aggressive harvesting destroyed the majority of its forests. Today both the alerce and the araucaria have been declared protected national monuments.

tiresome, but if you are a ski buff and are in the area, this little resort is worth the visit for its surrounding forest of araucaria and simply breathtaking views. (The road here is in bad shape, so bring a vehicle with chains and high clearance.) The center also has a ski school, equipment rental, and a restaurant and bar. Ticket prices are $30 (£20) Monday through Friday and $34 (£23) on weekends. The center offers dormitory-style lodging in two single-sex rooms with about 10 to 15 bunk beds without bedding for $11 (£7.30) per person (and two dormitories for 10 to 11 people for $17/£11 per person). Other lodging options are the **Apart Hotel Llaima** (five apartments with four beds each; $115/£77 a night), **Refugio Pehuén** (three units; $25–$30/£17–£20 double), and the **Refugio Los Paraguas** (one unit, six beds; $120/£80). Check www.skiaraucarias.cl for reservations.

An unpaved and poorly maintained road connects a Conaf (park service) **visitor center,** which is open daily from 9am to 1pm and 3 to 7pm (✆ **45/298213**), with the towns **Curacautín** in the north and **Melipeuco** in the south. The information center has interpretive displays highlighting the park's flora, fauna, and physical geology, including an interesting section devoted to volcanism. During the summer, park rangers offer informative talks and walks and a host of educational activities, which they post in the visitor center. (English-language talks can sometimes be arranged; send an e-mail to info@parquenacionalconguillio.cl, or check directly at the center.)

There's an easy, hour-long, self-guided trail that leaves from the Conaf center, but if you really want to get out and walk, you'll want to take the **Sierra Nevada trail.** This moderate 5-hour hike is the best in the park, taking visitors through thick forest and rising to two lookout points that offer sensational volcano and lake views before dropping back down to the Captrén Lagoon near the Conaf center. The trail head is on the western shore of Lake Conguillío, at the Conaf center. A second 5-hour hike along moderate terrain, **Los Carpinteros,** weaves its way through stands of araucaria trees that are several hundred—some more than 1,000—years old. This trail leaves from Laguna Captrén at the Conaf center.

GETTING THERE & BASICS If you plan to rent a vehicle, try to get one with a high clearance—it's not essential, but it helps. Most tour companies in Temuco plan excursions to this park. Bus service from Temuco's main terminal is available only to Curacautín and Melipeuco; from here you'll need to take a taxi or hitch a ride. The road is paved only to the park entrance, so during the winter, you'll usually need a 4×4 or tire chains to get to the ski center.

The park is officially open daily April through November from 8am to 11pm, and May through October 8:30am to 5pm—but you can really enter at any time of the day. In winter, the road through its eastern part isn't cleared, but it remains accessible—definitely take winter gear. The summer park entrance fee is $6 (£4) for adults and $2 (£1.30) for children (free for those under 12 years). There are a cafeteria and a store at Conaf's park information center in front of Lake Conguillío.

Corralco Ski Resort ★

This small resort (with one chairlift and one T-bar) in the Malalcahuello National Preserve is a good option for beginners and more of a novelty for experts. The eight runs on Lonquimay Volcano's treeless slope are relatively short and none tougher than intermediate level, so you might well long for a lift extending higher up toward the summit. But there are some off-*piste* possibilities and a few steep drops for snowboarders. It also has great views of the Llaima Volcano and the Andes along the border with Argentina, beyond the araucaria forest. Line up early or pack a lunch as the cafeteria is easily overwhelmed even on normal days. Lift fees are $40 (£27) per adult; $33 (£22) for seniors and children 11 and under. The hotel, however, has six fine rooms paneled in light wood amid the araucarias. Doubles with half-board are $168 (£84) per person Monday through Thursday and $214 (£143) Friday through Sunday (✆ **2/202-9326;** www.corralco.com). To get there, turn left 4km (6 miles) after passing the village of Malalcahuello on Rte. 181, continuing for another 4km (6 miles), then turn left again on the forest road.

Where to Stay & Dine

There are seven campsites along the shore of Lago Conguillío; backcountry camping is not permitted. Campsites cost about $18 (£12). From October to April, the park has cabins that go for an average of $50 (£33) per night; information about rentals can be found inside the store next to the visitor center in Sector Truful-Truful. A great option is one of the wooden cabins at **La Baita** (✆ **45/416410;** www.labaitaconguillio.cl), from $90 (£60) per night, located midway between Conaf and the town Melipeuco. Here you'll find a restaurant, a store, park information, and guided excursions such as hiking, alpine touring, and snowshoeing.

Hostería Donde Juancho ★★ Finds The little town of Lonquimay, surrounded by araucaria forest, sports this very charming little hotel, something between a bed-and-breakfast and a country inn. Considering Lonquimay's remoteness, Donde Juancho's quality is a real surprise. The second-floor rooms are cozy, carpeted, and heated with slow-burning wood stoves. If I had to nitpick, I'd say they're a little small and dark, but its prices make it an excellent value. Its restaurant, featuring hearty, succulent Chilean cuisine (that is, meats), is also very good.

O'Higgins 1130, Lonquimay. ✆ **45/891140.** www.dondejuancho.cl. 5 units. $28–$36 (£19–£24) double. No credit cards. **Amenities:** Restaurant; Wi-Fi. *In room:* TV, no phone.

Hotel Andenrose ★★ (Kids) (Value) Irrepressible host and owner Hans Schöndorfer built this contemporary Bavarian hotel in the Araucanian Andes himself after finding a spot along the Cautín River with a little beach to drop a kayak. The spotless hotel has a central seating area alongside a massive ceramic oven, and the midsize rooms are very cozy, shielded from the nightly cool by thermopane windows. All rooms have their own bathroom; a few, however, are across the hallway. The hotel has one three-bed room and one four-bed room. Some of the best food in the valley—including copious breakfasts—is prepared in the Andenrose's kitchen.

Rte. 181 Km 68.5, E of Curacautín. ✆ **9/869-1700.** www.andenrose.com. 7 units. $25–$45 (£17–£30) per person. AE, DC, MC, V. **Amenities:** Restaurant; kayaking; jeep tours; snowshoe rental; laundry service; riverfront beach. *In room:* No phone.

Hotel Termas de Manzanar A half-century of operations to its credit makes this one of the most traditional hotels in the area. Built in traditional stone and wood in 1954, its pink rooms could stand an upgrade; the cheaper rooms in particular can be drafty. The more expensive rooms are supplied with thermal water. Its great draw is the garden's thermal pools, more rustic than at Malalcahuello and quite attractive under the trees and open sky. It also has basic cement "hot tubs." Nonguests may use the facilities for a fee, so I'd consider staying at the Andenrose (earlier) or La Suizandina (later) and stopping by for a soak.

Rte. 181, Km 83. ✆ **45/881200.** www.termasdemanzanar.cl. 32 units. $130 (£87) double; $180 (£120) suite with Jacuzzi. Half- and full board available. AE, DC, MC, V. **Amenities:** Restaurant; bar; game room; TV room. *In room:* TV, safe, no phone.

La Suizandina ★★ (Finds) With the Swiss flag at the entrance in the picture, you might think you're in the Alps, unless one of the property's llamas ambles by. The two-building complex includes a rebuilt farmhouse with five rooms and a dorm-style guesthouse for up to 18 people. The midsize rooms feature hardwood floors with comfortable, duvet-clad wooden beds and the squeaky-clean bathrooms you'd expect from a Swiss family-run resort. The guesthouse, whose bunks continue in the same vein as those of the individual rooms, also has good-size kitchen facilities. All rooms are nonsmoking. It also runs a campsite and has a good restaurant.

Rte. 181, Km 83. ✆ **45/891140.** www.suizandina.com. 8 units. Prices per person: $26–$50 (£17–£33); double; dorms $22 (£15) per person; camping $10 (£6.70) per person. Half-board available. AE, DC, MC, V. **Amenities:** Restaurant; bikes; horseback riding; kayaking. *In room:* TV, safe, no phone.

Malalcahuello Hotel & Spa Resort ★★ The Conguillío area's top spa features a large, 1,300-sq.-m (14,000-sq.-ft.) glass-enclosed wellness area that belies its relatively small overall size of just 27 rooms on three floors. Grey stone, wood, and glass characterize the angular, modern hotel offering views of the Lonquimay volcano. In the large rooms, contemporary textile design meets more traditional wood furniture. Facilities are open to nonresidents, but the hotel imposes a limit on the number of people who can use it on a given day. Hence, it's a good idea to buy the passes ahead of your day of hiking or skiing. The staff is generally good, but can be a bit arrogant on an off day. The resort also has several five-person *cabañas* and six-person bungalows, each outfitted with Wi-Fi.

Rte. 181, Km 86, Malalcahuello. ✆ **2/415-8109** or 45/281166. www.malalcahuello.cl. 27 units. $250–$290 (£167–£193) double; $360–$476 (£240–£317) apts; $570 (£380) suites. AE, MC, V. **Amenities:** Restaurant; lobby bar; spa w/large indoor pool; game room; Wi-Fi in lobby. *In room:* TV/DVD player (by request), safe.

2 VILLARRICA & PUCON ★★

Villarrica: 25km (16 miles) W of Pucón, 764km (474 miles) S of Santiago; Pucón: 112km (69 miles) E of Temuco, 789km (489 miles) S of Santiago

Pucón is where the tourists head, but Villarrica is where the locals live. It's a quiet town that never really took off as a vacation resort, in spite of the fact that the view is so much better here, with the volcano rising majestically beyond the lake. There are a few good and inexpensive lodging options here, if you decide to leave the tourism hubbub of Pucón. But it's farther away from Villarrica and Huerquehue national parks and the ski resort.

Nationally and internationally known as the "Adventure Capital of Chile," Pucón offers a multitude of outdoor activities, including rafting, hiking, skiing, canyoning, kayaking, and fly-fishing. Yet what makes Pucón a great all-around destination is its flexibility. There's also an abundance of low-key activities, such as hot spring spas and scenic drives through gorgeous landscapes. Or you can just relax with a good book on the porch of a cabin or throw a towel on the beach and sun yourself, as hundreds do during the summer.

VILLARRICA

Villarrica does have a charm of its own; it's a more authentic Lake District pueblo, and some travelers find that aspect more appealing, especially in the summer. The center of town here hums with activity as regular townsfolk go about their daily business. The town is also closer to Temuco and attractions such as Lican Ray on Lake Calafquén, Panguipulli, and the Coñaripe and Geometric hot springs.

Essentials

GETTING THERE **Buses JAC** (✆ **45/411447**) leaves Villarrica every half-hour for Pucón from its location at Bilbao 610, near Pedro de Valdivia. In Pucón, JAC's location is Uruguay 505, near the hospital. The fare is $1.50 (£1). A taxi to or from Pucón costs about $10 (£6.70). For more information on getting to the region, see "Getting There" for Pucón, later.

VISITOR INFORMATION A good **tourism office** can be found at Av. Pedro de Valdivia 1070 (✆ **45/206619**). It's open daily from 8:30am to 11pm December 15 through March 15, and daily from 8:30am to 6:30pm the rest of the year; it often closes on winter afternoons when the weather is rotten. You can also visit **www.villarrica.com** for more information.

What to See & Do

You might consider a 2-hour trip to Villarrica to stroll the streets, have lunch, and drop in to visit the **Museo Histórico y Arqueológico,** Pedro de Valdivia 1050 (no phone), with displays of Mapuche items and trademark silver pieces and jewelry. Outside, you'll find an authentically thatched *ruca,* a traditional Mapuche home. The museum is open Monday through Friday from 9am to 1pm and 3 to 7:30pm, and the entrance fee is $1 (50p). The festival **Muestra Cultural Mapuche** takes place here in Villarrica from January to late February, with music, handicrafts, dancing, and other activities; for more information, call the visitor center at © **45/206618.**

HUIFQUENCO FUNDO ★★★ Whether you are staying in Villarrica or Pucón, a trip to the Huifquenco Farm, Camino Villarrica, Huifquenco at Km .5 (©/fax **45/415040;** www.fundohuifquenco.cl), is a must. Opened to visitors in 2002, this 862-hectare (2,129-acre) estate is the third largest in the region and boasts over 5,000 head of cattle, bulls, wild boar, llamas, and sheep, among other animals. Choose to tour the farm on your own horse or relax and enjoy the view in one of their antique carriages. A real-life *huaso* leads you along a magnificent tree-lined road, past lagoons, and along rolling meadows with fantastic volcano and lake views. Get a feel for farm life in the region; go fishing, cycling, or canoeing; or take in a rodeo show at the *media luna.* Finish off your tour with a Chilean-style barbecue. Full- and half-day tours are available, and special programs are available upon request. Contact the farm directly for transportation to Huifquenco and a bilingual guide.

Where to Stay

Hostería de la Colina ★, Las Colinas 115 (©/fax **45/411503;** www.hosteriadelacolina.com), is owned and managed by an American couple, Glen and Beverly Aldrich, who have lived in Chile for 16 years. The inn is located on a hill with a panoramic view of the lake and volcanoes and offers seven comfortable rooms in the main house and two cottages located in the peaceful gardens, as well as a Jacuzzi. The owners will help you plan your stay, and they serve hearty Chilean meals in the pleasant dining room. Doubles run from $70 to $90 (£47–£60); cottages start at $140 (£93). Rates include full breakfast.

Patagon Andino Hotel ★, Matta 320 (© **45/419978;** www.patagonandino.cl), is in a charming little house just off the park and can arrange just about any activity in the area. Doubles run $75 (£50). **Hostería Kiel,** General Körner 153 (© **45/411631;** fax 45/410925), has comfortable rooms ($40–$60/£27–£40 double) and a direct view of Volcán and Lake Villarrica that you can enjoy from your very own porch. Or try **Cabañas Monte Negro,** at Pratt and Montt streets (© **45/411371**); it charges $130 (£87) for six people (no credit cards), and has eight newer cabins near the lake with direct views of the volcano. Private parking or ample street parking is available and free.

Villarrica Park Lake Hotel ★★ Luxurious and expansive, this property strives to be the best in southern Chile. It has only 70 rooms, but it feels like a big corporate hotel, with its large lobby and aloof but polite staff. Extra-wide doors made of local wood lead into comfortable and spacious modern rooms, all with sliding French doors that open up onto a balcony with a view of the lake. The marble bathrooms come with a tub/shower combo and heated towel racks. The spa has an exquisite selection of facials and bodywork offerings. This is an excellent base for travelers who prefer large, full-service hotels, although you'd be well advised to book way in advance, as it occasionally fills up with corporate retreat groups for days at a time. Always request promotional rates when making your reservations.

Camino Pucón–Villarrica Km 13. © **45/450000.** Fax 45/450202. www.villarricaparklakehotel.cl. 70 units. $350 (£233) double; from $480 (£320) suite. AE, DC, MC, V. **Amenities:** Restaurant; bar; lounge; heated indoor pool; health club and spa; limited watersports equipment; concierge; business center; salon; room service; massage; laundry service; dry cleaning. *In room:* TV, fax, Internet, minibar, hair dryer, iron, safe.

Where to Dine

For excellent seafood dishes, try **El Rey de Marisco,** on the coast at Valentín Letelier 1030 (✆ **45/412093**), or **Hostería Kiel,** General Körner 153 (✆ **45/411631**), for simple Chilean fare and a superb view of Volcán Villarrica. **The Travellers,** Valentín Letelier 753 (✆ **45/413617**), has an international traveler's hostel vibe, and a menu to match, with Chinese, Indian, Mexican, Thai, and Chilean dishes, plus the ever-popular happy hour from 6 to 9:30pm. The only restaurant with a good view of the lake between Villarica and Pucón, **Martín Pescador,** Pedro Montt 40 (✆ **9/309-1848**), offers such exotic meats as wild boar and fine tuna steaks.

PUCON

Pucón is a picturesque little town almost entirely dependent on tourism, but, thankfully, it has not embellished its streets with gaudy tourist traps. Instead, a creative use of timber creates the architectural tone. During the early 1900s, Pucón's economy centered on the timber industry, but the town's fate as a travel destination was sealed when the first hotel went up in 1923, attracting hordes of fishermen. Ten years later, the government built the stately Hotel Pucón, drawing hundreds more visitors each year, at that time traveling here by boat from Villarrica. Today there are many lodging options and even more adventure outfitters ready to fill your days.

It is important to note that the summer season, particularly from December 15 to the end of February, as well as Easter week, is jam-packed with tourists. Hotel and business owners gleefully take advantage of this and jack up their prices, sometimes doubling their rates during that time.

Essentials

Getting There

BY PLANE Visitors normally fly into Temuco's **Maquehue Airport** (p. 245) and then arrange transportation for the 1- to 1½-hour ride into Villarrica or Pucón. Most hotels will arrange transportation for you, although it's usually at an additional cost. **Transfer & Turismo de la Araucanía** (✆ **45/339900**), a minivan service at the airport, will take a maximum of 10 guests (minimum four) to Pucón for $50 (£33). Pucón's airport is equipped to handle jets, but for the time being no airlines fly here.

BY CAR From the Pan-American Highway south of Temuco, follow the signs for Villarrica onto Rte. 199. The road is well marked and easy to follow. If coming from Valdivia, take Rte. 205 to the Carretera Panamericana Norte (Hwy. 5). Just past Loncoche, continue east, following signs for Villarrica and Pucón.

BY BUS **Tur Bus** (✆ **600/660-6600** toll free, or 2/270-7510; www.turbus.cl) offers service to Pucón from destinations such as Santiago, stopping first in Temuco and Villarrica. The trip is about 9 to 11 hours and generally a night journey; the cost is about $32 (£21) for an economy seat and $53 (£35) for an executive seat. **Buses JAC** (in Santiago, Av. Providencia 1072; ✆ **2/235-2484**) has service from Santiago to Pucón every half-hour from 6:30am to midnight from its Santiago terminal at Balmaceda and Aldunate (✆ **45/231330**).

Getting Around

There are dozens of tour companies providing transportation and tours to all points of interest around Pucón; they generally advertise everything in their front windows. However, this is another place where renting a car is a great option if you want to get out and

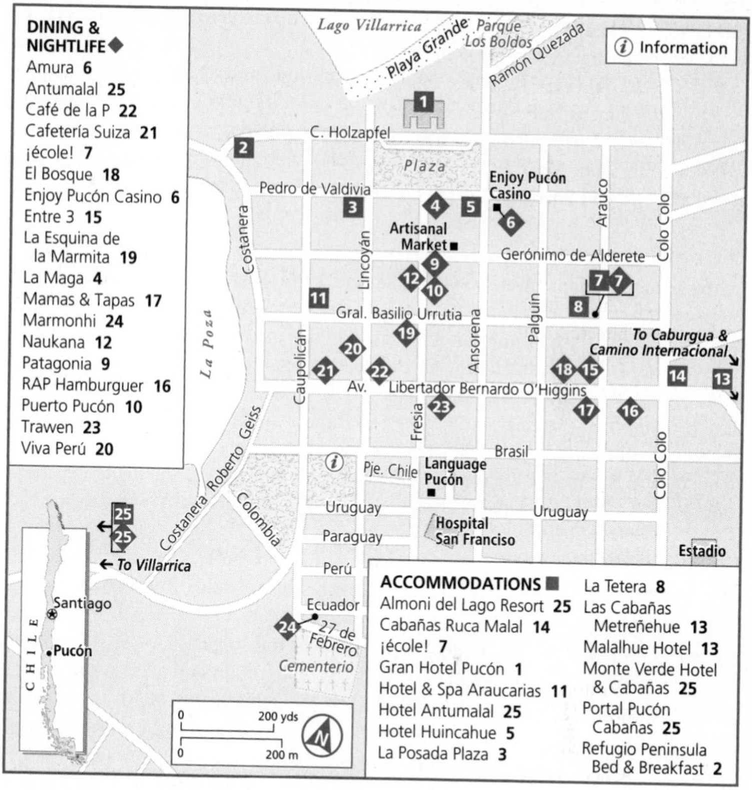

leisurely see the sights. In Temuco, **Hertz** has an office at Andrés Bello 792 (© 45/318585), and they operate a branch in Pucón at Ansorena 123—actually, an agency called **Enjoy Tour** (© 45/442303). In Pucón, try **Pucón Rent A Car,** Colo Colo 340 (© 45/443052); or **SPU Comercial Rent A Car,** 191 Ansorena (© 45/444485). **Sierra Nevada,** at the corner of O'Higgins and Palguin (© 45/444210), also rents cars and mountain bikes. Rates start at $45 (£30) per day for a small car.

Visitor Information

The **Chamber of Tourism** (© **45/441671**) operates a helpful office at the corner of Brasil and Caupolicán streets; it's open daily from 9am to 8pm December through March, and from 10am to 6:30pm the rest of the year. However, the staff does not speak English very well. The city of Pucón has an excellent website at **www.pucon.com**.

What to See & Do

You'll find shops everywhere in Pucón, but the best are on Fresia Street. Most sell some variation of adventure gear, wool sweaters and scarves, carvings, or jewelry from boutique designers. There's also an excellent **artisanal market** at Alderate between Fresia and

Ansorena (daily 10am–7pm) with several dozen small independent shops featuring handcrafted items—not the mass produced things you get in other Chilean shops—of surprisingly high quality. Brand names are not at all lost in Pucón though: North Face, Lacoste, Jack Wolfskin, and Crocs all have shops here.

If you're staying in Pucón longer than a few days and you'd like to learn a little of the local lingo, try **Language Pucón,** Uruguay 306 (✆ **45/444967;** www.languagepucon.com), which offers short but effective courses and home-stay opportunities. They also have a good book exchange in English and German.

For more things to see and do in this area, see "Hot Springs Outside Pucón" and "Natural Attractions Outside Pucón," later in this section.

Outdoor Activities

With so many outdoor adventures available here, it's no wonder there's a surplus of outfitters eager to meet the demand. Be very careful when selecting a tour operator in Pucón because few are 100% competent, and some are downright dangerous or simply don't have the years of experience in the area to provide responsible service. Ask about your guide's familiarity with the tour you are proposing to take (unbelievably, a few operators have periodically sent guides on trekking expeditions without having actually gotten to know the trail first) and what kind of experience and/or qualifications your guide has. Remember that you get what you pay for; be wary of seemingly fly-by-night operations. Most outfitters include insurance in the cost of a trip, but first verify what their policy covers.

Politur, O'Higgins 635 (✆ **45/441373;** www.politur.com), is a well-respected tour company that offers fishing expeditions, Mapuche-themed tours, and sightseeing trips around the Seven Lakes area, in addition to volcano ascents. They're slightly more expensive than other agencies but are worth it. **Aguaventura,** Palguín 336 (✆ **45/444246;** www.aguaventura.com), is run by a dynamic French group, and their main focus is snowboarding in the winter, with a shop that sells and rents boards, boots, and clothing; they also do volcano ascents with ski/snowboard descents, and rafting and kayaking, and they offer a half-day canyoneering and rappelling excursion. **Sol y Nieve,** Lincoyán 361 (✆ **45/444761;** www.solynievepucon.com), has been on the scene for quite a while, offering rafting and volcano ascents as well as fishing, airport transfers, and excursions in other destinations around Chile; however, there have been some complaints recently of lackluster service.

Trancura, O'Higgins 211-C (✆ **45/441189;** www.trancura.com), sells cheap trips to the masses, and they are best known for their rafting excursions, which they've been doing forever. Beyond that, I do not recommend any other trips with this company because of their yearly roster of inexperienced guides hired on the cheap. They do have ski and bike rentals, however, with low prices.

BIKING Several outfitters on the main street, O'Higgins, rent bicycles by the hour and provide trail information and guided tours. Bicycle rentals run an average of $8 (£5.30) for a half-day. You can also just pedal around town, or take a pleasant, easy ride around the wooded peninsula. **Miropucón,** Fresia 415, Local 6 (✆ **45/444874;** contacto@miropucon.cl), offers 3- and 4-hour medium-difficulty bike tours to the Ojos de Caburgua.

CLIMBING THE VOLCANO ★★★ An ascent of Volcán Villarrica is perhaps the most thrilling excursion available here—there's nothing like peering into this percolating, fuming crater—but you've got to be in decent shape to tackle it. The excursion begins early in the morning, and the long climb requires crampons and ice axes. Note that the descent has traditionally been a combination of walking and sliding on your behind in the snow, but so many have done this that the naturally formed "luge" run is now enormous, slippery, and fast, and people have been hurting themselves on it lately—so be cautious. Volcán Villarrica is perpetually on the verge of exploding, and sometimes trips are called off until the rumbling quiets down. Tour companies that offer this climb are **Politur** and **Sol y Nieve** (see earlier). The average cost is $90 (£60), including transfers, entrance fee, insurance, equipment, and guides, but not lunch.

FISHING ★ You can pick up your fishing license at the visitor center at Caupolicán and Brasil. Guided fishing expeditions typically go to the Trancura or the Liucura rivers. See a list of outfitters above for information, or try **Off Limits,** O'Higgins 560 (✆ **45/441210** or 9/949-2481; www.offlimits.cl).

FOUR TRACK TOURS These guided tours on 4×4 quad bikes are for people who either can't or don't want to walk through nature, and they are available in any kind of weather. Tours lead riders through Mapuche villages, native forests, and, on clear days, to points with impressive volcano views. Only one company offers this excursion (about $14/£9.30 per hr.): **Ronco Track,** O'Higgins 615 (✆ **45/441801;** www.roncotrack.cl).

GOLFING ★ Pucón's private 18-hole **Península de Pucón** golf course is open to the playing public. For information, call ✆ **45/443965,** ext 409. The cost is $46 (£31) for 18 holes. This is really the only way to get onto the private—and exclusive—peninsula that juts into the lake, by the way.

HIKING ★★ The two national parks, Villarrica and Huerquehue, and the Cañi nature reserve offer hiking trails that run from easy to difficult. An average excursion with an outfitter to Huerquehue, including transportation and a guided hike, costs about $24 (£16) per person. By far the best short-haul day hikes in the area are at Huerquehue and the Cañi nature reserve.

HORSEBACK RIDING ★ Half- and full-day horseback rides are offered throughout the area, including in the Villarrica National Park and the Liucura Valley. The **Centro de Turismo Huepil** (✆ **9/643-2673**) offers day and multiday horseback rides, including camping or a stay at the Termas de Huife, from a small ranch about a half-hour from Pucón (head east out of Pucón and then north toward Caburgua; take the eastern road toward Huife and keep your eyes open for the signs to Centro de Turismo Huepil). You'll need to make a reservation beforehand. All-inclusive multiday trips cost about $120 (£80) per person, per day. A wonderful couple, Rodolfo and Carolina, run this outfit. Rodolfo is a superb equestrian professor who used to train the Spanish Olympic team. Beginning riders are given an introductory course in the corral before setting out. Contact a tour agency for day rides in Villarrica Park, which go for about $65 (£43) for a full day. Tour agencies will also organize rides that leave from the **Rancho de Caballos** (✆ **45/441575**), near the Palguín thermal baths. If you're driving, the Rancho is at 30km (19 miles) on the Ruta International toward Argentina.

RAFTING & KAYAKING ★ Rafting season runs from September to April, although some areas might be safe to descend only from December to March. The two classic descents in the area are the 14km (8¾-mile) Trancura Alto, rated at Class III to IV, and the somewhat gentler Trancura Bajo, rated at Class II to III. Both trips are very popular and can get crowded in the summer. The 3-hour rafting trip on the Trancura Alto costs an average of $37 (£25); the 3-hour Trancura Bajo costs an average of $24 (£16). **Sol y Nieve** (see earlier) offers both trips. The rafting outfitter **Trancura** (see earlier) also offers an excursion rafting the more technical Maichin River, which includes a barbecue lunch. **Kayak Pucón** (✆ **45/716-2347;** www.kayakpucon.net) runs 3- to 15-day trips around Pucón to as far away as the Futaleufú that begin at $450 (£300) per person and include all food, accommodations, equipment, and transportation.

SKIING The **Centro de Ski Pucón** (✆ **45/441901;** www.skipucon.cl) gives skiers the opportunity to schuss down a smoking volcano—not something you can do every day. There's a sizable amount of terrain here, and it's all open-field skiing, but, regrettably, the owners (Gran Hotel Pucón; see review later) rarely open more than two of the five chairs, due to nothing else but laziness. You'll need to take a chairlift to the main lodge, which means that nonskiers, too, can enjoy the lovely views from the lodge's outdoor deck. There's a restaurant, child-care center, and store. The Centro has a ski school and ski equipment rental; there are slightly cheaper rentals from **Aguaventura, Sol y Nieve,** and **Trancura,** among other businesses along O'Higgins. Lift-ticket prices vary but average about $36 (£24) for a full-day pass. Most tour companies offer transport to and from the resort, and a shuttle goes every hour on the hour from the Gran Hotel Pucón. For more information, contact one of the tour operators above.

SWIMMING Pucón's **Lake Villarrica beach** ★, right in front of the Gran Hotel Pucón, is a hubbub of activity during the summer months and is the place for vacationers to see and be seen. Thousands of beach goers take up almost every inch of sand and the warm waters of Lago Villarica are filled with windsurfers, kayakers, boats, and swimmers.

Where to Stay

Pucón is chock-full of lodging options, nearly all of them good to excellent. If you're planning to spend more than several days in the region, you might consider renting one of the abundant *cabañas.* Keep in mind that Pucón is very busy during the summer, and accommodations need to be reserved well in advance for visits between December 15 and the end of February. Prices listed below show the range from low to high season; high season is from November to February, but verify each hotel's specific dates. You might consider visiting during the off-season, when lodging prices drop almost 50%; November and March are especially good months to visit.

Expensive

Gran Hotel Pucón (Kids) The Gran Hotel is a landmark built by the government in 1936 when fishing tourism began to take off in Pucón. It is a good choice for families, but otherwise I have mixed opinions about it. The owners renovated the premises fairly recently (and replaced a hideous peacock teal exterior with an insipid putty color), but one has the feeling they still have a long way to go, especially when it comes to service. The hotel's palatial hallways, stately dining areas, and lovely checkerboard patio give an aura of times gone by. Indeed, the old-world beauty of these common areas, with their marble and parquet floors, lofty ceilings, and flowing curtains, still looks scruffy. The rooms are not exactly noteworthy, but they are not bad, either: spacious, with comfortable beds and views of the volcano or the lake. The superior room has an alcove with one or two additional beds for kids; bathrooms are spacious and clean. The hotel is run somewhat like a cruise ship, with nightly dinner dances, stage shows, music, and comedy, as well as a team of activity directors who run a kids' "miniclub" and host classes for adults, such as cooking or tango. The hotel sits on the most popular beach in Pucón.

Clemente Holzapfel 190, Pucón. ✆/fax **45/913300**. www.granhotelpucon.cl. 133 units. $155–$265 (£103–£177) double. Kids 9 and under stay free in parent's room. AE, DC, MC, V. **Amenities:** Restaurant; outdoor cafe; bar; lounge; large outdoor pool and small indoor pool; health club; children's programs;

concierge; tour desk; room service; laundry service; dry cleaning. *In room:* TV, fax, Internet access, minibar, hair dryer, safe.

Hotel Antumalal ★★★ Moments This is simply one of the most lovely and unique hotels in Chile. Low-slung and literally built into a rocky slope, the Antumalal was designed to blend with its natural environment. It's retro-chic and exceptionally cozy, and the friendly, personal attention provided by the staff heightens a sense of intimacy with one's surroundings. The rooms are all the same size, and they are very comfortable, with honeyed-wood walls; a fireplace; a big, comfortable bed; and large panoramic windows that look out onto the same gorgeous view. Guests don't just walk into a room; they *sink* into it. There's also a Royal Cottage for rent that comes with two bedrooms, a living room, and fireplace—perfect for families or as a romantic bungalow for two.

The dining room not only serves up a spectacular view, but it also serves some of the best food in Pucón. Well-kept terraced gardens zigzag down the lakeshore, where guests have use of a private beach. A kidney-shape pool is half-hidden under a lawn-covered roof, and the tennis courts are a short walk away. It's all fit for a queen—indeed, Queen Elizabeth II graced the hotel with her presence several decades ago.

Camino Pucón–Villarrica, Km 2. ✆ **45/441011.** Fax 45/441013. www.antumalal.com. 16 units. $280 (£187) double; $363 (£242); family suite; $550 (£367) Chalet Royal. Rates include full breakfast. Half-board available. AE, DC, MC, V. **Amenities:** Restaurant (p. 265); bar; lounge; outdoor pool; tennis court; massage; laundry service. *In room:* TV, fax, Internet access, hair dryer, safe.

Hotel Huincahue ★ Finds If you like to be in the center of town, steps from all the shops and restaurants, in a quiet and sophisticated setting, then this is your best bet. The hotel sits right on the main plaza and has an elegant, homey feel to it. From the cozy lobby lounge with a fireplace and adjoining library to the peaceful pool in the lovely garden, this place feels more like a private mansion than a hotel. Rooms have pleasant beige carpets and nice wrought-iron and wood furniture, and a few have spectacular views of the volcano (room no. 202 is best). Second-floor rooms have small balconies. The marble bathrooms are large and many have windows as well. The staff tries hard to accommodate, but their English is minimal, so be patient.

Pedro de Valdivia 375. ✆/fax **45/443540** or 45/442728. www.hotelhuincahue.com. 20 units. $182–$195 double (£121–£130). Rates include continental breakfast. AE, MC, V. **Amenities:** Restaurant; bar; outdoor pool; room service; massage; babysitting; laundry service. *In room:* TV.

Moderate

Almoni del Lago Resort ★★ Finds Location is everything at the Almoni, with its lush, gorgeous grounds leading down to the lapping shores of Lake Villarrica just a few meters from the deck of your cabin. Cabins for two, four, and eight guests are available; ask for specials for multiday stays. Cabins are fully equipped, very comfortable, and elegant; guests are given their own remote gate opener to help control access. A kiosk sells basic food items and other sundries. Most *cabañas* have their own deck right on the water; others have a deck farther up the hill. Either way, the cabins are fairly close together, so you might end up getting to know your neighbor. Prices drop 50% in the off-season.

Camino Villarrica a Pucón, Km 19. ✆ **45/210676.** Fax 45/442304. www.almoni.cl. 8 *cabañas.* $66–$108 (£44–£72) *cabaña* for 2. MC, V. **Amenities:** Large outdoor pool; tennis courts. *In room:* TV, kitchen.

Hotel & Spa Araucarias The Hotel & Spa Araucarias is a good midrange option for its well-manicured grounds, indoor pool, outdoor deck, and extras such as an on-site gift shop. The size of the rooms is a little tight—not too much space to walk around in, but enough to open your suitcase. If you're looking for something a little more independent and spacious, try one of the four connected cabins in the back. The hotel has a "spa" room with a sauna and a heated indoor pool fitted with hydromassage lounges. The name comes from the araucaria trees that flank the entrance; there's also an araucaria sprouting from a grassy courtyard in the back. The hotel is within walking distance from the beach and is close to shops and restaurants.

Caupolicán 243, Pucón. ©/fax **45/441963.** www.araucarias.cl. 25 units. $90 (£60) double. Rates include continental breakfast. AE, DC, MC, V. **Amenities:** Restaurant; lounge; heated indoor pool; Jacuzzi; sauna; massage. *In room:* TV.

La Posada Plaza ★ This traditional hotel is housed in a 78-year-old home built by German immigrants. Everything about this old-fashioned hotel, from its exterior to its dining area, to its backyard swimming pool, is very attractive—except the rooms, that is, which are plain and inexplicably do not keep up the charm of the hotel's common areas. These old buildings always seem to come with fun house floors that creak and slant in every direction. All in all, it's a comfortable enough place to hang your hat for the evening, and it is located on the plaza 2 blocks from the beach.

Av. Pedro de Valdivia 191, Pucón. © **45/441088.** Fax 45/441762. www.plazapucon.cl. 17 units. $78–$92 (£52–£61) double. Rates include buffet breakfast. AE, DC, MC, V. **Amenities:** Restaurant; pool snack bar; lounge; large outdoor pool; laundry service. *In room:* TV.

Las Cabañas Metreñehue ★ Kids These pastoral *cabañas* are surrounded by dense forest and bordered by the thundering Trancura River, about a 10-minute drive from downtown Pucón, and are for those seeking a country ambience away from town. There are cabins built for seven guests; a few two-story cabins can fit eight. All are spacious and very comfortable, with wood-burning stoves, decks, and ample kitchens. Some come with bathtubs, and a few have giant picture windows; all have daily maid service. The two *cabañas* in the back have a great view of the volcano. Around the 3-hectare (7-acre) property are walking trails, a swimming pool, a volleyball court, a soccer field, and a river where guests can fish for trout. The cabins are popular with families in the summer, and sometimes large groups take advantage of the *quincho,* the poolside barbecue site. The German owners are gracious and multilingual, and live in the main house (and reception area), near the cabins. Parties of two to five will have to pay a $149/£99 six-guest rate during the summer.

Camino Pucón a Caburga, Km 10. ©/fax **45/441322.** www.metrenehue.com. 7 units. $60–$90 (£40–£60) for 2; $149 (£99) for 6. AE, DC, MC, V. **Amenities:** Restaurant; large outdoor pool; bikes; laundry service. *In room:* TV, kitchen.

Malalhue Hotel ★ This attractive, newer hotel is about a 15-minute walk from town, but it offers excellent value in handsome accommodations. It was designed to feel like a modern mountain lodge, made of volcanic rock and native wood, and is set on an open space in a residential area. The interiors are impeccably clean, and rooms are decorated with country furnishings. There's also a restaurant and a cozy lounge with a fireplace and couches. *Cabañas* have two bedrooms, a trundle bed in the living area, and a fully stocked kitchen. The location isn't ideal, but it is a good value nonetheless.

Camino Internacional 1615, Pucón. © **45/443130.** Fax 45/443132. www.malalhue.cl. 24 units, 3 *cabañas.* $95–$106 (£63–£71) double; $95–$151 (£63–£101). Rates include buffet breakfast. AE, DC, MC, V. **Amenities:** Restaurant; bar; lounge; room service. *In room:* TV.

Monte Verde Hotel & Cabañas ★★ Built in 2003 and tastefully designed using nearly every kind of wood available in the area (including recycled alerce), this six-room hotel is about 6km (3¾ miles) from Villarrica, meaning you'll need a taxi or rental car to get here. The hotel and *cabañas* are perched on a hill to afford views of the volcano and the lake. All rooms are decorated differently; four have king-size beds and all but one have private balconies with lake views. The bathrooms are decorated with old-fashioned sinks and bathtubs obtained from a turn-of-the-20th-century hotel in Villarrica. Attentive service and a complimentary bottle of red wine upon arrival are welcoming touches. A cozy lounge boasts a wood-burning fireplace and board games; during the high season, there are kayaks and boats available for guest use at the beach below and an outdoor pool, whirlpool, and hot tub. Reservations are necessary for the *cabañas,* which can sleep two to seven guests.

Camino Villarrica-Pucón Km 18. ✆ **45/441351.** Fax 45/443132. www.monteverdepucon.cl. 6 units, 14 *cabañas.* $160 (£107) double; $140–$280 (£93–£187) *cabaña.* Rates include buffet breakfast. AE, DC, MC, V. **Amenities:** Lounge; room service.

Inexpensive

Cabañas Ruca Malal ★ These custom-made, cozy wooden cabins are tucked away in a tiny forested lot at the bend where busy O'Higgins becomes the road to Caburga. The grounds, however, are peaceful, and they burst with bamboo, beech, magnolias, and rhododendron. The design of each cabin features log stairwells, carved headboards, and walls made of slabs of evergreen beech trunks cut lengthwise. They are well lit and have full-size kitchens and daily maid service. A wood-burning stove keeps the rooms toasty warm on cold days. In the center of the property is a kidney-shape swimming pool; there are also a Jacuzzi and sauna, but, unfortunately, you'll have to pay extra to use them. As with most cabins, those designed for four people mean one bedroom with a double bed and a trundle bed in the living area; book a cabin for six if you prefer two bedrooms. Those with a sweet tooth will love the on-site chocolate shop.

O'Higgins 770, Pucón. ✆/fax **45/442297.** www.rucamalal.cl. 10 units. $120 (£60) cabin for 4; $155 (£103) cabin for 6. MC, V. **Amenities:** Lounge; small outdoor pool; Jacuzzi; sauna; laundry service. *In room:* TV, kitchen.

¡école! ★ Value Nearly 40 partners own this pleasant hostel, which offers small but clean and comfortable rooms with beds blanketed with goose-down comforters. ¡école! sees a predominantly international crowd, from backpackers to families traveling on a budget. It has a very good vibe throughout and a nice outdoor patio with picnic tables. The hostel provides great reading material in the small lounge, from travel guides to environment-oriented literature, to logging protest rosters. The hostel is equal parts restaurant/lodging/ecology center, offering day trips to various areas, but especially to the private park Cañi, an araucaria reserve. It's very popular in the summer, when it's wise to book at least 1 or 2 weeks in advance. Note that some rooms are shared, meaning you may have to bunk with a stranger if the hostel fills up, although there are doubles located in the back for nonshared accommodations with a private bathroom.

General Urrutia 592, Pucón. ✆/fax **45/441675.** www.ecole.cl. 16 units. $50 (£33) double. Rates include continental breakfast. DC, MC, V. **Amenities:** Restaurant (p. 265).

La Tetera ★ Rooms at La Tetera are simple but meticulously clean, and shared bathrooms are not much of an issue, as they are just outside your door. It's all squeezed in pretty tight, but guests have use of a private, sunny common area with chairs and a picnic table, and a short walkway connects to an elevated wooden deck. A Swiss-Chilean couple own La Tetera; they offer a book exchange and good tourism information, and will arrange excursions and help with trip planning. La Tetera (the Tea Kettle) lives up to its name, with two menu pages of teas, along with sandwiches, daily specials, and pastries.

 A common area next to the cafe has the only TV in the place. The staff can arrange Spanish lessons, even if you're here for just a short time.

General Urrutia 580, Pucón. ✆/fax **45/441462.** www.tetera.cl. 6 units. $20–$34 (£13–£23) double. Rates include continental breakfast. No credit cards. **Amenities:** Restaurant; bar (for guests only).

Portal Pucón Cabañas Kids Fourteen of these newer wooden cabins are spread out over a large, grassy lot overlooking Lake Villarrica, and the remaining five (built in 2003) are across the road that separates the cabins from the beach. They are comfortable and relatively inexpensive, and a good bet for families with kids, especially for the pool, play area, "kids' clubhouse," and babysitting service. All cabins have tiny kitchens, living areas, wood-burning stoves, small decks with table and chairs, and sweeping views of the lake. However, five of the cabins *(cabañas chicas)* are large cabins split into two units, and are somewhat cramped. The cabins on the lakefront are the most spectacular for their views and have two bedrooms, one en suite, the other with bunk beds, and there is also a sofa bed in the living room. The spacious property features walking trails, and there's also a private beach and docking area a 5-minute walk down the hill and across the road. Portal Pucón is a 3-minute drive from downtown.

Camino Pucón–Villarrica, Km 4.5. ✆ **45/443322.** Fax 45/442498. www.portalpucon.cl. 19 units. $103 (£69) for 2; $185–$222 (£123–£148) for 4. AE, DC, MC, V. **Amenities:** Lounge; bar; large outdoor pool. *In room:* TV, kitchen.

Refugio Peninsula Bed & Breakfast ★ Of the three inexpensive options mentioned here, this hostel has the best location, a half-block walk from the shore and just a 100m (328-ft.) walk from the main beach in Pucón. Tucked away on a quiet corner on the lush peninsula side of town, the hostel offers shared accommodations, a few doubles, and a *cabaña* for five with a kitchenette, and all its furnishings and interiors are fresh and new. Like ¡école! this hostel has an outdoor patio; it also has a cozy, wood-hewn restaurant and bar for meals and drinks. Shared rooms (some with three beds, some with five) mean that you will bunk with a stranger on busy nights, but here each room has a private bathroom, unlike its competitors. There are also two double rooms for couples or a single seeking privacy. Service here is friendly.

Clemente Holzapfel 11, Pucón. ✆ **45/443398.** www.refugiopeninsula.cl. 8 units. $56 (£37) double; $95–$130 (£63–£87) *cabaña* for 5. Rates include continental breakfast (except *cabaña*). No credit cards. **Amenities:** Restaurant; bar (for guests only).

Where to Dine

Pucón has a good selection of cafes that serve *onces,* the popular late-afternoon coffee-and-cakes snack, in addition to a lunch menu. **Café de la P,** Lincoyán 395 (✆ **45/442018;** www.cafedelap.com), has a menu with sandwiches, cakes, coffee drinks, and cocktails. It's a nice place to unwind with a drink in the evening and is open until 4am in the summer. **Cafetería Suiza,** O'Higgins 116 (✆ **45/441241**), has a menu with everything from milkshakes to full-fledged entrees, and does a booming business with the Santiago crowd in the summer.

Patagonia ★★, Fresia 223 (✆ **45/443165**), holds the Cassis chocolate shop inside, and is a great place to get a tea and a piece of cake on a rainy day or a multiflavored ice-cream cone in the heat of the summer. Their outside patio is my favorite spot for *onces,* not to mention people-watching, as is the laid-back patio at California-style health food cafe **Trawen** (O'Higgins 311; ✆ **45/442024**). For Chilean comfort food, try **RAP Hamburguer** (✆ **45/443336**), at O'Higgins 619, which serves up massive burgers stacked with eggs, avocado, or whatever else you have in mind.

Expensive

Amura ★ INTERNATIONAL If you plan on spending lots of time at the town's casino, you'll want a place to refuel in between hitting the slots. This elegant contemporary restaurant that spills out onto the patio of Enjoy Pucón (see "Pucón After Dark," below) serves up everything from *onces* to sushi. They frequently have happy hour, buffet, and daily specials that are worth your consideration, as well as fine beef and fish dishes.

Ansorena 121. ✆ **45/550000.** Reservations recommended. Main courses $9–$22 (£4.50–£11). AE, DC, MC, V. Daily noon–4pm and 7pm–midnight.

Antumalal ★★ (Moments) INTERNATIONAL The Hotel Antumalal's restaurant serves some of the most flavorful cuisine in Pucón, with creative dishes that are well prepared and seasoned with herbs from an extensive garden. In fact, most of the vegetables used here are local and organic; the milk comes from the family's own dairy farm. Try a thinly sliced beef carpaccio followed by chicken stuffed with smoked salmon, grilled local trout, or any one of the pastas. There's a good selection of wine and an ultracool cocktail lounge for an after-dinner drink (but it's tiny and not a "happening" spot). It's worth a visit for the view of Lake Villarrica alone. This is my favorite dining experience in Pucón.

Camino Pucón–Villarrica, Km 2. ✆ **45/441011.** Fax 45/441013. Reservations recommended. Main courses $9–$12 (£6–£8). AE, DC, MC, V. Daily noon–4pm and 8–10pm.

La Maga ★★ URUGUAYAN/PARRILLA Undoubtedly the best *parrilla* in town, this restaurant originated in the beach town of Punta del Este, Uruguay. The food is excellent, especially the meat, chicken, and fish grilled on the giant barbecue on the patio. Order a bottle of wine and a large fresh salad, and watch the people go by the large picture windows overlooking the street. Try the grilled salmon with capers, if you're in the mood for fish. But, really, the best cuts here are the beef filets, known as *lomos,* served with mushrooms, Roquefort, or pepper sauce. The *bife de chorizo* (sirloin) is thick and tender. For dessert, the flan here stands out.

Fresia 125. ✆ **45/444277.** Main courses $9–$16 (£6–£11). AE, MC, V. Daily noon–4pm and 7pm–midnight.

Puerto Pucón (Finds) SPANISH Puerto Pucón pays homage to its owner's Spanish heritage through its design and well-made classics such as paella. Seafood is the focus here, and it is served in a multitude of ways: Have your razor clams, shrimp, and calamari sautéed in garlic or wrapped in a crepe and smothered in crab sauce. The atmosphere is typical Spanish, with white stucco walls, bullfight posters, flamenco-dancer fans, and racks of wine bottles; the fireplace is especially nice, and there's also a small bar. The sangria is excellent, and during warmer months, there's seating on the front deck, which can get packed.

Fresia 246. ✆ **45/441592.** Main courses $10–$14 (£6.70–£9.30). AE, MC, V. Daily 11am–3:30pm and 7–11:30pm (until 2am during summer).

Moderate

¡école! (Value) VEGETARIAN This vegetarian restaurant, inside the hotel of the same name, includes one salmon dish among heaps of such creative dishes as calzones, quiche, pizza, burritos, chop suey, and more. Sandwiches come on homemade bread, and the breakfast is the best in town, featuring an American-style breakfast as well as Mexican- and Chilean-style. ¡école! uses locally and organically grown products and buys whole-wheat flour and honey from a local farm. There are also fresh salads here. The outdoor patio is a lovely place to dine under the grapevine in good weather. The service is very slow and disorganized; they usually offer a shorter menu during the winter.

General Urrutia 592. ✆/fax **45/441675.** Main courses $6–$8 (£4–£5.30). MC, V. Daily 8am–11pm.

La Esquina de la Marmita ★ FONDUE Cozy and candlelit, La Marmita specializes in warm crocks of fondue, as well as the other Swiss favorite, *raclette.* Both involve a diner's participation, which usually makes for an amusing dinner—but if you are a fondue fan, you won't be as impressed here as in Europe, for example (the right cheeses aren't always available). Fondue can be ordered a variety of ways, with standard bread cubes, squares of breaded meat, or vegetables. A *raclette* runs along the same lines; diners heat cheese to eat with cured meats and potatoes; it's not as fun as fondue, but enjoyable nevertheless. Unfortunately, this restaurant closes during the winter, which is the perfect season for this kind of food.

Fresia 300. ✆ **45/442431.** Fondue for 2 $24 (£16). AE, DC, MC, V. Daily 7:30–11pm. Closed Apr–Nov.

Naukana ★ FUSION/ASIAN A trendsetter since it opened in 2001, Naukana offers a menu that spans the Spice Route from Arabia to Japan. The plates are small and meant for sharing over drinks. Vietnamese spring rolls, pad Thai, kebabs, and tempura are a great way to start the night off, and their Tibetan salmon in a sauce of cilantro, coconut, and peanut is a fine entree. There are decent vegetarian offerings too. Dark wood floors, walls, and furniture paired with contemporary art and splashes of deep red and candlelight lend the restaurant a romantic, almost woodsy vibe. There's a satellite restaurant in Santiago.

Fresia 236. ✆ **45/444677.** www.naukana.cl. Reservations recommended. Main courses $8–$10 (£5.30–£6.70). AE, DC, MC, V. Daily noon–4pm and 8–midnight.

Inexpensive

Marmonhi ★ (Finds) CHILEAN If you'd like to have lunch with the locals, then this place, a good 20-minute walk from the center of town, is worth the hike. The food is typically Chilean, prepared by the amiable Elena, who runs a tight ship. Many of Pucón's residents stop by here to pick up lunch or dinner for their families, although the simple dining room is pleasant for a leisurely meal, and there's a small patio for outdoor dining in good weather. Specials change daily, according to what Elena finds at the market. Vegetable or beef empanadas are a great start to the meal. Then order a big Chilean salad (fresh tomatoes and lots of sweet onion) and one of the special chicken or fish dishes. They're simply yet deliciously prepared: marinated and grilled and served with vegetables and rice. There's excellent baked lasagna as well. For dessert, have one of the decadent tarts that locals rave about, but skip the coffee, which is instant and tasteless.

Ecuador 175. ✆ **45/441972.** Main courses $3–$7 (£2–£4.70). AE, DC, MC, V. Daily noon–4pm and 7–10:30pm.

Viva Perú! ★★ (Kids) PERUVIAN This Peruvian restaurant is a favorite hangout for locals, offering warm, personalized service and tasty cuisine. For solo travelers, there is bar seating, and there is a patio with a volcano view. The restaurant specializes in *ceviche* and seafood *picoteos* (appetizer platters), which make an excellent accompaniment to a frosty pisco sour. Daily fixed-price lunch specials include a mixed salad, entree (steamed or grilled fish, pork loin, or chicken), and coffee for about $7 (£4.70). The restaurant offers one of the few kids' menus in the area. Try the sugary-sweet *suspiro limeño,* a creamy Peruvian traditional dessert.

Lincoyan 372. ✆/fax **45/444025.** Main courses $9–$14 (£6–£9.30). AE, MC, V. Daily noon–2am.

Pucón After Dark

Pucón's casino, **Enjoy Pucón** (✆ **45/550000**), can be found at Ansorena 121 and boasts three gaming rooms, the largest of which has slot machines. There's a good bar above their Aura restaurant here as well that appeals to all ages, and the place is open very late. For bars, **El Bosque,** O'Higgins 524 (✆/fax **45/444025;** closed Mon), is a popular local hangout that is open from 6pm until around 3am, and has Internet access and a good fusion-cuisine menu. **Mamas & Tapas** ★★, O'Higgins 597 (✆/fax **45/449002**), is a bar serving snacks and food; it has long been one of the most popular bars in Pucón. It gets packed in the summer and has excellent music, including DJs during peak season. Also try the rooftop patio at **Entre 3** (✆ **45/442032**), at the corner of O'Higgins and Arauco, where on warm summer nights the people-watching in the street below is as good as it gets.

HOT SPRINGS OUTSIDE PUCON

All the volcanic activity in the region means there's plenty of *baños termales,* or hot springs, that range from rustic rock pools to full-service spas with massage and saunas. Nothing beats a soothing soak after a long day packed with adventure. Also, like the Cañi Reserve, the hot springs make for a good rainy-day excursion. Apart from those listed below, you might consider nearby **Termas de Quimey Co** (31km/19 miles from Pucón; www.termasquimeyco.com), which opened in 2008, and the more rustic **Termas Los Pozones** ★ (Road to Huife, 34km/21 miles from Pucón; no phone), which is open 24 hours and popular with the younger crowd that wants to keep the party going after a night in Pucón's discos.

Termas de Huife ★ **Kids** Termas de Huife, a relaxing escape for the body and mind, is popular with tourists and locals alike for its idyllic thermal baths and setting. Nestled in a narrow valley on the shore of the transparent River Liucura, Huife operates as a full-service health spa for day visitors and guests who opt to spend the night in one of their *cabañas* or suites. This is one of my favorite *termas,* for both its cozy accommodations and gorgeous landscaping, complete with narrow canals that wind through the property and river-rock hot springs flanked by bamboo and palm fronds. The complex features two large outdoor thermal pools kept at 96° to 98°F (36°–37°C) and a cold-water pool, as well as private thermal bathtubs, individual whirlpools, and massage salons arranged around an airy atrium. Recently, a hydrotherapeutic pool was added. The four-person *cabañas* and double suites are housed in shingled, rust-colored buildings along the river, about a 2-minute walk from the main building. All come with wood-burning stoves, and the *cabañas* have a living area. The bathrooms deserve special mention for their Japanese-style sunken showers and bathtubs that run thermal water. The only complaint I have about this place is that it can be busy, and lots of families means lots of kids.

Road to Huife, 33km (20 miles) E of Pucón. ✆/fax **45/441222.** www.termashuife.cl. 10 units. $200–$240 (£133–£160) double. Day-use fee $13 (£8.70) adults, children 10 and under free. AE, DC, MC, V. Thermal baths daily 9am–8pm year-round. Take the road east out of Pucón toward Lago Caburgua until you see a sign for Huife, which turns off at the right onto an unnamed dirt road. Follow the road until you see the well-marked entrance for Termas de Huife. **Amenities:** Restaurant; cafeteria; 3 outdoor pools; exercise room; Jacuzzi; sauna; game room; massage. *In room:* TV, minibar, safe.

Termas de Menetúe In January 2008, Termas de Menetúe opened a dazzling indoor spa complex with two pools, sauna, massage tubs, mud baths, and massage rooms that is now the focus of this resort. The reception area and restaurant look out onto a giant grass-encircled swimming pool, and a short path takes visitors around to a woodsier setting, with one average-size pool serenaded by a gurgling waterfall. It's a relaxing, bucolic place with giant ferns and a gently flowing stream. The pine cabins are for two to six people and sit a bit too far from the complex. They come with a fully stocked kitchen and wood-burning stove. Menetúe rents bicycles and can point out a few trails for walking. A restaurant serves decent Chilean cuisine, and there's a snack bar near the second pool.

Camino Internacional, Km 30. ✆/fax **45/441877.** www.menetue.com. 6 *cabañas.* $170 (£113) *cabaña* for 2; full board. Day-use fee $16 (£11). No credit cards. Thermal baths Dec–Mar 9am–9pm; Apr–Nov 9am–6pm. **Amenities:** Restaurant; bar; 2 large outdoor pools; spa. *In room:* TV, kitchen.

Termas San Luis ★ Located high in the saddle of the Curarrehue Valley, the Termas San Luis is popular for its well-built thermal pools and view of Volcán Villarrica, but mostly for the rare paved access road that gets you there. The compact resort is centered on two swimming pools built with stone tiles, one outdoor and the other covered by a fiberglass shell much like a greenhouse; both are surrounded by plastic lounge chairs for reclining after a long soak. If you'd like to spend the night, San Luis has six wooden cabins perched on a slope overlooking, unfortunately, the parking lot, although a few are hidden behind trees. The cabins sleep four to six guests, meaning one double bed, three singles, and a living-room trundle bed. They are bright and very pleasant but can get very cold in the winter unless the wood-burning stove is continually stocked. The spa house features a tiny sauna and a massage salon at an additional cost. There is a restaurant here as well.

Ruta Internacional Pucón, Km 27. ✆ **45/412880.** www.termasdesanluis.cl. $140 (£93) double with half-board. Day-use fee $13 (£8.70) adults, $8 (£5.30) children. No credit cards. Thermal baths daily 9am–11pm summer; daily 10am–7pm winter. **Amenities:** Restaurant; large outdoor pool and large indoor pool; spa; sauna; limited room service; massage. *In room:* TV, kitchen.

NATURAL ATTRACTIONS OUTSIDE PUCON

Parque Nacional Huerquehue

Smaller than its rivals Conguillío and Villarrica, though no less attractive, Parque Nacional Huerquehue boasts the best short-haul hike in the area, the **Sendero Los Lagos.** This 12,500-hectare (30,875-acre) park opens as a steeply walled amphitheater draped in matted greenery and crowned by a forest of lanky araucaria trees. There are a handful of lakes here; the first you come upon is Lago Tinquilco, which is hemmed in by steep forested slopes. At the shore, you'll find a tiny, ramshackle village with homes built by German colonists in the early 1900s. A few residents offer cheap accommodations, but the best place to spend the night is in a campground near the entrance or at the Refugio Tinquilco (see "Where to Stay," later).

There's a self-guided trail called **Ñirrico** that is a quick 400m (1,312-ft.) walk, but if you're up for a vigorous hike, don't miss the spectacular **Tres Lagos** trail that begins at the northern tip of Lake Tinquilco. The path first passes the **Salto Nido de Aguila** waterfall, then winds through a forest of towering beech, climbing to a lookout point with a beautiful view of Lago Tinquilco and the Villarrica volcano. From here, the trail begins zigzagging up and up through groves of billowy ferns and more tall trees until finally (2–3 hr. later) arriving at the beautiful, araucaria-ringed **Lago Chico,** where you can take a cool dip. A relatively flat trail from here continues on to the nearby **Verde** and **Toro** lakes. Bring plenty of food and water, and come prepared with rain gear if the weather looks dubious.

On your way to or from the park, you can make a detour to the **Ojos de Caburga,** where two aqua-colored waterfalls crash into the tiny Laguna Azul. There are a few picnic tables here, and you can take a dip if the weather's nice. The turn-off point is about 15km (9¼ miles) from Pucón.

GETTING THERE & BASICS The park is 35km (22 miles) from Pucón. Buses JAC has daily service to the park (several times per day, depending on the season), and most tour companies offer minivan transportation and will arrange to pick you up later, should you decide to spend the night. If you're driving your own car, head out of Pucón on O'Higgins toward Lago Caburga, until you see the sign for Huerquehue that branches off to the right. From here it's a rutted dirt road that can be difficult to manage when muddy. Conaf charges $8 (£5.30) for adults and $4 (£2.70) for kids to enter; camping is $20 (£13); it's open daily from 8:30am to 6pm.

WHERE TO STAY Conaf has a campground near Lago Tinquilco and charges $28 (£19) per site, for a maximum of six people. The best option for a roof over your head is the attractive, barn-shaped **Refugio Tinquilco** (✆ **9/539-2728;** www.tinquilco.cl), a spacious lodge with bunks for $14 (£9.30) per person (you'll need your own sleeping bag), and regular rooms with bedding for $40 (£27) double. They also have a good restaurant and offer full pension for an additional $9 (£6).

Parque Nacional Villarrica

This gem of a park is home to three volcanoes: the show-stealer Villarrica, Quetrupillán, and Lanín. It's quite a large park, stretching 61,000 hectares (150,670 acres) to the Argentine border and that country's Parque Nacional Lanín, and is blanketed with a thick virgin forest of araucaria, evergreen, and deciduous beech. A bounty of activities is available year-round, including skiing and climbing to the crater of the volcano (see "Outdoor Activities" under "Pucón," earlier in this chapter), hiking, horseback riding, bird-watching, and more.

The park has three sectors. Most visitors to the park head to **Sector Rucapillán** (the Mapuche's name for Volcán Villarrica, meaning House of the Devil). Volcán Villarrica is one of the most active volcanoes in the world, having erupted 59 times from the 16th century until now. There are two trails here, the 15km (9.25-mile) **Sendero Challupén** that winds through lava fields and araucaria, and the 5km (3-mile) **Sendero El Glaciar Pichilancahue,** which takes visitors through native forest to a glacier. The park ranger booth at the entrance can point out how to get to the trail heads. You'll also find the interesting **Cuevas Volcánicas** in this sector. Ancient, viscous lava that flowed from the volcano created underground tunnels, 400m (1,312 ft.) of which have been strung with lights and fitted with walkways that allow you to tour their dark, dripping interiors. Visitors are provided with a hard hat; the cave's humid, cold air requires that you bring warm clothing, regardless of the season. There are also exhibits describing volcanism and bilingual tours. It's open daily from 10am to 8:30pm during the summer, and from 10am to 6:30pm during the winter; admission is a steep $6 (£4) for adults and $3 (£2) for children (✆ **45/442002**). Camping costs $18 (£12).

The second sector, **Quetrupillán,** is home to wilder, thicker vegetation and a multiple-day backpacking trail that wanders through virgin forest and past the **Termas de Palguín** (which is also accessible by road), a rustic hot springs. Here you'll also find several waterfalls, including the crashing **Salto el León.** There's a horse stable (see "Horseback Riding" under "Pucón," earlier in this chapter) that offers trips around the area. There is also an excellent day hike and the region's best thermal baths here (see the Villarrica loop drive mentioned in section 3). Finally, the third sector, **Puesco,** is accessed by Rte. 119 south of Curarrehue. There's a Conaf (park service) post and several hikes through the park's wildest terrain, including pine forests, lakes, and rugged mountains.

3 SIETE LAGOS: PANGUIPULLI & LICAN RAY

Panguipulli: 54km (33 miles) S of Villarrica; Lican Ray: 31km (19 miles) S of Villarrica

Few daylong sightseeing drives surpass the beauty of the **Siete Lagos (Seven Lakes)** region south of Pucón, where you can follow a half-paved, half-dirt loop around Lago Calafquén, with stops in the picturesque resort towns Panguipulli and Lican Ray. As its name implies, the region is home to seven lakes, one of which is across the border in Argentina, and all are set among rugged, verdant mountains that offer photo opportunities at every turn. Because this area is also home to Chile's best hot springs, Termas Geométricas, it makes sense to make a detour here. This can be done by driving to Coñaripe and heading left toward Parque Nacional Villarrica (follow signs for the park or Pualafquén). For a more adventurous drive, and only if you have a rental car with high clearance (4×4 is necessary during inclement weather), drive the highly recommended loop through the national park from the other direction, as described below.

DRIVING THE SIETE LAGOS ROUTE & THE LOOP THROUGH VILLARRICA NATIONAL PARK

Renting a car is the best option here, but all tour companies can put this excursion together for you. Ideally, these drives are best when the sun is shining, for maximum views; however, visiting the various hot springs and driving through dense forest is also a good way to pass a rainy day.

For the Siete Lagos route, head south from Villarrica toward Lican Ray and then through Coñaripe, circling the lake until reaching Panguipulli. From here, you take the paved road toward Lanco (although signs might say LICAN RAY as well) until you see the sign for Lican Ray and Villarrica. This rough dirt road continues to Villarrica (there's a good lookout point along the way) or forks to the right to Lican Ray, where you can again catch the paved road to Villarrica. Take a good look at the map before making any decisions; note that none of these roads is numbered or has a name. Of course, the trip can be done in the reverse direction, which might be more desirable for an afternoon soak at the hot springs just south of Coñaripe.

It's a little more difficult (read: potholes, slippery mud, and short, steep pitches), but the loop through Villarrica National Park is more desirable for its views of virgin forest of towering evergreen beech and monkey puzzle (araucaria) trees, a good day hike, and a visit to the Termas Geométricas. This route is for high-clearance vehicles (4×4 in wet conditions) and should be undertaken from the north through the south only. Leaving Pucón, head east toward Curarrehue and drive for 20km (12 miles), turning right at the sign for Palguín (30km/19 miles from Pucón). These hot springs have a small hotel and several thermal pools; however, the service here is surly and there are better hot springs in the area. Continue along the road until you reach the ranger station (37km/23 miles from Pucón; $6/£4 per-person entrance fee). There is a full-day hike here, the Los Nevados (16km/10 miles; about 10 hr. round-trip and moderate), but a preferred and shorter hike can be found about midway between the ranger station and Coñaripe, the

A Note on Camping

The road between Lican Ray and Coñaripe is full of campsites, some of which have showers and barbecue pits. Try **Cabañas y Camping Los Arrayanes Del Foresta** (✆ **45/431480** or 9/817-1796; www.arrayanesforesta.cl), 2km (1¼ miles) from Lican Ray, which has well-built sites ($34/£23) and is comfortable for 3 to 12 guests ($31–$96/£21–£64 winter; $58–$230/£39–£153 summer); check the website for exact prices at the time you'll be there.

Pichillancahue trail (6.6km/4 miles; about 4 hr. round-trip). This trail winds through dense virgin forest of the unusual, spindly monkey puzzle trees and has views of the surrounding volcanoes. The road from the ranger station to Coñaripe is about 27km (17 miles), with an obligatory stop at the most beautiful hot springs in the region, Termas Geométricas.

Termas de Coñaripe ★★ **Kids** These *termas* boast a privileged location in a narrow valley hemmed in by lush, steep mountains and Lago Pellaifa. The full-service hot springs complex has lodging and a restaurant, whereas the Termas Geométricas (see later) is more remote and puts you in the middle of more natural surroundings (but with fewer services). Coñaripe is handsomely built, with touches of Japanese design. There are four outdoor pools, one with a slide, and one indoor pool with whirlpool lounges and a waterfall. A babbling creek meanders through the property. The thermal spa's on-site trout fishery is fun for kids, as they can feed the fish. Inside the lobby and the hallways, the floors are made of a mosaic of cypress trunks. Rooms are carpeted and spacious, and suites come with a queen-size bed. If you require quiet, you might not want a room near the busy pool. The *cabañas* come with two rooms with double beds and one with two twins.

Along with all this beauty and the deluxe amenities comes the inevitable crush during the summer months, and it's not unusual for these hot springs to see almost 1,000 visitors per day at peak high season from January 1 to February 15. There are so many people that guests who have booked a few days often leave early, shell-shocked. During this time, there is a self-service cafeteria to alleviate the packed dining room at lunch; a restaurant serves Chilean food year-round. Off-season crowds drop dramatically, and during the winter you might have the place to yourself.

Camino Coñaripe to Liquiñe at Km 15. ✆ **45/431407.** Fax 45/411111. www.termasconaripe.cl. 10 units, 3 *cabañas,* 1 apt. $220 (£147) double standard with full board; $320 (£213) cabin with full board for 4. Day-use fee $14 (£9.30) adults, $8 (£5.30) children for use of outdoor pools, and an additional $4 (£2.70) for indoor pool. DC, MC, V. Thermal baths daily 9am–11pm year-round. **Amenities:** Restaurant; lounge; 4 outdoor pools and an indoor pool; tennis courts; exercise room; bike rental; game room; room service; massage; laundry service. *In room:* TV.

Termas Geométricas ★★★ **Moments** I can't stop raving about these hot springs. If you have the time, try to plan a visit here because they are one of the best in Chile. Designed by famed Chilean architect Germán de Sol (architect of the explora hotels), the hot springs are a delight. More than a dozen pools, made of handsome gray slate tiles, descend an emerald, jungle-draped ravine, each one linked by a winding boardwalk. Each pool has a changing room and bathroom, with creative touches such as grass roofs and stream-fed sink taps, all very minimalist and decidedly Japanese influenced. It is so utterly relaxing here that you could float until your skin wrinkles like a prune. At the end of the gently sloping boardwalk, you will be taken aback by the sight of a tremendous, crashing waterfall that seems almost too perfect—it is such an ideal spot for a hot springs that it is hard to believe the area wasn't capitalized on earlier. There is a small restaurant that serves coffee, cakes, and cheese sandwiches; you might want to bring your own picnic lunch if you want something more filling. The hot springs are open at night, too, lit by tiny candles resting on the top of the pool walls. It's not cheap, but it's money well spent.

12km (7½ miles) from Coñaripe on the road to Palguín. ✆ **2/214-1214** or 9/442-5420. Fax 2/214-1147. www.termasgeometricas.cl. $22 (£15) adults, $12 (£8) children 14 and under. Rate includes towel. No credit cards. Thermal baths daily 10am–10pm summer, 11am–8pm rest of year. **Amenities:** Cafe.

LICAN RAY

This tiny resort town hugs the shore of Lago Calafquén, offering toasty beaches made of black volcanic sand and a forested peninsula for a leisurely drive or stroll. The lake is warmer than others in the region and is, therefore, better suited for swimming; you can also rent a boat here. The name comes from Lican Rayén, a young Mapuche woman from the area who is said to have fallen in love with a Spanish soldier. The town was founded as a trading post, and today there are about 3,000 permanent residents, except for the period from December 15 to February 28, when the population doubles with the arrival of summer vacationers. The first weekend in January is the busiest time of year. There's also the **Noche Lacustre** the second week in February, when the bay fills with boats for a variety of contests and activities, followed by an evening fireworks display. Lican Ray is less crowded and less expensive than Pucón, and during the off-season you'll practically have the place to yourself.

There are a few places to stay here. South German–style **Hotel Becker,** Manquel 105 (✆ **45/431153;** www.hotelbecker-licanray.com), has modest but comfortable rooms, a restaurant, and a deck from which you can enjoy the lakefront view, charging $32 (£21) for a double in the off-season, $60 (£40) for a double in high season (includes breakfast). **Hostería Inaltulafquén,** Cacique Punulef 510 (✆ **45/431115;** fax 45/415813; jdf@universe.com), has good rooms and an even better dining area and deck, and it is ideally located across from the Playa Grande beach; it charges $46 (£31) per double. The *hostería* is run by two helpful Canadians, who also offer excursions. Another recommended hotel is the German run **Hostal Hoffman,** Camino a Coñaripe 100 (✆ **45/431109**), a small B&B with five basic rooms for $28 (£19) for a double (there's also a restaurant; no credit cards accepted). For dining, try the restaurant at the *hostería* or **Ñaños,** General Urrutia 105 (✆ **45/431026**), with an extensive menu that offers everything from barbecue meats to clay oven–baked pizzas, and a daily fixed-price lunch for $4 (£2.70). It also has outdoor seating during the summer but no lake view. For **visitor information,** go to General Urrutia 310 (in front of the plaza). In January and February, the office is open daily 9am to 11pm; during the rest of the year, it's open Monday through Thursday from 9am to 1pm and 3 to 6pm, Friday from 9am to 1pm and 3 to 5pm.

PANGUIPULLI

This little town with the impossible-to-pronounce name (try "Pan-gee-*poo*-yee") is spread across a cove on the shore of its eponymous lake. During the summer, Panguipulli's streets bloom a riot of colorful roses, which the town celebrates in February during the **Semana de las Rosas (Rose Week)** festival. During January and February, the town holds regular folkloric festivals, art exhibits, concerts, and more. Panguipulli was founded as a timber-shipping port and today has nearly 10,000 residents. The town's primary attraction is its charming church of **San Sebastián,** at Diego Portales and Bernardo O'Higgins (in front of the plaza). Mass is held from November to February Thursday and Saturday at 8pm, Sunday and holidays 8:30am and 11am; the church is open all day (no phone). The Swiss priest who initiated the building of this church in 1947 modeled its design after churches from his native country, with two latticed towers painted in creamy beige and red and topped off with black-shingled steeples. For visitor information, go to O'Higgins and Padre Sigisfredo streets in front of the plaza (Jan–Feb daily 9am–9pm; rest of the year Mon–Fri 9am–6pm).

The town is better visited as a day trip, but there is a remote lodge here that is a wonderful place to hole up in the middle of a forest and take part in a variety of outdoor excursions. The lodge is the **Hotel Riñimapu** (✆/fax **63/311388;** www.rinimapu.cl), located 27km (17 miles) south of Panguipulli and on the shore of Lago Riñihue. The Riñimapu draws guests from around the world for its fly-fishing, horseback riding, and hiking—but it is the tranquillity here that encourages guests to really lose themselves in the beauty of the surroundings. The woodsy lodge has 14 simple rooms and three suites, a restaurant, a bar, and a tennis court, and it charges $98 (£65) for a double. To get here, head south out of Panguipulli on the paved-then-dirt road toward Lago Riñihue, and continue for 20km (12 miles) until reaching the hotel; or contact the hotel for information about transfer shuttles from the Temuco or Pucón airports. If you want to stick to the town, try **Hotel & Restaurant Le Francais** (✆ **63/312496;** www.hotelelfrances.cl) at Martínez de Rozas 880, with nine cozy doubles ($70/£47 per night) and a decent French-Chilean restaurant.

HUILO HUILO

At the other, eastern end of Lake Panguipulli, the small Mocho-Choshuenco National Preserve protects the ecosystem of the volcanoes of the same name. A much larger, private preserve, Huilo Huilo stretches south from the narrow lake Pirihueico (the name means "water worm"). The 37m (121-ft.) Huilo Huilo waterfall dropping over a basalt lava deposit and the lower, wider Salto del Puma fall are the park's main features. The Choshuenco Volcano features the only snowboard park open year-round in Chile. Other local activities include horseback riding, zipline canopy riding at lofty, 70m (230 ft.) heights, rafting, and fishing. The private park also seeks to breed the highly endangered huemul, a deer similar to mule deer, and guanacos.

On the road leading to Puerto Fuy near Neltume sit several of Chile's most unique hotels. The aptly named **Montaña Mágica** ★ (✆ **63/197-2651;** www.huilohuilo.cl), or Magic Mountain, looks as if J.R.R. Tolkien himself designed it. A six-sided, cone-shaped little volcano of a stone building, water "erupts" from its summit, cascading down its sides. Each room is named for a different local species of bird and is on a different level as the interior spirals upwards. Each room is also slightly different, but they all have rustic, angular wood-paneled interiors in common. Beds are just a little on the soft side, and if you're tall, you should ask for a room farther down—it's a bit exaggerated to say the showers near the top are perfect for hobbits, but you get the picture. The restaurant has a similar, woodsy theme, featuring wild boar, and the hotel's service is quite good. Room prices range from $100 to $120 (£67–£80). Set 35 meters in the air amid the forest canopy, the bulb shaped **Hotel Baobab** ★ (✆ **63/197-2651;** www.huilohuilo.cl) has a massive oak tree that runs right through its center and a waterfall that runs down its side. The hotel features 55 artfully decorated rooms that run $110 (£73) per double, all inclusive.

This is also one of the more remote spots to cross into Argentina in the Lake District. By taking the ferry that travels the length of Lake Pirihueico in 1½ hours from Puerto Fuy, you'll cross to tiny Puerto Pirihueco, 11km (18 miles) from the border. From there, the resort town of San Martín de los Andes is another 47km (76 miles) alongside Lake Lacar, another narrow lake, lying entirely in the Lanín National Park. It's a good alternative to the more southern Andes lake crossing, considering it's not nearly as overwhelmed by tourists. Note there's no fuel beyond Panguipulli or Lican Ray. You can also reach Puerto Pirihueco via a secondary road through the Huilo Huilo preserve.

4 VALDIVIA ★

839km (520 miles) S of Santiago; 145km (90 miles) SW of Pucón

Valdivia is a university town on the waterfront of a winding delta, and it often receives mixed reviews from visitors. If you are not planning to visit the coast near Santiago and you are in Pucón for several days, consider a quick visit here or an overnight stay. There are regal homes built by German immigrants and a vibrant market on the water's edge, but it is as though every building from every decade from every architectural style were thrown in a bag, shaken up, and randomly scattered about the city—like in every Chilean city except La Serena. To top it off, a massive glass high-rise hotel and casino called the **Del Pacifico,** which looks like something out of Dubai, is being constructed right downtown and should be ready by late 2009; visit www.delpacifico.cl for info.

Valdivia does have more charm than Temuco and Puerto Montt, however, and there are many activities for kids here. The city is energetic, full of life, and very tenacious. Valdivia has suffered attacks, floods, fires, and the disastrous earthquake of 1960 that nearly drowned the city under 3m (9¾ ft.) of water (the strongest earthquake ever recorded). During World War II, Valdivia's German colonists were blacklisted, ruining the economy. So if Valdivia looks a little weary, well, it's understandable. There are tours here to visit the tiny towns and ancient forts at the mouth of the bay that protected the city from seafaring intruders. The market, where fishmongers peddle their catch of the day, and pelicans, cormorants, and fat sea lions wait for scraps, is a delight, and there are several good restaurants, opportunities to boat around the city's delta, and some of the best museums and galleries in Chile here, too.

Valdivia, with about 130,000 residents, is divided by a series of narrow rivers, notably the Río Valdivia and the Río Calle Calle, that wrap around the city's downtown area. These rivers have produced some of the world's top rowing athletes, and many mornings you can see spidery figures plying the glassy water. Across the Río Valdivia is the Isla Teja, a residential area that's home to the Universidad Austral de Chile. It is common to see students pedaling around town.

ESSENTIALS

Getting There

BY PLANE Valdivia's **Aeródromo Pichoy** (ZAL; ✆ **63/272295**), is about 32km (20 miles) northeast of the city. **LANExpress** (✆ **600/526-2000;** www.lan.com) has two daily flights from Santiago, one daily flight to Concepción, two weekly flights to Temuco, and one weekly flight to Puerto Montt. A **taxi** to town costs about $18 (£12), or you can catch a ride on one of **Transfer Valdivia's minibuses** for $6/£4 (✆ **63/225533**).

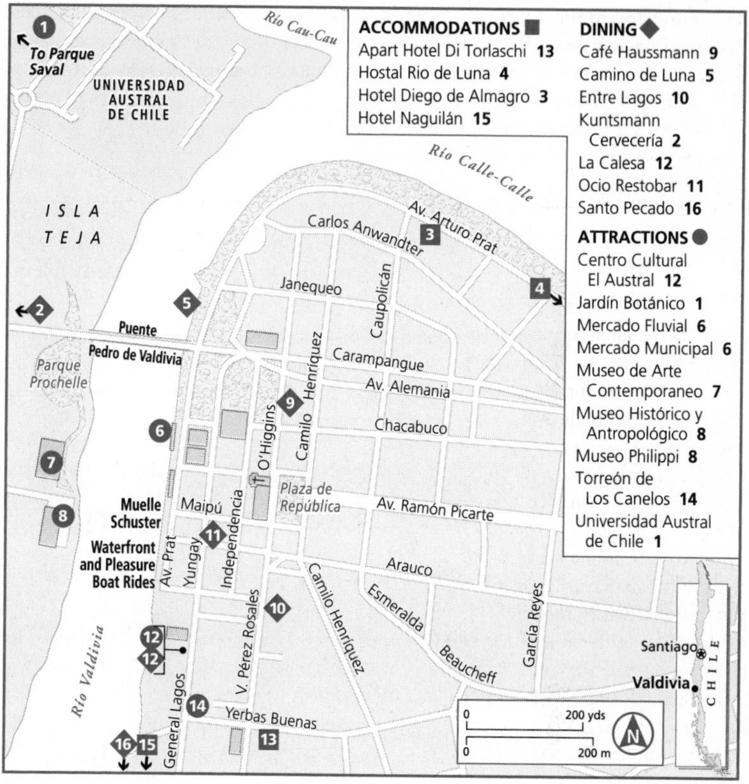

BY BUS The bus terminal is at Anwandter and Muñoz (✆ **63/212212**), and nearly every bus company passes through here; there are multiple daily trips from Pucón and Santiago. The average cost for a ticket from Santiago to Valdivia is $40 (£27); from Pucón to Valdivia, it is $6 (£4).

BY CAR From the Pan-American Highway, take Rte. 205 and follow the signs for Valdivia. A car is not really necessary in Valdivia, as most attractions can be reached by boat, foot, or taxi. It's about a 2-hour drive from Pucón, 1½ hours from Temuco, and 3 hours from Puerto Montt.

Visitor Information

Sernatur's helpful **Oficina de Turismo,** near Muelle Schuster at Arturo Prat 555 (✆ **63/215739**), has a well-stocked supply of brochures. The office hours from March to December are Monday through Thursday 8:30am to 5:30pm, and Friday from 8:30am to 4:30pm. January and February hours are Monday through Friday 8:30am to 7pm, Saturday and Sunday from 10am to 7pm. There's also an information kiosk at the bus terminal open daily from 8am to 9pm, and two websites with information at **www.valdiviachile.cl** and **www.valdivia.cl**.

SPECIAL EVENTS The city hosts a grand yearly event, the **Verano en Valdivia,** with several weeks of festivities that begin in January, culminating with the **Noche Valdiviana** on the third Saturday in February. On this evening, hundreds of floating candles and festively decorated boats fill the Río Valdivia; in the evening, the city puts on a fireworks display. Note that Valdivia is crowded during this time, so hotel reservations are essential. For event info, check out www.munivaldivia.cl.

Fast Facts Valdivia

Car Rental **Assef y Méndez Rent A Car** can be found at General Lagos 1335 (✆/fax **63/213205**), and **Hertz** at Ramón Picarte 640 (✆/fax **63/218316**); both have airport kiosks.

Currency Exchange *Casas de cambio* can be found at **La Reconquista** at Carampangue 325 (✆ **63/213305**), but banks **Banco Santander-Santiago,** Pérez Rosales 585, and **Corpbanca,** Ramón Picarte 370, have ATMs in addition to money exchange. Redbanc ATMs are in grocery stores, gas stations, and all banks throughout the city.

Hospital The Clínica Alemana can be found at Beaucheff 765 (✆ **63/246200**).

Internet Several spots for Internet access are near the plaza; try **Entel,** Vicente Pérez Rosales 601, no. 2.

Laundry Self-service Laundromats are **Lavamatic,** Walter Schmidt 305, no. 6 (✆ **63/211015**), and **Laverap,** Arauco 697, no. 2.

WHAT TO SEE & DO

The best tour is through Elisabeth Lajtonyi at **Outdoors Chile** (✆ **63/253377;** www.outdoors-chile.com). She can arrange your entire trip in Valdivia, from reserving hotels to airport transfers and personalized sightseeing tours.

Boat Trips

A delightful way to explore the Valdivia region is with one of the many boat tours that depart from the pier Muelle Schuster at the waterfront, including yachts, catamarans, and an antique steamer. Tours are in full swing during the summer, and although there's limited service during the off-season, it's possible for a group to hire a launch for a private trip. The most interesting journeys sail through the **Carlos Anwandter Nature Sanctuary** to the **San Luis de Alba de Cruces Fort** and to **Isla Mancera** and **Corral** to visit other 17th-century historic forts; both tours run about 5 to 6 hours round-trip and usually include meals. The Nature Sanctuary was created after the 1960 earthquake sank the banks of the Río Cruces, thereby spawning aquatic flora that, with the surrounding evergreen forest, is now home to more than 80 species of birds, including black-neck swans, red-gartered coots, and buff-necked ibis. Boating here is an excellent attraction for kids.

Embarcaciones Bahía (✆ **63/348727;** sergiosalgado60@yahoo.es) operates throughout the year with quick trips around Isla Teja ($8/£5.30 per person), and tours to Isla Mancera and Corral (see "Niebla, Corral & Isla Mancera," below) can be arranged during the off-season with a negotiated price or when there are enough passengers; children 9 and under ride free. Other trips to Isla Mancera and Corral are offered by **Orión III** (✆/fax **63/247896;** hetours@telsur.cl), which also includes a stop at the Isla Huapi Natural Park (also a convention center; www.islahuapi.cl); the price is $24 (£16) for adults, $18 (£12) for children ages 3 to 12. Prices include the trip, lunch on Isla Huapi, and afternoon tea on board. By far the most luxurious is the **Catamarán Marqués de Mancera** (✆ **63/249191;** www.marquesdemancera.cl), which offers Isla Mancera and Corral tours with lunch and snacks included, and evening dinner cruises (only specially organized for large groups); both cost from $24 (£16) per person.

The ***Vapor Collico,*** a completely restored 1907 German steamer, with tours to the Nature Sanctuary and historical sightseeing journeys along the Río Calle Calle and the Collico area, unfortunately, is currently out of service. Contact Sernatur for further information.

Other Attractions

The bustling **Mercado Fluvial** ★★, at Muelle Schuster (Av. Prat at Maipú), is the principal attraction in Valdivia and is worth a visit for the dozens of fishermen who hawk fresh conger eel, hake, and spindly king crabs in front of colorful fruit and vegetable stands. Take a peek behind the fish stands to view the lanky pelicans and enormous sea lions barking for handouts. Across the street, the **Mercado Municipal** holds few attractions apart from a couple of souvenir shops and decent, inexpensive restaurants. Hours for the various shops here are erratic, but they are generally open Monday through Sunday from 9am to 7:30pm, closing at 9pm in summer, with some restaurants open later.

A block up from the waterfront, turn right on Yungay and head south until the street changes into **General Lagos** at San Carlos. A pleasant stroll for several blocks along General Lagos offers picturesque evidence of German immigration to the area through the stately, historic homes that dot the street. The houses, built between 1840 and 1930, belonged to affluent families, and many have been restored and maintained, despite the various earthquakes and other natural disasters that have beset them since construction.

Take a step back in time at the **Centro Cultural El Austral** ★★, Yungay 733 (✆ **63/213658**), commonly known as the Casa Hoffman for the Thater-Hoffman family, who occupied the home from 1870 until 1980. It's open Tuesday through Sunday from 10am to 1pm and 4 to 6pm; admission is free. The first floor of this handsome building has been furnished to re-create the interior as it would have looked during the 19th century, complete with period antiques, paintings, and a few very garish chandeliers. Upstairs, the center holds temporary art exhibitions and painting, literature, and history classes. At the junction of General Lagos and Yerbas Buenas is the **Torreón de Los Canelos,** a 1781 defensive tower built to protect the southern end of the city—but if you're strapped for time, forget it.

Isla Teja

Isla Teja is a tranquil residential area across the bridge from downtown that is also home to the Universidad Austral de Chile and a splendid history museum, the **Museo Histórico y Antropológico,** Maurice van de Maele ★★ (✆ **63/212872;** www.museos austral.cl). It's open December 15 to March 15 Monday through Sunday from 10am to 8pm, and the rest of the year Tuesday through Sunday from 10am to 1pm and 2 to 6pm; admission is $3 (£2) adults, 75¢ (50p) children 12 and under. To get there, cross the Pedro de Valdivia Bridge, walk up a block, turn left, and continue for half a block. The museum is housed in the grand family home of Carl Anwandter, brewery owner and vociferous supporter and leader of German immigrants. Outside, two 19th-century carriages flank the entrance. Inside is a varied collection of antiques culled from local well-to-do families and notable figures such as Lord Cochrane (the noted admiral who helped secure independence for Chile, Peru, and Bolivia), including furniture (even a double piano), photos, letters, medals, and everyday objects. There are also a few conquest-era artifacts, such as a Spanish helmet, as well as an excellent display of Mapuche Indian silverwork, textiles, and tools. An interesting collection of sepia-toned photos depicts settlers' images of Mapuches.

The similarly themed **Museo Philippi** next door, inaugurated in January 2007 and housed in the transferred Schüler mansion, traces the history of German-born 19th-century explorer Rudolph Philippi and his descendents in unlocking Chile's natural secrets. You can view old watercolors, photographs, and letters, along with period furniture and scientific instruments; the museum is open during the same hours as the historical museum. Admission is $3 (£2).

Also along the waterfront, and occupying the old Kunstmann brewery across the street that was nearly demolished after the 1960 earthquake, is one of Chile's best art museums, the **Museo de Arte Contemporaneo** (✆ **63/221968;** www.macvaldivia.uach.cl), with excellent rotating displays of work by Chilean artists. It's open Tuesday to Sunday from 10am to 1pm and 3 to 6pm; admission $1 (70p).

Leaving the museum, turn right and continue north on Los Laureles until you reach the **Universidad Austral de Chile.** Once inside the campus, the road veers right; follow it and the signs to the **Jardín Botánico ★★**, a lovely botanical garden created in 1957 that features a labeled collection of native trees and vegetation from every region in Chile and around the world. It's open from October 15 to March 15 daily from 9am to 7:30pm, from March 16 to October 14 daily from 9am to 5pm. Cut west through the campus to Calle Los Lingues and turn right until you reach the gated entrance to **Parque Saval ★**, a sizable park with rodeo stands, a children's playground, a picnic area, and a small lagoon. Admission is 50¢ (25p) for adults, 20¢ (10p) for children, and it's open daily. From October to March, expositions, an arts-and-crafts fair, and agricultural demonstrations take place here.

Niebla, Corral & Isla Mancera

These three villages at the mouth of the bay were largely destroyed after the 1960 earthquake (on record as the strongest earthquake ever recorded). There's little left from that era, but what did survive were the relics of the 17th-century forts that once protected Valdivia from intruders, and a visit to these ancient relics, and the coastal views, makes for a very pleasant half-day trip—especially on a sunny day. If you are not planning to visit the coast near Santiago, do so here; there's enough to do and see to keep you occupied for at least a half-day, and Chile's only microbrewery is on the way back to town. Niebla lies 18km (11 miles) from Valdivia and is home to the **Castillo de la Pura y Limpia Concepción de Monfort de Lemus** (✆ **63/282084**), a defensive fort founded in 1671 and renovated in 1767. It's open November through March daily from 10am to 7pm, and April through October from 10am to 5:30pm; it's closed Monday. Admission is $1 (70p), and 50¢ (35p) for kids and seniors. The fort is carved partially out of rock and features details such as cannons and a powder room, as well as a small museum. The town itself is mostly a hodgepodge of seafood restaurants and tiny houses with the most privileged views anywhere in Chile. There's one great boutique hotel set right inside the curve in the center of town, **El Castillo** (✆ **63/282061;** www.hoteldelcastillo.com), with views of the water. Doubles run $82 (£55), including continental breakfast. To get there, take a private taxi for about $7 (£4.70), or grab a *colectivo* taxi (or *micro* bus) for $1 (70p) at the waterfront. In the summer, it is possible to take a tour boat to Niebla; in the off-season, you'll need to take the road. The trip takes about 15 minutes.

Across the bay sits **Corral** and the area's first and most powerful fort, the **Castillo San Sebastián de la Cruz** (✆ **63/471828**), built in 1645 and reinforced in 1764. It's open from November through March daily 9am to 6pm and April through October from Tuesday to Sunday 10am to 5:30pm; admission is $1.25 (85p). The city itself is a picturesque jumble of brightly painted wooden homes and fishing boats, an old German colony that never really recovered from the tidal wave that wiped out most of the town. To get to Corral, take a tour boat from Valdivia during high season, or take a ferry from the fishing dock just before entering Niebla (let your bus or taxi driver know you're getting off there). The mock soldier battle that once was the highlight of this attraction has been put on hold due to overenthusiastic actors mishandling gunpowder and shooting themselves in the foot; it remains to be seen if the ritual will continue anytime soon.

Either on the way to Corral or on the way back, ask to be dropped off at idyllic **Isla Mancera** (and ask to be picked up again!) for an easy stroll and a visit to the fort **Castillo de San Pedro de Alcántara** (✆ **63/212872**). Admission is $1 (70p), and it's open from November 15 to March 15 daily from 10am to 6pm, and Tuesday through Sunday from 10am to 5pm the rest of the year. It was built in 1645 and restored in 1680 and again in 1762 to house the Military Government of Valdivia. Inside the grounds are the crumbling ruins of the San Francisco Convent and an underground supply room. It is possible to walk the circumference of the island in 20 to 30 minutes, and there is a site for picnics with great views.

WHERE TO STAY

Expensive

Hotel Diego de Almagro ★ Opened in mid 2008 by a Chilean chain of the same name, the Diego de Almagro is in an attractive setting right where the river bends, giving ample water views from most rooms. Lost is the classic German feel, though this is the most modern of Valdivia's hotels by a mile and caters mostly to visiting execs. All rooms are spacious—about 30 square meters (322 sq. ft.)—and feature 25-inch LCD TVs that offset a rather run-of-the-mill contemporary decor.

Prat 433, Valdivia. ✆ **63/224744.** Fax 63/267000. www.dahoteles.com. 105 units. $149 (£99) double; includes breakfast buffet. AE, DC, MC, V. **Amenities:** Restaurant; bar; pool; sauna; gym; business center; room service; laundry service; Wi-Fi; parking. *In room:* TV, minifridge, safe.

Hotel Naguilán ★ (Moments) Although it sits about a 20-minute walk from the edge of downtown, the Hotel Naguilán boasts a pretty riverfront location and solid, attractive accommodations. The hotel is housed in an interesting structure (ca. 1890) that once held a shipbuilding business. All rooms face the Río Valdivia and the evening sunset; from here it's possible to watch waterfowl and colorful tugs and fishing skiffs motor by. Newer "Terrace" units sit directly on the riverbank and feature contemporary floral design in rich colors, classic furniture, ample bathrooms, and a terrace patio. The older wing is more economical and features a few dated items, such as 1960s lime-green carpeting, but the entire hotel is impeccably clean.

The staff offers professional and attentive service, and the hotel has a private dock from which guests board excursion boats. The Naguilán's restaurant, serving international cuisine, is one of the most attractive features of the property, with the river passing just outside the window.

General Lagos 1927, Valdivia. ✆ **63/212851.** Fax 63/219130. www.hotelnaguilan.com. 32 units. $94 (£63) standard double; $109 (£73) superior double. AE, DC, MC, V. **Amenities:** Restaurant; bar; pool; game room; concierge; room service; laundry service. *In room:* TV, minibar.

Moderate

Apart Hotel Di Torlaschi (Kids) (Value) These fully equipped *cabañas* feature charming exteriors; pleasant, well-lit kitchens; and a decent location on a residential street near downtown. They're also quiet due to the grammar schools at the front and side that empty at the end of the day. The friendly owners and staff strive to make guests feel at home here, and offer a wealth of tourism information. The 16 wood *cabañas* are situated around a courtyard walkway planted with climbing ivy. Guests park just outside their door, and there is a security gate that shuts during the evening. Each *cabaña* is identical, with two bedrooms upstairs (one comes with a double bed and the other with two twins) and a sofa that unfolds into a bed downstairs, with a maximum of six guests allowed. Kitchens come with a full-size fridge and microwave. These *cabañas* are popular with European visitors.

Yerbas Buenas 283, Valdivia. ✆ **63/224103.** Fax 63/224003. www.aparthotelitaliano.cl. 16 *cabañas.* $63 (£42) double. AE, DC, MC, V. **Amenities:** Tour desk; laundry service. *In room:* TV, kitchen.

Inexpensive

Hostal Rio de Luna ★ Amid several newer upscale hotels on the river and within walking distance from the bus station is this well-run inn that has been around for a few decades, but kept spotlessly clean and freshly painted. Rooms are utilitarian and lack polish, but are well put together with bluish grey floors, sky blue walls, and blue bedspreads. Room 11 on the top floor has the best views. While you eat your ham, cheese, toast and jam, and piece of pie for breakfast, you can watch the occasional row team advance by; it's a great way to start your day.

Prat 695, Valdivia. ✆ **63/253333.** www.hostalriodeluna.cl. 11 units. $42 (£28) double. Rates include breakfast. AE, DC, MC, V. **Amenities:** Restaurant; bar; Wi-Fi. *In room:* Fan, TV, CD player.

WHERE TO DINE

For an inexpensive meal, try the **Municipal Market** near the waterfront at Yungay and Libertad, where you'll find several basic restaurants with fresh seafood and Chilean specialties. Microbreweries have sprung up on the fringe of town to refresh the German brewing tradition; among them are **Calle Calle,** on Llanquahue s/n, 3km (2 miles) on the route to Osorno (✆ **63/226925**); and **J. Bello,** 8km (5 miles) on the route to Niebla (✆ **63/246751**). The most famous is Kunstmann (see review later).

Café Haussmann ★★ (Moments) CAFE The Haussmann is known for its *crudos* (steak tartare and raw onion spread on thin bread), which it has served since opening its doors in 1959. This tiny, old-fashioned cafe has just four booths and a counter, and is frequently packed with downtown workers. There are no frills, but there are good sandwiches, local color, and their own brand of beer, as well as Kuntzmann, on tap. It's *the* place for getting a feel for Valdivia's local flavor.

O'Higgins 394. ✆ **63/202219.** Sandwiches $3–$6 (£2–£4). MC, V. Mon–Sat 8am–9pm (summer until midnight).

Camino de Luna SEAFOOD The Camino de Luna serves excellent seafood and other dishes aboard a floating restaurant moored at the waterfront. The menu includes delicious fare such as seafood crepes, abalone stew, and *congrio* steamed in wine, bacon, asparagus, and herbs, as well as Greek and chef salads and a long list of terrific appetizers. Inside, the well-appointed, candlelit tables are much nicer than the pea-green facade and red Coca-Cola neon outside would indicate. The restaurant does sway when vessels speed by, but not much.

Costanera at Arturo Prat. ✆ **63/213788.** Main courses $8–$12 (£5.30–£8). AE, DC, MC, V. Daily 12:30–11pm.

Entre Lagos ★ Value CAFE Entre Lagos is one of the best-known shops in the region for its mouthwatering chocolates and colorful marzipan, and its neighboring cafe is equally good. Nothing on the menu is short of delicious, from the juicy sandwiches and french fries down to the heavenly cakes and frothy cappuccinos. The restaurant serves a dozen varieties of crepes, such as ham and cheese, and abalone and shrimp in a creamy crab sauce. Entre Lagos is a great spot for lunch or to relax for an afternoon *once* or coffee. It also offers a set menu for $6 (£4) that includes a main dish, dessert, and coffee.

Pérez Rosales 640. ✆ **63/212039.** www.entrelagos.cl. Main courses $8–$16 (£5.30–£11). AE, DC, MC, V. Mon–Sat 9am–10pm; Sun 10am–10pm.

Kunstmann Cervecería ★★ GERMAN/PUB FARE This is a nice place to stop on the way back from Niebla (see "Niebla, Corral & Isla Mancera," earlier); it's a 10-minute drive from town. The popular Kunstmann brewery serves four varieties of beer on tap (they'll let you sample before ordering) in a newer, microbrew-styled restaurant with wooden tables and soft, yellow light. The hearty fare includes appetizer platters of grilled meats and sausages, German-influenced dishes such as smoked pork loin with cabbage, and sandwiches, salads, and spaetzle. Kunstmann also has a small on-site brewery museum.

950 Rte. T-350. ✆/fax **63/292969.** www.lacerveceria.cl. Main courses $5–$10 (£3.30–£6.70). DC, MC, V. Daily noon–midnight.

La Calesa ★ Finds PERUVIAN Owned and operated by a Peruvian family, the cozy La Calesa features spicy cuisine served in the old Casa Kaheni, a gorgeous 19th-century home with high ceilings, wood floors, and antique furnishings. The menu features Peruvian fare along with several international dishes. Standouts include grilled beef tenderloin and sea bass in a cilantro sauce; *ají de gallina,* a spicy chicken and pepper sauce spread over rice; and any of the nightly specials. The pisco sours are very good, as is the wine selection. There's also a great wooden bar lit by giant windows looking out onto a garden and the river.

Yungay 735. ✆ **63/225467.** Reservations recommended for dinner. Main courses $8–$12 (£5.30–£8). AE, DC, MC, V. Mon–Fri noon–4pm and 8pm–midnight; Sat 8pm–midnight.

Santo Pecado ★★★ Value INTERNATIONAL This hipster-heavy lounge and restaurant, with colorful walls adorned with pop art, is my favorite restaurant in Valdivia for its eclectic menu. Standard bistro dishes, such as steak frites, are excellently prepared, and they don't shy away from more creative dishes such as a *Tortilla Iberíca* (a Spanish style omelet), crepes, chicken curry, and a mousse of pisco sour. *Tablas,* plates for sharing, pair well with a bottle of wine from their lengthy list.

Yungay 745. ✆ **63/239122.** www.santopecado.cl. Reservations recommended for dinner. Main courses $8–$12 (£5.30–£8). AE, DC, MC, V. Mon–Sat noon–4pm and 8pm–midnight.

Ocio Restobar ★ Finds FUSION Plank wood floors and exposed pipes give an industrial feel to this stylish restobar and lounge, an "it" spot for several years that gets packed on weekend nights. The food is lighter than other restaurants in town and ranges from maki rolls to empanadas. Most of the menu items make for perfect snacking food to go with drinks. Video installations and a DJ spinning rock and house music will keep you entertained.

Arauco 102. ✆ **63/239122.** www.ociorestobar.cl. Reservations recommended for dinner. Main courses $8–$12 (£5.30–£8). AE, DC, MC, V. Tues–Thurs 7pm–midnight; Fri–Sat 8pm–2am.

5 PUYEHUE ★

Termas de Puyehue: 73km (45 miles) E of Osorno, 95km (59 miles) W of Antillanca, 93km (58 miles) W of the Argentine border

This region is home to the long-standing **Termas de Puyehue** spa, the **Antillanca** ski and summer resort at the base of the Casablanca Volcano, and one of Chile's underrated national parks, **Puyehue.** It is a remarkably beautiful area, with thick groves of junglelike forest, emerald lakes, picture-perfect volcano backdrops, waterfalls, and roads narrowed by overgrown, enormous ferns. You won't find a tourist-oriented town here, such as Pucón or Puerto Varas, but there are several good lodging options in the area. You'll also find a fair number of outdoor activities, scenic drives, and one of the best lookout points in Chile, which can reached by car during the summer.

The Puyehue area is best suited as a diversion for travelers on their way to Argentina. I strongly recommend this journey; it is one of my favorite excursions in Chile, and visitors can even complete a "loop" through the lake districts of Argentina and Chile by booking a one-way ticket to Bariloche via the popular "lake crossing" (see "Parque Nacional Vicente Pérez Rosales & the Lake Crossing to Argentina," later in this chapter) and later returning to Chile via bus (or tour) to Puyehue, passing first through Villa la Angostura at the Argentina-Chile border and crossing at the international pass Cardenal Antonio Samoré, or vice versa. The scenery is just breathtaking.

The road from Osorno to Puyehue is rather flat and banal, but the scenery viewed when crossing from Villa Angostura to Puyehue is stunning. Note that during the winter, chains might be required when crossing the border. The city of Osorno is considered by Chileans as one of the least attractive cities in Chile, so consider it a transportation hub only.

GETTING THERE

BY PLANE **LAN Airlines** (✆ **600/526-2000;** www.lan.com) serves Osorno's **Aeródromo Cañal Bajo** (ZOS; ✆ **64/247555**), with two daily flights from Santiago; one flight stops first in Temuco. Osorno is a 1-hour drive from Puyehue. LAN has more frequent flights from Santiago to Puerto Montt, a 2-hour drive from Puyehue.

BY BUS Bus service from Osorno is provided by **Buses Puyehue,** with almost hourly trips to and from Puyehue, departing from the Terminal de Buses Rurales at Errázuriz 1300 (✆ **64/201237**). From Bariloche, Argentina, **Andes Mar** and **Río de la Plata** buses head to Osorno and stop along the highway near Puyehue or directly at the Hotel Termas de Puyehue. If you're trying to get to Puyehue from Puerto Montt, you'll need to transfer at Osorno. From Santiago, the buses run by **Tas Choapa** (to Bariloche) depart

Monday, Wednesday, and Friday, heading for Bariloche; they'll drop you off in Puyehue. From Puerto Varas, an excellent bilingual service, the Cruce TransAndino, offered by **LS Travel,** San José 130 (✆ **65/232424;** www.lstravel.com), takes visitors to Bariloche, leaving at 9:30am, stopping for a swim at the Termas Puyehue, passing through Villa la Angostura and on to Bariloche. The tour agency has an office in Bariloche at Mitre 83 (✆ **02944/434111**). The cost is $130 (£87) per person, with a minimum two guests (cheaper prices can be had for groups), and includes entrance fees and lunch.

BY CAR Termas de Puyehue is about 75km (47 miles) east from Osorno via Rte. 215. The border with Argentina, Control Fronterizo Cardenal Antonio Samoré, is open daily November through March from 8am to 9pm, and April through October from 8am to 7pm. The road is a bit curvy, and there are some potholes on the Chilean side, so drive slowly.

EXPLORING PUYEHUE NATIONAL PARK

Puyehue National Park (www.parquepuyehue.cl) is one of Chile's best-organized national parks, offering a variety of trails to suit all levels, well-placed park information centers, lodging, camping, restaurants, and hot springs. The 107,000-hectare (264,290-acre) park sits between the Caulle mountain range and the Puyehue Volcano, and is divided into three sectors: **Anticura, Aguas Calientes,** and **Antillanca.** Visitors head east toward Argentina to access Anticura, where they'll encounter a park ranger information station just before the border, as well as trail heads for day hikes and the 16km (10-mile) backpacker's trail up and around the Puyehue Volcano. There's also a self-guided, short hike to the Salto del Indio waterfall, where you'll see 800-year-old evergreen beech trees, known locally as *coigüe.*

To get to Antillanca, visitors pass first through the Aguas Calientes sector, where there are hot springs, 28 rustic cabins (five beds in each; all with kitchenettes) a restaurant, campgrounds, and a park information center (✆ **64/331710** or 64/331711). The most popular excursion in this region is the ascent to a spectacular lookout point atop the Raihuén crater, reached by foot or vehicle about 4km (2½ miles) past the Antillanca hotel and ski resort. This *mirador* can be reached only during temperate months (or during ski season via the center's ski lift) and is not worthwhile on a heavily overcast day. The view stretches into Argentina. The park ranger information stations are open daily from 9am to 1pm and 2 to 6pm, or you can contact Conaf for info (✆ **64/197-4573**). They sell an information packet about the region's flora and fauna, and issue fishing licenses. For information about day visits to the hot springs at Termas de Puyehue or Aguas Calientes, see "Where to Stay & Dine," later. To get here, you need to catch a bus in Osorno or book a tour with an operator out of Temuco, Puerto Montt, or Puerto Varas.

Other Attractions

Along the road to Puyehue, at about Km 25 on Rte. 215, just before the ramshackle town of Entre Lagos, is Chile's first car museum, the well-designed **Auto Museum Moncopulli** (✆ **64/210744;** www.moncopulli.cl). Admission is $4 (£2.70) adults, $2 (£1.30) students, and $1 (70p) kids; it's open from December through March 10am to 8pm, April through November 10am to 6pm. Owner Bernardo Eggers has assembled a collection of 42 Studebakers from the years 1928 to 1964, plus other vehicles, such as a 1928 Model A fire engine.

Aguas Calientes Turismo y Cabañas These A-frame cabins are a cheaper alternative to Termas de Puyehue and are owned by the same company. There's a hot spring/spa facility here, included in the price of the *cabañas,* and it can be used for the day for a fee. The *cabañas* sleep four to eight guests and are simple affairs with fully stocked, plain but decent kitchenettes (and *parrillas* for barbecues on the balcony). The drawback here is that the beds are really crammed into small spaces. Ask for a cabin with two floors; those come with separate living/eating areas. All cabins come with decks and a barbecue. There are also two nicely developed campgrounds here called Chanleufú and Los Derrumbes, with barbecue pits, free firewood, and a thermal spa. Los Derrumbes costs $20 (£13) for four campers, $4 (£2.70) each per extra camper; Chanleufú is $28 (£19) for four campers, $5 (£3.30) each extra camper.

The hot springs facility features indoor and outdoor pools (the outdoor pool is far nicer); there is also a picnic area. Day-use fees are $14 (£9.30) for adults and $7 (£4.70) for kids for the indoor pool; for the outdoor pool, they're $18 (£12) for adults, $11 (£7.30) for kids. A private herbal bath costs $15 (£10). Massages are $36 (£24) an hour.

Camino a Antillanca, Km 4. ✆/fax **64/236988** or 64/331700. www.termasaguascalientes.cl. 26 *cabañas.* $132 (£88) cabin for 2; $148 (£99) cabin for 4. AE, DC, MC, V. **Amenities:** Large outdoor pool and indoor pool; Jacuzzi; massage. *In room:* TV, kitchen.

Antillanca Hotel and Tourism Center ★ Rooms at the Antillanca Hotel are nothing to write home about, but the lovely surroundings at the resort make this one of Chile's gems—if you can hit it on a good weather day. The hotel could really stand to renovate its rooms, especially considering the price. Couples would do well to view the options, as the only room that comes with a double bed also comes with two twins and is considered a quadruple. The rooms are fairly spacious, but many are nothing more than dormitory style, with four bunks to a room and early 1980s furniture. If you're looking for something cheaper, you might consider the *refugio,* the slightly shabby, older wing of the hotel, popular with students and young adults for its rooms costing about a third less. The split-level lobby/restaurant/bar/lounge area is a delight, however—it's cozy and with character derived from pillars made of tree trunks that still have branches and a giant fireplace. There's also a deck for sunbathing and complimentary use of mountain bikes for registered guests.

Ski Resort: Lift tickets cost $34 (£23) adults ($29/£19 half-day), $28 (£19) students. Ski and snowboard equipment rental is available and sold in packages that include a lift ticket starting at $59 (£39) adults and $46 (£31) students. If you're not skiing but want to ride a chairlift to the top, the cost is $6 (£4).

Road to Antillanca, at about 12km (7½ miles) past Ñilque, or (in Osorno) O'Higgins 1073. ✆/fax **64/235114.** www.skiantillanca.com. 73 units. $41 (£27) double *refugio;* $67 (£45) double hotel. AE, DC, MC, V. **Amenities:** Restaurant; bar; lounge; exercise room; sauna; game room; room service; laundry service.

Termas Puyehue Wellnes & Spa Resort ★ Kids The large property features a view of Lake Puyehue and two attractively designed, enormous thermal pools, as well as massage rooms, mud baths, herbal baths, saunas, game rooms, and more. Though it was built between 1939 and 1942, the hotel has undergone substantial renovations and the addition of 55 roomy suites. Standard double rooms are disappointing, which is surprising for a hotel that esteems itself so highly. Perhaps the best lodging unit is their converted home on the shore of the lake.

This resort is a good option for skiers at Antillanca, or as a stop on the way to Argentina for a soak and lunch, because a night here as a "destination" is an overrated experience. The staff has no concept of customer service, and problems with plumbing have annoyed guests. But the activities and excursions offered, including horseback riding, trekking, mountain biking, windsurfing, fishing, tennis, and farm tours through organic gardens (all for an extra cost) might make a stay worthwhile. The spa facilities (which you can use even if you don't stay here) are more upscale than those at Aguas Calientes.

The costs charged to day visitors are $15 (£10) adults and $10 (£6.70) kids for the indoor pool, $10 (£6.70) adults and $6 (£4) kids for the outdoor pool. The indoor pool is open daily 8am to 9pm in summer, 8am to 8pm during the rest of the year; the spa is open 9am to 8pm year-round. Herbal, mud, sulfur, and marine salt baths cost $20 to $40 (£13–£27); reflexology and herbal therapy cost $10 to $40 (£6.70–£27).

Rte. 215, Km 76. ✆ **2/293-6000.** Fax 2/283-1010 or 64/23281 in Osorno. www.puyehue.cl. 137 units. $200 (£133) double with view of the forest; $230 (£153) double with view of the volcano. Rates are per person and include buffet breakfast. AE, DC, MC, V. **Amenities:** 3 restaurants; bar; lounge; large outdoor pool and large indoor pool; tennis courts; gym; spa; Jacuzzi; sauna; limited watersports equipment rental; bikes; game room; free Internet access; shopping arcade; gift shop; room service; massage; laundry service; dry cleaning. *In room:* TV, minibar.

6 AROUND LAGO LLANQUIHUE

Lago Llanquihue is the second-largest lake in Chile, a body of clear, shimmering water whose beauty is surpassed only by the 2,652m (8,699-ft.), perfectly conical, snowcapped Volcán Osorno (Orsono Volcano) that rises from its shore. The peaks of Calbuco, Tronador, and Puntiagudo add rugged beauty to the panorama, as do the rolling, lush hills that peek out from forested thickets along the perimeter of the lake. The jewel of this area is without a doubt the 231,000-hectare (570,570-acre) Vicente Pérez Rosales National Park, the oldest park in Chile and home to Volcán Osorno and the strangely hued emerald waters of Lago Todos los Santos.

This splendid countryside and the picturesque, German-influenced architecture of the homes and villages that ring Lago Llanquihue draw thousands of foreign visitors each year. Many adventure-seekers come to take part in the vast array of outdoor sports and excursions to be had here, including fly-fishing, rafting, volcano ascents, trekking, and just sightseeing. Puerto Varas is similar to Pucón, in that it offers a solid tourism infrastructure, with quality lodging and restaurants, nightlife, and several reliable outfitters and tour operators. I urge visitors to lodge in Puerto Varas, Frutillar, or Ensenada instead of Puerto Montt, as these three towns are far more attractive and closer to natural attractions than Puerto Montt. Puerto Octay, about 46km (29 miles) from Puerto Montt, is the most remote lodging option, a sublime little village with one lovely lodge on the shore of the lake.

FRUTILLAR & PUERTO OCTAY ★

58km (36 miles) S of Osorno; 46km (29 miles) N of Puerto Montt

Frutillar and Puerto Octay offer a rich example of the lovely architecture popular with German immigrants to the Lago Llanquihue area, and both boast dynamite views of the Osorno and Calbuco volcanoes. The towns are smaller than Puerto Varas and less touristy. For a soft adventure, the towns make an excellent day trip, and the coastal dirt road that connects the two is especially beautiful, with clapboard homes dotting the green

A Health Warning

Every January, this region is beset by horrid biting flies called *tábanos.* Avoid wearing dark clothing and any shiny object, which seem to attract them; they are also more prevalent on sunny days.

countryside—bring your camera. Apart from all this scenic beauty, there are a few museums documenting German immigration in the area.

Frutillar was founded in 1856 as an embarkation point with four piers. Later, the introduction of the railway created a spin-off town that sits high and back from the coast, effectively splitting the town in two: Frutillar Alto and Bajo, meaning "high" and "low," respectively. You'll drive straight through the ugly Alto section, a ratty collection of wooden homes and shops.

Puerto Octay was founded in the second half of the 19th century by German immigrants; folks in the region know it for its well-stocked general goods store—the only one in the region—run by Cristino Ochs. In fact, the name *Octay* comes from "donde Ochs hay," roughly translated as "you'll find it where Ochs is." Today there are only about 3,000 residents in this quaint little village, which can be reached by renting a car or with a tour (or bus if staying here). Two helpful websites are **www.frutillar.cl** and **www.puerto octay.cl**.

Essentials

GETTING THERE See the information under the "Puerto Varas" section, later.

VISITOR INFORMATION The **Oficina de Información Turística** is located along the coast at Costanera Philippi (✆ **65/421080**); it's open January through March daily from 8:30am to 1pm and 2 to 9pm. The **Oficina de Turismo Municipal** is open year-round and can be found at Av. Bernardo Philippi 753 (daily 8am–1pm and 2–5:30pm; ✆ **65/ 421685**).

What to See & Do

Excursions to **Parque Nacional Vicente Pérez Rosales** from Frutillar can be arranged by your hotel with a company such as **Alsur Expediciones** or **Aquamotion** out of Puerto Varas (see "Outdoor Activities" under "Puerto Varas," later). In Frutillar, spend an afternoon strolling the streets and enjoying the town's striking architecture. The town really gets hopping during the last week of January and first of February when it hosts, for 10 days, the **Semanas Musicales,** when hundreds of Chilean and foreign musicians come to participate in various classical music concerts. Call the administration in Osorno (✆ **65/ 421290**); tickets are never hard to come by. The hulking building that juts out on a pier onto the lake in Fruttilar southeast of the center, the **Teatro del Lago** (✆ **65/339-2293**), will be finished in 2010, though it's partly open and is already one of Chile's premier classical-music venues. Performances are held throughout the year. Check the website www.teatrodellago.cl for listings.

The two most-visited attractions in town are the **Museo de la Colonización Alemana de Frutillar** and the **Reserva Forestal Edmundo Winkler.** The museum (✆ **65/421142**) is located where Arturo Prat dead-ends at Avenida Vicente Pérez Rosales. Admission is $3 (£2) adults, $1 (70p) for kids 12 and under; it's open from April to November daily from 10am to 1pm and 2 to 6pm, and from December to March daily from 10am to 1pm and 2 to 8pm. It features a collection of 19th-century antiques, clothing, and artifacts gathered from various immigrant German families around the area.

The *reserva* (✆ **65/421291**) is run by the University of Chile and features a trail winding through native forest, giving visitors an idea of what the region looked like before immigrants went timber crazy and started chopping down trees. It's open year-round from 10am to 7pm; admission costs $2 (£1.30) for adults and $1 (70p) for kids. To get there, you'll have to walk a kilometer (a half-mile) up to the park from the entrance at Calle Caupolicán at the northern end of Avenida Philippi. You might also consider paying a visit to the town **cemetery,** which affords a panoramic view of the lake. To get there, continue farther north up Avenida Phillipi.

Where to Stay

Hotel Ayacara ★★ Finds The Ayacara is a top choice in Frutillar, housed in a superbly renovated 1910 antique home on the coast of Lago Llanquihue. The interior of the hotel is made of light wood, and this, coupled with large, plentiful windows, translates into bright accommodations. The rooms come with comfy beds, crisp linens, wood headboards, country furnishings, and antiques brought from Santiago and Chiloé. The Capitán room is the largest and has the best view. An attractive dining area serves dinner during the summer, and there's a small, ground-level outdoor deck and a TV/video lounge. The staff can arrange excursions around the area; fly-fishing excursions are their specialty.

Av. Philippi 1215, Frutillar. ✆/fax **65/421550.** www.hotelayacara.cl. 8 units. $100–$125 (£67–£83) double; $120–$140 (£80–£93) Capitán double. Rates include breakfast. AE, DC, MC, V. **Amenities:** Restaurant; bar; tour desk; Wi-Fi; laundry service. *In room*: TV.

Hotel & Cabañas Centinela ★★ Moments At the tip of a peninsula, at the end of a lush tree-lined dirt road, 10 minutes from town and right on the lake, you'll find this hidden gem with its own private beach. Originally built in 1914 as a bordello, it has long since been turned into a homey lodge with 12 rooms and 18 *cabañas.* Rooms in the main building are quaint, with thick beige berber carpets, down comforters, and antique furnishings. The restaurant serves excellent Chilean cuisine cooked by a well-known chef, Juan Pablo Moscoso; there's a daily fixed-price three-course meal for $14 (£9.30) for lunch and dinner. This place exudes charm, not luxury; there's no spa, but there's a rustic wood-fired hot tub. Six of the *cabañas* sit right on the water's edge; request nos. 21 to 26 when making your reservations, and you'll have the best views. The 12 A-frame *cabañas* that sit back from the water are pleasant for families and come with kitchenettes; all the *cabañas* have rather small bathrooms. The hotel's friendly staff can arrange for fishing trips, including fly-fishing expeditions; they can also arrange for free transfers from the airport.

Península de Centinela, Km 5, Puerto Octay. ✆/fax **64/391326.** www.hotelcentinela.cl. 30 units $129–$155 (£86–£103) double; from $119–$143 (£79–£95) *cabaña* for 4 people; $165 (£110) *cabaña* for 6 people. Rates include full breakfast. AE, DC, MC, V. **Amenities:** Restaurant; lounge; Jacuzzi; limited watersports equipment rental; free airport transfers. *In room:* Fridge (in *cabañas* only).

Hotel Elun ★★ This azure-colored hotel is a good bet for anyone seeking modern accommodations, a room with a view, and a quiet, forested location. The hotel, opened in 1999, is made almost entirely of light, polished wood and was designed to take full advantage of the views. The lounge, bar, and lobby sit under a slanted roof that ends with picture windows; there's also a deck, should you decide to lounge outside. Double standard rooms are decently sized and feature berber carpets and spick-and-span white bathrooms. The superiors are very large and come with a comfy easy chair and a table and chairs. Room no. 24 looks out over Frutillar. The hotel is attended by its owners, who will arrange excursions. A restaurant serves dinner during the summer, and breakfast can be ordered in your room.

200m (656 ft.) from start of Camino Punta Larga, at the southern end of Costanera Phillipi, Frutillar. ✆/fax **65/420055.** www.hotelelun.cl. 14 units. $100 (£67) double. Rates include breakfast. DC, MC, V. **Amenities:** Restaurant (summer only); lounge; bikes; tour desk; Internet access; room service; laundry service. *In room:* TV.

Hotel Klein Salzburg ★ Kids The Hotel Klein Salzburg is housed in a large wooden home built in 1911 and painted a spruce blue and white. It sits on the lakefront, but only one room has a view—the VIP room, larger than the rest and with a small balcony. The hotel has a lot of antique charm, complete with creaky wooden floors, but the decoration is as sugary sweet as the delicious cakes and tortes it serves in its tearoom: flowered wallpaper, duck motifs, and pink trim, all a tad cutesy, but not too overbearing. There are two small rooms for kids.

Av. Philippi 663, Frutillar. ✆ **65/421589.** Fax 65/421599. 8 units. $65–$72 (£43–£48) double; $80 (£53) suite. Rates include German breakfast. AE, DC, MC, V. **Amenities:** Restaurant; bar; laundry. *In room:* TV.

Hotel Residenz am See Value This pleasant wooden hotel is a steal in the low season when you factor in the lakefront view and its clean, comfortable accommodations. Run by an elderly German couple, the Residenz has rooms that range in size, and a few of the doubles are large enough to fit an extra twin bed. The rooms that look out onto the lake are slightly more expensive than those facing the back, but the rooms in the back receive glorious afternoon sun. The owners have a shop selling arts and crafts, and have decorated the place with woven wall hangings that are for sale. Downstairs there's a tea salon where guests are served German breakfast; in the afternoon, folks drop by for tea and homemade *küchen,* bread, pâté, and marmalade. They also arrange excursions.

Av. Philippi 539, Frutillar. ✆ **65/421539.** Fax 65/421858. www.hotelamsee.c. 6 units. $86 (£57) double; $140 (£93) suite. Rates include German breakfast. AE, DC, MC, V. **Amenities:** Restaurant. *In room:* TV.

Hotel Villa San Francisco ★ The Villa San Francisco sits high on a cliff and features a layout similar to the Hotel Elun (see earlier), with rooms that all face the lake, some with a view of the volcano. All of the rooms are identical, decorated with simple but attractive furnishings that include comfortable beds and wicker headboards. Some guests might find the rooms a little on the small side, but most come with a terrace and four have corner windows. The owners of this hotel have invested a great deal in gardens that surround the property. There's also a great barbecue area that sits on a grassy perch looking straight out toward the volcano, as does a pleasant glass-enclosed dining area. The staff will arrange excursions around the area for guests.

Av. Philippi 1503, Frutillar. ✆/fax **65/421531.** iberchile@telsur.cl. 15 units. $84 (£56) double. AE, MC, V. **Amenities:** Restaurant; bar. *In room:* TV.

Where to Dine

Club Alemán GERMAN/CHILEAN Nearly every city in the Lake District has a Club Alemán, and Frutillar is no exception. You'll find a few German dishes here, such as pork chops with sauerkraut, but the menu leans heavily toward traditional Chilean fare. Periodically, game specials such as duck and goose are on the menu, and there are set lunch menus for $6 (£4) on weekdays and $12 (£8) on Sunday that include a choice of fish or meat. The atmosphere here is congenial, and the service is very good.

Philippi 47. ✆ **65/421249.** Main courses $5–$10 (£3.30–£6.70). AE, DC, MC, V. Daily noon–4pm and 8pm–midnight.

El Ciervo CHILEAN This newer restaurant specializes in smoked meats and game, and lives up to its name (which means "deer" in Spanish) by offering a tasty grilled venison in pepper sauce. There are other delights, such as smoked pork chops Kassler with mashed potatoes and sauerkraut, filet mignon in a mushroom sauce, and pork leg pressure-cooked to tenderness and served with applesauce. Mounted deer antlers don't do much to add to the cold atmosphere. It's a good spot for lunch, as it serves lighter fare such as sandwiches. The specialties here include venison bourguignon and hazelnut venison, with potatoes, red cabbage, and apples.

San Martín 64. ✆ **65/420185.** Main courses $8–$15 (£5.30–£10). No credit cards. Mar–Nov noon–6pm; Dec–Feb 11am–midnight.

Guten Appetit GERMAN Beside the church, this rustic and popular eatery on the lakefront is not as touristy as some of the others nearby with similar menus. It's a good choice for reliable *onces* with *küchen* or strudel, as well as grilled trout and simple lunch plates. This restaurant also serves up a few German dishes and on some weekend nights hosts live music.

Balmaceda 98. ✆ **65/421145.** Main courses $4–$12 (£2–£6). AE, MC, V. Daily noon–4pm and 8pm–midnight.

PUERTO VARAS ★★

20km (12 miles) N of Puerto Montt; 996km (618 miles) S of Santiago

Puerto Varas is one of Chile's most charming villages, located on the shore of Lago Llanquihue. Like Pucón, it is an adventure travel hub, and it is also the gateway to the **Parque Nacional Vicente Pérez Rosales** (see "Parque Nacional Vicente Pérez Rosales & the Lake Crossing to Argentina," later in this section). Unlike its neighbor Puerto Montt, 20 minutes away, it is a spruce little town, with wood-shingled homes, a rose-encircled plaza, a handsomely designed casino, and an excellent tourism infrastructure that provides all the necessary services for visitors without seeming touristy. It can get crowded during the summer months, but not as busy as Pucón, seemingly because of its distance from Santiago. The city was built by the sweat and tenacity of German immigrants, and later it became a port for goods being shipped from the Lago Llanquihue area to Puerto Montt (mostly timber). Today most of the area's middle- and upper-middle-class residents call Puerto Varas home and commute to Puerto Montt and other surrounding places for work.

Essentials

Getting There

BY PLANE **El Tepual** airport (PMC; ✆ **65/294161**) is almost equidistant from Puerto Montt and Puerto Varas; it's about 25km (16 miles) from the airport to Puerto Varas. A taxi from the airport costs between $15 and $22 (£10–£15), or you can arrange a transfer with **ETM,** by either calling ahead or approaching their booth at the airport (✆ **32/294294**). They charge $20 (£13) for a car for a maximum of three people. Because there are fewer flights here, there normally are a few people waiting for a transfer, so the price can drop if there are others. **LANExpress** serves the El Tepual airport with nine daily flights from Santiago. **Sky Airline** (© **600/600-2828;** www.skyairline.cl) also has three daily flights to El Tepual airport. Ask your hotel about a transfer shuttle, as many include one in their price.

BY BUS The following buses offer service to and from major cities in southern Chile, including Santiago: **Buses Cruz del Sur,** San Francisco 1317 and Walker Martínez 239 (© **65/236969** or 65/231925); and **Buses Tas Choapa,** Walker Martínez 320 (© **65/233831**). Buses **Tas Choapa** and the Argentine company **Andesmar,** Walker Martinez 320 (© **65/233831;** www.andesmar.com.ar), have service to Bariloche, Argentina (Tas Choapa Thurs–Sun; Andesmar on Mon, Wed, and Fri). **Bus Norte,** Walker Martínez 239, has daily service to Bariloche (© **65/236969**).

BY CAR Puerto Varas is just 20km (12 miles) north of Puerto Montt and 88km (55 miles) south of Osorno via the Panamericana. There are two exits leading to Puerto Varas, and both deposit you downtown. To get to Frutillar, you need to get back on the Panamericana, go north, and take the exit for that town. There is about a $1.25 (85p) toll to enter the off-ramp, and another toll for about $2 (£1.30) to enter Puerto Montt.

Getting Around

BY BUS **Buses Cruz del Sur** offers transportation to Chiloé and nearly 20 daily trips to Puerto Montt, leaving from an office in Puerto Varas, at Walker Martínez 239 (© **65/236969** or 65/231925). There are also cheap minibuses that leave frequently from the corner of Del Salvador and San Pedro across from the pet shop, leaving you at the bus terminal in Puerto Montt. You'll also find minibuses at San Bernardo and Walker Martínez that go to Ensenada, Petrohué, and Lago Todos los Santos every day at 9:15, 11am, 2, and 4pm. **Andina del Sud,** Del Salvador 72 (© **65/232811;** fax 65/232511; www.andinadelsud.com), has daily trips to this area as well.

BY CAR Renting a car is perhaps the most enjoyable way (but also the most expensive) to see the surrounding area. In town, try **Adriazola Turismo Expediciones,** Santa Rosa 340 (© **65/233477;** www.adriazolaflyfishing.cl); **Hunter Rent a Car,** San José 130 (© **9/920-6888;** www.lstravel.com); or **Travel Sur** at San José 261 (© **65/236000;** www.travelsur.com), though prices are lower at the airport.

Visitor Information

The **Casa del Turista** tourism office can be found at the pier on the shore (© **65/237956;** www.puertovaras.org) and is open daily from December to March from 9am to 10pm, and the rest of the year daily from 9am to 1:30pm and 3 to 7pm.

Travel Sur exchanges dollars at its office on San José 261 (© **65/236000**).

What to See & Do

Puerto Varas is compact enough to explore by foot, which is the best way to view the wooden colonial homes built by German immigrants from 1910 until the 1940s. Eight of these homes have been declared national monuments, yet there are at least a dozen more constructed during the period of expansion that began with the installation of the railroad connecting Puerto Varas with Puerto Montt.

Walk up San Francisco from Del Salvador until you reach María Brunn, where you turn right to view the stately **Iglesia del Sagrado Corazón de Jesús,** built between 1915 and 1918. The neo-Romantic design of the church, made entirely of oak, was modeled after the Marienkirche in the Black Forest. Continue along María Brunn and turn right on Purísima, where you'll encounter the first group of colonial homes. The first is **Gasthof Haus** (1930), now run as a hotel; then **Casa Yunge** (1932), just past San Luis on the

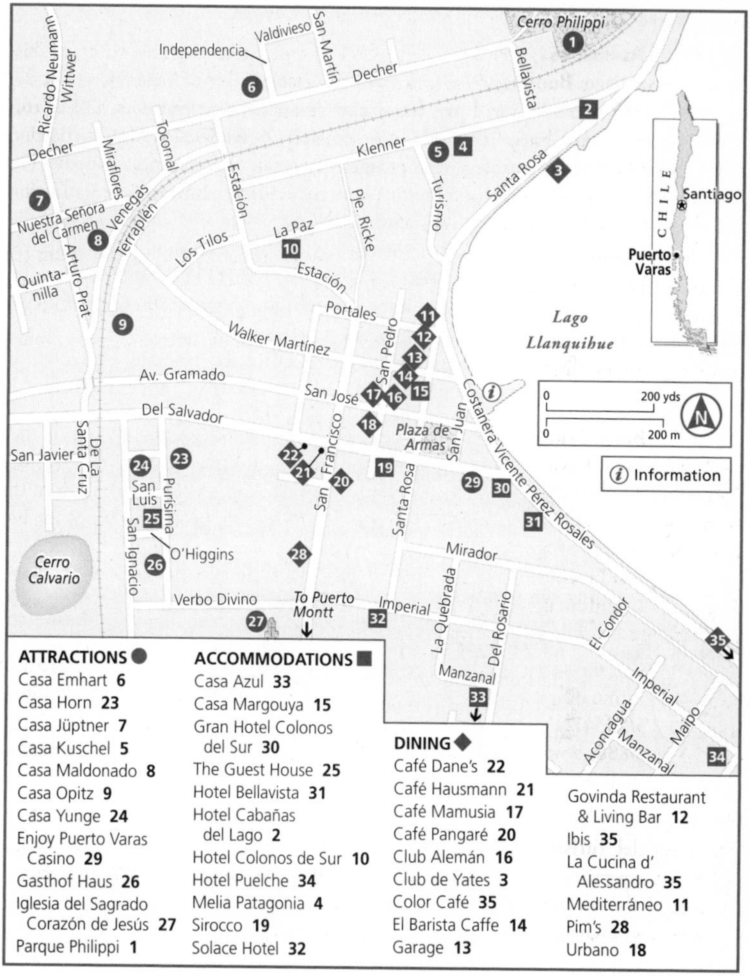

left; and on the right, **Casa Horn** (1925), where you turn left. If you'd like to see more, walk to Calle Dr. Giesseler and turn right, following the train tracks for several blocks, passing the **Casa Opitz** on the right (1913, and now a hotel) until you see **Casa Maldonado** (1915) on the left.

Turn left on Nuestra Señora del Carmen to view the five homes left and right, including the **Casa Jüptner** (1910). Double back and continue along Dr. Giesseler, turn left on Estación, and then right on Decher, passing the **Casa Emhart** (1920) and several other homes on the left. Continue through the forested road that winds up the hill to reach **Parque Philippi** (home to the giant cross, which is lit up at night and can be seen from downtown Puerto Varas), where you'll find an excellent lookout point. Double back, and turn left on Bellavista, right on Klenner, and left on Turismo; at the corner sits the eclectic **Casa Kuschel** (1910), with its Bavarian baroque tower. At the end of Turismo is the Avenida Costanera; turn right and stroll down the boardwalk.

Outdoor Activities

Tour companies and outfitters have changed ownership over the past few years, but, thankfully, many have matured and I can now recommend several with a clear conscience. **Aquamotion Expediciones,** San Pedro 422 (✆ **65/232747;** fax 65/235938; www.aquamotion.cl), is a professional, competent operation with a bilingual staff that can organize trekking, rafting the Petrohué, horseback riding, canyoneering, journeys to Chiloé, and much more. They also custom-plan excursions and offer packages that include accommodations; and they are better than their competition, CTS, across the street. **Tranco Expediciones,** San Pedro 422 (✆/fax **65/311311**), and Aquamotion Expediciones both offer ascents of Volcano Osorno, for about $180 (£120) for two, which includes gear, lunch, and transportation.

For city tours and sightseeing tours around the Lake District, including trips to Frutillar, Puyehue, and Chiloé, try **Andina del Sud,** Del Salvador 72 (✆ **65/232811;** fax 65/232511; www.andinadelsud.com). Andina del Sud is the company that provides boat excursions on Lago Todos los Santos and the Chilean leg of the lake crossing to Argentina (for information, see "Parque Nacional Vicente Pérez Rosales & the Lake Crossing to Argentina," later in this section).

For sightseeing trips to Bariloche via road, contact **LS Travel,** San José 130, Puerto Varas (✆ **65/232424;** www.lstravel.com).

BOATING During the summer, it is possible to rent kayaks and canoes at the pier, located near the main plaza. For a sailing cruise around Lago Llanquihue, try **Motovelero Capitán Haase** (✆ **65/235120;** fax 65/235166; www.teambuilding.cl). The amicable owner and captain offers one daily cruise aboard his "antique" yacht (built in 1998 to resemble a turn-of-the-20th-century boat) using antique designs. You can't miss it moored in the bay. "Sunset with the Captain," from 6:30 to 9:30pm, is a quiet, romantic trip using sails and no motor; the cost is $20 (£13) per person, which includes an open bar. Inquire about charters if you have a large group.

FISHING This region is very popular for fly-fishing, principally along the shores of Río Puelo, Río Maullín, and Río Petrohué—but there's fish in the lake, too. The best and most exclusive fishing expeditions are offered to guests at the Yan Kee Way Lodge (p. 299). There's also **Gray's Fly-Fishing Supplies,** which has two shops, at San José 192 and San Francisco 447 (✆ **65/310734;** www.grayfly.com). Gray's is a central hub for information, gear, and fishing licenses, and they can arrange day trips for river and lake fishing. Another good option for day trips is **Adriazola Fly Fishing,** Santa Rosa 340 (✆ **65/233477;** www.adriazolaflyfishing.com). The owner, Adrian, will custom-arrange any fly-fishing and trolling day tour with a bilingual guide. Both outfitters charge around $140 (£93) for a half-day and $300 (£200) for a full day (for two guests, including transportation, boat, lunch, wine, and fishing guides).

The exclusive, full-service **Río Puelo Lodge** (✆ **2/229-8533** in Santiago; fax 2/201-8042; www.riopuelolodge.cl) caters to fly-fishermen and hunters, but also offers horseback riding, boat rides, water-skiing, and more. The stately wood-and-stone lodge is tucked well into the backcountry on the shore of Lago Tagua Tagua, and it caters mainly to groups of guys who come to have fun in the backcountry. Packages average around

$350 (£233) per person per day, including meals, an open bar, guide, boats, horseback riding, trekking, and use of a heated pool. Ask about discounts for groups.

HORSEBACK RIDING **Campo Aventura,** San Bernardo 318, Puerto Varas (✆/fax **65/232910;** www.campo-aventura.com), offers horseback riding year-round, leaving from their well-designed camp in Valle Cochamó, south of the national park. Both day and multiday trips can be planned with the outfitters, with lodging in rustic shelters they have set up along the trail. Gear and bilingual guides are provided, and multiday trips are all-inclusive. Other tour companies, such as **Aquamotion** (✆ **65/232747;** www.aquamotion.cl), offer day horseback-riding trips in Vicente Pérez Rosales National Park, among other areas. Horseback riding through a forested area is a good option for a rainy day—just throw on a waterproof jacket and pants, and let the horse walk through the mud for you.

KAYAKING **Ko'Kayak,** a small outfit run by French kayak enthusiasts, is the best choice for kayaking both for the day and for multiday kayak/camping trips. They have a base in Ensenada at Km 40, but make a reservation at their main office at Casilla 898 (✆ **65/511648** or 9/310-5672; www.kokayak.com).

RAFTING Few rivers in the world provide rafters with such stunning scenery as the Río Petrohué, with frothy green waters that begin at Lago Todos los Santos and end at the Reloncaví Estuary. Rafters are treated to towering views of the volcanoes Osorno and Puntiagudo. The river is Class III and suitable for nearly everyone, but there are a few rapids to negotiate with sudden bursts of heavy paddling, so timid travelers might consult with their tour agency before signing up. For rafting, go to **AlSur Expediciones,** Del Salvador 100 (✆ **65/232300;** www.alsurexpeditions.com).

Shopping

There is an **arts and crafts fair** on the Del Salvador street side of the plaza. For high-end arts, clothing, and jewelry, head to **Primitiva,** Santa Rosa 302, or **Vicki Johnson,** Santa Rosa 318. The little wagons at the shore in front of the pier offer arts and crafts, but hours are erratic and most are open during the summer only.

Where to Stay

You'll find hotels and hostels in the town center area. Along the coast (both the Puerto Chico coast and all the way to Ensenada), it's mostly *cabañas,* cabins for two to eight people with living spaces and kitchenettes. The following are the best hotels available in the area, plus a couple of *cabañas* along the coast for those who want quiet accommodations in more bucolic settings. Ask where the *cabaña* is located on the complex when booking because many are filed in a row from the shore, meaning only the first two *cabañas* have a view. Also, some *cabañas* consider a fold-out couch bedding for two.

Expensive

Gran Hotel Colonos del Sur & Hotel Colonos de Sur ★★ Boasting a waterfront location next door to the casino and charming German colonial architecture, the Gran Colonos del Sur used to be a standard favorite among travelers to Puerto Varas, but has been edged out by the competition in recent years. A total reconstruction of Gran Hotel Colonos del Sur—involving many of the top designers in the country—is expected to make it one of the city's top hotels again by the project's end, in late 2009. Until then, you'll have to stay at the sister hotel, Hotel Colonos de Sur, which is less centrally located but has better panoramic views, cheery interiors, and an outdoor pool, along with lower prices. You can't miss the Hotel Colonos: It's a red-and-white building perched high on the hills just above downtown, with the giant sign HOTEL affixed to the roof. The corner rooms offer the best views, so try to get one of those.

Gran Hotel: Del Salvador 24, Puerto Varas. ✆ **65/233369** or for reservations 65/233039. Fax 65/233394. www.colonosdelsur.cl. Hotel Colonos de Sur: Estación 505. ✆ **65/235555.** www.colonosdelsur.cl. $120 (£80) double. AE, DC, MC, V. **Amenities:** Restaurant; bar; outdoor pool; Internet access and Wi-Fi; laundry service. *In room:* Cable TV, Internet access, minibar, fridge, hair dryer, safe.

Hotel Cabañas del Lago ★★ Kids Recent renovations and sweeping views of Puerto Varas and Volcán Osorno make Hotel Cabañas del Lago the highest-quality lodging available in town. The lakeview and park suites are luxuriously appointed and colossal in size; one could get lost in the bathroom alone. A junior suite is a slightly larger double and might be worth booking for the larger windows and better decorations. Doubles are not overly spacious and have cramped bathrooms, but curtains and bedding have been updated. Doubles with a lake view are the same price as rooms that overlook the *cabañas.*

The hotel takes advantage of its location, with lots of glass in its attractive lounge and restaurant, which, like all the rooms, sports a country decor. The common areas have the feel of a mountain lodge, complete with deer-antler chandeliers. There's also a large sun deck. The small two- to five-person *cabañas* are not as pleasant as the hotel rooms but are a bargain for a family of four, if you're willing to be a bit cramped. The excellent **El Mirador** serves wild game and other daily specials from an extensive menu. The hotel is a 2-block walk up from town.

Klenner 195, Puerto Varas. ✆ **65/232291.** Fax 65/232707. www.cabanasdellago.cl. 130 units, 13 *cabañas.* $138 (£92) double; $209 (£139) junior suite; $98 (£65) *cabañas* for up to 4 people. *Cabaña* rates do not include buffet breakfast. AE, DC, MC, V. **Amenities:** Restaurant; bar; lounge; indoor heated pool; sauna; game room; room service; babysitting; laundry service. *In room:* Cable TV, hair dryer, safe.

Hotel Puelche ★ Puerto Varas's first real boutique hotel has the look and feel of an upscale mountain lodge, albeit a smaller one. It lacks its own character, but does a decent job of imitating pricier accommodations with lots of space, quality bedding and bath accessories, big windows, and modern-day decor that isn't too over the top. Rooms vary considerably as a few have lake views, porches, and/or skylights. Puelche is in a quiet area on a hill southeast of the center, a longer walk than most, so having a car helps.

Imperial 695, Puerto Varas. ✆ **65/233600.** www.hotelpuelche.com. 21 units. $155 (£103) double standard; $175 (£117) double superior. AE, DC, MC, V. **Amenities:** Restaurant; bar; spa, parking. *In room:* TV, minifridge, hair dryer, safe.

Melia Patagonia Kids Spanish chain Melia's first foray into Chile opened in late 2007. It isn't technically located in Patagonia, so don't let the name fool you. It is set above the city of Puerto Varas, with premium views—in some of the rooms at least—of Lake Llanquihue and the Osorno Volcano. The decor throughout is tasteful and little touches, such as furs and Neruda's poetry adorning the walls, add to the mystique. Rooms are spacious, have personal Wi-Fi routers, and every amenity you could ask for, though many look out onto the parking lot. Service leaves something to be desired. You can occasionally find deals at the hotel when booking online that are 10% to 25% less than those listed.

Klenner 349. ✆ **65/201000.** Fax 65/201001. www.solmelia.com. 91 units. $214 (£143) double. AE, DC, MC, V. **Amenities:** Restaurant; bar; pool; gym; spa w/sauna; kids club; tour desk; Wi-Fi; laundry. *In room:* TV, Internet access, minibar, hair dryer, safe.

Moderate

The Guest House ★★ Finds Owned and operated by Vicki Johnson, an American who owns the crafts and foods store downtown (see "Shopping," earlier), this bed-and-breakfast is a more intimate hotel, located in a quiet residential area about a 4-block walk from the plaza. The hotel is housed in a 1926 renovated mansion, and, like most bed-and-breakfasts, the lodging experience here is a little like staying in one of your friends' homes, with a comfy living area decorated with art that has been collected, not store bought, and a collection of reading material; a dining area with one long, family-style table; and a big kitchen where you are given the opportunity to help out with the cooking, if you so wish. What's also special about the location of this B&B is that nearly all the homes that surround it are the lovely shingled style popular at the time of this home's inception. The rooms have high ceilings, comfortable beds, and a simple, clean decor.

O'Higgins 608, Puerto Varas. ✆ **65/231521.** Fax 65/232240. www.vicki-johnson.com/guesthouse. 10 units. $80 (£53) double standard. Rates include continental breakfast. AE, MC, V. **Amenities:** Room service; laundry.

Hotel Bellavista ★★ Value Another waterfront hotel with gorgeous views, the Bellavista recently renovated all of its guest rooms, giving it the edge on its competitors, Colonos and Cabañas del Lago (it used to be in competition with the Hotel Licarayen). The hardwood floors here aren't as cozy as the carpeted rooms found in other hotels; however, the fresh linens and handsome earth-toned decor are quite sophisticated, and their restaurant and bar is an inviting place to while away an hour with a coffee and admire the view of the volcano. There is also a cozy fireside lounge. There are four larger guest rooms that face a forested cliff for those seeking quieter accommodations, and, best of all, the duplex apartments for five to six people are the best in town: duplexes with two-storied, panoramic windows—good deals for a group of friends or families with kids. The Bellavista's restaurant has a good range of international dishes.

Av. Vicente Pérez Rosales 60, Puerto Varas. ✆ **65/232011.** Fax 65/232013. www.hotelbellavista.cl. 50 units. $125 (£83) double; from $184 (£123) suite. Rates include buffet breakfast. AE, DC, MC, V. **Amenities:** Restaurant; bar; lounge; sauna; laundry service. *In room:* TV, minibar, hair dryer, safe.

Sirocco ★★ This striking blue wood panel building hidden away down a small street is a nice midpoint between the massive resorts and the smaller *residenciales* that dominate downtown. Rooms and bathrooms are immaculately clean and cared for. The wood floors gleam and the paneled walls are painted in fresh earthy tones. While much of the furniture and photos follow a contemporary vein, the original architecture of the house is not lost. There's a fine restaurant serving Patagonian cuisine on the lobby level.

San Pedro 537, Puerto Varas. ✆ **65/232372.** www.sirocco.cl. 10 units. $82 (£55) double. Rates include breakfast. AE, DC, MC, V. **Amenities:** Restaurant; bar; Wi-Fi.

Solace Hotel ★ Value The Solace opened in May 2008 just 5 minutes from the center and has the feel, at least on the inside, of a smaller version of the Melia with a friendlier staff and better service. Most of the rooms get decent views of the lake, and you'll find the same level of high-tech amenities as the Melia, plus the same cozy beds and a similar decor, but for a third less of the price. Like most of the new constructions in Puerto Varas, this one lacks personality, however.

Imperial 211, Puerto Varas. ✆ **65/364100.** www.solacehotel.cl. 62 units. $110 (£73) double. Rates include buffet breakfast. AE, DC, MC, V. **Amenities:** Restaurant; bar; business center; Wi-Fi. *In room:* TV, minibar, hair dryer, safe.

Inexpensive

Casa Azul This German-Chilean budget/backpacker's hostel in a large, blue-and-red shingled house sits in a large garden a 10-minute walk from the center and 5 minutes to the lakefront. Rooms are entirely in wood from floor to walls to ceiling, featuring comfortable, modern beds—you get a bit of a contemporary farmhouse feeling here. Casa Azul has a four-bed dorm, singles and doubles with shared bathrooms, and doubles with private bathrooms. Its buffet breakfast is an additional $5 (£3.30). Reservations aren't guaranteed for stays of less than 2 nights.

Manzanal 66 and Rosario, Puerto Varas. ✆ **65/232904.** www.casaazul.net. 9 units. $40 (£27) double with shared bathroom; $32 (£21) double with private bathroom; $9 (£6) per person in dormitory. No credit cards. **Amenities:** Kitchen; laundry service; Internet access; Wi-Fi. *In room:* No phone.

Casa Margouya This hostel is in a well-situated area on Santa Rosa, close to everything and across the park from the beach. It's on the second floor, and there's a central living area with large tables and couches, and a kitchen that is open for guest use. It's a comfortable place and the service is friendly. There are five rooms, two of which have one double bed; the rest are shared accommodations that range in price according to the number of beds in the room. Bathrooms are clean but communal. This is a good place to meet other travelers. Breakfast is not included.

Santa Rosa 318, Puerto Varas. ✆ **65/237640.** www.margouya.com. 5 units. $33 (£22) double; $17 (£11) per person for shared rooms. No credit cards. **Amenities:** Kitchen. *In room:* No phone.

Where to Dine

Puerto Varas has many good to excellent restaurants, but the service in this area tends to be slow, so have patience. In addition to the restaurants below, there is **Pim's,** San Francisco 712 (✆ **65/233998**), a country-western–style pub with burgers, sandwiches, and such American-style appetizers as buffalo wings and salads. It is popular with locals, and the nighttime ambience is very lively. If you didn't get the chance to visit the landmark **Café Haussmann** in Valdivia (p. 280), you can try their famous crudos at their branch at San Francisco 644. Cutesy coffeehouses have also sprung up all over town, including the excellent **El Barista Caffe** (✆ **65/233130**), at Martínez 211, and **Café Pangaré** (✆ **65/231012**), at San Francisco 735.

Two good spots for a drink at night are the **Barómetro,** San Pedro 418 (✆ **65/236371**), with a rough-hewn wood bar and tree-trunk tables, a cozy atmosphere, and snacks; and the **Garage** (no phone; located on San José next to the Copec gas station), a two-story place with wood tables and electronic music that is popular with 20- and 30-somethings. **Urbano** (✆ **65/233081**), at San Pedro 516, is a trendier pub with grub and is occasionally home to DJs and acoustic music.

Café Dane's ★ Value CHILEAN/CAFE It's often hard to get a table during the lunch hour in this extremely popular restaurant. Dane's serves inexpensive, hearty food in good-size portions, plus mouthwatering desserts. The interior is simple and unassuming, and much of the food is standard Chilean fare, all of it good or very good. The fried empanadas, especially shellfish, deserve special mention. Dane's serves a daily set menu for $6 (£4) Monday through Saturday and $9 (£6) on Sunday, as well as a special dish, or *plato del día,* for $3.50 (£2.30). It's less busy before 1pm or after 3pm. You can also buy food to go from the front counter.

Del Salvador 441. ✆ **65/232371.** Main courses $4.50–$9 (£3–£6); sandwiches $3–$6.50 (£2–£4.30). No credit cards. Daily 7:45am–1am.

Café Mamusia (Value) CHILEAN/BAKERY The Mamusia is locally renowned for its delicious chocolates and pastries. The atmosphere is somewhat like a tearoom or ice-cream parlor, but there are delicious sandwiches, served on homemade bread, and full meals throughout the day as well, including typical Chilean favorites such as *pastel de choclo* and *escalopas,* as well as lasagna, pizza, and grilled meats and fish. Café Mamusia is also a good place for breakfast and serves a continental version for $5 (£3.30).

San José 316. ✆ **65/233343.** Main courses $6–$8 (£4–£5.30); sandwiches $5.50 (£3.70). MC, V. Summer daily 8:30am–2am; winter Mon–Fri 9am–10:30pm, Sat–Sun 10am–11pm.

Club Alemán GERMAN/CHILEAN This Club Alemán seems to offer more German specialties than its fellow clubs, with goose, duck, and bratwurst served with onions, potatoes, and applesauce; pork chops with caramelized onions and sauerkraut; goulash with spaetzle; steak tartare; and other dishes, in addition to Chilean favorites. Sandwiches are much cheaper than main dishes ($3–$6/£2–£4) and are substantial. There are also appetizing desserts, such as crepes *diplomático,* with bananas, ice cream, and chocolate sauce.

San José 415. ✆ **65/338291.** Main courses $8–$13 (£5.30–£8.70). DC, MC, V. Daily 11am–midnight.

Club de Yates Like its counterpart in Puerto Montt, this restaurant sits over the water on stilts, affording excellent views of Osorno Volcano and giving the sensation of being on a ship. The food here is better than at the Puerto Montt branch, although there are superior restaurants in town in terms of food quality. Club de Yates specializes in seafood, and the lengthy menu offers just about every kind of fish or shellfish cooked every way: grilled, sautéed, or fried, with sauces and your choice of a side dish. There are also good appetizers, such as Parmesan razor clams and, occasionally, *locos,* or abalone, and they serve enough meat dishes to satisfy those who aren't in the mood for seafood. The dining area is semiformal, with high ceilings and an airy atmosphere, but it is pleasurable and doesn't feel cold. Club de Yates often holds special events and large-scale lunches for cruise travelers who've docked in Puerto Montt, so they sometimes close to the public. This is a good restaurant if you are lodging downtown and do not feel like going very far.

Santa Rosa 161. ✆ **65/232000.** www.clubdeyates.cl/puertovaras.asp. Main courses $8–$16 (£5.30–£11). AE, DC, MC, V. Daily noon–4pm and 8pm–midnight.

Color Café ★ INTERNATIONAL The Color Café calls itself a wine restaurant, for it has more than 100 top wines on offer, plus a diverse menu. Clean, crisp interiors offset by contemporary oil paintings, a long bar, and a blazing, wood-burning stove set the ambience here. It's a bit of a walk from the town center (about 15–20 min.). The periodically changing menu features good bistro-style cuisine, including Caesar salads, soups, quiches, pastas, and main courses such as venison in a berry sauce and salmon *tataki.* This is a good place for a cocktail and an appetizer of regional smoked salmon.

Los Colonos 1005. ✆ **65/234311.** Main courses $8–$14 (£5.30–£9.30). AE, DC, MC, V. Dec–Mar daily noon–2am; Apr–Nov daily 8pm–midnight.

Govinda Restaurant & Living Bar ★★★ INTERNATIONAL The opening of this whimsical yet refined restaurant just off the lake has helped fill the shoes of the departed Merlin. The service is excellent and the atmosphere is delightful, with such funny touches as painted vines on the walls, handmade gnomes clinging to various lamps, and lots of cacti and potted plants. Some dishes, such as rolled chicken with *aji amarillo* (yellow chile) and *lomo saltado* (a beef stir-fry over french fries and rice), have a

Peruvian slant, and others, such as the lamb risotto or *merluzza* (white fish), have a more eclectic feel. Though the restaurant has a long cocktail and wine list, my vote is for the Cork artisanal beers on tap.

Santa Rosa 218. ✆ **65/233080.** www.govinda.cl. AE, DC, MC, V. Main courses $12–$22 (£8–£15). Apr–Nov Tues–Sat 6pm–1am; Dec–Mar 11am–1am.

Ibis ★★ INTERNATIONAL/CHILEAN This popular restaurant specializes in seafood and is one of Puerto Varas's best. Like a few of the aforementioned restaurants, it is about a 10-minute walk from the center. On offer is creative cuisine and a vast menu with dishes such as flambéed Ecuadorian shrimp in cognac; pistachio salmon; beef filet in a sauce of tomato, garlic, and chipotle pepper; and lamb chops with mint sauce. To begin, try a shellfish appetizer that the chef brings in fresh from the coast, and end the meal with crêpes Suzette. The eating area is small but warm and is decorated with crafts-oriented art; there's also a bar here. During the day, there is pleasant outdoor seating that overlooks the lake. The wine list also merits mention for its variety.

Av. Vicente Pérez Rosales 1117. ✆ **65/235533.** www.ibisrestaurant.cl. Main courses $7–$13 (£4.70–£8.70). AE, DC, MC, V. Daily 11:30am–3:30pm and 7:30pm–midnight.

La Cucina d' Alessandro ★ PIZZA/ITALIAN The authentic, fresh pastas and thin-crust pizzas at this restaurant are excellent because they are made by an Italian family who emigrated to Puerto Varas only a few years ago, bringing with them real Italian gastronomic know-how. The pizzas really shine here, and their special two-for-one pizza offer from 4 to 8pm every day makes this restaurant a good value. The restaurant has a cozy atmosphere and is housed in a typical shingled home across from the beach. There are a few wooden tables that are large enough for groups of six to eight diners. It's a 15-minute walk from downtown. Apart from pasta and pizza, La Cucina has good seafood dishes, and it is open all day. It's a tiny restaurant, so make reservations for dinner and come early for lunch.

Av. Vicente Perez Rosales 1290. ✆ **65/310583.** Main courses $5–$9 (£3.30–£6). No credit cards. Daily noon–midnight.

Mediterráneo ★ (Moments) INTERNATIONAL Boasting an excellent location right on the Costanera, this restaurant has a glass-enclosed terrace with water views. The cheerful orange tablecloths add to its brightness, as does the pleasant waitstaff. Mediterráneo is known for its imaginative dishes (think Chilean-Mediterranean fusion) that change weekly. The owners use mostly local produce, including spices bought from the Mapuche natives. Here, you'll find big, fresh salads mixing such ingredients as endives, Swiss cheese, anchovies, olives, and local mushrooms. For the main course, the venison here is excellent, served with a yummy zucchini gratin. Other standouts are the fresh sea bass with a caper white-wine sauce, and a delicious lamb cooked in a rosemary wine reduction and served with roasted potatoes. For dessert, try one of the fruit sorbets.

Santa Rosa 068, corner of Portales. ✆ **65/237268.** AE, DC, MC, V. Main courses $4–$25 (£2.70–£17). Apr–Nov daily noon–3:30pm and 7:30–11pm; Dec–Mar daily 10am–2am.

Puerto Varas After Dark

At night, the stately **Enjoy Puerto Varas Casino,** Del Salvador 021 (✆ **65/492000;** www.enjoy.cl), gives visitors a chance to depart with their travel money (or hopefully win enough for a hotel upgrade) via slot machines and gaming tables offering blackjack, baccarat, roulette, and more. The gaming salon is open daily from noon to 7am, the slot machine floor from noon to 5am, and every Monday the minimum bet drops to $1.50 (£1), and roulette to 30¢ (20p). The casino's bar and restaurants are open from noon to 4am, if you're looking for a midnight snack. It's quite an exciting place to be on weekends, and the decor is quite stylish.

A Side Trip from Puerto Varas to Ensenada

Ensenada is a tiny settlement at the base of Volcán Osorno. Its proximity to Petrohué and Lago Todos los Santos makes it a convenient point for lodging if you plan to spend a lot of time around the Vicente Pérez Rosales National Park. There is no town to speak of here, just a few vacation rentals, hotels, and a couple of shops. About 4km (2½ miles) outside Puerto Varas on the way to Ensenada is a Chilean rodeo *medialuna* (half-moon), where events are held during February and on Independence days, September 18 and 19. Check with the visitor's office if you are here during that time for this not-to-miss event that provides an in-depth look into Chilean rural culture.

GETTING THERE If you have your own vehicle, take the coastal road east out of Puerto Varas and continue for 46km (29 miles) until you reach Ensenada. In Puerto Varas, you'll find minibuses at the intersection of San Bernardo and Martínez that go to Ensenada, Petrohué, and Lago Todos los Santos every day at 9:15 and 11am, and 2 and 4pm. **Andina del Sud,** Del Salvador 72 (✆ **65/232811;** www.andinadelsud.com), has daily trips to this area as well.

Where to Stay

There are many *cabañas* on the shore; the **Cabañas Bahía Celeste** (✆ **9/873-6568;** www.bahiaceleste.cl) stand out. These self-service units have lake views, living areas, and kitchens for travelers seeking a little more freedom (although there are a few restaurants here if you would like to dine out at night). The *cabañas* are attractive stone-and-wood units on the lakeshore for two, four, or six guests. There is also maid service, and each *cabaña* comes with a wooden deck. Prices are $100 (£67) for a two-person cabin, $120 (£80) for a four-person cabin, and $140 (£93) for a six-person cabin.

As is true with the majority of hotels in rural settings (ecolodges, for example), the hotels in this area do not have TVs, though they have added Wi-Fi.

Hotel Ensenada ★ (Value) The Hotel Ensenada is a veritable museum, with a lobby jam-packed with colonial German antiques. The hotel itself is a living antique, built more than 100 years ago. Although it offers an acceptable level of comfort, the rooms do reflect the hotel's age. It's such a fun place, though, that most visitors, many of them foreigners, don't seem to mind. All rooms on the second floor have private bathrooms, and, for the most part, the rest share with just one other room. Rooms are sparsely decorated. If they're not too full, ask to see several rooms, as each one is differently sized. The hotel is situated on a 500-hectare (1,235-acre) private forest that's perfect for taking a stroll or riding a bike—which comes free with the room—and there's a tennis court, canoes, and motorboats. The old-fashioned kitchen serves simple Chilean cuisine with vegetables straight from the garden.

Ruta Internacional 225, Km 45. ✆ **65/212017.** Fax 65/212028. www.hotelensenada.cl. 23 units. $100 (£67) double; $150 (£100) double with volcano view. AE, DC, MC, V. Closed Mar–Sept. **Amenities:** Restaurant; lounge; bike rentals.

Yan Kee Way Lodge ★★★ (Moments) The name "Yan Kee Way" is a play on words, a gringo's pronunciation of Llanquihue, and it is owned and managed by an American. The owner could not have chosen a more picture-perfect site for this luxurious property: nestled in a thick forest of cinnamon-colored *arrayán* trees on the shore of Lago Llanquihue, and facing the astounding view of Osorno Volcano directly in front of the lodge.

The Yan Kee Way Lodge takes just eight fishermen on outings per day (the lodge capacity is higher, however) via inflatable boats, horseback, or walk-and-wade fishing. The best fishing season is from November to early May, yet fishermen have done well year-round—in fact, this lodge offers the best fly-fishing opportunities in the area because they can get to areas that are inaccessible to others. The hotel complex has independent units in standard rooms, two-story bungalows, and apartments; the latter are very spacious and good for a family or group of friends. Blending with the surroundings, each elegant building here is painted in tones of terra cotta and forest green, with contemporary decor such as ebony leather couches and furniture, and art imported from Mexico and Argentina. Service is attentive and very friendly, and the owner strives to provide the very best, including an extensive wine cellar with rare wines and the region's finest restaurant, Latitude 42 (see later).Yan Kee Way is not just a fly-fishing lodge, however, and they offer sport adventure all-inclusive packages, including rafting, mountain biking, hiking, and horseback riding. At the end of the day, many guests unwind in the spa or in the two wood-fired hot tubs that face the lake and the volcano.

Road to Ensenada E of Puerto Varas, Km 42. ✆ **65/212030.** Fax 65/212031. www.southernchilexp.com. 18 units. $270 (£180) double; $350 (£233) per person per day all-inclusive sport adventure package, which includes all meals and house wines with dinner and 20 activities from which to choose. AE, DC, MC, V. Amenities: Restaurant; bar; lounge; exercise room; spa; Jacuzzi; sauna; watersports equipment; free Internet access; room service; massage; laundry service. In room: Fridge, hair dryer, safe.

Where to Dine

Latitude 42 ★★★ (Moments INTERNATIONAL This is one of the finest restaurants in southern Chile, located right on the lake overlooking the volcano. The elegant decor features marble and brass chandeliers, fireplaces made of volcanic rock, orangey leather chairs, picture windows overlooking the water, a basement "cave" for wine tasting, and a cigar bar that sells Havanas. Service is superb. The chef uses only the highest-quality produce, mostly local and organic, to create the most tantalizing dishes. The salmon is smoked in-house using apple cider, and the meat is aged on the premises. Fish is brought daily from Puerto Varas and Puerto Montt, usually sea bass, salmon, and conger eel. Specials change daily and the entire menu changes occasionally throughout the year. The cellar houses outstanding wines, an impressive collection from over 40 vineyards. Pastries and desserts are also terrific; even the heavenly chestnut ice cream is homemade. The menu is surprisingly economical for the high quality of this restaurant. It is a good idea to make a reservation if you are not staying in the lodge.

In the Yan Kee Way Lodge, on the road to Ensenada, E of Puerto Varas, Km 42. ✆ **65/212030.** Reservations recommended. Main courses $10–$20 (£6.70–£13). AE, DC, MC, V. Daily noon–3pm and 7–10pm.

PARQUE NACIONAL VICENTE PEREZ ROSALES & THE LAKE CROSSING TO ARGENTINA

About 65km (40 miles) from Puerto Varas sits Chile's oldest national park, Vicente Pérez Rosales, founded in 1926. It covers an area of 251,000 hectares (619,970 acres), incorporating the park's centerpiece, **Lago Todos los Santos, Saltos de Petrohué,** and three commanding **volcanoes:** Osorno, Tronador, and Puntiagudo. The park is open daily from December to February 8:30am to 8pm, March to November 8:30am to 6:30pm; admission to Saltos de Petrohué is $4 (£2.70) adults, $3 (£2) kids. Conaf's **information center** (✆ **65/486115**) can be found toward the end of the road.

Tips Get on the Road

I have found that a better way than boat to travel from Puerto Varas to Bariloche is via the international highway (which is dirt is some areas), pausing for a stop at Termas de Puyehue, driving through the high Andes, dropping in through the picturesque village of Villa la Angostura, and finally circumnavigating the lake to arrive at Bariloche. Your car-rental agency can arrange the paperwork for you, or try a service such as **LS Travel** (✆ **65/232424;** www.lstravel.com).

By far the most popular excursions here are boat rides across the crème de menthe–colored waters of **Lago Todos los Santos,** and there are several options. **Turismo Peulla** (✆ **65/236150;** www.turismopeulla.cl) offers trips departing from Puerto Montt or Puerto Varas to Peulla on the far side of the lake.

From Petrohué, you can book a day trip to the Margarita island in the middle of the lake or cross to Peulla, a 1¾-hour crossing that departs daily at 10:30am October through April and in July; the rest of the year, the ship doesn't cross on Sundays.

Travelers may then return or continue on to Bariloche with the Argentine company **Cruce de Lagos** (✆ **65/236150;** www.crucedelagos.cl). **Andina del Sud** (the owner of Turismo Peulla) has a ticket office at the pier and an office in Puerto Varas, at Del Salvador 72 (✆ **65/232811;** $160–$190/£107–£127). This is a very popular and very touristy journey; though the trip to Bariloche offers rugged, panoramic views, the trip is not worth the money on stormy days. And too much of the cattle herd mentality exists here as tourist-weary guides shuttle passengers in and out quickly, over 50,000 per season. The ferry portions of this journey are broken up by short bus rides from one body of water to the other.

There are relatively few hiking trails in this national park. The shortest and most popular trail leads to the **Saltos de Petrohué,** located just before the lake (admission $4/£2.30). Here you'll find a wooden walkway that has been built above the start of the Río Petrohué; from here it is possible to watch the inky-green waters crash through lava channels formed after the 1850 eruption of Volcán Osorno. Apart from the one perfect photo opportunity of the crashing emerald water with the volcano in the background, there isn't really much to see here. If you're serious about backpacking, pick up a copy of the map *Ruta de los Jesuitas* for a description of longer trails in the park, one of which takes you as far as Lago Rupanco and Puerto Rico (the town, not the Caribbean island), where you can catch a bus to Osorno. Day hikes take visitors around the back of Volcán Osorno. One of my favorite treks here is a 1-night/2-day trek to the **Termas del Callao** thermal baths, the trail head of which is accessible only by boat. You can hire one of the boats at the dock (six-person maximum, $50/£33), or arrange a trip with **Expediciones Petrohué,** which will get you a guide and take care of gear and meals for the overnight stay. There is a rustic cabin at the hot springs; check with Expediciones before leaving for this trip to see if it is already booked. They also have rafting, 4×4 photo safaris, climbing, trekking, fly-fishing, and canyoneering opportunities. Expediciones organizes excursions for guests of the hotel and also for day visitors (Petrohué s/n, Rte. 225, Km 64, Parque Nacional; ✆ **65/212045;** www.petrohue.com), plus they have bike rentals.

Volcán Osorno Ski Resort ★ (✆ **65/233445;** www.volcanosorno.com) on the western slope of the volcano, with two basic chairlifts and a T-bar, is a small resort on the volcano of the same name. It has just 600 hectares (1,482 acres) of terrain, but there are sweeping views and runs apt for every level. This is not a ski resort that travelers head to Chile specifically for, such as Valle Nevado or Portillo; it's more of a novelty for those in the area during the mid-June to early October season. The snow can be armor piercing, as this side of the lake receives a lot of wind, and all the terrain is above tree level. Lift prices run $32 (£21) for a full day, $24 (£16) for a half-day, and $20 (£13) for students.

Where to Stay

Hotel Natura ★★ Finds Built in 2005 on the fringe of the forest and the floodplain near Peulla, this property is less of a lodge than its name suggests; in fact, the main building has the sort of traditional grand wood-and-stone style you see in much older hotels. Don't let that deter you. Rooms are chic and large; the matrimonial suit features a king-size bed, chimney, flat-screen TV, and a Jacuzzi, along with a balcony. The hotel also has a two-room family apartment, and 23 doubles with king-size beds. Irrespective of its traditional looks, it offers plenty of modern outdoor activities: canopying 15m (49 ft.) in the air over an 800m (half-mile) span, horseback riding, and fly-fishing. You can zoom down nearby rivers such as the Río Negro on a jet boat, and wind down with one of the 85 wines on the restaurant's list.

Lago Todos los Santos. ✆ **65/560483.** www.hotelnatura.cl. 45 units. $173 (£115) double; $202 (£135) triple. AE, MC, DC, V. **Amenities:** Restaurant; bar; gym; sauna; watersports equipment; game room; Internet access; Wi-Fi; massage; laundry service. *In room:* TV, hair dryer, safe, Internet access.

Hotel Peulla ★ Finds Passengers on the 2-day journey to Bariloche stop for the night at this giant lodge, which sits on the shore of Lago Todos los Santos inside the Vicente Pérez Rosales National Park. It's possible to spend several days here if you'd like, to take part in trekking (limited), fishing, kayaking, and horseback riding in the area. The lodge's remoteness is perhaps its biggest draw, surrounded as it is by thick forest and not much else. Built in 1896, the Peulla is a mountain lodge, with enormous dining rooms, roaring fireplaces, and lots of wood. It's an agreeable place, with a large patio and sprawling lawn, though it is older and not as exclusive as the price suggests. Guest rooms haven't really changed since the hotel was built; they are simple and slightly dark, with hardwood floors. Try reserving rooms at a lower rate through a travel agency.

Lago Todos los Santos. ✆ **65/232145** in Santiago. www.hotelpeulla.cl. 76 units. $170 (£113) double. AE, MC, V. **Amenities:** Restaurant; bar; gym; watersports equipment; game room; Internet access. *In room:* TV.

Petrohué Hotel & Cabañas ★★ The Hotel Petrohué (built to replace the previous lodge, which burned to the ground in 2002) puts travelers right where the outdoor action is, without having to commute from Puerto Varas—and the hotel has an outfitter with a range of daily activities. It sits perched above the shore of Todos los Santos Lake, within the confines of the national park, meaning it gets busy when the lake-crossing boat pulls in (but this doesn't last very long, as they're bussed out quickly). The forested location is gorgeous, even on a rainy day. The hotel itself is a tad austere, given its absence of homey touches such as artwork or plants, but the contemporary design of its interiors (stone, heavy wood beams, fresh white couches) is attractive, and the rooms are very comfortable, with crisp linens and panoramic windows. What's an even better idea is bunking up in one of their four cozy *cabañas* a little closer to the shore, all of which come with kitchenettes.

Petrohué s/n Rte. 225, Km 64, Parque Nacional. ✆ **65/212025.** www.hotelpetrohue.cl. 13 units, 4 cabins. $197 (£131) double; $208 (£139) double with half-board; $186 (£124) cabin for 4; $253 (£169) cabin for 8. AE, MC, V. **Amenities:** Restaurant; bar; lounge; outdoor pool; outdoor excursions; room service; laundry service. *In room:* Kitchenette in *cabañas*.

7 PUERTO MONTT

20km (12 miles) S of Puerto Varas; 1,016km (630 miles) S of Santiago

This port town of roughly 155,000 residents is the central hub for travelers headed to Lagos Llanquihue and Todos los Santos, Chiloé, and the parks Alerce Andino and Pumalín. It is also a major docking zone for dozens of large cruise companies circumnavigating the southern cone of South America and several ferry companies with southern destinations to Laguna San Rafael and Puerto Natales in Patagonia.

Puerto Montt was founded in 1853 by German immigrants and their stalwart promoter Vicente Pérez Rosales, who named the town after another promoter of immigration, President Manuel Montt. The waterfront here was rebuilt after the devastating earthquake of 1960, which destroyed the city's port, church, and neighborhood of Angelmó. Today it is the capital of Chile's southern Lake District, a thriving city that invests heavily in salmon farming, shipping, and tourism. There isn't much to see or do here, and most visitors head straight out of town upon arrival, but Puerto Montt's small downtown offers a quick, pleasant stroll on a sunny day, and there is an extensive outdoor market that sells Chilean handicrafts.

ESSENTIALS

Getting There

BY PLANE Puerto Montt's **El Tepual** airport (PMC; ✆ **65/294159**) is currently served by airlines **LANExpress** (✆ **600/526-2000;** www.lan.com) and **Sky** (✆ **600/600-2828;** www.skyairline.cl), with multiple daily flights to Santiago, Punta Arenas, Balmaceda (Coyhaique), and Temuco. An **ETM bus** from the airport to the city's downtown bus terminal costs $3 (£2); a taxi costs $13 (£8.70). Agree on the fare before getting into the cab. There are several **car-rental agencies** at the airport, including Hertz, Alamo, and Avis.

BY BUS Puerto Montt's main terminal is at the waterfront (Diego Portales s/n), a 10- to 15-minute walk from downtown, or there are taxis to transport you. Regular bus service to and from most major cities, including Santiago, is provided by **Cruz del Sur** (✆ **65/254731**), **Tur Bus** (✆ **65/253329**), **Tas Choapa** (✆ **65/254828**), and **Bus Norte** (✆ **65/252783**).

BY CAR The Pan-American Highway ends at Puerto Montt.

Getting Around

Puerto Montt is divided into *poblaciones,* or neighborhoods, scattered around the city's hilltops. From the city center to the east is the **Pelluco** district, where many of the city's good restaurants can be found, and to the west is the district **Angelmó,** with the city's fish market, port departures, and Feria Artesanal with great shopping; the two districts are connected by the coastal road Diego Portales. The city center is laid out on a grid system that abuts a steep cliff.

BY FOOT The city center is small enough to be seen on foot. The crafts market and fish market in Angelmó are a 20-minute walk from the center, but you can take a cab. You'll need a taxi to reach the Pelluco district.

BY BUS **Buses Cruz del Sur** (✆ **65/254731**) leaves for Puerto Varas 19 times daily from the bus terminal, and so do the independent white shuttle buses to the left of the coaches; look for the sign in the window that says PUERTO VARAS. Cruz del Sur also serves Chiloé, including Castro and Ancud, with 25 trips per day. **TransChiloé** (✆ **65/254934**) goes to Chiloé seven times per day from the terminal.

BY CAR This is one of those places where renting a car can come in handy, given the ample sightseeing opportunities and pleasant drives in the area. Local car-rental agencies in Puerto Montt include **Hertz,** Calle de Servicio 1031 (✆ **65/313445;** www.hertz.com); **Avis,** Benavente 670 (✆/fax **65/258199;** www.avischile.cl); and **Econo Rent,** Guillermo Gallardo 450 (✆ **65/254888;** econorent@telsur.cl). Hertz and Avis rent cars to travelers who wish to drive south along the Carretera Austral (see the "Driving the Carretera Austral" section in chapter 12, beginning on p. 328), and they can arrange to have the vehicle dropped off in Coyhaique. Some companies insist that you rent a 4×4 for the Carretera Austral (the importance of this during the summer is debatable; during the winter it could help if the road turns muddy). Calling the local office of each company is usually the best way to get bargain rates; but, in general, the rental drop-off fee is $500 (£333), in addition to the daily cost.

Visitor Information

The municipality has a small **tourist office** in the plaza at the corner of Antonio Varas and San Martín (✆ **65/261823**); it's open December through March daily from 9am to 9pm, and April through November Monday through Friday from 9am to 1pm and 2:30 to 7pm, Saturday and Sunday from 9am to 1pm. There is a largely unhelpful tourism kiosk in the main plaza (✆ **65/261808;** www.puertomonttchile.cl).

SPECIAL EVENTS During the second week of February, the city holds its annual **Semana Puertomontina** (www.puertomonttchile.cl), with weeklong festivities that culminate in a fireworks display over the bay celebrating Puerto Montt's anniversary. Throughout the summer, arts and crafts exhibits are held in public plazas.

Fast Facts Puerto Montt

Currency Exchange You can exchange currency at **Trans Afex,** Av. Diego Portales 516; **Cambios Inter,** Paseo Talca 84, Oficina 7 (✆ **64/253745**); **La Moneda de Oro,** in the bus terminal, Oficina 37; and **Eureka Tour,** Antonio Varas 445. Exchange houses are generally open Monday through Friday from 9am to 1pm and 2 to 6pm, Saturday from 9am to 2pm. For **ATMs,** look for banks at Urmeneta and Guillermo Gallardo downtown. Banks are open Monday through Friday from 9am to 2pm.

Hospital Try either **Hospital Base,** Seminario, s/n (✆ **65/261100**), or **Hospital de la Seguridad,** Panamericana 400 (✆ **65/257333**).

Internet Cafe Internet cafes come and go quickly, so it's best to walk Urmenta street and look for a sign or ask at your hotel. Try **Arroba Cibercafé,** Guillermo Gallardo 218-A, or **New Ciber,** San Martín 230. Internet service costs $1 (70p) per hour, but hotels now have Wi-Fi or free access for guests.

Laundry **Anny,** San Martín 167 (✆ **65/255397**); **Lavaseco Arcoiris,** San Martín 230; and **Lavatodo,** O'Higgins 231, are all spots to do your wash.

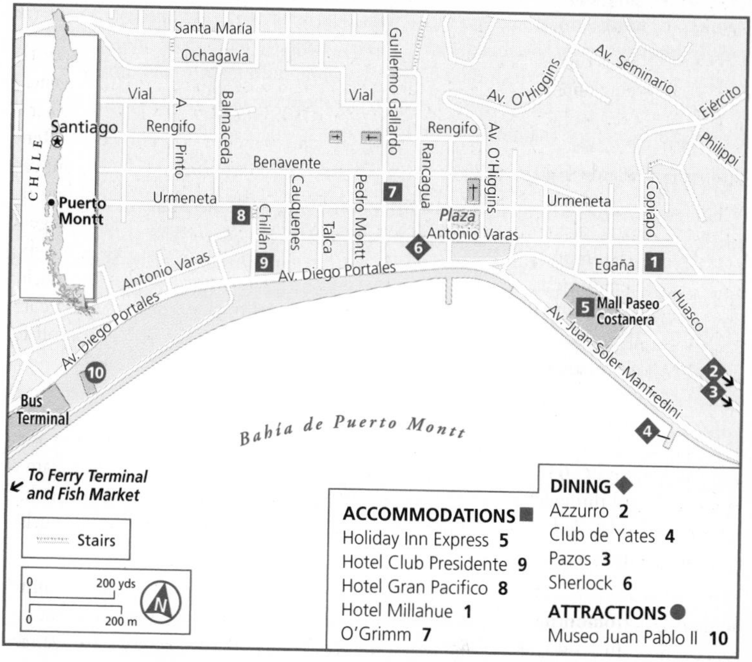

WHAT TO SEE & DO

The **Museo Juan Pablo II,** Av. Portales 991 (✆ **65/344457**), contains a medley of artifacts culled from this region. There's an interesting interpretive exhibit here of the Monte Verde archaeological dig that found bones estimated to be 12,000 years old. There's also an open-air railway exhibit next to the museum, but truthfully, the museum is worth a visit only if you have time to kill. It's open Monday through Friday from 9am to 7pm, Saturday and Sunday from 10am to 6pm. Admission is $1 (70p).

TOUR OPERATORS & TRAVEL AGENCIES **Ace Lagos Andinos,** Antonio Varas 445 (✆ **65/257686** or 9/707-9445), offers just about everything you could want, including tours to Vicente Pérez National Park, the Termas de Puyehue, and Chiloé; sightseeing tours around the circumference of Lago Llanquihue; 2-night treks around Volcán Osorno with an overnight in a family home; and more.

Andina del Sud, Antonio Varas 437 (✆ **65/257797;** www.andinadelsud.cl), is the tour agency with the monopoly on Lago Todos los Santos for the lake crossing to Bariloche; they also offer city tours and sightseeing journeys, and transportation service to attractions. **Travellers,** Bulnes 1009 (✆ **65/262099;** www.travellers.cl), is somewhat like a one-stop travel shop, with information and booking arrangements with nearly every outfitter, hotel, and program around Chile. Their location is far from the city center, though it is close to the arts and crafts market Feria Artesanal de Angelmó. They have a book exchange here, too.

SHOPPING Puerto Montt is a great place to pick up souvenirs. On Avenida Angelmó, from the bus terminal to the fish market, is the **Feria Artesanal de Angelmó** ★ (daily 9am–7pm, until 9pm in the summer), with dozens of stalls and specialty shops that peddle knitwear, ponchos, handicrafts, jewelry, regional foods, and more from areas around the Lake District, including Chiloé. It's about a 20-minute walk from the plaza, or you can take a taxi. There is also a large, tacky shopping mall south of the main plaza, with national and international chains.

WHERE TO STAY

While most visitors will prefer to stay in Puerto Varas, there are numerous inexpensive small hostels and *residenciales* in Puerto Montt that might be convenient if you're planning an early morning departure via plane, bus, or ferry. Among them, **House Rocco** at Pudeto 233 (✆ **65/272897;** www.hospedajerocco.cl) and **Casa Perla** at Trigal 312 (✆ **65/262104;** www.casaperla.com) cater to international visitors.

Expensive

Hotel Club Presidente ★ This well-tailored hotel's classic, nautical-themed design appeals equally to executives and tourists, and handy kitchenettes give guests a little extra freedom. Located on the waterfront, in a central location close to shops, the Presidente is on busy Avenida Portales, but double-paned windows keep noise to a minimum. All rooms have either queen-size or king-size beds. The doubles are spacious, but the superiors are much larger and worth the extra $5 (£3.30); they also have ocean views. Most come with a small loveseat and a table and chairs. The rooms are decorated with creams and terra cotta, striped curtains, and nubby bedspreads. A breakfast buffet is served daily in the comfortable restaurant/bar on the eighth floor.

Av. Diego Portales 664, Puerto Montt. ✆ **65/251666.** Fax 65/251669. www.presidente.cl. 50 units. $86–$111 (£57–£74) double. Rates include buffet breakfast. AE, DC, MC, V. **Amenities:** Restaurant; bar; small heated pool; sauna; business center; laundry service. *In room:* TV, kitchenette, safe.

Holiday Inn Express Yes, it's a Holiday Inn, but the location is excellent, the views outstanding, there are all the amenities you need, and this is the best hotel for business travelers in town. It opened in 2006 over the Paseo Costanera shopping center right on the waterfront. Big windows, about half of which look out onto the harbor, are the highlight of the otherwise average rooms, which feature standard Holiday Inn unadventurous beige walls, carpet, and bedding.

Av. Costanera s/n, Puerto Montt. ✆ **65/566000.** www.hiexpress.com. 105 units. $130 (£87) double. Rates include buffet breakfast. AE, DC, MC, V. **Amenities:** Restaurant; bar; exercise room; business center, Wi-Fi; room service. *In room:* TV, coffeemaker, hair dryer, safe.

Hotel Gran Pacífico ★ Opened in late 2001, the Gran Pacífico is the city's only luxurious hotel, and its imposing 10-story structure towers over the waterfront. The imitation Art Deco lobby is sleek and modern, with lots of wood and marble. The rooms follow the same motif and are spacious, modern, and very bright. They have wood headboards, off-yellow wallpaper, and large-screen TVs. Those overlooking the water have breathtaking views (request an upper-level oceanview floor when you check in). The marble bathrooms are a tad small, but the size of the room makes up for it. For such a high-caliber hotel, the staff is not too efficient, nor do they speak much English, so be patient.

Urmeneta 719, Puerto Montt. ✆ **65/482100.** Fax 65/292979. www.hotelgranpacifico.cl. 48 units. $126 (£84) double; $202 (£135) suite. AE, DC, MC, V. **Amenities:** Restaurant; bar; lounge; exercise room; sauna; business center; room service; laundry service. *In room:* TV, minibar, safe.

O'Grimm One of the city's most established hotels, the O'Grimm is run by a friendly English-speaking staff and is adjacent to the popular O'Grimm Pub. Rooms are of varying sizes and each comes with sleek black and gray furniture and dark satinlike bedspreads. There's no view to mention, really, and the rooms are not as inviting as the price may suggest. Bathrooms are small and aging, but clean. The restaurant, pub, and bustling atmosphere downstairs are pleasant, and there's live music most nights.

Guillermo Gallardo 211, Puerto Montt. ✆ **65/252845.** Fax 65/258600. www.ogrimm.com. 26 units. $90 (£60) double; from $100 (£67) suite. AE, DC, MC, V. **Amenities:** Restaurant; bar; business center w/Internet access. *In room:* TV, minibar, safe.

Moderate

Hotel Millahue This older hotel is not particularly fancy, but it does offer clean, large double rooms and friendly service. All double rooms are sized differently but priced the same, and rooms on the fourth and fifth floors are the nicest, especially those whose numbers end in 06 and 07. There's a dining area for breakfast and hearty, set-menu Chilean meals, should you decide to eat in. Beds are average but offer standard comfort. The hotel is run by its owner, a friendly woman who strives to make guests feel at home.

Copiapó 64, Puerto Montt. ✆ **65/253829.** Fax 65/256317. www.hotelmillahue.cl. 25 units. $48–$56 (£32–£37) double. Rates include breakfast. MC, V. **Amenities:** Restaurant; laundry service.

A Hotel Outside of Puerto Montt

The Cliffs Preserve ★★★ (Moments The Cliffs Preserve is set in as magical a setting as you will find in Chile. Their massive 8,000-acre property, in a suburb about an hour from Puerto Montt, is covered in primary coastal rainforest, and a number of active excursions are arranged by top guides and naturalists. Horseback riding, hiking, boat trips to see penguins, sea lions, otters, and whales—the world's largest blue whale nursery is not far off shore—and even heliskiing are offered. The resort is also actively involved with the local community of Los Muermos; it funds an orphanage there and the hotel property includes a home for the families of fishermen.

The huge and well-designed 2- to 4-suite villas, each with their own wood-fired hot tub, are isolated from each other and overlook a breathtaking sheltered beach. You can rent an entire villa, just a suite, or a suite with the use of a common area that includes a kitchen and living room. The cuisine and wine on offer at the restaurant are as good as any resort in Chile; produce comes from an organic farm on the property. An additional 12 smaller and less-expensive villas are currently under construction.

1 hr. W of Puerto Montt. ✆ **888/780-3011.** Fax 65/256317. www.cliffspreserve.cl. 16 units. $2,700 (£1,800) 4 nights/5 days per person Dec–Mar; $3,900 (£2,600) 4 nights/5 days per person Apr–Nov. Rates based on double occupancy; all-inclusive with meals, wine, excursions, spa treatment, laundry service, and transport. MC, V. **Amenities:** Restaurant; bar; pool; spa; Jacuzzi; sauna. *In room*: A/C, Wi-Fi.

WHERE TO DINE

Puerto Montt is Chile's seafood capital. If you're feeling adventurous, try a Chilean favorite, such as abalone, sea urchin, or the regional barnacle. And where better to see, smell, and taste these fruits of the sea than the **Fish Market of Angelmó,** located at the end of Avenida Angelmó, where the artisan market terminates? It's open Monday through Sunday from 10am to 8pm during the summer, until 6pm during the winter. Like most fish markets, it's a little grungy, but it's a colorful stop nevertheless and there are several restaurant stalls offering the freshest local specialties around. ***Be aware:*** There have been reports that a few food stalls like to overcharge tourists, so double-check your bill with the menu.

Apart from the restaurants below, there are a handful of inexpensive cafes in Puerto Montt, including **Café Central,** Rancagua 117 (✆ **65/482888**), and **Super Yoco,** Quillota 245 (✆ **65/252123**), which has lunches, empanadas, and appetizer platters. You'll find German pastries and beer from microbreweries at **Café Haussmann,** San Martín 185 (✆ **65/293380**) or **Club Alemán,** Varas 264 (✆ **65/252551**).

Azzurro ★ ITALIAN Fresh pasta served in rich sauces is this Italian eatery's mainstay, but that's not all they serve—the stuffed Roquefort chicken and pizzas are also very good. The folk-artsy blue dining area has a fun, pleasant atmosphere. The pastas are very good, such as lasagna, fettuccine, or cannelloni stuffed with crab and spinach, or with ricotta, walnuts, eggplant, and fresh basil, and a choice of 11 sauces.

Av. Inés Gallardo 146, Pelluco. ✆ **65/318989.** Reservations recommended Sat–Sun. Main courses $8–$12 (£5.30–£8). MC, V. Mon–Sat 1–3:30pm and 8pm–midnight; Sun 1–3:30pm.

Club de Yates ★ SEAFOOD The light-blue Club de Yates looks like a traditional seafood restaurant that sits out over the water like a pier. Inside, though, the atmosphere is white tablecloths, candlesticks, and sharp waiters in bow ties; it's one of the more elegant dining areas in town. This is a good place to come if you're looking for typical Chilean seafood dishes, such as razor clams broiled with Parmesan or sea bass *Margarita* (in a creamy shellfish sauce). It has a great waterfront view and is located about 1km (1/2 mile) from the plaza toward Pelluco.

Av. Juan Soler Manfredini 200. ✆ **65/282810.** Main courses $20–$25 (£13–£17). AE, DC, MC, V. Daily noon–4pm and 7:30pm–midnight.

Pazos CHILEAN This is the place to come if you're interested in sampling *curanto* but don't have time to make it to Chiloé. *Curanto* is that island's specialty, a mixture of mussels, clams, sausage, chicken, pork, beef, and a gooey pancake steamed in a large pot and served with a cup of broth. Pazos also serves a variety of other seafood items, such as sea urchin omelets and the shellfish cornucopia, *sopa marina.* The restaurant is on the waterfront in Pelluco, in a 90-year-old home. It's very popular with summer visitors to Puerto Montt.

Av. General Juan Soler Manfredini s/n, Balneario Pelluco. ✆ **65/252552.** Main courses $8–$12 (£5.30–£8). AE, DC, MC, V. Daily 12:15–3pm and 8:15–10pm.

Sherlock ★ Finds CHILEAN/PUB FARE The most happening place in Puerto Montt is this centrally located pub, cafe, and restaurant all rolled into one. There's lots of charm, a nice bar, and wood furniture, and it fills with locals at all hours of the day. This is a good place to get some local color, and they serve excellent homemade Chilean cuisine and delicious sandwiches. Try the albacore steak with a Chilean tomato-and-onion salad or the Sherlock sandwich with beef strips, tomato, corn, cheese, bacon, and grilled onion.

Antonio Varas 542. ✆ **65/288888.** Main courses $6–$10 (£4–£6.70); sandwiches $3–$5 (£2–£3.30). MC, V. Daily 9am–2am.

8 FERRY CROSSINGS TO THE CARRETERA AUSTRAL & CRUISES TO PATAGONIA THROUGH THE FJORDS

Few fjordlands in the world can match the elegant beauty of Chile's southern region. Its entire coast is composed of thousands of little-explored islands, canals, and sounds. A few companies offer trips through these remote channels south to Puerto Chacabuco in the

Aysén region, principally **Naviera Austral. Navimag** offers a popular trip through the southern fjords as far as Puerto Natales in Southern Patagonia, and to the Laguna San Rafael Glacier, as does the luxury liner ***Skorpios.*** (Please note that the itineraries can vary, and you need to reserve a berth well in advance of your trip.)

FERRY SERVICES Puerto Montt is the hub for ferries heading south. If you are planning a trip down the Carretera Austral, you'll need to travel to or from Puerto Montt or Chiloé by ferry (unless you enter through Argentina). During the summer, passengers and autos can cross to Pumalín Park and Caleta Gonzalo by ferry. This route is preferred but available only from December to March. For information about ferry crossings to Caleta Gonzalo as well as between La Arena and Puelche at the start of the Carretera Austral, see "Pumalín Park," in chapter 11.

To Chiloé, you need to head to Pargua west of Puerto Montt, see "Getting to the Island," in chapter 12. **Naviera Austral,** at Angelmó 2187 (in the ferry terminal or Terminal de Trasbordadores), in Puerto Montt (✆ **65/270400;** www.navieraustral.cl), offers ferry crossings to Chaitén on the Carretera Austral, the quickest and, in the end, the cheapest way to get a vehicle to the famed highway. Tickets cost $32 (£21) per passenger and $136 (£91) per car.

Navimag Ferries ★ Value Navimag offers 24-hour trips to Puerto Chacabuco in Aysén and 70-hour journeys to Puerto Natales, memorable for the sublime, pristine landscape, tiny outposts of civilization, and the camaraderie that grows between travelers. While you'll mostly travel through forested, sheltered channels dotted with cascades, it can get rough across the Golfo de Penas, where some passengers may suffer seasickness. The ships are passenger and freight ferries with a variety of cabins, from basic shared accommodations to higher-end cabins and low-end bunks separated only by curtains. Check the website for schedules and fares.

Offices in Puerto Montt, at Av. Angelmó 2187, in the Terminal de Transbordadores; ✆ **65/432300.** In Santiago, at El Bosque Norte 0440; ✆ 2/442-3120. www.navimag.com (online tickets). Prices vary but average $370–$1,800 (£247–£1,200) per person for the 4-night round-trip journey to Puerto Natales, and $76–$286 (£51–£191) per person for the 2-night round-trip journey to Puerto Chacabuco.

Nomads of the Seas ★★★ Moments This is one of the world's great small-scale luxury cruise-ship operators. The ship *Atmosphere*, which departs and returns from Puerto Montt, doesn't visit better-known sites, such as Laguna San Rafael, in an effort to journey to places with absolutely no other ships or tourists. Although the price tag is outrageous, it's a small price to pay to visit the farthest reaches of a wild and unruly Patagonia filled with glaciers, mountain lakes, snow-covered volcanoes, hot springs, and fjords that few others have ever laid eyes on. To accomplish this feat, the 159-ft. *Atmosphere* fuses nature and technology like few cruise ships have ever done. It carries an army of machinery including a Bell 407 helicopter (a second will be added in 2009), six custom-built jet boats, a Hurricane 920 RIB zodiac, four Helitour Mission zodiacs, various rescue boats, and top fly-fishing gear.

Even though it frequently charters rough seas, it's nothing but smooth sailing on this ship. Each of the 14 windowed cabins comes with such perks as soft beds with high thread-count sheets. The main deck combines a sleek circular bar, living space with plush designer couches and chairs, a small library, and elegant dining room. A "wet room" for gear and a spa area with hot tubs and Jacuzzis fill different levels on the back end of the ship. The eco-friendliness of this operation leaves something to be desired, however; this is one instance where being green might not be possible with the use of such high powered, gas-guzzling machines.

Nomads began offering 3-day gastronomic cruises near Puerto Montt and Chiloé in 2009, and is planning ground operations in the Andes and Atacama in 2010.

Del Inca 4446, Piso 4, Las Condes, Santiago. ✆ **2/414-4600** in Santiago. ✆ 866/790-4560 from U.S. and Canada. www.nomadsoftheseas.com. 14 units. $17,850 (£11,900) per person fly-fishing tour, $12,138 (£8,092) per person ecotourism tour Dec 27–Mar 14. $14,875 (£9,916) per person fly-fishing tour; $10,115 (£6,743) per person ecotourism tour Oct–Dec 27 and Mar 14–May. Rates include food and alcohol; excursions include use of helicopter and jet boats, plus transfers. **Amenities:** Restaurant; bar; Jacuzzi; library. *In room*: Hair dryer, safe.

Chiloé

The "Great Island of Chiloé" is a land of myths and magic—of emerald, rolling hills shrouded in mist, and tiny, picturesque coves that harbor a colorful palette of wooden fishing skiffs. This is Chile's second-largest island, located south of Puerto Montt with an eastern coast that faces the Gulf of Ancud and a western, wet Pacific shore. With the exception of a few small towns, the landscape here by and large is pastoral, with a deference to development that tends to make travelers feel as if they have been transported back a century. Across the island, wooden churches modeled after a Bavarian, neoclassic style appear like a beacon in every bay; they are so lovely and architecturally unique that UNESCO recently deemed them World Heritage sites.

Visually appealing as it is, Chiloé is truly defined by its people, the hardy, character-rich Chilotes, who can still be seen plowing their fields with oxen or pulling in their catch of the day the same way they have for centuries. Spanish conquistadors occupied Chiloé as early as 1567, followed by Jesuit missionaries and Spanish refugees pushed off the mainland by Mapuche Indian attacks. For 3 centuries, Chiloé was the only Spanish stronghold south of the Río Bio-Bío, and its isolation produced a singular culture among its residents, who, after so much time, are now a *mestizo* blend of Indian and Spanish blood. The Chilotes' rapid and closed speech, local slang, mythical folklore, and style of food, tools, and architecture were and still are uniquely different from their counterparts on the mainland. The downside of Chiloé's limited contact with the outside world is a dire poverty that has affected (and continues to affect) many of the island's residents. Most families eke out a living by relying on their own garden patch and livestock, animals that can be seen pecking and grazing along the side of the road. Off the main highway, it is as common to see residents traveling on horseback or by fishing boat as it is by vehicle.

I recommend a day or overnight trip to Chiloé rather than spending time in the grimy environs of Puerto Montt, but with one caveat: Rent a car. While the principal cities **Ancud** and **Castro** can be easily reached by bus, the true pleasure of visiting Chiloé is losing yourself on backcountry roads and discovering picturesque little bays and lookout points that are otherwise inaccessible by bus, and stopping at roadside stands for local cheese, fresh fish, and other delicacies. This chapter covers the highlights here, but the island is easy to navigate with a road map (see "Driving to & Around Chiloé," later). Chiloé also boasts the **Chiloé National Park,** where visitors can indulge themselves with a walk through primordial old-growth rainforest that once blanketed the island. The island's tourism infrastructure is improving, but visitors should still expect modest accommodations. The tedious rain that falls more than half the year here makes for soggy shoes and limited views; nevertheless, Chiloé rates as one of Chile's top attractions for its cultural value and natural beauty. Useful websites for information about Chiloé are **www.chiloe.cl** and **www.interpatagonia.cl**.

Tips: Driving to & Around Chiloé

Chiloé is a sightseer's paradise and, therefore, it is highly recommended that visitors rent a vehicle. You will be able to cover more ground and take full advantage of seemingly endless photo-worthy vista points, historic churches, and picturesque little villages. Hopping from island to island in a vehicle is a snap, and visitors can pack a lot of action into just 1 day. In years past, you would need to rent a car in Puerto Montt or Puerto Varas, where the rates are still the cheapest, though you would need to pay the $16 (£11) one-way ferry fee. Recently rental service became available in Castro at **Salfa** (Mistral 499; ✆ **65/630422**).

Local bus service from town to town is frequent and inexpensive. More information about bus service can be found in the sections for each specific town later. If you're driving your own rental car onto the ferry, don't line up behind the trucks and buses, but go to the front of the line and park to the left—that will make you visible to the ferry attendants, and they'll squeeze you onto the next available ferry.

Gas stations are sporadic. Fill up in Puerto Montt or Puerto Varas, and again in Ancud. If visiting the national park, fill up in Castro or Conchi.

EXPLORING THE ISLAND

Most visitors use Castro as a central base for exploring the island. I wouldn't really recommend a stay in Ancud unless you are short on time. Quellón is considered primarily a ferry departure point for Chaitén on the Carretera Austral (see chapter 12), but it may well emerge as a site for embarking on whale-watching in the coming years. On a clear day—not very often—one can see Volcán Osorno and the towering, snowcapped Andes in the distance.

You'll need a day or 2 to explore Castro, Dalcahue, Achao, and Conchi; a day to see the national park (more if you wish to do a long hike or camp out); and about a half-day to see Ancud (with a stop in Chacao). Also consider the new Tantauco Park at its southern tip, for which you should plan 2 days due to its difficult access.

GETTING TO THE ISLAND

BY BOAT Fortunately, the plan to build a giant bridge between the mainland and Chiloé—a surefire white elephant—has been scrapped. Meanwhile, two ferry companies operate continuously between Pargua (on the mainland) and Chacao (on the island), shuttling passengers and vehicles. If you are taking a bus to Chiloé, you won't need to worry about paying the fare because it's included in the price of the bus ticket; but if you've rented a car, the cost is $16 (£11) one-way. The ride lasts 30 to 40 minutes. (And, yes, there are toilets on board the ferry.) In compensation for the end of the plan to build the bridge, Santiago has promised to invest heavily in infrastructure on the island, so expect construction work through 2010.

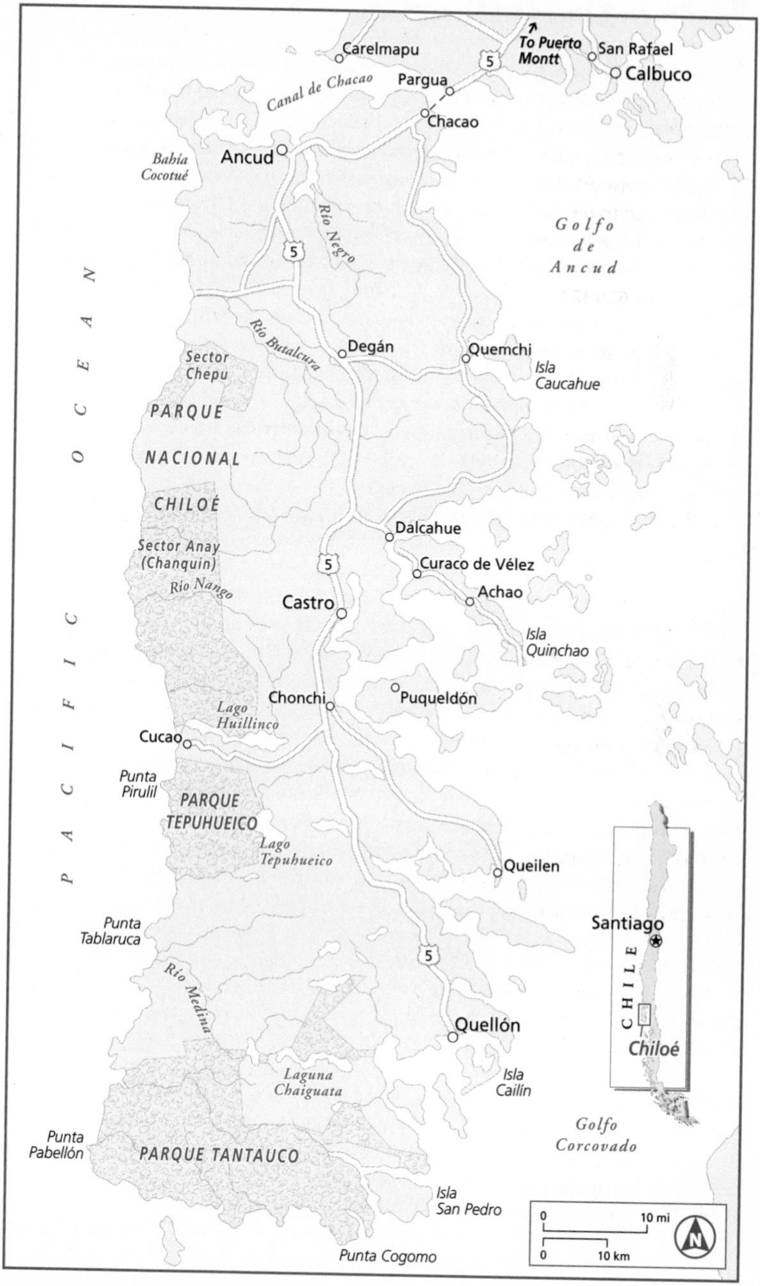

Carelmapu
To Puerto Montt
San Rafael
Calbuco
Canal de Chacao
Pargua
Chacao
5
Bahía Cocotué
Ancud
Río Negro
Golfo de Ancud
PACIFIC OCEAN
Río Butalcura
Degán
Quemchi
Isla Caucahue
Sector Chepu
PARQUE NACIONAL CHILOÉ
Sector Anay (Chanquin)
Río Nango
Dalcahue
Curaco de Vélez
Achao
Castro
Isla Quinchao
Puqueldón
Chonchi
Lago Huillinco
Cucao
Punta Pirulil
PARQUE TEPUHUEICO
Lago Tepuhueico
Queilen
Punta Tablaruca
Río Medina
Quellón
Isla Cailín
Laguna Chaiguata
Golfo Corcovado
Punta Pabellón
PARQUE TANTAUCO
Isla San Pedro
Punta Cogomo
Santiago
CHILE
Chiloé
0
10 mi
0
10 km
N

Chiloé's World Heritage Churches

Some 70 of Chiloé's churches, without a doubt, are the island's most singular attractions, and together with some in Germany, Norway, and the U.S., unique in having been built entirely of wood—no nails. The humble yet striking churches represent a rare form of architecture, the Chiloé "school" of religious architecture brought about by the fusion of European and indigenous cultural traditions, namely those of the Jesuit missionaries of the 17th and 18th centuries and the island's early inhabitants, the Chonos and Huilliches.

Jesuit missionaries first arrived on the island in 1608, conducting circular missions throughout the island wherein they traveled the archipelago throughout the year, stopping for several days at a mission site and spreading their brand of religion. But unlike other missionary groups, the Jesuits attempted to learn the languages and the cultural traditions of those they were hoping to convert. Thus, it was both their respect for traditional building methods and the Jesuits' absence for much of the year that afforded the indigenous peoples of the island the opportunity to lay such a heavy influence on the construction of each church.

The styles and layouts of the churches can be traced back to Europe: Chonchi's represents neoclassicism; the church in Nercón is neo-Renaissance; and in Achao, you'll find baroque, inspired by the first Bavarian Jesuits. However, the interiors and the locations chosen for each church reflect the inspiration of their local indigenous builders. A close look inside each church offers numerous examples of techniques that were borrowed from shipbuilding, such as wooden pegs and joints instead of nails. The center of the roof, if imagined inverted, often resembles the hull of a boat, with three naves to a church. Moreover, nearly all the chapels in Chiloé face the water, with central towers that functioned as beacons for sailors. The influence of the island's early maritime inhabitants continues to be a point of pride for those who call it home.

Although each church shares the same facade of semicircular arches, each church varies greatly in color and size, the latter representing what type of festivals were to be had at the church. The church at Achoa is the oldest and at Quinchao the largest, but the church at Tenaún, with its royal blue exterior—upon which are painted two large white stars—is probably the most impressive. Sixteen have been declared UNESCO World Heritage sites, but there are many more.

BY BUS Several companies provide service to Ancud, Castro, and Quellón from Puerto Montt, and even Santiago and Punta Arenas. In Puerto Montt, daily departures for Ancud and Castro leave from the bus terminal. **Cruz del Sur** (✆ **65/254731;** www.busescruzdelsur.cl) has 18 trips per day, **TransChiloé** (✆ **65/254934**) has seven trips per day, and **Queilén Bus** (✆ **65/253468**) has eight trips per day. From Puerto Varas, try **Cruz del Sur,** at San Francisco 1317, with five trips per day (✆ **65/236969**). **Cruz del**

Sur (✆ **2/779-0607**) offers three services per day from Santiago to Chiloé; the trip takes about 15 hours. Buses ride over on the ferry; you can remain in your seat or step out and walk around.

1 ANCUD

95km (59 miles) SE of Puerto Montt; 146km (91 miles) N of Castro

Ancud, home to 27,000 residents, was founded in 1767 as a fort to monitor passing sea traffic to and from Cape Horn. It was, for many years, the capital of Chiloé until the provincial government pulled up stakes and moved to Castro in 1982. Ancud is a bustling, rambling port town with much to see, but Castro is a more convenient base if you want to reach the island's outlying areas. This was the last Spanish outpost in Chile, and visitors can view the fort ruins here; there's also a good museum depicting Chilote history and culture.

ESSENTIALS

Getting There

BY BUS For regular bus service from Puerto Montt to Ancud, see "Getting to the Island," earlier. Ancud has a central bus station, the **Terminal Municipal,** at the intersection of Avenida Aníbal Pinto and Marcos Vera; from here, you'll need to take a taxi to the center of town, or a local bus headed toward the plaza. Frequent buses leave from this station for destinations such as Castro, Dalcahue, and Quellón; try **Cruz del Sur/ Transchiloé** (✆ **65/622265**) or **Queilén Bus** (✆ **65/621140**).

BY CAR **Rte. 5** (the Pan-American Hwy.) is a well-paved road that links Ancud with nearly every city on the island. The paved highway ends just south of Quellón.

Orientation

Ancud is spread across a minor peninsula, with the Canal de Chacao to the east and the Golfo de Quetalmahue to the west; it is 27km (17 miles) from the Chacao ferry dock. The city is not laid out on a regular grid pattern, and its crooked streets might easily confuse anyone driving into the city. Avenida Aníbal Pinto is the main entrance road that funnels drivers into the center of town. Most attractions are located within several blocks of the plaza.

Visitor Information

Sernatur's office is on the plaza, at Libertad 655 (✆ **65/622800;** fax 65/622665). It's open daily from 8:30am to 7pm during January and February; the rest of the year it's open Monday through Thursday from 8:30am to 5:30pm, Friday from 8:30am to 4:30pm, and closed on weekends.

SPECIAL EVENTS From the second week in January to the last week of February, the city hosts the "Different and Magical Summer of Ancud." The event kicks off with classical music concerts and a 3-day food and folklore festival at the Arena Gruesa (third week in January) and a shore-fishing contest (second week of February), and culminates with a fireworks display, again in Arena Gruesa (third week of February). For more information, call ✆ **65/628163** (municipal tourism information) or Sernatur (✆ **65/622800**).

Fast Facts Ancud

Currency Exchange There are no places to exchange money here, but there are a couple of ATMs on Ramírez, near the plaza.

Ferry Ferry tickets are paid for on board; for information, call **Navimag** (✆ **65/682207**) or **Transmarchilay** (✆ **65/270416**). Offices are located in Quellón.

Hospital The hospital is at Almirante Latorre 301 (✆ **65/622356**).

Internet Access Internet access can be found at **Entel,** on Pudeto 219 (on the Plaza, near Correos de Chile).

Laundry Laundry services are available at the **Clean Center,** Pudeto 45, half a block from the plaza.

WHAT TO SEE & DO

Fuerte San Antonio Built in 1770 and fortified with cannons aimed at the port entrance, Fort San Antonio was Spain's last stronghold in Chile after the War of Independence. The Spanish flag last flew here on January 19, 1826, and just 6 days later, Peru's El Callao surrendered, ending Spanish rule in South America forever. Okay, it's not much, but the site affords a sweeping ocean view, and the Hostería Ancud is next to the site if you're looking for a place for lunch.

San Antonio and Cochrane (below Hostería Ancud). No phone. Free admission. Daily 24 hrs.

Museo Regional de Ancud Audelio Bórquez Canobra ★★ Kids This handsome, well-designed museum features a wide variety of exhibits related to the history and culture of Chiloé. The museum includes a large courtyard with sculptures depicting the mythological characters that form part of Chilote folklore. Inside you'll find interactive displays designed for kids and a variety of archaeological items, such as Indian arrowheads and nautical pieces, as well as displays explaining the farming and wool-production techniques used by Chilotes. A permanent exhibit covers the entire span of Chiloé's history, from the pre-Columbian era to the 20th century. Temporary exhibits display photography, sculpture, and contemporary art.

Libertad 370. ✆ **65/622413.** Admission $2 (£1.30) adults, $1 (70p) children. Jan–Feb Mon–Sun 10:30am–7pm; Mar–Dec Mon–Fri 10:30am–12:30pm and 2:30–5:30pm, Sat–Sun 10am–2pm.

Shopping

For a selection of regional handicrafts, including knitwear, baskets, local foodstuffs, and carved wooden utensils and crafts, try the **Fería Rural y Artesanal,** between Prat and Dieiocho streets (no phone; Mon–Sat 8am–9:30pm, Sun and holidays 8:30am–7:30pm). For mouthwatering smoked salmon and other local foodstuffs, stop on your way in or out of Chiloé at **Die Raucherkate,** a German-owned smokery located about 2km (1¼ miles) before the Chacao ferry dock (✆ **9/444-5912**). There is a SMOKED SALMON sign that can be easy to miss, so keep your eyes peeled.

WHERE TO STAY

Moderate

Caulín Lodge ★★ Kids Finds The Caulín Lodge is not a woodsy hotel, but rather eight cabins fronting an isolated beach and backed by a forest called the Fundo Los Cisnes, a private ecological reserve. These features make Caulín the best choice for visitors who seek quiet, undeveloped surroundings. The cabins at Caulín are more suitable for visitors with a private vehicle because the hamlet of Caulín is about 25km (16 miles) from Ancud, although taxi service is available for a moderate $10 (£6.70). All wooden cabins face a splendid estuary that's home to flamingos and black-necked swans; the cabins are rustic but comfortable and clean, and have kitchens. Cabins have two or three bedrooms, one with a full-size bed and the other(s) with a twin and a bunk bed. The spacious living area has wood floors and is warmed by a *cancahua,* a ceramic fireplace typical of the region. There is a cozy rough-hewn wood pub/restaurant, although a few minutes' walk down the beach sits the popular Ostras Caulín (see "Where to Dine," later).

Road to Caulín, 9km (5½ miles) from port of Chacao. ✆ **9/330-1220.** www.caulinlodge.cl. 8 cabins. $80–$124 (£53–£83) cabin. AE, DC, MC, V. **Amenities:** Restaurant; outdoor pool; tennis court; sauna; horseback riding. *In room:* Kitchen.

Hostería Ancud ★★ Part of the Panamericana Hoteles chain, the Hostería Ancud is as upscale as it gets in Ancud, and it is the logical choice for travelers who are not comfortable sleeping in a hostel or a funky little hotel. It fronts the Gulf of Quetalmahue and is next to the ruins of the old Fort San Antonio. All rooms come with a partial view of the ocean, as does the airy, split-level lounge and restaurant and the large outdoor deck. Rooms are tight but offer all the necessary comforts. The interior bedroom walls are made of polished alerce logs, and the lobby is adorned with woodcarvings from the region. The *hostería* also has one of the better restaurants in town (see "Where to Dine," later), as well as a cozy bar with a giant fireplace.

San Antonio 30. ✆ **65/622340.** Fax 65/622350. www.hosteriaancud.com. 24 units. $86–$110 (£57–£73) double. AE, DC, MC, V. **Amenities:** Restaurant; bar; lounge, Wi-Fi. *In room:* TV.

Hotel Galeón Azul ★ Like the Hostería Ancud, this hotel's strength is its location—perched high on a cliff above the sea—and although the rooms are not nearly as nice, some travelers prefer the character of this bed-and-breakfast to that of the Ancud. With porthole windows, a nautical motif, and curved walls, the big, sunflower-yellow hotel feels somewhat like a ship—an aging ship, that is. Upstairs an intriguing, narrow hallway has a high ceiling that peaks into skylights. The hotel is next to the regional museum; large windows look out onto the museum's sculpture garden. The rooms have recently been recarpeted and bathrooms fitted with new showers; however, rooms are still drab and lifeless. The most attractive part of the hotel is its sunny restaurant, with glass walls that look out onto the ocean.

Av. Libertad 751. ✆ **65/622567.** Fax 65/622543. www.hotelgaleonazul.cl. 16 units. $120 (£80) double. No credit cards. **Amenities:** Restaurant, Wi-Fi. *In room:* TV, no phone in some units.

Inexpensive

Mundo Nuevo ★★ (Finds) This is a hostel? You might ask yourself this question while standing in front of the fine, three-story wooden building right on the waterfront overlooking the Ancud Bay. On a sunny day, you'll be tempted to look over the sea from the terrace alongside the entrance. The spotless, pastel yellow rooms are bright and airy except for one spectacular top-floor double featuring a wooden floor polished to a mirror finish and a boat-shaped double bed, under an angled, unpainted wooden ceiling. Prices include breakfast.

Costanera (Salvador Allende) 748. ✆ **65/628383.** www.newworld.cl. 12 units. Dorm $13 (£8.70) per person; double $16–$18 (£11–£12) with shared bathroom; double $20–$28 (£13–£19) with private bathroom. Rates include breakfast. No credit cards. **Amenities:** Restaurant; kitchen; bikes; trekking gear rental; organized tours; Internet access; Wi-Fi; laundry service; TV room. *In room:* No phone.

WHERE TO DINE

For good, inexpensive seafood meals, including Chilote dishes such as *curanto, carapacho,* and *cancato,* try **La Pincoya,** Av. Prat 61 (✆ **65/622613**), which also offers views of fishermen at the pier engaging in hectic business from their colorful fishing skiffs. One restaurant popular with tourists and locals alike is **Sacho** (✆ **65/622260**), which can be found inside the somewhat grungy market (Local 7). Across from the market is **El Cangrejo,** Dieciocho 155 (✆ **65/623091**), which serves dishes such as crab *carapacho* in a kitschy ambience. Reservations at these establishments are neither necessary nor accepted.

Expensive

Casa Mar ★ INTERNATIONAL This upscale two-level pub and restaurant, a block from Mundo Azul hostel on the waterfront, has the most international menu on the island. Chilean and Chilote staples, such as *lomo a la pobre* (steak topped with a fried egg) and *caldillo de congrio* (conger eel stew), are served along with farther-afield dishes such as Turkey curry, spaghetti, and sushi.

Costanera and Errázuriz. ✆ **65/624481.** Main courses $9–$16 (£6–£11). AE, DC, MC, V. Mon–Fri noon–late; Sat noon–7pm.

Hostería Ancud ★★ INTERNATIONAL/CHILEAN The expansive dining area here commands a superb view of the ocean, and there are good offerings from the menu that mix Chilean specialties with international dishes. Seafood such as oysters on the half-shell and king crab are offered as appetizers, as well as king crab casserole and conger eel with sea urchin sauce for entrees. Meat dishes include pork loin with mustard sauce and risotto. There's also a bar for a quiet evening drink. If weather permits, you can watch the sunset from the deck.

San Antonio 30. ✆ **65/622340.** Main courses $10–$14 (£6.70–£9.30). AE, DC, MC, V. Daily noon–11pm.

Moderate

Galeón Azul ★ CHILEAN The Galeón's yellow-painted dining area has sweeping ocean views, so be sure to get a table that sits up against the front windows. The menu here features several Chilote specials, such as *curanto,* as well as the standard Chilean fish and meat grilled and served with a choice of sauces. Try the salmon stuffed with ham and mushrooms or the garlicky *locos* (abalone).

Av. Libertad 751. ✆ **65/622567.** Main courses $10–$12 (£6.70–£8). No credit cards. Daily 11am–3pm and 7–11pm.

Kurantón ★★ CHILEAN As the name implies, this restaurant specializes in *curanto.* Other standards include *paila marina* (a fish stew), but what really stands out is their luscious, creamy *carapacho* that is speckled with crabmeat. The walls of Kurantón are covered with old photos and antiques, making for an amusing place to split a bottle of wine and sample local specialties.

Prat 94. ✆ **65/623090.** Main courses $8–$12 (£5.30–£8). MC, V. Daily noon–11pm.

Ostras Caulín ★ (Finds) CHILEAN/SEAFOOD Oyster lovers won't want to miss this tiny restaurant on the shore of Caulín, about 9km (5½ miles) from Chacao and 25km (16 miles) from Ancud (from the ferry, follow the signs and turn right onto a gravel road). The restaurant, with its hardwood floors and cheery red tablecloths, sits on an estuary where they farm their own oysters, and they offer three sizes: *especial, extra,* and *exportación,* all on the half-shell and all exceptionally fresh. The menu is really just oysters served fried, stewed, and cocktailed, but there is salmon and beef stew, too. Afternoon tea

"See Food" Everywhere: What to Eat on Chiloé

Part of the experience in Chiloé is sampling the local specialties of fish and shellfish dishes the Chilotes have invented over time. You'll commonly see dried and smoked mussels hanging in markets, but I haven't had the courage to try them yet. Another common sight (though common throughout Chile) is the ***cochayuyu,*** dried seaweed tied in bundles that Chileans use for stew. Chile's plentiful salmon farms are across the sound in the Andean fjords, and Chiloé has several oyster farms along its coast, so you'll see both items frequently on the menu.

Cancato Salmon stuffed with sausage, tomatoes, and cheese and steamed in tinfoil.

Carapacho A rich crab "casserole" with a breaded crust.

Curanto Perhaps the most famous dish here in Chiloé, traditionally prepared in a hole in the ground (similar to a New England clambake). First, hot rocks are placed in the hole and then layered with mussels, clams, beef, pork, chicken, sausage, and potatoes, and topped off with tasteless, chewy pancakes called ***milcaos.*** Most restaurants cook this dish in a pot and often call it ***pulmay;*** it is then served with a cup of broth. You are supposed to take a bite and then sip the broth; I recommend you just pour the broth over the meat and fish for a tastier meal.

is served with cakes and sandwiches daily from 3 to 7pm. The restaurant caters almost exclusively to visiting foreigners, so don't expect to mingle with locals here.

On the shore in Caulín. ✆/fax **9/643-7005.** www.ostrascaulin.cl. Main courses $7–$9 (£4.70–£6). AE, DC, MC, V. Daily 8am–10pm (until midnight Jan–Feb).

Inexpensive

Pastelería Pedersen ★ Finds CAFE/BAKERY This is the place to blow your diet. There are plenty of cakes and numerous tarts to choose from, but it's the raspberry-topped cheesecake, a perennial favorite, that often sells out. They serve a rare cup of decent Joe, too. The pastry house is located in an old home with plenty of windows from which to watch a storm come in over the sea.

Cochrane 470. ✆ **65/622642.** Slice of *küchen* $2 (£1.30). No credit cards. Daily noon–7pm.

2 CASTRO

146km (91 miles) S of Ancud; 99km (61 miles) N of Quellón

Castro is spread across a promontory on the eastern shore of Chiloé, midway between Ancud and Quellón. It is the capital of Chiloé, and Chile's third-oldest city, with about 29,000 inhabitants. Visitors to the island often choose Castro as a base for its central proximity to many attractions. While not the most architecturally charming of towns, Castro's shores are nonetheless interesting for their rickety homes on stilts, known as *palafitos,* and the main church, which is painted as colorfully as an Easter egg.

Getting There & Around

BY BUS You'll find the bus terminal at the corner of Esmeralda and Sotomayor. For buses to Dalcahue and Isla Quinchao, take **Buses Arriagada,** San Martín 681; for Dalcahue and Chonchi, take **Colectivos** from the Terminal Municipal; for Isla Lemuy, take **Buses Gallardo** from its office at San Martín 681; and for transportation to the national park, take **Buses Arroyo** or **Buses Ojeda** from the Terminal Municipal. The majority of these bus companies are independently owned and operated, so it's difficult to obtain reliable information about schedules and fares in advance. I recommend showing up at the terminal or checking at the tourist information kiosk (see "Visitor Information," below) to ask questions or book a tour.

BY CAR To get to Castro from Ancud, head south on the island's only highway for 146km (91 miles), and from Quellón, north on the highway for 99km (61 miles). The cheapest car rentals anywhere in Chiloé can be found at **Salfa** (Mistral 499; ✆ **65/630422**). Reserve well in advance, especially in the summer.

Visitor Information

A new municipal **tourism kiosk** (no phone; daily 9am–6pm) on the main plaza offers a decent selection of brochures and tourist information, and the staff is fairly good at answering any questions on travel in Chiloé. There are also scale models of a handful of the area's UNESCO churches, which are an interesting diversion.

SPECIAL EVENTS A weeklong gastronomic celebration takes place the third week in February, known as the **Festival Costumbrista Chilote.** If you like to eat, this enormous feast could very well be the highlight of your trip to Chiloé. The festival centers on traditional food and Chilote culture and mythological folklore, with men roasting meat over open fires and *curanto* simmering in grand cauldrons. Come hungry. For more information, call ✆ **65/633760.**

Fast Facts Castro

Currency Exchange **Julio Barrientos,** Chacabuco 286 (✆ **65/635079**), is open Monday through Friday from 9am to 1pm and 3 to 7pm, Saturday from 9am to 1pm; from December to March, they do not close for lunch. There are several ATMs in the downtown area.

Hospital Castro's hospital is **Augusta Rifat,** Freire 852 (✆ **65/632444**).

Internet Access Almost every hotel in Castro offers Internet access for its guests free of charge, though you can also try **Café de la Brújula,** O'Higgins 308 (✆ **65/633229**), open daily from 9am to 2am, or even better, the **Entel** office at Bernardo O'Higgins 480 (✆ **65/620271**), open daily from 10am to 6pm.

Laundry **Clean Center** is located at Balmaceda 230 (✆ **65/633132**).

Travel Agency LAN Airline's representative is **Turismo Pehuén,** Blanco 299 (✆ **65/635254;** www.turismopehuen.cl), open Monday through Friday from 9am to 1:30pm and 3 to 7pm, Saturday from 10am to 1pm; it's closed Sunday.

WHAT TO SEE & DO

You might begin a tour of Castro at the plaza and the neo-Gothic **Iglesia de San Francisco ★★**, painted in lilac and peachy-pink for Pope John Paul II's visit in 1987. Impossible to miss, the 1912 national monument glows on a dreary, gray Chiloé day (which is pretty much three-quarters of the year). Renovations of the church began in late 2008 and are set to continue throughout 2009; however, most of the work is on the facade and towers, so you can still get inside.

From there, head down Esmeralda toward the waterfront and drop by the town's small **Museo Municipal de Castro ★**, half a block from the plaza (© **65/635967**). It's open from January to February Monday through Saturday from 9:30am to 7pm, and Sunday from 10:30am to 1pm; from March to December Monday through Friday from 9:30am to 1pm and 3 to 6:30pm, Saturday from 9:30am to 1pm, and closed on Sunday. Admission is free, although a donation is encouraged. This earnest, small museum features displays of Chilote farming and household wooden implements that take visitors back in time to days when day-to-day living could be an arduous chore. There are also Indian artifacts such as arrowheads, bones, and *boleadoras;* scale models; and a dramatic photographic exhibit of the damage done to Castro after the 1960 earthquake and flood.

Castro's curious ***palafitos,*** ramshackle houses built near the shore but atop stilts over water, are a colorful attraction and a tourism favorite, in spite of the fact that locals consider *palifitos* a somewhat unsanitary mess. There are four main spots to view these architectural oddities. The first two sites are at the town entrance, the third site is on the coast at the end of San Martín, and the fourth is at the cove of the Castro Fjord, on the way out of town on Rte. 5.

A short taxi ride will take you to the **Parque Municipal,** home to the Costumbrista Festival in February and the **Museo de Arte Moderno (MAM; © 65/635454**). Admission is free, and it's open daily January and February from 10am to 6pm; November, December, and March from 11am to 2pm. It's closed April through October, but opening hours can randomly change. If the museum is closed, call to arrange a private viewing. If the weather is clear, visitors to the park are treated to stretching views of Castro and the Andes. MAM, housed in several renovated shingled barns, is one of the few contemporary art museums in the country, and it often hosts exhibitions by some of Chile's most prominent artists.

Shopping

The **Fería Artesanal,** on Lillo at the port, brings together dozens of artisans who offer a superb selection of hand-knitted woolen goods and handicrafts. Here you'll find the island's typical tightly woven ponchos; the raw wool used makes them water resistant. Vendors open their booths independently, and hours are roughly from 10am to 5pm April through November, and from 10am to 9pm December through March.

WHERE TO STAY

Moderate

Hostería Castro ★ This *hostería* is about as upscale as hotels get in Castro. Built in 1970, the Hostería Castro is solidly comfortable and clean, offering all the standard amenities of a midrange hotel; however, the rooms are cramped, and in more than a few it is difficult to walk around the bed. Ask to see several rooms, if you can, because a few are larger. Probably the best feature of the hotel is its cast-iron fireplace in the bar for cozying up with a pisco sour, and the decent bar/disco downstairs. The hotel overlooks the ocean, but only the rooms on the eastern side (rooms ending in odd numbers) have views of the water; rooms on the western side have a leafy view of a stand of trees. The white-tiled bathrooms are ample. The A-frame, shingled roof has a lengthy skylight that brightens the interior hallways. Service is friendly, and the bar is popular with traveling Europeans, as is Las Araucarias restaurant (see "Where to Dine," later). New suites and an indoor pool were being planned on my last visit.

Chacabuco 202. ✆ **65/632301.** Fax 65/635688. www.hosteriadecastro.cl. 29 units. $75–$90 (£50–£60) double. AE, DC, MC, V. **Amenities:** Restaurant; bar; Wi-Fi; room service; laundry service. *In room:* TV.

Unicornio Azul ★ Many people say this is the best place to stay in Castro. It's a fun place to stay, but don't expect regal comfort. Certainly, the hotel has character; it's housed in a pretty, large Victorian on the waterfront, with funky interiors decorated with framed prints of unicorns. The best rooms sit high above the main building facing out toward the water, and they come with tiny balconies and wooden floors. But they're unremarkable, and you have to hike up a long flight of stairs to get to them. Downstairs rooms are darker but newly carpeted, and a few come with bathtubs, unlike the rooms upstairs, which have showers only. The exterior is painted as pink as a Mary Kay Cadillac, and many of the wooden beams and floor-runner carpets are sugary shades of pink, too. Ongoing renovations have improved many of the mediocre rooms. The hotel has the same owners as Ancud's Hotel Galeón Azul (p. 317).

Pedro Montt 228. ✆ **65/632359.** Fax 65/632808. www.chiloeweb.com/pweb/unicornioazul. 18 units. $90–$100 (£60–£67) double. No credit cards. **Amenities:** Restaurant; bar; Wi-Fi. *In room:* TV, no phone in some units.

Inexpensive

Hostal Kolping ★ Value This hostel is a great value for the price, and really the best place to stay if you're looking for inexpensive lodging. The rooms are sunny and immaculately clean, and they come with beds with thick foam mattresses that are adequately comfortable. The rooms are all rather nondescript, but they are reasonably spacious and so are the bathrooms. A cheery dining area brightens gloomy days.

Chacabuco 217. ✆/fax **65/633273.** kolpingcastro@surnet.cl. 11 units. $28–$40 (£19–£27) double. No credit cards. **Amenities:** Lounge. *In room:* TV.

Palafitos Hostel ★★ Finds There's no better way to see Castro's signature architectural monuments than by staying in one. I have been waiting years for someone to open a hotel in a *palafito,* and finally it has happened in this restored house in the famous Gamboa district. The construction is wood from the floor to the ceiling and lots of windows let in ample light. The rooms are quite plain, with little more than a nightstand and lamp, though all have private bathrooms. Contemporary art adorns the walls throughout the building, plus there's a small lounge area with a wood-burning stove and an outdoor patio right over the water.

Ruqielme 1210, Gamboa. ✆ **65/531008.** www.palafitohostel.com. 9 units. $45–$60 (£30–£40) double. Rates include breakfast. No credit cards. **Amenities:** Wi-Fi; kitchen.

WHERE TO DINE

Several *palafitos* on the south side of downtown offer hearty local cuisine and a good way to view one from the inside. They're readily identifiable when they're serving meals. For a quick snack, on the corner across from the Cruz del Sur bus station, there is a small stand with a handful of women selling empanadas and *milcaos* (potato pancakes). For your comfort food fix, **La Piazza** (no phone), just off the square at the corner of Blanco and Esmeralda, is a decent option for pizza, pasta, and steaks.

Expensive

Kaweshkar Lounge VEGETARIAN/INTERNATIONAL This is one of several trendy pubs and lounges to have sprung up in Castro aimed at mostly backpackers and vacationing Chileans. The small, funky dining space serves mostly vegetarian and organic food, though they do offer some seafood dishes, sandwiches, and crepes. DJs spin on weekends, and they occasionally host live music in the basement.

Encalada 31. ✆ **56/85160475.** Main courses $8–$12 (£5.30–£8). No credit cards. Daily noon–4pm and 8pm–midnight.

Moderate

Las Araucarias ★ INTERNATIONAL/CHILEAN Las Araucarias is Hostería Castro's restaurant, and it is one of the top places to dine in town. The atmosphere is better during lunchtime, with the view and the airy interiors brought on by the two-story-high ceilings and a wall of windows; at night the dining room's airiness seems to encourage echoes, but it is comfortable nevertheless. The menu is steak and seafood, featuring Chilean classics and Chiloé specialties such as *carapacho* and *curanto.* There's also a wide selection of meat dishes, such as filet mignon wrapped in bacon and served with sautéed vegetables. You might want to call ahead; the hotel often has a buffet special that is usually themed (German food, for example), and although it is quite good, it might not be what you're in the mood for.

Chacabuco 202. ✆ **65/632301.** Fax 65/635688. Main courses $7–$10 (£4.70–£6.70). AE, DC, MC, V. Mon–Sat noon–midnight.

Octavio ★★ CHILEAN Octavio has the best atmosphere in Castro, with a wood-shingled, airy dining area that sits directly over the water, and a panorama of windows showcasing the view. The restaurant specializes in Chilote specials—it's known around town for its *curanto.* It also serves seafood specials such as *mariscal,* a shellfish stew made with onion and cilantro, and other typical Chilean dishes, such as breaded cutlets and filet mignon. Fish is delivered daily. This place has a simple menu and simple food, but it is all very good, including a few sandwiches and soups if you don't want a full meal. Octavio is typically more popular with visitors to Castro, while Sacho (see below) is more popular with locals, most likely because it is cheaper.

Pedro Montt 261. ✆ **65/632855.** Main courses $7–$10 (£4.70–£6.70). No credit cards. Daily 10am–midnight.

Sacho ★ (Value) SEAFOOD/CHILEAN It doesn't have the most eye-catching ambience, but Sacho serves some of the best cuisine in Castro, a fact clearly evident by the throngs of locals who patronize the restaurant daily. The upstairs dining room has large windows and a view of the water. The specialty here is seafood, and they serve the cheapest abalone *locos* I've seen anywhere in Chile. Try starting off with a plate of clams Sacho raw, steamed, or broiled, and served with onion, lemon, whiskey, and Parmesan; then follow it up with a *cancato.* Typically the only fish served here is *congrio* (conger eel) and salmon, but they do have hake and sea bass from December to March.

Thompson 213. ✆ **65/632079.** Main courses $8–$10 (£5.30–£6.70); $13 (£8.70) buffet first Sun of each month. No credit cards. Mar–Dec daily noon–4pm and 8pm–midnight; Jan–Feb daily noon–midnight.

Inexpensive

Años Luz Chiloé ★ Value INTERNATIONAL/PUB FARE Right on the main plaza, this is the most happening place in Castro. The attractive main dining area, with its hardwood floors, has windows looking out onto bustling San Martín Street, where locals sip coffee, pisco sours, and beer. A simple but delicious selection of salads, sandwiches, and a few meat dishes is served. The smoked salmon salad is yummy, with lots of fresh green lettuce and locally smoked salmon, and the steak and fries is the top choice for a main course. The back area has more of a pub feel, with tables closer together and local Castro "yuppies" drinking pint-size beers. The unusual bar area is carved out from a real wooden boat. Service tends to be slow.

San Martín 309. ✆ **65/532-700.** Main courses $6–$9 (£4–£6). MC, V. Daily 9:30am–midnight (Sat–Sun until 2–3am).

Café La Brújula del Cuerpo CAFE This sizable cafe on the plaza (the name translates as "the Body's Compass") is the social center for residents of Castro. It's perennially active thanks to its friendly service and extensive menu offering sandwiches, salads, main dishes, ice cream, desserts, espresso, and delicious fresh juices. The cafe/restaurant is open all day, and you'll often find travelers writing out postcards here. There's also one computer for Internet use.

O'Higgins 308. ✆ **65/633229.** Main courses $6–$9 (£4–£6); sandwiches $4–$6 (£2.70–£4). MC, V. Daily 11am–midnight.

3 EXCURSIONS BEYOND CASTRO

Few Chilean towns surpass the entrancing beauty of **Dalcahue, Achao,** and **Curaco de Vélez,** the latter two located on the **Isla Quinchao.** The towns and the countryside separating them are Chiloé highlights, offering lush scenery and a glimpse into the Chilote's culture and day-to-day life.

Just off Rte. 5, the island's only major highway, **Dalcahue** is a little town whose prosperity is best illustrated by the hustle and bustle of salmon industry workers at the pier, unloading and loading crates of fish byproducts to be processed. Dalcahue's other thriving industry (although on a smaller scale) is its **Feria Artesanal** ★★, located at the waterfront about 2 blocks southwest of the plaza. Every Thursday and Sunday, artisans drive or paddle in to Dalcahue from the surrounding area to hawk their knitwear, baskets, hand-carved wood items, clothing, and more. In a boat-shaped wooden building beside the restaurant, several relatively slick restaurants have been installed serving Chilote cuisine. **Sirena's** is the best of these.

At the plaza sits one of the larger Chiloé churches, with scalloped porticos. Across the plaza, on the corner, you'll find the tiny **Museo Histórico Etnográfico** ★, Pedro Montt 105 (✆ **65/642375**), which houses a cluttered array of stuffed birds and Indian and colonial-era artifacts. It's open daily from 9am to 5pm and admission is free. For directions to Dalcahue, see "Essentials" under Castro, earlier. All transportation stops in Dalcahue first before crossing over to Quinchao.

Several blocks away at Dalcahue's pier is the ferry to **Isla Quinchao.** The ferry makes the 5-minute ride almost continuously from 7am to 10:30pm every day ($8/£5.30 for cars round-trip). This is one of Chiloé's most populated islands, a magical landscape of plump, rolling hills, where smoke slowly wafts from clapboard homes and Chilote farmers can be seen tilling their land with oxen and a plow. The island also affords visitors with spectacular views of the Gulf of Ancud and the scattered, pint-size islands that sit between the Isla Quinchao and the mainland.

The first town you'll encounter upon exiting the ferry is **Curaco de Vélez,** a historic village whose former prosperity brought about by wool production and whaling can be witnessed through the grand, weather-beaten homes that line the streets. If you are hungry and are feeling adventuresome, follow the yellow OSTRAS street signs to an open-air restaurant, **Ostras El Trunco**, across the street from the water. Here you can slurp three different kinds of oysters, shucked right in front of you, for a quarter of the price you would pay back home.

Continue southeast along the island's single, unnamed main road to **Achao,** a former Jesuit colony founded in 1743 and home to the oldest church in Chiloé. Made entirely of cypress, alerce, and mañío, this church is as plain as a brown paper bag from the outside, but one step inside and all impressions change due to its multicolored interiors and whimsical decorations. Take a walk along the waterfront for people-watching, and bring your camera for the photo op along the shore, where red, yellow, and sky-blue fishing boats bob and dance in the bay. Throughout the Island of Quinchao, you'll find wooden gazebos atop well-designed lookout points along the road. Here's hoping the weather allows you to take full advantage of them. The homes in Achao are characterized by the region's penchant for adapting shingles into a variety of geometrical patterns, from concave to convex, circular to triangular, all nailed tightly together to keep the rain out. At the pier you can hire boatmen (be prepared to negotiate) to take you to some of the more remote islands such as Mechuque. If you have time, take a seat at **Mar y Velas,** in the building overlooking the harbor just steps away. It's known as one of the best traditional Chilote restaurants anywhere on the archipelago and serves some of the freshest mussels and clams around.

I recommend that you make the aforementioned destinations a priority, but if you still have enough time, try to make it to **Chonchi.** About 32km (20 miles) south of Castro, on the main highway, this pleasant town is home to the best-preserved 18th-century buildings on the island. The early prosperity brought on by the timber export industry (mostly cypress) at that time is reflected in the handsome wooden houses and buildings around town. Made from fermented cow's milk, *Licor de Oro* is as much a cultural experience as it is an intoxicating elixir. Chonchi has created a cottage industry out of this liqueur's production, and drinking it here is the norm. Made with fruits, herbs, or, in some cases, sugar and egg (think eggnog), the liqueur isn't as bad as you might think. You'll find it at Chonchi's *Fería,* located on the corner of Irarrázaval (along the coast) and Canessa streets. There is one decent lodging option if you want to stick around, **Esmeralda by the Sea** (✆ **65/671328;** www.esmeraldabythesea.cl), which charges $30 (£20) for a double.

Quellón, at the southern end of the Pan-American Highway, is another 72km (45 miles) south. It's not particularly attractive, but it's the departure (or arrival) port for ferries to Chaitén on the Carretera Austral or for the ferries that ply the fjords southwest to Puerto Chacabuco, a fantastic, 37-hour alternative to the more common trip directly from Puerto Montt. The latter is served by Aysén Express (✆ **65/680047** in Quellón, or 67/240956, Coyhaique head office), and Naviera Australon, Pedro Montt 457 (✆ **65/682207;** www.navieraustral.cl); reserve well in advance for either of the two. Quellón is also the departure point for boat trips to Inio in the Tantauco private preserve that takes up much of the island south of the town (see later). One of the most modern hotel options on the entire island is **Patagonia Insular** (Ladrilleros 1737; ✆ **65/681610;** www.patagoniainsular.cl; $75/£50 double) a Wi-Fi–enabled 30-room hotel that overlooks the water.

PARQUE NACIONAL DE CHILOE

Chiloé National Park, on the western coast of Chiloé, covers 43,000 hectares (106,000 acres) and is divided into three sectors: **Chanquin, Middle,** and **North.** This park's strong suit is its **short hikes** that allow you to savor the best the park has to offer; in fact, the 19km (12-mile) backpacker's hike is disappointing. Lodging at the park is a super deal, too, with attractive cabins for about $40 (£27) a night. The Chanquin sector is connected by a dirt road that branches off Rte. 5, about 35km (22 miles) south of Castro; this is where you'll find the Conaf ranger station and a visitor center. This is the only truly suitable part of the park for visiting, due to its easy access and good trail conditions (unlike the North, or "Chepu," sector). The Middle section (also referred to as "Metalqui") is a protected island with a large sea lion colony, but visitors are not allowed there.

For transportation to the national park, take **Buses Arroyo** or **Buses Ojeda** (no phone) from the Terminal Municipal. Buses depart once daily in low season and twice daily in high season, though schedules vary. The park is wild and wet—very, very wet—but it is one of the few places to see old-growth, thick rainforest bordering the coast. Many backpackers come in the summer to hike through the park's forest and along vast stretches of sandy beach that often peak into sand dunes.

Visitors first arrive at the tiny village of **Cucao,** the gateway to the national park, which was devastated by a 1960 tidal wave; today it is a collection of rickety homes. This is where you'll find the four **Cabañas Conaf,** each for six guests, and they have kitchenettes, so come prepared (✆ **65/532502;** pnchiloe@conaf.cl). After the suspension bridge, visitors will find the park interpretation center run by Conaf (Chile's national park service), which has environmental displays and information about hiking trails. From here hikers have an option of three trails. The short, though very informative (English-language signs are here) 770m (2,926-ft.) **Sendero El Tepual** winds through thick, humid tepú forest. The **Sendero Dunas de Cucao** is about 1.5km (a little less than 1 mile), and it passes alternately through dense vegetation and open stretches of sand dunes blanketed in golden grass.

Vast and desolate, this stretch of coastline is one of the most beautiful in Chile. If you are lucky and arrive at low tide, a handful of locals might be here digging *machas,* or razor clams, out of the sand, which they sell to buyers all the way to Puerto Montt. There is a 20km (12-mile) backpacker's trek via a long trail on the coast, which weaves in and out of evergreen forest and sandy beach until arriving at Conaf's backcountry refuge, **Cole-Cole.** In truth, the hike is overrated, but backpackers will enjoy camping out in this lovely environment. From here it's another 2 hours to Conaf's other refuge, **Anay.** The refuges are in bad condition, and it is recommended that you bring a tent. Parque Nacional Chiloé has a variety of campsites, and it is open every day from 9am to 7:30pm; admission is $2 (£1.30) adults, free for children.

South of the national park, a private preserve 30km (19 miles) southwest of Chonchi has recently been established. Called **Tepuhueico,** it features a lake and a fine eco-lodge of the same name, built in gray cypress wood in a style that reminds me of Le Corbusier (✆ **65/633958**). The lodge has seven doubles with en-suite bathrooms, along with two *cabañas.* Electrical light runs from 9pm to midnight. It has a hot tub in the garden and plenty of possibilities for hiking and fishing.

Another much larger but very remote private preserve, **Tantauco** ★★ opened here in 2005. Bought by billionaire entrepreneur and politician Sebastián Piñera, the park comprises some 100,000 hectares (250,000 acres), uninhabited except for the 30-family fishing hamlet of Inio on its southern coast. At press time, facilities were limited. One very rough road leads through a northern sliver to the Chaiguata and Chaiguaco lagoons, with one campground with 20 sites charging $10 (£6.70); at Inio, there's a campground with 15 sites, and a modern barbecue grill, for the same fee. A dozen hiking trails have been established in the park. One weekly boat heads to Inio from Quellón for $22 (£15). Information for the park is at Av. La Paz 68 in Quellón (✆ **65/680066;** www.parquetantauco.cl), open daily from 9am to 6pm. In Santiago, contact **Fundación Futuro,** Av. Apoquindo 3000, 19th floor (✆ **2/422-7322;** www.fundacionfuturo.cl/parque_chiloe.php).

SPORTS, GUIDED TOURS & OTHER ACTIVITIES

Turismo Pehuén, Blanco 299 in Castro (✆/fax **65/635254;** www.turismopehuen.cl), is the most reliable, respected agency in Chiloé, offering a variety of tours in the area that include hiking in the national park and guided visits to Dalcahue and Achao; and, during the summer only, horseback riding, boat tours, and overflight tours that give passengers an aerial view of the island. It's really the most complete tour agency; however, **Queilén Bus,** Villa Llau Llau s/n (✆ **65/632594;** fax 65/635600; queilenbus@surnet.cl), also offers guided tours around the area.

The calm, fairy-tale bays and coves of Chiloé and the emerald Andean fjords across the sound render this the best region in Chile for **sea kayaking** and **boating.** I strongly recommend that visitors interested in these sports consider the following two excellent tour operators that offer trips for several days or longer. These operators can customize trips according to your experience and stamina; in many cases, you don't need kayak experience at all, just a willingness to learn. Here are my picks.

Altué Expeditions is Chile's foremost tour operator for trekking, horseback riding, and kayaking, and their kayak center on the shore of Dalcahue, one of the prettiest areas of Chiloé, is the ideal base for practicing the sport. The center has a Chiloé-style shingled and very attractive lodge for overnight stays, and they plan longer journeys that include the Andean fjords and hot spring visits, using a Chilote boat as a support vessel (camping at night). There's a hot tub at the lodge, and they treat guests to a typical *curanto* meal while visiting. The superb crew is not only knowledgeable, but friendly, too. Trips around Chiloé archipelago last 4 days and 3 nights; trips including the Andean fjords last 9 days and 8 nights. Call or e-mail for pricing information, as group size is a factor in cost (✆ **2/233-2964** in Santiago, or 65/641110 in Chiloé; www.seakayakchile.com).

For kayaking, and especially sailing and soft-adventure nature and cultural tours, try the top-notch operation **Austral Adventures** (✆ **65/625977** or 9/642-8936; www.austral-adventures.com). The U.S./Chilean outfit specializes in luxury excursions around Chiloé and the Andean fjords, offering a 3-day/2-night round-trip "River and Sea kayaking in Chiloé" tour ($409/£273 per person) and a 6-day/5-night "Patagonian Fjords & the Wonders of the Chiloé Archipelago" tour ($1,775/£1,183 per person). Their tours include a bilingual guide, private transport from Ancud, and lodging and meals. For those short on time, Austral Adventures also offers some day options for $40 (£27) per person from Ancud, including a coastal hike and penguin colony (minimum four people), and sea kayaking the Ancud bay (minimum three people). In April and May, **Nomads of the Seas** (✆ **56/414-4600;** www.nomadsoftheseas.com) offers 3-day/2-night ultraluxurious gastronomic cruises with well-known Chilean chefs on board the *Atmosphere* cruise ship, which departs Puerto Montt and stops in Chiloé. Call or e-mail for pricing and schedules.

For boat trips that will take you to view **blue whales** in the December-to-February season, contact Carlos Villalobos at **Agencia Tic-Toc** (carlosv@surnet.cl) in Quellón. The cost is $120 (£80) per person, with a minimum of four passengers, for a full day excursion.

12

The Carretera Austral

South of Puerto Montt, the population thins and the vegetation thickens. This is the region of northwest Patagonia commonly called the "Carretera Austral," named for the dirt route that runs south to tiny Villa O'Higgins between 48° and 49° latitude. It's a 1,240km (769-mile) dirt-and-gravel road that bends and twists through thick virgin rainforest, past glacial-fed rivers and aquamarine lakes; jagged, white-capped peaks that rise above open valleys; and precipitous cliffs with cascading ribbons of waterfalls at every turn. If you like your scenery remote and rugged, this is the place for you. Though much less traveled than the famous Torres del Paine, in many ways, a journey down this "highway" is *the* quintessential Chilean road trip, and many of its natural attractions are as stunning as any you'll find farther south. There are also some of the country's best fly-fishing lodges, one of the world's top rivers for rafting, hot springs, and a sailing journey to one of Chile's most awe-inspiring glaciers. It is also home to fjords that are ideal for kayaking, and the rainforest jungle of Pumalín Park, which was severely affected by the May 2008 earthquake that wiped out the village of Chaitén.

The Carretera Austral runs from Puerto Montt in the north to **Villa O'Higgins** in the south, and passes through two regions: the southern portion of the **Región de Los Lagos** and the **Región de Aysén,** whose capital, **Coyhaique,** holds almost half the sparse population of the region, home to less than one person per square kilometer.

The area largely straddles the Andes, unlike most of Chile, where the range's summits form the eastern border.

A first few roads appeared in the 1930s, but before the mid-1970s, much of the area could only be reached by ferry or plane, and trucks servicing its tiny villages and fishing hamlets mostly had to enter from Argentina.

Worried about a very real threat of war with Argentina in the 1970s, then-dictator Augusto Pinochet sought to fortify Chile's presence in this isolated region by connecting the existing roads with the rest of the country. More than 30 years later and at a staggering cost above $300 million (and counting) and the lives of more than two dozen men, work continues.

1 DRIVING THE CARRETERA AUSTRAL ★★

Although it is possible to reach most destinations in this region by ferry, bus, or plane, road improvements and an expansion of services mean an increasing number of travelers are choosing to drive the Carretera Austral. It's not as enormous an undertaking as it sounds, but it can be costly, especially when you factor in the cost of ferry rides, drop-off fees (about $500/£333), and gas. Also, the remoteness and increasing popularity of the region among travelers makes it one of Chile's more expensive destinations.

Several agencies in Puerto Montt (at the airport) and Coyhaique offer one-way car rentals, and some allow you to cross into Argentina or leave the car as far away as Punta Arenas, Chile. (See "Essentials" under "Puerto Montt," in chapter 10.) Alternatively, you could rent a car in Coyhaique and drive north, stopping in Puyuhuapi before heading on

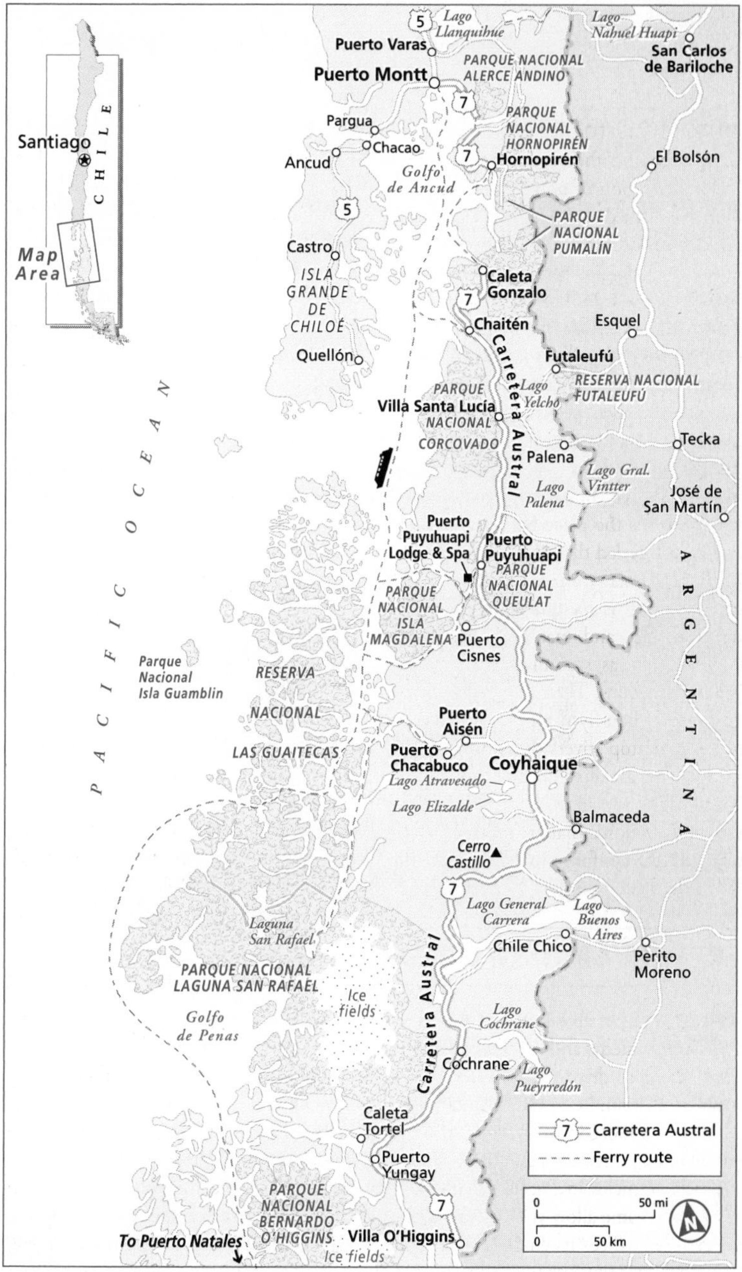
Lago Llanquihue
Lago Nahuel Huapi
Puerto Varas
Puerto Montt
PARQUE NACIONAL ALERCE ANDINO
San Carlos de Bariloche
PARQUE NACIONAL HORNOPIRÉN
Pargua
Chacao
Ancud
Hornopirén
El Bolsón
Golfo de Ancud
Santiago
CHILE
Map Area
PARQUE NACIONAL PUMALÍN
Castro
ISLA GRANDE DE CHILOÉ
Caleta Gonzalo
Chaitén
Esquel
Quellón
Futaleufú
RESERVA NACIONAL FUTALEUFÚ
Carretera Austral
Lago Yelcho
PARQUE NACIONAL CORCOVADO
Villa Santa Lucía
Palena
Tecka
Lago Gral. Vintter
Lago Palena
José de San Martín
PACIFIC OCEAN
Puerto Puyuhuapi Lodge & Spa
Puerto Puyuhuapi
PARQUE NACIONAL QUEULAT
PARQUE NACIONAL ISLA MAGDALENA
Puerto Cisnes
ARGENTINA
Parque Nacional Isla Guamblin
RESERVA NACIONAL LAS GUAITECAS
Puerto Aisén
Puerto Chacabuco
Coyhaique
Lago Atravesado
Lago Elizalde
Balmaceda
Cerro Castillo
Lago General Carrera
Lago Buenos Aires
Laguna San Rafael
Chile Chico
Perito Moreno
PARQUE NACIONAL LAGUNA SAN RAFAEL
Ice fields
Golfo de Penas
Lago Cochrane
Cochrane
Lago Pueyrredón
Caleta Tortel
Puerto Yungay
7 Carretera Austral
Ferry route
0 50 mi
0 50 km
N
PARQUE NACIONAL BERNARDO O'HIGGINS
To Puerto Natales
Villa O'Higgins
Ice fields

to Futaleufú. Although you'd have to backtrack to Coyhaique to return the car, this is a less expensive option, even if you pay the extra insurance necessary to return via Argentina. (See "Coyhaique," later in this chapter, for information.)

The most troublesome considerations are flat tires, slippery roads, and foul weather, any of which can strike at any time. Renting an extra spare tire is a wise add-on.

ESSENTIALS

FERRY CROSSINGS Make reservations for ferry services well in advance, as they tend to fill up, even during the low season. The trip from Puerto Montt to Chaitén requires a ferry crossing (ferries are in operation all year, though the frequency is less than in previous years). Contact **Naviera Austral** (© **65/270430;** www.navieraustral.cl) for information.

GAS Service stations can be found at reasonable intervals, and some smaller towns such as Futaleufú or Villa O'Higgins sell gas in jugs from stores or private residences, but some travelers feel safer carrying a backup canister of fuel. Canisters can be purchased from any service station or rented from any car rental agency.

CROSSING INTO ARGENTINA Drivers who head into Argentina must prove that they are the owner of their car, or have their rental agency set up the proper paperwork, which must be completed by your agency 48 hours in advance, to show you are driving a rental car. Extra insurance usually has to be purchased; check with the rental agency. The department store Falabella offers a 10-day plan for $37 (£25) and a 30-day plan for $60 (£40). Drivers must fill out a detailed form and are then given a copy to carry with them until crossing back into Chile.

ROAD CONDITIONS The Carretera Austral is made largely of dirt and gravel, which can get slippery during a storm. A 4×4 vehicle is necessary if going beyond any town center, especially if snow is in the forecast. Some rental agencies insist that you rent a truck with high clearance. Giant potholes are the exception, not the norm, but they can cause a car to spin out or even flip if driving too fast. For this reason, drivers are cautioned to keep their speed between 40kmph (25 mph) and 60kmph (37 mph). When it's wet or the road curves, you need to slow down even more.

HITCHHIKERS Road courtesy dictates that you might have to pick up a hitchhiker or two along the way. Most hitchhikers are humble local folk who simply do not have the means to get from place to place (during the summer many foreign backpackers try to get a lift, too). Use your own judgment. You should always lend a hand to anyone whose car has broken down.

GETTING AROUND BY BUS

There is inexpensive, frequent summer service and intermittent winter service to and from destinations along the Carretera Austral for those who choose not to drive. It takes longer, and you won't have the opportunity to stop at points of interest along the way, but every town has a tour operator that can usually get you to outlying sites for day trips. Also, the breathtaking scenery never fails to dazzle, even if you can't get off the bus.

The 5-hour journey from Puerto Montt to Hornopirén (for the summer-only ferry to Caleta Gonzalo) is no longer running due to the eruption of the Chaitén volcano in May 2008, and there is no telling when operations might resume. Call **Buses Fierro** (© **65/421522**) for updated information. Buses from Chaitén previously left for Futaleufú an average of five to six times per week during the summer, and about three times per week during the winter, though again, service has been significantly affected here; you should check on the present conditions before making any plans.

Buses from Chaitén to Coyhaique, stopping first in Puyuhuapi, used to leave up to four times per week year-round, though timetables will continue to be affected by the eruption. For information about buses from Chaitén, see "Getting There," under "Chaitén," later. Note that bus schedules are subject to change without notice.

2 PARQUE NACIONAL ALERCE ANDINO ★★

46km (29 miles) SE of Puerto Montt

The Carretera Austral is also known as Rte. 7, and it begins just outside the city limits of Puerto Montt, following the coast of Reloncaví Sound until it reaches **Parque Nacional Alerce Andino,** a place to indulge in quiet walks or canoe rides through dense forest. This 39,255-hectare (96,960-acre) park is home to the alerce, which is often compared to the sequoia for its thick diameter and height. These venerable giants can live more than 3,000 years, making them the second-oldest tree, after the American bristlecone pine. Heavy fines are levied against anyone caught harming or cutting one down, though a flourishing black market in the wood still threatens the trees even in some protected areas. Other species in the park include evergreen beech, mañío, canelo, ulmo, and thick crops of ferns. It can get pretty wet here year-round, so bring rain gear just in case.

The park itself is serviced by a rough dirt road that leads to a **Conaf guard station** in what's known as the **Chaica sector,** where there is a campground and the trail head for the half-hour round-trip walk to a waterfall and a fenced-off 3,000-year-old alerce tree. The walk to Laguna Chaiquenes is about 5.5km (3.5 miles), and to Lago Triángulo about 10km (6.25 miles) from the campground. Roads, trails, and campgrounds are often washed out or impeded by falling trees. Be sure to check for road conditions before heading out. For more information, contact the Conaf office in Puerto Montt, at Ochagavía 464 (✆ **65/254882;** www.conaf.cl).

The park's second sector, **Laguna Sargazo,** is at Lago Chapo, and it also has campgrounds and two muddy trails for day hikes through the park's rainforest, a section of which has a thick stand of alerce trees. This sector sees fewer visitors as it is more difficult to get to if you do not have your own vehicle; buses go only as far as Correntoso, a 2-hour walk from the park entrance (although it is possible to arrange a tour; see "Getting There," below). At the park ranger station here, it is possible to rent canoes for a paddle across Lago Chapo.

GETTING THERE

If driving, head south on Rte. 7, winding past tiny villages on the gravel road until you reach Chaica, about 35km (22 miles) from Puerto Montt, where a sign indicates the road to the park entrance at the left. The park ranger station is open from 9am to 5pm, so leave your car outside the gate if you plan to return later than 5pm. Travelers without a vehicle can take **Buses Fierro** (✆ **65/289024** or 65/253022) headed in the direction of Hornopirén from the main terminal in Puerto Montt (ask to be dropped off at Chaica); however, the bus (six daily services), which costs $3.50 (£2.30), leaves visitors at an entrance road 4km (2½ miles) from the park ranger station. You might consider hiring a tour operator to take a day trip or possibly to organize an advance pickup date if you plan to camp. To get to the Lago Chapo sector, head south on Rte. 7 for about 9km (5½ miles) to Chamiza; just before the bridge, take a left toward the town Correntoso and drive 19km (12 miles) to the park entrance. **Buses Fierro** (✆ **65/289024** or 65/253022) has two daily trips, costing $3 (£2), to Correntoso that leave from the main terminal in Puerto Montt; from here, it's a 2-hour walk to the park entrance. For tours to either of the park's sectors, try **Andina del Sud,** in Puerto Varas at Del Salvador 72 (✆ **65/232811;** www.andinadelsud.com); the company's main office is in Puerto Montt at Antonio Varas 437 (✆ **65/257797**).

WHERE TO STAY

Alerce Mountain Lodge ★★ Finds This quiet, remote lodge sits on the shore of a small lake—which must be crossed by a hand-drawn ferry—at the edge of the national park and is surrounded by dense stands of stately 1,000-year-old alerce trees. This is where you go to get away from crowds. The lodge is built almost entirely of handcrafted alerce logs, with giant trunks acting as pillars in the spacious, two-story lobby. The woodsy effect continues in the cozy rooms, which are decorated with local crafts and feature forest views. The cabins have a view of the lake and come with a living room and two bedrooms, and accommodate a maximum of six guests. One of the highlights at this lodge is that the surrounding trails are not open to the general public, so you'll have them to yourself. Bilingual guides lead horseback rides and day hikes that can last as long as 7 hours or as little as a half-hour.

Carretera Austral, Km 36. ✆/fax **65/286969.** www.mountainlodge.cl. 11 units, 3 *cabañas.* All-inclusive packages run per person, double occupancy: 2 nights/3 days $460 (£307); 3 nights/4 days $680 (£453). Inquire about other packages and off-season discounts. AE, DC, MC, V. **Amenities:** Restaurant; bar; Jacuzzi; sauna; game room.

3 PUMALIN PARK ★★

The Pumalín Park Project, the world's largest private nature reserve, spans roughly 300,000 hectares (742,000 acres) and incorporates temperate rainforest, glaciers, fjords, thundering waterfalls and rivers, and stands of ancient alerce trees. It's a marvelous place, a park that exists thanks to U.S. millionaire and philanthropist Douglas Tompkins, who bought his first chunk of land here in 1991.

The project has generated considerable controversy and will continue to do so for the foreseeable future. At its narrowest point, just 15km (9 miles) separate the Pacific from the Argentine border, and Chile has no shortage of politicians on all sides of the political spectrum to openly worry about a foreign citizen owning strategic lands. Many also question the idea of protecting an area on this scale rather than exploiting its resources in what is still an underdeveloped country.

Over 15 years since Tompkins started accumulating the properties, he continues in the spotlight. Major energy companies Endesa Chile and Colbún seek to develop the Aysén region's vast hydrology resources to supply power to central Chile, and the power lines would run through the park. The government, meanwhile, wants to complete the Carretera Austral by slicing through the park, an idea Tompkins criticizes as expensive and unnecessarily destructive, arguing for a road along the coast. He and his wife meanwhile have continued to buy land in Patagonia (see "To the End of the Road & Beyond," later in this chapter).

At the same time, the Pumalín Park has largely won acceptance, and was officially declared a nature sanctuary in 2005, run by Tompkins's foundation, the Conservation Land Trust. In May 2008, however, problems came from a new angle. The eruption of the Chiatén volcano almost completely destroyed the infrastructure of the entire southern end of the park, which was the main entrance and had some of the finest facilities in all of Chile. At press time, this meant closure for the entire 2008–09 season, perhaps longer. Major reconstruction is needed, including the road to the park from Chiatén. To top it off, this has been paired with the latest efforts of the Chilean government to build a road right through the center of the park, connecting the Carretera Austral with the rest of the mainland.

It is imperative that you get up-to-date information before visiting Pumalín Park. Most likely the majority of facilities should be in order by December 2009 for the start of the summer, though a number of factors are at play here, including how quickly the government will repair the roads. An alternative is to visit the region's fjords and the Cahuelmó hot springs in the northern sector of the park, which can done by rented boat, kayak, or tour only (see "Organized Tours," later).

VISITOR INFORMATION

For advance information about Pumalín Park, contact their U.S. office (✆ **415/229-9339;** www.parquepumalin.cl). Travelers coming from the north should stop at Pumalín's office in Puerto Varas at Klenner 299 (✆ **65/250079**).

GETTING THERE

Hornopirén can be reached by private vehicle; take Rte. 7 south from Puerto Montt for 45km (28 miles) until reaching La Arena, from which there is a 30-minute-long ferry that leaves nine times per day, year-round, to Puelche. South from La Arena, the ferry runs from 8am to 8pm; north from Puelche, it operates from 7:15am to 7:15pm (run by Transmarchilay's **Naviera Puelche;** ✆ **65/270000** in Puerto Montt). From here it is 55km (34 miles) to Hornopirén. Bus service to Hornopirén is offered from the Puerto Montt bus station by **Buses Fierro** (✆ **65/253022**), leaving three times per day (twice on Sun).

The southern entrance to the park at Caleta Gonzalo was severely affected during the May 2008 eruption and completely shut down through 2009. Contact the park office for the latest news. When things are again in working order, you can get to Caleta Gonzalo and the southern section of the park from either Chaitén in the south (see "Chaitén," later), or by a 6-hour ferry ride from Hornopirén. (In years past, during Jan and Feb, the ferry left daily at 3pm from Hornopirén and 9am from Caleta Gonzalo; the ride takes 5 hours and costs $17/£11 per person, plus $107/£71 for a private vehicle. Outside of Jan. and Feb., visitors will need to go first to Chaitén to visit Pumalín. Reservations are necessary for vehicles; contact **Transmarchilay,** at Av. Angelmo 2187 [✆ **65/270000;** www.transmarchilay.cl]).

WHAT TO SEE & DO

Once the park reopens, you will discover a magic kingdom that you have all to yourself. The fjords that plunge into the sea rival Norway's and are simply magnificent, and the remote, natural hot springs make for a divine way to end the day, especially if you've been kayaking. Of course, it rains profusely at times, and that can test your patience, especially when setting up camp. If you cannot stand the mud and watching your fingers turn to prunes, consider a boat trip with interior sleeping arrangements.

HIKING So far, the park has a dozen trails, ranging from lengthy, multiday ones to easy, short walks. At Caleta Gonzalo, trails include the 3-hour round-trip **Sendero**

Cascada, which meanders along a footpath and elevated walkways through dense vegetation before terminating at a crashing waterfall. The **Sendero Tronador,** 12km ($7^1/_2$ miles) south of Caleta Gonzalo, takes visitors across a suspension bridge and up, up, up a steep path and wooden stepladder to a lookout point, with views of Volcán Michimahuida, then down to a lake with a campground, taking, round-trip, about $3^1/_2$ hours. The **Sendero Los Alerces** is an easy 40-minute walk through old stands of alerce.

OTHER ACTIVITIES Pumalín offers **horse pack trips** and trips to the remote **Cahuelmó Hot Springs,** all with advance reservation only. You can also tour an **organic farm;** sign up for **boat trips** around the fjord and to the sea lion rookery; or take flights over the park. Contact the official outdoor operator for the park, **Alsur Expeditions** (see below). It offers daily transportation to the hot springs for an expensive $46 (£31).

ORGANIZED TOURS The northern section's hot springs and fjords are accessible only by boat. Tours can include kayaking, camping or on-ship lodging, and hiking. The park's "official" tour operator is **Alsur Expeditions,** in Puerto Varas at Del Salvador 100 (✆/fax **65/232300;** www.alsurexpeditions.com), which has horseback riding and trekking tours, specializing in sailing aboard their small yacht (Puerto Montt–Chiloé–Pumalín) or kayaking, using a Chiloé-style support boat. But the best sea kayaking is with **Altue Sea Kayaking,** based out of Santiago, at Encomenderos 83, Las Condes (✆ **2/233-2904;** www.seakayakchile.com), with outstanding kayak trips around Pumalín, which they normally combine with a kayak tour of Chiloé (where they own a coastal lodge). Altue also has a motorized support vehicle. **Austral Adventures,** Lord Cochrane 432, Ancud (✆ **65/625977;** www.austral-adventures.com), an American-owned operation based out of Chiloé, specializes in sailing, bird-watching, and fly-fishing journeys from Puerto Montt to Pumalín, including Chiloé, aboard their newer Chiloé-style boat. Lastly, the company **Yak Expeditions** focuses on kayaking and getting from one place to another by kayak and without a support boat. It is a quieter, more activity-oriented journey, with camping as lodging where there are no lodges (✆ **2/227-0427,** 9/892-8761, or 9/299-6487; www.yakexpediciones.cl).

WHERE TO STAY & DINE

Cabañas Caleta Gonzalo ★★★ These stylish yet rustic cabins are built for two to six guests and feature details like nubby bedspreads, gingham curtains, and carved wood cabinets (but no kitchenettes). The cabins are small but very cozy, with a double bed and twin on the bottom floor and two twins above in a loft; all are bright. Damages did occur here during the eruption of Chaitén, though they are expected to be open for the 2009–10 season.

The sites at **Camping Pumalín,** on the beautiful Fiordo Reñihué, are well-kept rooms with a fire pit (firewood costs extra), a sheltered area for cooking, bathrooms with cold-water showers, and an area for washing clothing; the cost is $3 (£2) per person. About 14km ($8^3/_4$ miles) south of Caleta Gonzalo is the **Cascadas Escondidas Campground,** with sheltered tent platforms, picnic tables, cold-water showers, bathrooms, and the trail head to three waterfalls. The cost to camp here is $10 (£6.70) per tent. There are more than 20 campsites throughout the park, many of them accessible by boat or by backpacking trail; consult the park for more information.

Caleta Gonzalo s/n. ✆ **65/250079,** or 415/229-9339 in the U.S. reservasalsur@surnet.cl (reservations). 7 units. $119 (£79) double. Extra person $10 (£6.70) each. AE, DC, MC, V. **Amenities:** Restaurant.

4 CHAITEN

420km (260 miles) N of Coyhaique

Chaitén was once the main jumping-off point for exploring Pumalín, Futaleufú, and the Carretera Austral; however, the May 5, 2008 eruption of the Chaitén volcano changed the face of this charming port village forever. When the first rumbles began, most residents thought **Volcán Michimahuida** was erupting, but they eventually realized the "extinct" **Volcán Chaitén,** which had been inactive for 10,000 years, was erupting. The town, a few days after being evacuated, was nearly wiped out when the water from a melting glacier mixed with significant ash deposits and a deluge ran right through the center of town. At press time, Chaitén remained buried and residents continued on in shelter homes set up in Puerto Montt. There was talk of rebuilding the town elsewhere and even vague plans from a Chilean businessman to turn the town into a self sustainable eco-community, though no steps in either direction had yet been taken.

If you visit town now, you will find a modern day Humberstone, Chile's UNESCO World Heritage ghost town in the north near Antofagasta. Some parts of the town survived under a coating of a few inches of ash, but those toward the river were more or less demolished. In a brief walk through town, you will see houses with missing walls and broken windows and some that have been moved completely off their hinges and torn apart. The beach, which used to sit right off the edge of town, has been extended for hundreds of meters into the bay. It is a sorrowing, eerie sight that reveals just a glimpse of the awesome power of Mother Nature.

As of December 2008, about 40 people were living in the village, with just a couple of small shops open and all restaurants still closed. Several hotels, such as Hotel Schilling and Cabañas Pudú, began taking guests on a temporary basis in December 2008, though there were still no phones, little electricity, and no running water. There is no telling when, or if, the town will fully rebuild. Before heading to Chaitén, it is important to get up-to-date information before showing up.

Note: As this book was going to press, more ash spewed from the Chaitén Volcano and sounded off fresh calls for the town to be permanently moved. Check with officials on the ground for the latest information before you visit.

GETTING THERE

BY BOAT **Naviera Austral,** at Angelmó 2187 in Puerto Montt (✆ **65/270000;** www.navieraustral.cl), used to run four weekly trips from Puerto Montt (10 hr.; one-way tickets from $24/£16) and three weekly trips from Castro, Chiloé (7 hr.; $22/£15), though service has been reduced significantly, down to as little as one trip per week in mid 2009. At press time, Naviera Austral could not confirm when services would return to normal. From Quellón, south of Castro, ferries cross to Chaitén twice a week; Naviera Austral's offices in Quellón are at Pedro Montt 457 (✆ **65/682207**). In early 2009 only passengers on vehicles were allowed on the ferries from Puerto Montt and Quellón; however, foot passengers could visit if they arranged their own transportation out, often by hitching a ride with other ferry passengers.

BY PLANE Several small airlines flew back and forth between Puerto Montt and Chaitén; however, after the May 2008 eruption all were shut down with little hope of returning anytime soon. Most were on shaky ground already, but damage to the airstrip and the lack of passengers was the last nail in the coffin.

BY BUS Bus schedules in this region are always subject to change, especially because traffic here has slowed to a trickle since the 2008 eruption. Both **Chaitur** (✆/fax **65/731429;** nchaitur@hotmail.com) and **B&V Tours** (✆ **65/731390**) have information about service to destinations such as Futaleufú, Puyuhuapi, and Coyhaique. Buses to all destinations used to leave daily, from December to March; from April to November, buses to Futaleufú leave six times weekly, and four times weekly to Coyhaique, with a stop at Puyuhuapi. The road to Caleta Gonzalo and Pumalín was still destroyed at press time and a long way from being rebuilt. Check with park officials for updated information on the route.

5 SOUTH FROM CHAITEN: FUTALEUFU ★

155km (96 miles) SE of Chaitén

The road south between Chaitén and Villa Santa Lucía, where drivers turn for Futaleufú, passes through mountain scenery that affords direct views of Volcán Michimahuida rising high above the wilderness, Yelcho Glacier, and Lago Yelcho. At 25km (16 miles), you'll arrive at Amarillo, a tiny village and the turnoff point for the 5km (3-mile) drive to Termas de Río Amarillo.

TERMAS DE RIO AMARILLO These hot springs have a large temperate pool along with several outdoor and private indoor pools ($6/£4; daily 9am–dusk). Check out Pumalín's website (www.parquepumalin.cl) for updated information about their trail to the Amarillo Valley that, in 2 hours, will take you to one of best campgrounds in the area, with extensive alpine and glacier views. Or lodge at the modest, family-run **Cabañas y Hospedaje Los Mañíos,** about 100m (328 ft.) from the hot springs, for $64 (£43) for a cabin for four, $73 (£49) for a cabin for six (✆ **65/731210**).

LAGO YELCHO

Farther south, the road curves past the northern shore of Lago Yelcho and the Yelcho en la Patagonia Lodge (see below), and at 60km (37 miles) crosses the Puente Ventisquero, which bridges a milky green river; this is where you'll find the trail head to **Yelcho Glacier.** To get there, take the short road before the bridge and then walk right at the almost imperceptible sign indicating the trail. A muddy 1½-hour hike takes you through dense forest to Yelcho Glacier. The 50km (31-mile) lake itself is a hub for fly-fishing (see the lodges listed below).

At Villa Santa Lucía, the Carretera Austral continues south to Puyuhuapi, but visitors should not miss a stay, or at the very least, a detour, to Futaleufú, an idyllic mountain town with adventure activities and one of the most challenging rivers to raft in the world. The road to Futaleufú is worth the trip itself for its majestic views at every turn, first winding around the southern end of Lago Yelcho, a hub of fly-fishing, before passing the Futaleufú River and lakes Lonconao and Espolón, and on to the emerald valley surrounding the town of Futaleufú.

An Adventure Lodge

Yelcho en la Patagonia Lodge ★★ (Finds The Yelcho Lodge is a remote tourism complex on the shore of the Lake Yelcho, a beautiful emerald lake bordered by tall peaks crowned with glaciers. It is the region's only complete resort, with woodsy, attractive accommodations and a full range of excursions, especially fly-fishing. Yelcho offers three options: suites, *cabañas* for four to six guests, and 15 well-equipped campsites complete with barbecues. The white, shingled *cabañas* come with spacious kitchens, but there's also a restaurant that serves gourmet cuisine as well as barbecue roasts. The cabins have a deck and barbecue and a view of the lake seen through a stand of *arrayán* trees; note that cabins for six mean two sleep in the living area. The lodge and the indoor accommodations have handsome two-tone floors made of mañío and alerce. The lodge offers excursions with bilingual guides for fly-fishing the Yelcho River and Lago Yelcho, locally renowned for its plentiful salmon and trout. Apart from fly-fishing (which costs $3,000/£2,000 per person for a 7-day/6-night package), the lodge also has treks to Yelcho Glacier, mountain biking, horseback riding, and visits to the Río Amarillo hot springs, Futaleufú, Chaitén, and Pumalín. The lodge will pick you up from nearly any nearby location.

Lago Yelcho, Km 54, Carretera Austral, Región X. ✆ **65/731337,** or 2/196-4187 in Santiago. www.yelcho.cl. 8 units, 6 *cabañas,* 15 campsites. $135 (£90) double; $184 (£123) *cabaña* for 4; $44 (£29) camping for 4. Rates include full breakfast (except *cabaña*). AE, DC, MC, V. **Amenities:** Restaurant; tours.

FUTALEUFÚ ★★★

155km (96 miles) SE of Chaitén; 196km (122 miles) NE of Puyuhuapi

Futaleufú is one of the prettiest villages in Chile, a town of 1,200 residents who live in colorful clapboard homes nestled in an awe-inspiring amphitheater of rugged, snow-capped mountains. Futaleufú sits at the junction of two rivers, the turquoise Río Espolón and its world-renowned cousin, the Río Futaleufú, whose white-water rapids are considered some of the most challenging on the globe. Every November to April, this quaint little town becomes the base for hundreds of rafters and kayakers who come to test their mettle on the "Fu," as it's colloquially known, although just as many come to fish, hike, mountain-bike, paddle a canoe, or raft the gentler Río Espolón. Futaleufú is just kilometers from the Argentine border; it's possible to get here by road from Puerto Montt by crossing into Argentina, a route sometimes preferred for its paved roads.

There are no banks or gas stations here in Futaleufú. However, residents do sell gas out of wine jugs and other unwieldy containers; just look for signs advertising BENCINA. Note that ash did blanket the town and surrounding area during the eruption of the Chiatén volcano in May 2008, though the minor damages have been dealt with and tourist operations are back to normal.

Getting There

BY PLANE Air service into Futaleufú has been shaky since the Chaitén eruption, though you can try **Aerotaxis del Sur** (✆ **65/252523** in Puerto Montt, or 65/731268 in Futaleufú; www.aerotaxisdelsur.cl) for charter flights from Puerto Montt, weather permitting. It's entirely feasible to fly into Esquel in Argentina from Buenos Aires and then travel by road 65km (40 miles) to Futaleufú; just be sure to factor in a possible delay at the border crossing and plenty of time to make the 3- to 4-hour journey.

BY BUS During the summer, bus service with **Chaitur** (✆ **65/731429;** nchaitur@hotmail.com) used to leave every afternoon at 3pm for the 4-hour journey ($10/£6.70); however, timetables have been affected by the eruption and you should now definitely check ahead for updated information. The same goes for **Turismo Pineda** (✆ **65/731298**), which typically runs a service from Chaitén to Futaleufú on Mondays, departing at 12:30pm, for $10 (£6.70). Winter service is sketchy; try calling **B&V Tours** in Chaitén to see if they have an upcoming trip (✆ **65/731390**). From Puerto Montt via

Argentina, **Turismo Futaleufú** (✆ **65/721215**) has a Tuesday trip for $42 (£28), returning Thursdays.

BY CAR From Chaitén, take Rte. 7 south and go left to Rte. 235 at Villa Santa Lucía. The road winds around the shore of Lago Yelcho until Puerto Ramírez, where you head northeast on Rte. 231 until you reach Futaleufú.

What to See & Do

Futaleufú was put on the map by travelers with one goal in mind: to raft or kayak the internationally famous Class V waters of the village's namesake river, although just as many come to enjoy the opportunities to fly-fish, horseback ride, or just hang out amid the pristine alpine setting here. The Futaleufú is one of the most challenging rivers in the world. You've got to be good—or at least be experienced—to tackle frothing white-water so wild that certain sections have been dubbed "Hell" and "The Terminator." But rafting and kayaking companies will accommodate more prudent guests with shorter sections of the river, and the nearby Río Espolón offers a gentler ride. A paddling trip in this region is undoubtedly one of the best far-flung adventures a traveler can have in Chile.

For **fishing licenses,** go to the municipal building at O'Higgins 596 (✆ **65/721241**); it's open April to November Monday through Friday from 8am to 1:30pm and 2:30 to 5pm, December to March Monday through Friday 9am to 7pm (outside the Municipalidad). For more information on fishing, see the "Fly-Fishing Lodges on the Carretera Austral" section later.

Where to Stay

Really, most visitors to this area join one of the organized trips mentioned in the "Rafting on the Río Futaleufú" box, below. Those with a rental vehicle will find a few local cabins or basic *hospedajes* during the summer in town, although for hotels it is slim if increasing pickings here, and you'll be charged a lot for what you get. Outside Futaleufú, there are several options for lodging, including campsites that dot the 78km (48-mile) road between here and Villa Santa Lucía. If you'd like to do a little fishing, check out the **Hostal Alexis** (✆ **65/731505**), located just before Puerto Ramírez and situated on the grassy bank of Lago Yelcho. There's a hotel in an old converted farmhouse and a dozen campsites with wooden half-walls that protect sites from the wind. You can fish directly from the shore here, but the owners also offer fishing excursions. It's open from November to April only ($28/£19 double). In town, decent budget accommodations include **Posada Ely** (✆ **65/721205;** fax 65/721308).

Hostería La Antigua Casona At over 60 years, this three-story building is one of the oldest in town, but has been restored and modernized. The ground floor houses its cafe, offering full meals by reservation only. It also sells local crafts. Rooms are on the top two floors, typically furnished in wood, with wool rugs and bedspreads. An affiliated property is the **Posada Anchileufú,** a country farmhouse 4.5km (3 miles) out of town to the northeast with slightly more upscale rooms. It has three rooms, but can offer two more rooms if a group wants to book the entire place.

Manuel Rodríguez 215, Futaleufú. ✆/fax **65/721311.** www.futaleufupatagonia.cl. 4 units. $65 (£43) double; $75 (£50) triple. AE, DC, MC, V. **Amenities:** Restaurant; bar. *In room:* No phone.

Hostería Río Grande This wooden, two-story *hostería* is popular with foreign tourists for its outdoorsy design and especially its restaurant and pub. It's one of the better hotels in town, but it has lost a lot of its energy of late, and it could really stand to be upgraded, as the rooms seem expensive for their dull, standard furnishings and office-building carpet. But the atmosphere is relaxed and guests can expect a standard level of comfort. There's also an apartment (but no kitchen) for six guests. The Río Grande's restaurant is the unofficial hangout spot in town, and it has a nice atmosphere for relaxing with a beer. There's seafood throughout the week, but try to make it on Wednesday or Saturday, when the restaurant receives its fresh fish delivery by air.

O'Higgins 397, Futaleufú. ✆/fax **65/721320.** www.pachile.com. 10 units, 1 apt for 6. $110 (£73) double; $130 (£87) triple; $180 (£120) apt for 6. AE, DC, MC, V. Closed June–Oct. **Amenities:** Restaurant; bar; extensive watersports equipment rental; bikes. *In room:* No phone.

Hotel El Barranco ★ This large, green-roofed, ranch-style building is probably the best place in town. Its rustic rooms are certainly the most attractive in Futaleufú, particularly the bathrooms, featuring wash basins placed on objects like a tree stump or on an antique sewing machine. Rooms have ash-colored carpeting; apart from that they're entirely in wood, with beams on the ceiling and white linens on box-spring beds. It has plenty of outdoor tours and activities to offer, including canyoning, fly-fishing, horseback riding, kayaking, rafting, and trekking; check the website for multiday packages up to a full week.

O'Higgins 172, Futaleufú. ✆/fax **65/721314.** www.elbarrancochile.cl. 10 units. $150 (£100) double. Half- and full board available. Rates include breakfast and bicycle use. AE, DC, MC, V. **Amenities:** Restaurant; bar; pool; bikes; laundry service. *In room:* Wi-Fi.

Posada La Gringa ★ Finds This attractive German-style clapboard hotel sits on a large grassy property with excellent views of the countryside stretched out before it. It is a cozy little place that makes you feel as if you are visiting someone's home, not a hotel. With well-maintained, clean, pleasant rooms, the hotel is open from November to March only, and the owner, "La Gringa," serves an excellent breakfast.

Sargento Aldea s/n, corner of Aldea, Futaleufú. ✆ **65/721260,** or 2/235-9187 in Santiago. www.lagringachile.com. 5 units. $82 (£55) double. Rates include full breakfast. No credit cards. Closed Apr–Oct. **Amenities:** Lounge. *In room:* No phone.

Where to Dine

El Barranco and the **Hostería Río Grande** are the better places to eat in town (see earlier), but you might also check out **Restaurant Escorpio,** Gabriela Mistral 225 (✆ **65/721228**), which offers about four choices per day of simple meat and seafood dishes (no credit cards accepted; daily 11am–2am). **Restaurante Futaleufú,** Pedro Aguirre Cerda 407 (✆ **65/721295**), has a short menu with 10 or so simple dishes that all cost the same ($7/£4.70; no credit cards accepted). Sample items include homemade spaghetti and chicken stewed with peas; there's also a range of sandwiches (daily 11am–1:30am).

CORCOVADO NATIONAL PARK

The Yelcho Glacier is largely inside the 209,623-hectare (517,990-acre) **Corcovado National Park,** established in 2005, but at press time without services or any trails beyond the access to the glacier. The park stretches almost from the Yelcho River south to the Río Rodríguez, skirted by the Carretera Austral along its eastern fringe. It features two volcanoes, the Corcovado with its angled summit and the Nevado, and is being developed for whale-watching—most famously in the amusingly named Tic Toc Bay—similarly to the Tantauco project on Chiloé across the Corcovado Gulf.

The nearest village to the bay is miniscule **Puerto Raúl Marín Balmaceda,** where the Palena River meets the ocean at the end of the road from La Junta. The road, however, doesn't quite reach it yet; there's a spot upstream on the Palena River where boats depart for the 40-minute trip to the village.

Several tour operators offer kayak trips down the river, and the estancia-type **Bahía Mala Lodge** 10km (6 miles) farther down the coast offers luxury accommodations and a variety of outdoor activities; it's owned and run by Belgian developers based in Buenos Aires (© **54-11/4311-1919;** www.burcoadventure.com). Visits to a few hot springs along the Palena are also available from Puerto Raúl Marín Balmaceda.

FLY-FISHING LODGES ON THE CARRETERA AUSTRAL

Anglers around the world consider Patagonia to be one of the last great regions for fly-fishing, especially now that fishing clubs, lodges, and private individuals have bought up stretches of some the best rivers in the U.S., strictly limiting access to some of the sweetest spots for casting a line. Some of the highest trout-yielding rivers in Patagonia see only a few dozen or so fly-fishermen per year, and, therefore, angling fanatics, some of Hollywood's biggest stars, and many international bigwigs (such as ex-president George H. W. Bush, Michael Douglas, Robert Redford, and Harrison Ford) pay a visit here to escape the crowds and be at one with nature.

The following list is a guide to the best lodges from Puerto Montt to Coyhaique. They aren't cheap; most run from $250 to $600 (£167–£400) per night per person, all-inclusive (nonfishing spouses sometimes pay less, and some offer "father-son" deals, so ask before booking). Typically, they cater to few guests—around 12 at most—though larger hotels also tend to offer fly-fishing excursions. All of the following rate three Frommer's stars (our highest ranking) for their one-of-a-kind location, direct access to prize streams and lakes, service, and friendliness.

El Patagon Lodge ★★★ Owned and operated by the first-class Yan Kee Way Lodge (p. 299) near Puerto Varas, El Patagon is nestled in the temperate rainforest south of Futaleufú and Palena, and it is a remote, rustic version of the aforementioned lodge. The area's trout-filled streams and lakes draw other fly-fishing guides with clients who must drive hours to reach the region, making this lodge's immediate access a bonus for longer fishing days. In fact, the American owners of this lodge purchased the land from a float pilot and fly-fishing enthusiast who sold his map of "secret" fishing spots along with the property. The property houses four rough-hewn wood cabins for a total of eight fly-fishing guests, plus an Oregon yurt dining room, and a sauna and hot tub perched high above the Figueroa River. There are also multiday fishing journeys outside the property, with horseback rides to remote fishing streams, and stays that combine local Chilean accommodations.

Región X, Latitude 44. © **65/212030.** www.southernchilexp.com. 7-night all-inclusive packages cost, per person, around $4,250 (£2,833) for fly-fishing; $3,100 (£2,067) for sport packages. AE, DC, MC, V. **Amenities:** Restaurant; bar; lounge; sauna; hot tub. *In room:* No phone.

Heart of Patagonia Lodge ★★★ This lodge is another American-owned lodge, this time an ex-editor of *Angling Report,* John Jenkins, who settled in this region in the late 1980s. The Heart of Patagonia caters predominately to foreigners. Jenkins decided to move his business from the outskirts of Coyhaique to save on drive time and take advantage of the morning and evening hatch, but the lodge is still close enough to town, if that is important to you. The lodge is in a remodeled home, originally built in the 1930s by an Austrian immigrant, and the owner has maintained the old-fashioned style

Rafting on the Río Futaleufú

The Futaleufú River is known as one of the best white-water rivers in the world, and an adventure down the rapids here rates as one of the highlights of a Chilean holiday. Tour operators can organize hard-adventure rafting expeditions, or shorter rafting on more mellow sections of the Futaleufú. There is also the Espolón River closer to town, which is suitable for light day rafting and kayaking trips (the **Hostería Río Grande,** see below, has sit-on-top kayak day rentals for the Espolón). The following three outfitters are the best around, and they offer weeklong all-inclusive packages that cost between $2,750 and $3,500 (£1,833–£2,333).

The rafting and kayaking company with the most experience and local knowledge is **Expediciones Chile,** run by American Olympic kayaker Chris Spelius. This outfit has one of the best-run all-inclusive trips here, with a series of lodges both in Futaleufú and in the surrounding backcountry; they're based at the three-story townhouse **Adventure Lodge,** Gabriela Mistral 296 (✆ **800/488-9082** in the U.S., or 65/721386 in Futaleufú; www.exchile.com). Expediciones Chile is, however, less of a lodge and more of an interconnected series of properties that include camping and the get-away-from-it-all cabins **CondorNest Ranch at Tres Campos.** These backcountry cabins are serviced by a staff that leaves every evening to ensure absolute privacy, and there are wood-fired saunas and massage service on the premises. Depending on your desire, Expediciones Chile can organize a week that can include rafting, kayaking, horseback riding, hiking, and fly-fishing. Contact them ahead of time for day trips if you are short on time.

Another outstanding pick is the all-inclusive rafting outfit **Earth River Expeditions** (✆ **800/643-2784;** www.earthriver.com), with a 400-hectare (1,000-acre) private ranch outside of Futaleufú fitted with camp-style lodging in lofty tree houses and "cliff dwellings" with tent platforms and sweeping views. They've been around for more than a decade, and, like Expediciones Chile, they boast superb guides whose local knowledge is as keen as their concern for safety. They also have outdoor hot tubs and massage services.

Lastly, try the rafting pros **Bío Bío Expeditions** (✆ **800/246-7238** in the U.S.; www.bbxrafting.com), a U.S.-based company with a passion for the Futaleufú. Like the other two outfits mentioned above, Bío Bío utilizes river-front lodging in the form of camping (on forest-canopied tent platforms) and cabins, and they combine a full-day horseback ride to a glacier to raft the river that runs from it. They also have a sauna and yoga classes.

with antiques and other homey touches. The lodge has good Chilean food as well as hiking and horseback riding options; it's probably the best lodge for those with nonfishing spouses.

18km (11 miles) from Puerto Aysén, road to Coyhaique. ✆ **67/334906.** www.heartofpatagonia.com. 6 units. 3-night all-inclusive packages cost, per person, $2,550 (£1,700) double with guide; 7-night all-inclusive packages cost, per person, $4,250 (£2,833) double with guide. Early season discounts available. No credit cards. **Amenities:** Restaurant; lounge. *In room:* No phone.

Isla Monita Lodge ★★★ (Moments) What is more exclusive than a fly-fishing lodge on a 112-hectare (277-acre) private island? This is not a lodge that is dependent on just one or two rivers; instead, the Isla Monita has access to some of the most diverse fly-fishing conditions found in Chile: the rivers Futaleufú, Palena Yelcho, Malito, and Verde, not to mention the lake the lodge sits on, the profoundly blue Lake Yelcho. All rivers are within a short drive from the lodge, and there are wading and floating excursions (32 boats in all) available. The lodge is owned by Chris Brown, an Englishman who has run this lodge since 1990, and there is room for just 12 guests. The idea at Isla Monita is that guests feel as if they are in their own home, and good food, privacy, and friendly service are the lodge's trademark. To get here, guests cross the lake by boat.

Lago Yelcho, Futaleufú, Región X. ✆ **800/245-1950** in the U.S., or 2/339-8465. www.islamonita.cl. 7-night all-inclusive packages (including guides, meals, laundry, and transportation to and from Chaitén) cost, per person, $4,495 (£2,997) Nov–Apr. No credit cards. **Amenities:** Restaurant; bar; lounge. *In room:* No phone.

La Posada de los Farios ★★★ Founded by a North American who came to Chile 16 years ago as a guide and never left, this lodge specializes in *farios,* or brown trout. The lodge is north of Coyhaique, in a refashioned country home on a private, tranquil ranch, and it caters predominately to foreigners. Nevertheless, the lodge keeps its roots firmly planted in the local culture, serving hearty Chilean cuisine and giving guests close access to rural folk whose traditional way of life has long disappeared in other parts of the world. Los Farios has a capacity of just six guests, who not only can take advantage of fishing rivers and lakes that are the secret of the guides, but also can navigate the fjords of Queulat National Park for saltwater fishing, if they are so interested. The lovely American/Chilean couple who runs this lodge provides very friendly, personal attention, and they arrange activities such as horseback riding, bird-watching, and more for non-fishing guests. The lodge is open from November to April.

Casilla 104, Coyhaique. ✆ **800/628-1447** in the U.S., or 67/236402. www.angleradventures.com. 5-night all-inclusive packages $3,040 (£2,027), per person, double occupancy. AE, DC, MC, V. **Amenities:** Restaurant; laundry service. *In room:* No phone.

Mincho's Lodge ★★★ No other fly-fishing lodge is as conveniently located as this one; it's even within (brisk) walking distance from the center of town—closer in comparison with La Pasarela (p. 352)—yet you can fish in the Simpson River below. The large, half-timbered building stretches along a forest hillside, its black and white colors giving it a bit of a Central European touch. It features one of the coziest lounges in Patagonia, with white sheepskin covers on sofas of the same color. The large rooms have gorgeous views of the pine forest and snowy Andes Mountains beyond; I'd say room 7 upstairs has the best view. Decor varies slightly, but basically rooms are white-walled with rustic, dark wood beams in ceilings and a Delft ceramic blue in plaid bed coverings and curtains and wood-burning stoves; the bathrooms have similar tones. Mincho's Lodge has the slight drawback of no longer being away from it all as other lodges and hotels have sprung up in the vicinity, but the lodge's guides can arrange tours to more remote spots. It's run by Chilean geologist Victoria Moya and golf champion Benjamín Astaburuaga.

Camino del Bosque 1170, .4km (1/4 mile) toward Teniente Vidal airstrip. ✆ **67/233273.** Fax 67/233240. www.minchoslodgepatagonia.com. 11 units. High-season $180 (£120) double. Rates include American breakfast. AE, DC, MC, V. **Amenities:** Restaurants; bar; lounge; transfers; room service; laundry service; nonsmoking rooms. *In room:* TV, minibar.

Patagonia Baker Lodge ★★★ This is one place really focused on fly-fishing enthusiasts' needs, from McKenzie drift boats to zodiacs to a tie-table in an upstairs lounge with a glacier view to sit down and prepare to outsmart the fish. The lodge rests on the waterfront of the Baker River, the most powerful in the country, but downstream of the planned dams. At this point, the crystal-clear river is relatively wide, nearing Lake Bertrand, and the lodge takes in the marvelous view of the forest, topped off by Andean glaciers. It has roughly 1,000 sq. m (10,764 sq. ft.) of floor space but just six double rooms, all with a river view. The white-shingle, green metal-roofed building is one-storied except for the double-story lounge, decorated with Gothic wall tapestries and featuring a terrace overlooking the river. The carpeted rooms are conservative in style, with comfortable beds, tan- and cream-colored walls, and wood-burning stoves. Fishing season runs from late October to late April. The lodge can receive up to 24 guests.

Carretera Austral, 2km (1¼ miles) S of Puerto Bertrand. ✆/fax **02/201-5503 in Santiago, or 67/411903.** www.pbl.cl. 6 units. All-inclusive $500 (£333) per person. No credit cards. **Amenities:** Restaurant; bar; Wi-Fi.

6 PUYUHUAPI ★

198km (123 miles) S of Chaitén; 222km (138 miles) N of Coyhaique

Chile's X Region ends just south of Villa Santa Lucía. The view in Region XI or Aysén (often spelled Aisén) begins to pick up farther along, until the scenery goes wild as the valley narrows and thick green rainforest rises steeply from the sides of the road, just outside the entrance of Parque Nacional Queulat. When the valley opens, the Seno Ventisquero (Glacier Sound) unfolds dramatically, revealing the charming town of Puerto Puyuhuapi on its shore, which was founded by four young German immigrant brothers and their families who set up camp here in 1935. They ran a surprisingly successful carpet factory, **Alfombras Puyuhuapi,** whose humble, shingled building you can still visit Monday through Friday from 8:30am to noon and 3 to 7pm, Saturday and Sunday 9am to noon. Admission is free (✆ **67/325131;** www.puyuhuapi.com). It really is worth a visit.

The most popular attractions in this region are **Parque Nacional Queulat** and the **Puyuhuapi Lodge & Spa** (see "Outside Puerto Puyuhuapi," later), just south and on the other side of the sound, a 5-minute boat ride away. If the Puyuhuapi Lodge's prices are beyond your limit, you might opt to stay at a more economical hotel in Puerto Puyuhuapi or, during the off-season, at El Pangue *cabañas,* and take a soak in the hot springs for the day; or visit the less luxurious but still charming springs at **Termas Ventisquero de Puyuhuapi** (✆ **67/325228;** $20/£13 per person; daily 9am–11pm), 6km/3¾ miles south of Puyuhuapi. You can then spend the following day at Parque Nacional Queulat.

PARQUE NACIONAL QUEULAT

Parque Nacional Queulat is one of Chile's least-explored national parks, due to its dense concentration of virgin rainforest—in fact, some areas of this park remain practically unexplored. Yet you can drive through the heart of it, and there are several lookout points reached by car or in brief to moderate walks. Be sure to keep your eyes open for the *pudú,* a miniature Chilean deer that is timid but, with luck, can be seen poking its head out of the forest near the road.

The 154,093-hectare (380,610-acre) park has several access points but few paths and no backpacking trails. If entering from the north, you first pass a turnoff that heads to the shore of **Lago Risopatrón,** which is within the park, and a very attractive camping spot at **Angostura** that charges $9 (£6) per site ($1.50/£1 for firewood and $4/£2.70 for a short boat ride). There's a 5.8km (3.5-mile) round-trip trail here that leads trekkers through rainforest and past Lago Los Pumas (a 4-hr. hike). Continuing south of Puerto Puyuhuapi, visitors arrive at the park's star attraction, the **Ventisquero Colgante,** a tremendous U-shape river of ice suspended hundreds of feet above a sheer granite wall. From the glacier, two powerful cascades fall into Laguna Témpanos below. Visitors can drive straight to a short trail that takes them to the glacier's lookout point at no charge. To get closer, cross the hanging bridge and take the **Sendero Mirador Ventisquero Colgante,** a moderate 3- to 4-hour hike (3.5 km/2.25 miles) that takes you to the lake below the glacier. The park service Conaf offers boat rides in this lake for about $4 (£2.70) per person; the park station is open daily November through March from 8:30am to 9pm, and April through October from 8:30am to 5:30pm. To camp in this area, the park charges $9 (£6) per site. For more information, contact Conaf's offices in Coyhaique at ✆ **67/212225** or 65/212142, or check the website at www.conaf.cl.

Farther south, the scenery becomes more rugged as the road takes visitors up the Cuesta de Queulat and to views of glacier-capped peaks, and then down again where the road passes the trail head to the **Sendero Río Cascada.** Even if you don't feel like walking the entire 1.7km (1-mile) trail, at least stop for a quick stroll through the enchanting forest. The trail leads to a granite amphitheater draped with braided waterfalls that fall into an ice-capped lake. Check with Conaf at the Ventisquero Colgante entrance for the status of a trail, or factor obstacles into your trip time. The station is open daily November through March from 8:30am to 9pm, and April through October from 8:30am to 5:30pm (✆ **67/212225** or 65/212142).

WHERE TO STAY & DINE

In Puerto Puyuhuapi

Try **Café Restaurant Rossbach,** Aysén s/n, next to the carpet factory (✆ **67/325203**), if you're looking for something to eat; cakes are the specialty here. **El Pangue** has a restaurant, but it's 18km (11 miles) away. Call beforehand to see if you can get a table (see "Outside Puerto Puyuhuapi," later).

Casa Ludwig★★ One of the few *residenciales* open most of the year (mid-Sept to Mar), Casa Ludwig can be found on the homestead of one of the original founders of the Puyuhuapi. It dates back more than 50 years, and was constructed entirely out of native woods. The rooms and furniture are on the older side, but well kept. Some rooms have bathrooms and some don't. They have a small rowboat for use to explore the bay.

Av. Otto Uebel 850, Puerto Puyuhuapi. ✆ **67/325220.** www.casaludwig.cl. 10 units. $55 (£37) double with private bathroom; $40 (£27) double with shared bathroom. Rates include breakfast. No credit cards. **Amenities:** Lounge. *In room:* No phone.

Hostería Alemana (Finds) The German woman who runs this hotel emigrated to Puerto Puyuhuapi more than 50 years ago, and her roots are reflected in the style of the establishment, including delicious breakfasts with sliced meats and *küchen.* The hotel is in a well-maintained, flower-bordered antique home that, at press time, just got a fresh coat of paint. Only one room comes with a private bathroom, and one triple comes with a wood-burning stove. All are spacious and scrubbed.

Av. Otto Uebel 450, Puerto Puyuhuapi. ✆ **67/325118.** hosteria_alemana@entelchile.net. 6 units. $49 (£33) double; $64 (£43) triple. Rates include full breakfast and dinner. No credit cards. **Amenities:** Lounge. *In room:* No phone.

Outside Puerto Puyuhuapi

Fjordo Queulat Ecolodge ★ This lodge that butts up against a fjord smack in the heart of the lush coastal rainforests of Parque Nacional Queulat features four fine cabins with hardwood floors and wood-burning stoves and one main, newer eco-chic clubhouse with a living and dining area. Bird-watching, fly-fishing, treks to the Moraine Hanging Glacier, kayaking through the fjords, visits to hot springs, and treks through the park are all offered separately, though package deals tend to be a better value. The lodge was listed for sale in 2009, though they were still taking reservations.

212 Km North of Coyhaique, Parque Nacional Queulat. ✆ **67/233-302.** www.queulatlodge.com. 6 units. $250 (£167) double. Rates include lunch and dinner. AE, DC, MC, V. **Amenities:** Restaurant; bar; tours, transfers.

Hotel y Cabañas El Pangue ★★ Kids Finds El Pangue is just kilometers from the edge of Parque Nacional Queulat, 30m (98 ft.) from Lago Risopatrón, and 18km (11 miles) from Puerto Puyuhuapi. Dense rainforest encircles the complex; a winding stream provides a fairy-tale spot for a quiet walk or a quick dip. Tremendous *nalca* plants abound on the property, some so large they'd serve as an umbrella. The staff is friendly and facilities are of good quality, and although the lodge focuses heavily on fly-fishing from November to May, other excursions include mountain biking, hiking, canoeing, and boat rides.

Lodging consists of cozy, attractive wood-paneled rooms that fit two to three guests and are good for families. There is also one "house" with a kitchen for seven guests; all cabins have kitchens. The open-room, split-level cabins have a small table and chairs and an extra bed/couch; bathrooms have sunken tubs. The main building houses an excellent restaurant, game room, and lounge; outside is a *quincho* where there are frequent lamb barbecues. As on a ranch, there are ducks, geese, pheasants, and chickens squawking from a fenced-in area. Off-season rates drop dramatically.

Carretera Austral Norte, Km 240, Región XI. ✆/fax **67/325128.** www.elpangue.cl. 12 units. $235–$280 (£157–£187) *cabañas* for 5; $130–$170 (£87–£113) exterior room double. Rates include buffet breakfast (*cabañas* excluded). AE, DC, MC, V (only during high season). **Amenities:** Restaurant; bar; lounge; outdoor heated pool; Jacuzzi; sauna; limited watersports equipment; mountain bike rental; game room; business center; room service; laundry service; Internet access.

Puyuhuapi Lodge & Spa ★★ Moments This is one of the best hotel/thermal spa complexes in Chile and draws visitors from around the globe for its remote, magnificent location, elegant design, thermal pools, and full-service spa. The hotel is nestled in thick rainforest on the shore of the Seno Ventisquero; to get here, guests must cross the sound via a 5-minute motorboat ride.

The baths were just a handful of ramshackle cabins until German immigrant Eberhard Kossmann bought the property and built this handsome complex of shingles and glass. There are however a few signs of wear and tear, and the cuisine might not meet the expectations of the gourmet palate. The nine large suites on the lakefront come with a deck that hangs out over the water during high tide. There are six newer, and smaller, nonsmoking suites that come with a similarly stylish decor (especially the "Captain's Suite"). Other options include duplexes, but they do not come with a kitchen stove or a view, and are on the small side.

Other indoor facilities include a pool, steam baths, whirlpools, and a gym that probably has the best view for a gym in Chile. Three outdoor thermal pools are accessible 24 hours a day, the smallest surrounded by ferns. Two paths run through the rainforest, and there's a pier where you can drop a kayak in the sound. But the big outdoor attractions here are Puyuhuapi's fly-fishing expeditions and the connection with *Patagonia Express,* a boat that takes visitors to Laguna San Rafael Glacier, an excellent option (see "Puerto Aysén, Puerto Chacabuco & Laguna San Rafael National Park," later in this chapter). Both are sold as packages. Guests typically fly into Balmaceda (Coyhaique) and transfer to the lodge by boat. If you're not staying at the hotel but want to use the facilities, there's an average charge of $36 (£24) adults, children $18 (£9) for day use of the spa; for the outdoor pools, adults pay $18 (£9), the price for kids is $9 (£4.50).

Bahía Dorita s/n, Puerto Puyuhuapi, Región XI. ✆/fax **2/225-6489** in Santiago, or 67/325103 in Puyuhuapi. www.patagonia-connection.com. 33 units. $140 (£93) double; 3-night packages, including the cruise to Laguna San Rafael, $1,760 (£880) per person high season, $1,540 (£1,027) low season; half-price for kids. Lunch and dinner $29 (£19) adults, $11(£7.30) children. AE, DC, MC, V. **Amenities:** Restaurant; bar; lounge; large indoor pool and 3 outdoor pools; spa; whirlpool; sauna; massage.

7 COYHAIQUE

222km (138 miles) S of Puyuhuapi; 774km (480 miles) N of Cochrane

Aysén includes natural preserves whose rivers and lakes draw thousands every year for superb fly-fishing opportunities. Visitors who are not traveling the Carretera Austral can fly into Coyhaique from Santiago or Puerto Montt; travel to southern Patagonia from here requires that you fly again to Punta Arenas, unless you have your own car and plan to take the long and gravelly road through flat Argentine pampa, enter via sea to Chacabuco, or hike in through remote Villa O'Higgins.

South out of Queulat, the scenery provokes oohs and ahhs at every turn. The pinnacle of Cerro Picacho comes into view before you enter Villa Amengual, a service village for farmers. Sadly, however, the scenery is marred at times by the terrible destruction wreaked by settlers who burned much of the area for pastureland. An ill-conceived law in 1937 provoked the ecological disaster as colonists could only receive title to the land if it was cleared of trees. Tall, slender evergreen beech tree trunks bleached silver from fire can still be seen poking out from regrowth forest or littered across grassy pastures in a messy testament to these gigantic fires, whose smoke billowed all the way to the Atlantic Ocean.

The road passes through numerous rinky-dink towns before arriving at a paved road that appears like a heaven-sent miracle after hundreds of kilometers of jarring washboard. At a junction south of Villa Mañihuales, drivers can head to Puerto Aysén and Puerto Chacabuco, the departure point for boat trips to Laguna San Rafael and Puerto Montt, and then southeast toward Coyhaique, passing first through the Reserva Nacional Río Simpson.

Founded in 1929, **Coyhaique** is a town that doesn't quite do justice to its stunning location beneath a towering basalt cliff called Cerro Mackay, surrounded by green rolling hills and pastures. This region of Patagonia takes a back seat to its southern counterpart around Torres del Paine, yet outside Coyhaique, new expeditions to unexplored areas start up every year; because of this, it's easy to get away from the crowds. The city is home to about 44,000 residents, almost half the population of the whole of Aysén. It's the only place in the region you'll find a full range of services; and, though it has a serious litter problem, it has so far managed to avoid most of the architectural sins of other Chilean

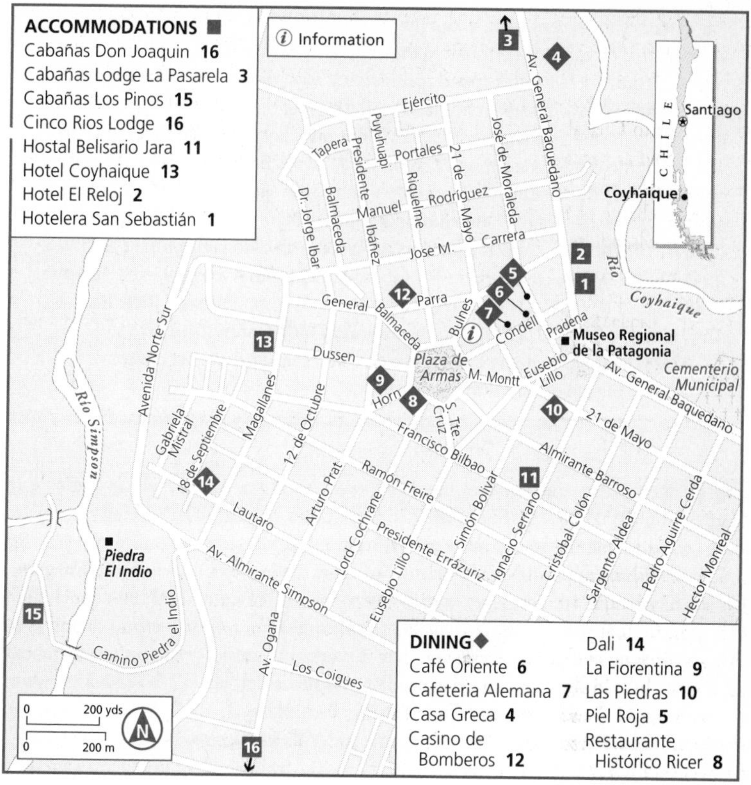

towns, offering some lovely views if you walk up some of the streets away from the center in the late afternoon. It also sits at the confluence of the Simpson and Coyhaique rivers, both renowned for trout and salmon fishing and a reason so many fly-fishing enthusiasts flock to this area. The other prime attraction here is the **Laguna San Rafael Glacier,** a colossal ice field that can be visited on a modest ship or a luxury liner from Puerto Chacabuco; there are also flyovers that provide unforgettable memories. Beyond fishing, visitors can choose from a wealth of activities within a short drive of the city.

ESSENTIALS

Getting There & Around

BY PLANE Coyhaique's **Aeropuerto de Balmaceda** (BBA; no phone) is a gorgeous 1-hour drive from downtown and is the landing and departure point for larger jets. **LAN Airlines** has two to three daily flights from Santiago, with a stop in either Puerto Montt or Temuco (there are no nonstops from Santiago); there's also one to two daily flights from Punta Arenas. The LAN office is at General Parra 402 (✆ **600/526-2000** toll-free; www.lan.com). **Sky Airline** has one or two daily flights depending on the season, with a

Car Rental for Local Trips & the Carretera Austral

Car rental is very expensive here, but there are plenty of offers; even the odd cafe has a pickup truck it will rent. Fortunately, the popularity of this trip has made competition fierce and prices have dropped considerably. Most require that you rent a truck if heading anywhere off paved roads (about $90/£60 per day for a truck, $120/£80 for a 4×4). **Hertz** (Balmeceda airport; ✆ **67/231648;** www.hertz.cl) or **Budget** (Errázuriz 454 and at the Balmeceda airport; ✆ **67/255171;** www.budget.cl) are here. For local rental, try: **AGS Rent a Car,** Av. Ogana 1298, and at the airport (✆/fax **67/231511;** agsrentacar@entelchile.net); **International,** General Parra 97 and at the airport (✆ **67/214770;** fax 67/212771); **Rent a Car Aysén,** Francisco Bilbao 926 (✆ **67/231532**); **Traeger,** Av. Baquedano 457 (✆/fax **67/231648;** www.traeger.cl); **Turismo Prado,** Av. 21 de Mayo 417 (✆ **67/231271;** ventas@turismoprado.cl); **Ricer Rent a Car,** Horn 48 (✆/fax **67/232920**); or **Automundo AVR,** Francisco Bilbao 510 (✆ **67/231621;** wfritsch@patagoniachile.cl). If you can't find what you want with these companies, request a list from Sernatur.

stop in Puerto Montt and several flights per week to Punta Arenas, which originate in Puerto Montt (Prat 203; ✆ **67/240827** in Coyhaique, or 600/600-2828 toll-free; www.skyairline.cl). Note that this airport doesn't have an ATM.

Charter flights (all small propeller planes) to closer destinations, such as Villa O'Higgins, Chile Chico, and Cochrane, leave from the **Aeródromo Teniente Vidal** (no phone), 7km (4¼ miles) outside town. Two charter-flight companies offer tourist overland flights, even over the Laguna San Rafael Glacier. Both are the same in terms of price and quality (about $1,000/£667 for 3 hr. for one to five people): **Aerotaxis del Sur** (✆ **67/252-253;** www.aerotaxisdelsur.cl) and **Empresas Don Carlos,** Baquedano 315 (✆ **67/232261;** www.doncarlos.cl). The latter also flies to Cochrane and Villa O'Higgins.

BY BOAT Some travelers arrive at Puerto Chacabuco by boat from Puerto Montt or Quellón on Chiloé and then transfer to Coyhaique. It is 67km (42 miles) to Coyhaique. For schedule information, see "Puerto Aysén, Puerto Chacabuco & Laguna San Rafael National Park," later in this chapter. In Coyhaique, **Navimag** is at Ibáñez 347 (✆ **67/233306;** www.navimag.cl).

BY BUS Coyhaique has a bus terminal at Lautaro and Magallanes streets and companies are gradually moving their offices there. For buses with a final destination in Chaitén, try **Buses Becker,** Presidente Ibáñez 358 (✆ **67/232167;** busesbecker@123.cl), which leaves on Monday, Thursday, and Saturday at 8am ($27/£18 one-way). For Puyuhuapi and La Junta, try **Buses Terraasutral** at the terminal (✆ **67/254335**), with buses daily at 6am, or **Buses Queulat** at Parra 329 (✆ **67/242626**), which connects with Futaleufú-bound buses on Wednesday, Friday, and Sunday departing at 8am. For Cochrane, take **Buses Don Carlos,** Arturo Prat 334 (✆ **67/522150;** www.doncarlos.cl), which leaves on Tuesday, Thursday, and Saturday at 9am ($18/£12). For Puerto Aysén and Chacabuco, take **Suray,** with 20 trips per day, at Prat 265 (✆ **67/238387**); or **Interlagos** at the Terminal (similar frequencies; ✆ **67/240840**). For Puerto Ibáñez, try **Minibus Don Tito,** Pasaje Curicó 619 (✆ **67/250280**).

BY CAR Heading south on Rte. 7, the highway comes to a fork—one paved road and one dirt. The choice here is clear, especially if you've been driving on gravel all day. The well-signed, paved route heads first toward Puerto Aysén and then heads southeast for a beautiful drive through the Río Simpson National Reserve before hitting town. At the city entrance, a sign points left for the center of town.

Orientation

Coyhaique has a pentagon-shape plaza—which happens to also be a Wi-Fi hotspot—in the northwest corner of town and many one-way streets that can easily confuse a visitor with a rental car. Most services and hotels are near the plaza, and you'll find it convenient to stick to walking downtown. The rest of the city is on a regular grid pattern.

Visitor Information

A helpful English-speaking staff can be found at the **Sernatur** office at Bulnes 35 (✆ **67/231752** or 67/240290; www.sernatur.cl); it's open January and February Monday through Friday from 8:30am to 8:30pm, Saturday and Sunday from 11am to 6pm; and March through December Monday through Friday from 8:30am to 5:30pm. Sernatur produces a glossy magazine packed with information about the region and full listings of services, and provides a brochure on fishing. Don't skip the **Oficina de Turismo Rural,** 2 blocks away on Ogana 1060 (✆ **67/214031;** www.rutatranspatagonia.cl), which is very helpful, offering contact information and a good brochure for even the remotest lodgings well beyond the end of the Carretera Austral. For information about the natural parks and preserves, you can try **Conaf**'s office at Los Coigües s/n (✆ **67/ 212125;** www.conaf.cl).

Fast Facts Coyhaique

Currency Exchange Options include **Turismo Prado,** Av. 21 de Mayo 417 (✆ **67/ 231271**), and **Emperador,** Freire 171 (✆ **67/233727**). Both are open Monday through Friday 9am to 1:30pm and 3 to 7pm, and Saturday 9am to 2pm.

Fishing Licenses **Departamento de Tránsito Municipalidad de Coyhaique,** Bilbao 357 (✆ **67/231788**), is open Monday through Friday from 9am to 1pm.

Hospital The city's Regional Hospital is at Jorge Ibar 0168 (✆ **67/219100**). For emergencies, dial ✆ **131,** as in every city in Chile.

Internet Access **Entel** has Internet access and a calling center at Prat 340. **Camello Patagón,** at Moraleda 463, has the best coffee to accompany your surfing, and cafes **Oriente** and **Alemana** (see later) have Wi-Fi.

Laundry Try **Lavaseco All Clean,** General Parra 55, no. 2 (✆ **67/219635**), or **QL,** Francisco Bilbao 160 (✆ **67/232266**).

Outdoor & Fishing Gear Go to **Ferretería La Nueva,** Condell 150 (✆ **67/231724;** no licenses given out here), or **Suraypesca**, Prat 267 (✆ **67/234088**), for outdoor and fishing gear. **Condor Explorer,** Dussen 357 (✆ **67/573634**), has mountaineering equipment.

Post Office Correos de Chile is at Cochrane 226 (✆ **67/231787**).

In Coyhaique

Museo del Maté This tiny museum on the road to the airport in the town of El Blanco is dedicated to the strong herbal tea called yerba mate, which is a far more popular drink in neighboring Argentina and Uruguay, especially among the gaucho community. The one room museum features old photos of the area, a variety of *guampa* gourds and *bombillas* (the metal straw used to drink mate). It's worth a quick look; vendors across the street sell mate for purchase.

Airport road, El Blanco. ✆ **67/213175.** Admission 70¢ (35p). Tues–Fri 11am–1pm and 3–6pm; Sat–Sun 11am–1pm and 3–7pm.

Museo Regional de la Patagonia ★ This small museum offers information about regional flora and fauna, with stuffed birds, armadillos, and turtles; rock and petrified wood samples; and an ethnographic exhibit featuring photographs, colonial machinery, and other antique items. There is also a photo exhibit of workmen building the Carretera Austral.

Av. Lillo 23, corner of Baquedano. ✆ **67/213175.** Admission 70¢ (35p) adults, free for kids. Mid-Dec to Feb daily 8:30am–8pm; Mar to mid-Dec Mon–Fri 8:30am–1:30pm and 2:15–5:30pm.

Reserva Nacional Coyhaique ★ You don't need to go far in Coyhaique to surround yourself in wilderness. This little preserve (2,670 hectares/6,595 acres) is just under 5km (3 miles) from town on the road to Puerto Aysén and is a good place to go for a light walk through native forest, have a picnic, or pitch a tent. A ranger station at the entrance has complete trail information. From here, a short trail leads to a campground and then continues to Laguna Verde, with picnic and camping areas. There is a longer trail called the Sendero Las Piedras, which rewards hikers with wide-open views of the surrounding area and city below. The reserve's proximity to the city means it's entirely feasible to walk there.

5km (3 miles) from Coyhaique on the road to Puerto Aysén. ✆ **67/212225.** www.conaf.cl. Admission $4 (£2.70) adults, $1 (70p) children; camping $9 (£6) for up to 6 people. Nov–Mar daily 8:30am–9pm; Apr–Oct daily 8:30am–5:30pm.

Reserva Nacional Río Simpson The only way to really see this reserve is by car—which you'll do anyway if you drive from Coyhaique to Puerto Aysén. The road winds along the shore of the Río Simpson, passing through impressive scenery and offering two crashing waterfalls, the Bridal Veil and the Virgin, which are signposted. There's also a museum here without anything of much interest and an information center. Unfortunately, trails in this reserve are not regularly maintained and are, therefore, tough to hike; inquire at the information center as to their status.

Road to Puerto Aysén, Km 37. ✆ **67/21222.** www.conaf.cl. Admission $2 (£1.30); camping $9 (£6). Nov–Mar daily 8:30am–9pm; Apr–Oct daily 8:30am–5:30pm. Information center daily 8:30am–1:30pm and 2:15–6:30pm.

Outdoor Activities in the Area

Tour operators plan day trips, multiday trips, and full expeditions to areas as far as the Southern Ice Field. **Adventure Expeditions Patagonia,** Riquelme 372 (✆ **67/219894;** www.adventurepatagonia.com), can put together unforgettable expeditions to areas rarely seen by travelers, including a hut-to-hut hiking expedition along the Aysén Glacier, a 14-day horseback-riding trip along the Pioneer Trail, and an "Ice to Ocean" 11-day horseback, hiking, and rafting adventure; they are highly recommended and they have an excellent staff of guides.

Andes Patagónicos, Horn 48, no. 11 (✆ **67/216711;** www.ap.cl), has tours around Coyhaique, such as trips to the Lake Carrera and the Capilla de Mármol; 5-day journeys to Caleta Tortal with stops at archaeological sites, immigrant posts, glaciers, and rivers; 1-day and multiday fly-fishing tours; trips to the Laguna San Rafael and Termas de Puyuhuapi; and more.

Condor Explorer, Dussen 357 (✆ **67/573634;** www.condorexplorer.com), specializes in mountaineering excursions, including the tough ones to the Northern Ice Field and San Lorenzo, and offers logistical support for overseas expeditions. It's one of few tour operators that are active year-round, offering ski treks/randonee, hiking, trekking, and horseback riding. Their agency has the sole mountaineering store in Coyhaique.

For a private fly-fishing guide, try **Expediciones Coyhaique,** Portales 195 (✆/fax **67/232300;** juliomeier@patagoniachile.cl). For sightseeing trips along the Carretera Austral and to Puerto Aysén, and trips to view Telhuelche Indian rock, try **Turismo Prado,** 21 de Mayo 417 (✆/fax **67/231271;** www.turismoprado.cl).

NOLS Patagonia, 11km (7 miles) south of Coyhaique (✆ **800/710-NOLS** [710-6657]; www.adventurepatagonia.com), is the Chilean branch of the U.S.-based National Outdoor Leadership School. Set on a 500-acre working organic farm, intensive training courses here range from 14- to 34-day kayaking and mountaineering trips ($3,330–$5,850/£2,200–£3,900) to semester-long wilderness courses that include studies in mountaineering, first aid, survival, and other outdoor activities.

FISHING Since their introduction in the late 1800s, trout and salmon have thrived in the crystalline waters in southern Chile, but nowhere in the country has fly-fishing taken off as it has here in the Aysén region. The burgeoning number of guides alone bears testament to the truth of this region's claim as one of the premier fishing destinations on the globe, drawing thousands of anglers from around the world to reel in 3-, 5-, and even 10-pounders. Even if you've never fished before, this might be your opportunity to try. Each tour operator has a list of its own fly-fishing guides in the Aysén region, some of whom work independently. If you're coming here mainly to fish, there are several full-service luxury lodges in the region. All have on-site guides, both Chilean and foreign, especially U.S. Most offer activities for nonangling spouses and friends (see the "Fly-Fishing Lodges on the Carretera Austral" section on p. 340).

Tour operators organize day, multiday, and weeklong excursions to fly-fishing spots such as the Simpson, Baker, and Nirehuao rivers, and Bertrand and General Carrera lakes. Some combine excursions with other activities, such as horseback riding or hiking.

HORSEBACK RIDING Trips often head to the Coyhaique Reserve and Lago Margaritas, but tour companies offer a variety of destinations. Some arrange all-inclusive, multiday trips; for this, try **Andes Patagónicos** (see earlier).

SKIING It's not a world-class ski resort (two T-bars are the lift service), but it can be fun to visit if you're here between June and September. The **Centro de Esquí El Fraile** (✆ **67/198-3007**) is 29km (18 miles) from Coyhaique, offering five ski runs serviced by two T-bars. It's a tiny resort but can make for a fun day in the snow, and it's one of the few resorts in Chile that has tree skiing. There are also cross-country skiing opportunities here. Tickets cost about $25 (£17) per day, and it's possible to rent equipment for an average of $16 (£11). **Andes Patagónicos** and **Condor Explorer** can get you there (see earlier).

WHERE TO STAY

There are many clean *residenciales* in Coyhaique that are inexpensive but pretty basic, and rooms are small and noisy; also, most have shared bathrooms and you must bring your own towel. **Residencial Mónica,** at Lillo 664, has a very attractive dark violet, shingled facade (✆ **67/234302**) and private bathrooms, while **Hostal Glady's,** at Parra 65 (✆ **67/245288;** patagoniagladys@hotmail.com), is both clean and friendly. Both hotels are a good notch above the rest, so book ahead. The backpacking crowd will like Spanish-owned lodge **Las Salamandras** (✆ **67/211865;** www.salamandras.cl), in the woods across the Simpson River, a 20-minute walk from town.

Expensive

Cabañas Lodge La Pasarela ★★ Moments These attached rooms and cabins nestled on the shore of Río Simpson (on the fork with Río Coyhaique) are good for those who'd like more rural surroundings. The complex is on the other side of the river, away from the main road, and to get there guests must first cross a wooden suspension bridge. Cabañas La Pasarela is geared toward fly-fishermen, with private guides from Chile and the U.S. But guests also like this lodge because you can fish right at the bank of the Río Simpson outside your door. All of the structures are made of cypress logs and have black, shingled roofs. In 2002, the main lobby, bar, and restaurant areas were refurbished and are now a bit more elegant than before, but the rooms are a bit on the dark side, with the exception of the new suites, which are worth a splurge for their pleasant decor, queen-size beds, and extras like a minibar. A pebbled walkway goes up to four A-frame *cabañas.* They arrange bilingual fly-fishing tours: $359 (£239) a day for two people, including transportation, fishing licenses, and lunch.

Km 2, road to Puerto Aysén, Coyhaique. ✆ **67/240700.** www.lapasarela.cl. 11 units. $130 (£87) double; $145 (£97) cabin for 5. Rates include buffet breakfast (except *cabaña*). AE, DC, MC, V. **Amenities:** Restaurant; bar; lounge; Internet access. *In room:* TV.

Cinco Rios Lodge ★★ This fine lodge opened in 2006 and is just a few kilometers outside of town on the road to the airport. It's close enough for quick drives into the city, but far enough away that you'll still soak in dramatic views and feel the vastness that is Patagonia. The six spacious contemporary cabins with floor-to-ceiling windows overlooking the Río Simpson are the best rooms in town. Their gourmet restaurant is worth a visit in its own right. Fly-fishing is the focus of the lodge, and they have special arrangements with *estancias* as far south as the Río Baker to use their properties for excursions. They also have a small fly-fishing lodge on the Argentine border, Estancia El Zorro.

Km 5 on the road to Balmaceda, Coyhaique. ✆ **67/244917.** www.cincorios.cl. 6 units. 6 days/7 nights $3,675 (£2,450) per person. Rates include all meals plus wine, transportation, tours/fishing. AE, DC, MC, V. Closed June–Oct. **Amenities:** Restaurant; bar; lounge; Wi-Fi; tours. *In room:* TV.

Hostal Belisario Jara ★ Value This boutique hotel is Coyhaique's best value lodging option. The charming design features honey-colored wood frames nailed together in varying angles, giving every room and sitting area a unique size and shape. The hotel is made of army-green stucco and windows aplenty, so it's bright and airy, and the crisp, white walls are accented here and there with local arts and crafts. Rooms are average size, some brighter than others, and all have carpeted floors. The softly lit dining area/bar is the highlight of the hotel, with a wooden table and chairs for relaxing fireside. French doors open out onto the front garden; the hotel sits on a busy street but is set back far enough so that you do not notice. The hotel has an apartment on the second floor of an old home on the main road, separate from the main building, which comes with a kitchen and can fit up to six. It arranges fly-fishing tours, car rental, and other expeditions.

Francisco Bilbao 662, Coyhaique. ✆/fax **67/234150.** www.belisariojara.itgo.com. 10 units. $98 (£65) double. Rates include buffet breakfast. No credit cards. **Amenities:** Bar; lounge; laundry service. *In room:* TV, Internet access.

Hotel Coyhaique (Kids) (Overrated) This ex-*hostería* is Coyhaique's largest hotel, and it sits in a quiet part of town surrounded by an unkempt, overgrown garden. Though it is a more traditional hotel than most in Coyhaique, the so-so quality offered by the Hotel Coyhaique makes it seem as if it has fallen on hard times but can't bear to lower its prices to reflect this. For the price, you'd be better off at the Belisario Jara. The hotel, however, has its own boat service to Laguna San Rafael Glacier, called the Iceberg Expedition, which is available for guests only. Their Patagonia Flash, a 3-day program with a visit to San Rafael, costs $847 (£565) per person based on double occupancy. Guest rooms are clean. Doubles come in two sizes; the matrimonial double with a full bed is larger than the double with two twins. A dark-wood lobby leads into the bar, and around the corner is a semiformal restaurant; there's a more casual restaurant downstairs with great views of the countryside. Outside there's a kidney-shape pool and lots of grass for kids to romp around in.

Magallanes 131, Coyhaique. ✆ **67/231137.** Fax 67/233274. www.hotelsa.cl. 40 units. $97 (£65) double; $188 (£125) suite. Rates include buffet breakfast. MC, V. **Amenities:** 2 restaurants; bar; lounge; outdoor pool; tour desk; transfers; room service; laundry service; nonsmoking rooms. *In room:* TV, minibar.

Moderate

Cabañas Don Joaquín ★ (Value) This group of modern two-story *cabañas,* nestled among the pine trees above the Simpson River, are fully equipped, including maid service, making them an upscale alternative to the nearby Las Salamandras. Polished tree-trunk–framed beds make the woodsy atmosphere even more rustic, as do the wood-burning furnaces. Some people like it so much they rent it for long periods of time, according to the Argentine administrator. The cabins are suitable for up to six people. Don Joaquín also has a good restaurant on the premises. For a group or family, this is a great value.

Camino Aeródromo Teniente. Vidal, Km 2, Coyhaique. ✆ **67/214553.** www.coyhaique.com. 9 units. $140 (£93) per bungalow. No credit cards. **Amenities:** Restaurant. *In room:* TV, kitchenette.

Cabañas Los Pinos ★ (Finds) These handcrafted log cabins are nestled in a pine forest on the shore of Río Simpson, about a 5-minute drive from downtown. There are cabins for three, four, or six people, each with a wood-burning stove; the cabin for six has one bedroom with a full-size bed and one with two bunks. All have shared bathrooms. The cabins for four are a little tight, but the charm of the place makes up for it. The cabin for six comes with a kitchen; the other two cabins share a separate eating area, which guests usually don't mind, considering the eating area is an idyllic little cabin with a beautiful view, great cooking facilities, and two tables for four. The couple who owns and runs the property is very friendly, and they have a vehicle for excursions.

Camino Teniente Vidal, Km 1.5, Parcela 5, Coyhaique. ✆ **67/234898.** www.lospinos-chile.com. 4 units. $46 (£31) cabin for 2; $82 (£55) cabin for 4; $90 (£60) cabin for 6. No credit cards. **Amenities:** Restaurant. *In room:* TV, kitchenette, no phone.

Hotel El Reloj ★ This bed-and-breakfast-style hotel is housed in a forest-green-and-lemon old home flanked by two *lenga* trees. The hotel is surrounded by an abundance of greenery, which is pleasant, but it shades the windows, so the rooms are fairly dark. The rooms are a little on the small side but are appealing; some have stone walls, and all have old wood floors. It's a cozy enough place and very clean. There's a common living area and a small restaurant serving local fare, such as wild hare, sheep cheese, and fresh salmon. The restaurant is open to the public, but limited seating keeps the numbers low.

Av. Baquedano 828. ✆/fax **67/231108.** www.elrelojhotel.cl. 13 units. $119 (£79) double. Rates include buffet breakfast. No credit cards. **Amenities:** Restaurant; lounge; bar; room service; laundry service. *In room:* TV.

Hotelera San Sebastián ★ This hotel's mustard exterior is so nondescript you might miss it the first time you pass by. Don't let the outside fool you: Inside, the rooms offer quality interiors, and all but one have lovely views of the Coyhaique River meandering through grassy countryside. The spacious bedrooms are tastefully painted in rose and cream, with matching linens and curtains, and are impeccably clean, as are the bathrooms. The hotel is on a busy street, but tucked away between two buildings and, therefore, it's very quiet.

Av. Baquedano 496, Coyhaique. ✆ **67/233427.** 7 units. $60–$90 (£40–£60) double. Rates include buffet breakfast. No credit cards. **Amenities:** Restaurant. *In room:* TV.

WHERE TO DINE

There are several cafes downtown that are good for a quick bite, such as **Café Oriente** (**✆ 67/231622**), Condell 201, with pizzas and sandwiches. The **Cafetería Alemana** (**✆ 67/231731**) is a very nice cafe almost next door, at Condell 119. It serves German specialties such as *küchen* and steak tartare, as well as sandwiches, pizzas, and a good fixed-price lunch for $7 (£4.70). Both are Wi-Fi hotspots.

Expensive

Dalí ★★★ SPANISH/INTERNATIONAL This trendy, 16-seat bistro reveals just how much Coyhaique is changing. A few years ago you would never find anything even remotely this hip in town. Chef Cristián Balboa, who lives upstairs, opened the restaurant and filled it with artistic flair and funky antiques in 2007. The sizeable wine list pairs well with their luscious rack of lamb, salmon and chorizo plate, and whatever else that's in season in Patagonia. The restaurant is hidden away in a residential area 5 blocks from the plaza. Just look for the oversized mural of Salvador Dalí.

82 Laurato. ✆ **67/245422.** Reservations required. Main courses $16–$25 (£11–£17). AE, DC, MC, V. Daily 7:30–11pm.

La Pasarela ★★ CHILEAN La Pasarela is about the best thing going in town. To get here, you need to take a taxi ride just outside town and across a wooden suspension bridge. The atmosphere is great: stone walls, wood beams, a roaring fireplace, and a comfortable bar for relaxing with a pisco sour. Through the windows, diners watch the Río Simpson rush by. The Pasarela is part of a *cabaña*/hotel complex and usually whips up specials according to the guests' whims. Standbys include grilled meats and pastas. There is usually a fixed-price meal for lunch and dinner, including appetizer, main dish, dessert, and coffee, for about $10 (£6.70) for lunch and $12 (£8) for dinner.

Road to Puerto Aysén, Km 2. ✆ **67/240700.** Reservations required. Main courses $13–$18 (£8.70–£12). AE, DC, MC, V. Daily 7:30am–midnight.

Las Piedras ★★ (Value) INTERNATIONAL This relatively new restaurant has something Coyhaique sorely needed: good food at decent prices, with a Patagonian grill for meats, seafood such as conger eel in chardonnay, or pielike *chupe* of king crab and crabmeat. It departs from the log cabin fashion in favor of a more generous, traditional restaurant layout, though keeping a few references to aboriginal culture in wall decorations (such as the ubiquitous guanaco) and adding modern touches in curved, polished walls and a flattened wood-paneled ceiling. Its *capilla de marmol* gin cocktail is interesting; it's a little sweet but its color spectacularly mimics the crystal waters of its namesake landmark.

21 de Mayo 655. ✆ **67/233243.** Main courses $8–$14 (£5.30–£9.30). AE, DC, MC, V. Daily noon–3pm and 7–10:30pm.

Moderate

La Fiorentina (Value) PIZZA/CHILEAN La Fiorentina serves a long list of pizzas and hearty, home-style dishes that can even be ordered to go—and stays open all day. The fixed-price lunch offers two selections and costs $7 (£4.70); it's very popular with the locals, who usually sit alone at lunchtime with their eyes glued to the TV blaring in one eating area. The atmosphere is very casual, and the service is friendly and attentive.

Arturo Prat 230. ✆ **67/238899.** Lunch $7 (£4.70); large pizza $11 (£7.30). MC, V. Mon–Sun 11am–11:30pm.

Piel Roja PUB FARE This pub is the liveliest night spot in town and is all right for a casual dinner such as quesadillas, burgers, sandwiches, and pastas; its more complex dishes don't really cut it. The funky interiors are embellished with iron and stained-glass lamps, tree-trunk tables and chairs, low lighting, and a long, winding wooden bar that is perfect for a solo traveler looking for a quick meal. Piel Roja is a good all-in-one place to grab a bite, relax with friends, have a few drinks, or go all night in the disco, as it stays open very late.

Moraleda 495. ✆ **67/237832.** Main courses $7–$10 (£4.70–£6.70). AE, DC, MC, V. Kitchen daily 5pm–midnight (bar and disco until 4am).

Restaurant Histórico Ricer ★ (Kids) CHILEAN/INTERNATIONAL This restaurant is a favorite with traveling gringos, and just about everyone else in town who can afford it, too. The large, pub-style restaurant is fashioned of logs, and a handcrafted wood staircase leads to a mellower, slightly more formal dining area upstairs. All in all, the food is decent, although terribly overpriced, and the service is absent-minded: Waitresses tend to group at the cash register and gossip rather than wait on tables. The fixed-price menu is a good deal at $7 (£4.70) and includes an appetizer, main course, and dessert, and the restaurant stays open very late.

Horn 48. ✆ **67/232920.** www.ap.cl/restaurante.htm. Main courses $8–$15 (£5.30–£10). AE, DC, MC, V. Daily 8:30am–2am (to 3am in summer).

Inexpensive

Casa Greca ★★★ (Finds) INTERNATIONAL You might wonder as you step into this house if you're not heading into a suburban residence by mistake, as this friendly restaurant's dining area is at the far end of a long corridor, opening out into a view over the valley beyond the pine trees. Contrary to what you might expect, La Greca has no Greek inclinations; its name comes from a Spanish term for geometrical designs, in this case from a typical, stylized guanaco suckling its young that you'll often see in the area. The food is decidedly international, with a tempting mix of Italian and Patagonian, as in the lamb goulash and gnocchi. I'd also wager their pisco sour is the best for hundreds of miles around. The ambience is upscale log cabin, with stone-baked pizza and a solid wine list.

Baquedano 22. ✆ **67/251483.** Main courses $6–$12 (£4–£8). No credit cards. Daily 7–11pm.

Casino de Bomberos (Finds) CHILEAN Chile's volunteer firemen need some way to make a buck, and here's their solution: Open a cafe in the fire station. The atmosphere is plain but fun, and the menu features such classic dishes as roasted chicken and calamari with tomato sauce. The food is tasty and the fixed-price lunch is cheap at $6 (£4), including a salad, soup, main dish, and dessert. On Sunday, there are baked and fried fresh empanadas.

General Parra 365. ✆ **67/231437.** Main courses $4–$6 (£2.70–£4). No credit cards. Daily noon–4pm and 7pm–midnight.

8 PUERTO AYSEN, PUERTO CHACABUCO & LAGUNA SAN RAFAEL NATIONAL PARK ★★★

Puerto Aysén: 68km (42 miles) W of Coyhaique

Puerto Aysén was a vigorous port town until the 1960s, when silt filled the harbor and ships were forced to move 16km (10 miles) away to Puerto Chacabuco. While it's in the midst of gorgeous landscape, it offers few attractions to the visitor. The same could be said for Puerto Chacabuco; however, the majority of visitors to this region pass through here at some point to catch a ship or ferry to Laguna San Rafael Glacier or to Puerto Montt. Most travelers arriving by ferry from Puerto Montt head straight to Coyhaique, and vice versa, but the full-day ferry ride to Laguna San Rafael leaves early and returns late, so many travelers find it convenient to spend a night here in Puerto Chacabuco.

It's recommended that you at least take a day trip to Puerto Aysén and Puerto Chacabuco, more than anything for the beautiful drive through the Reserva Nacional Río Simpson and the equally beautiful view of Aysén Sound at the journey's end. That said, both towns are a little scrappy, but the Hotel Loberías del Sur (see "Where to Stay & Dine," later) is a good spot for lunch before heading back to Coyhaique. If you don't have your own transportation, you can try **Buses Suray,** Eusebio Ibar 630 (✆ **67/336222**), which connects in Puerto Aysén for Coyhaique. The best bet is to call **Patagonia Austral,** Condell 149, no. 2 (✆/fax **67/239696;** ventas@australpatagonia.cl), which offers day trips around this area, especially bird-watching tours. The tours operate from November 15 to March 15 only, but the agency will arrange trips any time of the year for small groups. **Turismo Rucaray,** in Puerto Aysén, at Teniente Merino 840 (✆ **67/332862;** fax 67/332725; rucaray@entelchile.net), offers other excursions around the area and sells ferry tickets.

PARQUE NACIONAL LAGUNA SAN RAFAEL ★★★

If you're not planning a trip to the parks in southern Patagonia, Laguna San Rafael National Park is a must-see. It's the foremost attraction in the Aysén region, drawing thousands of visitors each year to be dazzled by the tremendous vertical walls of blue ice that flow 45km (28 miles) from the Northern Ice Field and stretch 4km (2½ miles) across the Laguna San Rafael. It's the closest sea-level ice field to the Equator. Around these walls, thousands of aquamarine icebergs float in soupy water, forming jagged sculptures.

The glacier is actually receding, and quite quickly; it may well stop dropping ice into the lagoon within only a few years, but in the meantime, you will likely see numerous, heavy chunks of ice plunging into the deep water. The first explorers here in 1800 described the glacier as having filled three-quarters of the lagoon; when you're here, you can appreciate how much has disappeared, and the speed at which it is shrinking is unsettling.

Laguna San Rafael National Park is a staggering 1.7 million hectares (4 million acres). Most of the park is inaccessible except by ship, on which visitors slowly cruise through narrow canals choked with thick vegetation. Like Torres del Paine, Laguna San Rafael is a UNESCO World Biosphere Reserve. Visitors set sail in Puerto Chacabuco or Puerto

Montt aboard an all-inclusive luxury liner or modest ferry for day and multiple-day trips.
The ship anchors near the glacier and passengers board zodiacs (inflatable motorized boats) for a closer look at the icebergs and the glacier, which in some places rises as high as 70m (230 ft.), rocked when the ice hits the water. A smaller fraction of visitors book an overflight excursion for a bird's-eye view of the glacier's entirety, which includes a touchdown at the park's center, near the glacier, for an hour-long visit.

Your best bet for clear skies is from November to March. Even on foul-weather days, the glacier is usually visible, as the clouds tend to hover just above it. Bring protective rain gear just in case, or inquire when booking a ticket, as many companies provide guests with impermeable jackets and pants.

Conaf administers the park and charges a $6 (£4) admission fee (ferry passengers do not pay; only those landing in planes do, but please donate something at the park ranger station anyway, as every bit of funding helps). Conaf offers several services at the park, including a boat ride near the glacier for $40 (£27) per person, and five sites for camping ($4/£2 per tent).

Ferry Journeys Through the Fjords to Laguna San Rafael ★★★

This extraordinary journey is about a 200km (124-mile) sail from Puerto Chacabuco, but many visitors leave from Puerto Montt for a round-trip journey or to disembark in Puerto Chacabuco. Some visitors plan a multiday journey to Laguna San Rafael as the focal point of a trip to Chile. When booking a trip, consider the journey's length and whether you will be traveling at night and, therefore, missing any portions of scenery. In addition to the companies below, **Navimag Ferries** (p. 309) offers round-trip cruises directly from Puerto Montt. Prices range from about $477 to $816 (£318–£544) per person.

Catamaranes del Sur ★ This catamaran service to Laguna San Rafael also owns the hotel at the port in Chacabuco, the Hostería Loberías del Sur, and they offer packages that include a stay here or 1-day journeys for travelers not lodging at the hotel. Catamaranes has its own private park, Aikén del Sur, which it visits for a half-day tour included in the 2- to 3-night packages. Also included in the packages is a typical Patagonian lamb barbecue. The company has a fleet of ships that are smaller and, therefore, offer a more personalized experience than the large Navimag ships, making this a good choice for day trips to the Laguna (the price is slightly higher than with Navimag). Trips include all meals, an open bar, onboard entertainment, and inflatable zodiac boat rides near the glacier.

In Santiago, Pedro de Valdivia 0210. ✆ **2/231-1902.** Fax 2/231-1993. www.catamaranesdelsur.cl. AE, DC, MC, V. Day trips $299 (£199) adults, $100 (£67) children; 3-night packages $1,080 (£720) per person based on double occupancy. Includes all meals, open bar, and excursions.

Patagonia Express ★★★ Patagonia Express works in conjunction with the Puyuhuapi Lodge & Spa (p. 345), leaving from Puerto Chacabuco and including a 2-night stay at the hotel and 1 night in Puerto Chacabuco. This is another premium excursion with sharp service and wonderful accommodations, but unlike Skorpios, you do not spend the night onboard the ship. It departs Tuesday and Saturday from September to April. During the entire long trip, the ship is kept amazingly spotless.

In Santiago, Fidel Oteíza 1921, no. 1006. ✆ **2/225-6489.** Fax 2/274-8111. www.patagonia-connection.com. AE, DC, MC, V. Prices average $1,650 (£1,100) per person for the 3-night package, including 1 night in Puerto Chacabuco and 2 nights at the Puyuhuapi Lodge & Spa; half-price for kids 15 and under. Includes all meals and excursions.

Skorpios ★★★ Skorpios is the upscale cruise service to Laguna San Rafael, offering deluxe onboard accommodations, great food, and all-around high quality. The rough-hewn wood cabins come with berths or full-size beds (or both, for families), in standard rooms or suites. The *Skorpios II* boards 130 people, although the trips are not usually heavily booked. Skorpios offers 7-day cruises along the eastern coast of Chiloé near Castro, then down to the glacier. On the return trip, the ship detours up the Fjord Quitralco to visit the remote hot springs there. Heading back to Puerto Montt, the ship cruises along the southern coast of Chiloé, stopping in Castro for an afternoon excursion. Skorpios offers service from September to May.

In Santiago, Augusto Leguía Norte 118, Las Condes. ✆ **2/231-1030.** Fax 2/232-2269. In Puerto Montt, Av. Angelmó 1660. ✆ **65/256619.** Fax 65/258315. www.skorpios.cl. AE, DC, MC, V. Cost for the 7-day/6-night journey is $1,050–$2,850 (£700–£1,900) per person. Prices include all meals, drinks, and excursions, and vary from high season to low season. Half-price for kids 11 and under in parent's room.

Overflight Trips to the Laguna San Rafael

A handful of companies arrange 2-hour overflight trips to the Laguna San Rafael, including disembarking near the glacier. It is a spectacular experience to view the glacier in its entirety (which means you won't want to do this trip on a cloudy day). These are charter flights, so you'll have to get a group together or fork over the entire price, but in a group, the price is competitive when you compare it with the cruises. Companies offering the service include **Don Carlos,** Subteniente Cruz 63 (✆ **67/231981;** www.doncarlos.cl); **Aerotaxis del Sur** (✆ **67/252253;** www.aerotaxisdelsur.cl); and **Transportes San Rafael,** 18 de Septiembre 469 (✆ **67/232048**). Conaf charges passengers $6 (£4) for admission to the park.

Where to Stay & Dine

Hotel Loberías del Sur ★★ Kids Puerto Chacabuco's shabbiness and stink belie its lovely location on the shore of Aysén Sound, and, thankfully, this hotel does it justice with wraparound windows in a large dining area and lounge. The Loberías del Sur is the obvious choice for its location right above the pier and because it is the only decent hotel in Puerto Chacabuco, though it is a bit overpriced. In fact, it's far more of a business hotel than a Patagonian lodge. This is where most travelers with ferry connections spend the night when they don't want to make the early morning journey from Coyhaique.

Carrera 50, Puerto Chacabuco, Región XI. ✆ **67/351115.** Fax 67/351188. www.catamaranesdelsur.cl. 60 units. $357 (£238) double. Rates include buffet breakfast. DC, MC, V. **Amenities:** Restaurant; bar; lounge; gym; sauna; game room; gift shop; business center; room service; laundry service. *In room:* TV, safe, hair dryer.

SOUTH FROM COYHAIQUE

A Sightseeing Excursion Around Lago Elizalde

The Seis Lagunas (Six Lagoons) and Lago Elizalde region just south of Coyhaique offers a sightseeing loop that passes through fertile, rolling farmland and forest, and past several picturesque lakes, all of which are known for outstanding fly-fishing. Because few people visit, this is a great place to escape the crowds. If you're tempted to stay and fish for a few days here, there are lodges that cater to this sport, described in "Fly-Fishing Lodges on the Carretera Austral" on p. 340. If you rent your own car, pick up a good map because many of these roads have no signs.

Leaving Coyhaique via the bridge near the Piedra del Indio (a rock outcrop that resembles the profile of an Indian), head first to Lago Atravesado, about 20km (12 miles) outside town. The road continues around the shore and across a bridge, and enters the Valle Laguna. From here, you'll want to turn back and drive the way you came until you spy a road to the right that heads through country fields, eventually passing the "six lagoons." Take the next right turn toward Lago Elizalde. This pretty, narrow lake set amid a thick forest of deciduous and evergreen beech is a great spot for picnicking and fishing. There is often a boat-rental concession here in the summer. There's a lodge here, but it's open only occasionally, usually when it books a large group. From here you'll need to turn back to return to Coyhaique; follow the sign for Villa Frei, which will lead you onto the paved road to Coyhaique instead of backtracking the entire route. Keep an eye open for El Salto, a crashing waterfall that freezes solid in the winter.

Reserva Nacional Cerro Castillo & Lago General Carrera ★★★

At a moderate 57km (35 miles) south of Coyhaique, this nature preserve protects a rough Andean scenery almost rivaling that of Torres del Paine. On a sunny day, you'll marvel at the 2,318m (7,603-ft.) **Cerro Castillo** or Castle Peak, named for the many granite needles that crown the summit, reminiscent of a medieval European fortress. The 179,550-hectare (443,678-acre) park holds glaciers, lagoons, and wildlife, including the rare huemul deer, along with several hiking trails. The Carretera Austral crosses the park, and tour operators from Coyhaique and around Lake General Carrera offer excursions. A great place to stop for a bite is **La Cocina de Sole,** where a young lady named Soledad whips up good sandwiches and simple lunches in a bus-turned-diner along the highway as it passes Villa Cerro Castillo. Don't miss the nearby **Manos de Cerro Castillo** national monument (admission $2/£1.30; daily 10am–6pm), about 5km/8 miles from town. Under a rocky ledge in view of the summit, it preserves some of the oldest artistic remains yet discovered in the Americas—some 10,000 years old. Here, Tehuelche tribespeople, including children, left red, black, and brown positive and negative handprints on the walls. It's a very touching, human spot.

Another 30km (19 miles) south by the most direct route, Chile shares its largest lake, the huge **Lago General Carrera,** with Argentina (where it is called Lago Buenos Aires). The landscape once again is gorgeous, with the water mostly a robin's-egg blue, surrounded by snow-capped mountains. Under mushroom-shaped islands, the lake features a series of marble caves polished and sculpted by centuries of wind and water, known as the marble "cathedrals" or "chapels." Their gray, yellow, or black-and-white swirls are a magnificent contrast to the blue water below. The best known is the **Capilla de Mármol** ★★, which is best visited by hiring a boatman in Puerto Río Tranquilo. There is a trailer just across from the gas station that sets up 1½-hour tours ($40/£27 per boat; up to 8 people), though they are highly dependent on the weather. Also consider visiting the less popular but larger islands from Puerto Sánchez; to get there, take the dirt road past Bahía Murta.

If the trip to the San Rafael glacier will bust your budget, head for the spectacular **Glaciar Los Leones**—like the former, part of the San Valentín Ice Field—which juts into the lake and river of the same name west of Puerto Río Tranquilo. Hire a guide as the trail to the Leones lakeshore is poorly marked, and you can hire a small boat to take you close to the glacier's face. It's a marvelous excursion, but it can be frigid in inclement weather. Other excursions include the **Exploradores Glacier,** easy to walk on, up Río Tranquilo. Those with a rental car might consider returning to Coyhaique by rounding the lake to **Chile Chico** on the Argentine border. From here, travelers must put their vehicle on a ferry, which crosses the lake and lands in Puerto Ibañez, from where drivers continue north to Coyhaique (reservations for cars are a good idea; contact **Motonave Pilchero at © 67/233466;** $4/£2.70 passengers, $35/£23 vehicles; one round-trip service Mon–Wed and Fri only from Puerto Ibáñez). This journey is for independent travelers with a fair amount of time.

Where to Stay

While good food other than hearty Patagonian barbecue is an issue in Aysén, quite a number of places to stay have sprung up recently in this area, from lakeshore *cabañas* to basic residences and some real gems. In Puerto Ibañez on the north shore, you can stay at the **Hostería Shehen Aike** (© **67/423284;** www.aike.cl). In Puerto Río Tranquilo (www.riotranquiloaysen.cl), two lakefront *hosterías* form bookends to the village. The first (from the north), **Hostería Costanera** (© **2/196-0072**), has better rooms with private bathrooms and lake views, but also a rudimentary gas station; the friendlier **Carretera Austral** (© **67/419500**) has better shared rooms with cleaner baths and a fine *cabaña*. On the south shore of the lake, on the road toward Chile Chico, consider the upscale **Mallín Colorado Eco-Lodge** (©/fax **2/234-1843;** www.mallincolorado.cl). In Chile Chico on the south shore, try the charming **Hostería de la Patagonia** (© **67/411337**), just outside town on the Camino Internacional; there are cheap, basic *residenciales* in the village.

To the south, on the shore of the lake of the same name, Puerto Bertrand holds several *residenciales* and the high-quality **Cabañas Campo Baker** (© **67/411447;** campobakerchile@123.cl), with fine views of the lake from most of the two-story bungalows and owned and run by fun and charming Italian Orlando Scarito; full board and multiday programs are available. The similar **Green Baker Lodge** (© **9/179116;** www.greenbakerlodge.cl) is a few kilometers away on the shore of the Baker River, "next door" to the **Patagonia Baker Lodge** (© **67/411913;** www.pbl.cl) and **Cabañas Rapidos del Rio Baker** (© **67/441-330**).

El Puesto ★★★ Finds One of Patagonia's top places to stay is this three-room boutique hotel in tiny Puerto Río Tranquilo, on Lake General Carrera. The boxy, contemporary building was built with native woods, with furniture upholstered in white helping to create a cozy, light atmosphere reminiscent of Scandinavian design. Rooms are similar, with one offering a terrace and another with a bunk bed best for a party of friends; you might find the triple just a tad on the small side. While not directly on the lakeshore, family-run El Puesto is the perfect place to relax after a day of wilderness activities, including hiking on glaciers, visits to the beautiful Capilla de Mármol, rock and ice climbing to fossil pits in Puerto Guadal, and soaring through forest canopies. El Puesto organizes 2- to 10-day tours, as well as dinners for groups.

Pedro Lagos 258, Puerto Río Tranquilo. © **02/196-4555.** www.elpuesto.cl. 3 units. $100 (£67) double. No credit cards. **Amenities:** Restaurant; Wi-Fi. *In room:* No phone.

Hacienda Tres Lagos ★★★ Nestled near the southwest corner of spectacular Lake General Carrera, this *estancia*-style luxury resort has a lake—and beach—of its own. Accommodations vary from hotel suites in the main lodge to family-oriented, independent *cabañas* to romantic luxury apartments, but all share the lakefront view of Lago Negro and the Patagonian Andes beyond, have balconies or terraces with rattan furniture, and are finely decorated with great attention to detail—guests even receive hotel iPods with speakers and music to suit the ambience.

The main complex has its own telescope for stargazing, a game room with pool table, darts, and Ping-Pong, plus a stone fireplace where they do *asados* (traditional Patagonian barbecues). As befits its location, it offers plenty of outdoor activities on foot, horseback, and boat, or farther afield to the Tamango Nature Preserve to try to glimpse the endangered huemul deer. And, while not a fly-fishing lodge per se, it also offers several fly-fishing and trawling excursions in the area and a 6-day/5-night tour, as well as packages with Puyuhuapi Spa & Lodge (p. 345).

Carretera Austral Sur Km 274, Cruce El Maitén, near Puerto Guadal. ✆ **02/333-4122.** www.haciendatreslagos.com. 20 units. $142–$194 (£95–£129) double. Rates include breakfast and afternoon tea. Full board available. AE, DC, MC, V. **Amenities:** Restaurant; bar; sauna; bikes; rowboats; massage; laundry service. *In room:* Minibar.

The Terra Luna Lodge ★ Kids This remote adventure lodge is owned by the French-Chilean outfitter company Azimut, which offers every kind of excursion throughout Chile. The lodge sits on a grassy slope above Lake General Carrera. Because the owners are renowned mountaineers and outdoors lovers, they can arrange serious adventure trips scaling regional peaks, long treks to glaciers, or rafting trips to the whitewater rapids of Río Baker. The lodging options consist of a spacious pine lodge with doubles and triples, a bungalow for four with a kitchenette, and another for two with a whirlpool, a "family" house for two to eight guests seeking total independence, and a low-cost cabin with bunks for two. Unfortunately, some visitors report the cuisine may not match the standard of the accommodations.

Km 1.5, Camino Puerto Guadal-Chile Chico. ✆ **67/431263,** or **2/235-1519.** www.terra-luna.cl. 4 apts with 3 rooms each, 3 cabins. $130 (£87) double (apt room); $170 (£113) for 4 people; all-inclusive packages run an average of 4 days/3 nights at $990 (£660) per double. All rates include breakfast. AE, MC, V. **Amenities:** Restaurant; Jacuzzi; sauna; kayak and bike rental; laundry service.

COCHRANE

It gets even remoter the farther south you travel. That may change over the next decade as a result of the giant hydroelectric projects planned along the Baker River, which has enough power to light up all of Belgium, tempting companies seeking to feed Chile's energy-guzzling economy. The number of residents could double temporarily for construction, worrying environmentalists. (See "Pumalín Park," earlier in this chapter.) In the meantime, **Cochrane** is the last place where you can reliably buy gas and get cash from an ATM; BancoEstado has an outlet on the main square. There are a few hotels and basic restaurants, but Cochrane is a rather gloomy, windswept place. The Esso station near the town's entrance has some information and brochures for travelers. Cochrane is the closest place from which to visit the **Estancia Valle Chacabuco,** a huemul and guanaco haven alongside the **Tamango** and **Jeinemeni** preserves, which the Conservación Patagónica Foundation, associated with Douglas Tompkins, bought in 2004 and seeks to transform into **Patagonia National Park** (www.conservacionpatagonica.org).

There are a number of decent places to stay here including the popular **Hosteria Lago Esmeralda** (San Valentín 141; ✆ **67/522621;** $20/£13 double) and larger, and more modern **Hotel Ultimo Paradiso** (Lago Brown 455; ✆ **67/522361;** $70/£47 double). The best place to eat is at **El Fogon** (San Valentín 651; ✆ **67/522322**), which serves Chilean standards and even has a few rooms in back. For supplies head to Casa Melero at Las Golondrinas 148, the very last place until Punta Arenas for fishing equipment, camping gear, most basic food stuffs, and wine.

Cochrane is the transportation "hub" for the limited southbound bus services: **Turismo Interlagos** (✆ **67/522606;** daily to Coyhaique at 9am), and **Don Carlos** at Prat 281 (✆ **67/522150;** Wed, Fri, and Sun to Coyhaique at 9:15am). **Los Ñadis** (✆ **67/211460**) heads to Villa O'Higgins Mondays and Thursdays and returns on Tuesdays and Fridays. **Buses Acuario 13,** Rio Baker 349 (✆ **67/522143**), runs to Caleta Tortel (3 hr.) Tuesday to Friday and Sunday at 9:15am. The frequency of buses drops significantly outside of the summer.

CALETA TORTEL

Continuing onward, the road narrows, but the scenery stays spectacular, passing through the Andes along multicolored peat bogs, finally descending into deep temperate rainforest. The road branches off to the remarkable little logging town of **Caleta Tortel ★★★**, an unreal, S-shaped place suspended somewhere between the steep slopes of a cypress rainforest and the pistachio green waters at the mouth of the Baker River, resembling a Patagonian Venice of sorts. Wood-shingled houses in bright or natural colors cling precariously to the hillside; cypress wood walkways and boats are the only ways to get around. Cars are banished to a lot at the end of the Carretera Austral—even the fire engine is a boat, just like in Venice. The scent of the planks and wood-burning stoves adds spice to the fresh mountain, forest, and sea air. There's little to do beyond exploring the boardwalk maze, though this can be as magical an experience as a walk through Torres del Paine. Hiking trails and fishermen's boats can take you to even more remote spots, including the **Montt** and **Steffens glaciers** and the **Isla de los Muertos;** check at the little municipality in Tortel for detailed information on how to get there. There are few *residenciales,* among them **Brisas del Sur**—a long walk from the parking lot and hence not a good choice for a brief stay—and **Don Adán** (both are reachable at **✆ 67/211876**) and **El Estilo** (no phone). For dining, **El Mirador** (no phone; above the Plaza de Armas) is the most formal restaurant with the best menu, though it tends to be pricey. **Sabores Locales,** up a narrow staircase (no phone; look for a sign on the waterfront), has cheaper meals, though the menu is simpler—comprising basically whatever they have fresh that day. There is an Entel office for phone calls on the plaza, and the library has free Internet service in 30-minute increments.

VILLA O'HIGGINS

A new ferry, **Padre Antonio Ronchi,** takes vehicles across the Bravo River from the hamlet of Puerto Yungay (summer hours: 10am, noon, and 6pm, returning at 11am, 1, and 7pm) for travelers heading on to the end of the road at **Villa O'Higgins,** an unattractive frontier outpost in a broad valley. It's like a mini-Cochrane with fewer services. The deep azure, multi-fingered lake by the same name is fed by the Southern Ice Field, the world's biggest non-polar mass of ice. Again, the landscape is marvelous, and hikers with plenty of time can cross into Argentina without too much trouble via lovely Laguna del Desierto, eventually ending up in El Calafate (see chapter 13). Tour outfitter **Hielo Sur/Villa O'Higgins** (**✆ 67/431821;** www.villaohiggins.com) offers boat trips to see glaciers and Mount Fitz Roy from the lake, and 1-day to 1-week hiking and horseback tours, including the crossing to El Calafate.

The area's next big attraction is a new **Cruce del Lagos** cruise from Villa O'Higgins to El Chaltén that avoids the cattle herd feel of the one from Puerto Montt to Bariloche—few realize that it even exists. The 50km (80-mile), 3½-hour, twice weekly journey ($35/£23) on the Quetru to the border at Candelario Mancilla passes Glaciar Chico and Glaciar O'Higgins, where you can either hike the 15km (24 miles) or hire a launch to Laguna del Desierto, where you can find buses to El Chaltén. The website has plenty of solid information (in Spanish), while the public library has free Internet service. The village has about a dozen basic places to stay. Check with the **Oficina de Turismo Rural** in Coyhaique (Ogana 1060; (**✆ 67/214031;** www.rutatranspatagonia.cl) for even more remote lodgings. Note that a road is being built near the ferry launch to Glacier Montt, about 70km/112 miles away, though it won't be finished until roughly 2012.

Southern Patagonia & Antarctica

Few places in the world have captivated the imagination of explorers and travelers like Patagonia has. Almost 500 years ago, the first Europeans sailed through on four ships captained by Ferdinand Magellan. But this vast region was one of the last on the planet to be settled and remains pristine and sparsely populated, protected by the harsh, cold climate. Sailors from around the world continue to test their luck and courage in these harrowing straits. Mountaineers stage elaborate excursions through rugged territories, only to be beaten back, like their predecessors, by unrelenting storms. What seduces so many people to Patagonia is the idea of the "remote"—indeed, the very notion of traveling to the End of the World. It is a seduction, but also an illusion. After all, on a globe, everywhere is both the center and the end of the Earth at the same time. And people do live here—very few people, but those who do are hardy survivors.

A harsh, wind-whipped climate and Patagonia's geological curiosities have produced some of the most beautiful natural attractions in the world: the granite towers of Torres del Paine and Mount Fitz Roy; the Northern and Southern Patagonian Ice Fields with their colossal glaciers (the greatest masses of ice and sweet water reserves outside the polar caps); the flat steppe broken by multicolored sedimentary bluffs; and the emerald fjords and lakes that glow an impossible sea-foam blue. In the end, this is what compels most travelers to plan a trip down here. Beyond landscapes, the region's cowboys (called *gauchos* in Argentina and *baqueanos* in Chile) lend a certain air of romanticism. Top the natural allure with an excellent array of new lodges and guiding services, and it's more appealing, and easier that ever, to journey to the "end of the world."

EXPLORING THE REGION

Despite its remoteness, Patagonia is surprisingly easy to travel. Once you get here, that is—airfare can be expensive, and flights are at least 4 hours from the major hubs of Santiago, Chile, or Buenos Aires, Argentina. Flying between Argentina and Chile is virtually impossible without returning via the national capitals. But, making use of increasingly excellent roads and traveling by local bus or car, it's entirely feasible to plan a circuit that loops through, for example, Ushuaia, Punta Arenas, Torres del Paine, and then El Calafate and El Chaltén. There's so much to see and do here, you'll really want to include a visit to this region in your trip to Chile, if possible.

How much time you plan on spending in Patagonia is entirely up to you. If you're planning a backpacking trip in Torres del Paine, for example, you'll want to spend between 5 and 10 days there; but those with plans for a few light walks and sightseeing drives in that national park might find that 2 to 3 days are enough. A quick trip to Patagonia might include 2 days in El Calafate, 3 in Torres del Paine, and a full day in Punta Arenas. A longer journey could begin with several days in El Chaltén, 2 in

Calling Between Chile & Argentina

One would think that two neighboring countries would offer low telephone rates for calls made from one to the other, but not so with Chile and Argentina. Visitors can expect to pay the same or higher rates as a call to the U.S., often around $2 (£1.30) per minute. When calling from Argentina to Chile, first dial **00-56,** then the area code and number. The prefix for Chilean cellphones is **09,** but callers from Argentina have to drop the 0; so to call a Chilean cellphone from Argentina, dial **00-56-9,** then the number.

When calling from Chile to Argentina, you must first call whichever carrier you're using (ask your host, your hotel, or at a calling center for the carrier prefix, usually **123, 181,** or **188**), followed by **0-54,** then the area code and number. Argentine area codes always begin with a 0 prefix, which you'll drop when dialing from Chile. For example, if dialing from Punta Arenas, Chile, to Ushuaia, Argentina, you'll dial 123 (or whichever carrier you're using), then 0-54-2901 and the number. When dialing Argentine cellphone numbers (which begin with 15), drop the 15 and replace it with the region's area code.

El Calafate, 5 in Torres del Paine, 1 in Puerto Natales, 1 in Punta Arenas, and a flight or cruise to Ushuaia for 3 to 4 days, returning over land or by plane. Remember, you need a day to get here from Santiago—it's a 4-hour flight to Punta Arenas alone.

Prices jump and crowds swell from early November to late March, and some businesses open during this time frame only. The busiest months are January and February, but these summer months are not necessarily the best months to visit Patagonia, as calmer weather usually prevails in October and from mid-March to late April. And winter travel is growing in popularity.

Note: Unless stated otherwise, hotel rates listed in this chapter are for high season (Oct–Mar) and include breakfast.

1 PUNTA ARENAS

254km (158 miles) SE of Puerto Natales; 3,090km (1,916 miles) S of Santiago

Punta Arenas, with a population of 113,000, is the capital of the Magellanic and Antarctic Region XII, and it is Patagonia's most important city, founded where the forest meets the steppe. The streets hum with activity, and its airport and seaports bustle with traffic. The town has made a living from coal mines, wool production, oil and natural gas, and fishing, and as a service center for cargo ships and the Chilean navy.

Punta Arenas' post-colonial wealth is reflected in the grand stone mansions that encircle the main plaza, which were built with earnings from the sheep *estancias* (ranches) of the late 1800s. Gold fever followed, and subsequently, hundreds of immigrants from Europe poured into the region from Britain, Germany, Yugoslavia, Russia, Spain, and Italy. Today Punta Arenas' streets are lined with residential homes with colorful, corrugated rooftops; business offices and hotels downtown; and an industrial port. The main waterfront area is undergoing a massive redevelopment project. The Magallanes region

Southern

Lago O'Higgins
Puerto Edén
Lago del Desierto
Lago San Martín
Lago Cardiel
Greg
ISLA WELLINGTON
Fitz Roy
El Chaltén
0 50 mi
0 50 km
N
Parque Nacional Bernardo O'Higgins
Parque Nacional Los Glaciares
Lago Viedma
Airport
Mountain
PACIFIC OCEAN
Lago Argentino
Glaciar Perito Moreno
El Calafate
Santa Cruz
Puerto Santa Cruz
Parque Nacional Torres del Paine
ARGENTINA
Bahía Grande
Cueva del Milodón
Coig
Reserva Nacional Alacalufes
Puerto Natales
Gallegos
Río Gallegos
CHILE
9
Parque Nacional Pali Aike
Punta Delgada
Estrecho de Magallanes
Penguin colony
Reserva Nacional Magallanes
Magallanes
Isla Magdalena
ATLANTIC OCEAN
Seno Otway
Punta Arenas
Porvenir
Estrecho de
Reserva Nacional Laguna Parrillar
Fuerte Bulnes
Camerón
ISLA GRANDE DE TIERRA DEL FUEGO
Parque Nacional Alberto de Agostini
Río Grande
Parque Nacional Tierra del Fuego
ARGENTINA
Lago Fagnano
Tolhuin
Ushuaia
Beagle Channel
Santiago
Buenos Aires
CHILE
ARGENTINA
Puerto Williams
Mar Chileno
Map Area
Parque Nacional Cabo de Hornos
Cabo de Hornes

onsiders itself somewhat of an independent republic due to its isolation from the rest of Chile—you'll see its attractive blue and yellow flag often—and this, in turn, has affected the personality of its people, an indefatigable bunch who brace themselves every summer against the gales that blow through this town like a hurricane. The wind, in fact, is so fierce at times that the city has fastened ropes around the plaza for people to hold on to. If that weren't enough, residents here now have to contend with a paper-thin ozone layer, which nearly dissipates for the summer around November.

Although for most travelers, Punta Arenas is simply an arrival and departure spot, the history of this region and the extremity of Punta Arenas' location on the famous Magellan Strait make for a fascinating place to explore. The most appealing reason to stop here is to visit one of the nearby penguin colonies (possible roughly from Oct–Mar). But if you have a few hours to kill, you'll find the human history on display in the mansions and museums also very intriguing and, in their own way, exotic.

ESSENTIALS

Getting There & Away

BY PLANE Punta Arenas' **Aeropuerto Presidente Ibáñez** (PUQ; ✆ **61/218131**) is 20km (12 miles) north of town, and, depending on the season, it's serviced with up to 10 flights per day from Santiago. **LAN,** Lautaro Navarro 999 (✆ **600/526-2000** or 61/241100; www.lan.com), has the most flights per day to both Santiago and Puerto Montt. They tend to be more expensive, but have been experimenting with rock-bottom prices for flights arriving or leaving in the wee hours of the morning. **Sky Airline,** Roca 935 (✆ **600/600-2828;** www.skyairline.cl), has one flight per day that is a bit of a milk-run, stopping twice en route. There is an ATM on the airport's ground floor.

LAN also offers three flights a week to Ushuaia, Argentina. The regional **Aerovías DAP,** O'Higgins 891 (✆ **61/223340;** www.aeroviasdap.cl), has six weekly flights to Porvenir and six flights a week to Puerto Williams as well. They also have charter flights to such places as Ushuaia and Antarctica, and charter sightseeing flights to Cape Horn and Torres del Paine.

To get to Punta Arenas from the airport, hire a taxi for about $10 (£6.70) or take one of the transfer services there (which can also arrange to take you back to the airport; their booths are at the baggage claim area). **Buses Transfer Austral** (✆ **61/229673;** www.transferaustral.com) has door-to-door service for $6 (£4) per person.

BY BUS From and to Puerto Natales: **Bus Sur,** José Menéndez 552 (✆ **61/614224;** www.bus-sur.cl), has four daily trips; **Buses Fernández,** Armando Sanhueza 745 (✆ **61/221812;** www.busesfernandez.com), has seven daily trips; and **Buses Pacheco,** Av. Colón 900 (✆ **61/242174;** www.busespacheco.com), has five daily trips. The cost is about $6 (£4), and the trip takes close to 4 hours.

To and from Ushuaia, Argentina: **Buses Tecni Austral,** Lautaro Navarro 975 (✆ **61/222078**), leaves Punta Arenas Tuesday, Thursday, and Saturday, and returns from Ushuaia on Monday, Wednesday, and Saturday; the cost for either is $45 (£30). **Buses Pacheco,** Av. Colón 900 (✆ **61/242174**), has direct service to Ushuaia on Monday, Wednesday, and Friday, and returns on Monday, Thursday, and Saturday, via Rio Grande. The direct trip to Ushuaia takes about 12 hours and costs $60 (£40).

BY CAR Rte. 9 is a paved road between Punta Arenas and Puerto Natales. Strong winds—and fog and ice in winter—often require that you exercise extreme caution when

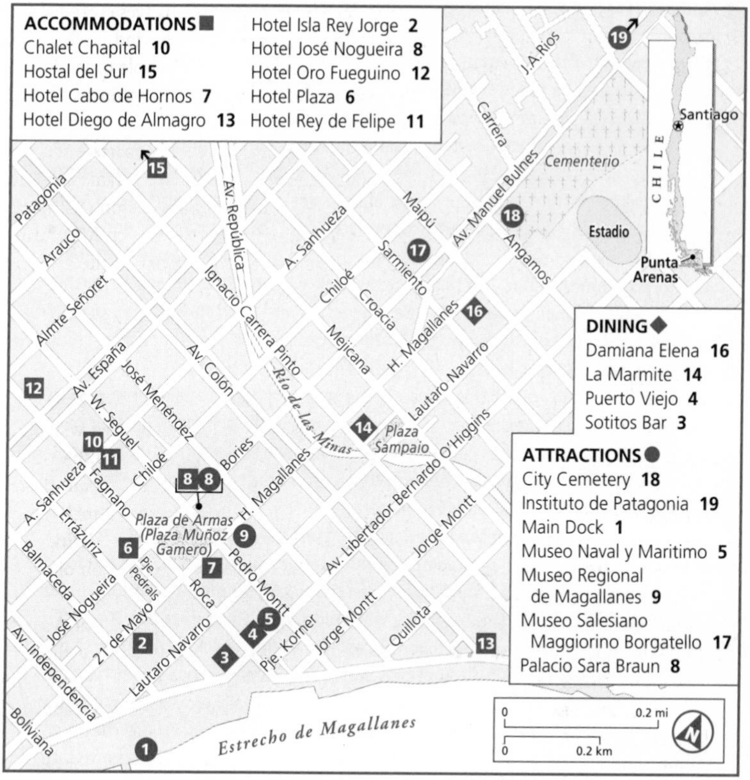

driving this route. To get to Tierra del Fuego, there are two options: Cross by ferry from Punta Arenas to Porvenir, or drive east on Rte. 255 to Rte. 277 and Punta Delgada for the ferry crossing there (for more information, see section 7, "Isla Navarino: Puerto Williams," later in this chapter). I recommend crossing Punta Delgada at least in one direction; the trip is shorter, more frequent, and will allow a detour to Pali Aike National Park and Estancia Lolita.

CAR RENTAL **International Rental Car,** Waldo Seguel 443 (✆ **61/225323;** www.international-rac.com), is a helpful and locally owned agency with an office at the airport. You can drop your car off in Puerto Natales or Coyhaique for an extra fee. Another option is **Southland Rentacar,** General de Canto 010 (✆ **61/241143;** www.southlandrentacar.com).

Getting Around

Downtown Punta Arenas is compact enough to explore on foot, but taxis are plentiful and you can hail one off the street—you'll find many around the Plaza de Armas. Travel

g from Punta Arenas to Ushuaia

…ro Australis runs an unforgettable journey between Punta Arenas and Ushuaia aboard its ships, the M/V *Mare Australis* and the *M/V Via Australis.* This cruise takes passengers to remote coves and narrow channels and fjords in Tierra del Fuego, and then heads into the Beagle Channel, ending at Ushuaia, Argentina. There's also a stop at the absolute end of the world, Cape Horn, although the chances that you will be able to get off the boat and touch *tierra firma* there aren't likely due to notorious winds. The trip can be done as a 4-night one-way from Punta Arenas or a 3-night one-way journey from Ushuaia. I recommend that you take just the one-way journey, ideally departing Punta Arenas, leaving you to explore a new city and then travel by air or land from there. It's a fantastic way to link both countries and turn your Patagonian itinerary into a loop.

What is unique about this cruise is the intimacy of a smaller ship and its solitary route that takes passengers to places in Tierra del Fuego that few have a chance to see. Passengers are shuttled to shore via zodiacs (motorized inflatable boats) for two daily excursions that can include visits to glaciers or a penguin colony, or walks to view elaborate beaver dams and lookouts. There are several excellent bilingual guides who give daily talks about the region's flora, fauna, history, and geology. Service is stiff but professional, and the food is quite good. The accommodations are comfortable, ranging from suites to simple cabins. In 2010, the company will introduce a third ship, the *M/V Stella Australis.* All-inclusive, per-person prices (excluding cocktails) range from \$1,930 to \$4,390 (£1,287–£2,927) one-way from Punta Arenas and \$1,440 to \$3,290 (£960–£2,193) one-way from Ushuaia. It's not really worth it to pay extra for an upper deck; second-floor berths at the front of the ship are the most stable, quiet, and comfortable. This cruise operates from early October to late April. For reservations or information, contact their U.S. offices in Miami, at 4014 Chase Ave., Ste. 215 (© **305/695-9615** or 877/678-3772; fax 305/534-9276), or in Santiago, at Av. El Bosque Norte 0440 (© **2/442-3110;** fax 2/203-5173); or visit www.australis.com.

anywhere within the city limits will not cost more than \$10 (£6.70); always confirm the fare with your driver before getting in the car. Cheap buses are also abundant and run either north–south on calles Bulnes and Noguiera or east–west along Independencia.

Visitor Information

There's an excellent **Oficina de Turismo** (© **61/200610**) inside a glass gazebo in the Plaza de Armas. The staff is helpful, and they sell a wide range of historical and anthropological literature and postcards. The office is open from December to March Monday through Friday from 8am to 5:30pm, Saturdays and Sundays from 9am to 2:30pm. From March through November, it's open weekdays only. **Sernatur**'s office at Lautaro Navarro 999 (© **61/225385;** www.sernatur.cl), on the other hand, is harried and inattentive; it's open Monday through Friday from 8:15am to 12:45pm and 2:30 to 7pm.

Fast Facts Punta Arenas

Currency Exchange Banks and currency exchange houses are mainly located on the 1000-block of Lautaro Navarro. Exchange money at **La Hermandad,** Lautaro Navarro 1099 (✆ **61/243991**); **Cambio de Moneda STP,** José Nogueira 1168 (✆ **61/223334**); or **Torres del Paine,** Lautaro Navarro 1013 (✆ **61/247675**). *Casas de cambio* are open Monday through Friday from 9am to 1pm and 3 to 7pm, and Saturday from 9am to 1pm.

For banks with 24-hour ATMs, go to **Banco Santander,** Magallanes 997 (✆ **61/201020**); **Banco de Chile,** Roca 864 (✆ **61/735433**); or **Banco de A. Edwards,** Plaza Muñoz Gamero 1055 (✆ **61/241175**). Banks are open Monday through Friday from 9am to 2pm.

Hospitals The local hospitals are **Hospital de las FF. AA. Cirujano Guzmán,** Avenida Manuel Bulnes and Guillermos (✆ **61/207500**); and **Clínica Magallanes,** Av. Manuel Bulnes 1448 (✆ **61/211527**).

Internet Access Try **Green Internet,** Jose Nogueira 1179 (✆ **61/617010**) or **Telefónica,** Bories 798 (✆ **61/248230**), open Monday through Friday from 9:30am to 5pm. There are also plenty of small Internet cafes, and Wi-Fi is widely available, including at the **Cyrano Café,** Bulnes 999 (✆ **61/242749**), and **Café Montt,** Pres. P Montt 976 (✆ **61/220381**).

Laundry Try **Lavandería Antártica,** Jorge Montt 664; **Autoservicio Lavasol,** O'Higgins 969; or **Lavandería Lavasuper,** José Nogueira 1595.

Pharmacy Go to **Farmacias Ahumada,** Bories 950 (✆ **61/220423**); **Farmacias Cruz Verde,** Bories 858 (✆ **61/246572**); or **Farmacia Salcobrand,** Bories 971 (✆ **61/240973**).

Post Office The central post office is at José Menéndez and Bories (✆ **61/222210**); hours are Monday through Friday from 9am to 6pm, and Saturday from 9am to 1pm.

WHAT TO SEE & DO

There are a surprising number of activities and sights to fill your day(s) while in Punta Arenas. When the wind is not overwhelming, it's a lovely town to stroll about. Begin your tour of Punta Arenas in the central **Plaza Muñoz Gamero,** where you'll find a bronze **sculpture** of Ferdinand Magellan donated by the region's long-ago wool czar José Menendez. Magellan is surrounded by lounging native Indians, one of whom has a shiny toe polished by the hundreds of visitors who kiss the nub each year; local lore here says that if you kiss the toe, you'll be lucky enough to visit Patagonia once again. The tranquil little plaza, delineated by cypress and other regional trees, has the visitor center gazebo, and several vendors here display crafts and souvenirs for sale. Around the plaza are old Punta Arenas' principal **mansions and edifices** from its boom times, which have, fortunately, been well kept over the decades.

From the plaza on Av. 21 de Mayo, head north toward Avenida Colón for a look at the **Teatro Municipal,** designed by the French architect Numa Mayer and modeled after the Teatro Colón in Buenos Aires. Head down to the waterfront and turn south toward the pier, where you'll find a 1913 clock imported from Germany that has a complete meteorological instrumentation and hands showing the moon's phases and a zodiac calendar. The entire port area is currently being redeveloped, with a giant new hotel and casino set to open in late 2009. There's also a lovely, new wide walkway and boulevard along the coast.

City Cemetery ★★ They say you can't really understand a culture until you see where they bury their dead, and in the case of the cemetery of Punta Arenas, this edict certainly rings true. The City Cemetery was opened by the Governor Señoret in 1894 and is fronted by a giant stone portico donated by Sara Braun in 1919. Inside this necropolis lies a veritable miniature city, with avenues that connect the magnificent tombs of the region's founding families, immigrant colonies, and civic workers, and a rather solemn tomb where lie the remains of the last Selk'nam Indians of Tierra del Fuego. It's a melancholic place, with lovely sculpted European cypress trees adding a gentle tone. The cemetery is about a 20-minute walk from the plaza, or a quick cab ride.

Av. Manuel Bulnes and Angamos. No phone. Free admission. Oct–Mar daily 7:30am–8pm; Apr–Sept daily 8am–6:30pm.

Instituto de la Patagonia/Museo del Recuerdo ★ The Instituto de Patagonia is run by the University of Magallanes and directed by the region's chief historian, Mateo Martinic. Here you'll find an engaging exhibit of colonial artifacts called the Museum of Memories. Antique machinery and horse-drawn carts are displayed around the lawn and encircled by several colonial buildings that have been lifted and transported here from ranches around the area. One cabin shows visitors what home life was like for a ranch hand, another has been set up to resemble a typical dry goods store, another is a garage with a 1908 Peugeot, and another is a carpenter's workshop. There's a library on the premises with a collection of books and maps on display and for sale. The museum is about 4km (2½ miles) out of town, so you'll need to take a taxi.

Av. Manuel Bulnes 01890. ✆ **61/217173.** Admission 70¢ (50p). Mon–Fri 8:30am–noon and 2:30–6pm; Sat 8:30am–noon; erratic hours and closing policies on Sun, so call ahead.

Museo Naval y Marítimo Punta Arenas' tribute to its seafaring history is this Naval and Maritime Museum. Here you'll find photos depicting the various ships and port activity over the past century, as well as small ship replicas and other artifacts. Although it's recently been updated and has an interesting new display on Shackleton, this museum is really recommended only for those with a strong interest in nautical-related items.

Pedro Montt 981. No phone. Admission $1 (70p). Tues–Sat 9:30am–12:30pm and 3–6pm.

Museo Salesiano Maggiorino Borgatello ★★ Kids This mesmerizing museum offers an insight into the Magellanic region's history, anthropology, ecology, and industrial history. That said, the lobby-level floor is packed with a fusty collection of stuffed and mounted birds and mammals that at turns feels almost macabre, considering that many have lost their shape; nevertheless, it allows you to fully appreciate the tremendous size of the condor and the puma. Several rooms in the museum display Indian hunting tools, ritual garments, jewelry, an Alacalufe bark canoe, and colonial and ranching implements, as well as the inevitable religious artifacts from the Catholic missionaries who played such a large role in the deterioration of native Indians' culture. Perhaps some of the most intriguing items on view here are the black-and-white photos of the early missionary Alberto d'Agostini.

Av. Manuel Bulnes and Maipú. ✆ **61/221001.** Admission $2.25 (£1.50). Tues–Sun 10am–12:30pm and 3–6pm.

Palacio Sara Braun & Museo Regional de Magallanes ★★ Moments These two attractions are testament to the staggering wealth produced by the region's vast 19th-century sheep and cattle *estancias*. The museums are the former residences of several members of the families Braun, Nogueira, and Menéndez, who believed that any far-flung, isolated locale could be tolerated if one were to "live splendidly and remain in constant contact with the outside world." And live splendidly they did in these veritable palaces, until the falling price of wool and the nationalization of *estancias* during the early 1970s forced the families to lose a large percentage of their holdings, and their descendants to relocate to places such as Buenos Aires.

The Palacio Sara Braun is now partially occupied by the Hotel José Nogueira and the Club de la Unión, a meeting area for the city's commercial and political leaders. The homes are national monuments, and both have been preserved in their original state, which allows visitors to appreciate the finest European craftsmanship available at the end of the 19th century. French architects planned the neoclassical exteriors, and craftsmen were brought from Europe to sculpt marble fireplaces and hand-paint walls to resemble marble and leather. The interior fixtures and furniture were also imported from Europe. For some visitors, the knowledge that these families to a large extent exterminated native Indians and suppressed labor movements in the region on their quest for wealth may temper the appreciation for the grandeur of these palaces. If one wants European grandeur, one normally goes to Europe, not to Patagonia. Still, both museums are really impressive.

Palacio Sara Braun: Plaza Muñoz Gamero 716. ✆ **61/248840.** Admission $2 (£1.35) adults, free for those 15 and under. Mon–Fri 3:30–8:30pm; Sun 11am–4pm. Museo Regional de Magallanes: Magallanes 949. ✆ **61/244216.** Admission $2 (£1.35) adults, 10¢ (6p) children 15 and under. Sun and holidays free. Nov–Apr Mon–Fri 10:30am–5:30pm; May–Oct daily 10:30am–2pm.

SHOPPING

Punta Arenas is home to a duty-free shopping center called the **Zona Franca,** with several blocks of shops hawking supposedly cheaper electronics, home appliances, imported foodstuffs, sporting goods, perfumes, clothing, toys, booze, and cigarettes. It's a massive shopping mall, with big-box stores a la North America. The savings here are very negligible, except for on alcohol, although there certainly is a lot on offer, including a few supermarkets. This does make it a fair place to stock up on supplies if you're planning a backpacking trip to Torres del Paine—otherwise, forget it. The Zona Franca is on Avenida Manuel Bulnes on the northern outskirts. It's open Monday through Saturday from 10am to 12:30pm and 3 to 8pm, and closed on holidays.

For regional crafts in town, try **Chile Típico,** Carrera Pinto 1015 (✆ **61/225827**), which has knitwear, carved-wood items, lapis lazuli, and more. For high-end, artsy-craftsy household items, such as picture frames, candles, throws, curtains, and the like, try **Almacén Antaño,** Colón 100 (✆ **61/227283**). Most afternoons see a collection of local artisans selling handicrafts in the city's main square, the Plaza de Armas. Look for wool sweaters and wooden toys there.

OUTDOOR ACTIVITIES

Few foreign travelers make it to Punta Arenas in winter, but if you do, there is a **ski resort** that operates from mid-June to mid-September: the **Centro de Esquí Cerro Mirador,** situated at the border of the Reserva Nacional Magallanes. It's notable more than anything else for its view of the Strait of Magellan, Tierra del Fuego, the Darwin Range of the Andes, and—on a clear day—Dawson Island. During the summer, they often run their only chairlift to carry you to the top of the peak, or you can hike the hill yourself. You can also take the chair up in winter to enjoy the view. The resort has 10 runs, ski rental, and a cafeteria. Ski lift tickets cost about $26 (£17); a ski rental package is $16 (£14). The resort (✆ **61/241479**) is just above town; to get here, take a taxi.

EXCURSIONS NEAR PUNTA ARENAS

Many tour operators run conventional city tours and trips to the penguin colonies, as well as short visits and multiday, all-inclusive trekking excursions to Torres del Paine National Park; but for excursions within the park I recommend that you stick with one of the outfitters listed under tour operators in the Puerto Natales section. A city tour here provides the historical background to this region and undoubtedly enriches a visitor's understanding of the hardship the immigrants and native aboriginals faced during the past century.

Turismo Yamana, Errázuriz 932 (✆ **61/710567;** www.yamana.cl), offers full-day city tours (about $75/£50 per person), penguin tours ($98/£65 per person), and tours to Pali Aike National Park ($275/£183 per person), as well as multiday kayaking and whale-watching expeditions. They also have an exhausting 14-hour "Torres del Paine in a day" tour ($417/£278 per person). Prices drop significantly for groups of four or more. The company also offers multiday trips to Lago Blanco in Tierra del Fuego for trekking, horseback riding, and fishing.

Turismo Comapa, Magallanes 990 (✆ **61/200200;** www.comapa.com), is the leader in town for conventional tours such as city tours and visits to the penguin colonies. **Turis Otway,** Mejicana 122 (✆ **61/224454**), also goes to the Seno Otway penguin colony for the bargain price of $25 (£17).

Turismo Viento Sur, 585 Fagnano (✆ **61/613845;** www.vientosur.com), is another respected company offering more outdoorsy excursions in and around Punta Arenas, including hiking to the San Isidro lighthouse, horseback riding, kayaking, fly-fishing, and bird-watching.

Fantastico Sur ★, José Menéndez 858 (✆ **61/615794;** www.fantasticosur.com), has naturalist tours including a day-long bird-watching tour where you can spot condors, penguins, waders, and passerines. They also have multiday naturalist tours of Patagonia, and their guides are passionate, professional, and superb.

Whale Sound, Lautaro Navarro 1163, 2nd floor (✆ **61/710511;** www.whalesound.com), is a new company offering multiday whale-watching tours in the distant waters off Carlos III Island, a breeding ground of the humpback whale. They also have a day-long helicopter whale-watching trip to the Francisco Coloane Marine Park, appealing if you have the time and, perhaps more importantly, the money. A 3-day, 2-night trip starts at $680 (£453) per person.

Fuerte Bulnes

In 1843, Captain Juan Williams, the naturalist Bernardo Philippi, 16 sailors and soldiers, and two women set sail from Ancud in Chiloé to the Strait of Magellan to plant the Chilean flag in this region before other powers could beat Chile to it. They chose a rocky promontory that dominated the strait and named it **Fuerte Bulnes.** Although this promontory was strategically appropriate for monitoring seafaring traffic, the location proved undesirable, and they pulled up stakes and moved 25km (16 miles) north, founding what is today Punta Arenas. In recognition of the historical value of Fuerte Bulnes, the Chilean government reconstructed the site in 1943, its centenary anniversary, and made it a national monument. At the gorgeous location, you'll find reconstructions of the log cabins that housed the settlers, a chapel, and several cannons. It is approximately 60km (37 miles) south of Punta Arenas on Rte. 9, the Panamericana. There are no set hours, and admission is free.

Just before Fuerte Bulnes is a short road leading to **Puerto Hambre.** The site was founded as Rey Felipe by Pedro Sarmiento de Gamboa in 1584, and settled by 103 colonists who were tragically stranded after tremendous storms prevented their ships from returning to shore. The name Puerto Hambre (Port Hunger) was given by the British captain Thomas Cavendish, who found only one survivor when he docked here in 1587 (the rest had died of starvation and exposure). In 1993, the Chilean ambassador José Miguel Barros found the plan for Rey Felipe in the library of the Institute of France in Paris, and it is the oldest known document of urban history in Chile. The only things you'll find here are a plaque and the remains of a chapel, but imagining yourself in the place of these settlers on this forsaken plot is worth the short detour from Fuerte Bulnes. Admission for both sites is free, with unspecified hours. To get here, sign up for a tour with Comapa or Viento Sur (see earlier).

Penguin Colonies & Estancia Lolita

If you have a day or a half-day to kill in Punta Arenas, from October through March, the most appealing activity is a visit to one of the penguin colonies at Seno Otway or Isla Magdalena. Both colonies allow visitors to get surprisingly close to the amusing Magellanic penguins (also called jackass penguins, for their characteristic bray) at their nesting sites. November through February provides the best viewing. Isla Magdalena is by far the best place to view the penguins, but the trip here involves a ferry ride and will take up more of your time and Isla Magdalena isn't open as long.

Penguins form lifelong partnerships and divide their chores equally: Every morning around 10am and in the afternoon around 5pm, the penguin couples change shifts—one heads out to fish, the other returns from fishing to take care of their young. When this changing of the guard begins, the penguins politely line up and waddle to and from the sea.

Seno Otway is accessible by road about 65km (40 miles) from Punta Arenas. A volunteer study group has developed the sight with roped walkways and lookout posts, including a peek-a-boo wall where you can watch the penguins diving into the ocean. Tours are offered in four languages, and there is a tiny cafe here, too. It's open October 15 to March 31 daily from 8am to 8pm. The best time to visit is between 9 and 10am and 5 and 7pm, when the majority of activity takes place (the crowds of visitors are thinner during the morning shift). Most tour companies in town (see earlier) will provide transportation with daily departures in the afternoons, but if you have a rental car you can go on your own. The cost of a tour here is about $12 to $15 (£8–£10), plus a $9 (£6) entrance fee (free for kids; © **61/224454;** www.turisotway.cl). It's open daily from 8am to 8pm. Give yourself 3 hours. Take Rte. 9 toward Puerto Natales, then turn left on the dirt road that branches out near the police checkpoint. Keep your eyes open for the ostrichlike Darwin's rhea on the ride here.

Isla Magdalena ★ is much larger than Seno Otway, with an estimated 150,000 penguins sharing nesting space with cormorants, compared to 3,000 penguins at Seno Otway. These penguins are more timid than those at Seno Otway, but the sight of so many of these birds bustling to and fro is decidedly more impressive. To get here, you need to take a ferry, which makes for a pleasant 5-hour afternoon excursion. **Turismo Comapa,** Av. Magallanes 990 (© **61/200200;** www.comapa.com), puts this tour together. Its boat, the *Barcaza Melinka,* departs from the pier at 4pm and returns at 9pm on Tuesday, Thursday, and Saturday, from late October to the end of March ($50/£33 for adults; $26/£17 for children under 12).

Estancia Lolita ★★ (✆ **61/233057;** www.faunapatagonica.com; adults $6/£4, children $4/£2.70) is a wildlife refuge and zoo for Patagonian fauna and the best place to view rarely seen species; it's 42km (16 miles) north of Punta Arenas. Josefina, a tame, rambunctious culpeo fox who loves to play with visitors, is one of the most charming living souls you'll meet in Patagonia. Guanacos, pumas (who seem happy enough, though their pens are on the small side) and other wild cats, and parrots and other endemic birds are among the denizens of the *estancia,* which has over 30 species in all. The refuge can provide lunch and arrange round-trip transportation, but it's on the expensive side.

Pali Aike National Park ★★

You may not be the only who finds the Patagonian steppe bleak and forlorn: In the language of the Aonikenk, or Tehuelches, the original inhabitants, the name Pali Aike means "Desolate Place." Though windswept and strewn with volcanic craters, the starkly beautiful area was inhabited thousands of years ago, with cracks in the lava forming caves that served as shelters and were excavated in the 1930s. The Cueva Fell has Stone Age cave paintings 9,000 years old. Fauna in the 5,000-hectare (12,350-acre) park include guanaco, fox, puma, armadillo, and waterfowl; Pali Aike also has several easy hikes, though the Cueva Pali Aike-Laguna Ana is a long 9km (5.5 miles). It's a fine side trip en route to or from Tierra del Fuego or Río Gallegos, but unless you have your own transportation, you'll need to book a tour in Punta Arenas, and you'll hardly see a thing on a foggy day. Note the minefields not far from the park entrance; the rustiness of the warning signs will chill your spine.

WHERE TO STAY

In general, lodging in Punta Arenas is expensive for the caliber of accommodations available. For hostels not mentioned below, however, check with the Tourism Office for recommendations. Note that many hotels are willing to negotiate a price. There is a massive new hotel and casino being completed near the port, slated to be opened in late 2009, though that date may change.

Expensive

Hotel Cabo de Hornos ★★ Punta Arenas' top hotel frankly has little competition. It's most conveniently located on the northeast corner of the plaza, and is comfortable and professionally run. The Cabo de Hornos sports an impressive, elegant, gray stone-clad reception and lounge area, very nicely decorated in a mixture of modern and rustic. A separate room, with a massive fireplace, is where stylish locals meet for a cocktail, coffee, or business lunch. Most rooms don't quite match the wow factor of the ground floor, being just a little on the small size. Top floor rooms have slanted ceilings and the best views.

Plaza Muñoz Gamero 1039, Punta Arenas. ✆ 61/715000. www.hoteles-australis.com. 111 units. $210 (£140) double; $290 (£193) triple. AE, DC, MC, V. Amenities: Restaurant; lounge; free Internet in business center; room service; laundry service. In room: TV, hair dryer, safe, Internet.

Hotel Diego de Almagro (Value) A new seven-story hotel that's part of a Holiday Inn–esque Chilean chain, this waterfront hotel is completely serviceable, if predictable and standard. It's the only hotel in town with an indoor pool. Rooms are sunny and clean; most have two double beds. Corner rooms have views of both the channel and town. Because it's still new, discounts are available year-round on the website.

Av. Colon 1920, Punta Arenas. ✆ 61/208800. www.dahoteles.com. 181 units. $165 (£110) double. AE, DC, MC, V. Amenities: Restaurant; pool; gym; sauna; games room. In room: TV, Internet access, minibar, safe.

Hotel Isla Rey Jorge ★★ Finds This hotel is housed in an antique English-style mansion, 2 blocks from the plaza. There's a compact lounge lit by a pergolalike glass ceiling, decorated with a blue country-style theme. Altogether, it's a lovable little hotel. The snug rooms (some are quite small) with angled eaves are just slightly dark but kept toasty warm. Rooms have a classic, executive-style decor, in navy blue and burgundy offset with brass details. The junior suites are the most spacious, with king-size beds and whirlpool tubs. The friendly staff let it be known that they rarely charge the advertised price, so always ask for a discount. Downstairs, in what was the brick-walled cellar, are an intimate restaurant and a popular pub.

Av. 21 de Mayo 1243, Punta Arenas. ✆/fax **61/248220.** www.islareyjorge.com. 25 units. $146 (£97) double; from $199 (£133) junior suite. AE, DC, MC, V. **Amenities:** Restaurant; pub; room service; laundry service. *In room:* TV.

Hotel José Nogueira This classic hotel is in the partially converted neoclassical mansion once owned by the widow of one of Punta Arenas' wealthiest entrepreneurs; half of the building is still run as a museum (p. 371). The mansion was built between 1894 and 1905 on a prominent corner across from the plaza, with materials imported entirely from Europe. The José Nogueira is appealing for its historical value but also offers old-world luxury. The rooms here are not as large as you would expect, but high ceilings accented by floor-to-ceiling curtains compensate for that. All are tastefully decorated, with oriental rugs and lithographs of local fauna; the marble bathrooms are sparkling. The Nogueira's singles are unusually spacious. The suites have ample bathrooms with Jacuzzi tubs and a living area in the open bedroom. Keeping with the old-fashioned theme, the maids here dress in long smocks. I find the hotel dark and stuffy, but it is more intimate than its neighbor, the Hotel Cabo de Hornos. The mansion's old "winter garden" is now a restaurant, La Pérgola, housed under the Nogueira's glass-enclosed terrace. Downstairs is a popular pub in what once was the wine cellar.

Bories 959, Punta Arenas. ✆ **61/711000.** Fax 61/711011. www.hotelnogueira.com. 22 units. $190 (£127) double; $290 (£193) suite. AE, DC, MC, V. **Amenities:** Restaurant; bar; room service; laundry service. *In room:* TV, minibar.

Rey de Felipe ★ Finds Little known, off the beaten-track, comfortable, and very quiet, this new hotel is cozy and private. There is an element of natural luxury here that stands out in Punta Arenas' hotel offerings. The spacious lobby has a giant fireplace and comfortable couches. Rooms are modern and plush, with natural colored carpets, and small details such as old maps decorate the walls. All have deep bathtubs and wooden bathroom counters. Service is a bit stiff, but that may be due to the fact that there's hardly ever anybody at this hotel. Rooms vary in size; if you want to ensure a big room be sure to ask. Located 3 blocks up the hill from the Plaza de Armas, it's farther from the water, so it's protected from the stormy weather.

Armando Sanhueza 965, Punta Arenas. ✆ **61/617500.** www.reydonfelipe.cl. 43 units. $145 (£97) single; $160 (£107) double; $210 (£140) suite. AE, DC, MC, V. **Amenities:** Restaurant; bar; gym; business center; Wi-Fi; laundry service. *In room*: TV, minibar, safe.

Moderate

Chalet Chapital (Value) A classic Punta Arenas mansion that was transformed into a simple, pleasant little inn, the best part of this hotel is the loving, friendly staff. Breakfasts, for example, are typically simple Chilean offerings. Rooms have comfortable beds, private bathrooms with hydro-massage showers, and nothing else fancy. There's a TV room downstairs. Like most small inns in town, it can be noisy when other guests get up early for excursions. This is a great midrange choice if you're not up for a hostel and your budget's not up for one of the hotels above.

Armando Sanhueza 974, Punta Arenas. © 61/730100. www.hotelchaletchapital.cl. 11 units. Double $85 (£57), triple $95 (£63). AE, DC, MC, V. Amenities: TV room, tourist agency.

Hostal Oro Fueguino ★ (Value) This hostel is a favorite with backpackers and budget travelers for its clean, comfortable rooms and friendly service. The interiors here are painted vibrant colors and decorated with folk art, and there are rooms for doubles, triples, and quadruples—all with private bathrooms. Their plant-filled, colorful dining room and lounge is a cozy spot to relax. The hostel is a 5-block walk up from the plaza; look for the bright yellow-and-aqua exterior.

Fagnano 356, Punta Arenas. © **61/249401.** www.orofueguino.cl. 12 units. $82 (£55) double with private bathroom. Rates include continental breakfast. AE, DC, MC, V. **Amenities:** Lounge; laundry. *In room:* TV.

Hotel Plaza Location and a certain faded charm make this a fair midrange option. On the southwest corner of the plaza across from the cathedral, this hotel has creaky wooden floors and high ceilings that hark back to better times a long, long time ago, with the interior less impressive than the grand, four-story exterior implies. Nevertheless, it's a decent place to stay, popular mostly with European tour groups. The carpeted, conservative rooms are good-size and beds with plaid coverings are very comfortable, and the Plaza boasts rooms for groups of up to five guests. It's a good value, though amenities are sparse.

José Nogueira 1116, Punta Arenas. ©/fax **61/241300.** www.hotelplaza.cl. 26 units. $107 (£71) double; $162 (£108) quintuple. AE, DC, MC, V. **Amenities:** Cafeteria; Internet; laundry service. *In room:* TV.

Inexpensive

Hostal del Sur (Value) This little hostel is tucked away on a residential street among a grove of pine trees, and it has been popularized by word of mouth. It is more of a family-style hostel, with exceptionally pleasant service and a friendly tan Labrador that welcomes you at the door. Simple yet clean rooms and private bathrooms in every room make this hostel a good value.

Mejicana 151, Punta Arenas. © **61/227249.** Fax 61/222282. 7 units. $45 (£30) double. No credit cards. **Amenities:** Lounge. *In room:* TV.

WHERE TO DINE

There are plenty of decent restaurants in Punta Arenas, most of which serve local fare such as lamb, king crab, and shellfish. The best strip of tourist-friendly restaurants is along O'Higgins. The major hotels have decent restaurants, if you feel like dining in. For a quick bite, head to a local favorite, the slightly overpriced diner-style **El Mercado,** Mejicana 617 (© **61/247415**). For pastas at a good price, try **O Sole Mio,** O'Higgins 974 (© **61/242026**). With a big menu and a lively bar, **La Luna,** O'Higgins 1017 (© **61/228555**) is laid-back and friendly. The liveliest cafe for drinks or sandwiches is the **Pub 1900,** at the corner of Bories and Colón (© **61/242759**); it is the social center for townsfolk here and it has giant windows for people-watching. The best casual spot for dinner and a pint of beer is **Santino,** Colón 657 (© **61/710882**), a spacious pub/restaurant that is the happening spot at night; they have sandwiches and simple Chilean dishes such as *lomo a lo pobre,* that heart-attack-on-a-plate dish of steak, fries, and a fried egg.

Damiana Elena ★★ Finds CONTEMPORARY CHILEAN With a menu that changes so frequently it's not even printed, and a packed house most nights, this may be the best restaurant in Punta Arenas. There are eight daily specials, usually including a seafood, meat, and pasta option. The chef's recommendation will be something like king crab cannelloni with artichokes and fine herbs. They've recently moved into a larger location, in a refurbished old house in a residential area, far from the touristy-strip on O'Higgins. The service (mostly bilingual!) is more youthful, relaxed, and friendly than in the other traditional restaurants in town. Upstairs is the nonsmoking section. There is also a large wine list, and a funky bar on the main floor.

Magallanes 341. © 61/222818. Reservations highly recommended. Main courses $12–$18 (£8–£12). AE, DC, MC, V. Mon–Sat 8pm–12:30am.

La Marmite ★★ REGIONAL CHILEAN/VEGETARIAN Focusing on unpretentious and fresh Chilean classics such as *curanto* (a traditional meal of fish and meat steamed over hot rocks in the ground), conger eel with quinoa, or the classic stew *charquicán* (made of beans, corn, potatoes and meat, and topped with a fried egg), La Marmite is funky and friendly. Located in a colorful heritage building, the restaurant's decor is slightly tongue-in-cheek, with random bits of ironic art displayed. Buns are warmed, and coffee is brewed on a giant wood-burning stove in the middle of the tables; great lunch specials are usually on offer. In a sea of conservatism, La Marmite is a happy and fun oasis. And they have real espresso, a novelty in Chile.

Plaza Sampaio 678. © 61/222056. Reservations recommended on weekends. Main courses $7–$19 (£4.70–£13). AE, DC, MC, V. Mon–Sat 12:30–3pm and 6:30–11:30pm, Sun 6:30–11:30pm.

Puerto Viejo ★ SEAFOOD/GRILL The slickest, coolest new restaurant in town is set to make the most of the new casino-hotel opening nearby at the port. Remodeled with a marine inspiration, the focus here is on food from the sea. Specialties include king crab, eel's cheeks in mustard sauce, and hake with cider and swordfish. At the back, Patagonian lamb roasts on a spit. There are also classic cuts of beef, and an excellent wine list heavy with Chilean cabernets sauvignon and sauvignon blanc.

O'Higgins 1166. © 66/225-103. Reservations recommended. Main courses $15–$22 (£10–£15). AE, DC, MC, V. Daily 8pm–12:30am.

Sotitos Bar ★ CHILEAN Don't be fooled by the plain green front and weathered sign: Sotitos has handsome semiformal interiors with brick walls and white linen tablecloths. A favorite for upper-class locals, Sotitos offers more menu items than most Chilean restaurants, including steak and seafood, local baked lamb, Valencia shellfish rice (which must be ordered ahead of time), pastas, and fresh salads. The key is that everything is of high quality, regardless of how simple the dish. The fish is very fresh. The service here, however, is only so-so. On Friday, Saturday, and Sunday, the restaurant fires up its *parrilla* (grill) for barbecued meats. There's a nonsmoking section up front, which is usually empty.

O'Higgins 1138. © **61/221061.** Reservations recommended. Main courses $12–$20 (£8–£13). AE, DC, MC, V. Mon–Sat 11:30am–3pm and 7–11:45pm.

PUNTA ARENAS AFTER DARK

The city has a handful of good bars and pubs, plus a few discos, which I recommend only if you like to hang out with teenagers and listen to bad techno music. One of the most popular places to get a drink is **Sotitos Bar** (see "Where to Dine," earlier), and it is especially suitable for large groups. Other popular spots are **Pub 1900** (see "Where to Dine," above) and **El Galeón,** Av. 21 de Mayo 1243, below the Hotel Isla Rey Jorge (✆ **61/222681**). The **Cabo de Hornos Hotel** (✆ **61/242134**), on the plaza, has a chic bar with a more somber atmosphere.

The **Cine Estrella,** Mejicana 777 (✆ **61/225630**), is the only cinema in town. Call or check newspaper listings to see what's playing.

2 PUERTO NATALES

254km (158 miles) NW of Punta Arenas; 115km (71 miles) S of Torres del Paine

Puerto Natales is a rambling town of 19,000, spread along the sloping coast of the Señoret Canal between the Ultima Esperanza Sound and the Almirante Montt Gulf. This is the jumping-off point for trips to Torres del Paine, and many visitors to the park will find themselves spending at least a night here. The town itself is a small center with rows and rows of weather-beaten tin and wooden houses. Within the ramshackle buildings are some truly cozy and delightful inns, cafes, and bistros. Puerto Natales has a frontier-town appeal and boasts a stunning location with grand views out onto a grassy peninsula and glacier-capped peaks in the distance. From May to September, the town virtually goes into hibernation, but come October, the town's streets are crowded with international tourists decked out in parkas and hiking boots on their way to or back from the park.

Puerto Natales was founded in 1911 as a port for the export of lamb's meat and wool. Tourism has now replaced wool and coal to dominate the economy, evident by the plethora of hostels, restaurants, and tour companies found here, though it appears the period of rapid growth is leveling off.

ESSENTIALS

Getting There

BY PLANE There is a tiny airport in Puerto Natales that operated sporadically in 2007 and 2008; but most flights were cancelled due to wind. Although there's always a possibility they'll give it another go, do not plan on being able to fly into Puerto Natales. The closest airports are in El Calafate, Argentina (4–5 hr.; p. 398) and Punta Arenas (3–4 hr.; p. 366).

BY BUS Puerto Natales is the hub for bus service to Torres del Paine National Park and El Calafate, Argentina. For information about bus service to and from Torres del Paine, see section 3, "Parque Nacional Torres del Paine," later in this chapter. There are frequent daily trips between Punta Arenas and Puerto Natales. In Puerto Natales, each bus company leaves from its own office.

TO AND FROM PUNTA ARENAS **Buses Fernández,** at Ramirez and Esmeralda streets (✆ **61/411111**), has seven daily trips; **Bus Sur,** Baquedano 668 (✆ **61/411859**), has two daily trips; **Buses Pacheco,** Baquedano 500 (✆ **61/414513**), has four daily trips (and the most comfortable buses); and **Transfer Austral,** Baquedano 414 (✆ **61/412616**), has two daily trips. The trip takes about 3 hours and the cost is about $6 to $8

(£4–£5.30) one-way. Reserve early during the busy season, as tickets sell out fast. Round-trip fares to Punta Arenas are a little cheaper. There is no central bus terminal in Puerto Natales; each bus company has a different office, although most are along Baquedano Street.

TO EL CALAFATE, ARGENTINA Options include **Buses Zaahj,** Arturo Prat 236 (✆ **61/412260;** www.turismozaahj.co.cl), departing at 8am Tuesdays, Thursdays, and Saturdays, and **Cootra,** Baquedano 456 (✆ **61/412785**), which leaves at 7:30am daily. The cost is $30 (£20) one-way. The trip takes 4 to 5 hours, depending on the traffic at the border crossing.

BY CAR Rte. 9 is a paved road that heads north from Punta Arenas. The drive is 254km (158 miles) and takes about 3 hours. If you're heading in from El Calafate, Argentina, you have your choice of two international borders: Cerro Castillo (otherwise known as Control Fronterizo Río Don Guillermo) or Río Turbio (otherwise known as Controles Fronterizos Dorotea y Laurita Casas Viejas). Both are the same in terms of road quality, but Río Turbio is busier, with Chileans heading to Argentina for cheaper goods and most of the bus traffic. Both are open 24 hours from September to May, and daily from 8am to 11pm the rest of the year. Gas is much cheaper in Argentina, so fill up there.

BY BOAT **Navimag** runs a popular 3-night ferry trip between Puerto Natales and Puerto Montt, cruising through the southern fjords of Chile. This journey passes through breathtaking (though repetitive) scenery, and it makes for an interesting way to leave from or head to Chile's Lake District. Navimag leaves Puerto Montt every Friday afternoon. Rates for private berth start at $610 (£407). Its offices in Puerto Natales are at Pedro Montt 308 (✆ **61/411642;** www.navimag.com).

Getting Around

Puerto Natales is built on a grid pattern, and you'll spend most of your time within a 5-block radius, from the coast up to the main plaza, Plaza de Armas, along which runs Calle Eberhard, the street where you'll find the post office and the town's yellow cathedral. Calle Eberhard dead-ends a block away at Blanco Encalada; this street, Avenida Manuel Bulnes (1 block to the right), and Baquedano (1 block up from Blanco Encalada) are the principal streets, with most of the supermarkets, banks, and tourism-oriented businesses. Along the shore of Puerto Natales runs Pedro Montt, also called the Costanera, which is an excellent place for a stroll.

All taxis charge a flat rate of $2 (£1.30) for trips within the town limits. They can be hailed off the street, or else found around the main plaza. Car rentals in Puerto Natales are offered by **International Rental Car** (✆ **61/228323;** www.international-rac.com), and **Amazing Patagonia,** Baquedano 558 (✆ **61/414949;** www.amazingpatagonia.com), among others. You don't need a car to get around the town, but a rental car can come in handy for longer-distance trips, including those into Torres del Paine National Park.

Visitor Information

Sernatur operates a well-stocked office on the Costanera at Pedro Montt and Philippi (✆ **61/412125;** www.sernatur.cl); it's open October through March Monday through Friday from 8:30am to 8pm, Saturday and Sunday from 9am to 1pm and 3 to 6pm. April through September, it's open Monday through Friday from 8:30am to 1pm and 3 to 6pm; it's closed on holidays. Better yet is the **Municipal Tourism office,** tucked in a corner of the historical museum at Bulnes 285 (✆ **61/414808**), with a wealth of information on lodgings, restaurants, and day trips; the staff here is far more helpful than at Sernatur. It's open Monday to Friday from 9am to 12:30pm and 2:30 to 6pm, and Saturdays from 3 to 6pm. **Conaf** has its park headquarters at O'Higgins 584 (✆ **61/411438;** www.conaf.cl), but you'll get better park information from a tour operator (see "Tour Operators & Adventure Travel Outfitters," later).

Fast Facts Puerto Natales

Camping Equipment If you don't feel like lugging your own camping gear down here, there are several agencies that rent equipment. Typical daily rental prices are two-person tents for $6 (£4), sleeping bags for $3 (£2), stoves for $1.50 (£1), sleeping mats for $1 (70p), and backpacks of various sizes for $3 (£2). During the high season, it's best to reserve these items ahead of time. **La Maddera Outdoor,** Arturo Prat 297 (✆ **61/413318;** www.lamadderaoutdoors.com), is recommended for its high-quality equipment, or try **Casa Cecilia,** at Tomás Rogers 60 (✆ **61/411797**).

Currency Exchange There are several exchange houses on Blanco Encalada; try **Mili,** Blanco Encalada 266 (✆ **61/411262;** Mon–Sat 10am–8pm). ATMs can be found at **Banco Santiago,** at the corner of Blanco Encalada and Bulnes, and **Banco Chile,** at Bulnes 544.

Hospital Frankly, the town's public hospital is horrible. It's on the corner of Pinto and O'Higgins (✆ **61/411583**). For major medical emergencies, it's best to get yourself to Punta Arenas.

Internet Access There are tons of cafes offering free Wi-Fi in Puerto Natales. And most hotels have a computer you can use. Also, try **Internet Melissa,** Blanco Encalada 258, and **Chilnet,** 343 Manuel Bulnes. Note that connections in Puerto Natales can be painfully slow.

Laundry The multilingual team at **ServiLaundry,** Prat 337 (✆ **61/412869**) gets your clothes back clean within 2 hours, and offers tourist information.

Pharmacy **Farmacias Marisol** is at Baquedano 331 (✆ **61/411591**).

Post Office The post office is on the Plaza de Armas, next to the cathedral (✆ **61/410202**); it's open Monday through Friday from 9am to 6pm, Saturday from 9am to 1pm.

WHAT TO SEE & DO

Tour Operators & Adventure Travel Outfitters

The many tour operators in Puerto Natales can be divided into two groups: conventional sightseeing day tours to Torres del Paine, Perito Moreno Glacier in Argentina's Los Glaciares National Park, the Cueva de Milodon, the Nordenskjöld Trail hike, and the icebergs at Lago Grey; and adventure travel outfitters that arrange multiday, all-inclusive excursions, including trekking the W or the Circuit (see "Exploring Torres del Paine" in section 3, later in this chapter) and climbing in Torres del Paine, kayaking the Río Serrano in Parque Nacional Bernardo O'Higgins, and taking horseback trips. Keep in mind that it's quite easy to arrange your own trekking journey in Torres del Paine; the bonus with these outfitters is that they carry the tents (which they'll set up) and food (which they'll cook). They also will pick you up from the airport and provide guided information about the flora and fauna of the park.

CONVENTIONAL DAY TOURS These tours are for people with a limited amount of time in the area. Tours typically leave at 7:30am, return around 7:30pm, and cost about $65 (£43) per person, not including lunch or park entrance fees. For day tours, try **Turismo Comapa,** Manuel Bulnes 533 (✆ **61/414300**), or **Viaterra,** Bulnes 632 (✆ **61/410775;** www.viaterra.cl); Viaterra has transfers from Punta Arenas directly to the park on a charter basis. Probably the most interesting way to see the Cueva de Milodon is with **Estancia Travel** (✆ **61/412221;** www.estanciatravel.com), which offers a horseback-riding trip there for $86 to $108 (£57–£72), including transfers, equipment, a bilingual guide, snacks, and a well-trained horse.

ADVENTURE TRAVEL Dozens of international adventure travel companies run trips to Torres del Paine, and most work with a local operator. You can save money by going directly to the operator. Most of the following ones offer custom packages. **Indómita,** Bories 206 (✆ **61/414525;** www.indomitapatagonia.com), is one of the most respected local outfitters for climbing, mountaineering, and kayaking. One of their most popular trips is a 3-day kayak descent of the River Serrano, with a paddle around Serrano Glacier. Partner **Antares,** Barros Arana 111 (✆ **61/414611;** www.antarespatagonia.com), focuses on the "softer" (meaning less strenuous and/or technical) side of adventure travel, with a variety of multiday trekking journeys through the park that can include horseback riding, kayaking, and sailing; and they have an office in the U.S. (✆ **800/267-6129**). **Chile Nativo Expeditions,** Eberhard 230 (✆ **61/411835** or toll-free from North America 800/649-8776; www.chilenativo.com), offers high-end trekking, bird-watching, and horseback-riding adventures outside of the more "touristy" areas. **Fantastico Sur** (✆ **61/615794;** www.fantasticosur.com) has wildlife-viewing tours, including a puma-watching tour that has a 70% guarantee of catching a glimpse of the elusive cat. **Onas,** Blanco Encalada and Eberhard (✆/fax **61/412707;** www.onaspatagonia.com), has a half-day zodiac trip down the Río Serrano; see "Getting There & Away" in section 3, later in this chapter.

EXCURSIONS NEAR PUERTO NATALES

Cueva de Milodon

In 1896, explorer Hermann Eberhard found a scrap of hairy skin and a few bones in a large cave near his property north of Puerto Natales that were later determined to be from a *Milodon,* a prehistoric, giant ground sloth. The story of the *Milodon* was popularized by Bruce Chatwin's travelogue *In Patagonia.* Although the *Milodon* is depicted in a full-size replica at the cave's entrance, most of the *Milodon*'s remains were shipped off to London, which means the real attraction is the 30m high (98-ft.), 200m deep (656-ft.) cave itself, which has a weird, shaggy roof and is surrounded by interesting conglomerate rock formations. There's an interpretative center with a few *Milodon* bones and a display showing the geological formation of the cave, as well as a historical display of the Indians who inhabited this and nearby caves as far back as 12,000 years ago. Its modern restaurant was designed to reflect the shape of the cave. While not too touristy, this attraction is recommended only if it's on your route, if you are interested in paleo-fauna, or if you've run out of things to do in Puerto Natales.

The cave is located 24km (15 miles) north of Puerto Natales, so you'll need your own car or a tour to get here. To get here, take the road to Torres del Paine; at 20km (12 miles), turn left, and then drive for 4km (2½ miles) to the cave's turnoff. The site is managed by Conaf and is open daily from 10am to 7pm; admission is $5 (£3.30) adults, $2.50 (£1.70) children (✆ **61/411843** in Puerto Natales).

Sailing to Parque Nacional Bernardo O'Higgins

This national park, tremendous in its size, is largely unreachable except for boat tours to the glaciers Balmaceda and Serrano, tours that involve kayaking (for kayaking trips, see Indómita under "Tour Operators & Adventure Travel Outfitters," earlier), and the Skorpios journey to the grand Pio XI glacier (see later). A low-key, traditional day trip takes travelers to the Serrano and Balmaceda glaciers, with a stop at the Monte Balmaceda Hostel and a short walk along the glacier and its iceberg-studded bay. The ride kicks off with a trip past the old mutton-canning factory, an *estancia,* and a cormorant nesting site, among other sites of interest. The return trip is a straight shot back to Natales—which can be repetitive, so bring a book in the event of boredom or bad weather. The trip is dull except for the glacier visits, and visitors are prone to being herded about.

Turismo 21 de Mayo, Eberhard 560 (✆ **61/411176;** www.turismo21demayo.cl), has a cutter and a yacht, and leaves daily (weather permitting) November through March and every Sunday from April to October (other days dependent on demand). The trip leaves at 8am, arriving at Serrano Glacier at 11:30am, where it stays for 1½ hours, returning at 5:30pm. They also offer custom-made charter rides for groups. **Nueva Galicia,** Eberhard 169 (✆ **61/412352;** nuevagalicia@terra.cl), takes visitors along a similar route aboard its wooden yacht of the same name, leaving at 7:45am and arriving at Serrano Glacier at 11am for a half-hour, then across the adjoining river to its lodge, the Hostería Monte Balmaceda. There visitors can take a walk around the self-guided nature trail, have lunch in the restaurant, and reboard, arriving at Puerto Natales at 5:30pm. Please note that the restaurant here serves tough, tasteless food, so you should bring a picnic, especially if the weather is pleasant. The luxury cruise company **Skorpios,** Agosto Leguia Norte 118 (✆ **2/477-1900** or 305/484-5357 in North America; www.skorpios.cl), has an all-inclusive 6-day journey from Puerto Natales to Pio XI Glacier, the largest and only "advancing" (some scientists call it "stable") glacier in the Southern Hemisphere. This glacier measures an astounding 6km (3¾ miles) in length and peaks in height at 75m (246 ft.); it is also the least-visited glacier, and this alone makes a visit all the more special. The size of the Pio XI simply dwarfs other glaciers, such as Glacier Grey in Torres del Paine. I recommend this journey for travelers who are not very physically active and who don't want to miss a visit to Torres del Paine but wish to add on a special journey to an out-of-the-way destination. Active travelers might get bored on a 6-day tour.

WHERE TO STAY

It seems that anyone and everyone who owns a home large enough to rent out a few rooms has decided to hang a HOSPEDAJE sign above their door. These simple, inexpensive accommodations can be found everywhere, but excellent higher-end (and more expensive) options are to be had as well. The high season in Puerto Natales is longer than in any other city in Chile—it's generally considered to run from October to April—and the price range shown reflects this.

Expensive

Altiplánico Sur ★★★ (Moments) One of several new options leaning heavily on contemporary style, the Altiplánico Sur is the southern brother of San Pedro's Altiplánico (p. 222), but sports completely different architecture. From the outside, it appears a bit reminiscent of a two-story brick school, but on approach, you'll see much of the property is in fact hidden underground with grass-covered roofs, and the exterior walls are made of a dark, unpainted adobe-type material. It shares a nearby stretch of waterfront property just north of town past the Remota (see later). Spacious on the inside, the ambience relies heavily on loft-style concrete, trimmed by zig-zagging wood and some metal decor. Views of the water, across the road, are lovely. Rooms, down the corridor, are good-size, comfortable, and feature such warm touches as plush sheepskins and bright cushions that offset other eye-catching but cooler materials. Bathrooms are similar—modern, functional, and elegant. Because they don't offer the all-inclusive packages that are so popular elsewhere, this is a good bet for independent travelers looking for a low-profile hotel.

Huerto Familiar 282, Puerto Natales. ✆ **61/412525.** www.altiplanico.cl. 22 units. $170 (£113) single; $180 (£120) double. AE, DC, MC, V. **Amenities:** Restaurant; bar; Jacuzzi; shop; Wi-Fi; room service; living room w/TV. *In room:* Safe.

Indigo ★★★ (Moments) The Indigo, Puerto Natales' sole boutique hotel, is a very cool and hip spot. Conveniently located both on the waterfront and in town, it also sports the finest views of the glaciers across the sound. Rooms are in the multistory, red-and-black ship container-inspired cube that overshadows the shingled former hostel, now with a funky lounge on the ground floor and a good restaurant on the top floor.

The hotel's divine top-level spa features three outdoor hot tubs. Even the sauna and massage areas offer views of the landscape. The airy, midsize rooms have fine views as well, exquisite bathrooms, and beds that feature crisp linens and wool blankets. The corner rooms are slightly larger, but still outdone by the suite, which features a large, freestanding white bathtub as its most distinguishing element. Many efforts have been made to keep the hotel eco-friendly, including through natural heat management, organic composting, an efficient waste water treatment system, and recycling. For location, views, and amenities, Indigo just slightly edges out Remota as the best place in town, and will be preferred by more independent travelers.

Ladrilleros 105, Puerto Natales. ✆ **61/413609.** www.indigopatagonia.com/uk/home. 29 units. $280 (£187) double; $378 (£252) suite. AE, DC, MC, V. **Amenities:** Restaurant; bar; sauna; tour services; Internet; Wi-Fi; massage. *In room:* Hair dryer.

Hotel CostAustralis ★★★ This hotel is certainly traditional, but compared to the other options (see above and below), it's conservative and dull. With a restaurant that recently doubled in size, the lobby, lounge, and main floor feel even larger and emptier, although there is a lovely view of the sunset. Spacious doubles come with a sea view or a somewhat depressing view of the buildings in the back; the 28 rooms on the fourth floor, though priced the same, are newer, with marble bathrooms and plenty of closet space, so ask for one. The price is fairly high, even by North American and European standards, and therefore might not be appealing to anyone who plans to arrive late and leave early. For its size, it best suits tour groups.

Pedro Montt 262, Puerto Natales. ✆ **61/412000.** Fax 61/411881. www.australis.com. 110 units. $248–$300 (£165–£200) double. AE, DC, MC, V. **Amenities:** 2 restaurants; bar; room service; laundry service. *In room:* TV, safe.

Remota ★★★ (Moments) You will either love or hate this hotel. The architecture alone is provocative, alternately uncomfortable and brilliant. Built by a renowned Chilean architect (the same who designed the explora) it's a unique mix of a bunker with a greenhouse, inspired by the *estancias* of Patagonia. Black and a bit forbidding from the outside, it's the complete opposite inside, featuring huge floor-to-ceiling windows that flood the white walls and columns with light amid a generous lounge and dining areas. Yellow cushions and huge fireplaces add to the coziness, while a collection of archaeological finds from around the country draw your eye (although they could use more explanation). Rooms feature native woods—wallboards even show off shreds of bark—along with washed cement floors and white ceilings. With natural grass on the roofs and energy-efficient lighting, Remota's design will please those looking to leave a small eco-footprint. Bathrooms have rainshower heads and deep tubs. Their all-inclusive packages (all meals, transfers, and excursions) tend to focus on lesser-traveled areas, and now include transfers from El Calafate, Argentina. Remota is the explora's top competition.

Huerto 279, 1.5km (less than a mile) N of Puerto Natales. ✆ **61/414040.** www.remota.cl. 77 units. 3-night package $1,548 (£1,032) per person double. Rates include excursions. AE, DC, MC, V. **Amenities:** Dining area; bar; indoor pool; bicycles; Wi-Fi; massage. *In room:* Hair dryer, safe.

Moderate

Aquaterra ★★ It is a fantasy many of us have, to open a small inn in a place we fell in love with while traveling. The three owners of Aquaterra did just that, trading the bustle of Santiago for this windy, quiet town, and travelers should be thankful, as the hotel is one of the best lodging options in town. The rooms are neither huge nor quiet, but they feature comfortable beds with marshmallowy down comforters accented with colorful woven throws. All rooms now have private bathrooms, and all rooms are flooded with light. There are two triples, at the same price as a double. The hotel's restaurant and tiny cafe with a wood-burning stove are cozy places to relax and read. What really stands out here is the pleasant, friendly service; there are also on-site massage services.

Av. Bulnes 299, Puerto Natales. ✆ **61/412239.** www.aquaterrapatagonia.com. 13 units. $155 (£103) double. DC, MC, V. **Amenities:** Restaurant; lounge; massage. *In room:* No phone.

Weskar Patagonian Lodge ★★ If your idea of the Patagonia experience is more rustic than hip, look no further than this hillside lodge above the waterfront, a 10-minute walk from town. Cozy and made of native lenga wood and stone, it has gabled oriels and fine views across the water and of the town itself. Though the hotel's exterior is rustic, the good-size rooms boast modern decor, with wooden headboards and colorful woolen bed covers on white linens. Two new "superior" doubles are bigger, with separated bathrooms. The dining area's tables are placed marvelously to take advantage of the views.

Rte. 9 Norte, Km 1, Puerto Natales. ✆ **61/414168.** www.weskar.cl. 22 units. $125 (£83) single; $160 (£107) double standard; $195 (£130) double superior. AE, DC, MC, V. **Amenities:** Restaurant; bar; Jacuzzi; excursions; Internet access; laundry service.

Inexpensive

Amerindia Hostel ★ If you are looking for a laid-back and friendly place to lay your head, this is a great choice. It's also a great option for more upscale backpackers. Rooms, tucked along a hallway at the back of a typical local home, are simple and warm. Some bathrooms have showers and some have tubs. Room 5 has a view of the water. The best part of Amerindia is the caring, utterly unpretentious staff, who will welcome you as if you were a member of their family.

Barros Arana 135, Puerto Natales. ✆ **61/411945.** www.hostelamerindia.com. 8 units. $52 (£35) double with shared bathroom; $70 (£47) double with private bathroom. No credit cards. **Amenities:** Breakfast room; gift shop; Internet access; laundry service; TV room.

Casa Cecilia (Value) Casa Cecilia is a budget favorite in Puerto Natales, consistently garnering rave reviews from guests for its full range of services, pleasant rooms, and delicious breakfasts. The front lobby acts as a travel agency of sorts, providing information, arranging excursions, and renting camping equipment; beyond that is a common area and a kitchen that guests can use—and they do. Rooms are stacked on two floors and encircle an atrium; some come with private bathrooms, some shared, and they are a good value for the price. Light flows into the rooms' windows from the interior atrium. The Swiss-Chilean couple (she's Cecilia) speaks several languages and both are very friendly. This hostel is popular with a wide range of ages and types.

Tomás Roger 60, Puerto Natales. ✆/fax **61/613560.** www.casaceciliahostal.com. 15 units. $49 (£33) double with shared bathroom; $59 (£39) double with private bathroom. AE, DC, MC, V. **Amenities:** Tour desk; Internet access; kitchen.

WHERE TO DINE

Along with the following restaurants, there are several that serve inexpensive fare. **Mesita Grande,** Arturo Prat 196 (✆ **61/411571**), is a popular place for pizzas, salads, and hanging out. **La Picada de Carlitos,** corner of Esmeralda and Blanca Encalada (✆ **61/411850**), has sandwiches, meat, and seafood dishes, and a daily set lunch for about $7 (£4.70).

Expensive

Angelica's MEDITERANEAN The menu here is long, and the service wonderfully friendly. Specialties include sea bass, hake, and the classic and warm Chilean seafood stew called *paila marina.* I loved the king crab cannelloni. There are also lots of fresh salads. This place tends toward the upscale, at least by Puerto Natales standards.

Bulnes 501. ✆ 61/410007. www.angelicas.cl. Main courses $12–$22 (£8–£15). AE, MC, V. Daily noon–3:30pm and 6pm–12:30am.

Cormoran de Las Rocas ★★ (Moments) SEAFOOD This is Puerto Natales' best seafood restaurant, and the top local choice for upscale dining. In a top-floor dining room designed to feel like a ship, the views are superb and the seafood-heavy menu large. Specialties include a king crab tart with four cheeses, rosemary octopus with a green apple salad, and salmon or hake in coconut and saffron sauce. For dessert, try the cheesecake with calafate sauce. Service is very professional. The bar offers lighter tapas, and is open late.

Miguel Sanchez 72. ✆ 61/413723. Main courses $12–$18 (£8–£12). AE, MC, V. Daily 12:30–3pm and 7:30–11pm.

Restaurant Última Esperanza ★★★ (Value) SEAFOOD This may not in fact be your last hope for a good meal, as the name implies. But it may well be the best in Chilean Patagonia, and it offers good food at competitive prices. Its location in a simple, half-timbered building near the square and its basic if conservative decor might not look like much, but it's what your taste buds say that counts. Above all, it prepares some of the best abalone, king crab, and *curanto* in the whole country. Try the poached conger eel in shellfish or king crab sauce. Magallanic lamb is also on the menu.

Eberhard 354. ✆ **61/411391.** restaurantultimaesperanza@hotmail.com. Main courses $12–$22 (£8–£15). AE, DC, MC, V. Daily noon–3:30pm and 6:30pm–midnight.

Moderate

Afrigonia ★★ FUSION One of the most interesting dining experiences in all of Chile is this tiny, unassuming spot that surprisingly blends Chilean cuisine with an East African influence. The curries and tandooris made here use real spices, and the *ceviche* in coconut milk with mango may be the best *ceviche* you'll have in Chile. It's small and very popular, so reserve ahead.

Eberhard 343. ✆ 61/412232. Reservations recommended. Main courses $9–$15 (£6–£10). No credit cards. Daily 7–11pm.

Inexpensive

El Living ★★ Finds CAFE/VEGETARIAN If you're looking for a friendly, comfortable place to kick back and spend the evening, then look no further. At El Living, run by a British expatriate couple who have lived in the area for more than a decade, you can lounge on a comfortable sofa with a pisco sour or have an excellent vegetarian dinner at one of their handmade wooden dining tables. The menu is simple and inexpensive but fresh and delicious. The Sweet and Sour Red Salad is a perfect mix of beetroot, red cabbage, kidney beans, and onion; the veggie burger is delicious and served on a wholewheat baguette. This is one of the only places in Chile that serves a peanut-butter-and-jelly sandwich. There's also French toast with fried bananas, and a variety of cakes baked daily. A full bar and wine list round out this excellent place.

Arturo Prat 156. ✆ **61/411140.** Main courses $9–$15 (£6–£10). No credit cards. Daily 11am–midnight.

PUERTO NATALES AFTER DARK

Little more than a few years ago, the only nightspot in Puerto Natales was a brothel. Now there are several bars where the party doesn't wind down until about 5am. **Toore Bar,** Eberhard 169 (no phone), is a hip new spot to sample a pisco sour. **The Pub El Bar de Ruperto,** Bulnes 310 (no phone), has pool tables and loud music. The bar and lounge at **Indigo,** Ladrilleros 105 (✆ **61/413609**), are good for a drink and view of the sunset.

3 PARQUE NACIONAL TORRES DEL PAINE ★★★

113km (70 miles) N of Puerto Natales; 360km (223 miles) NW of Punta Arenas

This is Chile's prized jewel, a national park so magnificent that few in the world can claim a rank in its class. Granite peaks and towers soar from sea level to upward of 2,800m (9,184 ft.). Golden pampas and the rolling steppes are home to llamalike guanacos and more than 100 species of colorful birds, such as parakeets, flamingos, and ostrich-like rheas. During the spring, Chilean firebush blooms a riotous red, and during the autumn, the park's beech trees change to crimson, sunflower, and orange. A fierce wind screams through this region during the spring and summer, and yet flora such as the delicate porcelain orchids and ladyslippers somehow weather the inhospitable terrain. Electric-blue icebergs cleave from Glacier Grey. Resident *baqueanos* ride atop sheepskin saddles. Condors float effortlessly even on the windiest day. This park is not someplace you just visit; it is something you experience.

Although it sits next to the Andes, the Torres del Paine is a separate geologic formation created roughly 3 million years ago when bubbling magma began growing and pushing its way up, taking a thick sedimentary layer with it. Glaciation and severe climate weathered away the softer rock, leaving the spectacular Paine Massif whose prominent features are the *Cuernos* (which means "horns") and the one-of-a-kind *Torres*—three salmon-colored, spherical granite towers. The black sedimentary rock is visible on the upper reaches of the elegant Cuernos, named for the two spires that rise from the outer sides of its amphitheater. *Paine* is the Tehuelche Indian word for "blue," and it brings to mind the varying shades found in the lakes that surround this massif—among them the milky, turquoise waters of Lagos Nordenskjöld and Pehoé. Backing the Paine Massif are several glaciers that descend from the Southern Ice Field.

Torres del Paine was once a collection of *estancias* and small-time ranches; they were forced out with the creation of the park in 1959. The park has since grown to its present size of 242,242 hectares (598,338 acres), and in 1978 was declared a World Biosphere Reserve by UNESCO for its singular beauty and ecology. This park is a backpacker's dream, but just as many visitors find pleasure staying in lodges here and taking day hikes and horseback rides—even those with a short amount of time here are blown away by a 1-day visit. There are options for everyone, part of the reason the number of visitors to this park is growing by nearly 10,000 per year.

ESSENTIALS

When To Come & What To Bring

This is not the easiest of national parks to visit. The climate in the park can be abominable, with wind speeds that can peak at 161kmph (100 mph) and rain and snow even in the middle of summer. On average, the windiest days happen between mid-November and mid-March, but the only predictable thing about the weather here is its unpredictability. ***Note:*** Come with your expectations in check—it's not uncommon to spend a week here and not see the towers even once due to bad weather.

Spring is a beautiful time for budding flowers and birds; during the fall, the beech forests turn colors, which can be especially striking on walks up to the Towers and to the glacier. The winter is surprisingly temperate, with relatively few snowstorms and no wind—but short days. You'll need to stay in a hotel during the winter, but you'll practically have the park to yourself. Summer is, ironically, the worst time to come, especially from late December to mid-February, when the wind blows at full fury and crowds descend upon the park. When the wind blows, it can make even a short walk a rather scary experience or just drive you nuts—just try to go with it, not fight it, and revel in the excitement of the extreme environment that makes Patagonia what it is.

I can't stress enough the importance of bringing the right gear, especially waterproof hiking boots (if you plan to do any trekking), weatherproof outerwear, and warm layers, even in the summer. The ozone problem is acute here, so you'll need sunscreen, sunglasses, and a hat as well.

Visitor & Park Entrance Information

Your visit to Torres del Paine will require logistical planning, unless you've left it up to an all-inclusive tour or hotel. Begin your research at **www.torresdelpaine.cl**, an English-language overview of the park and its surroundings, including maps, activities information, events, photos, hotel overviews and links, and more. The park service, Conaf, has a relatively unhelpful Spanish-only website at **www.conaf.cl**.

The park's administration and visitor center can be reached at ✆ **61/691931;** it's located at the southern end of the park. The park is open year-round from 8:30am to 10:30pm. The entry fee is $30 (£20) for adults; during the winter, the cost is $16 (£11) adults. If staying outside the park, get your ticket stamped for multiple visits.

Many travelers are unaware of the enormous amount of time it takes to get to Torres del Paine. There are no direct transportation services from the airport in Punta Arenas to the park, except with package tours and hotels that have their own vehicles, or by chartering an auto or van (try **Viaterra; © 61/410775;** www.viaterra.cl). The earliest flight from Santiago to Punta Arenas arrives at around noon; from there it's a 3-hour drive to Puerto Natales. The last bus to the park leaves at 2:30pm for the 2-hour journey to the east side of the park. Thanks to a new road, the west side (where such lodgings as explora, Patagonia Camp, and Hosteria Lago Grey are) is now only 1 hour from Puerto Natales. If you're relying on bus transportation (and if you are not staying at an all-inclusive hotel), you will likely need to spend the night in Puerto Natales. If you've arranged a package tour or hotel stay that picks you up at the airport, remember that the 3- to 5-hour trip from here can be very tiring if you've just taken a 4-hour flight from Santiago.

BY BUS Several companies offer daily service from October to April. During the low season, only Bus Sur offers service to the park. Buses to Torres del Paine enter through the Laguna Amarga ranger station, stop at the Pudeto catamaran dock, and terminate at the park administration center. If you're going directly to the Torres trail head at Hostería Las Torres, there are minivan transfers waiting at the Laguna Amarga station that charge about $5 (£3.30) one-way. The return times given below are when the bus leaves from the park administration center; the bus will pass through the Laguna Amarga station about 45 minutes later.

Trans Via Paine, Bulnes 516 (**© 61/413672**), leaves daily at 7:30am via Laguna Amarga. **Gomez,** Arturo Prat 234 (**© 61/411971**), also leaves at 7:30am, returning from the administration building at 1pm. **Buses JB,** Arturo Prat 258 (**© 61/410242**), departs also at 7:30am, returning at 1pm. The cost is around $16 (£11) one-way.

BY TOUR VAN If you don't have much time to spend in the park or would like to get there at your own pace, check into the minivan tour services that plan stops at the Salto Grande waterfall and carry on to Lago Grey for a walk along the beach to view giant icebergs (see "Tour Operators & Adventure Travel Outfitters" in section 2, earlier in this chapter).

BY CAR Heading north on Pedro Montt out of town, follow the dirt road for 51km (32 miles) until you reach Cerro Castillo. From here the road turns left and heads 47km (29 miles) toward the park (keep your eyes open for another left turn that is signposted TORRES DEL PAINE). You'll come to a fork in the road; one road leads to the Lago Sarmiento Conaf station, another to the Laguna Amarga station. If you are planning to head to the Torres trail head and Hostería Las Torres hotel complex on your way out, then take the Lago Sarmiento entrance; it's faster, and you'll get to view the striking blue waters of Lago Sarmiento. You can park your car at the Hostería Las Torres, the park administration center, the Pudeto catamaran dock, or the Lago Grey ranger station. To get to the western side of the park (to such places as Lago Grey and Lago Pehoe, and to hotels such as explora and Patagonia Camp), take a left just north of town toward the Cueva de Milodón cave, and continue north to the Conaf Station. Check with the park service at www.conaf.cl or ask your rental-car agency for updated road information.

CROSSING LAGO PEHOE BY CATAMARAN Day hikes to the Glacier Grey trail and backpackers taking the W or Circuit trails will need to cross Lake Pehoé at some point aboard a catamaran, about a 45-minute ride. The cost is $22 (£15) one-way or $36 (£24) round-trip. Buses from Puerto Natales are timed to drop off and pick up passengers in conjunction with the catamaran (Nov 15–Mar 15 leaving Pudeto at 9:30am, noon, and 6pm, and from Pehoé at 10am, 12:30, and 6:30pm; Oct 16–30 and Mar 16–30 from Pudeto at noon and 6pm, and Pehoé at 12:30 and 6pm; Oct 1–15 and Apr, from Pudeto at noon, from Pehoé at 12:30pm; closed May–Sept). Hikers walking the entire round-trip Glacier Grey trail can do so only taking the 9:30am boat and returning at 6:30pm from mid-November to March 15.

GETTING TO THE PARK BY BOAT Zodiac-catamaran combinations that take visitors from Puerto Natales through the Ultima Esperanza Sound and up the Río Serrano, or vice versa, are available. This is an interesting alternative to getting to the park via bus or van, but it's an all-day affair. Also, you'll need to arrange transportation with your hotel to or from the administration office. Along the winding turquoise river, visitors are taken through territory that rivals Alaska, past the Tyndall and Geike glaciers, and eventually to Serrano Glacier. Here they disembark for a walk up to the ice, then board another boat for a 3¹/₂-hour ride to Puerto Natales. The one-way ride costs $95 (£43) per person, depending on the season. You can also do a round-trip journey leaving from and returning to the park for about $68 (£45). See "Tour Operators & Adventure Travel Outfitters" in section 2, earlier in this chapter, for more information. **Onas**'s zodiac is an adventure, and their guides are fun (✆/fax **61/614300;** www.onaspatagonia.com).

Active travelers will be interested in following the same Río Serrano route but by **kayak,** about a 3-day journey. This trip is suitable for travelers on their way back to Puerto Natales, to take advantage of the river's downward current; at night, travelers camp out on shore. Check with **Indomita** (✆ **61/413247;** www.indomitapatagonia.com), on Bories 206, in Puerto Natales.

EXPLORING TORRES DEL PAINE

Trails

Torres del Paine has something for everyone, from easy, well-trammeled trails to remote walks through relatively people-free wilderness. Which path you choose depends on how much time you have and what kind of walking you're up for. If you have only a few days, I suggest you stick to the major highlights. If you have a week or more, consider a horseback-riding trip to the base of Mount Donoso, or a bird-watching trip through the Pingo Valley, or a walk to the Valle de Silencio beyond the Towers. The best way to plan a multiday hike is to begin at Hostería Las Torres, reached from the Laguna Amarga ranger station, although it is just as feasible to start at Lago Pehoé by catamaran and begin the trip up to the glacier or French Valley. Pick up one of **JLM's Torres del Paine maps** (sold at most bookstores and at the park entrance), or download a map from **www.torres delpaine.com** to begin planning your itinerary. Walking times shown below are average. The minimum number of days shown assumes walking 4 to 8 hours a day; plan for extra days if you want to take it easy, and factor 1 or 2 days for bad weather.

Long-Haul Overnight Hikes

The Circuit ★★★ The Circuit is a spectacular, long-haul backpacking trip that takes hikers around the entire Paine Massif. It can be done in two ways: with or without the W included. Including the W, you'll need 8 to 11 days; without it, from 4 to 7 days. The Circuit is less traveled than the W because it's longer and requires that you camp out at least twice. I don't recommend doing this trail if you have only 4 or 5 days. This trail is for serious backpackers only because it involves several difficult hikes up and down steep, rough terrain and over fallen tree trunks. You'll be rewarded for your effort with dazzling views of terrain that varies from grassy meadows and winding rivers to thick virgin beech forest, snowcapped peaks, and, best of all, the awe-inspiring view of Glacier Grey seen from atop the John Garner Pass. Always do this trail counterclockwise for easier ascents and with the scenery before you.

If you're here during the high season and want to get away from crowds, you might contemplate walking the first portion of this trail, beginning at Laguna Azul. This is the old trail, and it more or less parallels the Circuit, but on the other side of the river, passing the baqueano post La Victorina, the only remaining building of an old *estancia.* At Refugio Dickson, you'll have to cross the river in the *refugio*'s dinghy for $4 (£2.70). To get to Laguna Azul, you'll need to hitchhike or arrange private transportation. Do not underestimate the isolation of most of this hike—snowstorms, injuries, not having enough food—a lot can go wrong on this trek, so be fully prepared.

Approx. 60km (37 miles) total. Beginning at Laguna Amarga or Hostería Las Torres. Terrain ranges from easy–difficult.

The W ★★ This segment of the Paine Massif is so called because hikers are taken along a trail that forms a W, up three valleys. This trail leads to the park's major geological features—the Torres, the Cuernos, and Glacier Grey—and it's the preferred multiday hike for its relatively short hauls and a time frame that requires 4 to 5 days. In addition, those who prefer not to camp or carry more gear than a sleeping bag, food, and their personal goods can stay in the various *refugios* along the way. Most hikers begin at Hostería Las Torres and start with a day-walk up to the Torres. From here, hikers head to the Los Cuernos *refugio* and spend the night, or continue on to the Italiano campsite near the base of the valley; then they walk up to French Valley. The next stop is Pehoé *refugio,* where most spend the night before hiking up to Glacier Grey. It's best to spend a night at Refugio Grey and return to the Pehoé *refugio* the next day. From here, take the catamaran across Lago Pehoé to an awaiting bus back to Puerto Natales.

Approx. 56km (35 miles) total. Beginning at Hostería Las Torres or Refugio Pehoé. Terrain ranges from easy–difficult.

Day Hikes

These hikes run from easy to difficult, either within the W or from various trail heads throughout the park. Again, the times given are estimates for the average walker.

Glacier Grey Hike here for an up-close look at the face of Glacier Grey, though warm summers of late have sent the glacier retreating. There aren't as many steep climbs as the trail to Las Torres, but it takes longer to get there (about 3½ hr.). I recommend that hikers in the summer walk this lovely trail to the glacier lookout point, then take the boat back to Hostería Grey (see "Excursions around Glacier Grey," later). The walk takes hikers through thick forest and stunning views of the Southern Ice Field and the icebergs slowly making their way down Lago Grey. A turnoff just before the lookout point takes you to Refugio Grey.

3½ hr. one-way. Difficult.

Lago Grey (Moments) Not only is this the easiest walk in the park, but it also is one of the most dramatic for the gigantic blue icebergs that rest along the shore of Lago Grey. A flat walk across the sandy shore of the lake takes visitors to a peninsula for a short hike to a lookout point with Glacier Grey in the far distance. This walk begins near the Hostería Lago Grey; they also offer a recommended boat ride that weaves past icebergs and then takes passengers to the face of the glacier (see "Excursions around Glacier Grey," below).

1–2 hr. Easy.

Lago Pingo (Finds) Lago Pingo consistently sees fewer hikers and is an excellent spot for bird-watching for the variety of species that flock to this part of the park. The trail begins as an easy walk through a pleasant valley, past an old baqueano post. From here the trail heads through forest and undulating terrain, and past the Pingo Cascade until it eventually reaches another old baqueano post, the run-down but picturesque Zapata *refugio.* You can make this trail as long or as short as you'd like; the return is back along the same trail. The trail leaves from the same parking lot as the Lago Grey trail.

1–4 hr. one-way. Easy–moderate.

Las Torres (The Towers) ★★ The trail to view the soaring granite Towers is a classic hike in the park but certainly not the easiest. Those who are in decent shape will not want to miss this exhilarating trek. The trail leaves from the Hostería Las Torres and begins with a steep 45-minute ascent, followed by up-and-down terrain for 1½ hours to another 45-minute steep ascent up a slippery granite moraine. Midway is the Refugio Chileno, where you can stop for a coffee or spend the night. Don't give up—the Torres do not come into full view until the very end.

3 hr. one-way. Difficult.

Mirador Nordenskjöld The trail head for this walk begins near the Pudeto catamaran dock. This trail begins with an up-close visit to the crashing Salto Grande waterfall. Then it winds through Antarctic beech and thorny bush to a lookout point with dramatic views into the French Valley and the Cuernos, looking over Lago Nordenskjöld. This trail is a good place to see wildflowers in the spring, but it can get really windy in late summer. Most day tours of the park include this hike.

1 hr. one-way. Easy.

Valle Francés (French Valley) There are several ways to hike this trail. From Refugio Pehoé, you'll pass by the blue waters of Lake Skottsberg and through groves of Chilean firebush and open views of the granite spires behind Los Cuernos. From Refugio Los Cuernos, you won't see French Valley until you're in it. A short walk through the campground leads hikers to direct views of the hanging glacier that descends from Paine Grande, and enthusiastic hikers can continue the steep climb up into the valley itself for a view of French Valley's enormous granite amphitheater.

2½–4½ hr. one-way. Moderate–difficult.

Other Outdoor Activities in the Park

A **horseback ride** in Torres del Paine can be one of the most enjoyable ways to see the park. Both Hotel Las Torres and Explora have their own stables, but only the hotel has daily horseback rides, even to the Refugios Chileno and Los Cuernos (✆/fax **61/363636;** www.lastorres.com). The full-day trips cost $125 (£83) per person, and they leave from the hotel. Your hotel can reserve a horseback ride leaving from the concession-run stable near the administration center, too. For multiday horseback-riding trips, contact **Chile Nativo Expeditions,** Eberhart 230 (✆ **61/411835** in Chile or 800/649-8776 in the U.S.; www.chilenativo.com). Chile Nativo can plan custom-made journeys within the park and to little-known areas, some of which include an introduction to the *baqueano* and *estancia* (ranching) way of life. Most trips require prior experience.

EXCURSIONS AROUND GLACIER GREY

A surprisingly accessible and electrifying excursion in the park is taking a crampon-shoed **walk across the quickly disappearing Glacier Grey.** Trips begin from the Refugio Grey with a 15-minute zodiac boat ride to the starting point on the western arm of the glacier. The excursion is a full-day trip, so the only way to participate is to lodge at the *refugio.* Guests are provided with full equipment, including crampons, ice axes, ropes, and harnesses, and are given basic ice-climbing instructions. Visitors who have taken this hike have consistently given it rave reviews for the chance to peer into deep blue crevasses and explore the glacier's otherworldly contours up close.

Now that the glacier has receded, the best way to view it up close is to ride **Hostería Grey's half-day boat ride,** which takes passengers past floating icebergs and directly to the face of the glacier. Passengers ride round-trip from the shore at Lake Grey; hikers can take the Pehoé ferry, walk approximately 4 hours to the Grey *refugio,* and then ride back on the Hostería Grey boat ($65/£43 one-way), and transfer to the administration center and wait for a bus to drop them back at their hotel (though most hotels will arrange pickup for this excursion). The price is $85 (£57) round-trip and $51 (£34) one-way, and there are two trips leaving daily, at 8:30am and 3:30pm. Best of all, the journey runs year-round. Reservations are imperative, as are transfer reservations from the administration center; contact the *hostería* at © **61/410220** or www.turismolagogrey.com. Travelers who are not lodging at the Refugio Grey may take the early boat from the Hostería Grey, participate in the glacier walk (see above), and head back with the late boat.

WHERE TO STAY & DINE

Beyond the hotels listed in greater detail here, there are several rural hotels between Puerto Natales, Cerro Castillo, and the park itself. For travelers with a vehicle at their disposal, these lodgings are more moderately priced and hence a good option as park entrance fees are valid for multiple entries, if you don't mind a fair amount of driving. Among them, consider the half-timbered **Hotel Posada Tres Pasos** ★, between Natales and Cerro Castillo (© **61/245494** or 2/196-9630; www.hotel3pasos.cl), built in 1904 and visited by Nobel Prize Laureate Gabriela Mistral. At the new development outside

Tips — Advance Planning

Due to the soaring popularity of Torres del Paine, it is recommended that travelers book well in advance if planning on visiting the park between late November and late March. Nearly every business now has a website or, at the very least, an e-mail address, so trip planning is easier than ever. Hotels can be booked directly, and often they offer their own transportation from the airport or, at the very least, can recommend a service to call or e-mail. One-stop agencies such as **Fantastico Sur** (Sarmiento 846, in Punta Arenas; © **61/613410;** www.fantasticosur.com) and **Chile Native** (Eberhard 230, in Puerto Natales; © **61/411835,** or toll-free from North America 800/649-8776**;** www.chilenativo.com), are good places for *refugio* reservations, horseback-riding trips, or camping equipment rentals, and they can sometimes offer lower hotel rates at *hosterías* in the park. They can also solve tricky transfer problems.

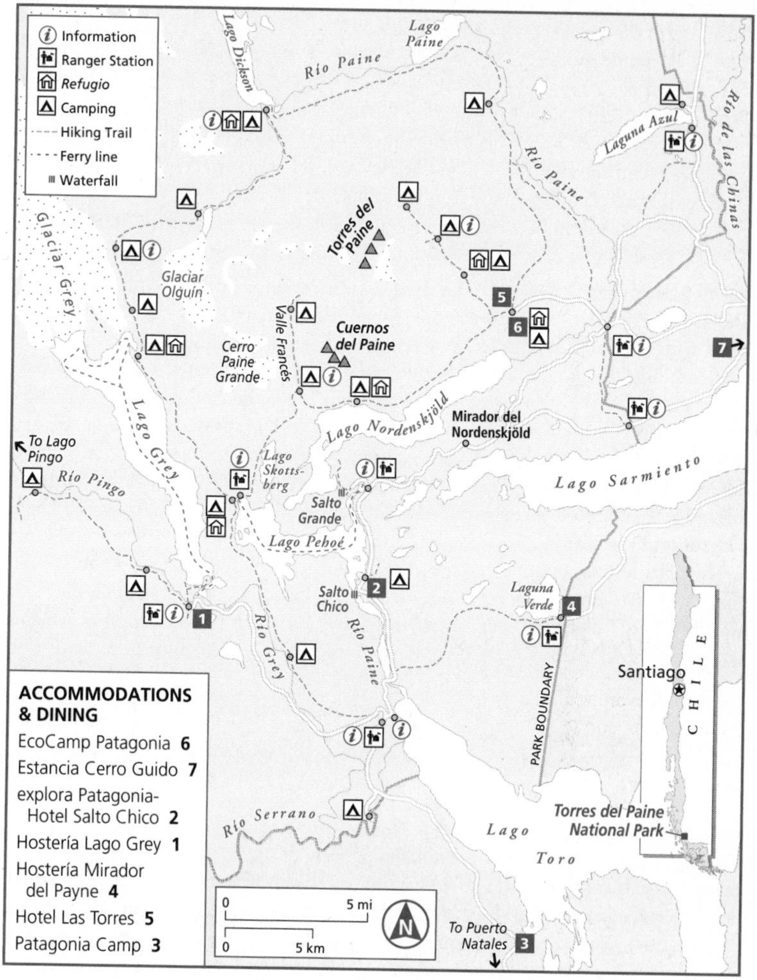

the far southwest limits of the park is the sprawling **Hotel Río Serrano** ★ (✆ **61/240528;** www.hotelrioserrano.cl), a giant complex with a whopping 105 rooms and nice views of the Paine Massif. Another option is the *estancia* lodging operated by Baqueano Zamora, Baquedano 534 in Puerto Natales (✆ **61/613521;** www.baqueanozamora.com), including **Tercera Barranca** 20km (12 miles) from Laguna Amarga.

Hotels & Hosterias

Hostería Lago Grey ★ This spruce little white *hostería* is tucked within a beech forest, looking out onto the beach at Lago Grey and the astounding blue icebergs that drift to its shore. It's well on the other side of the park, but the view is better here than at the Hostería Las Torres (below), and they have a transfer van and guides for excursions to all reaches of the park, for an extra cost. The 30 recently spruced-up rooms are spread out from a main common area, a thoroughly enjoyable place to relax, with a restaurant, outdoor deck, and lounge area. The price suggests more luxurious rooms, but the walls are a tad thin and have little decoration. Also, when the wind whips up, this side of the park is colder. Another problem is that nothing is included except for breakfast; expect to rack up quite a bill on expensive "extras," such as transfers and other meals. On the plus side, there are plenty of trails that branch out from here, including the stroll along the beach out to the Pingo Valley and the strenuous hike up to Mirador Ferrier.

Office in Punta Arenas, Lautaro Navarro 1077. ✆ **61/712100.** 30 units. $315 (£210) double. AE, DC, MC, V. **Amenities:** Restaurant; lounge; tours.

Hotel Las Torres ★★ Kids This used to be an original working cattle *estancia*, sitting at the trail head to the Torres. But due to recent expansion, it's now a full-blown hotel, with the traffic to match. The complex includes a low-slung, ranch-style hotel, a two-story hotel wing next door, a large campground, and a hostel. In the afternoon, horses and the odd cow graze just outside your hotel room door, making this a fun place for kids. This is an ideal lodge for horseback-riding enthusiasts due to their on-site stables, and its access to the Towers is convenient; however, it is a long drive to the other side of the park, and rooms have no views. Las Torres also has a small spa, with mud therapy and massage treatments, as well as a sauna. The buffet-style restaurant is above par, but pricey at $35 (£23) per person for dinner.

The hotel offers expensive packages that include guided tours, meals, and transportation, much like explora, and excellent off-season trips to little-explored areas. Packages run from 3 to 7 nights, or you can pay separately for day trips. Try spending 2 nights here and 2 at Hostería Lago Grey, thereby avoiding the steep price of an excursion there.

Office in Punta Arenas, Sarmiento 846. ✆/fax **61/363636.** www.lastorres.com. 84 units. $305 (£203) double. Rates include buffet breakfast. 4-night packages per person, double occupancy, are from $1,674 (£1,116). AE, DC, MC, V. **Amenities:** Restaurant; lounge; horseback riding; tour desk; room service; laundry service.

Hostería Mirador del Payne ★ This *hostería* is part of an historic *estancia* just outside the park, and it boasts a commanding view of the Paine Massif rising behind a grassy field and Lake Verde. If you really want to get away from crowds, this is your hotel, although it doesn't put you directly near the park's trail heads. The rooms are in a unit separate from the main lodge, which has a restaurant, bar, and fireside lounge. The *hostería* offers horseback-riding opportunities that include a chance to corral cattle and assist with other ranch duties. Access to the *hostería* is via one of two ways: by a road that branches off before arriving at the park or by a moderate 2-hour trail that leads to the park administration center. Guests arrive by road, but more than a few opt to end their stay here with a horseback ride to the park administration center to continue on to another hotel within the park's boundaries.

Office in Punta Arenas, Fagnano 585. ✆ **61/228712.** www.miradordelpayne.com. 20 units. Nov–Mar 15 $245 (£163) double; Mar 16–Oct $200 (£133) double. AE, DC, MC, V. **Amenities:** Restaurant; bar; lounge; tours; laundry service.

explora Patagonia—Hotel Salto Chico ★★★ Moments Explora in Patagonia has garnered more fame than any other hotel in Chile, and deservedly so. It's a one-stop shop for an unforgettable experience. Few hotels in the world offer as stunning a view as does explora, perched above the milky, turquoise waters of Lago Pehoé and facing the dramatic granite amphitheater of the Paine massif. It is terribly expensive, but worth the splurge if you can afford it. Explora's style is comfortable elegance, and its handsome interiors belie the contemporary exterior: softly curving blond-wood walls built entirely from native deciduous beech, a band of picture windows wrapping around the full front of the building, and large windows in each room. The furniture was handcrafted using local wood, and the crisp guest rooms are accented with Spanish checkered linens, handsome slate-tiled bathrooms, and warming racks for drying gear. Explora now has 50 rooms, making it more of a hotel than a cozy mountain inn.

The hotel has begun completing certification with the LEED (Leadership in Energy and Environmental Design) body to recognize its many efforts to promote sustainability. All-inclusive prices cover airport transfers, meals, open bar, and excursions, on regular 4-day rotations. Excursions range from easy half-day walks to photo safaris. The set menu is limited to two choices, generally a meat and vegetarian dish, and it must be said that the food quality has at times been uneven—but never bad, and the food is remarkably fresh given the extreme distances from any decent market.. Americans make up a full 60% of the guests, who typically indulge in the open bar, make new friends, and leave thrilled with their visit. Guests will want to consider explora's "Viajes," add-on journeys to Chaltén and the Fitz Roy National Park and Calafate, both in Argentina.

In Santiago, Américo Vespucio Sur 80, 5th floor. © **866/750-6699** in the U.S., or 2/206-6060 in Santiago. Fax 2/228-4655. www.explora.com. 50 units. Package rates are per person, double occupancy: 4 nights/3 days from $2,476 (£1,650); 6 nights/7 days from $4,400 (£2,933). Rates include all meals, excursions, transportation, gear, and guides. AE, DC, MC, V. **Amenities:** Restaurant; bar; lounge; large indoor pool; outdoor Jacuzzi; shop; sauna; massage.

Estancia Cerro Guido ★★★ Moments This luxurious lodge may be a fair distance from the park proper, but it's the only top hotel with a view of the distinctive Torres, from its perspective due west across the plains. It also has a marvelous view of the vast steppe, and of Sierra Baquedano to the east, and is one of the only properties by the park to offer an authentic *estancia* experience. While the sheep ranch covers a vast 100,000 hectares (247,000 acres) between the park and Argentine border and includes the entire village of Cerro Guido, the facilities themselves include two *estancia* buildings formerly occupied by the administrators and owners, a dining area, and a few service areas such as a horse stable. The finest view of the Torres is from the excellent restaurant, which has barbecue facilities indoors and out. Rooms, with fine polished hardwood floors, are furnished largely according to the lodge's original, country English-style, early-20th-century decor, with the nicest being the superior rooms in the former administrator's mansion; at a 10% higher price, they're larger and have fireplaces along with central heating. It's the perfect place for a genuine dive into Patagonia's rural traditions, and Cerro Guido now offers 2- to 4-day all-inclusive packages that allow guests to take sheep-shearing tours and personal guided horseback and hiking excursions to the park, as well as to a nearby aboriginal gravesite with a spectacular view.

Cerro Guido. © **61/411818.** www.cerroguido.cl. 15 units. $236 (£157) standard double, $305 (£203) superior double; 4-day all-inclusive package including excursions and meals for $1,950 (£1,300) per person. AE, DC, MC, V. **Amenities:** Restaurant; bar; lounge; tours; Wi-Fi. *In room:* Hair dryer, safe.

Patagonia Camp ★★ Kids Moments The most appealing new lodging option in the area is a camp for grownups. With a mountaineer's heart and a luxury bent, this is not a

Moments **Dome, Sweet Dome: Patagonia's EcoCamp**

Somewhere between a lodge and a tent, the accommodations at EcoCamp Patagonia (© 800/901-6987 in the U.S., or 2/232-9878 in Chile; www.ecocamp.travel), across from Hotel Las Torres, are a series of permanent domes that offer refuge for budget-minded, eco-friendly travelers. You'll get a real bed under a real roof, but no electricity and shared outhouse-style toilets. The "Suite domes" have running water. Each dome sleeps two, and all have composting toilets. Meals are held in the "dining dome," and there's a cozy "living dome" for chilling out. All lodging is based on all-inclusive packages, starting at $1,059 (£706) per person for 4 days.

hotel, it's an experience in nature. Set on a slope above Lago del Toro, with stunning views of the Paine massif, it feels similar to safari camps found in the African savannah. There are 18 wood-framed *yurts* (Mongolian-inspired wood-framed tents) situated along wooden walkways tucked inside a beech forest. Incredibly bright, cozy, and plush, the yurts have such high-end touches as woven blankets, central heating, deep tubs, and copper showerheads. If the night's clear, you'll have delightful stargazing from your bed; if you have trouble sleeping, you may curse the way the tents flap loudly during strong storms. Still, the atmosphere is incredibly natural, secluded, and romantic. In the main lodge, meals (and pisco sours) are served. Their all-inclusive packages, again, mirror those of explora, but Patagonia Camp is much more quiet and intimate.

Hernando de Aguirre 414, Santiago. © **2/335-6898.** www.patagoniacamp.com. 18 units. 3-night programs $2,110 (£1,406) single, $1,410 (£940) double. Rates include all meals, excursions, transfers in/out, guides. AE, DC, MC, V. **Amenities:** Restaurant; library.

Refugios & Hostels

Five cabinlike lodging units and one hostel, all with shared accommodations, are distributed along the park's Circuit and W trails, and they are moderately priced sleeping options for backpackers who are not interested in pitching a tent. Although most have bedding or sleeping bags for an expensive rental price, your best bet is to bring your own. The price, at $40 (£17) on average per night (about $63/£32 for room and full board), may seem steep for a simple dorm bed (or $80/£53 for full board); still, it is a far cry cheaper than many shared accommodations in national parks in the U.S. All come with hot showers, a simple cafe, and a common area for hiding out from bad weather. Meals served here are simply prepared but hearty, or alternatively, guests can bring their own food and cook. Each *refugio* has rooms with two to six bunks, which you'll have to share with strangers when they're full. During the high season, consider booking weeks in advance, although many visitors have reported luck when calling just a few days beforehand (due to cancellations). All agencies in Puerto Natales and Punta Arenas book reservations and issue vouchers, but the best bet is to call or e-mail (see info below). There is a scrappy *refugio* near the park administration center, with two rows of sleeping berths that I do not recommend except in an emergency situation. This *refugio* is on a first-come, first-served basis.

The first three *refugios* are owned and operated by **Fantástico Sur,** a division of the Hostería las Torres. They can be booked by contacting ✆/fax **61/360361** or by visiting www.wcircuit.com:

- **Refugio El Chileno.** This is the least-frequented *refugio* because it is located halfway up to the Towers (most do the trail as a day hike). Hikers will find it more convenient to stow their stuff in the campground at the *hostería,* but, then again, this *refugio* puts you away from the hubbub below, and is the best place to stay if you want to see the sun rise on the Torres.
- **Refugio Los Cuernos.** This may be the park's loveliest *refugio,* located at the base of the Cuernos. The wood structure (which miraculously holds up to some of the strongest winds in the park) has two walls of windows that look out onto Lago Nordenskjöld.
- **Refugio Torres.** This *albergue* (lodge) is the largest and most full-service *refugio* in the park; it sits near the Hostería Las Torres. This is also the trail head for the W-circuit and the Full Circuit. You may dine in the hotel or eat simple fare in the *refugio* itself. Horseback rides can be taken from here.

All three of the following *refugios* can be reserved at ✆ **61/412742** or online at www.verticepatagonia.cl.

- **Lodge Paine Grande.** This hostel-like "lodge" replaces the old *refugio* Pehoé, at the busiest intersection in the park. It is the hub for several of the trail heads to the park administration center, Glacier Grey, and French Valley, as well as the docking site for the catamaran. Utilitarian in style, the hostel has 60 beds, two lounges, and a cafeteria that can serve 120 people. Day walks to Glacier Grey and French Valley can be taken from here.
- **Refugio Dickson.** This is one of the park's loneliest *refugios,* due to its location well on the other side of the park (part of the Circuit trail). There are a lot of mosquitoes in the summer, but you can't beat the rugged location on a grassy glacial moraine, facing Dickson Glacier.
- **Refugio Grey.** Tucked in a forest on the shore of Lago Grey, this log-cabin *refugio* is a 10-minute walk to the lookout point for the glacier. It's a cold but refreshing setting, and it has a cozy fireside seating area. This is a good base for taking a walking tour on the glacier (see "Excursions around Glacier Grey," above).

Camping

Torres del Paine has a well-designed campground system with free and concession-run sites. All *refugios* have a campground, too, and these and other concession sites charge about $15 (£10) per person, which includes hot showers, clean bathrooms, and an indoor dining area to escape bad weather and eat under a roof. The site at Las Torres provides barbecues and firewood. Free campgrounds are run by Conaf, and they can get a little dingy, with deplorable outhouses. Beginning in March, mice become a problem for campers, so always leave food well stored or hanging from a tree branch. The JLM hiking map (available at every bookstore, airport, kiosk, and travel agency, and at the park entrance) denotes which campgrounds are free and which charge a fee.

4 EL CALAFATE, ARGENTINA ★★

222km (138 miles) S of El Chaltén; 2,727km (1,691 miles) SW of Buenos Aires

El Calafate is a tourist-oriented town that hugs the shore of turquoise Lago Argentino, a location that, combined with the town's leafy streets, gives it the feel of an oasis in the desert pampa of this region. The town depends almost entirely on its neighboring natural wonder, Perito Moreno Glacier, for tourism. Thousands of visitors come for the chance to stand face to face with this tremendous wall of ice, one of the few glaciers on the Southern Patagonian Icefield that isn't retreating.

El Calafate was named for the calafate bush found throughout Patagonia that produces a sweet berry commonly used in syrups and jams. As the economy in Buenos Aires struggled after 2002, many Argentines fled to the countryside and some came here, to El Calafate, to build inns and open tourist services. The town itself is quite a pleasant little place, but you won't find many attractions here—they are all within the confines of Los Glaciares National Park. What you will find are several good restaurants and a charming main street lined with boutiques boasting fine leather goods and shops selling locally manufactured chocolates, jams, and delicious caramel cookies called *alfajores.*

ESSENTIALS

Getting There

BY PLANE From late October through March, El Calafate's **Aeropuerto Lago Argentino (FTE; © 2902/491220)** is a busy spot. Service is from Argentine destinations only: **Aerolíneas Argentinas/Austral** (**© 0810/222-86527;** www.aerolineas.com.ar) has daily flights from Buenos Aires, as well as a daily flight from Bariloche, Trelew, and Ushuaia. There are flights arriving directly from Ezeiza International Airport in Buenos Aires during the high season (before, most flights left from Aeroparque, downtown); be sure to specify which airport you'd like to fly from. **LAN Argentina** (**© 0810/999-9526**) flies from Buenos Aires daily, with two flights on Saturdays and Sundays. Four of the weekly flights continue on to Ushuaia.

Aerovías Dap, Av. del Libertador 1329 in Calafate (**© 61/223340;** www.aeroviasdap.cl), has charter-only flights from Punta Arenas.

From the airport, **Ves Patagonia** (**© 02902/494355**) operates a bus to all the hotels in town for $8 (£5.30); they can also pick you up for your return trip if you call 24 hours ahead. A taxi into town should cost no more than $28 (£19) for up to four people.

BY BUS El Calafate has a bus terminal on Julio A. Roca, reached by taking the stairs up from the main street, Avenida del Libertador. To and from Puerto Natales, Chile: **Buses Sur** (**© 02902/491631**) and **Turismo Zaahj** (**© 02902/491631;** www.turismozaahj.co.cl) have a daily bus departing Puerto Natales at 8am, returning also at 8am ($30/£20 per leg); **Cootra** (**© 02902/491444**) also has daily buses departing Puerto Natales at 8:30am. The trip takes 5 to 6 hours, depending on how long you get held up at the border. To get to El Chaltén, take **Chaltén Travel,** which leaves daily at 8am, 1 (Dec–Feb only), and 6:30pm, and returns from Chaltén at 7:30am, 1:30 (Dec–Feb only), and 6pm (**© 02902/491833**), or **Caltur** (**© 02902/491842**), which departs El Calafate at 7:30am and 6:30pm.

BY CAR In summer only, from just outside Torres del Paine National Park, you can cross through the border at Cerro Castillo, which will lead you to the famous Rte. Nacional 40 and up to the paved portion of Rte. 11. During the rest of the year, take the

Ruta 40: The Road South

The mighty and legendary **Ruta 40** is one of the world's great adventure drives. It takes you along the eastern slope of the Andes from the top of Argentina all the way to the bottom of Patagonia. In Argentine Patagonia, travelers can link El Calafate and the glacier with the Lakes District hub of Bariloche in at least 2 days. **Chalten Travel** (✆ **02902/492212;** www.chaltentravel.com) heads north in a 2-day trip that includes a night in a rustic hotel. The trip starts at $130/£87. Don't even think of making this expedition on your own without a 4×4 in excellent condition, stocked with all the necessary supplies. This land is Patagonia truly off the beaten track.

border crossing at Rio Turbio, which leads from Rte. 9 straight to Puerto Natales. The drive from Puerto Natales is roughly 4 to 5 hours, not including time spent at the border checkpoint.

Getting Around

For information about transportation to and from Perito Moreno Glacier, see "Parque Nacional Los Glaciares," later in this section. If you'd like to rent a car, you can do so at **Servi-Car,** Av. Del Libertador 1341 (✆ **2902/492634;** www.servicar4x4.com.ar); they are the local agents for Dollar Rental Car. Or try **Fiorasi Rentacar,** Av. Del Libertador 1341 (✆ **2902/495330;** www.fiorasirenacar.com). Rates begin at $70 (£47) per day, including insurance and taxes.

Visitor Information

The city's **visitor information kiosk** can be found inside the bus terminal. It offers an ample amount of printed material and staff can assist in planning a trip to Perito Moreno Glacier. It's open October through April daily from 8am to 11pm, and May through September daily from 8am to 8pm (✆ **02902/491090**).

A good website to check for information is **www.elcalafate.com.ar/english.html.**

WHAT TO SEE & DO

El Calafate serves mostly as a service town for visitors on their way to visit the glaciers (see "Parque Nacional Los Glaciares," later in this section), but it does present a pleasant main avenue for a stroll, and as expected, there are lots of souvenirs, bookstores, and crafts shops to keep you occupied.

Near El Calafate

For information about visiting the glaciers and the national park, see "Parque Nacional Los Glaciares," later in this section.

HORSEBACK RIDING **Cabalgata en Patagonia,** Av. Del Libertador 4315 (✆ **2902/493278;** cabalgataenpatagonia@cotecal.com.ar), offers two horseback-riding options: a 2-hour ride to Bahía Redonda for a panoramic view of El Calafate ($70/£47) and a full-day trip bordering Lago Argentino, with an optional stop at the Walicho Caves, where one can supposedly view Indian "paintings," which are billed as real but are really reproductions as the originals have been badly damaged. This tour costs $133 (£89) per person and includes lunch and transfer to the hotel. Book directly or with a travel agency.

A Half-Day in El Calafate

Because of flight or bus schedules, as well as tour schedules (most day tours leave once a day around 9am), many people are "stuck" in El Calafate the day they arrive or depart. Below are some options for things to see if you just have a half-day in town.

- Who knew there were flamingos in Patagonia? Take your binoculars and stroll along the shallow shore of Laguna Nimez, on the western edge of town for some surprisingly world-class **bird-watching.** Other birds include cauquén geese, black-necked swans, and ibis birds.
- Slated to open in late 2009, the new **Glaciarium** (www.glaciarium.com) will be a state-of-the-art glaciology facility calling itself a "Museum of Patagonian Ice." It'll certainly be worth a visit.
- **Centro de Interpretacion Historica Calafate,** Avenida Brown and Bonarelli (✆ **2902/492799**), is an exhibition center that covers 14,000 years of history. It's 5 blocks from downtown, and is open Monday to Friday from 8am to 7pm, and weekends from 10am to 1pm and 3 to 7pm.
- Let your inner *gaucho* ride free on a half-day horseback-riding trip. See below for details on outfitters.
- The *estancia* **El Galpón del Glaciar** (see below) has afternoon sheep-shearing shows and evening folklore dinner shows. See below for details.

VISITING AN ESTANCIA As the world's wool market declines, many of the *estancias* (ranches) in Patagonia have opened their doors to tourists, including some very close to El Calafate. Most offer lodging as well. The **El Galpón del Glaciar** (20km/12½ miles from El Calafate; ✆ **2902/491793;** www.elgalpondelglaciar.com.ar) has day tours. **Estancia Alta Vista** ★★ (35km/22 miles from El Calafate; ✆ **2902/491247;** www.hosteriaaltavista.com.ar) is part of the Estancia Anita, which has more than 75,000 hectares in the surroundings of El Calafate and has long been the most influential *estancia* in the area, and **Estancia Nibepo Aike** (56km/35 miles from El Calafate; ✆ **2902/422626;** www.nibepoaike.com.ar) is quite rustic but gets you on a still-working *estancia* dedicated to cattle and sheep raising.

WHERE TO STAY

The main issue to resolve when selecting lodging in El Calafate is if you want to stay in town or not. A slew of inns are within walking distance of the main drag, Avenida Del Libertador, which is great for strollers and shoppers. Another group of inns are about 10 to 15 minutes away from town; most of these hotels offer complimentary shuttles to town, and have better views of the lake. Finally, there are options significantly far from town, which will appeal to those looking to relax and stay still.

Remote Hotels

Eolo Patagonia's Spirit ★★ (Finds) Built around a protected courtyard, Eolo is upscale through and through, yet casual and comfortable. Expansive cream-colored rooms have huge windows and a mixture of new and antique furnishings. Bathrooms have refurbished mirrors, vanities, and deep tubs with windows looking out to the vastness. The corner suite has a view of the Torres del Paine on a clear day. No matter which way you look, there are sublime expanses outside with no trace of civilization in sight. Only 25km (15 miles) from El Calafate, and en route to the Perito Moreno Glacier, the location is convenient to town, the airport, and the main tourist attractions, making it the best place to base a trip lasting from 3 to 5 days. Most people come here on an all-inclusive package that includes transfers and all meals, as well as trekking, bird-watching, and horseback riding. But you can always just relax by the indoor heated pool. The unpretentious and flexible staff will call you by name and make you feel at home. For a place with only 17 rooms, Eolo offers a remarkably complete experience.

Rte. 11, Km 23, El Calafate. ✆ **02902/492042** or ✆ 11/4700-0075 for reservations in Buenos Aires. www.eolo.com.ar. 17 units. 2-night packages start at $720 (£480) per person based on double occupancy; 4-night packages start at $1,120 (£747) per person based on double occupancy. Rates include all meals, airport transfers, excursions. AE, MC, V. **Amenities:** Restaurant; lounge; indoor pool; sauna; guided excursions; Internet access; library; TV room. *In room:* Safe.

Estancia Cristina ★★★ **Moments** If seclusion is the new luxury, this *estancia* is the ultimate indulgence. Situated at the far end of the north arm of Lago Argentino, it's the well-preserved former ranching outpost of the Masters family, early-20th-century British pioneers. To get here, you take a spectacular 3-hour boat trip, sailing past floating icebergs and the enormous Upsala Glacier. One- and two-night packages allow you to choose from a selection of day excursions, such as treks, bird-watching, or a wonderful horseback ride. Upon return, you'll have the place to yourself, once the day-trippers have headed back to town. Relax in a soaker tub, explore the Masters family museum, roam the English gardens, or sidle up to the bar for a glass of *vino tinto.* Twelve rooms have been designed to resemble the older ranch buildings, with light green roofs and white walls. Inside, they're clean, spacious, and fresh, with large beds and huge bay windows that open onto the Cerro Norte. The food is excellent, and the service is friendly and charming. The modern facilities (the hotel opened in 2005) don't detract from the history or majestic setting of the place. If you can splurge for just 1 night in Argentine Patagonia, do it here.

9 de Julio 69, El Calafate. ✆ **02902/491133,** reservations ✆ 2902/491133. www.estanciacristina.com. From $635 (£423) per person double. Rates include all meals, excursions, and transfers. AE, MC, V. **Amenities:** Restaurant; bar; hiking trails; Internet access; library; museum. *In room:* Safe.

Hotels In & Closer to Town

Expensive

Casa los Sauces Not only is the current President of Argentina, Cristina Fernandez de Kirchner, the owner and next-door neighbor of this exclusive boutique hotel, but she was also the interior designer. And she's obviously got good taste, exemplified in the genteel country style that oozes through the five separate houses dotting this green property by the lake. It's all very refined, luxurious, but, frankly, snobby. There's a large staff ready to wait on you, from offering glasses of champagne at check-in or a ride in a golf cart to massages and private transfers. The 38 über-plush suites are each drastically different in style. There is a minimum 2-night stay; most guests come here as part of an all-inclusive program. For a taste of the exclusivity, come for dinner at the excellent restaurant, La Comarca.

Los Gauchos 1352–1370, El Calafate. ✆ **11/4348-5288** in Buenos Aires, or 2902/495584. www.casalossauces.com. 38 units. All-inclusive program from $600 (£400) per person per night; $360 ($240) per person per night in bed-and-breakfast program. AE, DC MC, V. **Amenities:** Restaurant; bar; spa; bikes; games room; transfers; Wi-Fi; archery; reading room. *In room*: Minibar, safe.

Deep in the Heart of Patagonia: Hosteria Helginfors

Remote, warm, and widely admired, **Hosteria Helsingfors,** open from October to March, is a wilderness lodge located on the shore of Lago Viedma about 150km (93 miles) from El Calafate in a rarely visited corner of Los Glaciares National Park. It's a great spot for hikes and horseback riding. On a clear day, it has amazing views of FitzRoy. With a lovely main lodge and endless miles of untouched wilderness at its doorstep, Helsingfors also offers cozy lodging and fine dining. For more information, contact their offices in Buenos Aires at Av. Cordoba 827, 11th floor (✆/fax **011/4315-1222;** www.helsingfors.com.ar).

Hotel Edenia ★ A very comfortable and functional hotel on the outskirts of town, the view out your window just may include an iceberg or two here. Rooms are similar to what you'd find in a classy business hotel, with crisp linens, satellite TV, a workable desk, and individually controlled heaters. Bathrooms are large and have heated floors. Edenia's best asset, though, is its friendly, multilingual staff who'll welcome you with a glass of champagne, and take good care of you as you rush in and out from the many excursions typical of a visit to El Calafate.

Punta Soberana, Manzana 642, El Calafate. ✆ **02902/497021.** Fax 2902/496210. www.edeniahoteles.com.ar. 68 units. $147–$256 (£98–£171) double. AE, MC, V. **Amenities:** Restaurant; bar; gym; transfers; Wi-Fi; room service; laundry; library. *In room*: Satellite TV, hair dryer, safe.

Kau Yatun Hotel del Campo ★ Long before El Calafate was a major tourist destination, it was the heart of a rugged area populated by remote *estancias* (ranches). Kau Yatun is a sprawling inn located on the Estancia 25 de Mayo, only 5 blocks from El Calafate's main drag. It has a lovely country charm, with generous green spaces, quiet corners, and a relaxed air. Rooms are very large, with thick walls and ceilings. Bathrooms, likewise, are very large but are dated. The restaurant and bar are both pricey, but breakfasts are generous. Out back, besides 7 hectares of natural paradise, is an excellent Argentine parrilla. If you're in El Calafate for an extended stay, you'll be glad you chose Kau Yatun.

Estancia 25 de Mayo, El Calafate. ✆ **02902/491059** or in Buenos Aires 11/4523-5894. Fax 11/4523-5894. www.kauyatun.com. 44 units. $170–$210 (£113–£140) double; $300 (£200) triple. AE, MC, V. **Amenities:** 2 restaurants; bar; bike rentals; excursions; transfers; boutique; library. *In room*: Wi-Fi, hair dryer, safe.

Moderate

Hostería Sierra Nevada ★ Finds This charming *hostería* is a 15-minute walk from all the town's shops and restaurants. It's right on the lake, and every room comes with a water view. Built in 2000, the two-story building has a pleasant expansiveness to it, and the rooms are fresh and modern, with wrought-iron furniture, firm mattresses, and beautiful granite-tiled bathrooms and showers. Large French doors in each room slide open to reveal the garden and the lake just beyond. Walls are thin. Most of the guests here are South American, so the staff members don't speak much English, but they're friendly and pleasant and will try their best.

Libertador 1888, El Calafate. ✆ **02902/493129.** www.sierranevada.com.ar. 18 units. $180 (£120) double. MC, V. **Amenities:** Restaurant; bar. *In room:* TV, safe.

Patagonia Rebelde (Moments) History buffs will love the heritage items on display in this train-themed tin-walled *hostería* on the hill above town. Every item has a story behind it: The main room floors are recycled from a Buenos Aires *conventillo* (a high-density building that housed many families during the 19th century), furniture is from auctions, even key chains are from old train cars. Some guests may find it noisy. Rooms are small but bright, with yellow walls and refurbished bureaus. All have stand-up showers only. The suite, in the corner, is slightly bigger and brighter.

José R. Haro 442, esq. Jean Mermoz, El Calafate. ✆ **02902/494495.** www.patagoniarebelde.com. 12 units. $118 (£79) double; $132 (£88) suite. MC, V. **Amenities:** Bar; Wi-Fi; library. *In room*: Hair dryer.

Kau Kaleshen (Value) With an excellent location just a block and a half from the main drag, the Kau Kaleshen *hostería* is a simple inn. It's been around long enough to feel warm and authentic. Rooms are all located around the tranquil back garden, some on a two-story yellow-walled building (the top-floor rooms have better circulation, which is particularly important here). They all have rustic brick walls and ceramic floors; everything is done up rather smartly if simply. Clean white bathrooms are also simple, with stand-up showers only. There is a lovely teahouse out front where breakfast is served.

Gobernador Gregores 1256, El Calafate. ✆ **02902/491188.** www.losglaciares.com/kaukaleshen. $80 (£53) double. **Amenities:** Teahouse; tour desk; Internet access (free in lounge); laundry service. *In room*: Hair dryer.

Inexpensive

America del Sur Hostel ★ With a friendly vibe and nightly all-you-can-eat *asados* (barbecues) for only $16 (£11), this is a great budget option. Located a 7-minute walk up the hill from downtown, it affords a lovely panoramic view. Guests have the choice of a simple bunk bed in a shared room that sleeps up to four people at a time, or one of the newer doubles with private bathrooms. All dorm rooms have private lockers and bathrooms with separate tubs, showers, and toilets that allow for some privacy in an otherwise shared room. The big common living room has a fabulous panoramic view and a cozy wood-burning fireplace, making it a great place to mix and mingle with other travelers.

Puerto Deseado 153, El Calafate. ✆ **02902/493523.** www.americahostel.com.ar. 60 beds. $65 (£43) double; $16 (£11) bed in shared room. No credit cards. **Amenities:** Restaurant; kitchen; transfers; Internet access; laundry; luggage storage. *In room:* Lockers.

Casa de Grillos B and B (Finds) This small inn, 8 blocks from Avenida del Libertador in the old, rural part of town, is in one of El Calafate's only lush, green areas. Steps from Laguna Nimez and the shores of Lago Argentino, it's somewhat of an oasis and a nice choice for nature lovers who still want the convenience of being within walking distance from town. It's a true bed-and-breakfast, in that a lovely couple rents a handful of rooms in their home. Rooms are cozy but simple; two of the four have private bathrooms (the other two rooms share). There is a lovely common area for TV watching, Internet surfing, and visiting.

Los Condores 1215, esq. Las Bandurrias, El Calafate. ✆ **02902/491160.** www.casadegrillos.com.ar. 5 units. $55–$75 (£37–£50) double. No credit cards. **Amenities:** Internet access (free in lobby); library.

WHERE TO DINE

If you're just looking for a pleasant place away from the main street crowds in which to unwind with a cup of tea, then try **Kau Kaleshen** (see above). Located in a charming house on a side street, this teahouse is open daily from 5pm to midnight and offers a

"Te Completo" for $14 (£9.30) that includes your choice of either tea or specialty coffee, along with homemade breads and jam, a selection of pastries, and toasted sandwiches. Or try the interesting **Borges & Alvarez Libro-Bar,** Av. del Libertador 1015 (© **02902/491464**), which has a fantastic selection of books to peruse while you sip a *café con leche.*

Expensive

Casimiro Biguá ★★ Moments REGIONAL CHILEAN This sleek wine bar and restaurant is the best restaurant in El Calafate. The chic and modern black-and-white decor, thick tablecloths, flickering candles on every table, and young and energetic waitstaff make this place a winner. You can sample one of the many wines while enjoying an appetizer platter of regional Patagonian specialties such as smoked trout, smoked wild boar, and a variety of cheeses. Main courses change frequently but usually range from a simple steak to an elaborate pasta with salmon, cream, and capers in white-wine sauce; there's always a chicken and seafood offering as well. The menu combines Argentine classics such as empanadas and beef with fusion-style dishes such as sesame tuna. It's also an excellent place to try a glass of dry Argentine sparkling wine. A few doors down is the sister restaurant, the town's most upscale steakhouse, Casimiro Biguá Parrilla. And farther down is a new Italian-inspired Trattoria.

Av. del Libertador 963. © **02902/492590.** Reservations recommended. Main courses $10–$22 (£6.70–£15). AE, MC, V. Daily 10am–1am.

La Posta ★★★ ARGENTINE In a building next to the Posada Los Alamos hotel, La Posta is El Calafate's most upscale restaurant, serving great cuisine and choice wines in a cozy, candlelit environment. The menu, printed in four languages, offers well-prepared dishes that effectively blend Argentine and international-flavored fare, such as beef filled with goat's cheese, grilled trout with vegetables, king's crab soufflé, and homemade pasta. Desserts are superb.

Gobernador Moyano and Bustillo. © **02902/491144.** Reservations recommended in high season. Main courses $16–$26 (£11–£17). AE, DC, MC, V. Daily 7pm–midnight.

Moderate

La Cocina ★ Value ITALIAN This recently expanded restaurant serves bistro-style food, including fresh pastas such as raviolis and fettuccine, fresh trout, and meats prepared simply but well. Try the crepes stuffed with vegetables (known as *cannelloni*) or combinations such as ham and cheese, or meat items such as steak with a pepper-and-mustard sauce. There's a huge list of pasta options as well. Of all the restaurants on the main street with a similar appearance, La Cocina is without a doubt the best. There is something here for everyone, and when it's busy, the friendly staff maintains an upbeat vibe.

Av. del Libertador 1245. © **02902/491758.** Main courses $10–$19 (£6.70–£13). MC, V. Tues–Sun noon–3:30pm and 7pm–midnight.

La Tablita ★★ Value PARRILLA/STEAK This is 100% typical Argentine food—the stuff that families from Iguazú to Ushuaia enjoy on any given Sunday afternoon. Carnivores need look no further. La Tablita is all about meat, and it's one of the local favorites in town for its heaping platters and giant *parrilladas* (mixed grills) that come sizzling to your table on their own minibarbecues. The *parrilladas* for two cost $30 (£20), but they really serve three diners, given the size and assortment of chicken, sausage, beef, lamb, and a few innards you may or may not recognize. The filet mignon is incredibly tender here; at $9 (£6), it's one of the least expensive filets that I've ever had. The sunny, airy restaurant can be found on the other side of the bridge that spans the Arroyo Calafate, about a 2-minute walk from downtown.

Coronel Rosales 24. ✆ **02902/491065.** Reservations highly recommended. Main courses $13–$17 (£8.70–£11). AE, MC, V. Daily 11am–3pm and 7pm–midnight (Wed closed for lunch).

Pura Vida ★ Finds VEGETARIAN/REGIONAL CHILEAN The friendliest place in town is a short walk from downtown but is worth finding. Set in a woodsy location overlooking the lake, this is the best place in El Calafate for home-style cuisine, and offers good options for vegetarians. Try the delicious pumpkin soup or the gnocchi in saffron sauce. If you want to try a regional specialty, then go for the *cazuela de cordero* (hearty lamb stew with mushrooms). For dessert, both the rice pudding and the pumpkin ice cream are delicious. Fresh fruit shakes, sandwiches, and afternoon tea with homemade rolls and jams are also offered. The service is laid-back, the crowd is young and relaxed, and the view of the lake is divine.

Av. del Libertador 1876. ✆ **02902/493356.** Main courses $8–$17 (£5.30–£11). No credit cards. Daily 7:30pm–midnight.

Inexpensive

Casablanca CAFE/PUB FARE The Casablanca is the local hangout for a beer and a quick meal, and one of the few places around where you can grab a meal at odd hours. There's a wooden bar and a dining area with tile floors and metal chairs and tables, and an elevated TV that's usually on. The menu is mostly pizzas, sandwiches, and empanadas, but the sandwiches are your best bet here. This is a good spot for writing out postcards and sipping a cold beer on a warm afternoon.

Av. 21 de Mayo and Av. del Libertador 1202. ✆ **02902/491402.** Main courses $6–$16 (£2–£3); sandwiches $4.50–$8 (£3–£5.30). No credit cards. Daily 10am–3am.

Viva la Pepa ★ Kids LIGHT FARE A new spot that has fun vibes and healthy lighter options, Viva la Pepa specializes in crepes (both savory and sweet), salads, and sandwiches. Lots of juices, and a hearty breakfast, are also available. Hang out in the afternoon on the outdoor patio, or indoors with a sweet treat.

Emilio Amado 833. ✆ **02902/491880.** Main courses $5–$12 (£3.30–£8). No credit cards. Daily 9am–11pm.

PARQUE NACIONAL LOS GLACIARES ★★★

The Los Glaciares National Park covers 600,000 hectares (1.5 million acres) of rugged land that stretches vertically along the crest of the Andes and spills east into flat pampa. Most of Los Glaciares is inaccessible to visitors except for the park's two dramatic highlights: the granite needles, such as Fitz Roy near El Chaltén (covered in "El Chaltén & Mt. Fitz Roy, Argentina," later), and this region's magnificent Perito Moreno Glacier. The park is also home to thundering rivers, blue lakes, and thick beech forest. Los Glaciares National Park was formed in 1937 and declared a World Heritage region by UNESCO in 1981.

Named after famed Argentine scientist Francisco "Perito" Moreno ("perito" is the title given to someone considered an expert in his or her field), the famous glacier Perito Moreno is a must-see, as important to Argentine culture and tourism as Iguazú Falls or the Casa Rosada. Few natural wonders in South America are as spectacular or as easily accessed as this glacier, and unlike the hundreds of glaciers that drain from the Southern Patagonian Ice Field, Perito Moreno is one of the few that are not receding. Scientists like to say it is "stable," and it generally cycles through growing toward the Península Magallanes, touching land, and forming a dam in Lago Argentino, then receding with a majestic "dam break." Perito Moreno is usually reliable for sending a few huge chunks hurling into the channel throughout the day, especially around sunset, when movements lead to plenty of snapping, cracking, and splashing ice.

What impresses visitors most is the sheer size of Perito Moreno Glacier, a wall of jagged blue ice measuring 4,500m (14,760 ft.) across and soaring 60m (197 ft.) above the channel. To give you some perspective of its length: You could fit the entire city of Buenos Aires on it. From the parking lot on the Península Magallanes, a series of newly improved boardwalks descend, which take visitors directly to the glacier's face. It's truly an unforgettable, spellbinding experience, particularly at dusk, when the sun colors the ice red and shadows turn deep blue. There are opportunities to join an organized group for a walk on the glacier, as well as boat journeys that leave from Puerto Banderas for visits to the neighboring glaciers Upsala and Spegazzini. From El Chaltén, you can visit the nearby Viedma glacier.

Essentials

At Km 49 (30 miles) from El Calafate, you'll pass through the park's entrance, where there's an information booth with erratic hours (✆ **02902/491005**). The entrance fee is $10 (£6.70) per person. If you're looking for information about the park and the glacier, pick up an interpretive guide or book from one of the bookstores or tourist shops along Avenida del Libertador in El Calafate. There is a restaurant near the principal lookout platform near the glacier and a good, though expensive, restaurant inside the Los Notros hotel (see "Where to Stay Near the Glacier," later).

Getting There

BY CAR Following Avenida del Libertador west out of town, the route turns into a mostly paved road. From here it's 80km (50 miles) to the glacier.

BY TAXI OR REMISE If you want to see the glacier at your own pace, hire a taxi or *remise* (a radio taxi). The cost averages $70 (£47) for two, $75 (£50) for three, and $100 (£67) for four, although many taxi companies will negotiate a price. Be sure to agree on an estimated amount of time spent at the glacier, and remember that the park entrance fee of $10 (£6.70) is not included.

BY ORGANIZED TOUR Several companies offer transportation to and from the glacier, such as **Infinito Sud,** Pasaje los Cerezos 74 (✆ **02902/493032;** www.infinitosud.com); **Caltur,** Av. del Libertador 1177 (✆ **02902/491368;** www.caltur.com.ar); and **Los Glaciares Turismo,** Av. Almirante Brown 1188 (✆ **02902/491159**). These minivan and bus services provide bilingual guides and leave around 9am and again at around 2:30pm, spending an average of 4 hours at the peninsula; the cost is $30 to $50 (£20–£33) per person, not including lunch. For a more personalized tour—a private car with driver and a bilingual, licensed guide—contact **SurTurismo,** Av. Del Libertador 1226 (✆ **02902/491266;** suring@cotecal.com.ar); they can arrange for a half-day trip costing $70 to $105 (£47–£70) for two people (prices vary with the seasons).

Outdoor Activities

There are several exciting activities in this region. **"Minitrekking"** (although there is nothing "mini" about it) takes guests of all ages and abilities for a walk upon the glacier. The trip begins with a 20-minute boat ride across the Brazo Rico, followed by a 30-minute walk to the glacier. From here guests are outfitted with crampons and other safety gear, and then they spend approximately 1 1/2 hours atop the ice, complete with a stop for a whiskey on the thousand-year-old "rocks." This great trip gives visitors the chance to peer into the electric-blue crevasses of the glacier and fully appreciate its size. More experienced, fit, and adventurous visitors can opt for the **Big Ice ★★** option, which has a more technical approach and gives you much more time (upwards of 4 hr.) to walk on the glacier. Both Big Ice and Minitrekking are organized exclusively by **Hielo y Aventura,** which has its main office at Av. del Libertador 935 (✆ **02902/492205;** www.hieloyaventura.com). Big Ice costs $175 (£117), including the transfer from El Calafate. Minitrekking will run you $135 (£90) with transfer. Remember, you have to bring your own lunch from town, and don't forget sunscreen.

Fernandez Campbell, Av. Del Libertador 867 (✆ **02902/491105;** www.solopatagonia.com), offers visitors navigation trips through the Brazo Rico to the face of Perito Moreno for $50 (£33), departing hourly from 10:30am to 3:30pm from the Muelle Moreno port next to the glacier's visitor center. Their **Todo Glaciares ★★** trip departs from Puerto Punta Bandera and visits the Spegazzini (the tallest glacier in the park), Uspala (the largest), and Onelli glaciers for $295 (£197).

Where to Stay near the Glacier

Los Notros ★★★ (**Moments**) Few hotels in Argentina (or in the world) boast as spectacular a view as Los Notros—but it doesn't come cheap, and it's not quite up to the standards of explora on the Chilean side. This luxury lodge sits high on a slope looking out at Perito Moreno Glacier, and all common areas and rooms have been fitted with picture windows to really soak up the marvelous sight. Although the rough-hewn wood exteriors give the hotel the feel of a mountain lodge, the interior decor is contemporary. Each room is slightly different, with such personal touches as antique lamps and regional photos; crocheted or gingham bedspreads; lilac, peach, or lemon-yellow walls; padded floral headboards or iron bed frames; and tweedy brown or raspberry corduroy chairs. Bathrooms are gleaming white, but smallish in standard rooms. The older "Cascada bungalow" rooms have very thin walls; if you're a light sleeper, be sure to request a top-floor room or a room in the newer "Premium" (and more expensive) wing. Inside the main building is a large, chic, and expansive restaurant that serves creative regional cuisine. Upstairs is an airy lounge area with chaise longues positioned in front of panoramic windows; here you'll find a TV room with a selection of nature videos.

Main office in Buenos Aires: Santa Fe 1461, 3rd floor. ✆ **11/5277-8200.** Fax 11/5277-8222. www.losnotros.com. 32 units. $1,287 (£858) per person for 2-night package Cascada bungalow; $1,752 (£1,168) per person for 2-night package in double superior; $2,054 (£1,369) per person for 2-night package in double premium. Rates include all meals, park entrance, excursions, and transfers. Room-only rates available by request only, depending on availability. AE, DC, MC, V. **Amenities:** Restaurant; bar; lounge w/TV; tour desk; room service; laundry service. *In room:* Minibar, Jacuzzi (in Premium rooms).

5 EL CHALTEN & MT. FITZ ROY, ARGENTINA ★★

222km (138 miles) N of El Calafate

El Chaltén is a rugged village of about 800 residents whose lifeblood, like El Calafate's, depends entirely on the throng of visitors who come each summer. This is the second-most-visited region of Argentina's Los Glaciares National Park and quite possibly its most exquisite, for the singular nature of the granite spires that shoot up, torpedolike, above massive tongues of ice that descend from the Southern Patagonian Ice Field. In the world of mountaineering, these sheer and ice-encrusted peaks are considered some of the most formidable challenges on the planet, and they draw hundreds of climbers here every year. The valleys beneath them provide absolutely world-class trekking trails that any hiker can enjoy.

Just 10 years ago, El Chaltén counted just a dozen houses and a hostel or two, but the Fitz Roy massif's rugged beauty and great hiking opportunities have created somewhat of a boomtown. The town sits nestled in a circular rock outcrop at the base of the Fitz Roy and is fronted by the vast, dry steppe. Visitors use El Chaltén either as a base from which to take day hikes or as an overnight stop before setting off for a multiday backpacking trip.

ESSENTIALS

Getting There

BY PLANE All transportation to El Chaltén originates from El Calafate, which has daily plane service from Ushuaia and Buenos Aires. From El Calafate, you need to take a bus or rent a car; the trip takes from 2½ to 3 hours.

BY CAR From El Calafate, take Rte. Nacional 11 west for 30km (19 miles) and turn left on Rte. Nacional 40 north. Turn again, heading northwest, on Rte. 23 to El Chaltén. The road is almost completely paved.

BY BUS Buses from El Calafate leave from the bus terminal, and all cost about $50 (£33) round-trip. A giant new bus terminal is being built in El Chaltén at the entrance to town. In the meantime, buses continue to use their normal drop-off/pickup locations listed here. **Chaltén Travel,** with offices in El Chaltén, at Avenida Guemes and Lago del Desierto (✆ **02962/493092;** www.chaltentravel.com), leaves El Calafate daily at 8am and 6:30pm year-round, and at 1pm during January and February only, and El Chaltén at 7:30am and 6pm daily year-round, and at 1pm in January and February only, departing from the Rancho Grande hostel, Av. San Martín 724. Chaltén Travel can arrange private tours and day trips to outlying destinations such as Patagonian ranches, as well as summer-only transportation up Rte. 40 for those crossing into Chile. **Caltur,** which leaves from El Chaltén's Hostería Fitz Roy at Av. San Martín 520 (✆ **02962/493062;** www.caltur.com.ar), leaves El Calafate daily at 7:30am and 6:30pm, and leaves El Chaltén at 3pm.

Visitor Information

There is a $10 (£6.70) fee to enter the park, which is charged when buses stop at the APN Intendencia (park service) at the entrance to town (✆ **2902/493004**). Park wardens give a good intro to the park in English. El Chaltén also has a well-organized visitor center at the town's entrance—the **Comisión de Fomento,** Perito Moreno and Avenida Güemes (✆ **02962/493011**), open daily from 8am to 8pm. Here you'll find maps, pamphlets, and brief interpretive displays about the region's flora and fauna. In El Calafate, the **APN Intendencia** (park service) has its offices at Av. del Libertador 1302, with a visitor center that is open daily from 9am to 3pm (✆ **02902/491005**).

Note: There is currently no ATM in El Chaltén and many places won't accept credit cards. Be sure to stop at a bank in El Calafate before making the trip here.

OUTDOOR ACTIVITIES

TOUR OPERATORS **Fitz Roy Expediciones** ★★, Av. San Martin 56 (✆/fax **02962/493017;** www.fitzroyexpediciones.com.ar), offers heaps of excursions, including a full-day excursion trekking through Valle de Río Fitz Roy combined with ice climbing at Glacier Torre. No experience is necessary, but they do ask that you be in fit condition. On a stormy day, their excursion to Lago del Desierto is a good option, and they also set up "self-guided" backpacking trips that include food and tents. It's a good budget-friendly way to get into the backcountry. **Mountaineering Patagonia,** Av. San Martin 16 (✆ **2962/493194;** www.mountaineeringpatagonia.com), also offers guided treks and mountaineering trips in the area. **PatagoniaAventura,** Av. San Martin 56 (✆ **2962/493110;** www.patagonia-aventura.com), currently runs the outstanding ice-treks on nearby Viedma Glacier.

HIKING & CAMPING If you're planning on doing any hiking in the park, you'll want to pick up a copy of Zagier & Urruty's trekking map, *Monte Fitz Roy & Cerro Torre,* available at most bookstores and tourist shops in El Calafate and El Chaltén. You'll also need to register at the park service office at the entrance to El Chaltén. Day hiking is superb here; you won't find a well-defined overnight circuit here as you will in Torres del Paine, but there is a loop of sorts, and all stretches of this 3- to 4-day loop can be done one leg at a time on day hikes. Trails here run from easy to difficult and take anywhere from 4 to 10 hours to complete.

One of the most spectacular day hikes, which can also be done as an overnight, 2-day hike, is the 19km (12-mile) trail to the **Mirador Maestri** above Laguna Torre. It offers exhilarating views of the spire Cerro Torre needlelike granite peak. The hike takes 6 to 7½ hours to complete and is classified as challenging, although the first three hours could be considered easy. It's possible to camp nearby at the D'Agostini campground (formerly Bridwell). A more demanding, though beautiful, trail heads to several campsites and eventually the **Laguna de los Tres,** where there is a lookout point for views of Mount Fitz Roy. If you're in decent shape, you can do the round-trip hike to Laguna de los Tres in a day. Campgrounds inside the park's boundaries are free but do not have services; paid campgrounds (outside the park) have water, and some have showers. I also recommend a trip to the lovely tree-lined Laguna del Desierto, the scene of several border skirmishes between Chile and Argentina; border crossings on foot to Villa O'Higgins and the Carretera Austral in Chile are possible beyond the lake (see chapter 12).

HORSEBACK RIDING There's nothing like horseback riding in Patagonia, and one recommended outfitter offers several day excursions. **El Relincho,** Av. San Martín 545 (✆ **02962/493007**), has been operating *cabalgatas* (horseback rides) for many years from their stable in "downtown" El Chaltén.

WHERE TO STAY

Very Expensive

Los Cerros del Chaltén ★★★ The owners of the drop-dead gorgeous Los Notros facing Perito Moreno Glacier have launched this premium inn on a small hill above the village, with grand views over the mountains, and offering all-inclusive programs similar to Los Notros. The rates include transfers from El Calafate or Los Notros, meals, taxes, and a choice of guided excursions, including treks, hikes, and 4×4 rides. The exterior, built in a bit of a plain, chalet style, isn't that impressive. The carpeted rooms, mostly decorated in olive hues, exude a modern but conservative style, with king-size beds and trendy, elegant bathrooms featuring a whirlpool and shower. The website sometimes has special offers, including extra nights for a multinight booking.

El Chaltén s/n. ✆ **11/5277-8200** or 02962/493182. www.loscerrosdelchalten.com. 44 units. $452–$561 (£301–£374) double; 2-night all-inclusive packages $836–$1,422 (£557–£948). AE, MC, V. **Amenities:** Restaurant; bar; spa; Internet access; boutique; laundry service. *In room:* Minibar, hair dryer.

Expensive

El Puma ★ El Puma is one of the originals in El Chaltén. The hotel sits back from the main road and faces out toward snowy peaks, although without a view of Fitz Roy. Inside, warm beige walls and wooden beams interplay with brick. Although the common areas have terra-cotta ceramic floors, all rooms are carpeted. Rooms are bright, but their decor and their bathrooms are frankly outdated. The inn relies heavily on repeat bookings from foreign agencies. The cozy lounge has a few chairs that face a roaring fire. There's also an eating area with wooden tables and a small bar. Service here is relaxed and very friendly.

Lionel Terray 212, El Chaltén. ✆ **02962/493095.** Fax 02962/493017. www.hosteriaelpuma.com.ar. 12 units. $160 (£107) double; $200 (£133) half-board. MC, V. Closed Apr–Oct. **Amenities:** Restaurant; bar; excursions; transfers included; laundry service; Wi-Fi. *In room*: Hair dryer.

Hostería El Pilar The Hostería El Pilar is 17km (10 miles) from El Chaltén toward Lago del Desierto, putting guests far from restaurants and shops. But the lovely, peaceful surroundings are what many guests look for when they come to visit the national park. The yellow-walled and red-roofed El Pilar was once an *estancia;* now it's tastefully and simply decorated with just enough detail to not distract you from the outdoors. The lounge offers a few couches and a fireplace, and is a comfy spot to relax and read a book. Rooms are unadorned but attractive, with peach walls, comfortable beds, and sunlight that streams through half-curtained windows. Guests normally take their meals at the hotel's restaurant, which serves great regional-inspired cuisine. The hotel offers guided excursions and is located next to several trail heads. If you're driving here, keep an eye open for the sign to this hotel because it's easy to miss.

Rte. Provincial 23, 17km (10 miles) from El Chaltén. ✆/fax **02962/493002.** www.hosteriaelpilar.com.ar. 10 units. $155 (£103) double. No credit cards. Closed May–Sept. **Amenities:** Restaurant; bar; lounge; transfers from El Chalten included in rates.

Senderos Hosteria ★★ Finds A lovely mountain lodge, this new inn has superb service, cozy rooms (the nicest ones have wooden ceilings) and great service. Built with traditional Patagonian architecture (tin and wood), rooms are bright and sunny. There's a gentle luxury that is just upscale enough for this informal town. Top-floor rooms are the quietest. The location, on the edge of town facing the new bus terminal, isn't the best, and landscaping is a problem. But inside, there is a lot of heart, warmth, and good vibes. Their restaurant is superb.

Perito Moreno s/n, El Chaltén. ✆ **2962/493336.** www.senderoshosteria.com.ar. 21 units. $132–$156 (£88–£104) double; $170–$210 (£113–£140) suite. MC, V. **Amenities:** Restaurant; wine bar; transfers; reading room; DVD room. *In room*: Hair dryer.

Moderate

In-Land-Sis ★ Value A fresh new spot in town that's run by two funky young mountain lovers, this is just a small step up from a hostel and particularly appealing to young couples on a budget. There are eight doubles, each with a private bathroom. Four have double beds, and four have bunk beds squished in. All have views of the peaks; room 6 has a great view of Fitz Roy. It's clean and friendly. Discounts are given to those who pay in cash.

Lago del Desierto 480, El Chaltén. ✆ **02962/493276.** www.inlandsis.com.ar. 8 units. $70 (£47) double with queen bed; $55 (£37) double with bunk bed. AE, MC, V. **Amenities:** Small restaurant; Internet access; laundry service.

Inexpensive

Nothafagus B&B ★ Value Owned and operated by a down-to-earth local couple, this B&B is bright, sunny, and well priced. There are seven simple and clean rooms; three are doubles with private bathrooms, and four have shared bathrooms and a mix of beds. The upstairs triple has a huge bathroom. If you like the unpretentiousness of a hostel but want something more mature and quieter (although walls are a bit thin), this is a great choice. There is also a cozy reading room, and a hearty breakfast is included in the rates.

Calle 10 y Riquelme, El Chaltén. ✆ **2962/493087.** www.elchalten.com/nothofagus. 7 units. $35 (£23) with shared bathroom; $65 (£43) with private bathroom. Rates include breakfast. No credit cards. Open Oct–Apr; rest of the year with reservations only. **Amenities:** Breakfast room; laundry service; library.

WHERE TO DINE

El Chaltén has some excellent dining options. For food and ambience try the climber's hangout **Patagonicus,** M.M de Güemes 140 (✆ **02966/493025**). Patagonicus serves mostly pizza and enormous salads in a woodsy dining area; no credit cards are accepted. **Fuegia** ★, San Martín 342 (✆ **2962/493243**), has an eclectic, global menu including coconut chicken with cashews and excellent salads. There are also good vegetarian options. In a ramshackle old house loaded with character, **Ruca Mahuida,** at Lionel Terray 55 (✆ **2962/493018**), has the feel of an old alpine hut. The food is pure Patagonian, with stews, trout, and hearty pastas to fill you up after a day on the trail. Diners gather around a handful of tables, making this a great spot to make new friends. Reservations are recommended. For a funky scene with cool music and creative food, head to **Estepa,** at the corner of Cerro Solo and Antonio Rojo (✆ **2962/493069**). The lamb in soft mint sauce, pizzas, and pumpkin sorrentinos are superb.

6 TIERRA DEL FUEGO ★★

Ushuaia: 461km (286 miles) SW of Punta Arenas; 594km (368 miles) S of Río Gallegos

"Where there's smoke, there's fire," thought Magellan in 1520 when he named this island for the smoke rising from the native Selknams' campsites. And more fire came: Settlement in the 19th century meant death for the four native groups on Tierra del Fuego, bordering on genocide despite the brave efforts of Anglican and Catholic missionaries to protect them.

The border between Chile and Argentina slices the main island in half, with far more people living on the Argentine side in Río Grande, Ushuaia, and little Tolhuin. The southern tip of the Americas peters out into a series of archipelagos besides the main island, ending at Cape Horn. There's plenty of hiking and fly-fishing available, along with winter sports near Ushuaia.

The name *Ushuaia* comes from the Yamana Indian language meaning "bay penetrating westward," a fairly simple appellation for a city situated in such a spectacular location. It's the southernmost city in the world (although the naval base and town Puerto Williams is farther south across the channel). Ushuaia is encircled by a range of rugged peaks and fronted by the Beagle Channel. The view across the channel to Chile's Navarino Island is spellbinding, the mountains on that side reminiscent of Torres del Paine. To the west of Ushuaia, the Darwin Range offers more gorgeous mountains.

Founded in the late 1800s, Ushuaia was a penal colony until 1947. The region grew as a result of immigration from Britain, Croatia, Italy, and Spain, and migration from the Argentine mainland, with government incentives such as tax-free duty on many goods being part of the draw. Today the city has about 70,000 residents. Ushuaia is a great destination with plenty of activities, and many use the city as a jumping-off point for trips to Antarctica or sailing trips around Cape Horn.

ESSENTIALS

Getting There

BY PLANE The **International Airport Malvinas Argentinas** is 5km (3 miles) from the city (USH; ✆ **02901/431232**). There is no bus service to town, but cab fares are only about $7 (£4.70). Always ask for a quote before accepting a ride. **Aerolíneas Argentinas** (✆ **0800/222-86527** or 2901/437265; www.aerolineas.com.ar) operates four or five daily flights to Buenos Aires, one of which leaves from Ezeiza and stops in El Calafate. The average round-trip fare is $500 (£333). Frequency increases from November to March, when there's also a daily flight from Río Gallegos and twice-weekly flights from Trelew. **LAN Argentina** (✆ **0810/999-9526** or 2901/424244) flies from B.A. daily via El Calafate. They also fly from Santiago via Punta Arenas on Wednesday, Friday, and Sunday. **Aerovías DAP,** Deloqui 575 (✆ **2901/431110;** www.aeroviasdap.cl), runs charter flights from Punta Arenas and over Cape Horn. It costs around $3,000 (£2,000) for a group of seven people (round-trip), leaving whenever you want.

BY BUS There is no bus station in the city. Buses usually stop at the port (Maipú and Fadul). The service from Punta Arenas, Chile, costs $30 to $40 (£20–£27) and takes about 12 hours. **Tecni Austral** (✆ **2901/431408** in Ushuaia, or 61/613423 in Punta Arenas) leaves Mondays, Wednesdays, and Saturdays at 5:30am; tickets are sold in Ushuaia, from the Tolkar office at Roca 157, and in Punta Arenas, at Lautaro Navarro 975. **Pacheco,** San Martín 1267 (✆ **2901/437727;** www.busespacheco.com), has trips to Punta Arenas via Río Grande, leaving on Monday, Thursday, and Sunday at 9am; it costs $54 (£36). To go to Río Grande, try **Lider LTD, Transporte Montiel,** or **Tecni Austral.** They offer eight daily departures, and the $18 (£12) trip takes around 4 hours.

BY BOAT The company **Crucero Australis** operates a cruise to Ushuaia from Punta Arenas and vice versa aboard its ships the M/V *Mare Australis* and M/V *Via Australis;* departures are Saturday from Punta Arenas and Wednesday from Ushuaia, from late September to April. If you have the time, this is a recommended journey for any age, and it's covered in the box "Cruising from Punta Arenas to Ushuaia" on p. 368.

Getting Around

BY CAR Everything in and around Ushuaia is easily accessible via bus or taxi or by using an inexpensive shuttle or tour service, so renting a car is not necessary. However, with more and more of the top hotels being built on the far outskirts of town, having a car will help you to explore these more rural areas. **Hertz,** San Martín 245 (✆ **2901/437529;** www.hertz.com), has an office in town right next to the Crucero Australis office and another at the airport. Or try **Avis,** Godoy 46 (✆ **2901/436665;** www.avis.com), which drops its prices for multiday rentals. **Cardos Rent A Car** is at Av. San Martín 845 (✆ **2901/436388**).

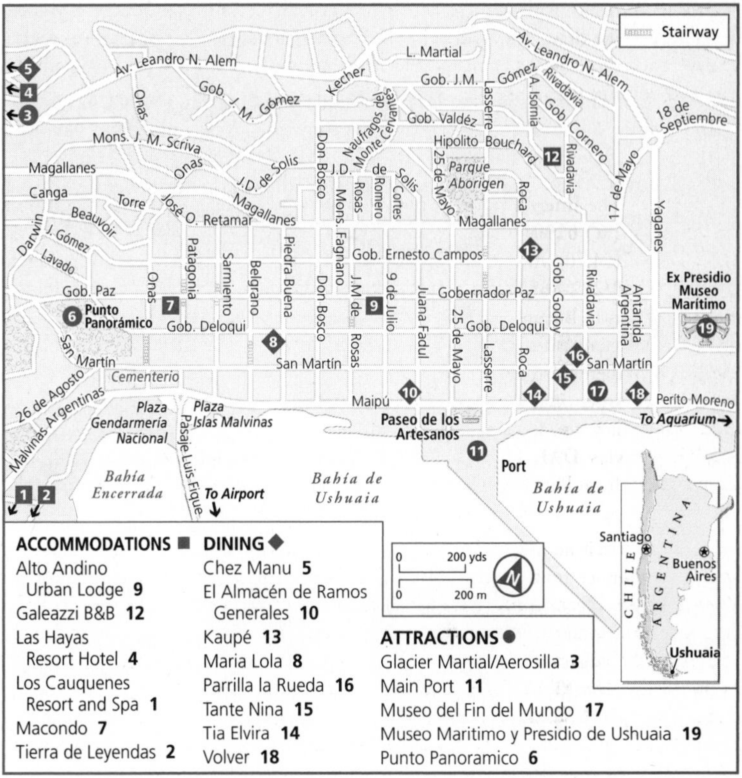

Visitor Information

The **Subsecretaría de Turismo** has a helpful, well-stocked office at San Martín 674 (✆ **02901/432001;** fax 02901/434550; www.e-ushuaia.com). They also have a counter at the airport that is open to assist passengers on all arriving flights and a booth at the main pier. The offices are open Monday through Friday from 8am to 10pm, Saturdays and Sundays from 9am to 8pm. Remember to check for crossings to Isla Navarino in Chile across the Beagle Channel. The national park administration office can be found at San Martín 1395 (✆ **02901/421315;** Mon–Fri 9am–3pm).

Fast Facts Ushuaia

Currency Exchange **Thaler,** Av. San Martín 788 (✆ **2901/421911**), is an old-fashioned currency exchange house. **Banco Sud,** Maipu 781 (✆ **02901/424323**), and **Banco Nación,** San Martín 190 (✆ **02901/422896**), both exchange currency and have 24-hour ATMs.

Laundry **Los Tres Angeles,** Rosas 139, is open Monday through Saturday from 9am to 8pm.

Pharmacy **Andina,** San Martín 638 (✆ **02901/423431**), is open 24 hours a day.

Post Office **Correo Argentino** is at San Martín and Godoy (✆ **02901/421347**), and is open Monday through Friday from 9am to 7pm, Saturday from 9am to 1pm; the private postal company **OCA** is at Maipú and Av. 9 de Julio (✆ **02901/424729**), open Monday through Saturday from 9am to 6pm.

Travel Agency/Credit Cards **American Express** travel and credit card services are provided by All Patagonia, Juana Fadul 60 (✆ **02901/433622**).

WHAT TO SEE & DO

In & Around Ushuaia

The best way to get oriented and get a feel for the landscape is to take a walk to the city park and up to the **Punto Panorámico,** a great lookout point where you get sweeping views of the city and the channel. The trail begins at the southwestern end of Avenida del Libertador and is free.

Acuario de Ushuaia ★ Finds If the idea of jumping into the frigid waters of the channel is out of the question, visit this basic but highly interesting aquarium on the east side of town for a look at what it's like under the surface of the Beagle Channel. Be warned: You might be charmed by the king crabs and refuse to eat one again. It's a little expensive, but the aquarium gets top marks for environmental awareness, and was born from local, grass-roots efforts, receiving no government funds; except for injured animals, all specimens are returned to the water after a few months on display. You'll want to take a taxi as it's on the channel, 3km (2 miles) east of downtown.

Av. Perito Moreno 2564, 3km (2 miles) from town. ✆ **02901/422980.** www.ushuaiaaquarium.com. Admission $14 (£9.30) adults, $6 (£4) children 4–16, free for children 3 and under; group discounts available. Daily noon–8pm.

Glaciar Martial ★ Martial Glacier is a pleasant excursion that sits in Ushuaia's backyard. Avenida Luis Fernando Martial winds 7km (4¹/₄ miles) up from town to the base of a beautiful mountain amphitheater, where you'll find a chairlift that takes visitors to the small Martial Glacier. It's a long walk up the road, and there are no buses to take you there. Visitors usually hire a taxi for $12 (£8) and walk all the way back down, or arrange for the driver to pick them up later. At the base of the chairlift or *aerosilla,* don't miss a stop at **La Cabaña ★** (✆ **02901/424257**), an excellent teahouse with a wraparound outdoor deck and mouthwatering cakes and pastries.

Av. Luis Fernando Martial, 7km (4¹/₄ miles) from town. No phone. Admission $14 (£9.30) adults, $3 (£2) children 8 and under. Daily 10:30am–5:30pm.

Museo del Fin de Mundo ★ The main room of this museum has an assortment of Indian hunting tools and colonial maritime instruments. There's also a natural history display of stuffed birds and a "grandfather's room" set up to resemble an old general store, packed with antique products. But the strength of this museum is its 60 history and nature videos available for viewing and its reference library with more than 3,650 volumes, including a fascinating birth record. Its store has an excellent range of books about Patagonia for sale.

Maipú 172. ✆ **02901/421863.** Admission $8 (£5.30) adults, $2 (£1.30) students, free for children 13 and under. Daily 9am–8pm. Guided tours daily at 10:30am, and 3 and 6pm.

Museo Marítimo y Presidio de Ushuaia ★★ (Moments) Ushuaia was founded primarily thanks to the penal colony set up here in the late 1800s for hundreds of Argentina's most dangerous criminals. The rehabilitation system consisted of forced labor to build piers and buildings, and creative workshops for teaching carpentry, music, tailoring, and other trades—all of which, coincidentally, fueled the local economy. The museum offers a fascinating look into prisoners' and prison workers' lives through interpretive displays and artifacts. There's a restaurant here, with "prison" meals and other theme items. It really is an outstanding museum experience.

Yaganes and Gobernador Paz. ✆ **02901/437481.** Admission $17 (£11) adults, free for children 4 and under. Daily 9am–8pm. Guided tours at 11:30am and 6pm.

Outdoor Activities

BOATING The best way to explore the Beagle Channel is by boat. Numerous companies offer a variety of trips, usually in modern catamarans with excellent guides. Many of them run kiosks near the pier; you'll see a cluster of them by the water. The most popular excursion is a half-day cruise of the Beagle Channel to view sea lions, penguins, and more. **Canoero Catamaranes** (✆ **2901/433893;** www.catamaranescanoero.com.ar) has a variety of options ranging from 2½ hours to 8 hours, on four different boats. **Motonave Barracuda** (✆ **2901/437066**) leaves twice daily for its 3-hour trip around the channel for $45 (£30) per person, stopping at Isla de Lobos, Isla de Pájaros, and a lighthouse. **Motovelero Tres Marías** (✆ **2901/421897**) also leaves twice daily and sails to the same location; they accommodate a maximum of nine guests at a time, and they add an hour-long walk, crab fishing, cognac, and an underwater camera to the package, for $36 (£24) per person.

From November through February, most companies visit the teeming penguin colony and pull the boats up to the shore where travelers can close in tight to watch these marvelous animals. It costs $75 (£50). **Pira Tur,** B. Yaganes Casa 127 (✆ **2901/15604646**), offers walking tours onto the colony with controlled groups. **Motovelero Patagonia Explorer** (✆ **2901/15465842**) has an 18-passenger maximum and leaves daily; it visits the sea lion colony and includes a walk on the Isla Bridges for $50 (£33). This company also works with the Aventuras Isla Verde in the park for a full-day sail; inquire at their kiosk. **Ushuaia Boating,** Gob. Godoy 190 (✆ **2901/436193;** www.ushuaiaboating.com.ar), operates a small, speedy zodiac ferry to Chilean Puerto Williams. It costs $240 (£160) round-trip.

FISHING For a fishing license and information, go to the **Club de Pesca y Caza,** Av. Maipú 822 (no phone). The cost is about $15 (£10) for foreigners per day. Tierra del Fuego's northern area, around the Río Grande, has some of the absolute finest fly-fishing in the entire world, known mainly for its monster sea brown trout. For information on high-end, all-inclusive fishing packages at some outstanding lodges, contact **The Flyshop, Inc.,** 4140 Churn Creek Rd., Redding, CA 96002 (✆ **800/669-3474** or 530/222-3555; fax 530/222-3572; www.theflyshop.com) or **Nervous Waters,** Figueroa Alcorta 3351, Buenos Aires, Argentina (✆ **877/637-8420** in the U.S. or 54-11/4801-1008; www.nervouswaters.com).

SKIING Ushuaia's ski resort, **Cerro Castor** (✆ **02901/499301;** www.cerrocastor.com), is surprisingly good, with more than 400 skiable hectares (988 acres), 15 runs, three quad chairs and one double, a lodge/restaurant, and a slope-side bar. Day tickets cost $23 to $33 (£15–£22), depending on low or high season, and the resort is open from June 15 to October 15. Ticket prices drop for multiday stays, but you can also easily stay in town. To get there, take the shuttle buses **Pasarela** (✆ **02901/433712**); the fare is $12 (£8). The beautiful Andean valley in which the resort is based also has several places for cross-country skiing and taking a fast, bumpy spin on a dogsled through the forests and glades.

Tour Operators

All Patagonia Viajes y Turismo, Juana Fadul 60 (✆ **02901/433622;** www.allpatagonia.com), is the local American Express travel representative and acts as a clearinghouse for everything: If they don't offer it themselves, they'll arrange an excursion with other outfitters, and they can reserve excursions in other destinations in Argentina and Chile. All Patagonia offers three glacier walks for those in physically good shape, scenic flights over Tierra del Fuego, and treks and drives in its Land Rover with nature guides. If you're not sure what you want, start here. **Canal Fun & Nature,** Rivadavía 82 (✆ **02901/437395;** www.canalfun.com), is a great company with excellent guides who provide 4×4 trips and walks culminating with a barbecue, as well as kayaking and nighttime beaver-watching, and they'll custom-build a trip for you. **Rumbo Sur,** San Martín 350 (✆ **02901/422275;** www.rumbosur.com.ar), and **Tolkeyen,** Av. de Los Ñires 2015 (✆ **02901/437073;** www.tolkeyenpatagonia.com), are two operators that deal with larger groups and arrange more classic excursions, such as a city tour and guided visits to the national park and Lagos Escondido and Fagnano.

Excursions near Ushuaia

One of the most intriguing destinations around Ushuaia is the **Estancia Harberton,** the first ranch founded in Tierra del Fuego. It is now run as a museum. The ranch is located on the shore of the Beagle Channel and can be reached by road or boat. The entrance fee is $9 (£6) for adults, free for children under 14. It's open daily from 10am to 7pm. Transportation to the *estancia,* 90km (56 miles) from Ushuaia, is provided by most travel agencies in town, for an average cost of $65 (£43) per person plus the entrance fee, provided you are a group of four or more. Roughly from October to April, several tour companies offer a catamaran ride to the *estancia,* a 6-hour excursion for $85 (£57) per person; try **All Patagonia,** Juana Fadul 60 (✆ **02901/433622**). Tour groups will also arrange a boat excursion to a **penguin colony** from the *estancia,* an add-on excursion that costs about $67 (£45) per person.

Parque Nacional Tierra del Fuego

Parque Nacional Tierra del Fuego was created in 1960 to protect a 63,000-hectare (155,610-acre) chunk of Patagonian wilderness that includes mighty peaks, crystalline rivers, black-water swamps, and forests of lenga, or deciduous beech along the border with Chile, where private parks are being developed. Only 2,000 hectares (4,940 acres) are designated as recreation areas, part of which offer a chance to view the prolific dam building carried out by beavers introduced to Tierra del Fuego in the 1950s.

Views of the Beagle Channel and the Darwin Range on both sides of the border are the park's main attractions, and it offers easy and medium day hikes to get out and stretch your legs, breathe some fresh air, take a boat ride, or bird-watch. Also, there are areas

A Ride in the Park

If you don't feel like walking but still want to take in the sights at Parque Nacional Tierra del Fuego, you can ride **El Tren del Fin del Mundo,** a vapor locomotive replica of the train used to shuttle prisoners to the forest to chop wood (✆ **2901/431600;** www.trendelfindelmundo.com.ar). Be warned that it's a touristy experience, however. The train departs from its station (which features a souvenir shop and cafe) near the park entrance three times daily. I recommend just going one way, as the return trip is tediously slow. And don't bother with first class—the added cost only gets you a light snack and souvenir. The 1-hour, 50-minute round-trip coach journey costs $30 (£20) for adults, $43 (£29) for first class, $7 (£4.70) for passengers 4 to 14, and is free for children under 4.

where the road runs through thick beech forest and then abruptly opens into wide views of mountains whose dramatic height can be viewed from sea level to more than 2,000m (6,560 ft.). Anglers can fish for trout here in the park but must first pick up a license at the **National Park Administration office,** San Martín 1395 (✆ **02901/421315;** Mon–Fri 9am–3pm), in Ushuaia. The park service issues maps at the park entrance showing the walking trails here, ranging from 300m (984 ft.) to 8km (5 miles); admission into the park is $10 (£6.70). Parque Nacional Tierra del Fuego is 11km (6¾ miles) west of Ushuaia on Rte. Nacional 3. Camping in the park is free; there are no services, but potable water is available. At the end of the road to Lago Roca, there is a snack bar/restaurant. At Bahía Ensenada, you'll find boats that take visitors to Isla Redonda, where there are several walking trails. The cost is about $12 (£8), or $19 (£13) with a guide. All tour companies offer guided trips to the park, but if you just need transportation there, call shuttle bus company **Pasarela** (✆ **02901/433712**).

WHERE TO STAY

Accommodations are not cheap in Ushuaia, and quality is often not on par with price. Below are some of the best values that can be found here.

Very Expensive

Las Hayas Resort Hotel ★ For years, this was the top hotel in Ushuaia, on the road to Glacier Martial. It has traditionally welcomed all VIPs, major events, and appealed to those looking for old-world elegance. Times have changed, however, and the market is much more competitive. Las Hayas needs to up the ante to stay at the top. A major plus is the location, which yields sweeping views of the town and the Beagle Channel. It's at least 3km (1¾ miles) from downtown, however, so you'll need to take a cab, hike, or use one of the hotel's summer-only transfer shuttles. The sumptuous lounge stretches the length of the building; here you'll find a clubby bar, formal restaurant, and fireside sitting area. The large, but not deluxe, rooms are decorated with rich tapestries, upholstered walls, and big and bright bathrooms. A glass-enclosed walkway leads to an outstanding spa, swimming pool, and an indoor squash court; the hotel also offers automatic membership at the local golf club. The owner promotes an air of genteel exclusivity, making the hotel less family friendly. Luis Martial, the gourmet restaurant on-site, changes its menu weekly but specializes in black hake and king crab dishes.

Av. Luis Fernando Martial 1650, Ushuaia. ✆ **2901/430710.** Fax 2901/430719. www.lashayas.com. 102 units. $315 (£210) double; $421–$632 (£281–£421) suite. AE, DC, MC, V. **Amenities:** 2 restaurants; bar; lounge; indoor swimming pool; exercise room; Jacuzzi; sauna; concierge; room service; massage; laundry service; dry cleaning. *In room:* TV, hair dryer, safe.

Expensive

Los Cauquenes Resort and Spa ★★ Kids Ushuaia's newest luxury hotel has an outstanding location, perched right on the Beagle Channel and meters from the beach. The red roofed, beechwood and stone-walled main building looks like a mountain lodge. The lobby has massive windows, comfortable oversized wool and leather furniture, and a giant fireplace. For a hotel with only 60 rooms, there are a lot of amenities, including the area's top spa and an acclaimed restaurant. Opt for a superior room, as it'll be large and have bright windows overlooking the channel—standards often have little or no views. Suites have wooden terraces, and all have modern bathrooms with marble and stainless steel fixtures. Staff members will try very hard to exceed your expectations. There are 10 daily transfers into town, although after a busy day exploring the area, you may not want to go anywhere. The six cabins on site work well for families on extended stays.

Calle Reinamora 3462, Ushuaia. ✆ **2901/41300** or 11/4735-2648 in Buenos Aires. www.loscauquenes.com. 60 units. $294–$331 (£196–£221) double, $553 (£369) junior suite with ocean view. AE, MC, V. **Amenities:** Restaurant; wine bar; in/out pool; gym; spa; business center; babysitting service; laundry service; Wi-Fi. *In room*: Satellite TV, minibar, safe.

Tierra de Leyendas ★★ This delightful establishment quickly gained a reputation as one of the best boutique hotels in Argentina, if not South America, when it opened in early 2005. The entire bottom floor is designed according to an open plan, comprising a lounge room, restaurant, and reception with huge windows overlooking the bay. A rust-colored sofa contrasts nicely with olive-green walls and a corn-yellow staircase. The attention to detail is incredible; the sheepskin seat covers are combed every day, and breakfast is delivered every morning with a note explaining a local anecdote (playing off the "legends" in the hotel's name). The dining room tables are minimuseum exhibits with indigenous arrowheads and flints encased beneath the glass dining surface. The five rooms are all named after a local fable; my favorite is the Los Yamanas room, with its stunning view and incredibly relaxing, giant hot tub. If you decide to lodge elsewhere, at least book a table here to experience the excellent cooking. Like other hotels in the area (Las Yamanas, Los Cauquenes), Tierra de Leyendas is on the outskirts of town; it's a $4 (£2.70) taxi ride into town.

Calle Sin Nombre 2387, Ushuaia. ✆ **2901/443565.** www.tierradeleyendas.com.ar. 5 units. $195 (£130) double. AE, MC, V. **Amenities:** Restaurant; bar; Wi-Fi; room service; DVD library. *In room:* TV/DVD, Jacuzzi.

Moderate

Alto Andino Urban Lodge Value Probably the best value in all of Ushuaia can be found at this new apart-hotel. Get in while it's still new. Funky modern art welcomes you in the lobby. Then head up the escalator to one of 10 standard doubles. For just a bit more, you can get a suite, which comes with a sofa bed and kitchenette. All rooms are done in shades of rusted red and chocolate brown. Be sure to ask for a third-floor room for views. The eight "aparts" sleep four and have simple kitchenettes. Breakfast is served in a sunny, bright space on the top floor. Out back is a new backpacker's hostel called "Freestyle," which has bunks in shared dorms for $16 (£11).

Gobernador Pax 868, Ushuaia. © 2901/430920. www.altoandinohotel.com. 18 units. $100 (£67) d... $120 (£80) double suite; $140 (£93) four-person apart with kitchenette. AE, MC, V. Amenities: Bar; Wi... In room: TV, minibar, safe.

Macondo This stylish green-roofed boutique hotel has a young, bohemian feel, without sacrificing elegance. Wall-to-wall Georgian windows surround the common room, with a black stone floor and colorful, cubed armchairs. Spacious bedrooms have a loftlike feel, with red roof beams and rafters. Bathrooms are fair-sized with shower enclosures and wooden platforms. Stairs are in the style of a fire escape, leading you down to a second denlike common room with more couches and mattresses. Simple, modern, and attractive, this hotel also boasts a good central location with a great view.

Gobernador Paz 1410, Ushuaia. ©/fax **02901/437576.** www.macondohouse.com. 7 units. $115 (£77) double. AE, DC, MC, V. **Amenities:** Free Internet access and Wi-Fi; room service; laundry service; TV room.

Inexpensive

Galeazzi–Basily B&B (Value) Sixteen years ago, Frances Basily's hospitality so overwhelmed an American house guest that he raved she should start a bed-and-breakfast. Twenty minutes after he had left, Frances received a knock on the door, and it was two strangers inquiring about a room, recommended by the insistent American. "They had prices and everything! What could I do?" she asks. Since then, Frances and her husband Alejandro have been receiving a steady stream of guests, some lodging in the family home and others in well-appointed cabins out back. The house itself is tall, with a picket fence out front guarding a small forest of beech trees. A wooden walkway leads you into a comfortable, if somewhat worn, suburban home of white walls, plants, family photos, and a long dining room table. The house rooms are small and basic and a little gloomy. They offer two single beds and a shared bathroom. The cabins are much more spacious with lots more light. Yet you do not come here for simple luxury, but for a much more elusive sense of welcome and belonging. Everyone in the family speaks perfect English, and they're all very engaging and helpful.

Gob. Valdez 323, Ushuaia. © **02901/423213.** www.avesdelsur.com.ar. 5 shared units. $55 (£37) double; $95 (£63) cabin for up to 4. No credit cards. **Amenities:** Lounge; bike rental; Internet access; kitchen.

WHERE TO DINE

A dozen cafes can be found on Avenida del Libertador between Godoy and Rosas, all of which offer inexpensive sandwiches and quick meals. The most popular among them is **Tante Sara,** San Martín 701 (© **02901/433710**), where a two-course meal of salad and ravioli or gnocchi costs $8 (£5.30). A block away, the **Tante Sara Café** is the place to sip coffee with locals in the afternoons. In addition to the restaurants listed below, you might consider the **Hotel Los Cauquenes** (© **2901/441300**). It offers great views and gourmet dining, as well as fixed meals and weekly changing menus.

Expensive

Chez Manu ★ (Finds) SEAFOOD/FRENCH The Chez Manu offers great food and even better views seen through a generous supply of windows. Manu, the French chef who run this restaurant, stays true to his roots with a menu that offers French-style cooking using fresh local ingredients. Dishes include black hake cooked with anise and herbs, or Fueguian lamb. Ask about the catch of the day, usually a cold-water fish from the bay such as abejado or a merlooza from Chile. The side dishes include a delicious eggplant ratatouille, made with extra-virgin olive oil and herbes de Provence. The wine list cellent regional dry whites. Note that service is so-so and the decor te.

rtial 2135. ✆ **02970/432253.** Main courses $10–$12 (£6.70–£8). AE, MC, V. Daily –midnight.

ant ★★★ Moments ARGENTINE Gourmets take note: This is one of the best restaurants in South America, for its superb cuisine, lovely view, and warm, attentive service. In 2005, Argentina's gourmet association named it the best restaurant in the country. The menu is brief, but the offerings are delicious. Don't start your meal without ordering a sumptuous appetizer of king crab wrapped in a crepe and bathed in saffron sauce. Main courses include seafood, beef, and chicken dishes, such as tenderloin beef in a plum sauce or a subtly flavored sea bass steamed in parchment paper. Kaupé offers a special "sampler" with appetizers, a main dish, wine, dessert, and coffee for $38 (£25) per person. The extensive gourmet wine list ranges in price from $14 to $58 (£9.30–£39); there's also wine by the glass. Finish it all off with a sorbet in a frothy champagne sauce. Kaupé's dining area is cozy, and its candlelit tables exude romance.

Roca 470. ✆ **02901/422704.** www.kaupe.com.ar. Reservations recommended Sat–Sun. Main courses $14–$27 (£9.30–£18). AE, MC, V. Mon–Sat 6:30–11pm (extended hours during high season).

Tante Nina ★ Finds SEAFOOD/ARGENTINE Tante Nina can't help but appeal to tourists. It has great views, an ideal location, and a friendly atmosphere. The elegant dining room has huge picture windows overlooking the bay, handsome wooden chairs, and white tablecloths. Specialties are the seafood casseroles (known as *cazuelas*), most of which come with fresh king crab (all for $16/£11). There's a delicious Hungarian-style *cazuela* with king crab, tomatoes, cream, and mushrooms; a long list of fish prepared many different ways; and grilled chicken, tenderloin, and even a pickled Patagonian rabbit, for the terribly adventurous. For dessert, try the homemade almond ice cream or the luscious lemon sorbet. Service here is refined, if slightly aloof, and diners tend to be on the older side.

Gobernador Godoy 15. ✆ **02901/432444.** www.tanteninarestaurant.com.ar. Reservations recommended for dinner in high season. Main courses $12–$28 (£8–£19). AE, MC, V. Daily 11am–3pm and 7pm–midnight.

Volver ARGENTINE Even if you don't eat here, don't fail to stop by just to see this crazy, kitschy restaurant on the waterfront. Volver is inside a century-old yellow tin-pan house. Old newspapers and signs wallpaper the interiors, which are also packed with oddball memorabilia, photos, gadgets, trinkets, spider crabs swimming in tanks, and antiques. The food is pretty good, too, boasting regional dishes such as trout, crab, lamb, plus homemade pastas. King crab is served in a dozen different ways, including in soups, casseroles, or simply with a side sauce. The desserts are primarily crepes with such local fruits as calafate. My only complaint is that service can often be absent-minded or hurried.

Maipú 37. ✆ **02901/423977.** Main courses $15–$24 (£10–£16). MC, V. Tues–Sun noon–3pm; daily 7:30pm–midnight.

Moderate

El Almacén de Ramos General ★★ COFFEEHOUSE/DELI This recently renovated, 103-year-old general store has a relaxing appeal and huge personality. It's been lovingly and passionately restored; there are pieces of Ushuaia's amazing heritage all around. Family portraits of the original owners hang in a side room, and a piano sits in the corner, along with old-fashioned typewriters. Situated in front of the port, the restaurant offers cheese platters and generous king crab salads. They have outstanding breads and sweet treats made by a fantastic French baker, too. I recommend the paninis, fisherman's salad, and the superb cheese boards. It makes for the perfect midmorning coffee stop or last stop on land before boarding a cruise. The wine list is excellent and includes a deservedly pricey Cheval des Andes. In keeping with its old-world vibe, the coffeehouse also serves as a bakery, a chic ladies' fashion store, and bar with draft beer.

Maipú 749. ✆ **02901/424317.** www.ramosgeneralesushuaia.com. Main courses $7–$19 (£4.70–£13). AE, MC, V. Daily 9:30am–12:30am.

Parrilla la Rueda ★ PARRILLA A long line of parrillas (steakhouse grills) stretches along the far east end of the main drag, San Martín. All offer "all you can eat" buffet-style service. By far the best of the bunch is La Rueda. Lamb, beef, and chicken are all slow-roasted on the grill, then offered table by table. There's also a large salad bar and friendly, unpretentious service from people who honestly care that you enjoy your meal. Eat as much as you can for $18 (£12), with a dessert such as homemade *flan* (crème caramel) included.

San Martín 193. ✆ **2901/436540.** Main courses $15–$21 (£10–£14). MC, V. Daily noon–11pm.

Tía Elvira Restaurante ARGENTINE/BISTRO Tía Elvira is part restaurant and part minimuseum, with walls adorned with antique photos of the region and various artifacts its owners have collected during its 30 years in business. The menu features fairly straightforward Argentine dishes, such as grilled meats, but the restaurant serves mostly simply prepared seafood, including king crab, trout, sea bass, and cod in a variety of sauces, such as Roquefort or Parmesan. There's also a list of homemade pastas, including lasagna and stuffed cannelloni. The restaurant is on the waterfront, with up-close views of the canal and the pier, and caters mostly to foreign tourists.

Maipú 349. ✆ **02901/424725.** www.tiaelvira.com.ar. Main courses $14–$22 (£9.30–£15). MC, V. Daily noon–3pm and 7–11:30pm.

Inexpensive

Maria Lola ★ (Kids) ARGENTINE This laid-back, relaxing restaurant is situated on a hill, 4 blocks from main street San Martín. In a modern house with large windows, it overlooks the bay, with the town's clapboard church in the foreground. The dining area is large and spacious, and the decor is modern if a little bare. The clientele are a healthy mix of locals and visitors. There's a kids' menu, so families come for the early sitting (before 9pm). All come for a seafood menu, which includes the ubiquitous king crab, homemade pasta, and enormous desserts of cream and fresh fruit. There's a new wine list and sommelier. Maria Lola may not leave you speechless gastronomically, but it makes for very pleasant evening dining. Its charm is in its understatement.

Deloqui 1048. ✆ **2901/421185.** www.marialolaresto.com.ar. Main courses $7–$16 (£4.70–£11). AE, MC, V. Mon–Sat noon–3pm and 7pm–midnight. Reservations recommended.

7 ISLA NAVARINO: PUERTO WILLIAMS

287km (178 miles) SE of Punta Arenas; 3,240km (2,013 miles) S of Santiago

Puerto Williams is the southernmost town in the world, though it functions primarily as a naval base with a population of less than 2,500 residents. The town occupies the northern shore of Isla Navarino in the Beagle Channel, an altogether enchanting location framed by towering granite needles called the "Teeth of Navarino." These peaks are being called the "next Torres del Paine." It's much more wild, remote, and "undiscovered" here than it is across the channel in Argentina's Ushuaia, and Puerto Williams has little tourism infrastructure. It's hard to get here, but it can be even harder to leave. Storms and wind often cancel any boat or air service.

Apart from a few hiking trails and a museum, there's not a lot to do here, but adventurers setting out for or returning from sailing and kayaking trips around Cape Horn use the town as a base. And really, there is a certain cachet to setting foot in this isolated village and knowing you're at the end of the world. The best way to visit Puerto Williams is via ship, ranging from a zodiac that whizzes across the Beagle Channel (in good weather only) to regular service cargo ships. The Yamana culture, who so perplexed the first Europeans with their ability to withstand the harsh environment with little clothing, is long gone, but visitors may still view the last vestiges of their settlements and a well-designed anthropological museum in town. Plans are in the works to expand the airport, start a ferry service from Ushuaia, and to finally bring Internet to the town. In the meantime, it's a sleepy place.

GETTING THERE

BY PLANE **Aerovías DAP,** O'Higgins 891 (✆ **61/223340** in Punta Arenas, 61/621051 in Puerto Williams; www.aeroviasdap.cl), runs a handful of flights per week from Punta Arenas, Chile. Contact DAP for information about occasional flights from Ushuaia to Puerto Williams. DAP also has charter flights, and overland flights to Cape Horn from Punta Arenas.

BY BOAT There are possibilities to get here crossing the Beagle Channel from Ushuaia. **Ushuaia Boating,** Gob. Godoy 190, Ushuaia (✆ **2901/436193;** www.ushuaiaboating.com.ar), runs a small, speedy zodiac service to and from Puerto Williams, whenever they have enough people to fill the boat (a minimum of three is needed)—and whenever weather permits, for $130 (£87) one-way and $240 (£160) round-trip. The passenger and cargo ferry **Transbordadora Austral Broom** offers cheaper passage to Puerto Williams with a 34-hour journey from Punta Arenas (Av. Bulnes 05075; ✆ **61/218100;** www.tabsa.cl). During the summer, the ferry leaves Punta Arenas four times a month on Wednesday and returns on Saturday; sleeping arrangements consist of reclining seats ($175/£116 adult one-way) and bunks ($210/£140 adult one-way). Kids receive a 50% discount.

Victory Adventure Expeditions, based out of Puerto Williams at Teniente Munoz 118, no. 70 (✆ **61/621010;** www.victory-cruises.com), specializes in sailing journeys around the Beagle Channel and Cape Horn, and as far away as Antarctica. The schooner-style ships are not luxurious, but they are warm and comfortable, and their small size allows for a more intimate, hands-on journey than the *Australis* cruises. A 7-day trip starts at $3,100 (£2,066) per person. **Sea & Ice & Mountains,** in Puerto Williams (in the Coiron Guesthouse; ✆ **61/621150;** www.simltd.com), is a German-run agency with a 6-passenger and 12-passenger yacht that takes visitors on 5- to 12-day journeys around Cape Horn and past the Darwin mountain range; contact the agency for prices. For general travel agency needs, including city tours, airline tickets, and hotel reservations, contact **Turismo Akainij,** Uspashum 156 (✆ **61/21327;** www.turismoakainij.cl).

WHAT TO SEE & DO

The **Museo Martin Gusinde,** Aragay 01 (✆ **61/621043**), features a good collection of Yaghan and Yamana Indian artifacts, ethnographic exhibits, and stuffed birds and animals. The museum's docent is an anthropologist, naturalist, and all-around expert in the region; he is usually on hand to provide tours in the area. The museum is open Monday through Thursday and Saturday from 10am to 1pm and 3 to 6pm.

About 3km (1¾ miles) southeast of Puerto Williams on the main road, at the La Virgen cascade, is a medium-level **hiking trail** with an exhilarating, sweeping panorama of the Beagle Channel, the Dientes de Navarino mountain range, and Puerto Williams. The hike takes 3 hours round-trip. One of Chile's best backpacking trails, the **Dientes de Navarino Circuit ★★**, is here, thanks to an Australian who blazed the trail in 1991. The circuit is 53km (33 miles) in length and takes 4 days minimum to walk, with a difficulty level of medium to high, and the mountains are very remote. The trail is open only from late November to April; otherwise, snow makes this walk dangerous and disorienting. The best map is JLM's *Tierra del Fuego* map, sold in most shops and bookstores. The last descendents of the Yamana Indians live at Villa Ukike to the west of town. Attempts are underway to rescue what can be salvaged of their culture, including their language. They sell crafts in the **Centro de Artesanía Yamana Kipa-Akar.** A little farther west are the **Omora botanical gardens** (www.cabodehornos.org), a project to study and protect the world's southernmost forests.

WHERE TO STAY & DINE

Dining and accommodations pickings here are slim but reasonably priced; you won't find luxury hotels in Puerto Williams except for the new 24-room **Hotel Lakutaia** at Seno Lauta s/n (✆ **61/621733;** www.lakutaia.cl), with all-inclusive multiday programs starting at $1,970 (£1,313) for 5 days/4 nights. Basic, clean accommodations can be found at the **Hostería Camblor,** Calle Patricio Capdeville (✆ **61/621033;** hosteriacamblor@hotmail.com), which has six newer rooms for $38 to $58 (£25–£39) per person; some rooms come with a kitchenette. The Camblor also has a restaurant that occasionally serves as the local disco on Friday and Saturday nights, so noise could be a problem.

For dining, try the convivial **Club de Yates Micalvi** (✆ **61/621042**), housed in an old supply ship that is docked at the pier, which serves as the meeting spot for an international crowd of adventurers sailing around Cape Horn. Also try the Hostería Camblor's restaurant (see earlier), **Los Dientes de Navarino** (✆ **61/621074**), on the plaza, or **Restaurant Cabo de Hornos,** Ricardo Maragano 146 (on the second floor; ✆ **61/621067**), for Chilean specialties.

8 ANTARCTICA

It may be the coldest spot on the planet, but it's a hot destination for travelers seeking the next great adventure. Antarctica is its own continent, but the hook of the Antarctic Peninsula is closest to the tip of South America, and, therefore, the majority of people depart for Antarctica from Ushuaia.

Antarctica is home to exotic wildlife and landscapes that are equally savage and beautiful. Be prepared for ice like you've never seen it: monumental peacock-blue icebergs shaped in surreal formations, craggy glaciers that crash into the sea, sheer ice-encrusted walls that form magnificent canals, and jagged peaks that jut out of icy fields. A major highlight here are the penguins—colonies of several hundred thousand can be found nesting and chattering away throughout the area. Humpback, orca, and minke whales are often spotted nosing out of the frigid water, as are elephant, Weddell, leopard, and crabeater seals. Bird-watchers can spend hours studying the variety of unique seabirds, including petrels and albatrosses.

Its remoteness alone is enough to compel many people to travel here. Like the early explorers who first visited this faraway continent in the 1800s, travelers today revel in the chance to venture to a pristine region where relatively few humans have stepped foot before. But this comes at a price: No matter how you get here, it's expensive, and the tediously long traveling time (unless you take a brief and expensive plane trip from Chile) and sometimes uncomfortable conditions are also part of the price you'll pay. Nevertheless, many of Antarctica's roughly 45,000 yearly visitors would agree that the effort is worth it.

For information on sustainable travel and limits on the number of visitors to Antarctica, see p. 45 in "Planning Your Trip to Chile."

A BRIEF HISTORY

The history of exploration and the discovery of the Antarctic continent are littered with claims, counterclaims, tall tales, intrigue, and suffering. Captain James Cook discovered the South Sandwich and South Georgia islands (a part of Antarctica, these islands are a British possession) in 1773, but he never spotted the Antarctic continent. He did, however, set off a seal-hunting frenzy after providing reports of the large colonies he found there, and it's estimated that sealers discovered around a third of the islands in the region. Two sealers were the first to actually step foot on the continent: the American John Davis at Hughes Bay in 1821, and the British James Weddell at Saddle Island in 1823. During a scientific expedition in 1840, the American navy lieutenant Charles Wilkes finally concluded that Antarctica was not a series of islands and ice packs, but rather a contiguous landmass.

The South Pole was not reached until 90 years later, on December 4, 1911, by Norwegian Roald Amundsen and his well-prepared five-man team. Though Amundsen's arrival at the pole accounted for one of the most remarkable expeditions ever to be completed by man, his feat at the time was eclipsed by the tragic finale of an expedition led by his rival, the British captain Robert Scott. Scott arrived at the pole 33 days later, only to find Amundsen's tent and a note. Scott and his party, already suffering from scurvy and exposure, finally froze to death on their return trip, just 18km (11 miles) from their ship.

No other destination has held such an adventurous cachet for explorers. One of the greatest adventures ever recorded was in 1915, led by the Irish explorer Ernest Shackleton, who pronounced Antarctica "the last great journey left to man." Shackleton attempted to cross the Antarctic continent but never achieved his goal: Pack ice trapped and sank his boat. The entire party miraculously survived for a year on a diet of penguin and seal before Shackleton sailed to South Georgia Island in a lifeboat to get help.

Today 27 nations send personnel to Antarctica to perform seasonal and year-round research. The population varies from 4,000 people in the summer to roughly 1,000 in the winter. There are a total of 42 stations that operate year-round, and an additional 32 that operate during the summer only. The stations study world climactic changes, and in 1985, researchers at the British Halley station discovered a growing hole in the ozone layer.

PLANNING YOUR TRIP TO ANTARCTICA

Visitor Information

A number of websites offer helpful information about Antarctica. A few of the best include:

- **www.iaato.org**: This is the official website of the International Association Antarctic Treaty Organization, the only governing body in Antarctica (although it is more akin to a gentleman's treaty among all nations with bases here). It is important that your tour group be a member of the IAATO, International Association of Antarctica Tour Operators. Most cruise operators are members. Membership in the organization ensures a safe and environmentally responsible visit to Antarctica. Statistics, general information, and news can be found on this website.

- **www.discoveringantarctica.com.uk**: This educational site has the nuts and bolts behind natural and human life on the frozen continent.
- **www.antarcticconnection.com**: This site offers travel information, tour operator links, and Antarctica-related items for sale, including maps and videos.

Entry Requirements

No single country claims Antarctica as its territory, so visas are not necessary, but you will need a passport for unscheduled stops and your first stop in Chile or Argentina (see chapter 3 for information about entry requirements).

When to Go

Tours to Antarctica are conducted between late November and March—after March, temperatures dip to lows of –100°F (–38°C) and the sun disappears until September. The opposite is true of the summer (Dec–Mar), and visitors can expect sunlight up to a maximum of 18 to 24 hours a day, depending on where you are in Antarctica. Summer temperatures near the Antarctic Peninsula vary between lows of 5° to 10°F (–15° to –12°C) and highs of 35° to 60°F (2°–16°C).

What you see during your journey to Antarctica may depend on when you go. November is the mating season for penguins and other birds, and visitors can view the offspring in December and January. The best time for whale-watching is during February and March.

Safety

EXTREME WEATHER Cold temperatures, the wind-chill factor, and perspiration all conspire to prohibit the body from keeping itself warm in Antarctica's conditions. Travelers, therefore, need to outfit themselves in the highest-quality outdoor clothing available. Tour operators are constantly amazed at how underprepared visitors to Antarctica are, and they, therefore, will provide you with a packing checklist. Ask your tour company if it provides its guests with waterproof outerwear or if you are expected to bring your own. Additionally, the thin ozone layer and the glare from snow, water, and ice make a high-factor sunscreen, a hat, and sunglasses absolutely imperative.

SPECIAL HEALTH CONCERNS *Everyone* should bring anti–motion sickness medication on a trip to Antarctica. If you suffer from a special health problem or are taking prescription medication, bring a signed and dated letter from your physician for medical authorities in case of an emergency. Delays of up to 4 weeks have been known to happen on guided trips to the interior, so visitors should seriously consider the extremity of such a trip, submit themselves to a full medical exam before their departure, and bring the quantity of medication necessary for a long delay.

MEDIAL SAFETY & EVACUATION INSURANCE All passenger ships have an onboard physician in the event of a medical problem or emergency; in any case, passengers should discuss an evacuation policy with each operator. Emergency evacuation can be hindered by poor weather conditions, and anyone with an unstable medical condition needs to keep this in mind. Also, check your health insurance to verify that it includes evacuation because it can be unbelievably expensive—from the Shetland Islands alone, it costs $35,000 (£23,333) to evacuate one person.

GETTING THERE

By Ship

Few would have guessed that the collapse of the Soviet Union in the early 1990s would be the catalyst to spawn tourism in Antarctica. But when Russian scientific ship crews found themselves without a budget, they spruced up the ships' interiors and began renting the vessels out to tour operators on a rotating basis. These ships (as well as others that have since come on the market) are specially built for polar seas, complete with antiroll stabilizers and ice-strengthened hulls. A few of these ships have icebreakers that can chip through just about anything.

Before you go, it helps to know that a tour's itinerary is a rough guide of what to expect on your journey. Turbulent weather and ice conditions can cause delays or detours. Wildlife sightings may prompt your group to linger longer in one area than the next. The ship's crew and the expedition leader of your tour will keep you informed of any changes to the program.

Typical Itineraries

A journey's length is the determining factor for which stops are made. Tour companies offer roughly similar trajectories for cruises to Antarctica, with the exception of a few over-the-top cruises. (Got a month and $37,000/£24,600? Then you might join Quark Expedition's semi-circumnavigation of Antarctica.) Apart from the destinations listed below, cruises attempt a landing at research stations when convenient. Most Antarctic cruises leave from Ushuaia, Argentina, although a tiny fraction leave from New Zealand. The Ushuaia departure point is the quickest way to reach Antarctica. Although Chile used to be a departure site for Antarctica, few (if any) travelers now leave from Chile; those who do make the journey aboard a military ship. Plan to leave from Ushuaia.

Remember to factor in 2 days (4 in total for the return trip, if traveling to the Antarctic Peninsula) to cross the Drake Passage, during which time you'll not do much more than hang out, relax, take part in educational lectures, and suffer through occasional bouts of seasickness. Cruises typically last 8 to 13 days for the Antarctic Peninsula, and 18 to 21 days for journeys that include the Subantarctic Islands. Seasoned travelers have frequently said that 8-day trips are not much of a value; consider tacking on 2 extra days for a 10-day trip.

THE ANTARCTIC PENINSULA This is the easiest site to visit in Antarctica, and due to its rich variety of wildlife and dramatic scenery, it makes for a magnificent introduction to the "White Continent." If you have a short amount of time and/or a limited budget, these trips are for you.

All tours head from Ushuaia through the Drake Passage. First stop is at the **South Shetland Islands.** Historically, sealers and whalers used these islands as a base; today they're home to research stations, colonies of elephant seals, and a variety of nesting penguins and sea birds. Popular sites here are **King Island, Livingston Island,** and **Deception Cove,** a collapsed, active volcanic crater with bubbling pools of thermal water.

Tours continue on to the eastern side of the Antarctic Peninsula, with a variety of stops to view wildlife such as Weddell and leopard seals and vast colonies of Adélie, chinstrap, and Gentoo penguins. At the peninsula, sites such as the **Lemaire** and **Neumayar** channels afford camera-worthy views of narrow, sheer-walled canals made of ice and rock. At **Paradise Harbor,** calving icebergs theatrically crash from the harbor's main glacier, and throughout the area, outlandishly shaped gigantic icebergs float by. Other popular stops include **Port Lockroy,** a former British base that is now run as a museum; **Cuverville** and **Rongé** islands, with their penguin colonies; and **Elephant Island,** named for the huge, sluglike elephant seals that inhabit it.

THE POLAR CIRCLE Ships with ice-breaking capabilities can transport guests past the Antarctic Circle, below 66 degrees and into the zone of 24-hour sunlight. The highlight here is **Marguerite Bay,** with its abundant orca, minke, and humpback whales, and multitudinous Adélie penguins. These cruises typically stop for a fascinating tour of research stations, both ultramodern and abandoned ones.

THE WEST SIDE & THE WEDDELL SEA Longer tours to the peninsula might include visits to its west side, known as "iceberg alley" for the mammoth, tabular chunks of ice floating slowly by. Stops include the rarely visited **Paulet Island,** an intriguing crater island, and **James Ross** and **Vega** islands, known for their nesting colonies of Adélie penguins.

An even longer trip (or simply a different itinerary) takes travelers to the distant **Weddell Sea,** which is blanketed with a vast expanse of pack ice, looking much like a frozen sea. But that's just one of the highlights here; the real reason visitors pay extra time and money to reach this white wonderland is because of the colonies of emperor penguins that reside here. Rugged mountains and glaciers are also part of the view.

SUBANTARCTIC ISLANDS Tours to the Subantarctic Islands begin or end with a trip to the Antarctic Peninsula and the Shetland Islands, which is the reason these tours run 18 to 21 days. A few of these faraway islands are little-visited by tourists, and they instill a sense of adventure in the traveler for their remoteness and fascinating geography, not to mention their important historical aspects.

The first stop is usually the **Falkland (Malvinas) Islands,** to view bird life, especially king penguins, and to tour the Victorian port town of Stanley. Some tours fly directly from Santiago, Chile, to the Falklands and begin the sailing journey there.

South Georgia Island is surely one of the most magnificent places on Earth and is, therefore, a highlight of this trip. The island is home to a staggering array of wildlife and dramatic landscapes made of rugged peaks, fjords, and beaches. South Georgia Island is also subject to unpredictable weather, and, therefore, trip landings here are at risk of being canceled far more frequently than at other sites. Some tours tack on visits to the **South Orkney Islands** (with their dense area of Antarctic hairgrass—an indigenous flowering plant) and the actively volcanic **South Sandwich Islands.**

Tour Operators

Prices vary depending on the length of the trip, the company you choose, and the sleeping arrangements you require. A 9-day journey in a room with three bunks and a shared bathroom runs about $3,500 (£2,333) per person, and a 21-day journey with lodging in a corner-window suite runs between $12,000 and $26,000 (£8,000–£17,300) per person. Shop around to find something to suit your needs and budget.

Prices include passage, meals, guides, and all excursions. Some tours offer scuba diving, kayaking, overflights, or alpine trekking, usually at an additional cost. When researching trips, also consider the size of the ship: Tour companies offer space for anywhere from 50 to 600 passengers. Most travelers like to share their space with fewer people; although some enjoy the camaraderie of a crowd, more than 100 to 150 guests is just too many. The International Association Antarctic Treaty Organization limits landings to 100 people, meaning large ships must conduct landings in turns. The main reason this is done is to limit the ecological "footprint" of visits to this extremely fragile environment. The smaller cruises are more eco-friendly.

Tips Last-Minute Reduced Fares to Antarctica

Several travel agencies in Ushuaia offer reduced fares for last-minute bookings made about 15 to just a few days before a cruise's departure date, with prices 10% to 50% lower than the advertised rate. Two agencies to try are **Rumbo Sur,** Av. San Martín 350, Ushuaia, Argentina (© **2901/422441;** fax 2901/430699; www.rumbosur.com.ar); and **All Patagonia,** Juana Fadul 60, Ushuaia, Argentina (© **2901/433622;** fax 2901/430707; www.allpatagonia.com). Both offer a variety of expeditions from a handful of operators. Note that the best deals on discounted rates tend to occur in late November and early December, before the onset of the high travel season in Southern Argentina.

With the soaring fuel prices in 2008, most companies began adding fuel surcharges that were not confirmed until the day of boarding.

A few well-known tour operators include:

- **Abercrombie & Kent** (© **800/544-7016** or 630/954-2944; fax 630/954-3324; www.abercrombiekent.com): Like Quark, A&K offers deluxe journeys, with trips that run from 11 to 20 days.
- **Antarctica Cruises** (© **54-11/4806-6326;** fax 54-11/4804-9474; www.antarctica cruises.com.ar): Based in Buenos Aires, owners Zelfa Silva and her husband Gunnar are seasoned Antarctica travelers and expert trip-planning consultants.
- **Antarctic Shipping** (© **877/972-3531;** www.antarctic.cl): This Chilean-owned company has won praise for its small vessel trips to the Antarctic.
- **Antarpply Expedition** (© **54-2901/433636;** fax 54-2901/437728; www.antarpply.com): From their office in Ushuaia, Antarrply runs 10-night, 11-day cruises that start at $6,410 (£4,273).
- **Aurora Expeditions** (© **61-2/9252-1033;** fax 61-2/9252-1373; www.aurora expeditions.com.au): This is an Australian company with a variety of educational, photographic, and climbing tours for small groups.
- **Fathom Expeditions** (© **800/621-0176** or 416/646-2688; www.fathomexpeditions.com.au): A Canadian company that is run by former expedition leaders, Fathom's trips tend to be a bit longer, and a bit less hurried.
- **Lindblad Expeditions** (© **800/397-3348** or 206/403-1525; www.expeditions.com): This venerable Swedish-run company was the first to bring tourists to Antarctica. In 2008, they launched the *National Geographic Explorer.* It offers 11- to 28-day tours, with trekking.
- **Oceanwide Expeditions** (© **31-118/410410** or 800/453-7245; www.oceanwide-expeditions.com): This Dutch company operates a variety of journeys aboard its own ship.
- **Peregrine Adventures** (© **1300/854444** in Australia, or 613/9662-2700 outside Australia; fax 03/9662-2442; www.peregrine.net.au): This Australian company is the only operator that doesn't charge solo travelers a single supplement.
- **Quark Expeditions** (© **800/356-5699** or 203/852-5580; www.quarkexpeditions.com): This highly esteemed company offers the industry's most outrageous trips. A 12-day trip leaving from Ushuaia to Antarctica is priced from $4,900 (£3,266).

By Plane

Apart from working for a research station, one of the few ways to get out and really explore the Antarctic continent is by plane, and there are a handful of companies that offer a small selection of astonishing and out-of-this-world journeys to the Antarctic interior and beyond.

Flights to the Antarctic can be divided into two distinct categories: flights that access man-made airstrips on certain islands close to the peninsula, and flights that penetrate the frigid interior, relying on natural ice and snow runways for landing areas. The logistics involved in flying to the Antarctic are complicated, to say the least, and fuel becomes an issue. Make no mistake, air travel to the Antarctic is a serious undertaking; but the rewards can be unforgettable.

From Punta Arenas, Chile, King George Island on the peninsula is the preferred destination. The island houses a number of research stations, some of which can be visited, and it boasts extraordinary wildlife and sightseeing opportunities. The average stay is 1 or 2 days, but weather delays can alter itineraries.

The severity of the landscape and the remoteness of the interior of the Antarctic continent call for special considerations when planning and preparing for an unexpectedly prolonged stay. All travelers attempting a trip to the interior should be aware of the extreme climatic conditions. Travel delays caused by severe weather are the norm. These trips, however, represent adventure travel in its purest form.

Tour Operators

Prices vary depending on the company and destination. In general, flights to the peninsula are cheaper than those to the interior. These all-inclusive trips can cost anywhere from $12,000 to $30,000 (£8,000–£20,000) per person, depending on the destination. Logistical support for extended expeditions can easily run to over $40,000 (£26,600). Prices typically include transportation, meals, and guides.

- **Adventure Network International** (© 801/266-4876; fax 801/266-1592; www.adventure-network.com): This company began as a private plane service for climbers headed for Vinson Massif, the highest peak in Antarctica. They now include several 7- to 22-day tours, such as flights to the South Pole and the Transantarctic and Ellsworth mountain ranges, an emperor penguin safari, and a 60-day ski trip to the South Pole. Activities planned during these trips can include hiking, skiing, and skidoo trips; overnight camping; ice hockey; igloo building; and just about anything else related to ice.
- **Aerovías DAP** (© **61/223340;** fax 61/221693; www.aeroviasdap.cl): This small Chilean airline specializes in charter flights to the peninsula, in particular King George Island.
- **Antarctica XXI S.A.** (© **61/614100;** fax 61/614105; www.aeroviasdap.cl): This Chilean company offers 6-day trips that include daily flights. It departs from Punta Arenas and is based out of King George Island.

14

Easter Island

Easter Island is the most isolated inhabited island in the world. Called "Rapa Nui" by the local population and "Isla de Pascua" by Chileans, the island's name comes from its discovery by Dutch explorers on Easter Sunday in 1722. At 3,540km (2,200 miles) west of continental Chile, and 2,075km (1,290 miles) east of the closest body of land, Pitcairn Island, it is difficult to fathom the remoteness of this island, which is no larger than the District of Columbia. A visit to this ethereal land will exceed every expectation you've held—and then some. The island is a veritable living museum that will fascinate and enrapture you, and make you wish you'd planned a few more days to soak up the indelible magic that makes this one of Chile's most special destinations.

Of course, the island's famous moai sculptures that stand like mute sentinels are the first thing that you'll think of when you picture Easter Island, but really there is so much more here: 20,000 archaeological sites, a rich culture of truly beautiful people, dramatic views of volcanic craters, scuba diving in crystalline waters, white-sand beaches, and that unmistakable hang-loose island vibe that makes you want to throw your agenda away after day one.

The Rapa Nui are Polynesian descendents who, according to the most recent studies, arrived at the island some time around the 8th century. Legend has it that it was King Hotu Matu'a who first arrived here on a double-hulled canoe with his extended family; researchers believe they most likely came from the Marquesas, Cook, or Pitcairn islands. The population flourished and created a society characterized by a written language and megalithic art, including moais and petroglyphs. But it all went horribly wrong when the Rapa Nui deforested the island and population exploded, bringing about war and starvation. The first Europeans here found a culture in decline. Many were carted off to work on the guano islands in Peru in the 19th century or died in epidemics. Catholic missionaries came next and destroyed much of their cultural art, including their *Rongo-Rongo* written tablets; and experts have been unable to decipher the few that remain. Nevertheless, the Rapa Nui are experiencing a cultural renaissance, and they take great pride in their culture and native language, which they habitually speak among themselves, in addition to Spanish.

The climate here is marine subtropical, with temperatures between 60°F (16°C) during the winter (July–Aug), and 82°F (28°C) during the summer (Jan–Feb). The island has a persistent breeze that can make it feel cooler, especially if it's raining, so bring a sweater or light jacket. Downpours can occur at any time, but generally May is considered the wettest month. High season is December through March. It is recommended that you spend at least 4 days here given the travel distance and the wealth of things to see and do.

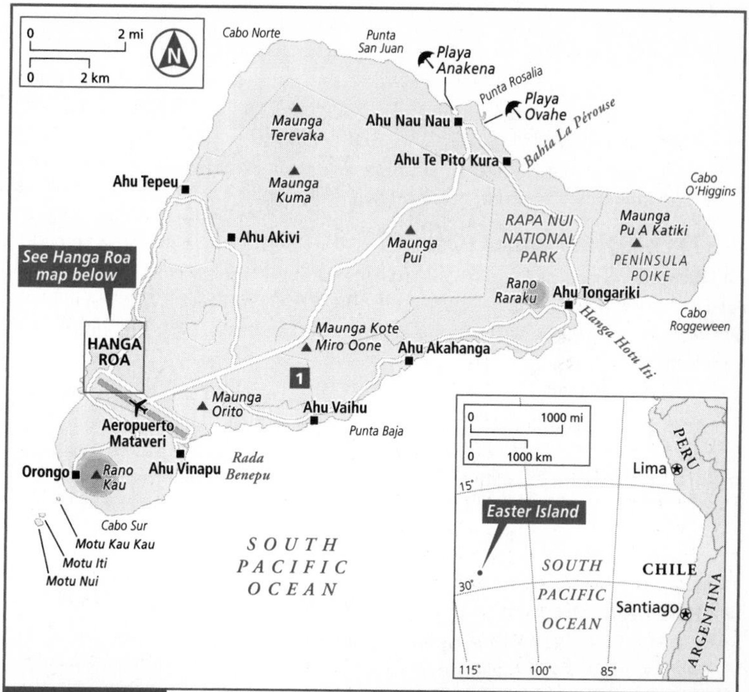
0 2 mi
0 2 km
N
Cabo Norte
Punta San Juan
Playa Anakena
Punta Rosalia
Playa Ovahe
Ahu Nau Nau
Bahía La Pérouse
Maunga Terevaka
Ahu Te Pito Kura
Maunga Kuma
Ahu Tepeu
Cabo O'Higgins
Ahu Akivi
Maunga Pui
RAPA NUI NATIONAL PARK
Maunga Pu A Katiki
PENÍNSULA POIKE
See Hanga Roa map below
Rano Raraku
Ahu Tongariki
Cabo Roggeween
Hanga Hotu Iti
HANGA ROA
Maunga Kote Miro Oone
Ahu Akahanga
1
Maunga Orito
Ahu Vaihu
Punta Baja
Aeropuerto Mataveri
Rada Benepu
Orongo
Rano Kau
Ahu Vinapu
Cabo Sur
Motu Kau Kau
Motu Iti
Motu Nui
SOUTH PACIFIC OCEAN
0 1000 mi
0 1000 km
15°
PERU
Lima
Easter Island
CHILE
SOUTH PACIFIC OCEAN
Santiago
ARGENTINA
30°
115°
100°
85°

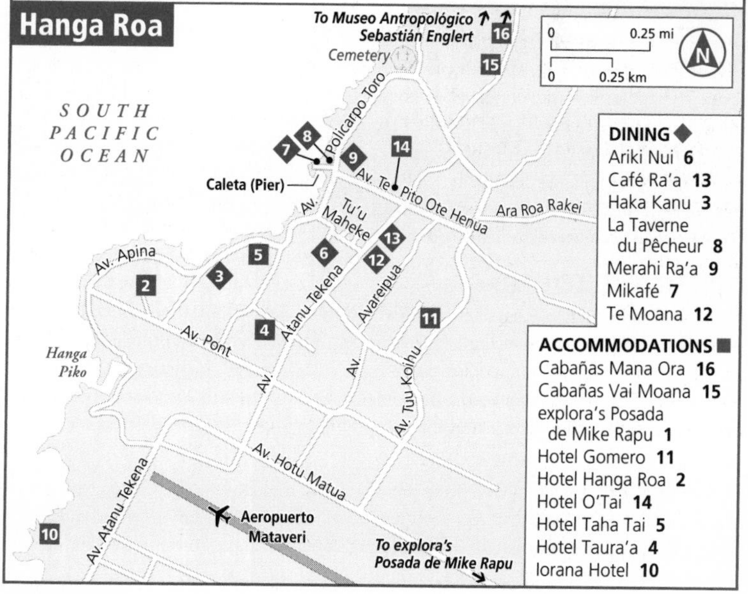
Hanga Roa
To Museo Antropológico Sebastián Englert
16
15
Cemetery
0 0.25 mi
0 0.25 km
N
SOUTH PACIFIC OCEAN
Policarpo Toro
Caleta (Pier)
Av. Te Pito Ote Henua
Ara Roa Rakei
Av. Tu'u Maheke
Av. Apina
Av. Atanu Tekena
Avareipua
Av. Pont
Av. Tuu Koihu
Hanga Piko
Av. Hotu Matua
Av. Atanu Tekena
Aeropuerto Mataveri
To explora's Posada de Mike Rapu
DINING
Ariki Nui 6
Café Ra'a 13
Haka Kanu 3
La Taverne du Pêcheur 8
Merahi Ra'a 9
Mikafé 7
Te Moana 12
ACCOMMODATIONS
Cabañas Mana Ora 16
Cabañas Vai Moana 15
explora's Posada de Mike Rapu 1
Hotel Gomero 11
Hotel Hanga Roa 2
Hotel O'Tai 14
Hotel Taha Tai 5
Hotel Taura'a 4
Iorana Hotel 10

1 ESSENTIALS

GETTING THERE

Easter Island's **Mataveri International Airport** in Hanga Roa is served by **LAN Airlines** only (IPC; ✆ **866/435-9526** in the U.S., or 600/526-2000 in Chile; www.lan.com), with daily flights (except Mon and Thurs) and two flights on Wednesday and Sunday. This flight carries on to Papeete, Tahiti, twice a week on Wednesday and Sunday. Most hotels pick you up at the airport and greet you with a garland of flowers.

VISITOR INFORMATION

The **Sernatur** office is at Avenida Policarpo Toro at Tuu Maheke (✆ **32/210-0255**); it's open weekdays from 8:30am to 1:30pm and 2:30 to 5:30pm. They also have an information desk at the airport that is open daily when flights arrive. You'll find information galore here, plus maps.

SPECIAL EVENTS Tapatai, held since 1975 for 2 weeks in late January and early February, is the largest cultural gathering and celebration of Rapa Nui culture. Craft expositions, horse races, fishing and swimming competitions, and dance and theater performances make up this festival. A few of the more unusual and interesting events are the Tau'a, a tortora reed raft race held inside the Rano Raraku volcano, and the Haka Pei, where contestants slide down a mountain on a banana tree trunk and try to stay on the longest. The festival culminates in the crowning of a queen.

ORIENTATION

Easter Island measures just 168 sq. km (65 sq. miles), and there is only one village, **Hanga Roa.** The island is roughly triangular in shape, with each point dominated by an extinct volcano: Maunga Terevaka at the northern point, Maunga Pu A Katiki on the eastern edge at the Poike Peninsula, and Rano Kau, a vast crater on the southern edge next to Hanga Roa. The island is principally composed of a wide, grassy expanse and about 70 smaller volcanic craters and cones, as well as lava beds peppered with so many volcanic chunks of rock that it is said that certain areas "bloom" stones. Most of the island's roads are paved, with the exception of the western coast and the road to Ahu Akivi. Given the island's relative lack of significant coral reef, the pounding ocean has created towering, sheer sea cliffs in some areas. The island's two beaches, Anakena and Ovahe, are located on the northeast coast.

GETTING AROUND

BY FOOT Hanga Roa is small enough to be seen on foot. Throughout the island, there are walking trails (not very well marked, however) that can be found principally in flatter areas, providing easy to moderate treks. Some tour guides, including those used at explora (p. 394), traverse between archaeological sites on the west coast or the Rano Kau volcano. None of the hikes are that intense, and if you have the time there is not a more beautiful way to see the island.

BY CAR Renting a vehicle is a great way to get out and explore the island at your own pace. Rental agencies ask that you keep your speed down to 30kph (19 mph) outside of Hanga Roa, which is a smart idea considering that animals are often found on or near the island's roads. Also, rental agencies do not offer insurance.

The following car rental agencies can deliver a vehicle to the airport for your arrival, or you can pick up a rental in town: **Rent a Car Insular** (✆ **32/210-0480;** www.renta-insular.com) and **Oceanic Rent a Car** (✆ **32/210-0985;** www.oceanicrapanui.cl), which also rents 4×4s, motorcycles, and ATVs. Book a reservation in advance or race to rent a vehicle upon arrival, as they do sell out.

BY TAXI Taxis charge about $3 (£2) for local destinations. Call **Radiotaxi Avareipua** (✆ **32/210-0700** or 32/221-0398).

Fast Facts Easter Island

Banks There is a 24-hour ATM at Banco Estado across the street from Sernatur on Tu'u Maheke (✆ **32/276-5500**). However, the machine only accepts Cirrus network cards (like MasterCard); Visa/Plus cardholders need to have a bank representative run their card through the bank system in order to receive cash, which can also be done at Honu Vaikava on Atamu Tekena (✆ **32/255-1950**). A Banco Santander was being constructed near the harbor and should be running by mid-2009 and will have a 24-hour Visa/Plus ATM. Bank hours are Monday through Friday from 8am to 1pm.

Emergencies For a **police** emergency, call ✆ **133.** For **fire,** call ✆ **132.** To call an **ambulance,** dial ✆ **131.**

Hospital The **Hospital Hanga Roa** (✆ **32/210-0183**) has basic medical services, but more serious cases need to be treated back on the mainland.

Internet Access Most hotels have an Internet station and even Wi-Fi. Or try **Isl@ net** next to the plaza, open daily from 9:30am to 10pm (Sat–Sun open at 10am). **Rapu Call** (✆ **32/255-1600**) has a call center and Internet services.

Laundry Most hotels will do your washing for you at a fairly reasonable price. Or try **Lavandería Tea Nui,** at Avenida Atamu Tekena s/n, Monday through Saturday from 10am to 1:30pm and 4 to 8pm.

Pharmacies **Farmacias Cruz Verde** (✆ **32/255-1540**) is at Atamu Tekena s/n and open Monday through Saturday from 9am to 1pm and 4:30 to 8pm.

Post Office The post office is on Avenida Te Pito o Te Henua s/n (across from the Hotel O'tai) and is open weekdays from 9am to 1pm and 2:30 to 6pm.

Telephone The country code for Chile is 56, and the city code for Hanga Roa is 32. Note that all phone numbers are now prefixed with a 2 for a seven-digit phone number, but many published numbers still do not reflect this (for example, 32/005555 is now 32/200-5555).

2 HANGA ROA

Hanga Roa is the only town on Easter Island, and virtually all of the island's 3,800 residents live here. In spite of LAN Airlines increasing its flights to seven per week, bringing in more and more tourists, Hanga Roa still holds on to its quintessentially laid-back ambience. Many of the town's roads outside of the main commercial area are unpaved,

The Mysterious Moais

Where moais came from and how they were made and moved to their final resting ground is clear, but *why* still ranks as one of the world's great mysteries. The Rapa Nui carved moais from compressed volcanic ash found on the slopes of the Rano Raraku crater; today there are more than 850 moais spread around the island, either erected atop an ahu, left lying in transit to an ahu, or half-finished in the Rano quarry. Moais average 4m (13 ft.) in size and weigh an average of 12 tons; the largest moai, Te Tokanga, reached 21m (71 ft.), but was never finished and remains in the Rano quarry. It is generally believed that the statues were commemorative images of family or clan leaders, even though the moais are not portraits of individuals but instead abstract designs with angular faces and long bodies. Why they chose this design and what their obsession with the moais was are unclear, but what is known is that the transportation of the moais atop tree trunks is a principal factor in the widespread deforestation of the island that stressed the environment and the community and led to eventual war and the destruction and toppling over of the moais. The moais you see erected today are thanks to the restoration efforts of archaeologists.

and laws prohibiting ownership by nonislanders means the town has grown organically and has thus far avoided encroachment by high-rise resorts and chain stores. It's not a terribly sophisticated place, but then that is part of its appeal. Nearly all of Hanga Roa's residents earn a living from tourism, and the "downtown" area is replete with simple hotels and guesthouses, shops, tour companies, and restaurants. You don't need a car to see Hanga Roa, just your feet, and part of the enjoyment of visiting is simply strolling around and taking in the town's mellow charm.

While here, you'll want to visit the **Museo Antopológico Sebastián Englert** in the Tahai Sector (© **32/255-1020;** www.museorapanui.cl; Tues–Fri 9:30am–12:30pm and 2–5:30pm, Sat–Sun 9:30am–12:30pm; admission $2/£1.30), and the **Biblioteca William Mulloy** (Tues–Sat 9:30am–12:30pm). The museum focuses more on ethnology than archaeology, but there is a tiny display of artifact replicas. The museum's bookstore and the excellent Mulloy library are stocked with diverse literature and photo books about Easter Island. They occasionally hold free lectures in both English and Spanish on recent archaeological research and theories. Also worth visiting, especially during Mass on Sundays (in both Rapu Nui and Spanish) is the **Iglesia Hanga Roa,** located at Te Pito o Te Henua and Tu'u Koihu streets. Inside are intricate wood carvings that illustrate the adaptation of Rapa Nui culture to Catholicism, while outside to the right are the tombs dating back to the mid-1800s of several important Catholic priests who lived on the island.

The best displays of moais lie scattered around the island, but there are two broken moai at **Ahu Tautira** overlooking the Caleta Hanga Roa harbor, where there are several of the best cafes and restaurants and both dive shops. If you look around under the dive boats, you can usually spot a green sea turtle floundering about.

For a better archaeological excursion near town, visit one of the island's best reconstructions of an ahu (ceremonial altar) at **Ahu Tahai,** past the island's colorful cemetery and near the museum. There are actually three ahus here: The first is **Ahu Vai Uri,** with five reconstructed moai, followed by the solitary Tahai moai, and the **Ahu Ko Te Riko,** with its topknot and coral and obsidian eyes. The moais front a grassy expanse with stone walls and a canoe ramp; here you'll also see the oval foundations of a *hare paenga,* or "boathouse," so-called for the traditional home's resemblance to a capsized boat. There is no better place to watch a sunset than at Tahai, so bring your camera and join your tourist brethren for a superb photo session.

There are fine beaches at Anakena and Ovahe, but **Playa Pea** near the harbor has a rock pool for swimming.

WHERE TO STAY

Lodging on Easter Island is overpriced for what you get, and no hotel other than explora's Posada de Mike Rapu can be considered higher than a middle-range hotel. Every hotel is about the same: a moderately comfortable bed, nightstand, maybe a television and desk, ceramic floors, and cheap linens. Even the most basic hotels charge at least $60 (£40) a night, and anything less than that can be pretty grim. All hotels on the island are located in Hanga Roa, but some are a 10- to 15-minute walk to restaurants and services. All lodging options include breakfast in the price, and most can organize tours and set up rental vehicles. As a last resort, you can usually find locals selling rooms in small *residenciales* and family homes waiting arriving flights.

Very Expensive

explora's Posada de Mike Rapu ★★★ *Moments* The combination of breathtaking nearby archaeology, spaceshiplike architecture, and fine food and drinks leaves most visitors to this hotel, a recent replacement of the island's smaller explora hotel, in awe. Many of their treks, led by native Rapa Nui guides and capped at a maximum of 8 people, are rarely done by other operators and they even have exclusive access to several trails. Excursions are so superbly timed that you rarely encounter the hordes of bus tours that plague most sites. While the price to stay here is high, it includes all excursions (two a day) plus contemporary Pacific Rim meals and all drinks, not to mention the best rooms on the entire island. The high-ceilinged guest rooms are set six to a building and utilize lots of wood, volcanic stone, and glass, offering distant ocean views over the pastoral setting just a 15-minute ride from town. Each room also features ambient lighting, linen bedspreads draped over ultra comfortable beds, and lavish bathrooms. Little extras such as the amuse-bouche and pisco sours that are passed out after excursions are the ahu topping on one fine moai. The hotel was also recently the first in Latin America to garner LEED certification from the U.S. Green Building Council.

6 km from Hanga Roa; Te Miro Oone Sector, s/n. ✆ **866/750-6699** in the U.S., 2/206-6060 in Santiago. Fax 2/228-4655. www.explora.com. 30 units. 3 nights $2,280–$3,030 (£1,520–£2,020) per person; 4 nights $3,040–$4,040 (£2,027–£2,693) per person; 5 nights $3,710–$4,915 (£2,473–£3,277) per person; 7 nights $4,949–$6,440 (£3,299–£4,293) per person. AE, DC, MC, V. Rates based on double occupancy. **Amenities:** Restaurant; bar; pool, Jacuzzis, spa; all transportation, transfers, guided excursions; free Wi-Fi; laundry service. *In room:* Hair dryer, safe.

Expensive

Hotel Hanga Roa Throughout the past several years this hotel, owned by the same family as Termas de Puyehue (p. 284), has been in various stages of renovations, with only a handful of rooms open at any given time. At the end of 2008 it shut its doors completely to undergo a complete overhaul. It will reopen in December 2009 with a new theater, museum, pool, plus dozens of new guest rooms and cabañas. Though it isn't comparable to the explora in terms of luxury and service, it promises to become the center of tourist activity on the island and the best option in this price range.

Av. Pont s/n. ✆ **32/210-0299.** Fax 2/210-0695. www.hotelhangaroa.cl. AE, DC, MC, V. Check the website or call for rates and service information.

Hotel O'Tai ★★ The Hotel O'Tai and the Taura'a (below) are the best hotels in this category. The O'Tai's central location and palm-fringed swimming pool are definite perks. The guest rooms are nothing to write home about, but they are spacious, and there is an overall cleanliness to the establishment and a staff that provides cheery service. Guest rooms are set back from the street motel-like and surrounded by lush gardens. Most doubles come with a sliding glass door and a sitting area terrace, and there are rooms designed for groups in which five guest rooms center around a common seating area.

Te Pito o Te Henua s/n. ✆ **32/210-0250.** Fax 2/210-0482. www.hotelotai.com. 41 units. $135 (£90) standard double; $165 (£110) superior double. AE, DC, MC, V. **Amenities:** Restaurant; bar; outdoor pool; laundry service. *In room:* A/C (superior rooms only), safe.

Hotel Taha Tai ★ One of the largest, full-service hotel complexes on the island, the glossy Taha Tai has as much style as a hospital, but it's well run by a friendly staff and kept spotlessly clean. Rooms 17 to 26 have views of the ocean for no additional cost, so try to nab one. The cabins are smallish and not much of a value. The restaurant has excellent views of the sea, and there are many soothing common spaces for just hanging out.

Av. Policarpo Toro. ✆/fax **32/255-1192.** www.hotel-tahatai.co.cl. 40 units. $165 (£110) double. AE, DC, MC, V. **Amenities:** Restaurant; bar; outdoor pool; tour desk; gift shop. *In room:* TV, safe, no phone.

Hotel Taura'a ★★ This is the kind of hotel you could recommend again and again and feel good about it, considering its consistent service, sparkling clean guest rooms, and neatly manicured grounds. The Taura'a isn't even really a hotel; it's a small B&B in a converted home with extra units added on, tucked away off the main street. Guest rooms have fresh linens, quality beds, wicker furniture, and a small terrace. For the price, rooms are basic by U.S. standards, but they are tastefully decorated enough to put them a step above other rooms in Hanga Roa. What's really worth mentioning is the attentive service provided by the good-natured and helpful owners, the Aussie Bill and his Rapa Nui wife Edith, not to mention their tail-wagging, friendly dogs.

Atamu Tekena s/n. ✆ **32/210-0463.** Fax 2/255-1310. www.tauraahotel.cl. 31 units. $140 (£93) double. AE, DC, MC, V. **Amenities:** Restaurant; bar; pool; tour desk; free Wi-Fi; laundry. *In room:* A/C, minibar, coffeemaker.

Iorana Hotel The rooms need a serious makeover—the property looks like it hasn't been touched since they opened 2 decades ago—general character is severely lacking, service tends to be mediocre, and the property is a long way from town, but the view from Iorana is spectacular enough to make up for these faults. This large hotel is wedged between the airport and the Rano Kau crater on a dramatic bluff overlooking an inspiring stretch of Pacific coast. The standard rooms are a bit dingy and lack A/C, and though the superior rooms and suites are more spacious, they're still unspectacular.

Av. Ana Magaro s/n. ✆ **32/2100-608.** www.iroanahotel.cl. 52 units. $145 (£97) standard; $180 (£120) superior; $190 (£127) suite. AE, MC, V. **Amenities:** Restaurant; bar; 2 pools; tennis court; tour desk; free airport transfers; laundry service. *In room:* A/C (in superior and suites), TV, safe, Jacuzzi (in suites).

Moderate

Cabañas Mana Ora ★ A cabin at Mana Ora is ideal for DIY travelers with their own rental car; it comes with fully stocked kitchenettes, a deck that faces the distant ocean and the afternoon sunset, and it's located in a more rural setting about 10 minutes outside of town. The cabins here are simple, made of wood and artistically decorated with local art and colorful cushions. There is one bedroom and a sofa bed. Stock up on food in town, or better yet, bring cheaper supplies with you from Santiago.

Sector Hinere. ✆ **32/210-0769.** www.manaora.cl. 3 units. $105 (£70) for 2 people. No credit cards. **Amenities:** Laundry. *In room:* Kitchenette, no phone.

Cabañas Vai Moana ★ Finds Set behind a rock wall and nestled in a sylvan garden near the ocean, these *cabañas* are an utterly delightful place to stay, though high demand has caused them to jack up their prices significantly. While the staff offers a gracious welcome, the owner is grumpy and his negativity can put a damper on your experience if you're unlucky enough to be here when he's on duty. Both standard and superior rooms are simple units without much flair, but the premises are kept clean, and they are grouped together in detached units of two rooms each and spaced down the well-manicured property. Most units have sunny terraces that are ideal for relaxing and feeling the ocean breeze. The Vai Moana is located next to the museum and is a good 15-minute walk to the main street.

Atamu Tekena s/n. ✆ **32/210-0626.** www.via-moana.cl. 19 units. $144 (£96) standard double; $180 (£120) superior double. Rates include breakfast. AE, DC, MC, V. **Amenities:** Restaurant; organized tours; laundry service. *In room:* Minibar, no phone.

Hotel Gomero ★★ Just 2 blocks from the main street lies this little gem of a moderate hotel, known for its bright, spacious rooms and trim grounds that wrap around a swimming pool. Given the preponderance of frilly bedspreads and curtains, it's nothing fancy in terms of style, but the owners have added touches of local Rapa Nui art throughout the property.

Av. Tu'u Koihu s/n. ✆ **32/210-0313.** www.hotelgomero.com. 13 units. $120 (£80) double; $150 (£100) superior. Rates include breakfast. AE, MC, V. **Amenities:** Pool, restaurant; bar; tour desk; airport transfers; laundry service. *In room:* A/C (superior), minibar, safe.

WHERE TO DINE

Easter Island is the place to savor Pacific fish—you simply ask what's fresh and order it. The restaurant Merahi Ra'a has a menu with photos of Easter Island's native fish types. A popular side dish is *camote,* which is similar to a sweet potato, and taro, a starchy root. Another in-and-out cheap meal can be found at **Motu Hava,** in a converted trailer on Policarpo Toro street next to the school playing field, with fresh *ceviche,* sandwiches, and simple pasta dishes. Lastly, **Empanadas Tía Berta** serves fabulous fried empanadas made of tuna, seafood, cheese, and meat, and salads and simple dishes. Look for the sign on the main street Atamu Tekena on your left-hand side almost before reaching the gas station.

Expensive

Haka Kanu ★★ CONTEMPORARY PACIFIC RIM Haku Kanu was called El Jardin de Mau before being taken over by new owners in 2008 and given a fresh contemporary feel. The ambience of this cafe is so enjoyable, it is almost worth visiting for this aspect alone. It is bright and airy, with an artsy decor and an outdoor patio that offers a view of the ocean crashing against the shore. The cafe serves melt-in-your-mouth tuna sashimi, along with grilled fish, steaks, and pasta. This is also a good spot for an afternoon coffee or glass of wine, and the service is friendly. Note that the patio can be windy on some days.

Ave. Policarpo Toro s/n. ✆ **32/255-1677.** Reservations not accepted. Main courses $11–$17 (£7.30–£11). AE, DC, MC, V. Daily 10:30am–10pm.

La Taverne du Pêcheur ★★ Finds FRENCH/PACIFIC RIM Yearning to splurge? This is Easter Island's best and most expensive restaurant, serving meals prepared with the freshest, highest quality ingredients available. Owned and operated by a grouchy French chef who married a local woman, the specialty here is seafood such as *rape rape* (local lobster, costing $48–$77/£24–£39 depending on size), sea urchin, dorado, and seafood platters with all this plus mussels and shrimp. La Taverne also imports its meat from Argentina, and serves dishes such as entrecote with pepper or Roquefort sauce. Every dish is lavishly presented on giant platters and served with a variety of accompaniments like camote, taro, potato, and vegetables—truthfully, the portions are almost too big—apart from the steaks. The wine list is excellent but outrageously expensive. In spite of the prices, La Taverne's atmosphere leans more toward rusticity, with rough-hewn wood interiors, lots of plants, and softly lit, boothlike seating. With chocolate marble cake, sorbets, and crepes on offer, you'll want to save room for dessert. The restaurant sits at the harbor beside the dive shops.

Av. Te Pito o Te Henua s/n. ✆ **32/210-0619.** Reservations recommended for dinner. Main courses $15–$23 (£10–£15). AE, DC, MC, V. Mon–Sat noon–3pm and 6–11pm. Closed May–June.

Te Moana ★ CONTEMPORARY PACIFIC RIM The Te Moana is one of the coziest spots for a meal. The ambience is stylish rusticity, built of wood, bamboo, and volcanic rock, and there is a tiny patio for watching street life parade by. Te Moana is known for its coconut milk *ceviche.* On the whole the food is good, not great, with standouts such as Thai fish soup, fish in green curry with rice noodles and veggies, shrimp tempura, and a surf-and-turf platter with a T-bone or entrecote steak and seafood. Te Moana occasionally hosts live music during the evenings.

Av. Atamu Tekena s/n. ✆ **32/255-1578.** Reservations not accepted. Main courses $13–$30 (£8.70–£20). MC, V. Mon–Sat 6:30pm–1:30am.

Moderate

Ariki Nui ★ PACIFIC RIM/CHILEAN This restaurant is where you go for exotic meat dishes such as grilled wild boar or ostrich stroganoff. Like many restaurants on the island, much more thought was put into the concept of this restaurant than in the actual execution of its cuisine, but nevertheless the food is better than at other restaurants, and the Kon-Tiki ambience of bamboo, low-slung ceilings, and glass walls backed by green tree fronds is cool and relaxing. A good bet for a group is their Ariki Nui platter with mixed seafood such as tempura, *ceviche,* and carpaccio, and they have fresh salads and some pasta dishes. Note that every Monday, Thursday, and Saturday at 9pm the restaurant hosts a special *curanto* (seafood and meat steamed over hot rocks in the ground), followed by the folkloric dance show Matatoa; the cost is $48 (£24) for dinner and the show, or $19 (£9.50) for the show only.

Oho Vehi s/n. ✆ **32/255-2017.** Main courses $13–$16 (£8.70–£11). No credit cards. Daily 11:30am–3:30pm and 6:30–11:30pm.

Merahi Ra'a ★ Value PACIFIC RIM/CHILEAN As a *picada* (Spanish for a dive), there isn't much ambience here, but this little eatery is an excellent spot for lunch for their reasonable prices and ultrafresh fish served in a variety of ways, including scallop and tuna carpaccio. I love their tuna *ceviche,* as it has just the right tanginess and comes with a green salad and *camote* (sweet potato). Meals here are nearly abundant enough for two diners. The restaurant has outdoor and indoor seating and is owner attended. Merahi Ra'a is located by the harbor.

Av. Te Pito o Te Henua s/n. ✆ **32/255-1125.** Reservations not accepted. Main courses $8–$14 (£5.30–£9.30). No credit cards. Fri–Wed noon–10pm.

Inexpensive

Café Ra'a ★★★ CAFE One of the most popular cafes in town, the small patio of the Café Ra'a is almost always packed with visitors and locals soaking in the vibe and gossiping. Most come for the best breakfast on the island, with everything from pancakes and *küchen* to eggs to real coffee. The reasonably priced dinner and lunch menus feature fettuccine, tuna carpaccio, seafood soups, and sandwiches.

Av. Atamu Tekena s/n. ✆ **32/551-1530.** Reservations not accepted. Main courses $8–$15 (£5.30–£10). MC, V. Daily 8am–8pm.

Mikafé ★★ CAFE/DESSERT This island patio hangout opened in December 2007 beside Mike Rapu's dive shop and looks out over the "hustle and bustle" of the harbor. Their artisanal ice creams in flavors such as banana, passion fruit, camote, and taro are the main objective here, particularly on hot days. They also offer a decent tea menu, brewed coffees, *küchen,* hot cakes, and sandwiches.

Caleta Hanga Roa. ✆ **32/255-1055.** Reservations not accepted. Main courses $5–$12 (£3.30–£8). No credit cards. Mon–Sat 9am–1:30pm and 4:30–9pm.

3 PARQUE NACIONAL RAPA NUI

Nearly all of Easter Island is within the confines of Parque Nacional Rapa Nui, in an effort to protect the island's moais, petroglyphs, beaches, and 20,000 archaeological sites. **Conaf** (✆ **32/210-0236;** www.conaf.cl) administers the park and charges a $10 (£6.70) entrance fee at their office in Orongo that is good for all sites during the length of your stay. The best way to tour archaeological sites is with a knowledgeable guide, but plenty of travelers go it alone and at their own pace with a rental car. Either way, if it's high season, reconsider taking a tour with a large group as it seems to spoil the mysterious ambience of the island. ***Important note:*** It is imperative that travelers understand that all archaeological sites and the moai statues and their ahu platforms are considered sacred and should not be walked upon or altered in any way.

The best tour guides in the area are bilingual Ramon Edmunds and Josie Nahoe Mulloy, who form **Haumaka Archeological Tours** (✆ **32/210-0274;** haumaka@entel-chile.net); unfortunately they can be quite busy during high season, so contact them well in advance. **Aku Aku Turismo** (✆ **32/210-0770;** www.akuakuturismo.cl) is a competent tour operator with bilingual guides and large group half-day tours around the island, including boat tours and horseback riding.

EXPLORING THE ISLAND

The South Coast

Begin your tour of the island by heading early to the **Rano Rakaru** crater ★★★, the quarry and birthplace of the island's moais, and undeniably Easter Island's most extraordinary site. Before reaching Rano Rakaru, you'll pass two ahus, **Ahu Vaihu** and **Ahu**

Akahanga, with their toppled-over moais; scattered along the road to Rano Rakaru there are dozens of prone moais abandoned midway to their final resting place. To say that the approach to Rano Rakaru is an emotive experience is an understatement—the most common reaction is an expletive! Scattered about the crater's slope are upright, half-buried moais, and even more half-finished moais attached to the matrix rock—in all, nearly 400 moais of all shapes and sizes can be viewed here in varying states of completion. There is a ranger's station here and picnic tables under eucalyptus trees. Follow the path along the slope to "El Gigante," the largest moai on the island at 21m (71 ft.). A short but steep path leads up to the crater's edge and into its interior, where you can view more moais and the crater's freshwater lake, and grasp your first view of the famous **Ahu Tongariki** moai site ★★★. Located at the shoreline east of Rano Rakaru's sheer volcanic walls, Ahu Tongariki is the largest collection of erect moais on the island, 15 statues in all, the tallest reaching 6.6m (22 ft.). Tongariki is a captivating place—together with Rano Rakaru you'll want to spend your entire day exploring both.

At the eastern tip of Easter Island is the **Poike Peninsula** ★, a high plateau formed by the extinct volcano **Maunga Pu A Katiki.** There is no road access here and few travelers take the time to visit the peninsula, except to hike or horseback ride.

South of Hanga Roa

The **Rano Kau** volcano ★★★ and its crater is the island's most impressive natural attraction—prepare to be left breathless as you stand before it. The crater measures 1.6km (1 mile) in diameter and has steep slopes that descend to a reed-choked lake (which you can walk to if you're in shape). It is possible to follow a path around the crater, but it will take the better part of a day. To get here, drive or walk (about an hour). Clinging to the crater's edge and fronting the steep coastal escarpment is **Orongo,** the ceremonial and ritual site dedicated to the Birdman cult. This annual ritual was a brutal competition whereby men battled to obtain the first egg laid by the sooty tern, which nested on the islet **Motu Nui.** The men would descend the rocky cliff, swim through shark-infested waters, and wait for days or weeks until the first egg was found. The winner, or his "sponsor," would swim back with the egg in a head strap, and spend the following year in seclusion while his family was granted special status to dominate others. The reconstructed, stone slab structures at Orongo demonstrate clearly how ritual participants lived during the ceremony. Also here are basalt rocks with beautifully carved petroglyphs depicting half-human, half-bird figures.

Closer to Hanga Roa, about a half-hour walk south from town, is **Ana Kai Tangata** ★, a sea-cliff cave used as a refuge during days of social conflict. Inside the cave is what remains of rather remarkable prehistoric paintings of birds.

Southeast of Hanga Roa, following the road at the end of the airstrip, is the island's most curious ahu, **Vinapu** ★. The perfectly symmetrical stones used to build the ahu platform gave rise to the theory that the people of Easter Island came from South America, due to the platform's similarity to stonework seen in Peru.

North of Hanga Roa

Following the rough coastal route north out of Hanga Roa will take you to the **Caverna Dos Ventanas** ★★, or the "Cave of Two Windows." Unfortunately, it's difficult to find. Drive a little less than 3km (2 miles) until you are parallel to two offshore islets; there's usually a rock cairn here indicating the turnoff, or maybe another car or van will guide you as to where the cave's entrance lies. The cave entrance is a small hole in the ground, but it leads to two fantastic cliff openings (bring a flashlight) where you can watch the crashing sea. Farther north lies **Ahu Tepeu** ★, a well-built ahu whose moai lies fallen over. Scattered around this area are the foundations of the *hare paenga* boat houses, and reconstructions of chicken coops and walled gardens.

More cave dwellings lie at **Ana Te Pahu** ★. Follow the poorly marked road from Ahu Tepeu until you see lots of greenery, which is a garden planted with typical root vegetables and bananas, and the cave's entrance. These caves provided refuge for people escaping island battles, and are made from lava tubes. Note that it is common for travelers to hike or bike to Ahu Tepeu and the Dos Ventanas caves.

Farther inland, seven finely reconstructed moais can be viewed at **Ahu Akivi** ★★. These are the only moais that face out to sea, and oriented toward the summer solstice. From here, a rutted road leads up to **Maunga Terevaka** ★★, the highest point on the island. From this point it is possible to see the island in its entirety. The road's closed to traffic, although some locals still sneak up in a 4×4. Hiking here takes about 1 to 1[bf]1/2 hours, depending if you walk the road from Akivi or from the other entrance near Vaitea. Heading south on the road from Ahu Akivi, you'll see a turnoff to **Puna Pau** ★, the quarry for the *pukao,* or topknot that some moais sport. There are two dozen half-finished topknots here, and a splendid view of Hanga Roa and the coastline.

The Northeast Coast

Come here to relax. The island's two beaches, **Anakena** and **Ovahe** ★★★, can be found here, and they are dreamy, with cerulean sea lapping at white sand. Anakena is the larger beach, and legend holds that this is where King Hotu Matu'a landed when he arrived at Easter Island. You'll find a few shacks selling grilled meats, snacks, beverages, and beer here. Overlooking the beach are **Ahu Ature Huki,** with one moai, and **Ahu Nau Nau** ★★, with seven moais etched with petroglyphs, and four of which have topknots. Ovahe has pinkish sand and is backed by a cliff and is usually less crowded than Anakena, but it is best before the sun hides behind the cliff.

Worth exploring is **Ahu Te Pito Kura** ★★, named for a perfectly rounded and magnetic boulder here that local lore says was brought over by King Hotu Matu'a, as there is no other rock like it on the island. The name means the "navel of the earth," and it was the name of the island before it was called Rapa Nui. The ahu here once supported the largest moai to have been transported to an ahu, measuring 10m (33 ft.) and lying face down, with his topknot knocked off. Following the coast east on foot will take you past a rich assortment of boathouse foundations, chicken coops, and even an ancient observatory.

OTHER ACTIVITIES

Outdoor Fun

BIKING Rent a bike from one of the many shops on the main street Atamu Tokena (around $15–$20/£10–£13 per day).

HORSEBACK RIDING Riding horseback is one of the most enjoyable ways to see Easter Island. Although you can hire a horse for an hour or so and limit the ride to sites around town, a more thrilling, full-day journey is up to the top of the volcano Terevaka, the highest point of the island. **Piti Pont** is the person to call (✆ **32/210-0664** or 9/574-0582).

KAYAKING, SURFING & OTHER WATERSPORTS Rent boards and kayaks at Orca Diving Center's **Hare Orca** shop (✆ **32/255-0375;** www.seemorca.cl), and pick up information about the best spots to do both. Surfboards rent for $20 (£13) a day and single ocean kayaks and bodyboards for $15 (£10) a day.

SCUBA DIVING & SNORKELING The waters off Easter Island are some of the bluest—and clearest—in the world, providing scuba divers with up to *60m (200 ft.)* of visibility. Diving here is in open-sea conditions, with limited coral reef. You won't see the throngs of sea life found at other South Pacific destinations, but you will see wild volcanic landscapes such as sheer cliffs, ledges, arches, caves, and possibly the moai that Mike Rapu sunk 25m below sea level in honor of his ancestors. Water temperatures that average 65° to 80°F (18°–27°C) oblige divers to wear a wetsuit. Absolute beginners can join in, too, with a guide-assisted Discovery Dive, or an easygoing snorkeling trip (Mike Rapu's trips even include a Rapa Nui lunch). If you're up for it, don't miss this fascinating underwater opportunity. You'll find two companies at the harbor; both are reputable operations with high-quality dive masters, and both offer PADI scuba classes. **Mike Rapu Diving Center** (© **32/255-1055;** www.mikerapu.cl) is owned by "Mike," a Rapa Nui co-owner of explora's Casas Rapa Nui and the South American breath-holding champion; **Orca Diving Center** (© **32/255-0375;** www.seemorca.cl) is owned by a French diver who arrived here in 1978 with Jacques Cousteau and stayed.

Shopping

Souvenir shops line the streets Atamu Tekena and Te Pito o Henua. There are two large markets—the **Feria Municipal** at the corner of Atamu Tekena and Tu'u Maheke, and the **Mercado Artesanal** at Roa Rakei and Tu'u Koihu. Both are open Monday through Saturday in the morning and afternoon. A more unusual craft workshop is the **town prison,** about 2km from town near the airport—ask for directions or better yet take a taxi. Many of the same quality wood carvings and knickknacks you will see in the markets are sold at this popular tourist attraction for much less money, and they're bought directly from the prisoners who carve them. The internationally recognized carver Luis Hey sells his pricey yet high quality crafts at **Arte Pahika,** on Avenida Atamu Tekena. Kava Kava and Moko statues made of endemic wood run between $200 and $1,500 (£133–£1,000). For upscale home accessories, woven baskets, silver jewelry, native art, and textiles that you won't find in the markets, head to **Honu Vaikava** at Atamu Tekena.

Hanga Roa After Dark

Hanga Roa's two funky nightclubs are a riot, and really ignite on weekends—just don't show up before midnight or you might be sipping your rum and Coke alone. **Toroko,** on Avenida Policarpo Toro, has music and dancing, and a mellow atmosphere and is one of the older hangouts in town. The new "it" spot is **Topatangi** ★ on Avenida Atamu Tekena (© **32/255-1554**), with a huge dance floor that gets packed late nights with young Rapa Nuis girls and guys, along with a smattering of gringos, there to dance to a mix of live music and recorded hits. It's open from Thursday to Saturday from 10pm until the early morning.

The dance troupe **Kari Kari** puts on a thoroughly entertaining Rapa Nui folkloric show 3 nights a week, showcasing native dance, elaborate costumes, and music. Check with your hotel for times and dates as they change periodically. They used to perform at the Hotel Hanga Roa, but since it closed for renovations, they have been performing elsewhere and have a new theater on Atanu Tekana that should be ready by mid-2009.

Appendix A: Fast Facts, Toll-Free Numbers & Websites

1 FAST FACTS: CHILE

ATM NETWORKS/CASHPOINTS See "Money & Costs," p. 40.

BUSINESS HOURS Banks are open Monday through Friday from 9am to 2pm, and are closed on Saturday and Sunday. Many commercial offices close for a long lunch hour, which can vary from business to business. Generally, hours are Monday through Friday from 10am to 7pm, closing for lunch around 1 or 1:30pm and reopening at 2:30 or 3pm.

CAR RENTALS See "Airline & Car Rental Phone Numbers & Websites," p. 446.

DRINKING LAWS The legal age for purchase and consumption of alcoholic beverages is 18; alcohol is sold every day of the year, with the exception of general elections.

DRIVING RULES See "Getting There and Getting Around," p. 36.

ELECTRICITY Chile's electricity standard is 220 volts/50Hz. Electrical sockets have two openings for tubular pins, not flat prongs; adapters are available from most travel stores. Always bring a **connection kit** of the right power and phone adapters, a spare phone cord, and a spare Ethernet network cable—or find out whether your hotel supplies them to guests.

EMBASSIES & CONSULATES The only U.S. representative in Chile is the **U.S. Embassy** in Santiago, located at Av. Andrés Bello 2800 (✆ **2/232-2600;** www.usembassy.cl). The **Canadian Embassy** is at Nuevo Tajamar 481, 12th floor (✆ **2/362-9660;** www.dfait-maeci.gc.ca/chile). The **British Embassy** can be found at El Bosque Norte 0125 (✆ **2/370-4100;** www.britemb.cl). The **Australian Embassy** is at Isidora Goyenechea 3621 (✆ **2/550-3500;** www.chile.embassy.gov.au). The **New Zealand Embassy** is at Av. Golf 99, no. 703 (✆ **2/290-9800;** www.nzembassy.com/chile).

EMERGENCIES You'll want to contact the staff if something happens to you in your hotel. Otherwise, for a police emergency, call ✆ **133.** For fire, call ✆ **132.** To call an ambulance, dial ✆ **131.**

GASOLINE (PETROL) At press time, in Chile, the cost of gasoline was $1.17 (78p) per liter. Taxes are already included in the printed price. One U.S. gallon equals 3.8 liters or .85 imperial gallons.

INSURANCE **Medical Insurance** For travel overseas, most U.S. health plans (including Medicare and Medicaid) do not provide coverage, and the ones that do often require you to pay for services up front and reimburse you only after you return home.

As a safety net, you may want to buy travel medical insurance, particularly if you're traveling to a remote or high-risk area where emergency evacuation might be necessary. If you require additional medical insurance, try **MEDEX Assistance** (✆ **410/453-6300;** www.medexassist.com) or **Travel Assistance International** (✆ **800/821-2828;** www.travelassistance.com; for general information on services, call the company's **Worldwide Assistance Services, Inc.,** at ✆ **800/777-8710**).

Canadians should check with their provincial health plan offices or call **Health Canada** (✆ **866/225-0709;** www.hc-sc.gc.ca) to find out the extent of their coverage and what documentation and receipts they must take home in case they are treated overseas.

Travelers from the U.K. should carry their European Health Insurance Card (EHIC), which replaced the E111 form as proof of entitlement to free/reduced cost medical treatment abroad (✆ **0845 606 2030;** www.ehic.org.uk). Note, however, that the EHIC covers only "necessary medical treatment;" for repatriation costs, lost money, baggage, or cancellation, travel insurance from a reputable company should always be sought (www.travelinsuranceweb.com).

TRAVEL INSURANCE The cost of travel insurance varies widely, depending on the destination, the cost and length of your trip, your age and health, and the type of trip you're taking, but expect to pay between 5% and 8% of the vacation itself. You can get estimates from various providers through **InsureMyTrip.com**. Enter your trip cost and dates, your age, and other information, for prices from more than a dozen companies.

U.K. citizens and their families who make more than one trip abroad per year may find an annual travel insurance policy works out cheaper. Check **www.moneysupermarket.com**, which compares prices across a wide range of providers for single- and multitrip policies.

Most big travel agencies offer their own insurance and will probably try to sell you their package when you book a holiday. Think before you sign. **Britain's Consumers' Association** recommends that you insist on seeing the policy and reading the fine print before buying travel insurance. **The Association of British Insurers** (✆ **020/7600-3333;** www.abi.org.uk) gives advice by phone and publishes Holiday Insurance, a free guide to policy provisions and prices. You might also shop around for better deals: Try **Columbus Direct** (✆ **0870/033-9988;** www.columbusdirect.net).

TRIP CANCELLATION INSURANCE Trip-cancellation insurance will help retrieve your money if you have to back out of a trip or depart early, or if your travel supplier goes bankrupt. Trip cancellation traditionally covers such events as sickness, natural disasters, and Department of State advisories. The latest news in trip-cancellation insurance is the availability of **expanded hurricane coverage** and the **"any-reason"** cancellation coverage—which costs more but covers cancellations made for any reason. You won't get back 100% of your prepaid trip cost, but you'll be refunded a substantial portion. **TravelSafe** (✆ 888/885-7233; www.travelsafe.com) offers both types of coverage. Expedia also offers any-reason cancellation coverage for its air-hotel packages. For details, contact one of the following recommended insurers: **Access America** (✆ 866/807-3982; www.accessamerica.com); **Travel Guard International** (✆ 800/826-4919; www.travelguard.com); **Travel Insured International** (✆ 800/243-3174; www.travelinsured.com); and **Travelex Insurance Services** (✆ 888/457-4602; www.travelex-insurance.com).

INTERNET ACCESS See "Staying Connected."

LANGUAGE Spanish is the official language of Chile. Many Chileans in the tourism industry and in major cities speak basic English, but don't count on it. Try to learn even a dozen basic Spanish phrases before arriving; *Frommer's Spanish PhraseFinder & Dictionary* will facilitate your trip tremendously. See also "Appendix B: Glossary of Spanish Terms & Phrases."

LOST & FOUND Be sure to tell all of your credit card companies the minute you discover your wallet has been lost or stolen, and file a report at the nearest police precinct. Your credit card company or insurer may require a police report number or record of the loss. Most credit card companies have an emergency toll-free number to call if your card is lost or stolen; they may be able to wire you a cash advance immediately or deliver an emergency credit card in a day or two.

If you need emergency cash over the weekend when all banks and American Express offices are closed, you can have money wired to you via **Western Union** (✆ **800/325-6000;** www.westernunion.com).

MAIL The postal service, called **Correos de Chile** (✆ **800/267736** or 2/956-0200; www.correosdechile.cl), is very reliable and offers regular and certified mail. Prices for a letter under 20 grams are, respectively, 400 pesos and 925 pesos (70¢/50p and $1.60/£1.05). For express mail services, try **FedEx** (www.fedex.cl) or **DHL** (www.dhl.cl), both of which have several locations in Santiago and around Chile.

NEWSPAPERS & MAGAZINES The major dailies are the conservative *El Mercurio* and the more moderate *La Tercera,* and the left-leaning *La Nación.* The newspaper *La Segunda* is an afternoon paper with scant news and screaming headlines; *La Cuarta* is a sensationalistic rag but a lot of fun to read if you know anything about Chilean politics or celebrities. Another fun read is *The Clinic,* a satirical weekly named for the London hospital where Pinochet was arrested. You'll find 2-day-old editions of the *New York Times* and North American and European magazines at one of two kiosks in downtown. Both are located on the pedestrian walkway Ahumada (Metro: Univ. de Chile) on the right-hand side when heading up from Avenida Alameda: One is a half-block from Avenida Alameda (this kiosk has cheaper prices), and the other is at Húerfanos. Most kiosks around Santiago sell English editions of *Time* and *Newsweek,* and *The Economist.*

PASSPORTS The websites listed provide downloadable passport applications as well as the current fees for processing applications. For an up-to-date, country-by-country listing of passport requirements around the world, go to the "International Travel" tab of the U.S. Department of State at **http://travel.state.gov**.

FOR RESIDENTS OF AUSTRALIA You can pick up an application from your local post office or any branch of Passports Australia, but you must schedule an interview at the passport office to present your application materials. Call the **Australian Passport Information Service** at ✆ **131-232,** or visit the government website at www.passports.gov.au.

FOR RESIDENTS OF CANADA Passport applications are available at travel agencies throughout Canada or from the central **Passport Office,** Dept. of Foreign Affairs and International Trade, Ottawa, ON K1A 0G3 (✆ **800/567-6868;** www.ppt.gc.ca). ***Note:*** Canadian children who travel must have their own passport. However, if you hold a valid Canadian passport issued before December 11, 2001, that bears the name of your child, the passport remains valid for you and your child until it expires.

FOR RESIDENTS OF IRELAND You can apply for a 10-year passport at the **Passport Office,** Setanta Centre, Molesworth Street, Dublin 2 (✆ **01/671-1633;** www.irlgov.ie/iveagh). Those under age 18 and over 65 must apply for a 3-year passport. You can also apply at 1A South Mall, Cork (✆ **21/494-4700**) or at most main post offices.

FOR RESIDENTS OF NEW ZEALAND You can pick up a passport application at any New Zealand Passports Office or download it from the website. Contact the **Passports Office** at ✆ **0800/225-050** in New Zealand or 04/474-8100, or log on to www.passports.govt.nz.

FOR RESIDENTS OF THE UNITED KINGDOM To pick up an application for a standard 10-year passport (5-yr. passport for children under 16), visit your nearest passport office, major post office, or travel agency; or contact the **United Kingdom Passport Service** at ✆ **0870/521-0410** or search its website at www.ukpa.gov.uk.

FOR RESIDENTS OF THE UNITED STATES Whether you're applying in person or by mail, you can download passport applications from the U.S. Department of State website at **http://travel.state.gov**. To find your regional passport office, either check the U.S. Department of State website or call the **National Passport Information Center** toll-free number (✆ **877/487-2778**) for automated information.

SMOKING Traditionally laissez faire when it comes to smoking regulations, in 2006, Chile introduced stringent new laws requiring restaurants to provide designated nonsmoking areas and a prohibition of cigarette sales within 300 feet of schools. It is not unusual for Chileans to light up between courses and a lack of social etiquette toward nonsmokers certainly still prevails. Most upscale and boutique hotels don't allow smoking.

TIME Chile is 4 hours behind Greenwich Mean Time (GMT) from the first Sunday in October until the second Sunday in March; the country is 6 hours behind during the rest of the year. An easy way to remember the time zone switch is that from mid-March to mid-October, Chile is in the same time zone as the eastern U.S. or 5 hours behind Greenwich Mean Time; from mid-October to mid-March, Chile is 2 hours ahead of the eastern seaboard of the U.S.

TIPPING The customary tip in restaurants is 10%. Taxi drivers do not receive tips, nor do hair stylists. Bellhops should be tipped $2 to $3 (£1.30–£2). Gas stations are full-serve, and attendants are tipped $1.25 to $2.50 (85p–£1.70).

2 AIRLINE & CAR RENTAL PHONE NUMBERS & WEBSITES

MAJOR U.S. AIRLINES

American Airlines
www.aa.com

Continental Airlines
www.continental.com

United Airlines
www.united.com

US Airways
www.usairways.com

MAJOR INTERNATIONAL AIRLINES

Aeroméxico
www.aeromexico.com

Air New Zealand
www.airnewzealand.com

British Airways
www.british-airways.com

LAN Airlines
www.lanchile.com

Qantas Airways
www.qantas.com

South African Airways
www.flysaa.com

MAJOR DOMESTIC AIRLINES

Air Comet (formerly Aerolíneas del Sur)
✆ 600/625-0000 (in Chile)
www.aircomet.cl

LANExpress
✆ 800/735-5526 (in the U.S.)
✆ 2/687-2400 (in Chile)
www.lan.com

Sky Airlines
✆ 866/501-4679 (in the U.S.)
✆ 2/353-3169 (in Chile)
www.skyairline.cl

CAR RENTAL AGENCIES

Advantage
www.advantagerentacar.com

Alamo
www.alamo.com

Avis
www.avis.com

Budget
www.budget.com

Dollar
www.dollar.com

Enterprise
www.enterprise.com

Hertz
www.hertz.com

National
www.nationalcar.com

Payless
www.paylesscarrental.com

Thrifty
www.thrifty.com

Appendix B: Glossary of Spanish Terms & Phrases

The official language of Chile is Spanish, and few Chileans outside of the tourism industry speak more than rudimentary English—so bone up on a few handy phrases before arriving. Chileans appreciate the effort, and really, part of the fun of traveling is learning the local lingo.

That said, even Spanish speakers have a difficult time understanding singsong, high-pitched Chilean Spanish, which has grown to be known as *chilensis* for its rapid-fire delivery and heavy use of local phrases and slang. The most notable peculiarity about Chilean Spanish is the merge of the formal *vosotros* with the casual *tu* verb forms, which over the centuries has created a verb tense unique to this country. Chileans use *"tu estas,"* or *"tu comes,"* but it's very common to hear instead *"tu estai"* or *"tu comai."* This *-ai* ending is used in very informal settings; most popular is the greeting, *"¿Como estai?"* Another oddity in Chilean Spanish is *"pues,"* which puts emphasis on a word, and is more commonly shortened to *"poh,"* as in *"Sí, poh,"* meaning "Well *yes!*" Words that end in *-ado* or *-ido* typically drop the "d," so that *pelado* becomes *"pelao."* Chileans also drop the "s" in words, so that *más* becomes *"ma."*

While some Latin countries such as Argentina have virtually dropped the *usted* verb form except in the most formal of occasions, Chileans use the *usted* form habitually. Waiters, doormen, strangers, and any new business associate should be greeted with *usted* until you become better acquainted.

1 BASIC WORDS & PHRASES

GREETINGS & FORMALITIES

English	Spanish	Pronunciation
Hello	**Buenos días**	*bweh*-nohss *dee*-ahss
How are you?	**¿Cómo está usted?**	*koh*-moh ehss-*tah* oo-*stehd*
Very well	**Muy bien**	mwee byehn
Thank you	**Gracias**	*grah*-syahss
Good-bye	**Adiós**	ad-*dyohss*
Please	**Por favor**	pohr fah-*vohr*
Yes	**Sí**	see
No	**No**	noh

English	Spanish	Pronunciation
My name is . . .	**Me llamo . . .**	meh *yah*-mo
And yours?	**¿Y usted?**	ee oos-*tehd*
It's a pleasure to meet you.	Es un placer conocerle.	ehs oon plah-sehr koh-noh-*sehr*-leh
No problem.	**No hay problema.**	noh aye proh-*bleh*-mah

LANGUAGE DIFFICULTIES

English	Spanish	Pronunciation
Excuse me (to get by someone).	**Perdóneme.**	pehr-*doh*-neh-meh
Excuse me (to begin a question)	**Disculpe**	dees-*kool*-peh
Do you speak English?	¿Habla usted inglés?	ah-blah oo-stehd een-*glehss*
I don't understand Spanish very well.	No (lo) entiendo muy bien el Español.	noh (loh) ehn-tyehn-do mwee byehn el ehss-pah-nyohl
Would you spell that?	¿Puede deletrear eso?	pweh-deh deh-leh-treh-ahr eh-so
Would you please repeat that?	¿Puede repetir, por favor?	pweh-deh rreh-peh-teer pohr fah-vohr
What does ___ mean?	**¿Que significa ___?**	Keh seeg-*nee*-fee-ka
Would you speak slower please?	¿Puede hablar un poco más lento?	pweh-deh ah-blahr oon poh-koh mahs lehn-to

DIRECTIONS & TRAVEL

English	Spanish	Pronunciation
Where is . . . ?	**¿Dónde está . . . ?**	*dohn*-deh ehss-*tah*
the station	**la estación**	la ehss-*tah*-syohn
the bus stop	**la parada**	la pah-*rah*-dah
a hotel	**un hotel**	oon oh-*tehl*
a restaurant	**un restaurante**	oon res-tow-*rahn*-teh
the toilet	**el baño**	el *bah*-nyo
To the right	**A la derecha**	ah lah deh-*reh*-chah
To the left	**A la izquierda**	ah lah ees-*kyehr*-dah
Straight ahead	**Adelante**	ah-deh-*lahn*-teh
How do I get to . . . ?	**Cómo llego a . . . ?**	*koh*-mo *ye*-go a . . .
Is it far?	**Está lejos?**	es-*ta le*-hos
What time does leave/arrive?	**¿A qué hora sale/llega**	ah keh *o*-ra *sa*-le/*ye*-ga
the flight	**el vuelo**	el *vweh*-loh
the train	**el tren**	el tren

KEY QUESTIONS

English	Spanish	Pronunciation
Who?	**¿Quién? ¿Quiénes?**	*kyehn? kyeh*-nehs?
What?	**¿Qué?**	keh
When?	¿Cuándo?	*kwahn*-doh
Where?	¿Dónde?	*dohn*-deh
Why?	¿Por qué?	pohr-*keh*
How?	¿Como?	*koh*-moh
Which?	**¿Cuál?**	*kwahl*
How many?/ How much?	**¿Cuánto?/ ¿Cuántos?**	*kwahn*-toh/ *kwahn*-tohs

SHOPPING & DINING

English	Spanish	Pronunciation
I would like	**Quiero**	*kyeh*-roh
to eat	**comer**	ko-*mehr*
a room	**una habitación**	*oo*-nah ah-bee-tah-*syohn*
the check	**la cuenta**	la *kwen*-tah
the Laundromat	**la lavanderia**	la-ven-da-*re*-ah
the pharmacy	**la farmacia**	la far-ma-*cee*-ah
the ATM	**Ee cajero automático**	el ka-*heh*-roh ow-to-*mah*-tee-ko
I'm looking for a size . . .	**Busco una talla . . .**	*boos*-koh *oo*-nah *tah*-yah
small	**pequeño**	peh-*keh*-nyoh
medium	**mediano**	meh-*dyah*-noh
large	**grande**	*grahn*-deh
How much is it?	**¿Cuánto cuesta?**	*kwahn*-toh *kwe*-sta
Can I see it?	**Puedo verlo/a?**	*pweh*-doh *ver*-lo
I'll take it	**Lo llevo**	lo *ye*-voh
Breakfast	**Desayuno**	deh-sah-*yoo*-noh
Lunch	**Comida**	coh-*mee*-dah
Dinner	**Cena**	seh-nah
A menu please?	**¿Una carta por favor?**	*oo*-nah *kahr*-ta pohr fah-vohr
What do you recommend?	**¿Qué recomienda usted?**	*keh* reh-koh-*myehn*-dah oos-*tehd*

WHO

English	Spanish	Pronunciation
I	**yo**	yoh
you	**usted/tú**	oos-*tehd*/too
him	**él**	ehl
her	**ella**	*eh*-yah

English	Spanish	Pronunciation
us	**nosotros**	noh-*soh*-trohs
them	**ellos/ellas**	*eh*-yohs, *eh*-yahs

WHEN

English	Spanish	Pronunciation
now	**ahora**	ah-*oh*-rah
later	**después**	dehs-*pwehs*
in a minute	**en un minuto**	ehn oon mee-*noo*-toh
today	**hoy**	oy
tomorrow	**mañana**	mah-*nyah*-nah
yesterday	**ayer**	ah-*yehr*
in a week	**en una semana**	ehn *oo*-nah seh-*mah*-nah
at	**a las**	ah lahs

NUMBERS

0 cero
1 uno (*oo*-noh)
2 dos (dohss)
3 tres (trehss)
4 cuatro (*kwah*-troh)
5 cinco (*seen*-koh)
6 seis (sayss)
7 siete (*syeh*-teh)
8 ocho (*oh*-choh)
9 nueve (*nweh*-beh)
10 diez (dyehss)
11 once (*ohn*-seh)
12 doce (*doh*-seh)
13 trece (*treh*-seh)
14 catorce (kah-*tohr*-seh)
15 quince (*keen*-seh)
16 dieciséis (dyeh-see-*seh*-ees)
17 diecisiete (dyeh-see-*syeh*-teh)
18 dieciocho (dyeh-*syoh*-choh)
19 diecinueve (dyeh-see-*nweh*-veh)
20 veinte (*beh*-een-teh)
21 veintiuno (beh-een-*tyoo*-noh)
30 treinta (*treh*-een-tah)
40 cuarenta (kwah-*ren*-tah)
50 cincuenta (seen-*kwehn*-tah)
60 sesenta (seh-*sehn*-tah)
70 setenta (seh-*tehn*-tah)
80 ochenta (o-*chehn*-tah)
90 noventa (noh-*behn*-tah)
100 cien (syehn)
200 doscientos (doh-*syehn*-tohs)
500 quinientos (ken-ee-*en*-tos)
1,000 mil (meel)
5,000 cinco mil (*seen*-koh meel)

DAYS OF THE WEEK

English	Spanish	Pronunciation
Monday	**Lunes**	*loo*-nehss
Tuesday	**Martes**	*mahr*-tehss
Wednesday	**Miércoles**	*myehr*-koh-lehs
Thursday	**Jueves**	*wheh*-behss
Friday	**Viernes**	*byehr*-nehss
Saturday	**Sábado**	*sah*-bah-doh
Sunday	**Domingo**	doh-*meen*-goh

2 CHILEAN MENU GLOSSARY

GENERAL TERMS

Lomo Beef/steak
Pan Bread
Pollo Chicken
Postre Dessert
Huevos Eggs
Pescado Fish
Fruta Fruit
Cordero Lamb
Carne Meat
Cerdo/puerco Pork
Papas Potatoes
Papas fritas French fries
Arroz Rice
Asado Roast
Ensalada Salad]
Mariscos Seafood
Camarones Shrimp
Sopa (chupe) Soup
Camote Sweet potato
Verduras Vegetables

MEAT

Adobo Meat dish in a spicy chili sauce
Alpaca Alpaca steak
Anticuchos Shish kebab
Cabrito Goat
Carne de res Beef
Chicharrones Fried pork skins
Conejo Rabbit
Cordero Lamb
Empanada Pastry turnover filled with meat, vegetables, fruit, manjar blanco, or sometimes nothing at all
Estofado Stew
Lomo asado Roast beef
Parrillada Grilled meats
Pato Duck
Pollo a la brasa Spit-roasted chicken
Venado Venison

SEAFOOD

Corvina Sea bass
Langosta Lobster
Langostinos Prawns
Lenguado Sole
Mero Mediterranean grouper
Paiche Large Amazon fish
Tollo Spotted dogfish

BEVERAGES

Cerveza Beer
Refresco Mixed fruit juice
Jugo Juice
Leche Milk
Gaseosa Soft drink
Agua Water
  con gas carbonated
  sin gas still
Vino Wine
Cóctel/trago Cocktail

3 SOME TYPICAL CHILEAN WORDS & PHRASES

Al tiro Right away

¿Cachai? You know? Do you get it?

Choro Good, as in "Cool!"

Cuico/a Wealthy elite, snob

Curado/a Drunk

Ene A lot

Fome Boring

Guagua Baby

Harto Many, a lot

Huevón/ona Idiot, stupid person; can be used as an insult but is peppered innocuously in all Chilean speech, somewhat like "dude"

La Caña Hangover

Lucas 1,000; used like "bucks" for money

Oye! "Listen!"; used to get someone's attention

Paco Cop

Pega Work, job

Pesado Boring, stick in the mud, or an annoying person

Polera T-shirt

Pololo/a Boyfriend/girlfriend

Por si acaso Just in case

Rasca Tacky, low class (other common words for this are *ordinario* or *roto*)

¿Te fijas? Do you see? Do you get it?

INDEX

Frommer's® Complete Travel Guides

Alaska
Amalfi Coast
American Southwest
Amsterdam
Argentina
Arizona
Atlanta
Australia
Austria
Bahamas
Barcelona
Beijing
Belgium, Holland & Luxembourg
Belize
Bermuda
Boston
Brazil
British Columbia & the Canadian Rockies
Brussels & Bruges
Budapest & the Best of Hungary
Buenos Aires
Calgary
California
Canada
Cancún, Cozumel & the Yucatán
Cape Cod, Nantucket & Martha's Vineyard
Caribbean
Caribbean Ports of Call
Carolinas & Georgia
Chicago
Chile & Easter Island
China
Colorado
Costa Rica
Croatia
Cuba
Denmark
Denver, Boulder & Colorado Springs
Eastern Europe
Ecuador & the Galapagos Islands
Edinburgh & Glasgow
England
Europe
Europe by Rail
Florence, Tuscany & Umbria
Florida
France
Germany
Greece
Greek Islands
Guatemala
Hawaii
Hong Kong
Honolulu, Waikiki & Oahu
India
Ireland
Israel
Italy
Jamaica
Japan
Kauai
Las Vegas
London
Los Angeles
Los Cabos & Baja
Madrid
Maine Coast
Maryland & Delaware
Maui
Mexico
Montana & Wyoming
Montréal & Québec City
Morocco
Moscow & St. Petersburg
Munich & the Bavarian Alps
Nashville & Memphis
New England
Newfoundland & Labrador
New Mexico
New Orleans
New York City
New York State
New Zealand
Northern Italy
Norway
Nova Scotia, New Brunswick & Prince Edward Island
Oregon
Paris
Peru
Philadelphia & the Amish Country
Portugal
Prague & the Best of the Czech Republic
Provence & the Riviera
Puerto Rico
Rome
San Antonio & Austin
San Diego
San Francisco
Santa Fe, Taos & Albuquerque
Scandinavia
Scotland
Seattle
Seville, Granada & the Best of Andalusia
Shanghai
Sicily
Singapore & Malaysia
South Africa
South America
South Florida
South Korea
South Pacific
Southeast Asia
Spain
Sweden
Switzerland
Tahiti & French Polynesia
Texas
Thailand
Tokyo
Toronto
Turkey
USA
Utah
Vancouver & Victoria
Vermont, New Hampshire & Maine
Vienna & the Danube Valley
Vietnam
Virgin Islands
Virginia
Walt Disney World® & Orlando
Washington, D.C.
Washington State

Frommer's® Day by Day Guides

Amsterdam
Barcelona
Beijing
Boston
Cancun & the Yucatan
Chicago
Florence & Tuscany
Hong Kong
Honolulu & Oahu
London
Maui
Montréal
Napa & Sonoma
New York City
Paris
Provence & the Riviera
Rome
San Francisco
Venice
Washington D.C.

Pauline Frommer's Guides: See More. Spend Less.

Alaska
Hawaii
Italy
Las Vegas
London
New York City
Paris
Walt Disney World®
Washington D.C.